Jesus and Purity *Halakhah*

Itero

Reprints in the Service of the Scholarly Community

www.ehs.se/itero

Series Editor

Thomas Kazen

No. 2

Thomas Kazen

Jesus and Purity *Halakhah*

Was Jesus Indifferent to Impurity?

Enskilda Högskolan Stockholm
2021

Itero – Reprints in the Service of the Scholarly Community

Books still in demand should not get out of print, and with today's techniques there is no defence. With the reprint series *Itero*, the Biblical Studies department at Stockholm School of Theology would like to make books available for free online and at a very low cost in print. Part of the background is the fact that several faculty members have published their studies in series that were cancelled. With the publishing market in constant flux, series migrate, and volumes still in demand can suddenly become unavailable. This is unsatisfactory. In collaboration with the authors, we are now republishing a number of such volumes and we will consider publishing other out-of-print titles, for which authors hold the copyright. This is entirely a non-profit project. Files may be downloaded at www.ehs.se/itero and books can be bought through most major internet bookshops.

University College Stockholm – Stockholm School of Theology

University College Stockholm (Enskilda Högskolan Stockholm) is a major Swedish provider of education in Human Rights and Democracy, as well as in Theology/Religious Studies. EHS offers Bachelor's Master's and Doctoral programmes. The university college was founded in 1993 through a merger of educational institutions with roots dating back to 1866. Stockholm School of Theology is the common designation for the two theological departments: Religious Studies and Theology, and Eastern Christian Studies. Stockholm School of Human Rights and Democracy is the designation for the programmes in Human Rights and Democracy.

Reprint edition. Previously published by Almqvist & Wiksell International and by Eisenbrauns.

ISBN: 978-91-88906-14-4

Cover design by Carl Johan Berglund. Typeset in EB Garamond.
Printed by BoD – Books on Demand, Norderstedt, Germany.

Stockholm School of Theology
University College Stockholm
Åkeshovsvägen 29, 168 39 Bromma, Sweden
www.ehs.se

Preface to the Itero Reprint Edition

The present book is my Uppsala dissertation from 2002 in the corrected reprint version which was republished in 2010 with some minor corrections. There still seems to be a certain demand for the book, but it suddenly went out of print when the ConBNT series changed home. Hence another reprint.

If I were to properly revise this book, there are more things I would like to adjust than I did in 2010, but that would require major reworking and is not the purpose of this series. The point is for the book to remain available. Readers who want to know how my thoughts on purity and impurity have developed through more than two decades are referred to *Issues of Impurity in Early Judaism* (Eisenbrauns 2010, republished in the present series, too) and *Impurity and Purification in Early Judaism and the Jesus Tradition* (SBL Press 2021). Towards the end of the first chapter of *Impurity and Purification*, I discuss whether my views are more nuanced today and reflect on the occasional misunderstanding that I was arguing for an indifferent Jesus. Anyone who reads *Jesus and Purity* Halakhah carefully will see that I do not – also note the title's question mark! – but in *Impurity and Purification* I clarify my stance further on a number of issues.

The pictures that were originally found in the book were few and the files are no longer available, so they are not included in this edition. Adding new ones would only incur further work and expenses. Today, high-resolution photographs of ancient texts and archaeological artifacts, as well as everything else related to ritual purity practices, are easily available on the internet.

From the Foreword to the corrected reprint edition (2010)

When my study on Jesus and purity *halakhah* was first published in 2002 by Almqvist & Wiksell International, I had too little faith. Interest in purity issues apparently surpassed the number of copies we decided upon. The book is now out of print. The Swedish series Coniectanea Biblica was recently taken over by Eisenbrauns and I am grateful for their willingness to print the book anew and very quickly at that.

The present version is basically a corrected reprint, not a new edition. In addition to correcting a number of typos and a few unfortunate mistakes or unintended expressions, I have only made changes with regard to one issue; the idea that the saying in Mk 7:15 has been preserved in a more original form in Mt 15:11 and *Gos. Thom.* 14. While I used to agree with this idea, I am no longer able to defend it, nor do I think that it is necessary in arguing for an underlying dialectical negation expressing relative priority rather than opposition. This has resulted in some changes on pp. 66–67 and 228–229. A fuller argument will, however, have to await another occasion. In all other respects, the text basically stands as in the 2002 edition. Any interaction with more recent literature ... or update of the bibliography will have to await a truly new edition or another book.

From the Acknowledgements to the original edition (2002)

I want to express my sincere gratitude to all those who contributed to this study. As long as I remember, the interpretation of Jesus' behaviour and attitude has interested me, and for several years I have found the puzzling process, through which Judaism and Christianity parted, fascinating.

Professor Kari Syreeni urged me to choose a topic at an early stage, while research was still a part-time hobby, and he encouraged me to take on the subject of purity. His support and willingness to discuss various issues has been invaluable, and his keen eye has noticed numerous possibilities for improvement. The members of the New Testament Seminar in Uppsala have provided friendship and constructive criticism. It has been a privilege to belong to such a group. Helpful friends and colleagues have assisted in various matters. Helpful librarians have obtained unavailable books from somewhere, in spite of database breakdowns and bureaucratic acquisition policies.

I am also grateful for economic support from SKY:s Stipendiefond during the first years when I lacked financing, as well as this last year, to cover some of the printing expenses.

Bromma in November 2021

Thomas Kazen

Contents

PART THREE: EXPLANATORY MODELS

Figures:

Abbreviations

AASF Annales Academiae Scientiarum Fennicae
ABD *The Anchor Bible Dictionary*
ANRW *Aufstieg und Niedergang der römischen Welt*
ASOR American Schools of Oriental Research
BAR *Biblical Archaeology Review*
BETL Bibliotheca ephemeridum theologicarum lovaniensium
BJRL *Bulletin of the John Rylands University Library of Manchester*
BTB *Biblical Theology Bulletin*
BWANT Beiträge zur Wissenschaft vom alten und neuen Testament
BZ *Biblische Zeitschrift*
CBQ *Catholic Biblical Quarterly*
ConBNT Coniectanea Biblica New Testament Series
DDR *The Damascus Documents Reconsidered* (Broshi)
DJBP *Dictionary of Judaism in the Biblical Period, 450 B.C.E. to 600 C.E.*
DJD *Discoveries in the Judaean Desert*
DSD *Dead Sea Discoveries*
DSS Dead Sea Scrolls
DSS GM *The Dead Sea Scrolls Translated* (García Martínez)
DSSSE *The Dead Sea Scrolls Study Edition* (García Martínez and Tigchelaar)
DTT *Dansk Teologisk Tidsskrift*
EDSS *Encyclopedia of the Dead Sea Scrolls*
EJ *Encyclopaedia Judaica*
EKK Evangelisch-katolischer Kommentar zum Neuen Testament
ETL *Ephemerides Theologicae Lovanienses*
FRLANT Forschungen zur Religion und Literatur des Alten und Neuen Testaments
HTR *Harvard Theological Review*
HUCA *Hebrew Union College Annual*
IEJ *Israel Exploration Journal*
IG *Inscriptiones Graecae*
JAAR *Journal of the American Academy of Religion*
JBL *Journal of Biblical Literature*
JJS *Journal of Jewish Studies*
JJSoc *Jewish Journal of Sociology*
JPS The Jewish Publication Society
JQR *Jewish Quarterly Review*
JSJ *Journal for the Study of Judaism in the Persian, Hellenistic, and Roman Periods*
JSJSup Supplements to the Journal for the Study of Judaism
JSNT *Journal for the Study of the New Testament*
JSNTSup Journal for the Study of the New Testament Supplement Series
JSOT *Journal for the Study of the Old Testament*
JSOTSup Journal for the Study of the Old Testament Supplement Series
JSPSup Journal for the Study of the Pseudepigrapha Supplement Series
JTS *Journal of Theological Studies*
KEK Meyer's Kritisch-Exegetischer Kommentar über das Neue Testament
LCL Loeb Classical Library
NEAEHL *The New Encyclopedia of Archaeological Excavations in the Holy Land*
NICOT The New International Commentary on the Old Testament
NIGTC New International Greek Testament Commentary

NovT	*Novum Testamentum*
NTS	*New Testament Studies*
NTT	*Norsk Teologisk Tidsskrift*
PEQ	*Palestinian Exploration Quarterly*
PGM	*Papyri Graecae Magicae*
RB	*Revue Biblique*
RevQ	*Revue de Qumran*
RevScRel	*Revue des Sciences Religieuses*
RGG	*Die Religion in Geschichte und Gegenwart*
SAC	Studies in Antiquity and Christianity
SANT	Studien zum Alten und Neuen Testament
SB	Strack-Billerbeck: *Kommentar zum Neuen Testament aus Talmud und Midrasch*
SBL	Society of Biblical Literature
SEÅ	*Svensk Exegetisk Årsbok*
SFSHJ	South Florida Studies in the History of Judaism
SJLA	Studies in Judaism in Late Aniquity
SJT	*Scottish Journal of Theology*
SNTS	Society for New Testament Studies
SNTSMS	Society for New Testament Studies Monograph Series
STDJ	Studies on the Texts of the Desert of Judah
STK	*Svensk Teologisk Kvartalstidsskrift*
TQ	*Die Texte aus Qumran* (Lohse)
ÜTY	*Übersetzung des Talmud Yerushalmi*
TWAT	*Theologisches Wörterbuch zum Alten Testament*
VT	*Vetus Testamentum*
WUNT	Wissenschaftliche Untersuchungen zum Neuen Testament
ZD	*The Zadokite Documents* (Rabin)
ZNW	*Zeitschrift für die Neutestamentliche Wissenschaft und die Kunde der Älteren Kirche*
ZTK	*Zeitschrift für Theologie und Kirche*

Notes on editions, translations, transliteration and references

Unless otherwise stated, quotations from Qumran texts are taken from the *DSSSE*. In cases where readings and reconstructions differ on details which have a bearing on the argument of this study, the *editio princeps* (*DJD*) and/or other editions are consulted and quoted. The *Mishnah* is quoted in the edition of Beer, Holzmann, Rengstorf and Rost, the LXX in Rahlfs' edition, and other Greek texts are taken from LCL editions, when nothing else is indicated. For all other sources, the bibliography provides information about the editions used. In ambiguous cases information is provided in the footnotes. For the convenience of the reader, lengthy source text quotations are usually translated, at least in a footnote.

All translations of biblical texts are made by the author unless otherwise stated. When nothing else is indicated, translations of Qumran texts are taken from the *DSSSE*, and translations of Greek texts from LCL editions. Rabbinic texts are usually quoted from Neusner's translations. Again, the bibliography and/or footnotes provide information about translations of other texts.

Transliteration of Hebrew terms are simplified and usually follow the general-purpose style recommended in the *SBL Handbook of Style* (1999). However, orthography rather than pronunciation is reflected in the case of certain spirant consonants: hence *zab*, not *zav*.

References follow the *SBL Handbook*, with some exceptions: for certain books of the Bible and tractates of the *Mishnah*, *Tosefta*, and *Talmudim*, shortened and simplified abbreviations are used (e.g. Ez, Mk, *mAZ*). Columns in Qumran references are marked with Arabic numerals. There should be no doubt, however, as to what sources are intended.

PART ONE:

INITIAL POSITIONS

Chapter I
Jesus and purity: an introduction

How did Jesus relate to impurity? Did he discard the impurity concept altogether or was it an obvious and natural part of his Jewish faith and life? Perhaps he advocated another or different type of purity?

Ritual or cultic purity played an important role in Jewish society and life during the Second Temple period, and differences in purity *halakhah* were one of the factors that distinguished various movements. Purity is a crucial issue in any attempt to interpret the historical Jesus within his contemporary context.

This study is an attempt to examine and explain Jesus' attitude to impurity, in spite of methodological limits and historical difficulties. It is part of the latest, or "third" phase of historical Jesus research, in which Jesus' social and cultural context is given prominence. Thus it is necessary to give equal weight to an investigation of the historical Jesus and a discussion of contemporary Jewish purity *halakhah*.[1] Too often, in matters of "Jesus and the Law," New Testament scholars have engaged in Jesus, employing meticulous exegetical workmanship, while mostly relying on experts on Judaism for legal matters. In the past, this could at times result in prejudiced portraits based on an uncritical use of Strack-Billerbeck-like compilations of rabbinic material. Today, when many of these experts are Jewish scholars, the pictures usually become more balanced. Without denying my immense debt to scholars on Judaism, even less pretending to be one myself, I find it necessary for a student of the historical Jesus to become engaged with the primary materials relating to legal matters. This conviction has influenced the form and content of the present study.

I.1 The idea of impurity

The Jewish impurity system

The Jewish purity concept is a ritual or cultic one, having nothing to do with modern notions of hygiene. Interpretations in terms of hygiene belong almost exclusively to the modern era, and were in the past often coupled with attempts to find rational explanations for otherwise incomprehensible rules. Before this

[1] Since readers may range from students of the historical Jesus not especially acquainted with purity laws, to scholars of Jewish *halakhah* not particularly interested in historical Jesus research, this study includes overviews of what may be obvious to some, but not to others.

more or less modern interpretation, purity rules were often understood and/or explained allegorically.[2]

The concept of purity, in various forms, is found in several cultures, and has received a number of religious and socio-anthropological explanations. Most scholars think that the idea of impurity had an *origin* with a strong demonic strain, even in ancient Israel, although overt demonic traits faded away or were remoulded, becoming more and more incompatible with emerging monotheism. Comparative studies of ancient Near Eastern and Mediterranean religious concepts and rites confirm this.[3] Comparative studies and anthropology have also shed light on the possible *function* of impurity rules, protecting and preserving order in society.[4] The ground-breaking research of Mary Douglas has provided comparisons with various tribal religions.[5] Impurity as a system has been studied not only in Judaism, but also in Zoroastrianism and comparisons have been made between these systems, and to some extent with impurity in Islam.[6]

In the present study, I do not discuss origin or function primarily, but limit myself to an analysis of the actual interpretation and implementation of various impurity rules during the Second Temple period. In doing so, questions of origin and function will at times surface, but their role is subordinate. I do not aim to "explain" impurity.

The Jewish impurity system is based upon legal material in Leviticus and Numbers. The concept of purity is actually used in three different and to some

---

[2] It is true that some sort of hygienic explanations for the food laws are found with Maimonides and Nahmanides, but clear hygienic theories are found only from the 19th century and onwards. Cf. Houston 1993, 69–70. As explanations they are obviously anachronistic, but persist with fundamentalists and with those who see "human societies as acquiring adaptive behaviour by an unconscious process similar (it seems) to Darwinian natural selection" (70). One or both of these opinions can be detected in popular interpretation.

Purity rules were explained allegorically by Jews even before the time of Philo. Cf. Neusner 1973a, 44–50 for a discussion and references to the *Letter of Aristeas* and various passages from Philo. Note that Philo, at a distance from the temple, gave the purity laws an allegorical explanation, while still applying them literally. After the destruction of the temple, we find allegorical interpretations both with the church fathers and in rabbinic Judaism. For a mention of patristic sources and a discussion of the view of Origen, see Rouwhorst 2000, 181–190.

[3] Cf. Kaufmann 1960 [1937–1948], 101–108, 113ff; B. Levine 1974, 77–91; Milgrom 1991, 42–44, 1067–1084. Cf. Neusner 1973a, 12, who suggests that impurity in its origin was associated with loathing.

[4] Cf. Eilberg-Schwartz 1990, 177–216.

[5] Douglas 1966; 1982 [1970]. Douglas has subsequently revised her views, emphasizing the differences between taboo systems around the world and defilement in Judaism, suggesting that the purity laws of Leviticus and Numbers do not organize social categories (1993, 152–157).

[6] Cf. Boyce 1975, 294–324; Choksy 1989; Lazarus-Yafeh 1984; Reinhart 1990; Neusner 1994, xi–25. Neusner's systemic study of purity in rabbinic Judaism is supposed to be followed by a similar study by A. V. Williams on Zoroastrianism, as well as a study on comparisons and contrasts, which do not seem to have been published yet. For discussions about pollution in Greek and Roman society, cf. Parker 1983 and Wagenvoort 1947.

extent independent contexts: the food laws distinguishing between clean and unclean animals (Lev 11), impurity as a contact-contagion and a state which is dealt with by purifications (Lev 12–15; Num 19), and the polluting effect of certain grave sins (Lev 18–20).[7] The present work deals primarily with the second type of impurity; the first one receives little attention in this study, while the third use of impurity terminology is given some attention in Chapter V, inasmuch as it has some bearing on Jesus' attitude to purity *halakhah*.

Impurity bears a negative correspondence to holiness; that which is unclean and that which is holy must be kept separate. Impurity can thus constitute a threat to the sanctuary, but it is also dealt with in situations which have no intrinsic relationship to the temple.[8] Impurity regulations were developed continuously and were differently interpreted by first-century religious groups such as the Pharisees and the Qumran sectarians, and further elaborated on by the rabbis, as attested in the *Mishnah.*[9] Tendencies to expand or restrict the scope of purity can be traced in biblical legislation as well as in later texts.[10] Non-priestly perspectives are at times found in biblical, Hellenistic and rabbinic material.

Impurity is seen as transmitted by certain sources: the corpse, "leprosy" (certain skin diseases, discolorations and fungi etc.), and different "flows" (menstruation, post-natal bleeding, pathological genital discharges). It can be transmitted to people and objects (utensils, food, clothes and liquids), and different items are susceptible to different degrees. Possible means of transfer are mainly through touch, but also, in some cases, through air, moist (liquid), pressure and overhang. Impurity is removed by various purification rites, mainly through sacrifices, immersion and waiting for sunset.[11]

In the biblical system, the human corpse is the most serious source of impurity. Contact with a corpse contaminates persons and object with a seven-day impurity. Similarly, a seven-day purification period is required of "lepers" and dischargers if or when their symptoms cease. Seven days is likewise the period of impurity for menstruants, and it motivates the length of the first stage, that of

[7] There is, however, a certain amount of overlap. The rules about animal carcasses are integrated with the food laws in Lev 11, although they belong rather to the second class. Certain sexual relationships are discussed within the framework of both the second and third set of rules. Cf. below, 210f.

[8] Cf. Oppenheimer 1977, 52–55.

[9] For comprehensive descriptions of the idea of purity in Judaism, see for example *EJ* 13: 1405–1414; Oppenheimer 1977, 51–62; Booth 1986, 118–130; Harrington 1993, 28–43.

[10] For tendencies in biblical legislation depending on differences between P and H sources, see Milgrom 1991, 997–999; cf. 316–318, 13–35; 2000a, 1319–1367; Knohl 1995, 180–186; See below, 73f, 147ff, 213, 214ff, for further discussion.

[11] In certain cases by various rites such as the bird rite (Lev 14:1–7, 49–53) or the ashes from a red cow (Num 19:2–10).

actual impurity, for the parturient, at least in case of a male child.[12] While they are in their original state of impurity "lepers," dischargers and corpse-contaminated persons may contaminate other persons and objects with a one-day impurity.[13]

A simplified overview of the biblical system is illustrated in fig. 1:

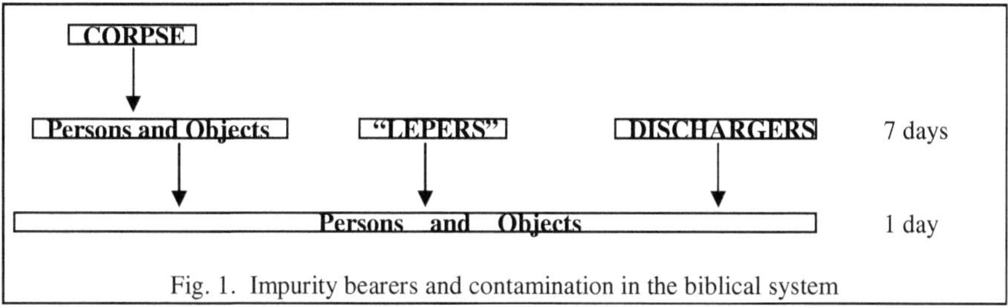

Fig. 1. Impurity bearers and contamination in the biblical system

In the figure above, the three main sources of impurity are indicated with upper-case letters. As is clear from the figure, the human corpse belongs to a separate category, as compared with the other sources, since contact with a corpse, or even presence within the same room as a corpse, conveys a seven-day impurity to people and objects. This means that corpse-impure persons and objects may contaminate other persons and objects with a one-day impurity, in basically the same way as do "lepers" and dischargers.[14] As long as their symptoms persist, "lepers" and dischargers, similarly to the corpse, are constant sources of impurity,[15] although they convey only a one-day impurity to other persons and objects. If or when their symptoms cease, they enter a seven-day purification period similar to that of corpse-impure persons.

Purity laws during the Second Temple period

The biblical system of purity contains a large number of details and exceptions, some of which will be discussed in this study. The different rules were variously interpreted and developed, until a climax was reached in the mishnaic system. In the *Mishnah*, a whole order of tractates (*Toharot*) is dedicated to purity. After the Tannaitic period, however, the interest in impurity rules de-

[12] Num 19:11–22; Lev 12:1; 14:8–9; 15:13; 19, 28.

[13] This applies to animal carcasses too (Lev 11:24–40), which contaminate persons and objects with a one-day impurity.

[14] In addition, dischargers contaminate their beds and seats, so that these items convey contamination just as the persons themselves, transmitting a one-day impurity by contact to other persons and objects. The semen-emitter (nocturnal emission) is an exception, since he becomes impure for only one day (together with clothes in contact with the semen), and does not contaminate others (Lev 15:16–17).

[15] Note that this applies neither to the menstruant or the parturient, whose bleedings are natural, temporary and transient (Lev 12:2; 15:19), nor to the male with nocturnal emissions, whose impurity lasts only one day (Lev 15:16).

clined, and to this day it is only in the area of menstruation that purity rules have played any significant role in Judaism.[16]

Scholars have developed detailed charts for illustrating chains of contamination and degrees of impurity within different systems: the biblical, the sectarian at Qumran, and the rabbinic.[17] All such charts are constructions, based on textual evidence of different kinds, and sometimes in part on conjecture, but for many purposes helpful. Fig. 2 is a simplified chart, illustrating the "rabbinic system," deduced from various mishnaic passages.[18]

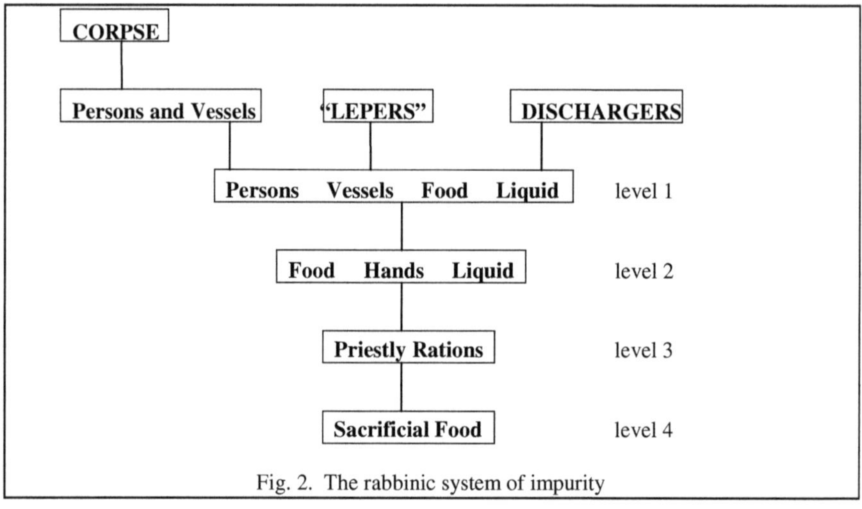

Fig. 2. The rabbinic system of impurity

In the rabbinic tradition, the biblical customs were systematized, defined, developed and ordered, although not in a modern way and never put into a neat chart. Various ordering principles were at work, at times in conflict with each other. Corpse-impure people and vessels, "lepers" and dischargers were called

[16] This can partly be explained due to the lack of means of purification after the destruction of the temple. The *Talmudim* contain *Gemara* for no tractate of the order of *Toharot*, except for *Niddah*. Cf. below, 350.

[17] David P. Wright 1987; Milgrom 1991; Harrington 1993.

[18] Cf. Harrington 1993, 149, 203, 240, 245. The picture omits a number of anomalies, some of which are already found in biblical legislation, e.g. *midras* impurity, intercourse with a female discharger, etc. Vessels refer to "rinsable vessels" (including clothes), of which earthenware belongs to a special category, and from which certain materials are excluded. This restriction of the range of susceptible objects results from the fact that the Rabbis harmonized or "homogenized" the system to a high degree, often promoting leniency. In this case, Lev 11:24–40 provided a definition of which objects could be contaminated. The rules about the discharger's bed and chair contaminating just like the discharger him/herself (not included in the simplified chart above), were extended to apply to the "leper" as well (*mZab* 5:6). For further details, see the more elaborated charts (79, 82) and the extended discussion in Chapters III and IV.

"fathers" of impurity,[19] and the corpse itself "father of fathers." Different levels of impurity were allowed for, based on either the contamination potential of the source or the susceptibility of various items. While all levels (1–4) involved a one-day impurity, that which belonged to the cultic realm was more susceptible to impurity than ordinary food or people. Objects susceptible to impurity were limited to rinsable vessels. Hands and liquids were given a special place. These details and developments are important for evaluating Jesus' attitude to impurity, and will be further discussed in Chapter III.

The mishnaic system of purity represents an ideal reconstruction at the end of the Tannaitic period (ca. 200 CE). We cannot surmise that it gives us a correct picture of the state of development at the end of the Second Temple period. Opinions differ as to how mishnaic traditions should be used and what methods be employed in order to extract early traditions and legal practices from the time of the Second Temple.[20]

Hence the *extent* to which purity regulations were developed and adhered to among Jews at the time of Jesus is debated.[21] Nevertheless, most scholars agree that purity was becoming an increasingly important issue in Second Temple Judaism.[22] Even if we can no longer determine exactly to what extent purity regulations were developed and to what degree they were kept among the populace at large, there is enough evidence of the importance of purity to most or all of the religious groups in first-century Palestine. The *Mishnah* is not our only source, but a careful comparison with passages from intertestamental literature, Philo, Josephus, the gospels, and not least the legal texts from Qumran, will yield sufficient results for tracing the purity *halakhah* to provide the context for the stance of the historical Jesus. I am operating on the conviction that it is possible to discover enough about contemporary purity practices to evaluate Jesus' attitude.

I.2 Jesus' attitude

The problem

This study aims at an historical reconstruction of how a particular first-century Galilean Jew related to contemporary purity codes. By defining the aim in this way, I have already indicated that I regard differentiation within Second Temple

[19] In the rabbinic system, fathers of impurity also include other items, such as chairs, beds and saddles of "lepers" and dischargers, as well as semen. Cf. *mKel* 1:1–4.
[20] Cf. below, 51–55.
[21] Cf. Booth 1986; Sanders 1990.
[22] E.g. Neusner 1973a, 32–71; Westerholm 1978, 62–67; Sanders 1992, 218f; Harrington 1993, 4; *tShabb* 1:14; cf. *yShabb* 1:3.

Judaism to be an important factor, and that I find it necessary to consider the historical Jesus within his religious and socio-cultural milieu.

It is the contention of this study that purity rules influenced the life of ordinary people at the end of the Second Temple period.[23] For some people, such as individuals suffering from skin diseases or constant discharges, it meant certain restrictions on interacting with others. Although gentiles were not formally unclean in themselves according to biblical law, they were regarded unclean in a transferred sense, and were by the first century CE regarded literally so, at least by some Jews.[24]

Ascertaining Jesus' attitude is thus not mainly a question about theory or theology, but a question about practice. How did Jesus act? To state my conclusions in advance, the analyses in this study indicate a seeming indifference on Jesus' part to certain purity issues. However, it is not satisfactory, and perhaps not even possible, only to describe actions, without somehow interpreting them. Jesus' seemingly indifferent stance towards various purity issues demands, if not an explanation of his motives, at least an interpretation within his cultural and religious context. I attempt, in this study, both to discover Jesus' way of conduct, and to provide plausible interpretations or explanatory models for Jesus' attitude to impurity.

During the first century CE, religious developments within Second Temple Judaism resulted in the two major movements of rabbinic Judaism and the Christian church. These two emerging religions were taking very different stances towards the role and function of the Torah, particularly in respect to covenant conditions and group boundaries. Although subsequent discussions between Jews and Christians concerned different areas of the law, the idea of purity is important, since it could be seen as representing an attitude towards the Torah as a whole.[25] The Christian church often referred to Jesus for its stance on issues separating it from Judaism. The subject matter of the present study may be useful in evaluating the role of the historical Jesus in this development.

Sources

The sources available for the historical Jesus in general are limited in scope as well as ideologically biased. In addition to the four "canonical" gospels, we may find traditions with historical traces in the *Gospel of Thomas* and in certain ancient papyrus and parchment fragments. A few scattered reminiscences may be found in the letters of Paul and in the writings of early church fathers.

---

[23] Saldarini 1988, 212–220, 290–291; Sanders 1992, 214–222.

[24] Harrington 1993, 37, 40. For various views on gentile impurity, cf. Alon 1977, 146–189; Hayes 1999; Klawans 2000, 43f, 80–82, 134f.

[25] See for example John K. Riches' (1980, 112–144) choice of purity in discussing Jesus and the law.

In addition to direct traditions about Jesus, or references to him, there are a number of sources which can be drawn upon for reconstructing the context in which Jesus must have lived and worked. These include a vast number of ancient religious and historical texts, as well as archaeological findings. Among these, the Hebrew Bible, Josephus, Tannaitic traditions, texts from Qumran and certain material artefacts relevant to purity practice (such as *miqvaot* and stone vessels) are of considerable importance for this study.

For direct evidence about Jesus, however, the gospels must provide the greater part of the material. I follow a broad consensus of taking the synoptic tradition as a departure point for reconstructing the historical Jesus. This does not mean that the synoptics always have priority over Johannine traditions for historical reminiscences, but that the special character of the Fourth Gospel is acknowledged. Every gospel has its own bias and theology, however, although this is manifest to various degrees. In tracing useful data for historical reconstruction I use Johannine traditions too, but they are not my point of departure.

In examining Jesus' attitude to impurity, I make use of various traditions: synoptic, Johannine, and possibly independent material. I discuss some Thomas traditions as possibly independent, but I do not regard the *Gospel of Thomas* as necessarily containing more ancient and superior traditions compared with other gospels. When discussing synoptic material I work primarily with Markan and Q traditions, since I accept the basic outline of the two-source theory. This does not mean that I always assume an unqualified Markan priority, nor that I entertain a *naive* belief in Markan stories as possessing a higher degree of unspecified "authenticity." I do at times argue for other versions than Mark's reflecting a more ancient rendering, and I am quite aware that Mark's bias, be it theological or otherwise, may at times be as strong as that of the Fourth Gospel. I am also reluctant to adopt speculative reconstructions of hypothetical sources such as Q. Nevertheless, I find no convincing alternative to the idea that the gospels of Matthew and Luke are based on mainly two sources: one which must have been quite similar to what we now call the gospel of Mark, the other which has not (yet?) been identified, but which at least contained some non-Markan sayings material and was common to both of them.

Contents and structure

Since this investigation is part of "the quest" for the historical Jesus, I am bound to take a stand on several issues of method. Because of the famous (or infamous) history of historical Jesus research, I find it necessary, however, to discuss the limits and possibilities of historical reconstruction in a separate chapter, including criteria, methodology and a history of research.

Questions of method are thus to be found in Chapter II, in relation to a short discussion of historical Jesus research. I do not attempt to give a full survey of the quest, but rather to deal with such aspects in particular which have a bearing on questions pertaining to the present study. Hence I will discuss the question of continuity versus discontinuity between Jesus and Judaism, and between Jesus and the early Christian movement. Closely intertwined is the discussion of reliable criteria for deciding what material should be used for reconstructing Jesus' attitudes. For reasons which will become clearer below, it is difficult to construct a secure foundation for building a reconstruction by separating so-called "authentic" sayings from others. I will argue for giving more emphasis to traditions about Jesus' deeds than has been done in the past, and I will take as my point of departure traditions which do not seem to reflect conflicts in the early church. Questions of criteria and method are not presented in isolation, however, but in relation to a broader discussion about historical reconstruction in general.

Having discussed preliminary matters and questions of method in the first two chapters, I turn to a reconstruction of Jesus' attitude in the second part of the study. Chapter III discusses Jesus and various legal issues, including the difficulties in identifying his opponents, important points of conflict, and contemporary legal practices. The two most conspicuous areas are the Sabbath and purity. In both cases, scholars have focused almost exclusively on conflict stories, which in the case of purity may lead to a digression from, or at worst, a confusion of the issues at stake. I attempt to show that what is at stake, even in Mk 7, is not food, but the overarching concept of bodily transferrable impurity. In the fourth chapter, I argue for the use of Markan non-conflict traditions containing implicit purity issues, as a point of departure for tracing Jesus' attitude to such impurities. This chapter contains a major part of my textual analyses, and discusses the three major sources of impurity: "leprosy," discharges, and the human corpse. From these analyses of the Jesus tradition and legal texts, I suggest some conclusions about Jesus' conduct or attitude to impurity.

The third part of this study is an attempt to provide a number of explanatory models for Jesus' behaviour. These suggestions do not aim at interpreting Jesus' mind, but rather at understanding his attitude within an historical context. The three suggested explanations are not mutually exclusive, but rather complementary. In Chapter V I discuss moral connotations in the impurity concept and their roots in biblical legislation. It is possible to see a trajectory through prophetic and wisdom literature, to Qumran and John the Baptizer. Jesus' relationship to the Baptizer and baptism in the context of various rites of purification are issues which must be taken into account. In Chapter VI I discuss diversity within Second Temple Judaism. It is important to look not only at differences between religious groups such as Pharisees, Sadducees and the Qumran sectarians, but also at regional differences, as a relevant background when interpreting Jesus' attitude to impurity. A Galilean perspective in particular might yield some interesting results, and archaeological findings as well as sociological and anthropological considerations are of some importance for a full picture. Finally, in Chapter VII, I discuss possible links between Jesus' attitude to impurity and his activity as an exorcist coupled with his message about God's kingdom. The connection between impurity and possession, suggested by the terminology ("unclean spirits"), is traced far back in Israelite religion, and has left imprints in Second Temple Judaism as well. The link between Jesus' exorcisms and the kingdom makes it possible to interpret his attitude to impurity in a power perspective.

In the conclusion I combine my results into an interpretation of how the historical Jesus related to contemporary concepts of impurity. I make no other claims for that interpretation except as a tentative reconstruction. I hope, however, that the reader will find it plausible and coherent.

Finally, something must be said about the choice of structure for this study. Since I have chosen to engage with primary material, this study is shot through with textual analyses, not only of gospel traditions, but of various texts relevant for legal matters. The legal discussions at times abound with detail. One obvious possibility in a study like this would have been to separate the analyses of textual gospel traditions from the discussion of legal issues.[26] Another similar but not identical division would be that between an analysis of literary or narrative material and historical reconstruction.[27] This might give a neat and square impression but is not entirely satisfactory. Such divisions tend to become strained. Gospel traditions raise questions about legal issues, and legal texts and historical contexts shed light on the Jesus tradition. There is a constant and mutual interplay. I have preferred to use a "process structure" which reflects the line of argument; the aim is that the reasoning should be "unfolding." This means, however, that I do not discuss purity *halakhah* in a single section, but return to it repeatedly, when this is warranted by the texts and topics relating to Jesus' attitude. The latter thus set the agenda, and I do not aim to cover all aspects of purity law. The disadvantage of such a structure is that at times a particular argument may presuppose earlier discussions, and may be carried over in a subsequent chapter or section. This may cause some inconvenience for the kangaroo reader, but I attempt to minimize it by frequent references in the footnotes, and by indices at the end.

[26] Cf. Booth 1986.
[27] Cf. Freyne 1988a.

Chapter II
Jesus and history: problems and possibilities

II.1 The historical Jesus and purity

The quest for the "historical Jesus" is a perilous task, as has already been recognized by Martin Kähler.[1] Is it at all possible to get behind the gospel stories without simply exchanging the interpretative framework of the gospel redactor for one's own? What modern interpretative tendencies, or biases, contribute to the immense interest in the "historical Jesus?" In this chapter, I discuss some hermeneutical problems and methodological limits of historical Jesus research and relate these to various interpretations of Jesus' attitude to impurity, as well as to my own methodology.[2]

Trends and tendencies in the "quests"

The first period in "the Quest of the historical Jesus,"[3] today often called "the liberal quest," took its lead from H. S. Reimarus' rationalistic criticism and distinction between the Jesus of history and the Christ of the church.[4] Reimarus' discussion about the *intention* of Jesus and his disciples became important for subsequent research. This project of liberal theology was mainly limited to German Protestantism, with the unspoken aim of making Jesus *meaningful* for modern Europeans. From it emerged a teacher of truths, a Jesus of eternal ethics, whose message conformed not to the church, but to a surprisingly high degree to contemporary cultural Protestantism. Jesus was imagined in sharp contrast to legalistic Pharisees or apocalyptic enthusiasts. In order to fit with European, liberal and rational ideals, he was severed from his Jewish roots. He could hardly have been a Jew at all.[5]

---

[1] Kähler 1988 [1896]. Note for example Kähler's discussion about the impossibility of an investigation going beyond the *forms* of human inner experience to the *content* of Jesus' inner life (52f), or his discussion about historical work becoming an ideological tool (55f).

[2] For surveys of the "quest" for the historical Jesus and its development since the 18th century, the reader is referred to numerous overviews which have been published, e.g. Riches 1993, 14–30, 89–124; Theissen and Merz 1998 [1996], 1–13; Holmberg 2001, 165–223 (including a list of overviews, 207–208, n.2). A future standard work will probably be *The Historical Jesus in the Twentieth Century* of which the first volume (Weaver 1999) covers the period 1900–1950. Forthcoming volumes will cover 1951–1980 (Baasland) and 1981–2000 (Charlesworth).

[3] The English title of Schweitzer's thesis *Von Reimarus zu Wrede*.

[4] *Von dem Zwecke Jesu und seiner Jünger*, published posthumously by Lessing, in the 1770s.

[5] Cf. Harnack's interpretation, which amounts to a serious distortion of Jewish religion. The Jews, according to Harnack, "thought of God as of a despot guarding the ceremonial obser-

This paradigm was challenged around the turn of the nineteenth century, initially by Johannes Weiss, but principally by Albert Schweitzer, who emphasized Jesus' apocalyptic traits.[6] In spite of their criticism of the liberals for reflecting contemporary values and questions, they could not live with their own reconstructions, but ended up in a way playing the same game as did liberal theology. It was not Jesus' apocalyptic understanding of the kingdom, but rather his ideas about religious and ethical fellowship, which were of abiding value.[7] Schweitzer turns into an almost existentialist preacher in his attempts to extract meaning from an enigmatic and uncomprehensible figure.[8]

Although Rudolf Bultmann and other form critics in the 1920s gave historical research a new turn by seriously questioning the (previously more or less assumed) reliability of the gospel sources, they agreed with Schweitzer that historical knowledge of Jesus was not important to Christian faith. Relevance and meaning was found not in historical Jewish traits, such as apocalypticism, but in modern reinterpretations of Jesus' challenge and man's response.

In spite of the fact that several British scholars claimed that form critical methods verified rather than discredited the general historicity of gospel traditions,[9] the German scepticism towards finding material with a genuine *Sitz im Leben Jesu* meant that little historical research about Jesus was done until the 1950s. At that time a growing reaction among students of Bultmann resulted in several studies of Jesus.[10] It was Ernst Käsemann who most clearly pointed out the risk of divorcing Christian faith from its historical roots. The question of continuity between Jesus and the church came into focus.[11]

The "New Quest" was gradually embraced by a number of New Testament scholars from different countries, and has continued until this day. Although at least one early participant, Ernst Fuchs, did emphasize the traditions of Jesus' *actions* (as being less prone to change by early church influence than his

---

vances in His household; he [Jesus] breathed in the presence of God. They saw Him only in His law, which they had converted into a labyrinth of dark defiles, blind alleys and secret passages; he saw and felt Him everywhere" A. von Harnack, *What is Christianity?* (London, 1901 [Berlin 1900], 50, quoted in Riches 1993, 19.

[6] J. Weiss 1900, 64f, 175–178; Schweitzer 1936 [1906], 350ff.

[7] Dunn 1991, 6; J. Weiss 1892, 66f.

[8] "He comes to us as One unknown, without a name, as of old, by the lake-side, He came to those men who knew Him not. He speaks to us the same word: "Follow thou me!" and sets us to the tasks which He has to fulfil for our time. He commands. And to those who obey Him, whether they be wise or simple, He will reveal Himself in the toils, the conflicts, the sufferings which they shall pass through in His fellowship, and, as an ineffable mystery, they shall learn in their own experience Who He is." Schweitzer 1936 [1906], 401.

[9] Esp. V. Taylor 1935 [1933], cf. the statement on p. vi; cf. Dodd 1963, 1–9, 427f; 1971, 17–36.

[10] Bornkamm 1960 [1956]; Conzelmann 1959; Fuchs 1956. Meanwhile, some Jewish scholars (Klausner, Montefiore, Eisler) had published; cf. Theissen and Merz 1998 [1996], 8f.

[11] Käsemann 1954, 125–152 (English tr. in Käsemann 1965, 15–47).

words),[12] the main focus during this period was on reconstructing the genuine *words* of Jesus, by removing redactional layers and applying certain criteria. Among these, the criterion of multiple attestation and the criterion of coherence have been influential tools,[13] but the most important and controversial is the criterion of dissimilarity or discontinuity, which has had the effect, when strictly applied, of once more severing Jesus from his Jewish roots. It can possibly be used to verify, but hardly to falsify a saying. If no saying corresponding either with contemporary Judaism or with the early church could be genuine, any continuity between Jesus and his cultural and religious environment must by definition be ruled out from the very beginning.[14]

This peculiar characteristic of the "New Quest" is perhaps best explained by a heritage from Schweitzer and Bultmann of regarding Jesus as an "unknown" or incomprehensible figure. It did not, however, result in a particularly *historical* picture.[15] In a way, one could say that the "New Quest" ended where the liberal Quest did: with a non-historical Jesus, seen in continuity neither with Judaism, nor with the early church. However, there are positive things to be said. Many of the criteria developed are used today, but usually with more refinement and discrimination than at an earlier stage.[16] The question of continuity or discontinuity between Jesus and his Jewish environment has not been totally absent from the "New Quest" either. The judgement that the "New Quest" attempted to liberate Jesus from his Jewishness[17] is not entirely correct when other than German scholarship of the Bultmannian school is taken into account. James Robinson wrote in 1959, expounding his programme for a new quest, about "a considerable body of material about Jesus whose historicity tends to be generally accepted" and "whose historicity is conceivable in terms of Jesus' Jewish, Palestinian background."[18] Unfortunately, the Jewish traits of the historical Jesus did not gain sufficient attention until the end of the 1970s.

Whether the latest phase of historical Jesus research should be termed the "Third Quest" is open to debate. While a new turn is definitely to be observed, this phase is more continuous with preceding research than is often supposed.

---

[12] Fuchs 1956, 220ff.

[13] E.g. Perrin 1969, 71.

[14] Cf. Holmberg 1995, 29; Holmén 1999, 50f.

[15] German scholars of this period emphasized the non-Jewish traits of Jesus, except for Joachim Jeremias (cf. Jeremias 1972 [1947] and Jeremias 1971). As John Riches remarks, many of them viewed Judaism through Lutheran-Pauline eyes, and interpreted the message of Jesus with the help of existentialist philosophy, adding little that was new to the understanding of the Jewish world (Riches 1993, 91–92). Holmberg is probably right in detecting a measure of antisemitism in the assumption that Jesus differed totally from his Jewish contemporaries (Holmberg 1995, 28).

[16] Cf. Meier 1991, 167–184.

[17] Holmberg 1995, 43.

[18] Robinson 1959, 104. Cf. the attention paid to Jewish sources by Jeremias 1972 [1947].

An increase in knowledge about Judaism is usually presented as one important condition for the third phase.[19] This is obviously true, to the extent that knowledge usually increases and understanding develops. In this respect, the works of Martin Hengel and Jacob Neusner gave important impetus to subsequent research. Hengel's *Judentum und Hellenismus* in 1968 focused on the Jewish context of Jesus, and the place of Judaism within the larger context of the Hellenistic world.[20] From the early 1970s, Neusner has, through his numerous critical investigations into rabbinic traditions, drawn attention to the need for differentiation in rabbinic material, especially with a view to the importance of the year 70 CE for the development of rabbinic Judaism.[21]

There is little to be said about new sources. Rabbinic and apocryphal materials were there already during the original quest, and both the Qumran scrolls and the Nag Hammadi library were discovered before the "New Quest" was initiated. Even if much of this material only gradually became generally available, James Robinson's discussion from 1959 seems almost up to date: the Qumran texts "are not so much new sources for the life of Jesus as new arguments; except that the arguments are not new;" from the *Gospel of Thomas* one could expect "an increase in the quantity of authentic sayings of Jesus," but this material would basically be similar in character to material already available from some of the Oxyrhynchus Papyri.[22] This is not to deny the importance of later analyses of materials from these two libraries for historical Jesus research. But unless the "New Quest" is regarded as an enterprise of the "post-Bultmannians" only, there is more reason to speak of the third phase as a development than as a fresh start.

Just as important for this third phase are historiographical conditions, as pointed out by Holmberg.[23] Ben F. Meyer, building upon Bernard Lonergan's criticism, is one of the first to analyse and reject "the many reductionistic philosophies which, whether or not they have won the historians' conscious agreements, have exercised a decisive remote control over historical-Jesus work."[24] The two main characteristics of this reductionism are the view of the universe as a closed system and the assumption that judgement of the past is limited by present experience (Troeltsch's principle of analogy).[25] It is interesting to note, however, that when several participants in the "New Quest" discuss Jesus' self-understanding, this is in effect the beginning of a loosening of a strictly "scien-

---

[19] Cf. Riches 1993, 91f; Holmberg 1995, 29f.

[20] The second edition came in 1973 and was published in English the subsequent year.

[21] Neusner 1971.

[22] Robinson, 1959, 59–63. Quotation from pp. 62–63. Robinson is discussing Ethelbert Stauffer's *Jesus: Gestalt und Geschichte*, Bern: Francke, 1957.

[23] Holmberg 2001, 192f.

[24] B. Meyer 1979, 16. Holmberg (2001, 192) notes Meyer's allusion on Reimarus' title (*The Aims of Jesus*).

[25] B. Meyer 1979, 16–17.

tific" view of causation.[26] Hence James Robinson discusses twenty years before Meyer "a new concept of history and self" as one of the characteristics of the "New Quest" in comparison with the 19th century enterprise. Says Robinson:

> Today history is increasingly understood as essentially the unique and creative, whose reality would not *be* apart from the event in which it becomes, and whose truth could not be *known* by Platonic recollection or inference from a rational principle, but only through historical encounter. History is the act of intention, the commitment, the meaning for the participants, behind the external occurrence. In such intention and commitment the self of the participant actualizes itself, and in this act of self-actualization the self is revealed. Hence it is the task of modern historiography to grasp such acts of intention, such commitments, such meaning, such self-actualization; and it is the task of modern biography to lay hold of the selfhood which is therein revealed.[27]

While a less reductionist attitude can be seen to have been initiated already during an earlier period, the influence of social sciences on biblical studies in general, and historical Jesus research in particular, during the last decades of the 20th century, is unparalleled. Methods and terminology from sociology and cultural anthropology came to be used in numerous studies. Some of these will be discussed below. It is, however, not too difficult to see in this development a natural supplementing of the interest in contexts and environments which followed in the wake of redaction criticism. In secular history, interaction between sociology and history had already been established since the time of Marx and Weber.[28]

From the very brief discussion above, it should be clear why I presently prefer to speak about a third phase rather than the "Third Quest." This is not to deny the importance of new directions in contemporary research, but only to underscore continuity with the past. It could well be that the shift in methodology, which Dagmar Winter and Gerd Theissen trace in their recent study *Die Kriterienfrage in der Jesusforschung,*[29] will come to be seen as the main distinctive qualification for regarding the third phase as an altogether new start. This shift, however, still has the character of scattered attempts to go beyond the methodological restrictions of earlier periods, but not yet showing the characteristics of a conscious and comprehensive programme.

A Jewish Jesus

The most obvious trend in the latest phase of historical Jesus research is the emphasis on, and the importance ascribed, to the Jewish context of Jesus. One of the most problematic results of the quest from its very beginning was that

---

[26] Cf. the discussion below, 37–39.

[27] Robinson 1959, 67–68.

[28] The "deficit" on sociological perspectives in New Testament studies before the 1970s is discussed in Holmberg 1990, 1ff. Cf. also the overview in Elliott 1995 [1993], 17–35.

[29] Theissen and Winter 1997. The shift in methodology will be further discussed below, 25–34.

Jesus was severed from his Jewish heritage. Since the early works of Hengel and Neusner, not to mention Jeremias, there has been an increasing focus, however, on the Jewishness of Jesus. Holmberg speaks about the sluice-gates being opened for a flood of investigations stressing Jesus' Jewishness, and the social and political dimensions of his activity interacting with contemporary Palestinian circumstances.[30]

The awareness of the importance of Jesus' Jewish environment has manifested itself in various ways. Sometimes the pendulum has swung toward the effect of Jesus being presented as having no substantial conflicts with mainstream Judaism. Geza Vermes is one example of such a view. The Jesus of his trilogy[31] is being executed with no compelling reason.[32] While Vermes claims that Jesus had no serious disputes about biblical law,[33] he admits a lax attitude to ritual impurity.[34] A similar view is found in David Flusser, who claims that Jesus was scrupulous in keeping the law, and that the disputes ascribed to him in the gospels "touch on minutiae" only.[35] He actually bridged the differences between the Schools of Hillel and Shammai, and there is simply "no difference between the views of Jesus and authentic Jewish traditions."[36]

Ed Sanders can be seen as part of the same trend, although taking into account not only the religious, but also the social and political context of Jesus. There is, however, very little room for conflict or tension.[37] This is linked with Sanders' criticism of a traditional Lutheran and pietistic interpretation of Judaism as a legalistic religion, based on earning salvation by merits. According to Sanders, Judaism was based on grace and election, and the covenant law stipulated mutual obligations. Sanders' key concept for describing Second Temple Judaism is "covenantal nomism" and Jesus is placed within the framework of Jewish restoration theology. Sanders has been extremely important for counteracting a prejudiced general view of Judaism, but he does not reflect so much on differentiation within Jewish society. By avoiding polarization, Sanders presents quite a harmonious picture of a Jesus within mainstream Judaism.[38] Although he finds most of the legal disputes in the gospels inauthentic, he discusses them for the sake of argument, and concludes that the synoptic Jesus

[30] Holmberg 1995, 43. The tendency could be illustrated by the titles of Vermes 1973 (*Jesus the Jew*) or Charlesworth 1988 (*Jesus Within Judaism*). For a survey of historical Jesus-research from the perspective of his Jewishness, see Moxnes 2002.

[31] Vermes 1973b; 1983 and 1993.

[32] Vermes 1993, ix–x.

[33] Vermes 1993, 21–26. It should be noted that Vermes does not explicitly discuss bodily impurity here, but focuses rather on food laws.

[34] Vermes 1973b, 81.

[35] Flusser 1987, 22.

[36] Flusser 1987, 25.

[37] Sanders 1985.

[38] Sanders 1985, 267ff, 290ff, 335–340; cf. 1990, 90–96.

was law-abiding.[39] We know of "no substantial dispute about the law, nor of any substantial conflict with the Pharisees."[40] Sanders is one of the few New Testament exegetes who discusses purity at length,[41] and with a vast knowledge of primary sources. He concludes, however, that "it is incorrect to make purity the issue between Jesus and his critics."[42]

Of the same opinion, although not with the cogent arguments of Sanders, is Paula Fredriksen, who thinks that Jesus' adherence to purity rules is taken for granted in the sources, and supported by arguments *ex silentio*. The "loudness of this silence"[43] is heard in logia about offerings and mentions of pilgrimages and paschal meals, which suggest that Jesus purified himself and took impurity rules for granted. Fredriksen suggests that Jesus' observance of purity rules is implicit in several traditions where the material is not construed as conflict stories.[44]

The denial of any substantial conflict between Jesus and his contemporaries on legal issues is not a necessary effect of this trend, however. A second line of interpretation emanating from the increased consciousness about the Jewish context of Jesus, and of utmost importance for subsequent research, was initiated by Gerd Theissen. Theissen's outline of a sociology of the Jesus movement[45] has influenced almost a generation of scholars. Although his reconstruction of the Jesus movement as wandering charismatics supported by groups of resident villagers does not convince every scholar, his attempt to tie the Jesus movement to social and political circumstances of that day has found many followers. Theissen's analysis can be summarized in two points:

> first, that we have to see first-century Palestinian society as undergoing a deep social crisis, stemming from the prolonged erosion of Jewish norms by foreign domination and occupation; and, second, that we need to see the Jewish renewal movement as part of a pattern of social responses to such a situation. This, of course, leaves the way clear for asking how Jesus himself with his own particular vision and activity relates to the Jewish renewal movement of which he was a part.[46]

While Theissen did not at first attempt a direct reconstruction of the historical Jesus,[47] his insights and methods were applied by other scholars. One of

---

[39] Sanders 1990, 1, 90.

[40] Sanders 1985, 292.

[41] Most of *Jewish Law from Jesus to the Mishnah* (1990) is occupied with purity issues.

[42] Sanders 1985, 199. Cf. 1985, 209f, 290f; 1990, 29–42.

[43] Fredriksen 2000, 206.

[44] Fredriksen 2000, 197–207. Although purity issues are dealt with in only a few pages, the centrality of purity for Fredriksen's reconstruction is evident from her fictional description of the boy Jesus' visit to the temple, and the subsequent chapter on Jewish adherence to the Torah, which concentrates on purity.

[45] Theissen 1978 [1977].

[46] Riches 1993, 96.

[47] In a subsequent book, *Der Schatten des Galiläers* (1986; English tr. 1987), Theissen made a sort of indirect reconstruction; Jesus is traced but never confronted. Theissen has recently sub-

them is Marcus Borg, who develops the idea of how tension grew in Jewish society, because of increasing segregation. Borg argues that the common denominator for the Jewish renewal movements was the quest for holiness, understood as separation from that which was impure. The purpose of this holiness policy was to unite Israel against external threats, and it was a necessary prerequisite for having a relationship to God, which is most clearly seen in the *haburot* of the Pharisees.[48] According to their view, the land was being defiled by the mere presence of the Romans, since holy land should be owned by Jews and all its produce should be tithed. Borg sees a Pharisaic programme for Israel, in which *imitatio dei* was at the core: "Be holy as I am holy." This policy, however, created division within the people itself and growing hostility toward Rome. Because of the Pharisaic holiness programme the nation faced political and national ruin. Jesus' "programme" was, according to Borg, also built on the *imitatio dei*, but with God understood as mercy: "Be merciful, as your father is merciful." This policy would save the people from catastrophe, since it integrated the outcasts and lowered tension between the people and the occupying Romans.[49]

Another scholar discussing Jesus in a contemporary social and political context is John Riches. Riches is more coherent than Borg,[50] and not as dependent on Theissen, but starts out from a discussion about language and principles of religious change.[51] He nevertheless comes up with a similar picture of a society under pressure,[52] and a similar suggestion: Jesus had a strategy for handling social and political tension which was notably different from the various programmes of resistance found with other groups.[53] Purity becomes a central issue in Riches' reconstruction, and he suggests that Jesus did not rework, but simply discarded, the notion of purity as unusable, because it created barriers.[54]

A third line of interpretation emphasizing the contemporary context of Jesus gives priority to a Galilean perspective. An influence from Theissen's sociological approach, especially the picture of the Jesus movement as itinerant, supported by local communities, can be detected in several reconstructions. In addition, archaeological evidence usually plays an important role for proponents of a Galilean Jesus.

---

mitted a very short, direct reconstruction in narrative form in Theissen and Merz 1998 [1996], 569–572.

[48] The question of *haburot*, and whether they were Pharisaic, is discussed below, 47, 87, 272.

[49] Borg 1984.

[50] Cf. Borg's attempt to include a non-eschatological characterization of Jesus as a "Holy man" in his reconstruction, which is not fully integrated with the social and political figure.

[51] Riches 1980, 20–43.

[52] Cf. the subtitle of Riches' subsequent book (1990): *First century Judaism in crisis*.

[53] Riches 1980, 168f.

[54] Riches 1980, 112–144.

Seán Freyne's thorough study on the social, political, economical and religous conditions in Galilee during the period of the Second Temple[55] formed the groundwork for his *Galilee, Jesus and the Gospels*,[56] as well as numerous articles, in which he increasingly brings in archaeological evidence.[57] In his description of the Galilean context of Jesus, he discusses differences between rural and urban environments, and brings into focus possible tension between peripheral areas and central Judaea. Freyne concentrates on Galilee and does not attempt a thorough reconstruction of the historical Jesus, but he suggests that Jesus could have presented a possible alternative to Pharisaism in a Galilean context.[58] In matters of law, "[l]ife-experience rather than text was for him decisive,"[59] and the Galilean cultural experience made it possible to maintain allegiance to the Jewish faith without necessarily adhering to halakhic detail.[60] However, Freyne never deals explicitly with purity issues.

Richard Horsley has a similar approach, but produces somewhat different results. After his first sociological investigations of the historical Jesus,[61] Horsley published two works on Galilee which dealt not only with social, political, economical and religious aspects, but also with archaeological evidence.[62] Horsley describes a Galilee characterized by much social, political and economic tension. He emphasizes more than does Freyne the conflict between rural peasants and urban elites.[63] Horsley regards Hellenistic influence in the countryside as minimal, and claims that Galilee had an unbroken heritage of ancient northern Israelite traditions.[64] He does not believe in the picture of Jesus as a Cynic preacher, nor even as a "wandering charismatic." Jesus is rather to be seen as "the prophetic leader of a movement of Israelite renewal based in the villages,"[65] who attempted a reorganization in order to achieve an egalitarian society. Like Freyne, Horsley does not give a comprehensive picture of Jesus, but suggests that conflicts between Jesus and his opponents may be understood according to the anthropological distinction between great and little tradition, where Galilean ancient popular tradition clashed with official Jerusalem Torah.[66] However, Horsley does not deal with purity as a separate issue.

---

[55] Freyne 1998 [1980].
[56] Freyne 1988a.
[57] Collected in Freyne 2000.
[58] Freyne 1998 [1980], 329–334.
[59] Freyne 1988a, 254.
[60] Freyne 1988a, 254ff, 261f.
[61] Horsley 1987 and 1989.
[62] Horsley 1995 and 1996.
[63] Horsley 1995, 202ff; 1996, 76f., 83f.
[64] Horsley 1996, 15–42, 122, 171–175.
[65] Horsley 1996, 189.
[66] Horsley 1996, 182–184.

There are also various reconstructions of a Cynic-like Jesus, which could be regarded as a digression from the Galilean line of interpretation. This picture is elaborated on by John Dominic Crossan and Burton Mack.[67] For both of them, it is connected to their views on Jesus' teaching. In the case of Mack, the material on which he builds his case is a reconstruction of the Q source, while Crossan makes his own reconstruction of the earliest Jesus tradition by a kind of "stratigraphy"[68] in which he divides his materials in four chronological strata.[69] Crossan builds his reconstruction primarily on what he judges to be the earliest stratum, and only on materials with "multiple, or at least plural independent attestations in the primary stratum."[70] This is a rather innovative method, which has been seriously criticized.[71] Crossan calls Jesus a "peasant Jewish Cynic," with the condition, however, that "Jewish" is not forgotten. Jesus is seen as representing a rural, oral and popular type of inclusive Judaism, akin to Cynicism. His was a specific social vision of "religious and economic egalitarianism."[72] Mack, on the other hand, regards Jesus more distinctly as a Cynic sage, in a thoroughly hellenized Galilee, relatively distanced from the Jewish social world.[73] He had no explicit purpose; in a sense he was aimless.[74] Starting with a Galilean setting we have again moved away from a Jewish context.[75] Neither

---

[67] Crossan 1991; Mack 1993. Other advocates for a Cynic Jesus include Downing 1988 and 1992; Vaage 1994.

[68] In addition to the canonical gospels, Crossan includes extra-canonical materials such as the *Gospel of Thomas*, the *Egerton Gospel*, the *Gospel of Peter*, the *Gospel of the Hebrews*, etc.

[69] Crossan 1991, 427–450 (Appendix I).

[70] Crossan 1994, xiii.

[71] Theissen and Winter 1997, 15–16, 246. Crossan's early dating of certain extra-canonical traditions is not commonly accepted by New Testament scholars and the high value ascribed to the *Gospel of Thomas*, in combination with the principle of multiple attestation, gives this disputed document too much influence on what is deemed authentic. This is not least observed in Crossan's judgement on Jesus and eschatology (1991, 282f).

[72] Crossan 1991, 421–422, Cf. 1994, 102–122. Note that Crossan does not presuppose direct influence or even knowledge of Cynicism on the part of Jesus. "Maybe he had never even heard of the Cynics and was just reinventing the Cynic wheel all by himself" (1994, 122).

[73] Mack's hellenized Galilee is hardly a credible construction. This applies to several "Cynic" reconstructions of Galilean society. For a further discussion, see below, 277–286.

[74] Mack 1988, 53–77. Cf. Borg 1994, 21–23.

[75] We have also returned to the lack of eschatology which characterized the liberal Jesus of the nineteenth century. Neither Mack, Crossan, Horsley, nor Borg regard apocalyptic eschatology as part of genuine Jesus tradition. This is a notable trait of several American scholars associated with the Jesus Seminar, such as Robert Funk, who claims that "the overpowering vision of Jesus was translated back into the ordinary apocalyptic expectations of that time" (1996, 254). One condition for this development seems to be the earlier work of British scholars, such as C. H. Dodd and G. B. Caird. Dodd's concept of "realized eschatology" which he subsequently revised and imbued with greater nuance (1961 [1935], 41f; cf. Dodd 1953, 447 n.1, where he acknowledges the problems of the term and expresses preference for Jeremias' suggestion: "sich realisierende Eschatologie," had it been translatable), and Caird's arguments from non-literal metaphorical language that NT eschatological sayings should not be taken actually to refer to the end of the world (1980, 243–271) are more balanced and less one-sided. J. P. Meier's

Mack, nor Crossan devote much attention to the question of Jesus' attitude to impurity.

Jesus and purity issues

I think that the recent emphasis on the Jewishness of Jesus in general, including his Galilean context, is important in tracing his relationship to Jewish law and purity rules, in spite of the fact that most Galilean approaches deal very little with questions of law and purity. All three of the above-mentioned lines of interpretation offer important contributions to a search for Jesus' attitude to impurity. Among the scholars mentioned in the previous section, it is only Sanders, however, who discusses Jesus and purity issues at length.

Gospel traditions about purity and impurity have of course been examined by a number of exegetes who cannot easily be identified with any of the three above-mentioned lines of interpretation. The majority of studies have primarily discussed the logia in Mk 7 about hand-washing and eating,[76] often as part of a wider treatment of Jesus' attitude to the Torah.[77]

An important contribution was Stephen Westerholm's 1978 study on Jesus' attitude to legal issues.[78] Although he concentrates on Mk 7 in the section on purity, Westerholm initially discusses the purity system briefly, and identifies several of the major problems involved: the difficulty of finding a *rationale* behind purity laws, the threat involved in impurity, the demand for purity in view of sanctuary visits and in ordinary life, the question of whether Pharisees ate their ordinary food in purity, as well as the problematic relationship between Pharisees, *haberim* and common people (*ammei ha-arets*).[79] Westerholm does note various gospel traditions which involve implicit purity issues.[80] Seeing no need "to weigh the historicity of these accounts," yet regarding them as "at least typical of Jesus' ministry," he nevertheless dismisses them too lightly, claiming that "they tell us in any case very little."[81] From Jesus' table-fellowship and traditions in Mk 7, Westerholm concludes, however, that Jesus shows an "apparent indifference," to be explained by a different conception of God's will, not as statutory law, but as an attitude of the heart.[82]

---

comment is relevant, that "a Baptist with a message of future eschatology on one side of Jesus and a church with a message of future eschatology on the other side of Jesus makes a Jesus totally bereft of future eschatology a suspicious figure from the start" (1994, 9).

[76] E.g. Paschen 1970, 155–200; Lambrecht 1977; Hübner 1986 [1973].

[77] E.g. Banks 1975, 132–146; Hübner 1986 [1973], 142–195.

[78] Westerholm 1978, 62–91.

[79] Westerholm 1978, 62–67.

[80] I.e. the three major traditions to be used as springboards in my study (Mk 1:40–45; 5:25–34; 5:21–24, 35–43) as well as Mk 14:3. Westerholm 1978, 68.

[81] Westerholm 1978, 69.

[82] Westerholm 1978, 90f.

A major study of Mk 7 was Roger Booth's (1986) *Jesus and the Laws of Purity*. Booth makes a serious attempt to interpret this gospel tradition by *both* a thorough tradition- and redaction-historical exposition *and* an initiated discussion of the legal situation, based on primary sources. Booth interprets the crucial logion about what makes man unclean, in a relative sense, and suggests a fairly detailed reconstruction of the state of hand-washing *halakhah* at the time of Jesus.[83] In the end, the basic issue is seen to be not one of food *per se*, but of bodily communicable impurity, which could contaminate food.[84]

Booth has been followed recently by Jesper Svartvik, whose dissertation deals with Mk 7:1–23, mainly from the perspectives of genre and reception history. When Svartvik turns to the historical context, he agrees with Booth that the issue is not food laws, but food contaminated by the main sources of bodily impurity, via the hands.[85] The intent of the "cardinal saying" (Mk 7:15) is in the end to warn against the evil tongue (לשון הרע) or malicious gossip.[86]

Since detailed studies of Mk 7 often show that the underlying issue is not one of food, but of ritual impurity understood as a bodily state and a contact-contagion, one would expect this issue to receive more attention. While there is a good number of studies of ritual purity in Judaism,[87] studies of Jesus' attitude to purity *halakhah* from a general perspective are scarce. William Loader discusses possible purity issues in various Markan traditions in the course of his voluminous study about Jesus and the law, but concludes that Mark shows no interest in and no concern for the various purity issues raised by the narrative.[88] A recent study with a section on impurity, which does start out with its sources and discusses Jesus' contacts with unclean people before turning to food laws, is Tom Holmén's dissertation about Jesus and the Covenant.[89] Holmén suggests that behind the lack of interest in purity matters, found in part of the tradition, we can detect a disinterest on the part of Jesus. Holmén refers to the fact that Jesus frequently came into contact with unclean people, while there is no evidence that he engaged in purification rites.[90] Holmén's assertion that unclean people included sinners, Gentiles, diseased and possessed, is not supported by evidence, however. And to claim that "[w]e do not need to bother with the numerous, different understandings of the issue,"[91] nor do we need to

[83] In this respect Booth's reconstruction turns out to be too speculative. For further discussion about Booth's interpretations, see Chapter III.
[84] Cf. Booth 1986, 205–210.
[85] Svartvik 2000, 370ff.
[86] Svartvik 2000, 375–402.
[87] Cf. the vast production of Jacob Neusner, e.g. Neusner 1973a, 1974–1977, 1994; David P. Wright 1987; Milgrom 1991; Harrington 1993; Maccoby 1999.
[88] Loader 1997, 20–26, 59–65.
[89] Holmén 2001, 221–251.
[90] Holmén 2001, 233–236, 250f.
[91] Holmén 2001, 250.

find out what type of interpretations were dominating, is not satisfactory even for Holmén's purpose of establishing path markers for covenant loyalty, and much less so in an attempt to study Jesus' attitude to ritual impurity.

One of the few pictures of Jesus in which purity is an important factor is the reconstruction by Bruce Chilton. According to Chilton, purity was of systemic importance for Second Temple Judaism.[92] Jesus possessed a dynamic type of purity, capable of resisting various forms of uncleanness.[93] Although he sees Jesus as a religious reformer who can be understood only from the viewpoint of the Jewish system of purity, Chilton is not primarily interested in different sources of impurity and contemporary purity *halakhah*. He thinks that Jesus had a particular theory of purity and advocated an eschatological purity programme, with the social meal as a focus. Jesus took up the authority assigned to priests and pronounced people pure, but he based purity on forgiveness, and demonstrated it through table fellowship. This purity made people entitled to participate in the sacrificial cult. In this Jesus opposed common views on how purity was achieved and on forgiveness as a *result* of sacrifice.[94] Chilton clearly wants to interpret Jesus within a Jewish context in which purity and sacrifice are placed in focus. He objects to distortions of Jesus' position which claim that he would have been concerned only with moral matters as opposed to cultic, or that which is within as opposed to that which is outside a person.[95] He sees his task as "to rescue the West from a Jesus whose avowed purpose is to ridicule Judaism."[96] The problem of Chilton's picture, however, is his highly speculative exegesis and detailed reconstructions. This is especially evident when Chilton explains the ultimate goal of Jesus' programme: people are made pure through his prounouncements and through table fellowship, which entitles them to sacrifice; the sacrifices should, however, be their own possessions and not exchanged for money.[97] Finally, when this "*halakhah*" of Jesus was not accepted, he allowed the meal not only to establish the purity required for sacrifice, but to become itself a substitute for sacrifice.[98] Chilton's reconstruction is thus highly original, excessively speculative and difficult to accept on several points. The emphasis on purity as important for interpreting Jesus within his context is reasonable and the suggestion about a dynamic type of purity is inter-

---

[92] Chilton 1994, 13ff. Chilton criticizes Sanders for minimizing the significance of purity and for ignoring the link between purity and temple (Chilton and Evans 1997, 224, 230).
[93] Chilton 1999, 234.
[94] Chilton 1994, 34; 1992, 121–136, 147, 150.
[95] Chilton 1994, 35f.
[96] Chilton and Evans 1997, 317.
[97] "To eat forgivingly and to offer of one's own in the Temple was to anticipate the ultimate banquet with the patriarchs within the kingdom of God" (Chilton 1992, 150).
[98] Chilton actually thinks that the reason Jesus was arrested and executed was that he provoked the religious authorities by practising this substitution meal inside Jerusalem (Chilton 1992, 137–154; 1994, 63–74).

esting, and is found in a few other exegetes too.[99] It must be corroborated by other evidence, however, to gain wider credibility.[100]

From the survey above we can see that there is a need for a study on Jesus' attitude to ritual impurity, i.e. impurity as a bodily state and a contact-contagion, which takes into account both narrative and sayings material, and does not use the conflict story in Mk 7 as its main source or point of origin. Such a study would actually be excpected from John P. Meier's fourth volume of *A Marginal Jew*, which is supposed to deal at length with Jesus' attitude to matters of law. Meier's careful method[101] and his virtually monographic treatment of miracles and John the Baptizer within the scope of his second volume,[102] give reason to hope for an exhaustive discussion of Jesus and purity as well. Meier's fourth volume still belongs to the future, however, at the time of this study.

II.2 Continuity and authentic traditions

In the brief survey above, we have seen a "Jewish trend" in Jesus research, although not uniform. Looking at Jesus within his Jewish context is necessary for a fair reconstruction of how he related to concepts of impurity, but does not answer questions of the extent to which his own views were continuous or discontinuous with a particular variety of contemporary Judaism. What methods are to be used in ascertaining Jesus' attitudes, and what results are we to expect? The first part of this question will be dealt with by turning to a discussion of the classical New Quest criteria and the role of redaction criticism. The second part will be addressed with a discussion of historical constraints and reasonable expectations.

More than a problem of criteria

I have already mentioned above the three most important "criteria of authenticity," which came to be used in redaction criticism. These were, following Norman Perrin's vocabulary, the criterion of dissimilarity, the criterion of multiple attestation and the criterion of coherence.[103] A number of other debatable criteria have also been used, for example criteria of Palestinian environment, vivid-

[99] Cf. the view of Berger 1988, 239–246; Holmberg 2001, 71f.

[100] Cf. below, Chapter VII.

[101] Meier uses traditional methods to separate reliable traditions from later redaction mainly with the help of "New Quest" criteria, but he discusses their use and value at length in vol. 1 (Meier 1991); and he also builds on sociological and anthropological insights of the third phase, which is hinted at in the very title: *A Marginal Jew*. Cf. the discussion about criteria and redaction below.

[102] Meier 1994.

[103] Perrin 1969, 71.

ness of speech, or Aramaic influences. Today there is a change taking place in the use of and value ascribed to the different criteria which are inherited from the New Quest.

In their recent discussion, Theissen and Winter sort out the criteria used by different scholars and found in different lists, by assigning them to one of three categories: *Quellenwertargumente, Besonderheitsindizien* and *Echtheitskriterien.* Only in the last category do we find genuine criteria of authenticity. The other two categories are used to support criteria of authenticity from both sides. *Quellenwertargumente* are used to sort out traditions and texts in which we can expect to find genuine traditions from Jesus. This category includes arguments about age, Palestinian character, or the independence of at least two traditions (i.e. the criterion of multiple attestation). Such arguments can only be used negatively, to deny authenticity, but never by themselves establish it. *Besonderheitsindizien* are logically dependent on the criterion of dissimilarity, and denote special or strange traits in the Jesus traditions, such as the use of *Amen*, the form of the antitheses, or the "son of man" expression. These arguments do not by themselves establish authenticity, but they presuppose that proper criteria of authenticity have been applied.[104]

In a narrow sense, the criteria of authenticity are seen, then, as only two: the criterion of dissimilarity and the criterion of coherence. The criterion of dissimilarity says in brief that only sayings not paralleled in contemporary Judaism or reflected in (i.e. suspected of having been created by) the early church, are to be considered as originating with Jesus. This criterion is thus seen to have two edges: one towards Judaism and the other towards the church. The criterion of coherence can, in the words of John Meier,

> be brought to play only after a certain amount of historical material has been isolated by previous criteria. The criterion of coherence holds that other sayings and deeds of Jesus that fit in well with the preliminary "data base" established ... have a good chance of being historical.[105]

Hence this criterion is dependent on the criterion of dissimilarity, which has thus become the most important, but also the most questioned of the two. It can be criticized for a number of reasons. Perhaps the most devastating criticism has to do with the way in which the criterion of dissimilarity demands an historical reconstruction in which Jesus is separated from his Jewish context,[106] at the same time as his influence on the early church is minimized. The criterion of dissimilarity necessitates a discussion on continuity versus discontinuity between Jesus and his context.

---

[104] Theissen and Winter 1997, 8–19.

[105] Meier 1991, 176.

[106] Cf. B. Meyer 1979, 86; Holmén 1999, 51ff.

Other criticisms can be outlined briefly.[107] One concerns the vagueness in the concept of dissimilarity. It can be applied more or less strictly, and even its most eager adherents confess that it must be used with discrimination.[108] Another has to do with our incomplete knowledge of Judaism, which means that what is today deemed original with Jesus, could tomorrow become known as part of first-century Jewish culture or religion.[109] A third objection is that we have very little knowledge about the interests of the church between 70 and 100 CE.[110] A fourth points out the impossibility for an historical individual to ascertain uniqueness in comparison with her/his followers.[111] A fifth point of critique questions the conclusions drawn from an established dissimilarity, in which peripheral or accidental details may be mistaken for important characteristics of the historical Jesus. We may thus end up with a caricature.[112]

The problems of the New Quest's most important criterion have been dealt with differently among scholars, during the third phase. John P. Meier supplements the three traditional criteria with two others: the criterion of embarrassment and the criterion of rejection and execution. Concerning the latter, he admits its difference in character to the other four, but stresses that there were reasons for Jesus being executed, which must be accounted for in an historical reconstruction. The criterion of rejection and execution could be seen as a particular development of the criterion of dissimilarity, in view of many recent attempts to depict Jesus as fully in accord with common Judaism.[113] The criterion of embarrassment, however, is Meier's first and perhaps most important one.[114] It can be seen as a development of the criterion of dissimilarity, this time with regard to the early church.[115] It centres on those details in the gospels which for various reasons could have caused embarrassment in the early church, but were retained in the tradition. In addition to these five primary criteria, Meier mentions others, which he, however, regards as secondary or dubious.[116]

Words are not enough

---

[107] For summaries, see Meier 1991, 171–174; Theissen and Winter 1997, 139, 157f.

[108] To blame the problems experienced with this criterion on misuse only, as does Jürgen Becker, is ill-advised. "The criticism that this criterion has attracted, when examined by the light of the day, speaks only to its misuse as the only criterion rather than to its use to secure a beginning nucleus of material." 1998 [1996], 14.

[109] Meier 1991, 172f; Hooker 1972, 575.

[110] Sanders 1985, 16.

[111] Meier 1991, 174.

[112] Meier 1991, 172.

[113] Meier 1991, 177.

[114] For this criterion Meier refers to Schillebeeckx and B. Meyer (Meier 1991, 168–171).

[115] Cf. Holmén 1999, 60, 75. It would be a mistake, however, to regard Meier's criterion of embarrassment as identical with, or including all instances of dissimilarity with Christianity.

[116] Meier 1991, 178–184.

Much of the work of both the New Quest and the third phase has aimed at retrieving the genuine *words* of Jesus. Whether a traditional form and redaction critical study, a "red-letter edition" of the Jesus Seminar,[117] the earliest Q-version or a collection of materials belonging to the "earliest stratum," it is all a matter of words. Although committed to the quest of the historical Jesus, many scholars have become more and more sceptical of this enterprise.

Discussing methodology, John Riches points out that even Bultmann did not go by rigid criteria when judging the authenticity of particular sayings. Although no single word of Jesus can be proved authentic, "one may point to a whole series of words found in the oldest stratum of tradition which do give us a consistent representation of the historical message of Jesus."[118] Hence:

> To talk thus of looking for a group of sayings, is, I think, a useful corrective to speaking of two separate 'criteria', viz. of dissimilarity and coherence, for judging the authenticity of any given saying. It is not simply a matter of finding individual sayings which are beyond doubt authentic and moving out from these to those which are closest to them. What one is looking for is a *group* of sayings sufficiently distinctive that, although one cannot be sure of the authenticity of any one of them, one can say with some confidence that, taken as a group they present characteristic features of Jesus' teaching.[119]

Referring to the form critics, Riches specifies this body of sayings as containing the three categories of prophetic-apocalyptic, legal-ethical and wisdom material. His conclusions, however, are that even if we are confident about a certain group of sayings which could be attributed to Jesus, we still "need to look at the reliability of the narrative material in more detail."[120]

This seems to express one trend in third phase historical Jesus research. The problems of retrieving the words of Jesus are not seen to be problems of criteria only; and the problems of reconstructing a picture of the historical Jesus are not seen to be only a matter of authenticity of sayings. Many scholars consider a reconstruction of Jesus' words as too shaky a ground for reconstructing an historical figure of Jesus. They would rather begin with those "facts" about Jesus' life on which there is general agreement,[121] and then move on cautiously with an historical investigation characterized by careful reasoning and plausible argumentation.

Ed Sanders represents such a position. He does not believe in building upon certain genuine words of Jesus, since there is no real consensus about which

---

[117] The results of this original task of the Seminar is found in Funk 1993. Subsequently, the Jesus Seminar has turned to Jesus' actions as well, as accounted for in Funk 1998.

[118] Rudolph Bultmann, "The Study of the Synoptic Gospels" in R. Bultmann and K. Kundsin, *Form Criticism: Two Essays on New Testament Research* (New York: Harper, 1934), 61, quoted in Riches 1980, 49.

[119] Riches 1980, 53.

[120] Riches 1980, 55, 60.

[121] Cf. Riches' list of "what appear to be the main points of agreement and disagreement," in 1993, 121.

they are and what Jesus meant by them. One must rather "construct hypotheses which, on the one hand, do rest on material generally considered reliable without, on the other hand, being totally dependent on the authenticity of any given pericope."[122] The most secure evidence on which people can agree more easily consists of *facts* about Jesus, rather than individual logia. In arguing this, Sanders is leaning on Ernst Fuchs, who suggested a similar way of procedure in the 1950s, beginning with a framework built primarily on narrative traditions, and supplementing it secondarily with sayings traditions.[123]

While not giving priority to one over the other, Meier's methodology is in some aspects similar to that of Sanders. Although Meier usually discusses sayings material and narrative traditions separately,[124] he consciously emphasizes both sayings and deeds as objects for applying the various criteria,[125] which results in an overall picture based on both types of material equally. I think there is a point to relating narrative traditions and logia more closely, so that the constant interplay in which the interpretation of one is informed by the other, is made clear.

The shift in attitude and method which is taking place is not always consciously stated. This is noted and systematized by Theissen and Winter. In discussing problems with the concept of authenticity, they point out the difference between an authentic thing and an authentic word. Since words of Jesus always belong to contexts which influence their meaning, we are not really looking for the letters but for the sense of a word.[126] We cannot deal with Jesus' words in isolation from possible contexts, from other words or from some sort of picture of his person.[127] The same is true of the acts of Jesus. The historicity of a certain act is judged differently depending on how that act is interpreted, i.e. what sense is given to it; and interpretation is dependent on the interpreter's total picture.[128] Thus it is more fruitful to discuss the authenticity of a *Gesamtbild* than of separate words and deeds.

---

[122] Sanders 1985, 3. A similar position is taken by e.g. René Kieffer (1991, 216–217). Several American scholars working on the historical Jesus, while still reconstructing bodies of genuine sayings, do in effect work from similar presuppositions.

[123] Sanders 1985, 5. Cf. Fuchs 1956. 220ff. Note, however, Meier's criticism of Sanders for not following his own programme. "Sander's presentation has weight only because he meshes the deeds and sayings of Jesus..." (Meier 1994, 474, n.97).

[124] As in vol. 2 (1994) when sayings about exorcisms are discussed in Chapter 16, while narrative traditions about exorcisms are dealt with in Chapter 20.

[125] Meier 1991, 187, n.8; 1994, 5f.

[126] Cf. the discussion about words and meaning in Riches 1980, 29–43.

[127] Theissen and Winter 1997, 194–198. Of course, the basic fact that Jesus probably spoke in Aramaic must be mentioned. There can never be a question of retrieving the *ipsissima verba*, Aramaic words spoken in a Palestinian context, when what we have are Greek words fitted into a later early church context. Cf. Perrot 1979, 48.

[128] Theissen and Winter 1997, 198–201.

> Forschungslogisch stehen bei der Rekonstruktion eines historischen Jesusbildes keineswegs Authentizitätsurteile über einzelne Traditionen am Anfang, aus denen wir dann induktiv ein Gesamtbild zusammensetzen. Vielmehr sind Urteile über Einzeltraditionen von einem Gesamtbild von Jesu abhängig, mag dies auch noch so vage und offen sein.[129]

In the end, then, we can actually be more certain of general statements about Jesus' work and teaching than of many single words or acts.[130] This insight is applied in the present study. I am not building a case for Jesus' view on impurity by relying on the alleged authenticity of particular logia. I do give weight to individual traditions, but interpreted within a total picture. What this means in practice will become clearer in subsequent chapters.

Tradition is redaction too

Whether words or deeds are discussed, the results of a reconstruction of the historical Jesus are often dependent on advanced exercises of separating "original" material from various layers of additions and redaction which communities, later transmitters or final redactors have added. This is often a necessary road, but has its pitfalls. Several exegetes have attempted to identify pre-Markan units, suggesting a plausible *Sitz im Leben*,[131] and the method is used for studying Jesus' relationship to the *Torah* and his attitude to impurity from the perspective of Mk 7 in a number of studies.[132] The very terms "tradition" and "redaction" are ambiguous, however. When working with Matthean or Lukan materials from the stance of the two-source theory, the distinction seems fairly simple, at least at first sight. Tradition denotes what Matthew or Luke took over from Mark or Q. Redaction is their respective adjustments, bridges and additions.

Any student of redaction criticism knows that the method is more complicated, not least where Markan material is concerned. In the case of Mark particularly, there is no safe way of judging what is original and what is added. In addition, it is reasonable to suppose that the material has gone through various stages of redaction, and the chain of transmission is at best conjectural. John Donahue discusses various aspects and limitations of redaction criticism, pointing out that

---

[129] Theissen and Winter 1997, 205.

[130] Theissen and Winter 1997, 204–205. Such an approach is found already with an early participant in the third phase of the quest, Charles Perrot, who refuses to build upon the alleged authenticity of single events, but looks for discrepancy and discontinuity as signs of early Christian *anamnèse*, which could provide something of a total picture (Perrot 1979, 59, 61–64).

[131] Cf. Kuhn 1971. For a fairly balanced and convincing redaction critical discussion, which nevertheless gives evidence for the diverse results and arbitrary nature of delimitations and evaluations, see Dunn 1990.

[132] Cf. Hübner 1986 [1973]; Lambrecht 1977; Sariola 1990. Cf. the detailed redaction critical study by Kertelge (1970) on Jesus' miracles in the gospel of Mark, also relevant to the subject matter of the present study.

> traditions rarely exist in the form postulated by Markan editorial critics, nor does 'editing' involve the kind of activities often postulated for Markan editing. The Gospel of Mark presents a paradox. Most of it is 'tradition', that is, it was put together by Mark out of pre-existing materials; all of it is composition, that is, Mark retold every story and probably recast every incident in terms of his theological and rhetorical purpose. Though it may be possible to determine in general the shape or thrust of a tradition used by Mark, for example, in the case of parables, the miracle stories, or the passion narrative, the attempt to determine his purpose from a study of minute and hypothetical alterations of a reconstructed tradition has resulted in so many contradictory statements that it is obviously flawed.[133]

Donahue's reasoning shows that the separation of tradition from redaction is strained and that in a case such as Mark, the task is hazardous, whether the primary goal is to identify original traditions or to determine the purpose of the redactor. The two tasks are constantly interdependent.

Kari Syreeni suggests that tradition and redaction must be understood as different ways of approaching the text, belonging to different methods.[134] The common separation of the two misses the point. This does not mean that the two concepts and their respective viewpoints cannot be used, but that a separation can be upheld as an ideal only at the cost of confusion.[135] In reality, a particular tradition is seen as a redaction of some earlier material, and the result of a redactional process at one level may function as tradition at another. The distinction depends on the perspective chosen. With this in mind, I suggest that redaction-critical techniques may be used, to a moderate extent, not for isolating "genuine" source material on which to build a case, but for identifying obvious intent and strong bias in a particular text in order to find remains from earlier levels. Redaction criticism is one possible tool for distinguishing that which more reasonably or plausibly reflects Jesus' attitude from that which does so less reasonably. I will thus use the terms tradition and redaction, but not as absolutes. Early materials are interpretative too.

Constraints and plausibility

From the previous discussion of criteria and redaction, we realize the importance of finding a balance between the ideas of continuity and discontinuity when evaluating Jesus' relationship to his historical context.

It is unreasonable to expect a person with strong convictions to separate him or herself totally from the social, cultural and religious context. Nor is it reasonable to expect such a person to fully conform to all rules and patterns of behaviour that govern the environment. Even a "reformer" deviating greatly from tradition will usually stay within certain limits; otherwise communication be-

---

[133] Donahue 1994, 40.

[134] I.e. tradition belongs to traditio-historical explanation, while redaction is a term for detailed redaction-critical study (Syreeni 1987, 10).

[135] Syreeni 1987, 10f.

comes impossible. The question is to what extent such a person will deviate or conform. This depends to a large degree on the options available.

In 1980, Anthony Harvey developed the idea that the actions open to an individual are dependent on contemporary role expectations. These constraints of history can be stretched to some extent by certain individuals, but not totally transgressed without loss of communication. In his research for the historical Jesus, Harvey investigates six such constraints: politics (crucifixion), the law, the concept of time and end, the miracle-maker, messianic expectations and monotheism.[136]

Discussing constraints is one fruitful attempt to deal with the question of continuity versus discontinuity. In dealing with the relationship between Jesus and Judaism and the early church respectively, it is not uncommon to emphasize continuity with one at the cost of the other. There is reason, however, to expect both contact and contrast between Jesus and Judaism, as well as between Jesus and the early church. The contrast was enough to cause conflict, but the contact was enough to ensure communication.

Exploring the social and cultural constraints of a given time or situation may help to determine what is possible, probable or reasonable.[137] In their discussion of criteria, Theissen and Winter suggest a *criterion of historical plausibility* as a corrective to the criterion of dissimilarity. *Das historische Plausibilitätskriterium* is in effect a comprehensive formula, including several traditional criteria used in historical Jesus research, the criteria of dissimilarity and coherence being foremost. At the same time it takes seriously the need to distinguish between and thoroughly deal with questions of continuity and discontinuity between Jesus and his Jewish context on one hand, and the evolving church on the other.[138] Theissen and Winter divide their criteria in two: a criterion of *Kontextplausibilität* and a criterion of *Wirkungsplausibilität*.

Kontextplausibilität deals with Jesus' relationship to his Jewish environment. It has two aspects: *Kontextentsprechung* and *Kontextuelle Individualität*. *Kontextentsprechung* requires that what Jesus wished and said must have been compatible with Judaism in Galilee during the first half of the first century. The

---

[136] Harvey 1982.

[137] However, as Riches points out in the context of Jesus' attitude to the Law, "what is possible by way of innovation within a given cultural matrix ... requires more than commonsense to answer." Relating Jesus to such a complex matrix as that of Judaism and Christianity during the first centuries can hardly be done, according to Riches, "without some understanding of the nature of religious change in general and of the details of this process of change in particular" (Riches 1993, 123–124). An answer must "be consistent with what we can learn about religious change and innovation from other times and places: attention to the work of religious historians, anthropologists and sociologists of religion will be of considerable assistance. It must also fit into a broader hypothesis about the development of Christianity and rabbinic Judaism in the first and second centuries" (123).

[138] Theissen and Winter 1997, 215–217.

requirements of *Kontextuelle Individualität* demand that what Jesus wished and did must be recognizable as an individual phenomenon within the frames of contemporary Judaism.

Wirkungsplausibilität deals with Jesus' effects on early Christianity. It has two aspects as well: *Tendenzwidrigkeit* and *Quellenkohärenz*. *Tendenzwidrigkeit* means that information within the Jesus tradition, which differs from the interest of early Christian sources, but is still retained in tradition, can be regarded as historically plausible in proportion to how much it differs.[139] *Quellenkohärenz* means that the coherence of single elements from independent and diverging traditions, different strata and different *Gattungen* within the Jesus tradition, create historical plausibility.[140]

The result of Theissen and Winter's scheme is that a reconstruction of the historical Jesus must at the same time provide room for an individual personality within the contemporary Jewish context, and be compatible with the ensuing Christian *Wirkungsgeschichte*.

> Wir sehen in dieser Formulierung eines Kriteriums historischer Gesamtplausibilität kein zusätzliches (drittes) Kriterum neben Wirkungs- und Kontextplausibilität, sondern eine in allen Kriterien, Quellenwertargumenten und Besonderheitsindizien wirksame regulative Idee.[141]

Theissen and Winter's criterion of historical plausibility is an all-inclusive and perhaps somewhat cumbersome structure. It is, however, in part construed from observations of how historical Jesus research has actually been done during the latest phase of the quest. It is thus a summary, but also a correction of past practices, and a programme for how the authors think the quest should be properly handled. For these reasons, and in comparison with the traditional criteria, the criterion of historical plausibility should perhaps be regarded not as a criterion proper, but rather as a programme for future research. It is perhaps somewhat biased: in the way it is formulated, it does not give much room for Jesus deviating from his Jewish context. If the emphasis on Christian *Wirkungsgeschichte* is brought forward as a counter-argument, one could ask whether Theissen and Winter's all-inclusive criterion is aimed at harmonizing evidence a bit, at the cost of losing sight of diversity and conflict. This might be an unintended side-effect of trying to bring everything under one roof. In spite of this, there is reason to take Theissen and Winter's suggestions seriously. Historical Jesus research in the future will have to take their criterion of historical plausibility into account.

I agree with Theissen and Winter about the need to balance continuity and discontinuity. I am suspicious when the discontinuity between Jesus and either Judaism or the church is too heavily emphasized. I am likewise suspicious

---

[139] Cf. Meier's criterion of embarrassment (1991, 168–171).

[140] Theissen and Winter 1997, 216.

[141] Theissen and Winter 1997, 217.

when continuity is emphasized to such a degree that hardly any room is left for differences or conflicts. I am suspicious when the potential of the individual to deviate from the norm is minimized, so that Jesus is portrayed as having almost no substantial conflicts with contemporary Judaism. In the present study I am arguing for an attitude of Jesus towards impurity which is firmly rooted in his Jewish context, but at the same time deviates from certain norms, enough to cause conflict. Without exaggerating the discontinuous element, one could profitably argue that the most *interesting* questions in the quest for the historical Jesus do not concern the similarities and points of agreement between Jesus and his social, cultural and religious context, but rather the differences and areas of contention. *Where* did he differ, *how* did he differ and, if possible, *why* did he differ from his environment? Such questions can be asked without the risk of distortion, only when Jesus' basic continuity with Judaism is given due place. From such a stance, the subject matter of this study, *Jesus and purity halakhah*, becomes highly significant. Before turning to the subject matter in detail, however, it is necessary to discuss the possibilities of historical reconstruction in general.

II.3 The limits of historical reconstruction

History is more than facts

When Leopold von Ranke in 1824, protesting against moralizing history, called historians to the task of showing "how it really was," he could not anticipate what effect this "not very profound aphorism"[142] would have. This call became the creed of positivist historians up to our time, and has had much influence on historical exegesis in the theological field. The development of hermeneutics since Schleiermacher and Dilthey should have warned historians that things were not that easy, and some did heed that warning. In 1910, Carl Becker discussed the relationship of fact to theory, and in the 1930s and 1940s historians questioned Ranke and advocated a relativistic position.[143] It was not until the 1960s and onwards, however, with the rise of tendencies which subsequently came to be labelled postmodernism, that the old paradigm was seriously challenged.[144]

---

[142] Carr 1961, 3. The oft-quoted phrase "wie es eigentlich gewesen," was coined by Ranke in the preface to the first edition of his *Geschichten der romanischen und germanischen Völker* (Ranke 1874 [1824], vii). For a discussion of Ranke and the "cult" which evolved around him, especially in America, see Iggers 1962.

[143] C. Becker 1910. Together with Becker, Raymond Martin mentions Crane Brinton in 1939. Martin 1995, 325–326.

[144] Appleby, Hunt and Jacob 1994, 198–237.

In an historical *Gesamtbild* of Jesus, the total picture is informed by single traditions, but those traditions are at the same time interpreted in light of the present total picture. Such an hermeneutical circle highlights the element of interpretation, in which the interpreter's role becomes clear. The interpreter's pre-understanding influences interpretation of "facts," but it is also informed by, and continuously developed, or sometimes altered by, those facts.[145]

The traditional distinction between facts and interpretation thus becomes inadequate. History is more than a pile of objective facts. Interpretation enters into the very choice of facts; which details or observations are to be seen as relevant for the quest? The historian must evaluate in order to know what to record.[146] In his classical book *What is History?*, Edward Carr claimed that history becomes a "continuous process of interaction between the historian and his facts, an unending dialogue between the present and the past."[147]

If historical reconstruction is more of a discussion than a recording of what actually happened, what claims could then be made for accuracy or objectivity? Carr's conclusion is that since social sciences, including history, cannot work with an epistemology which totally separates subject from object, objectivity in history "cannot be an objectivity of fact, but only of relation, of the relation between fact and interpretation, between past, present and future." The concept of absolute truth is no longer relevant.[148]

This is in essence the way in which Appleby, Hunt and Jacob, in their much-cited book *Telling the Truth about History,* describe their own theory of historical objectivity, in their attempts to find a middle way between traditional positivist and post-modern relativist history. They "have redefined historical objectivity as an interactive relationship between an inquiring subject and an external object."[149] Their "ally in the campaign against relativism" is what they, referring to the philosopher Hilary Putnam, call "practical realism."[150] This is

[145] Jeanrond 1991, 5–6, 139–140.

[146] Carr 1961, 3, 15. Carr also refers to Carl Becker's dictum (1910, 528), that "the facts of history do not exist for any historian till he creates them," although he does not himself seem to endorse such a radical standpoint. Carr's own picturesque and metaphorical description merits citation: "When you read a work of history, always listen out for the buzzing. If you can detect none, either you are tone deaf or your historian is a dull dog. The facts are really not at all like fish on the fishmonger's slab. They are like fish swimming about in a vast and sometimes inaccessible ocean; and what the historian catches will depend, partly on chance, but mainly on what part of the ocean he chooses to fish in and what tackle he chooses to use—these two factors being, of course, determined by the kind of fish he wants to catch. By and large, the historian will get the kind of facts he wants. History means interpretation." (1961, 18).

[147] Carr 1961, 24.

[148] Carr 1961, 114.

[149] Appleby, Hunt and Jacob 1994, 259.

[150] Appleby, Hunt and Jacob 1994, 247–251. Practical realism understands that the meanings of words do not "lock on to objects of the external world and fix reality for all time," but is wrought out in response to things outside, and develops "through an interaction with the objective world" (247). There is an element of circularity here, which belongs to the conditions of

in fact a "common-sense" epistemological view, which "endorses knowability experienced by human agents able to use language."[151]

A somewhat different approach is taken by Mark Bevir.[152] While the idea of a given past is untenable, because we do not have pure experiences,[153] objectivity does not even in natural sciences refer to giving conclusive answers, but to presenting the best available theories.[154] "This suggests that objectivity rests not on conclusive tests against a given past, but on a process of comparison between rival theories." Objectivity thus becomes a matter of criticizing and comparing what Bevir calls "rival webs of interpretations in terms of agreed facts," i.e. pieces of evidence accepted by most people.[155] In the context of historical Jesus research, this brings to mind Sanders' programme: to base reconstruction on "almost indisputable facts," and to "construct hypotheses which, on the one hand, do rest on material generally considered reliable without, on the other hand, being totally dependent on the authenticity of any given pericope."[156] Bevir admits the circularity of such a process, since interpretations determine the nature of what they explain, but he claims that since critics can always confront a theory with other facts, "criticism gives facts a relative autonomy which prevents the process of comparing interpretations in terms of facts from being purely circular."[157] Objectivity is thus seen as a product of intellectual honesty in dealing with criticism.

In dealing with scepticism, Bevir agrees that because our perceptions are not foolproof, any *individual* interpretation may be false, and we cannot verify or falsify any particular fact. However, because of the nature of our being in the world, we learn that our perceptions are *generally* reliable, and we have reason to regard as true those facts which we usually agree upon. Concludes Bevir:

> Our interaction with our environment secures the broad content of our perception, not particular instances of our perception. This is why we can accept criteria for comparing rival webs of interpretations, but not a logic of either vindication or refutation for evaluating individual interpretations.[158]

---

human knowledge and communication. The historian will have to accept these terms, not giving up reconstruction aiming at accuracy, while being aware of its tentativeness.

[151] Appleby, Hunt and Jacob 1994, 251. Cf. Raymond Martin's comment in his review of *Telling the Truth about History,* that most sceptics or relativists do not in actual fact act as if they fully believed in scepticism (Martin 1995, 325–327).

[152] Bevir 1994, 328–344.

[153] "The nature of a perception depends on the perceiver." Thus empiricism is false, and "objectivity cannot rely on a logic of vindication or refutation." Bevir 1994, 330, 331.

[154] Cf. the view of McCullagh 1998, 129–133, 307–309.

[155] Bevir 1994, 332, 333.

[156] Sanders 1985, 11, 3. Cf. Perrot 1979, 59, 71.

[157] Bevir 1994, 335.

[158] Bevir 1994, 341.

Bevir's argument is in a sense an interesting parallel to the comments by Theissen and Winter, reflecting the actual state of research in the quest for the historical Jesus, "dass wir bei den allgemeineren Aussagen über Wirken und Lehre Jesu sicherer sind als bei vielen Einzelurteilen."[159] The problems and possibilities in the quest for Jesus are the same as in any historical research.

Causation, intention, and "thick description"

Bound up with interpretation is the problem of causality.[160] What do we think that we are explaining when attempting historical reconstruction? Are we describing a causal chain or just overstating an observable correlation of events?

When dealing with Jesus' relationship to the early church, the question of causation is often relevant. To what extent did Jesus' words and actions determine subsequent development in the Christian movement? To what extent did that development take place independently of the historical Jesus? Interpretations differ, but few would deny at least some causal arguments.

When dealing with Jesus' relationship to his Jewish context, however, causation might not always be the best model. While scholars applying sociological methods might describe Jesus' behaviour as being "caused" by different social, political or economical factors, cultural anthropologists would rather give "thick descriptions." This expression, which was used by the anthropologist Clifford Geertz, and became popular among historians in the 1970s and 1980s, refers to the trend not of attempting to explain different phenomena *out of*, but of understanding them *within* a particular cultural context.[161] Says Geertz:

> culture is not a power, something to which social event, behaviours, institutions, or processes can be causally attributed; it is a context, something within which they can be intelligibly—that is, thickly—described."[162]

While they concede that such an approach does not necessarily rule out an interest in social or economic explanations, Appleby, Hunt and Jacob warn that culture as a category may run the

> risk of encompassing everything and thus, in a sense, explaining nothing; what can it mean to say that everything is due to culture? Should historians concentrate on offering thick descriptions and forget about causal analysis?[163]

A problem in this discussion might be deficient definitions. Causation is usually taken to refer to a chain of events, in which every link is dependent on the previous one. Such a view is usually based on experience from natural science.

---

[159] Theissen and Winter 1997, 204–205.
[160] Carr 1961, 101.
[161] Appleby, Hunt and Jacob 1994, 217–223. "When swimming in culture, neither causes nor effects could be distinguished." (223).
[162] Geertz 1973, 14.
[163] Appleby, Hunt and Jacob 1994, 223.

But this is not the only way to define causation. While some deny that social sciences and history can yield causal knowledge proper, and others claim that a concept of causality in history and social sciences must be very different from that in natural science, still others find dual accounts of causality implausible.[164] Many acknowledge, however, that historical explanations rest on different kind of generalizations than those law-like ones of natural science. Alasdair Macintyre points out that "[w]e never in citing a cause simply seek to explain why a particular revolution or famine or war happened; we seek to explain why that revolution or that famine or that war happened rather than something else."[165] And he gives a possible definition:

> A cause is what makes *any* outcome different from what it would otherwise have been. Such an outcome is always the product of the conjunction of the causal agencies already at work and some intervening cause or causes.[166]

When studying the historical Jesus, we see that thick descriptions have become common during the last phase of research. At the same time, questions about what caused certain courses of action in the life of Jesus, such as his mission, his exorcisms or his so-called "cleansing" of the temple, are often discussed. Such questions come close to questions of teleology—in the case of Jesus, questions of *why* he acted as he did, i.e. the old question from Reimarus and onwards about the aims and intentions of Jesus, which has been increasingly taken up during the third phase of Jesus research. While some still avoid dealing with it and others try to draw a line between a legitimate quest for Jesus' intentions and an illegitimate search for his self-understanding, it is nevertheless becoming a part of historical Jesus research once more.[167]

Historical interpretation, to Meyer, is the discovery of what historical agents actually intended.[168] Citing Collingwood, he claims that "for the historian there is no difference between discovering what happened and why it happened."[169] Intention is thus crucial for interpretation.

---

[164] Cf. Macintyre 1976, 137–158, 138–139.

[165] Macintyre 1976, 147. "To give a causal explanation we therefore need at least four related terms: there is first of all that which intervenes, secondly that state of affairs which is interfered with by the intervention, thirdly the actual effect of the intervention and fourthly the outcome that would have prevailed but for the intervention. Causality is a relationship between at least four items, not two." (147–148).

[166] Macintyre 1976, 150. Cf. the very similar statement of Ben Meyer, in 1979, 78: "The aim of finding out why this went forward and that did not, though a project of no little interest, is also one of considerable dimensions and difficulty. We call it 'historical explanation'."

[167] It is discussed by B. Meyer (1979) but avoided by Sanders (1985). Cf. Holmberg 2001, 205f.

[168] B. Meyer distinguishes between historical interpretation, which answers questions of what an historical agent intended, and historical explanation, which attempts to answer why a particular intention (act or event intended) was carried through or came to grief (B. Meyer 1979, 77–78).

[169] Collingwood 1946, 175f; B. Meyer 1979, 87. Referring to the work of a detective, or court practice, Meyer shows how the possible motives of a suspected murderer can give an interpreta-

A thorough discussion of intention and causation, which would take us back at least to Kant and Hegel[170] is neither possible, nor necessary within the scope of this study. Suffice it to mention G. H. von Wright's discussion about historical explanation as characterized by a combination of causal and teleological procedures. The event to be explained and the previous event(s) are often logically independent of each other, not connected by any general law, but through statements forming the premises of a practical inference.[171]

Hence the opposition of causation and thick description could be seen as exaggerated. It should be possible to reconstruct an historical figure of Jesus within Jewish contemporary culture, without claiming too much in terms of causes and effects, and yet regard such a reconstruction as part of an historical explanation.

Getting down to what?—authenticity, reality and *rétrodiction*

In historical Jesus research, historical reconstruction depends almost exclusively on literary texts. Much work since the beginning of the New Quest has aimed at "getting down," i.e. retrieving genuine sayings and reconstructing the most "authentic" traditions about Jesus' acts.

The concept of authenticity is problematic. Theissen and Winter point out that a notion of religious truth has been linked to the idea of authenticity since the Middle Ages. This easily leads to false expectations of historical Jesus research to produce "'glaubenskrisenfeste' Ergebnisse."[172] Together with the popular conception, still shared by some scholars, of "authentic" traditions being accounts of "what really happened," and containing the very words of Jesus, such expectations have seriously impaired the cause of historical Jesus research.

If the idea of authenticity has proved to be confusing, and if facts are not what we thought they were, but dependent as we have seen on the interpreter, what are we then trying to retrieve? We cannot expect to isolate either the very words or the very voice of Jesus, but as long as we are aware of the conditions for historical work, it is possible to reconstruct the history of Jesus in part. It is important, however, as Charles Perrot has pointed out, not to confuse history in its literary form, contained in a narrative text, and that which actually happened in the past.[173] With all the tools available, we can only come down to the earli-

---

tion of available evidence, and actually sometimes establish or confirm facts. "'[W]hy it happened' enters as a factor into the hypothesis of what happened." (88).

[170] Kant regarded causality and teleology as two kinds of explanation which could not be unified in a common principle. Hegel found the language of causality inadequate in history, since human actions usually are motivated by purposes. Historical actions can be explained or understood only when translated into the language of teleology. Cf. Riedel 1976, 11f., 14f.

[171] G. H. von Wright 1971, 96–103, 132–143; cf. Riedel 1976, 13ff.

[172] Theissen and Winter 1997, 195.

[173] Perrot 1979, 61.

est possible layer of tradition, the earliest interpretation, not to the event itself. Language will always remain between the event and the historian: "La rétrodiction historique ne restitue pas la vie."[174]

The concept of authenticity is ambiguous and must be used with discrimination. Whether we refer to literary or historical "authenticity," it is a matter of reconstruction, not re-creation. Historical Jesus research is never a matter of re-creating a bygone reality, but of tracing an early *rétrodiction*, to some degree based on early memories of Jesus, reflecting the symbolic world or the ideology of the tradition bearers.[175] With these conditions spelled out, historical reconstruction is possible, when carried out in a careful and discriminate way. It must, however, emanate from a *Gesamtbild* of Jesus, "ses gestes et ses comportements décisifs"[176] rather than from isolated sayings or traditions.

Summary: A case for the historical Jesus as conscious reconstruction

In this chapter I have attempted to trace the development of historical Jesus research and its methods, with a view to the task of the present study: to discuss Jesus' attitude to contemporary purity *halakhah*.

We have seen that traditional methods and historical reconstructions have their limits. In spite of this, I have argued that it is both reasonable and possible to conduct historical investigations about Jesus from Nazareth. Various criteria can be used, not for establishing a narrow database of "authentic" traditions, but to provide material for an ongoing dialogue between singular traditions and a *Gesamtbild* of Jesus. Redaction-critical tools can be employed, not for discovering the "original" saying or narrative, or finding out what "really happened," but for tracing early interpretations and memories.

Throughout this chapter we have come across the circular nature of all historical investigation. There is a constant interplay between the interpreter and the questions posed, between facts and interpretation, between why and what, between hypotheses and criticism. This should not be seen as a problem but as a necessary condition of historical research. What should be required of the scholar, however, is awareness of the range and complexity of the questions.

The historian's questions, says Meyer, are not those of the author but of the investigator. The unknown to be known is not the data of the text, but some-

---

174 Perrot 1979, 63.

175 Cf. Syreeni 1999, 37–40, about the symbolic world, the site of ideology, hiding itself partly in the text world.

176 Perrot 1979, 71.

thing behind the text which can be reached through a selection of data.[177] Meyer seems in part to be aiming at the distinction between using a text as a source or as remains.[178] In seeking to establish Jesus' attitude to purity in the present study, I do not primarily want to know what message Mark or a particular pre-Markan tradition tried to convey with a certain saying or miracle story, but I hope to discover something about the historical Jesus which may not be the primary message of the text. This is possible by posing questions of the texts (and other remains, such as archaeological findings), and since the texts do not usually provide straight answers, the interpreter must suggest them. The interpreter must, however, verify them too. If this is done with convincing arguments within the framework of a credible *Gesamtbild* of Jesus, the suggestions put forward should be considered. It is the aim of this study to make a conscious reconstruction of how Jesus related to concepts of impurity, and to argue the case plausibly.

---

[177] B. Meyer 1979, 90–91. I do not agree, however, with Meyer's claim that this does not apply to the exegete but marks a difference between exegetes and historians.
[178] Cf. Torstendahl 1971, 80–87.

PART TWO:

LAW, PURITY AND BODY

Chapter III
Jesus and the law: much debated conflict stories

III.1 Evaluating legal issues

Identifying Jesus' adversaries

In the previous chapter I discussed the recent trend of placing Jesus more firmly within Judaism. The pendulum has swung, so that Jesus is often pictured in basic agreement with his contemporary co-religionists on most questions. With this development, however, we run the risk of reducing conflicts between Jesus and some of his contemporaries to matters of minor disagreements only; unless all gospel traditions about such conflicts are no more than creations of the early church,[1] and Jesus' execution is to be seen merely as an unfortunate misunderstanding,[2] we must reckon with some substantial points of dissent between Jesus and his adversaries.

Who were these adversaries? In the Synoptic Gospels they are usually called Φαρισαῖοι[3] and/or γραμματεῖς,[4] and a couple of times in Matthew, Φαρισαῖοι καὶ Σαδδουκαῖοι.[5] Outside of Matthew, the Sadducees figure only once, by themselves, and in a Jerusalem setting.[6] Jesus' enemies in Jerusalem (also mentioned in the predictions about his coming suffering), are otherwise called οἱ ἀρχιερεῖς καὶ οἱ γραμματεῖς, sometimes also οἱ πρεσβύτεροι.[7] Since all synoptics are dependent on the Markan one-year frame, there is only one visit to Jerusalem, when Jesus is executed. This means that the Pharisees are pictured as Jesus' chief opponents during the main part of his activity. Although they

[1] Cf. Bultmann 1972 [1921], 39–54; Dibelius, 1961 [1919], 22–34.

[2] Vermes 1993, ix–x.

[3] Mk 2:23 par; 3:6 par; 7:1 par; 8:11, 15; 10:2 par; 12:13; 14:43. In the context of Jesus' arrest and death, the Pharisees figure only once in Mark and once in Matthew (Mk 14:43; Mt 27:62). Matthew and Luke denounce Pharisees (Mt 23; Lk 11), but Luke has in addition certain passages in which friendly Pharisees are mentioned (7:36; 11:37; 14:1).

[4] Mk 3:22; 7:1 par; 12:28, 38. The scribes are said to have come from Jerusalem, or appear in Jerusalem. Matthew does not mention scribes in the context of Jesus' death.

[5] Mt 3:7; 16:1, 6, 11, 12.

[6] Mk 12:18 par.

[7] Mk 8:31 par; 10:33 par; 11:27; 14:1 par; 14:53 par; 15:1 par; 15:31 par. In some of these cases οἱ πρεσβύτεροι are added to the high priests and scribes, sometimes the scribes are exchanged for the elders.

are often coupled with scribes,[8] the two must not be equated. A Pharisee was identified with a party, a religio-political faction; a scribe had a particular occupation. Scribes were at times Pharisees, but could be otherwise. This explains the expression γραμματεῖς τῶν Φαρισαίων in Mark.[9]

It is possible that the Pharisees were not at all Jesus' most *dangerous* adversaries. In the passion story they hardly figure at all.[10] It might have been people of the temple establishment, Sadducees and priests, who were his fiercest opponents. This is a reasonable supposition if we reckon with several visits to Jerusalem, i.e. a time frame other than Mark's. In that case, Jesus would not have been unknown in Jerusalem.[11] The Romans should not be forgotten, although they cannot be discussed at length here. It could well be that Jesus was perceived as more of a threat to the Romans than the gospels tend to admit. The Christian communities within which the Synoptic Gospels were formed would not, however, have had their main conflicts with the Jerusalem establishment, but with local Jewish leaders and teachers, at a time when Pharisaism, together with other pious strains of Judaism, were beginning to coalesce into the rabbinic movement. Nor did subsequent conflicts between the church and Rome concern the type of religious questions that became hotbeds in the relationship between Christians and Jews. Hence it was only natural for early Christians to identify the Pharisees as Jesus' main adversaries.[12]

The Pharisaic movement is generally seen as the dominant group in the Yavnean reconstruction of Judaism, and Hillelites are viewed as the group gradually gaining predominance at Yavneh, while Shammaites seem to have been more influential before 70 CE.[13] It is often taken for granted that the pre-70 sages mentioned in the *Mishnah* were Pharisees, belonging to the two schools of Hillel and Shammai. Such a view is found in Neusner, although he is aware that the two "Houses" are never mentioned in any other extant contemporary document.[14] A Pharisaic identity is nowhere explicitly stated in the texts, except for Gamaliel I and his son Simeon, who are designated Pharisees by the New Testament and by Josephus.[15] Even Hillel himself, as Günther Stemberger notes, is

---

[8] E.g. Mk 2:16 par; 7:1 par; especially in the woes, denouncing Pharisees (cf. n.3 above), in Mt 23. Luke has here and elsewhere νομικοί instead of scribes (Lk 7:30; 11:45, 46, 52; 14:3).
[9] Mk 2:16 par.
[10] Only in Mt 21:45 (parable of wicked tenants—Mk has simply "they"), Mt 27:62 (a legendary, polemical story, in which they, together with the high priests, ask Pilate for grave guards), and in Mk 14:43 (where they are co-organizers of the mob arresting Jesus). Cf. Meier 2001, 339.
[11] Cf. K. L. Schmidt 1919, 301ff; Meier 1991, 403–409.
[12] Cf. Saldarini 1988 or Stemberger 1995 [1991], for various groups and their relative influence.
[13] Neusner 1971, 3: 317ff.
[14] Neusner 1979, 93.
[15] Acts 5:34; Josephus, *Life*, 190–191. Josephus' reference to the Pharisees Samaias and Pollion in *Ant.* 15:2–4 could be interpreted as Shammai and Abtalion, but this is denied by Neusner (1971, 1: 159).

not mentioned anywhere before the *Mishnah*, nor is Johanan ben Zakkai.[16] The latter seems actually to be identified with the Sadducees, or at least to be distanced from the Pharisees in *mYad* 4:6.[17] Neusner later admits some of these problems, and actually hesitates to speak of the precursors of rabbinic Judaism as Pharisees.[18]

If the rabbinic literature does not expressly identify its early sages as Pharisees, it does use the term *perushim* (פְּרוּשִׁם), although sometimes negatively, with other meanings, such as sectarians, ascetics or heretics.[19] The term is simply multivalent in rabbinic sources. The suggestion of Ellis Rivkin to sort out passages where *perushim* are confronted with *tsedukim* (צְדוּקִים),[20] is helpful, but not decisive, since the latter term could carry several meanings too.[21]

In attempting to sort out the different uses of *pharisaioi* and *perushim* in Josephus, the New Testament and rabbinic texts, John Bowker suggests that there was a transition from the "Pharisees" as a name of a larger group, to a later situation, when it was rejected and applied to others.[22] The Rabbis referred to their predecessors as *hakamim* (sages), and these overlap to some extent with Josephus' *pharisaioi*.[23] Although Pharisaic views dominated in the emerging rabbinic movement, the name came to be used for those adhering to stricter views, and eventually as a derogatory term.

Such a usage might have originated before 70 CE. The *hakamic* movement seems to have been originally in close contact with the people, offering a seri-

---

[16] Stemberger 1995 [1991], 39. For an overview of the evidence (or lack of evidence) for identifying various figures as Pharisees, especially in Josephus, see Sievers 1997.

[17] "Say Sadducees: "We complain against you, Pharisees. For you say, 'Holy Scriptures impart uncleanness to hands, but the books of Homer do not impart uncleanness to hands.'" Said Rabban Yohanan b. Zakkai, "And do we have against the Pharisees only this matter alone? Lo, they say, 'The bones of an ass are clean, but the bones of Yohanan, high priest, are unclean.'" ..." *mYad* 4:6. But this could be a case of irony.

[18] Neusner 1988, 70f.

[19] E.g. *mSot* 3:4, explained in the *Babylonian Talmud bSot* 22b as seven types of problematic *perushim*. See also *tBer* 3:25, associating the *perushim* with the *minim* (heretics), in interpreting the 18 blessings. Note that the meaning of the root פרש has to do with separation (A. Baumgarten 1991, 110; Rivkin 1978, 162–173).

[20] Rivkin 1978, 131–138.

[21] A. Baumgarten 1991, 111–112.

[22] Bowker 1973, 15.

[23] The *hakamim* are contrasted sometimes with priests, sometimes with Sadducees, and sometimes with *perushim*, but there are also texts associating, although not identifying them with the *perushim* (*bNid* 33b, 34a; cf. Bowker 1973, 7, 12). A possible explanation is that at an early stage, the *hakamic* movement was called *perushim/pharisaioi*, as distinct from other groups, such as Essenes or Sadducees. The name had perhaps initially been a designation by the opponents of the movement (Cf. Bowker 1973, 19f). As the new leadership in Yavneh, after the destruction of Jerusalem and the temple, included people of several backgrounds, *perushim* was avoided as a self-designation. Cf. Rivkin (1978, 158f., 177) who suggests that the term *perushim* originally was a nickname given by the Sadducees, and hence avoided later as a (self)designation except in traditions about controversies between Pharisees and Sadducees.

ous possibility of "holiness in the world," exercising extensive influence, as well as receiving considerable support. According to Bowker's interpretation, the *hakamim* sometimes supported the customs of the people against the religious establishment, but this did not mean that the people at large adopted the *hakamic* way of life, which led to something of both an alliance and a tension with the *ammei ha-arets*, and conflicts among the *hakamim*, concerning the extent to which ordinary people should be expected to understand and apply their detailed interpretation.[24] Such tensions could be seen both in the division between *bet Hillel* and *bet Shammai*,[25] and in the development of *haburot*.[26] There is thus a development to be traced from a basic *hakamic* vision that holiness should be possible for all, to a situation with degrees of holiness and separate associations. Jesus is to be situated in the context of this transition, which in part explains the mixed picture of Pharisees in the gospels.[27]

Roger Booth takes a similar position, regarding the *haberim* as a movement within a movement,[28] but his reconstruction is somewhat different, taking "Pharisees" as a generic term, including a number of sub-groups.[29] He suggests that *perushim/pharisaioi* could *at times* be used in the *Mishnah* and the gospels where *haberim* are meant rather than Pharisees in general.

There is a problem in talking about real or normal Pharisees in contrast to extremists, however. Although we may exchange Pharisees in the broad sense with *hakamim*, nothing much is gained, since it is often not evident how passages using *perushim/pharisaioi* should be interpreted and classified. We will simply have to continue using the term Pharisees, with an enhanced awareness of the diversity and development of the movement.

---

[24] Bowker 1973, 29ff.

[25] Bowker 1973, 32f.

[26] Bowker 1973, 35f. See the discussions below about the *ammei ha-arets* and about the need for *haburot* being due to ordinary people's inconsistency in legal observance (266–273). Cf. Westerholm 1978, 65.

[27] Bowker 1973, 35f; 38ff.

[28] Against Finkelstein 1938, 1: 76 and Jeremias 1971, 118, who regard all Pharisees as *haberim*.

[29] Booth takes *perushim/pharisaioi* to "indicate a general class within which lie at least four species: those who joined *haburoth*, the better to observe the law; the extreme Pharisees, who are condemned in the *Talmud* and gospels for their ostentation and hypocrisy; the 'ordinary' Pharisees who tried to observe the law binding upon all, but did not take upon themselves the additional legal obligations accepted by the *haberim*; and the *hakamim*, or Sages who upheld the oral law against the Sadducees, and made both the laws which are generally applicable, and the laws applicable only to persons of particular status, such as priests, Nazirites or *haberim*; the hallmark of the *hakamim* was not, however, the strict purity of the *haberim*, but devotion to the traditional law. Confusion is caused because the generic term is probably used to refer to the species..." (Booth 1986, 193). Doubts must be raised concerning Booth's detailed classification, especially in subordinating the *hakamim* to Pharisees in general. The problem with detailed reconstructions is that they are almost bound to be false on some points. The alternative, when evidence is scanty and/or ambiguous, is to remain with a general but blurred picture.

At the same time, we need to be able to discuss the general trend or current in legal interpretation and development of which Pharisaism was an important part. Possibly we could talk about a *hakamic*, or perhaps *hasidic* current, in contrast to a Zadokite one.[30] However, these designations are not unproblematic either, in what they imply about origins and delimitations. I will continue to use "Pharisees," but in discussing the legal trend or development which the Pharisees in particular embodied, I rather prefer to talk about an "expansionist current."[31]

The theory of Pharisaic dominance at Yavneh has certain evidence to speak for it. Josephus' view on the power of the Pharisees, especially in his later work *Antiquities*, is best explained as reflecting historical circumstances and power relationships at the end of the first century CE.[32] Reasoning in a similar way, the "developed" picture of the Pharisees in the polemical Gospel of Matthew testifies to their being the dominant Jewish adversaries of the Syrian church in the 80s.[33] While they may not have been that dominant in Jewish society at the time of Jesus, they may have been his most important adversaries. This depends on how the points of conflict are identified.

Identifying points of conflict

If the task of defining the adversaries of Jesus is difficult, disentangling the questions of dissent is more so. Two main areas stand out: the temple and the Torah. It is a widely held idea that Jesus was in trouble with the temple authorities because of his attitudes and actions. There is no consensus, though, about what the conflicts consisted of in detail. The idea that Jesus was opposed to the temple cult in principle is rejected by most scholars. From a socio-economic perspective, he has been seen as protesting against profits and unfair conditions in trade with sacrificial animals and money exchange.[34] Sanders thinks that Jesus publicly threatened the destruction of the temple as part of his restoration theology.[35] Chilton sees Jesus' "cleansing" of the temple as neither a protest against sacrifice, nor a threat of destruction, but as an occupation, insisting that "Israelites should offer of their own produce in God's house."[36]

The lack of consensus applies even more to the question of Jesus' attitude to the Torah. In the case of the temple, gospel material is fairly limited, and re-

---

[30] Cf. J. Baumgarten on the Sadducees and Qumran sectarians as "Zadokite" groups, 1980, 170.

[31] Cf. Alon 1977, 232ff; See below, 158–161, 188–189, 293–296.

[32] *Ant.* 18: 15, 17; Meier 2001, 302f.

[33] Cf. the principled way of reasoning about another ideological trait in the gospel of Matthew, i.e. the ambivalent characterization of Peter, in Syreeni 2000, 183f. "Matthew seems to promote an *ideological* stance addressing the contemporary *historical* situation" (184).

[34] Cf. Jeremias 1971, 145; Hooker 1991, 263f.

[35] Sanders 1985, 75.

[36] Chilton and Evans 1997, 199–200. Cf. Chilton 1992, 111, 135f.

lates to an institution which, at the stage of final gospel redaction, no longer existed.[37] As for the Torah, the situation is different. At the time of gospel redaction, Christian communities as well as Jewish opponents related to the Torah in diverse ways. Not a meagre amount of gospel material relates to Jesus' attitude to the Torah, either explicitly or implicitly. Implications vary, according to the stance taken by different gospel communities/authors, and depending on what type of relationship or conflicts they had with contemporary and local Jewish tradition. Matthew's Jesus has a more condemnatory attitude to Pharisees, while he is less careless about legal matters, as compared with the Jesus of Mark.[38] What about the historical Jesus? Scholarly consensus is absent. Traditionally, Jesus has been seen as opposing the Torah. But with an increased interest in the Jewish context, Jesus has been interpreted as more or less in accord with Jewish law. Many of the recent reconstructions picture Jesus as fully observant, with no quarrels about legal matters. The different options in discussing Jesus and the Torah could be structured as follows: 1) Jesus was explicitly opposing or abrogating the Torah in principle, emphasizing ethics instead of ritual.[39] 2) Jesus was explicitly opposing certain commandments, emphasizing his own authority.[40] 3) Jesus was defending the biblical law against human tradition.[41] 4) Jesus was in his teaching and actions implicitly opposing the Torah, without fully realizing what he did or what consequences could result.[42] 5) Jesus was not opposed to the Torah; he differed on certain points of interpretation, but was fully observant.[43]

The two concepts of temple and Torah are interrelated. Although the Torah functioned without the temple after 70 CE, the two presuppose each other during the period of the Second Temple, and to a large extent continued to do so in the minds of the Rabbis of the *Mishnah*. The temple service was an important part of the Torah, and much of the Torah, especially purity rules, were geared towards the temple, although not exclusively. If Jesus was involved in quarrels concerning the temple system or temple service, it is likely that he was involved in some disagreements about the Torah as well. Disagreements were common, however, and a key question is whether Jesus dissented in any remarkable way, when compared with the differing interpretations and ensuing discussions be-

---

[37] Mark is the only gospel which at times is considered to have received its final form before 70 CE. For a discussion of the dating of the gospel of Mark before or after the destruction of Jerusalem, see Hooker 1991, 5–8.

[38] Mt 23; cf. the legal arguments in Mt 12:1–14 with the "careless" attitude in Mk 2:23–3:6.

[39] Käsemann 1965 [1954], 39ff; Lambrecht 1977, 76f; Schweizer 1971 [1967], 72f, 145ff, 151f, 234.

[40] Banks 1975, 262f; Cf. Loader's description of Mark's Jesus, 1997, 37f, 134f, 510. This is not, however, Loader's picture of the *historical* Jesus.

[41] Jeremias 1971, 204–211.

[42] Dodd 1971, 70, 77. Cf. the discussion in Sanders 1985, 56.

[43] Sanders 1985, 245–269; Vermes 1993, 11–45.

tween Pharisaic schools, or between Pharisees, Sadducees and Essenes. Even if it is unlikely that dissensions between Jesus and his contemporaries about the law directly caused his death, we cannot infer from this that they were not serious, but we should regard them as important clues for understanding an attitude or a general posture of Jesus, which could allow for or explain the actions which eventually led to his execution.

Sanders discusses such questions at length in the introductory chapter of his *Jesus and Judaism.*[44] Referring to Klausner and Vermes, he argues that "those who presumably know the most about Judaism, and about the law in particular—Jewish scholars—do not find any substantial points of disagreement between Jesus and his contemporaries."[45] The argument is generalizing and problematic; with a similar reasoning, Christians would by nature have more knowledge about the historical Jesus, or at least about the earliest Christianity, than Jews. I am dubious of Sanders' claim that a view of Jesus as opposing parts of the Torah in such a way as to cause Christianity's subsequent break with Judaism, without intending it, must be based on a nineteenth-century conception of Jesus as the first modern man.[46] There are other options. It is not uncommon for religious reformers to challenge questions which are perceived as principal, without having a previous intention of breaking with tradition or founding a new movement.

An obvious reason for Sanders to minimize Jesus' conflicts about the law, while emphasizing the temple incident, is his intention to show that Second Temple Judaism was tolerant, and Jesus could not have been *killed* because of legal dissension.[47] Although Sanders may well be right about the reasons for Jesus' execution, this does not mean that Jesus was not in conflict with other groups about the Torah, or that such dissensions are not interesting or important for understanding the historical Jesus. The question of execution is not the only important one. I do not believe that once we have explained the reasons for Jesus' execution we have necessarily explained his most important or most interesting traits.

Thus, while placing Jesus fully within his Jewish context, I would give more room than do several recent interpreters for differences between Jesus and some of his contemporaries in attitude to the Torah. I am dealing with Jesus and purity in an attempt to understand, sort out and explain the background and nature of such differences. Purity, together with sabbath, divorce, fasting and attitudes to parents and family have often been regarded as "test cases" for establishing

---

[44] Sanders 1985, 23–58. Sanders focuses on the cause of Jesus' death, and gives an overview of the discussion from Schweitzer to Vermes.

[45] Sanders 1985, 55.

[46] Sanders 1985, 56, 34.

[47] Sanders 1990, 42. This purpose shapes Sanders' questions and makes him seek answers which at times inhibit discussions in other directions. Cf. Moxnes 1995, 146ff, about Sanders' programmatic meta-narrative.

Jesus' attitude to the Torah. Of these, sabbath and purity can be considered major issues.[48]

To be able to discuss such issues it is necessary to evaluate relevant Jesus-traditions, ask what legal interpretations were established in the first century, find out to what extent such laws were applied or adhered to, and within that context interpret the traditions.[49]

Identifying contemporary legal material

The discussion about legal traditions in Second Temple Judaism is complex, to say the least. Contemporary *legal* texts are available from the probably Essene sect in Qumran only.[50] As for Pharisaic *halakhah* we are restricted to rabbinic material, of which the earliest is the *Mishnah* (ca. 200 CE). We do have references to the Pharisees in Josephus[51] and the gospels, but they are problematic for reasons of bias, and they are not legal texts, although the gospels sometimes refer to legal discussions. We know nothing of Sadducean *halakhah*, except through polemical rabbinic references, which may refer to later heretics.[52] Both Josephus and Philo refer at times to legal practices, but without identifying them with any particular group.[53]

The gospel stories' portrayal of the Pharisees as Jesus' main adversaries is especially evident in conflicts about sabbath and purity. Thus it becomes crucial to discuss the role and *halakhah* of the Pharisees. Too many scholars in the past have followed the path of Billerbeck in reading rabbinic materials from later centuries as commentaries on the New Testament. While this is not as common today, there are still numerous unfounded presuppositions around when rabbinic texts are utilized.

Jacob Neusner's research in the 1970s about the Pharisees in rabbinic tradition was ground-breaking. While Neusner has been criticized for not being

---

[48] Theissen and Merz 1998 [1996], 365, 370; Cf. the subjects treated by Westerholm 1978.

[49] Cf. the programme followed by Booth in 1986, 18–19.

[50] E.g. the *Damascus Document* (CD—generally Essene?), the *Community Rule* (1QS), the *Temple Scroll* (11Q19), and Halakhic texts from cave 4: 4QMMT (4Q394–399), 4Q Ordinances (4Q159, 513, 514), 4Q Tohorot (4Q274–280), etc.

[51] For Josephus on the Pharisees, see *Ant.* 13:171–173, 288–300, 399–411; 15:2–4, 368–371; 17:41–46; 18:11–17; *J.W.* 1:107–114, 571; 2:162–166, 411–417; *Life* 10–12; 21; 189–198. Relevant passages collected in Bowker 1973, 77–98. Cf. Meier 2001, 301f, for a list of various interpretations. Josephus at times refers to the Pharisees' theology, but rarely to their *halakhah*.

[52] Sadducees are often called "Boethusians" in rabbinic sources. For a discussion of Sadducean halakhah, see Wassén 1991, 127–146; for early rabbinic material, see *tHag* 3:35; *mYad* 4:6–7; *tYad* 2:20; *tRosHas* 1:15; *tSanh* 6:6; *mPar* 3:7–8; *tPar* 3:7; *tNid* 5:2; *tYom* 1:8. Josephus' references to the Sadducees are juxtaposed with several of his references to the Pharisees, and follow the same pattern, not discussing points of *halakhah*. We are only informed about general differences in attitude to oral law (cf. *Ant.* 13:297–298). Cf. Meier 2001, 399–406.

[53] A "Philonic halakhah" can be deduced from Philo's texts, e.g. in Belkin 1940.

consistent, his form-critical approach has been fruitful.[54] In *The Rabbinic Traditions about the Pharisees before 70*, Neusner thoroughly analyzes all rabbinic traditions referring to the pre-70 masters and the houses of Hillel and Shammai, finding a limited number of *types* of materials, and a few clear-cut *forms,* which characterize Yavnean transmitters of tradition.[55] Traditions are then sorted through verification or attestation. When a tradition about pre-70 masters is commented on by a named later rabbi, it is deemed to have been available at the time of that rabbi. Pre-70 traditions verified by rabbis belonging to the Yavnean stratum (70–125 CE) could thus be regarded as having strong claims for reliability. This does not mean, however, that we have pre-70 formulations, or that details or positions are verified, but only the *themes* of law.[56]

When such a theme, subject, or as Meier puts it, a similar "cluster of concerns" is also attested by various gospel traditions, it was very likely an issue for discussion between Jesus and his adversaries. Meier identifies three such clusters in the area of purity: rules concerning food and vessels containing food and liquids, rules concerning corpses and tombs, and purity or sanctity of the cult apparatus.[57]

The point is that the legal subject (not the details) of early traditions, verified by Yavnean Tannaim, ought to have been present in pre-70 Judaism. To put it another way, a legal praxis which is assumed in such a discussion, must have been present at least during the end of the Second Temple period.[58] This is especially the case when such subjects are attested by early gospel traditions.

Neusner's method of attestation is not without problems.[59] Booth gives more weight to reconstructing a logical development of a legal concept, using attributions of sayings as support for, or detraction from, conclusions thus reached, and mentions that Neusner has moved towards such a standpoint too.[60] Sanders points out that the *stam*, i.e. the anonymous layer in the *Mishnah*,

[54] Sanders, among others, regards the approach as sound in principle, even if he does not always accept Neusner's conclusions (Sanders 1990, 172f). For a review of Neusner's early method together with a critique, cf. Saldarini 1977, 263–269.

[55] Neusner 1971, 3: 99–100 etc.

[56] Neusner 1971, 3: 180ff, 284ff.

[57] Meier 2001, 320f, with references to Mk 7:1–23; Mt 23:16–22, 25–28; *mOr* 2:12; *tAZ* 4:9; *mYad* 4:6–7; *tHag* 3:35; *mSheq* 6:1; *mKer* 1:7. Meier points out that this is an application of the criterion of multiple attestation.

[58] Sanders 1990, 171f. While Neusner applying his method concludes that many rabbinic developments, especially in the area of purity, were in existence already with pre-70 Pharisees, Sanders seemingly downplays the evidence, in his attempt to show that Pharisees were nothing like their caricatures, but were responsible religious people, and hence could not have had any serious quarrels with Jesus (Sanders 1990, 23, 252). Both use basically the same method though, taking for granted the continuity between Pharisaism and rabbinic literature.

[59] Saldarini 1977, 263–269.

[60] Booth 1986, 143f, referring to Neusner 1974–1977, 18: 161.

which Neusner generally regards as late, sometimes may in fact represent very early traditions.[61] The general idea, however, is similar.

This means that although rabbinic literature neither gives a clear identification of different Jewish first-century groups, nor provides any systematic information about legal differences between them, it can nevertheless be used to trace a number of legal views which are presupposed in further post-70 development and thus ought to have been current before 70 CE. Although we cannot automatically claim that such views were Pharisaic, we can assume that certain basic views were present before the destruction of the Second Temple. But were such views entertained by Pharisees or by several groups? Or were they presupposed only by a couple of small, sect-like Jerusalemite "Houses" of legal scholars? Were they taken for granted by the common people?[62]

Our precise knowledge of these matters is limited by the nature of available sources. In spite of this, the situation is not as precarious as it might seem. Rivkins' method is not without value. The *Mishnah*'s use of צְדוּקִים is not *as* multivalent as its use of פְּרוּשִׁים. The fact that several positions which are attributed to the Sadducees in the *Mishnah* are seen to have been held by the Qumran sectarians,[63] is most easily explained not by assuming that the *Mishnah* uses צְדוּקִים for Essenes, but by similarities between specific interpretations of the Torah between Essenes and Sadducees.[64] Such observation rather strengthen theories about the two groups sharing many principles of legal interpretation, the main differences being questions of priesthood and temple cult, calendar issues, as well as strictness of law.

In addition to this, halakhic texts from Qumran witness to differences between Essene sectarians and others. These others could admittedly be thought of as either Sadducees or Pharisees. However, the state of *tebul yom*, as well as the rule about flowing liquids, which apparently were not accepted in Qumran, but by the recipients of the letter 4QMMT, show that the recipients must either have been Pharisees, or that views we generally ascribe to Pharisees must have been common or dominating.[65]

This is supported by archaeological findings of ritual baths or immersion pools (*miqvaot*), both in Jerusalem and elsewhere. Many of the *miqvaot* found in the poorer parts of Jerusalem, as well as elsewhere in the country, were connected by a pipe to an upper storage pool (*otsar*), while all *miqvaot* in Qumran, and almost every *miqveh* in the upper city of Jerusalem, where the aristocrats lived, lacked such storage pools. This is evidence for similarities in interpreta-

---

[61] Sanders 1990, 167, referring to J.N. Epstein.

[62] Cf. the caveats mentioned by Meier 2001, 305–310.

[63] E.g. on questions of *tebul yom*, *nitsoq*, bones of animals etc. J. Baumgarten 1980, 157–170.

[64] A. Baumgarten 1991, 112; Schiffman 1994, 299.

[65] 4QMMT B13–16, 55–58. J. Baumgarten 1980; Schiffman 1994, n.61. The concept of *tebul yom* (i.e. becoming pure by immersion during day time, without waiting for sunset) will be further discussed below, 76–81. For a discussion about flowing liquids, see 83f.

tion between Essenes and Sadducees, and shows the storage pool as a Pharisaic invention, which became an influential practice.[66] It is taken for granted in the *Mishnah*, which shows the preponderance of Pharisaic traits in rabbinic Judaism.[67] There seems to be ample evidence for similarities between Essenes and Sadducees in matters of *halakhah*, although they differed in strictness and attitude, while Pharisees differed and developed their *halakhah* partly along other routes.

Thus I find it reasonable that the current, which dominated in the rabbinic movement after 70 CE, was at least *fairly* influential even before 70 CE. I also find it reasonable to think that the fairly influential Jewish current which figures in the Jesus tradition as his adversaries, and are usually named Pharisees, were basically similar in matters of law to the highly influential Pharisees known to the gospel writers (and Josephus) at the end of the first century. Thus I assume links between the influential Jewish legal interpreters in the Jesus tradition and the subsequent Yavnean rabbinic movement. We must always question whether a particular legal discussion of the *Mishnah* would have evolved already at the time of Jesus. However, since the continuous interpretative activity in rabbinic Judaism did not have as its aim the multiplication of rules, but rather should be characterized as a defining enterprise, which aimed at leniency and practicability, the assumption that the topical issue as such must not have been taken so seriously, but must have been treated with more leniency and less exactitude by pre-70 Pharisaic or other legal tradition, than by later rabbinic rulings, is simply unfounded.[68]

Hence some conclusions about legal interpretation can be drawn from rabbinic material where Pharisees and Sadducees figure together (Rivkin), and where the opinions of pre-70 sages or the schools of Hillel and Shammai figure, especially when verified by Yavnean authorities (Neusner), as to what views were *presupposed*, i.e. what general views or concepts were current and influential before 70 CE. Logical development, as well as the anonymous layer, ought to be taken into account as well, and this evidence should, when possible, be corroborated by comparisons with Qumran texts, Pseudepigraphic material, Philo, Josephus, and archaeology. It should also be noted that the gospels are sometimes more suited for verifying rabbinic material than vice versa.[69] When practices and topics or themes are broadly attested, there are good reasons to

[66] Sanders 1990, 214–227; 1992, 222–229. For further discussion about *immersion pools*, see below, 74–76, 259, 281.

[67] *mMiq* 6:8. The designation *otsar* (אוֹצָר) for the storage pool is of a later date.

[68] Since the Amoraim attempted to limit corpse-impurity, due to the lack of proper means of purification after the fall of the temple, it is rather to be expected that pre-70 Pharisaic interpretation was in certain ways stricter than that of the *Mishnah*.

[69] Cf. Piattelli and Jackson 1996, 37f; Segal 1990, xv–xvi. Segal comments: "Rather, a commentary to the Mishnah should be written, using the New Testament as marginalia that demonstrates antiquity" (xv).

think that such views were current and influential with the people, i.e. fairly common, at the beginning of the first century CE, at least in Jerusalem and its Judaean surroundings.[70]

The Sabbath as a test case

Since, apart from purity, Jesus' attitude to the Sabbath is the other major legal issue, I will briefly turn to that subject to test how some of the tools just discussed can be used, and to highlight certain questions which are relevant in dealing with purity. The obvious synoptic texts about Jesus and the sabbath are the much debated conflict stories in Mk 2:23–28 par. (plucking of corn) and Mk 3:1–6 par. (healing of man with withered hand). In addition to these traditions, a couple of Lukan healing stories, similar to the withered hand tradition, are relevant (Lk 13:10–17; 14:1–6). Usually the saying in Lk 6:5D is also discussed in this context.[71]

Most scholars agree that "the Sabbath was generally observed very strictly"[72] during the Second Temple period. 1 Maccabees and Josephus are often cited as evidence.[73] Examples of strict Sabbath rules are found in *Jubilees*[74] and the *Damascus Document*,[75] and the Pharisees are supposed to have developed more lenient interpretations. An example of this is the rabbinic concept of *erub*, which made it possible to fictionally unite courtyards in an alley, to allow the carrying of items within that area during the Sabbath. Discussions about making an *erub* are the subject of a whole tractate in the *Mishnah*, and the concept of *erub* is taken for granted. Several rabbinic traditions about the Houses and pre-70 sages discussing *erub*, with Yavnean or Ushan verification, are mentioned by Neusner.[76] There is good reason to believe that the idea of *erub* was known and practised by some before the fall of the temple. Such a conclusion is supported by comparisons with the Sabbath laws in *Jubilees* (before 100 BCE), which prohibit carrying anything from house to house,[77] and in CD (ca. 100 BCE), according to which "no-one should remove anything from the house to outside, or from outside to the house."[78] Such legislative interpretation of the

[70] The discussion about Galilee and regional differences will be presented in Chapter VI.
[71] Cf. studies of Rordorf 1962; Westerholm 1978, 92–103; Back 1995.
[72] Sanders 1990, 7.
[73] 1 Macc. 2:29–41 about Israelites refusing warfare on Sabbath, which resulted in a massacre. As a result the group around Mattathias resolved to fight in self-defence even on the Sabbath. Josephus *J.W.* 1:57–60 about John Hyrcanus ending an important siege, because the sabbath year was approaching.
[74] *Jub.* 2:25–33 and 50:6–13.
[75] CD 10:14–11:18.
[76] Neusner 1971, 3: 226, 232. Examples of mishnaic traiditions verified by Yavnean Tannaim are *mErub* 1:2 and 6:2.
[77] *Jub.* 2:30; 50:8.
[78] CD 11:7–8.

Sabbath laws can be seen as an intended contrast to an emerging concept of *erub* among Pharisees. The phrase אל יתערב איש מרצונו בשבת in the very context (CD 11:4) could readily be interpreted as a prohibition of making an *erub* on Sabbath. The interpretation has been dismissed for reasons of grammar,[79] or emended to read יתרעב (fast)[80], but the latter is gainsaid by one of the new fragments of CD from cave 4, which reads יתערב as do the Cairo Genizah copies.[81] While the issue cannot be settled conclusively, there is good reason to follow Günther Stemberger in regarding CD 11:4 as opposing the idea of *erub*.[82] Together with the statement from *mErub* 6:2, implying that Sadducees did not accept the idea either, we receive a fairly clear picture of general differences in outlook during the period before 70 CE.

This discussion shows that it is sometimes possible to reconstruct the legal situation during the time of the Second Temple by combining data from rabbinic texts with other (earlier) evidence. When looking at Jesus' attitude to the sabbath, the particular topic of *erub* is not discussed, and thus of no relevance, except as an example showing the relative degree of development and differentiation of contemporary sabbath *halakhah* among various groups.

An issue of direct importance for studying the historical Jesus is the definition of work (מלאכה). In *mShabb* 7:2 a list of 39 forbidden categories of acts of labour is given. These include among others reaping and threshing. The prohibition of work is biblical and was taken for granted by all Jews.[83] We do not know the degree of definition during the time of Jesus, but comparisons between the sabbath rules in CD, which are dated at least a century before Jesus, and the extremely detailed discussions in the *Mishnah*, give some hints. We can at least expect the topics of CD being discussed during the first century, although Pharisaic rulings may well have been more lenient than those of the Essenes.[84] Topics discussed in CD include walking (no more than 1000 cubits outside the dwelling-place; later the *Mishnah* allowed 2000 cubits[85]), preparing food, carrying things, and, especially interesting in view of the Jesus tradition,

---

[79] Schiffman 1975, 109–110. Schiffman claims that the hitpael form cannot have the required meaning, and translates "no one shall enter partnership…," which according to Stemberger is "also not without problems" (Stemberger 1995 [1991], 75, n.73).

[80] Suggested by Rabin 1954 (*ZD*), 54–55, n.4.3, from a conjecture by Lévi. This emendation is accepted by García Martínez 1996 (*DSS* GM), but not by Lohse 1971 (*TQ*).

[81] See 4Q271 5 1:1 (formerly 4Q268 3 1:1). Cf. Doering 1997, 256, n.24. García Martínez translates even this fragment: "no one should fast…" in *DSS* GM, but modifies this in *DSSSE* to "No-[one] should intermingle" in agreement with J. Baumgarten's translation in *DJD* 18: 181. Baumgarten refers to intermingling (התערב) in the context of ritual purity, but this is strained as the explicit textual context is that of Sabbath *halakhah*.

[82] Stemberger 1995 [1991], 75.

[83] Ex. 31:12–17; 35:1–3; Num 15:32–36.

[84] Cf. Dunn 1990, 17–18.

[85] CD 10:21; *mSot* 5:3.

eating what is lost in the field and helping an animal out of a well or a pit.[86] In all the above-mentioned matters the (probably) Essene legislation of CD is very strict. While Pharisaic interpretations a hundred years later might have been more lenient, they should have included at least those topics, as well as a somewhat more developed discussion. But opinions differ as to which standpoints should be ascribed to the Pharisees of Jesus' time.

As a result, gospel traditions about Jesus and the sabbath are judged according to the interpreter's opinion of contemporary Pharisaic interpretation. In addition, redaction-critical reconstructions are often crucial. This is especially apparent when dealing with the Markan key texts (2:23–28; 3:1–6). They are often seen as part of a larger pre-Markan unit (2:1–3:6) of five conflict stories. While some scholars doubt the possibilities of isolating such units in Mark,[87] others find the exercise rewarding.[88]

This is not the place to make a detailed review of different interpretations.[89] It is enough for my purpose to note some of the diversity of opinion regarding the two above-mentioned Markan traditions and their synoptic parallels. Jesus' behaviour is often seen as ambiguous. Although he was involved in conflicts about the Sabbath, he did not openly reject it. Scholarly opinions differ, however, about Jesus' aim. Was he primarily against scribal or Pharisaic *halakhah*, but in favour of the biblical command?[90] Or did his criticism of halakhic interpretation imply an attack on the Sabbath commandment itself?[91] Or did his attitude reveal a different understanding of the will of God, and a denial of the function of biblical rules as literally binding statutes?[92] Some do not see any ambiguous behaviour, but regard Jesus as law-abiding, having no substantial conflicts with other pious Jews.[93]

Does Mark try to portray Jesus as upholding the Law? According to William Loader this is the case. He regards the section 2:1–3:6 as being governed by 1:39–45, where he claims that Jesus is presented as Torah observant.[94] Mark's Jesus is a figure of authority, who does not act contrary to the Torah.[95] Synoptic comparisons show, however, that Matthew did not seem to understand Mark in that way. Although Mark's Jesus defends the corn field incident by referring to David's action in the temple, Matthew apparently did not regard such a defence as valid, but supplied it with a comparison with the Sabbath-breaking of temple

[86] CD 10:14–11:18.
[87] Cf. Hooker 1991, 11; Kiilunen 1985, 249–266.
[88] For a discussion and a list of differing views, see Hultgren 1979, 151f., 166–167, n.1,2.
[89] For a history of interpretations, see Back 1995, 2–13.
[90] Jeremias 1971, 209.
[91] Rordorf 1962, 63.
[92] Westerholm 1978, 102f.
[93] Sanders 1990, 23; 1985, 266f. Vermes 1993, 11–45.
[94] Loader 1997, 26, 28, 37. For a discussion of Mark 1:39–45, see below, 100–107.
[95] Loader 1997, 35–37.

priests and a quotation from Hosea, as well as eliminating the relativizing saying about the Sabbath being made for man (Mt 12:5–7). In the subsequent healing story this tendency is even more evident, since Matthew substitutes the provocative and polarizing saying about saving life or killing, with a rabbinic-like *qal wa-homer* argument, comparing a sheep in a pit with the disabled man, thus justifying Jesus' action (Mt 12:11–12). This is Q-material, which is also used by Luke in one of his two additional Sabbath healing stories (Lk 14:1–6). It is evident that Matthew has a strong interest in adjusting the Markan Jesus to handle Sabbath law more responsibly. This is probably to be understood in light of Matthew's particular context with its strong polemical interest.[96]

It seems that Mark depicts Jesus as not necessarily non-observant, but seemingly careless in action and argument. Against this picture that of Q could be set up, which originally may have been tied to healing stories, as in Luke, but definitely not to the Markan cornfield incident. Which picture would be closest to the historical Jesus? Are they actually incompatible?

To attempt an answer, scholars often combine form and redaction criticism with a discussion of the legal context. As for the cornfield incident, there are three possible answers which have been considered original: the David story, the saying about the Sabbath being made for man, and/or the saying about the lordship of the Son of Man over the Sabbath. The first answer does not really fit the story. Some regard this as disqualifying, while others think it is the point. The second answer has parallels in rabbinic literature, which make it possible to argue either way. The third is often seen as a secondary commentary on the story.[97] The story itself, however, involves accusations about doing forbidden work. What is it about? Suggestions have varied: walking too far, making a path, stealing crops or harvesting. Walking distance was an issue, not only among Essenes, but generally.[98] Making a path is an unlikely candidate, as well as stealing crops; it was permitted to pick some ears of corn.[99] Harvesting seems to be the obvious crime, in the Lukan version possibly threshing as well.[100] It is reasonable to assume that plucking corn would be regarded as work, at least by some Jews. But the David story which is told in defence, is about eating. This could point at a further possibility. The *Damascus Document* prohibits eating what is lost in the field on Sabbath (CD 10:22–23), possibly in line with Ex 16:26. In *mPes* 4:8 picking up fruit on the Sabbath is condemned. Evidence is too slight, however, for drawing any conclusions as to general practice at the time of Jesus. It is possible, however, that the David

[96] But Westerholm denies that Matthew's Jesus is arguing the legality of the case. "The appeal is rather to actual practice, in which common sense and compassion rather than rules of *halakhah* must often have determined behaviour." (1978, 101).
[97] Back 1995, 91–95.
[98] Mishnaic discussions to this effect (*mSot* 5:3) are verified by Acts 1:12.
[99] Deut 23:25.
[100] Loader 1997, 33

story was originally intended not to "fit" the incident as a legal analogy, but only to convey the message: David also transgressed a legal precept because of hunger, so what?

In the subsequent healing story, Jesus' question ignores the issue of what constitutes work and what could be left for another day.[101] The issue here is clearly healing as forbidden work. There are numerous examples in later rabbinic literature of how treatment of diseases on the Sabbath was regarded: minor cures were not allowed, but when life was in danger it superseded the Sabbath.[102] However, we know almost nothing from other sources about actual practice during the Second Temple period. Several gospel traditions suggest that not only Pharisees, but religious leaders in general were against Jesus healing unnecessarily on the Sabbath. Do they reflect a pre-70 context?

As for the Q parable about a human or an animal having fallen into a well or a pit, there are interesting parallels in Essene literature. An animal which falls into a well or a pit should not be lifted up on the Sabbath (CD 11:13–14.) A human being who had fallen into water could be assisted only if it was possible without using tools/utensils of any kind (CD 11:16–17, 4Q265 7 1:7–8). There is a rabbinic discussion in the *Tosefta* about what to do with an animal in such a situation. It should be provided with food, but not lifted up.[103] It is thus a real possibility that the legal answer to Jesus' parable in Lk 14 would be that the animal should not be pulled out. However, in view of the argument in Lk 13:10–17 about watering animals on the Sabbath, Lk 14:5 may be understood less as a legal argument than a pragmatic appeal to how the hearers would actually behave.[104]

It is common to interpret Jesus' behaviour on the Sabbath as an expression of a concern for human need, and an emphasis on its priority. Many scholars find this explanation insufficient, and discuss his understanding of authority and the will of God.[105] Some, however, find no conflict between the actions of Jesus and Jewish legal tradition at all.[106] The cornfield incident is at times seen as unhistorical,[107] while the healing stories are nothing to quarrel about, since no work was being done, only words were spoken.[108]

A major problem is that all gospel traditions about Jesus and the Sabbath are conflict stories. Although every tradition is influenced by its context and his-

---

[101] Loader 1997, 36.

[102] *mShabb* 14:3f; *mYoma* 8:6; Sanders 1990, 13; Westerholm 1978, 95; Back 1995, 46–49.

[103] *tShabb* 14:3; cf. *bShabb* 128b. Schiffman 1975, 122.

[104] Westerholm 1978, 101.

[105] Westerholm 1978, 102f.

[106] Vermes 1973, 22ff.

[107] Hultgren 1979, 115; Sanders 1985, 266. Loader, in contrast, finds it credible (1997, 51).

[108] Sanders 1985, 266; 1993, 215. The issue can hardly be dismissed so simply; it seems as if healing itself (except in case of danger of life) was understood as transgressing the Sabbath, and Jesus' defence supposes a transgression. Cf. Back 1995, 46–49, 82f, 90.

tory, conflict stories can be thought to reflect debates and concerns of a later time to a greater extent than other traditions. Since Bultmann, these stories have been suspected of being no more than church creations.[109] The obvious fact that a tradition has been shaped by a particular *Sitz im Leben* in the early church, does not exclude an historical basis,[110] but when the shaping context is polemical or apologetic, the tradition is difficult to penetrate. Speculations about pre-Markan stages complicate matters further. A conflict story may reflect a Markan gentile setting, while part of it is seen as a pre-Markan tradition shaped by a Jewish-Christian church. There may be further layers as well. This is only to be expected, but it complicates historical investigation.

Discussing the Sabbath, testing some tools for identifying legal interpretations and conditions before 70 CE, and evaluating relevant gospel traditions, we have seen that the combination of legal and textual data may lead to overall interpretations. In the case of the Sabbath, however, we see that reconstructions of Jesus' attitude are made especially difficult by the relevant traditions consisting exclusively of conflict stories, shaped by their *Sitz im Leben*, reflecting both internal and external struggles of the early church. As will be seen below, the problems are usually the same in the traditional search for Jesus' attitude to purity, based on Mark 7.

III.2 Mark 7, hand-washing, and the impurity system

Structure and content

Turning to Jesus and purity, we are faced with a complex situation. The text usually discussed is Mark 7:1–23 with its Matthean parallel (15:1–20). The text is problematic, however, since it obviously consists of different parts, with certain discrepancies between the various traditions.[111] The first part concerns ritual hand-washing before eating, and is a question from the Pharisees to Jesus about the behaviour of some of his disciples (7:1–5). Jesus' answer deals with God's commandments as opposed to the tradition (παράδοσις) of the elders, and includes a quotation from Isa 29:13, close to the LXX version (7:6–8). The following argument is about vows (*korban*), and is supposed to illustrate how Pharisees allow their παράδοσις to override the law of God concerning parents (7:9–13). The question of hand-washing and eating is left behind, and in addition, vows depend on biblical law too (Num 30:3; Deut 23:21). After this, Jesus calls upon the crowd again (πάλιν, but the crowd has not been mentioned until now!), explaining that "there is nothing outside of man, going into him, which

[109] Bultmann 1972 [1921], 39ff, 51.
[110] Cf. V. Taylor 1935 [1933], 41ff.
[111] For a survey of the problems involved, see Booth 1986, 23–53.

can defile him, but that which is going out of man is what defiles man" (7:14–15). This is followed by a further explanation to the disciples, in the form of "secret teaching" in the house. Now it is evidently a question neither of hand-washing nor of vows, but of food, which cannot defile a person, since it does not go into man's heart but passes via the stomach to the latrine (7:17–19). To this is added what is obviously a redactor's comment: καθαρίζων πάντα τὰ βρώματα, usually translated "by this he declared all food clean" (19c). Finally, things which defile a man are supplied in a list of vices (7:20–23).

Obvious problems concern the relationship between the hand-washing incident, the *korban* section, the logion about what goes into and out of man, and the discussion about defiled food. In addition to problems relating to the tradition-history and redaction of the text, there are questions concerning the historical plausibility of different traditions. Did hand-washing before ordinary meals belong to the "tradition of the elders," and was it practised by people generally or at least by some Pharisees at the time of Jesus? Did Jews of that time generally immerse themselves and their utensils to the extent that Mark claims? Did the attitude to vows, attributed to the Pharisees in the *korban* section, prevail during the same period?[112] Did the historical Jesus question the idea of purity as such? Did he discuss questions of clean and unclean food? Would that have been possible in a Palestinian Jewish context?

Mark 7:1–23 has been dealt with by numerous scholars.[113] While the text has been regarded in the past as providing an example of Jesus' radical, anti-legal attitude, more recent studies tend to emphasize the Jewishness of Jesus, and tone down conflict.[114]

In the Markan context, this text is placed between the story of the feeding of 5000, with its many Israel motifs and images, and the doublet story of feeding 4000, with its Gentile allusions. Mark probably says something about the place of Gentiles in the church by his structure, and the issue of purity and food laws was important in this context.[115]

Just as in the previous section about the Sabbath, we are dealing with a conflict story. Possibly, such *Streitgespräche* might originally have formed a unity.[116] In their present context, however, they are made part of a narrative, and have probably been re-worked a number of times. During this process, they have been shaped and interpreted by later situations and conflicts in the early church. Finally, they have been redacted, to fit into a gospel narrative.

---

[112] Cf. Westerholm 1978, 72–73.

[113] E.g. Lambrecht 1977, 24–82; Banks 1975, 132–146; Hübner 1986 [1973], 142–175; Westerholm 1978, 62–91; Sariola 1990, 23–73; Booth 1986. For an overview of interpretations and positions on tradition and redaction, see Lambrecht 1977, 28–39.

[114] For an example of the former, see Hübner 1986 [1973], 142–195; cf. Käsemann 1965 [1954], 39f. For an example of the latter, see Booth 1986.

[115] Loader 1997, 67ff.

[116] Berger 1972, 461; but note Kiilunen 1985, 249–266.

Several redaction critical studies have attempted to disentangle Mark 7:1–23. As I have already declared my misgivings about the possibilities of overly detailed redaction critical exercises on Markan material,[117] I am sceptical of the results of some of these studies.[118] Their results on fine points are often contradictory. But apart from this I find a general outline and discussion, to which we will now turn, both possible and necessary.

Tradition, redaction, and authenticity

According to Bultmann, conflict dialogues in the gospels are imaginary scenes illustrating a principle, which the early church ascribed to Jesus. There is accordingly no point in asking about the authenticity of questions and answers in such a dialogue.[119]

It should be self-evident that the conflict story in Mark 7, as we now have it, has been shaped within the context of the early church. The final form ought to stem from a Hellenistic milieu, since the Isaiah quotation is closer to the LXX than to the MT.[120] It has been seen as an apologetic text, composed to defend the church against Jewish criticism.[121] The fact that "some" of Jesus disciples are accused could be taken as an indication of later conflicts, in which some Christians did not conform to Jewish standards of purity.[122] This does not mean that the story must necessarily have *originated* in the early church. To *prove* this to be the case might be as precarious a task as attempting the opposite.[123] Although Mark probably had an interest in adapting his traditions to fit contemporary church controversies, I agree with Anthony Harvey that "it is hardly conceivable that the whole picture of an ongoing controversy between Jesus and the sages of his time is fictional."[124] Still, the pointed conflict setting in Mark 7 is a major problem when this text is used to reconstruct the attitude of the historical Jesus to issues of purity, especially since the hand-washing question seems to be used to provide an occasion for questioning legal tradition in general, within the conflict story form.[125]

---

[117] Cf. above, 25–31.

[118] Both Sariola's and Booth's conclusions seem to me a bit too detailed (Sariola 1990, 49–52; Booth 1986, 23–53). However, I find Booth's tradition history more convincing (55–114).

[119] Bultmann 1972 [1921], 39.

[120] Hultgren 1979, 117.

[121] Hultgren 1979, 118.

[122] Hultgren 1979, 143, n.86; Cf. the cornfield incident, where the behaviour of the disciples is similarly the cause of accusations, Mk 2:23–28.

[123] Booth 1986, 76; Loader 1997, 72. Hultgren, in 1979, 198, hardly discusses the possible historical background of the conflict stories, but claims that church conflicts could not have been the *only* creative impulses in the shaping of those traditions.

[124] Harvey 1982, 51.

[125] Hultgren 1979, 118.

Roger Booth, in his thorough treatment of Mark 7:1–23, discusses the history of pre-Markan tradition (ch. 2), after having first separated Markan redaction from tradition (ch. 1). Booth regards the explanation in vv 3–4 about the Pharisaic purifications, as well as all references to παράδοσις, as Markan redaction. The opposition of παράδοσις to the commandments of God is not considered pre-Markan.[126] His reconstruction of the pre-Markan text seems to me basically sound, although conclusions about details could be questioned.[127] Most scholars agree to vv 3–4, as well as v 19c being Mark's comments.[128] Quite a few would also regard the dichotomy between traditions of men and commandments of God as late.[129]

Booth's division of the pre-Markan material into sections is useful for further discussion. These are an Introduction (1,2,5), the Question (5), the Isaiah Reply (6,7), the *Korban* Reply (9–12), the Purity Reply (14,15), a Scene-change (17), the Medical Explanation (18,19) and the Ethical Explanation (20–22).[130] His position is that the earliest form of the question consisted of the second limb only (hand-washing), while the first limb ("why do your disciples not live according to the tradition of the elders?") reflects Mark's "editorial hostility towards the traditional law in vv 3 and 4."[131] The question about hand-washing, however, could hardly have been created by Mark or the early church, since this was not an issue in that later context. To this question belongs the Purity Reply, which fits, and should be interpreted in a relative sense (i.e. things outside cannot defile *as much as* things inside a man).[132] The Medical and Ethical Explanations are seen by Booth as later teachings, added by the church; the Medical Explanation does not suit a Jewish environment, but has its origin in a totally different conceptual world. The Isaiah and *Korban* Replies were used as separate units in early church polemics. The *korban* discussion and the hand-washing dispute could both go back to the historical Jesus, but the two units did not originally belong together.[133]

There is much to support Booth's general reconstruction. It is obvious that the text consists of several separate passages.[134] At the same time it is possible to see one "original" tradition (7:1,[2,]5,15) rather than two, into which material

---

126 Booth 1986, 23–53.

127 Booth 1986, 52–53

128 Loader 1997, 71; Cf Sariola's comments about a sarcastic tone in vv 3–4, 1990, 46; Hübner 1986 [1973], 155, n.48; Booth 1986, 35f, 49f.

129 Cf. Lambrecht 1977, 51; Loader 1997, 72f.

130 Booth 1986, 61–62. In most verses, certain words or phrases are excluded as Markan redaction, but such details are accounted for only when they have a bearing upon my discussion.

131 Booth 1986, 65, against Hübner, who regards the discussion about the authority of the tradition of the elders as the oldest tradition (1986 [1973], 146).

132 Booth 1986, 67, 69ff; for a discussion about a relative sense, see below, 65–67.

133 Booth 1986, 71, 72, 74, 96.

134 Westerholm (1978, 72) notes the separate introductory formulas (vv 6,9,14,18,20), as evidence for the passages hanging together very loosely.

has been inserted with the aim of generalizing Jewish behaviour and opposing παράδοσις to divine commandments.[135]

Mark's generalizing tendencies are clearly seen in v3, where he explains the demand for hand-washing with a reference to the tradition of the elders, which the Pharisees and *all the Jews* keep. The παράδοσις referred to is otherwise usually seen as typical for the Pharisees as *distinct* from other Jews.[136] As for hand-washing in particular, the extent to which it was practised generally will be discussed below. However, from Mark's statement only, we would suspect that hand-washing was practised by some group of Jews at the time of Jesus, and possibly by an increasing number at the time of Mark. An increasing adherence to Pharisean *halakhah* towards the 70s would also explain v 13b ("And you do many such similar things") as a Markan expansion.

The Markan generalizations suggest that Christians rather than Jews are obedient to God's will.[137] Hence "all Jews" follow "human rules," while Jesus' disciples obey God's commandment. The opposition probably reflects arguments between Christians and Jews in the period between Jesus and Mark.[138] A prooftext from Isa 29:13 is used as evidence. The Hebrew וַתְּהִי יִרְאָתָם אֹתִי מִצְוַת אֲנָשִׁים מְלֻמָּדָה (and their fear of me is a taught rule of men) is different in meaning from the LXX μάτην δὲ σέβονται με διδάσκοντες ἐντάλματα ἀνθρώπων καὶ διδασκαλίας (in vain they worship me, teaching precepts of men, and teachings), which is much closer to the Markan text and context. Since Isa 29:10ff was used frequently by the early church, "especially for attacking legalistic religion,"[139] there are good reasons for not considering the Isaiah Reply as going back to the historical Jesus.

In the *korban* section, the new introductory formula in v 9 suggests that either the Isaiah Reply or the *Korban* Reply are not original in the context.[140] While Westerholm opts for the *Korban* Reply as representing the actual answer of Jesus to the hand-washing dispute, I think the easier solution is to regard it as possibly going back to the historical Jesus, but not belonging to the context of hand-washing.[141] Mark uses the tradition, however, as an example of typical Pharisaic hypocrisy.

---

[135] Berger 1972, 464; against Sariola 1990, 49.

[136] Kieffer 1995, 679.

[137] Cf. the Sabbath controversies in Mk 2:23–3:6.

[138] Hooker 1991, 174.

[139] Westerholm 1978, 76. Westerholm notes Rom 9:20; 11:8; 1Cor 1:19; Col 2:22.

[140] Westerholm 1978, 75.

[141] Westerholm 1978, 80. The *korban* unit has been much discussed in the context of oaths. Cf. Sanders 1990, 51–57; Westerholm 1978, 76–78, cf. 104–113. Oaths were in principle binding, and biblical law was strict (Num 30:3; Deut 23:21). Sanders notes the strict position of Philo (*Hypothetica* 7:3–5). There is a rabbinic discussion, explicitly dealing with the problem of vows which affect one's parents (*mNed* 5:6; 9:1). The problem was apparently known, and provisions were made for releasing a person from a vow in certain circumstances, although opinions among rabbinic authorities varied. In *mNed* 9:1, "the sages" forbid the release of vows

The Jesus logion in 7:15[142] is a *mashal*-like response, similar to those in Mk 2:1–3:6, and is often regarded as the original answer, belonging to the conflict story about hand-washing.[143] Most exegetes consider this saying to originate with the historical Jesus,[144] and Booth attempts to reconstruct its earliest form.[145] Doubts have been raised concerning its authenticity, especially by Heikki Räisänen, who does not regard the purity logion as original with Jesus, mainly due to its lack of *wirkungsgeschichte*. Subsequent conflicts in the early church (during the period between Jesus and Mark) are considered incomprehensible if Jesus had expressed himself as clearly as in Mk 7:15. The saying could possibly have had its origin in a Q saying about the inside and the outside, similar to Mt 23:25, which was radicalized in the church at a late stage, when Christians were looking for justification for the path already taken, in relationship to gentiles.[146] The lack of *wirkungsgeschichte* is embarrassing, and references to Rom 14:14 are not conclusive.[147] The most convincing explanations, however, place the saying in a context *not* of clean and unclean foods (in the sense of Lev 11:1–23), but of ritual hand-washing, and interpret it in a relative sense. The Markan interpretation (Mk 7:19c) of the purity logion might not have occurred at an earlier stage, before it was combined with other material, as in Mark's redaction.[148] This suggestion is even more credible if the saying was understood in a relative sense, or even had a more relative original form. This is the approach of several scholars.[149]

---

interfering with the command to honour parents, while later in the passage "the sages" agree to R. Eliezer's opinion that it should be possible. Westerholm's interpretation is plausible: earlier Pharisaic teachers did not free people from vows, but in the time of Eliezer (early Yavnean period) the matter was being discussed (1978, 77–78; Westerholm refers to Neusner 1973b, 2: 110, 311 for support). Cf. Hübner's comment (1986 [1973], 150f.) that release of vows probably was not permitted at the time of Jesus—why should we otherwise have a tradition suggesting legal fiction instead of release in *mNed* 5:6? Jesus could thus be seen as putting his finger on a conflict between two laws, which was real and later given a rabbinic solution. (Jesus' solution, however, seems to point in a different direction.) Sanders' claim, that the discussion in Mk 7:9–13 fits into a picture of Jesus as opposing only Pharisaic interpretation of the law, is questionable. The opposition of human traditions with divine law suits later church polemics better.

[142] οὐδέν ἐστιν ἔξωθεν τοῦ ἀνθρώπου εἰσπορευόμενον εἰς αὐτὸν ὃ δύναται κοινῶνται αὐτόν, ἀλλὰ τὰ ἐκ τοῦ ἀνθρώπου ἐκπορευόμενά ἐστιν τὰ κοινοῦντα τὸν ἄνθρωπον. "There is nothing outside of man, going into him, which can defile him, but that from man going out of him is that which defiles man."

[143] Loader 1997, 75. Against Bultmann (1972 [1921], 17f), who considers v 15 to be an authentic tradition to which other material was attached.

[144] Kieffer 1995, 683; Booth 1986, 112ff.

[145] Booth 1986, 68–71, 74.

[146] Räisänen 1986, 209ff, 218, 219ff. For a thorough discussion of the (lack of) *wirkungsgeschichte*, see Svartvik 2000, 109–204.

[147] Booth 1986, 100; Svartvik 2000, 115f.

[148] This suggestion is supported by the need for quotations from Scripture for the argument.

[149] Loader 1997, 76; Westerholm 1978, 83; Booth 1986, 69ff. Hooker (1991, 179) also suggests a relative interpretation of the *korban* passage: "the question is therefore not one of Law

A relative interpretation finds support in Semitic idiom. The οὐ ... ἀλλά construction could be seen as reflecting a Semitic dialectic negation, meaning "not so much as," or "rather."[150] Furthermore, the context favours such a reading.[151] A possible rendering would be: "A man is not so much defiled by that which enters him from outside as he is by that which comes from within."[152] A relative reading is denied by Räisänen, who thinks that

> "it would be methodologically plausible to *give precedence to an interpretation which takes the wording of the saying literally, if it is able to combine an anti-Torah orientation with other data,* in particular with the absence of influence upon subsequent developments."[153]

While he admits that the saying might have been slightly changed from an original form more like that of Mt 15:11, he finds that this makes no difference in meaning and content.[154] I share the surprise of James Dunn at such a verdict.[155] The difference could be exactly that of a relative meaning. Dunn makes an interesting comparison between versions of the purity logion in Mark, Matthew and Thomas, suggesting that the latter versions (Mt 15:11 and *Gos.Thom.* 14) are dependent on a Q tradition, similar to the alternative Markan version in Mk 7:18b and 20b,[156] which contains more semitic traits than Mk 7:15.[157] Dunn thinks that Jesus' saying is most closely reflected in Mt 15:11, but then elaborated on (probably in a Hellenistic-Jewish Christian context[158]), and "7.15 is an interpretative rendering of that earlier saying which embodies the more radical interpretation found also separately in 7.19c."[159] While this is tempting, Matthew's focus on the "mouth" (cf. vv. 17–18) reveals his version to be sec-

---

versus tradition at all, but rather of the relative weight to be given to different parts of the Law..." (177).

150 Westerholm 1978, 83f; Booth 1986, 69f.

151 Booth 1986, 69–70.

152 Westerholm 1978, 83.

153 Räisänen 1986, 226.

154 Räisänen 1986, 224.

155 Dunn 1990, 41.

156 Dunn 1990, 44. οὐ τὸ εἰσερχόμενον εἰς τὸ στόμα κοινοῖ τὸν ἄνθρωπον, ἀλλὰ τὸ ἐκπορευόμενον ἐκ τοῦ στόματος τοῦτο κοινοῖ τὸν ἄνθρωπον (Mt 15:11); **ⲡⲉⲧⲛⲁⲃⲱⲕ ⲅⲁⲣ ⲉϩⲟⲩⲛ ϩⲛ̄ ⲧⲉⲧⲛ̄ⲧⲁⲡⲣⲟ ϥⲛⲁϫⲱϩⲙ̄ ⲧⲏⲩⲧⲛ̄ ⲁⲛ ⲁⲗⲗⲁ ⲡⲉⲧⲛ̄ⲛⲏⲩ ⲉⲃⲟⲗ ϩⲛ̄ ⲧⲉⲧⲛ̄ⲧⲁⲡⲣⲟ ⲛ̄ⲧⲟϥ ⲡⲉⲧⲛⲁϫⲁϩⲙ̄ ⲧⲏⲩⲧⲛ̄** (*Gos.Thom.* 14); πᾶν τὸ ἔξωθεν εἰσπορευόμενον εἰς τὸν ἄνθρωπον οὐ δύναται αὐτὸν κοινῶσαι ... τὸ ἐκ τοῦ ἀνθρώπου εκπορευόμενον, ἐκεῖνο κοινοῖ τὸν ἄνθρωπον (Mk 7:18b, 20b).

157 Dunn points out that both Paschen (1970, 173ff) and Hübner (1986 [1973], 165ff) argue for vv 18b and 20b preserving elements closer to an underlying Aramaic saying, than does v 15 (Dunn 1990, 55, n.21).

158 Booth 1986, 89f.

159 Dunn 1990, 51. Although Räisänen (1986, 238–239) suggests that the saying was created in an emancipated Jewish Christian group engaged in a Gentile mission, he also considers the possibility of a remoulding of some version of Mt 23:25f.

ondary.[160] No recourse to Matthew is necessary, however, for a hypothesis of a dialectical negation underlying the Markan text. An original saying with a relative meaning would explain both a pre-Markan association with the hand-washing tradition and Mark's redactional use of it for other purposes.

Hand-washing and eating at the time of Jesus

As we have seen above, there are good reasons for regarding Jesus' saying in Mk 7:15 as having an historical basis. Although originally it might not necessarily have been attached to any of the traditions in Mk 7, it certainly did not refer to the food laws (Lev 11). Looking for a context, hand-washing, or transmission of impurity in general, is a likely candidate. The discussion about clean and unclean food in the early church was mainly another issue (i.e. pork, as well as sacrificial meat), and I will not pursue the discussion about subsequent Christian interpretation any further. Since my chief interest in this study concerns Jesus' attitude to bodily transmittable impurities, I find the saying in 7:15 important for other reasons. If taken as responding to the issue of hand-washing and interpreted in a relative sense, it implies a seemingly indifferent attitude of Jesus towards bodily impurity. Such an interpretation is dependent, however, on hand-washing being a halakhic custom, practised at least to some extent at the time of Jesus.

The *Mishnah* tractate *Yadayim* discusses hand-washing in detail and at length. The custom of washing hands before meals is taken for granted, and in the context it is clear that the issue is purity of food.[161] A preoccupation with hands is similarly revealed in *mBer* 8:2–3, where the presupposition is that defilement of food during meals should be avoided.[162] Most scholars during the nineteenth century took for granted that this was the state of *halakhah* during the time of Jesus, although the *Mishnah* was not finally redacted until ca. 200 CE.

The standard view had already been questioned by Adolf Büchler in 1906, in his work on the Galilean *am ha-arets*. Büchler claimed that hand-washing was practised by Hillel and Shammai in connection with *qodoshim* (sacrificial food) only. While he admits that purity was observed for eating *hullin* (ordinary food) already in temple times, Büchler suggests that this was practised by a few individuals as a voluntary act of piety only, not as a halakhic rule, and mainly by Shammaites, who were the originators of the halakhah, which was accepted in Yavneh by the school of Gamaliel, around 100 CE. Most rabbinic references to

---

[160] On this point I am taking a different stance today than in the 2002 edition.

[161] I.e. purity of priestly food (heave-offering or *terumah* [תְּרוּמָה]), and ordinary, unconsecrated food (*hullin* [חוּלִּין]). The mishnaic discussions have nothing to do with the question of clean and unclean animals, mentioned above. The idea of eating pork was totally excluded, and would not turn up as a matter for discussion. *mYad* 1:1–2; 3:1–2; cf. *mZab* 5:12.

[162] This is clear from the explanation in the *Tosefta* (*tBer* 6(5):2–3). Alon 1977, 210.

hand-washing, however, concern *terumah* rather than *hullin*. This means that almost all references refer to priests, and further developments belong mainly to the Ushan period.[163]

Büchler's view was not generally accepted and has been refuted by Gedalyahu Alon.[164] Alon claimed that purity was not practised only in the area of temple and priests during the Second Temple period,[165] nor was the preparation of *hullin* in purity "the practice of the few, but was a religious custom observed by all the Associates." Alon seems to regard the *haberim* as a large group during the time of the temple. But he also suggests the possibility of this being a custom of all Israelites, "only the Associates took it upon themselves to keep the observance scrupulously."[166] Alon finds the suggestion far-fetched that the sages of Usha should have given lots of new and more stringent *halakhot*, not based on earlier tradition.[167] While Hillelites and Shammaites differ about the *order* of the washing of hands at meals, the disagreements about details show that the practice is presupposed. Although hand-washing for *hullin* was not accepted by *all* sages or practised by *all* Israel in the days of Jesus (the gospels thus make exaggerating generalizations), "it is not possible to reject the premise that essentially this precept was in force already prior to the Destruction, even though it was uncertain and subject to dispute."[168] I actually find Alon fairly balanced. During the same period, Louis Finkelstein and Joachim Jeremias, among others, treat purity of food as a membership requirement for Pharisees in general, thus virtually equating the Pharisees with *haberim*.[169] Alon does not make such claims.

Jacob Neusner has repeatedly described the Pharisees of the first century as a pure food association, who, since the time of Hillel, turned more towards piety than politics, and aspired to priestly sanctity. The main means of achieving this was through the meal, i.e. handling and eating *hullin* in a state of purity.[170] There is, however, an ambiguity in Neusner's descriptions of the predecessors

---

[163] Büchler 1968 [1906], 83ff, 130ff.

[164] Alon 1977. The articles in this English translation were collected and published in the 1950s (in Hebrew) after Alon's death, but the relevant articles referred to here were published in *Tarbiz* in 1937–1938.

[165] Alon 1977, 190f.

[166] Alon 1977, 209. For the possibility of tensions between stricter groups and ordinary people being due not to the difference between observance and non-observance, but rather to the degree of *consistency* in observance, see below, 72, 86–87, 269–272.

[167] Alon 1977, 214. Cf. the discussion above about an increasing leniency coupled with an identifying and detail-producing process, 54, 55. Cf. below, 110, 116, 154–156.

[168] Alon 1977, 219, 221f. Quote from 221–222.

[169] Sanders 1990, 152, referring to Finkelstein 1938, 1: 77, and Jeremias 1958 [1923], IIB: 251, 266. Pharisaic groups are discussed above, 44–48, and in the summary below, 86–88.

[170] Neusner 1979, 14; Neusner 1971, 3: 288: "Eating one's secular, that is, unconsecrated, food in a state of ritual purity as if one were a Temple priest in the cult was one of the two significations of party membership."

of the mishnaic rabbis living like priests, as well as in his hesitance sometimes to identify them outright with the Pharisees. He considers them to be a group consisting of ordinary Israelites pretending to be, or wanting to live as priests, while knowing they were not priests and not claiming to be the new priests.[171]

This is the point at which Sanders aims his criticism of Neusner. Much of Sanders' discussion is centred on refuting Neusner's claim that the Pharisees tried to keep priestly purity laws outside of the temple, applying them to their meal. The polemic against Neusner is inherent in the title of Sanders' essay: "Did the Pharisees Eat Ordinary Food in Purity?"[172] Says Sanders: "The full analogy between the altar and the common table which Neusner proposes is neither implied in Leviticus nor specified in Pharisaic material."[173] In this Sanders is right, and it is regrettable that the discussion has received such a polemical note, with an unfortunate formulation restricting its scope. "Living like priests" is to me more of a later construction, attempting to explain a phenomenon. Sanders can easily show that Pharisees did not live like priests, since they did not avoid corpse-impurity for all but next of kin.[174] And one could furthermore claim that they did not eat like priests either, since they could eat their food after immersion, while priests could not, in case of impurity, eat until evening, since a *tebul yom* contaminated *terumah*.[175] This is not the point, however, since we have traces of a phenomenon that needs explanation, not denial. Despite Sanders' criticism, Neusner's observation that two thirds of all rabbinic pericopes from pre-70 authorities, which are verified according to his method, relate to matters of food and table fellowship, cannot be lightly dismissed.[176] Sanders admits, and even returns several times to the judgment, that the Pharisees did make *minor symbolic gestures* towards living like priests. In this he comes closer to Neusner than he would like to, and thus has to emphasize "how minor the gesture was," stressing that the Pharisees did not accept the antisocial aspects of the priestly law.[177]

It would perhaps be better to drop the discussion about living or eating "like priests." It is evident that many Jews, including the Pharisees of the Second Temple period, strove for a higher degree of holiness than the Torah prescribed

---

[171] Neusner 1974–1977, 22: 106, 108.

[172] Sanders 1990, 131–254.

[173] Sanders 1990, 176.

[174] Sanders 1990, 187, referring to Lev. 21:1–3.

[175] Maccoby 1999, 209f. Cf. Booth 1986, 201.

[176] Neusner 1971, 3: 297ff. Cf. Sanders 1990, 177f.

[177] Sanders 1990, 192. This last point has to do with Sanders' overarching aim, to defend the Pharisees against their caricatures (cf. 252f). In this context Sanders seems to downplay evidence for the Pharisees separating themselves from other people. He admits that "Pharisees did not, at least on average, eat with people below them on the purity scale." But he thinks that "Christian scholars make too much of this. ... In real life, most people do not eat with most other people. In communities today where Methodists, for example, have church suppers, usually there are only Methodists there" (1990, 441). This is not, however, a useful analogy.

for a lay Israelite.[178] This might be explained as adapting to priestly customs; that is not a *rationale* for the behaviour or development, however, but an interpretative description. What could later be seen as a partial likeness is not necessarily an adequate explanation of origin.

The custom of washing hands is sometimes seen as originating with regulations for priest, such as those of Ex 30:18–21, about the bronze basin.[179] Priests should wash hands and feet before ministering in the tabernacle. This does not refer to eating, however. As stated above, the whole mishnaic tractate of *Yadayim* presupposes hand-washing before eating, the question being under what circumstances and in what manner.

Another possible context for the origin of a hand-washing practice is the separation of *terumah* by ordinary Israelites. This is, according to Sanders, not a biblical requirement, but pre-Pharisaic passages such as Judith 11:13 and Isa 66:20 testify to the view that ordinary people must not touch *terumah*, and that offerings were brought to the temple in pure vessels. Sanders thinks that hand-washing before separating *terumah* was introduced by the time of Shammai and Hillel.[180] It is clearly taken for granted in the *Mishnah* (*mToh* 10:4). Harrington argues that the prohibition for impure people to touch *terumah* was not a late innovation, but is made clear by Lev 7:19 and 22:3. According to the latter passage, defiling priestly food resulted in *karet*, being cut off from God's presence.[181] The unanswered questions, however, are how a state pure enough for separating *terumah* was achieved, and at what time hand-washing became a means for achieving such a state.

Turning from the question of priests' food (*terumah*) to ordinary food (*hullin*), another possible origin for the custom of hand-washing should be mentioned. In Lev 15:11 the *zab* is seen as transmitting impurity by touch, unless he has washed his hands. Although referring to the *zab* only and not belonging to a context of food, we nevertheless have a rule regarding hand-washing from a time far before that of Hillel and Shammai. In the case of a *zab*, hand-washing protected that which he touched from defilement. This has possibly been a precedent for an expanded hand-washing practice in a context where concern for purity increased and the impurity system expanded. At the time of the *Mishnah*, it seems as if hand-washing was used to protect food from contamination; since hands can be separately made impure (*mYad* 3:1–2), they are able to contaminate *terumah* (*mZab* 5:12), those who eat food made unclean are themselves made unclean (*mToh* 2:2), and there are numerous regulations for how to purify hands (*mYadayim*). The *Tosefta* gives some further clarification. A *haber* undertakes to eat *hullin* in purity (*tDem* 2:2), and an *am ha-arets* is de-

[178] Cf. Harrington 1993, 281.
[179] Cf. Booth 1986, 158.
[180] Sanders 1990, 30.
[181] Harrington 1993, 277f.

fined by R. Meir as one who does not eat *hullin* in a state of purity (*tAZ* 3 (4):10).[182] But the reader can easily see the missing link: in what way, if at all, do impure hands contaminate *ordinary* food (*hullin*), and at what time did such a view arise? There is a *baraitha* in *bShabb* 14b, claiming that Shammai and Hillel decreed impurity for hands. There is a saying in *mPar* 11:4–5 which seems to state that a person who has immersed himself or herself does not render *hullin* unclean. There is, however, no mention of hands in that context. I agree with Sanders, that although the authors of the *Mishnah* evidently took hand-washing seriously, and although some apparently practised it in Jesus' day, we do not know the chain of tradition from those who began observing the practice to the *Mishnah*.[183] But I do not agree with him that this proves that "failure to wash hands before eating would not have been much of an issue," and that neglecting it was "not serious in the least."[184]

Sanders' reconstruction is that many people in Jesus' time thought that priests should wash hands before eating *terumah*. Some people undertook to be trustworthy handlers of priests' food and also washed their hands before handling *terumah*. A small number of *haberim* probably adopted the practice of eating *hullin* in a state of purity, i.e. they washed their hands before eating. This was eventually made into normative practice by the Rabbis, but before 70 CE the common people did not accept it.[185] The main reason for this should have been, according to Sanders, practical. Accepting priestly purity laws for ordinary food would mean that certain impure people had to starve.[186] This is apparently exaggerated. It would only mean that people suffering from impurities which could not be dealt with in a *miqveh* at once (*yoledot*, *niddot*, *zabim*), could not eat their food in purity during this period. But Sanders finds it hard to

---

[182] Cf. Harrington 1993, 273ff.

[183] Sanders 1990, 185.

[184] Sanders 1990, 40, 90. Sanders' argument aims at proving that the Pharisees, or even the *haberim*, would not have regarded Jesus as a sinner, even if he did not follow their rules, since they did not regard such rules as binding on others (1985, 185ff). Unfortunately there are missing links in Sanders' argument just as there are in the mishnaic evidence. Sanders' argument runs as follows: 1) Tiberias was built on a graveyard and its people were constantly impure. 2) Jesus did not go there and tell them that "they were fine just as they were." 3) Hand-washing was a minor matter to most Jews. Hence Jesus could not have had any serious dispute with his contemporaries over laws of purity (1990, 40f).

[185] Sanders 1985, 185f. Sanders' explanation for people not accepting such a practice is that "had they done so they would have met one of the requirements of the *ḥaberim*. But their failure to be *ḥaberim* in this way, as in others, did not make them sinners" (1985, 186). And further: "While the *ḥaberim* undertook to observe special purity rules, there is no evidence that they thought that those who did not do so were sinners, and there should certainly be no reason to single out Jesus' disciples for criticism. Jesus and his disciples were obviously not *ḥaberim*, but that put them in the vast majority" (1985, 265f). It should be possible to argue that Jesus or ordinary people were not regarded as sinners, however, without underestimating the increase in purity aspirations among people in general.

[186] Sanders 1990, 149ff, 174ff.

believe that even Pharisees or priests really followed many of the purity rules. He actually says that they would have done so if it had been possible, but since the rules were so impractical they probably did not do it.[187] Sanders' own evidence for people in general striving for purity in the Second Temple period,[188] is good reason for believing that many aspired to as high a level of purity as possible. I suggest that what distinguished the stricter current from the rest was the latter's *lack of consistency*, which caused the former group to regard many Israelites as not "trustworthy." This division could also explain ambiguities in the mishnaic legislation, for example regulations for handling *terumah* in purity. It has been suggested that the "only possible reason for having special rules about heave offering" was that Pharisees did not handle their own common food with as high a degree of purity.[189] Another equally plausible reason, however, would be that everyone was *obliged* to take care when handling heave offering (*terumah*), while not everybody managed to be consistent about his/her own food. And the mishnaic legislation is specific about *terumah*, since it would be a transgression to defile it.[190]

An expansionist purity practice in Second Temple Judaism

Inherent in this discussion about whether *hullin* as well as *terumah* should be eaten in a state of purity, is the larger question about the place of purity in Second Temple Judaism. Is purity to be explained as a concern for the temple only,

---

[187] Sanders 1990, 160ff, 232ff. Questioning whether priests kept their wives separate during menstruation or after child-birth, Sanders remarks "Some were quite poor and would have found it very hard to keep this law—hard to find the extra space, the extra furniture and the extra food (their wives had to eat something)" (1990, 233). While I have empathy for the poor priests, I do not believe that the premises on which the conclusion rests are true. That poverty is no hindrance for adherence to a strict purity *halakhah* is empirically demonstrated by the isolation of menstruants, parturients and corpse impure among the Falashas. Cf. Leslau 1951, xivf; 1957, 91f; Semi 1985, 105ff; Corinaldi 1995, 117ff; Corinaldi 1998, 75ff. Isolation of menstruants to various degrees is found in several sectarian traditions at different points in time, such as the Karaites, Samaritans and Kurdish Jews (cf. Corinaldi 1998, 77, n.109 and 110; Milgrom 1991, 765); cf. Zoroastrian practices (Milgrom 1991, 952).

[188] Sanders 1990, 184; 1992, 218f, 229.

[189] Sanders 1990, 234.

[190] Cf. Alon's view that the eating of *hullin* in purity was a widespread custom, was regarded as obligatory, and was taught as established *halakhah*, but the eating of defiled *hullin* was nevertheless not absolutely forbidden (1977, 207).

In view of the problems in assessing the legal situation during Jesus' time, Westerholm is making it too simple when he says, referring to Shammai and Hillel declaring hands as unclean (*bShabb* 14b), and discussing hand-washing and the mixing of cups (*mBer* 8:2, 4), that "we need not doubt that the practice of washing the hands before eating ordinary meals was observed in the time of Jesus at least by the adherents of the Pharisaic schools" (Westerholm 1978, 73). In the end, however, he might in this case come closer to the truth than Sanders, who agrees that hand-washing was practised by Pharisees from the time of Hillel, but *only* in the contexts of *terumah*, sabbath and festival meals, scriptures and prayer (Sanders 1990, 228ff).

or as a concern of everyday life? The evidence is ambiguous. On the one hand, purity legislation in the *Mishnah* often refers to priests, temple offerings and *terumah.*[191] This is in accord with much of the biblical motivation for purity (Lev 7:19–21; 12:4; 15:31; 21:4; 22:4–8). Purity is important because of the holiness of the temple and God's presence in the midst of Israel. But at the same time it is clear that purity was a desirable state for many people during the first century, regardless of whether they were going to visit the temple or separate *terumah* in the near future. Evidence for this is found in both Philo and Josephus.[192] Although such a position could have been reinforced after the fall of the temple, it existed well before, and is just as much motivated by biblical legislation (Lev 11; 13; 18:19–28). In view of this, it is clear that people were expected to purify themselves of all types of defilement, even in contexts outside the temple.[193] Failure to fulfil the prescribed purification rituals was considered a sin.[194]

These somewhat conflicting pieces of evidence are best explained by different traditions in the Pentateuch. Alon speaks about a restrictionist and an expansionist tendency in rabbinic Judaism which both find scriptural support, since there is a duality in the Torah.[195] Jacob Milgrom agrees with Alon that there are (in Milgrom's terms) minimalist and maximalist trends in the biblical material, but explains this as a result of different sources.[196] Leviticus is mainly construed from a Priestly source, P (1–16), and a Holiness source, H (17–26).[197]

---

[191] Later, when most purity practices of the *Mishnah* were abandoned (except for those of *Niddah*), this became the general interpretation. Cf. Maimonides: "Whatever is written in Scripture and in traditional teaching about the laws relating to things unclean and things clean is relevant only to the Temple and to its Hallowed Things and to heave offerings and second tithe, for it warns those who are unclean against entering the Temple or eating in uncleanness anything that is hallowed or heave offering or tithe. But no such prohibition applies to common food, and it is permissible to eat common food that is unclean and to drink liquids that are unclean." *Mishneh Torah* 10 (Book of Cleanness), part 6 (The Uncleanness of Foodstuffs), 16:8.

[192] That purity was regarded as a positive good, pursued for its own sake, is argued by Sanders 1990, 184. Cf. statements of Josephus (*Ag. Ap.* 2:205) and of Philo (*Spec. Laws* 3:205f) about corpse impurity, which point to the obligation to purify oneself, quite apart from temple matters. See Alon 1977, 226ff and Oppenheimer 1977, 54. Cf. Maimonides' comment, juxtaposed to the passage quoted in the previous note, about "the pious of former times" who "used to eat their common food in conditions of cleanness, and all their days they were wary of every uncleanness." *Mishneh Torah* 10. 6. 16:12.

[193] Westerholm 1978, 64; but cf. the hesitance of Booth 1986, 152f.

[194] Milgrom 1991, 310ff; Sanders 1985, 184.

[195] Alon 1977, 232f.

[196] Milgrom 1990a, 85ff. Cf. Booth's comments about the Priestly Code accentuating the "connection of the purity rules with the Temple because of its priestly authorship," while "neither the Covenant Code in Exodus nor the Deuteronomic Code states the defilement of the tabernacle to be the reason for the avoidance of impurity" (1986, 152).

[197] Milgrom 1991, 1f, 13. In addition, parts of *Exodus* and *Numbers* should be assigned to P, as well as some material in Lev 23. H has redacted P and supplied several interpolations in Lev 1–

The holiness source posits the holiness of the land and deals with the avoidance of impurity outside of the camp or the temple city. It takes an expansionist view regarding impurity. The division is not between priests and lay people, but between a P source, which limits impurity to the sanctuary and its surroundings, and an H source, which extends the sacred sphere to the land of Israel, and hence to all Israelites.[198] The existence of different strata in the Pentateuch, especially in *Leviticus*, may explain the ambiguity not only in biblical legislation, but in later interpretation. It seems as if both restrictionist and expansionist views of purity, based on scriptural interpretation, were current during Second Temple times. Such a diversity in practice and interpretation might explain some of the ambiguity in Tannaitic material; the *Mishnah* and the *Tosefta* do not reflect one clear and unitary tradition. In early rabbinic tradition there was room for *both* restrictionist and expansionist attitudes to impurity. This should be compared with the Qumran sectarians, who *combined* a restrictionist with an expansionist position: in one sense all Israel was holy, but only the members were considered a true remnant; in another sense holiness was limited to the sanctuary and its city, but within the temple city it was expanded, so that its residents must live "priestly."[199]

With this in view, rabbinic material should not be pressed into the service of *one* perspective, when it could more easily fit into another.[200] It is reasonable to suppose that restrictionist and expansionist views were parts of first-century Jewish society, and that there were, within the expansionist current, several subgroups with somewhat differing standards.

We see that purity outside of the temple was already an issue early in the Second Temple period, and that the area of impurity was constantly expanded by one current in Judaism. Such expansion, however, was not without problems. Sanders is right when he notes all sorts of ensuing practical problems and inconveniences. It does not follow from this, however, that hardly anybody should have adhered to an expansionist interpretation in real life.[201] Detailed restrictions and definitions of modes of transfer and degrees of susceptibility were needed to make it possible and practicable to remain in, or restore a state of purity. Perhaps the most important development which made it possible to implement an expansionist view of impurity in practice, was the *miqveh*—the immersion pool. The large number of *miqvaot* found by archaeologists, dating

---

16, as well as editorial comments throughout the Pentateuch (13, 61ff). Cf. Harrington 1993, 5. For a comprehensive discussion of the H source, see Milgrom 2000a, 1319–1367.

[198] Milgrom 1990a, 86.

[199] Milgrom 1990a, 88f, with references to CD 4:6; 8:28; 1QS 1:12–13; 2:9, 16; 5:13, 18; 8:17, 21, 24; 1QM 12:1; 11Q19 [11QT] 45:7–12; 48:7, 15–17.

[200] Cf. the remarks by Alon 1977, 206.

[201] Sanders returns repeatedly to the impracticability of following purity laws, as an an argument against an influential expansionist current. See 1990, 149, 160f, 174f, 233 (cf. above, 72, n.187).

mostly from the first century CE, supports the view that purity was a concern of more than a few. More than three hundred such stepped pools have been found in many places, such as Jericho, Sepphoris, Gamla, Matsada, and Qumran. The largest number of pools was found in Jerusalem, and several were situated near the entrance to the temple.[202] None of these pools are drained. Some of them are single, with no source of running water. These are most common in the Upper City, in Sepphoris, and in some of Herod's palaces. Others are connected to an upper, unstepped storage pool (*otsar*), from which additional rain water could be supplied during the dry season, without "drawn water" being added.[203] Such "twin" pools have been found in almost all places, except in Qumran, and they fit with the rabbinic requirements for valid immersion pools, which are described and presupposed in the *Mishnah* tractate *Miqvaot*.[204] Reasonable conclusions from these findings are that immersion was a wide-spread custom; it was practised before entering the temple, but also, at least by parts of the population, in circumstances apart from the temple, and in locations far from it; some people, perhaps the majority of the rich priestly aristocracy, as Sanders has suggested,[205] did not follow the practice attested by later mishnaic regulations which prohibited adding "drawn water" to a *miqveh*, while another part of the population did. This means that at least the basic outline of the rabbinic rules for immersion existed in Jesus' time, and it is not very far-fetched to interpret the storage pool as "Pharisaic," while Sadducees and Essenes seem to have accepted single *miqvaot*.[206]

The fairly wide-spread use of *miqvaot* made an expansionist view of impurity possible to implement. In biblical legislation, immersion was required for major impurities, and it was coupled with waiting for sunset.[207] As sources of

---

[202] Mazar 1975, 146f; Avigad 1984 [1980], 139–143, 160; Reich 1993; Sanders 1990, 214–227, 355 n.28; 1992, 222–230. *Miqvaot* had been found earlier, but were not identified as such until the 1963–1964 excavation season on Matsada. Sanders 1990, 215f. For a different evaluation, identifying fewer pools as ritual baths, see H. Eshel 1997; B.G. Wright 1997.

[203] For still water to be considered valid for purification, it must not, according to expansionist views, go below a certain quantity and it should be collected by natural means (cf. Harrington 1993, 132–139); Sanders 1990, 214–226; Regev 2000, 236, n.38.

[204] Sanders 1990, 223ff. Cf. photographs above, 42. There are also pools provided by a constant flow of spring water, especially in Jericho. Maybe the "twin" pools in Jericho were built while the Pharisees were in favour with the Hasmoneans. Single pools have been found in Jericho as well, and in one case a storage pool was filled with rubble and the channel blocked up, which could imply a change in practice (218, 219, 223); cf. Reich 1981; Netzer 1982.

[205] Sanders 1990, 218ff.

[206] An interesting feature of some public pools is the division of steps, or cutting of a second set of steps, which made it possible to descend impure and come out pure, without touching others on their way down. Reich 1981, 52; 1984; Sanders 1990, 217f; 1992, 225. See the discussion of *Papyrus Oxyrhynchus 840*, below, 256–260.

[207] Lev 11:24, 27, 28, 39, 40; 15:5–7, 18, 20, 27. Details for different types of impurities and their purification are dealt with in the following chapter. While immersion is not expressly stated, Milgrom and Harrington argue for the phrase יִטְמָא עַד־הָעָרֶב ("he will be impure until

impurity were defined, modes of transfer expanded, and chains of transmission further developed, the *miqveh* made frequent and regular immersions possible. In spite of this, an expansionist view would have made purity difficult to maintain within the bounds of normal social life. This can be deduced from the expansionist legislation of the *Temple Scroll*. Although some of it relates to an ideal Jerusalem, and therefore prescribes for example a three-day exclusion from the temple city after a seminal emission and sexual intercourse,[208] and a seven-day exclusion for a *zab*,[209] rules for the ordinary city seem to allow purifying persons to remain at home and eat ordinary food.[210] In case of severe seven-day impurities, one had to immerse on the first, third and seventh day. The first-day ablution might have served to remove a degree of impurity, which made it possible to remain within the city/settlement and eat food.[211] But the *Temple Scroll* stresses, for light as well as severe impurities, that they last until the evening, i.e. at sunset. (11Q19 [11QT] 49–51). And since immersion and sunset belong together, the purifying person could not eat pure food until after sunset.[212] This meant that even contact with light impurities and normal sexual relations caused real inconveniences for expansionists, in spite of a system of purification by immersion. The withdrawal of the Qumran sectarians testifies to this. Within the community it was easier to avoid impurity, but outside the Qumran community, life should have become just as impracticable as Sanders believes it would have been for anyone being particular about purity.

What made an expansionist view on purity possible within the bounds of normal society was, in addition to the *miqveh*, the concept of *tebul yom*. This rabbinic interpretation of the relationship between immersion and sunset meant that by immersion the impurity of a person was lessened by one degree at once, even before sunset.[213] The person purified by immersion, waiting for sunset was called a *tebul yom*. This concept must be seen as an early one, in view of the probably polemical emphasis on sunset in the above-mentioned passages from the *Temple Scroll*, and especially in 4QMMT B15.[214] It made it possible

the evening"), as always implying immersion (Milgrom 1991, 667; Harrington 1993, 117ff). Harrington points to Lev 11:39–40 and 17:15, which both use the phrase in the same context, while only the latter text mentions immersion.

208 J. Baumgarten 1980, 159. 11Q19 [11QT] 45:7–12.

209 11Q19 [11QT] 45:15–18: probably for the purifying "leper" and the corpse-impure as well.

210 Harrington 1993, 65.

211 Cf. Milgrom 1990a, 512–18; Harrington 1993, 60, 76, 77. Cf. Philo, who seems to presuppose a first-day immersion, *Spec.Laws* 3:206–207.

212 This is made clear by halakhic texts such as 4QMMT B15 and 4Q514 1 1:3–10. The latter text deals specifically with the "temporally impure" (lines 5 and 8: טמאי הימים), and mentions "whoever has not started to cleanse himself" (line 4: [איש] אשר לא החל לטהור).

213 For a discussion of degrees, see below, 78–81. Texts referring to immersion, but not mentioning sunset, could be used for justifying the concept of *tebul yom*. Lev 14:8; 15:13; 16:28.

214 4QMMT is a letter singling out points of dissent between the addressees and the originating group. The position that the priest conducting the red cow rite must be pure by sunset, and not

to maintain a high standard of purity while living in a mixed community; meals could be eaten in purity before evening (except for the consumption of *terumah* and *qodoshim*, i.e. priests' food), and normal marital life would be possible without too many restrictions, permitting "access to the non-sacrificial purities abounding in Jerusalem."[215]

Sanders thinks that for this to have worked, Pharisees should have immersed every morning, which they did not do according to the "morning bathers," who complain about them because of this negligence (*tYad* 2:20). He rather thinks most of them, Pharisees and priests alike, immersed themselves together with their clothes, beddings and chairs once a month, after their wives' period of menstruation.[216] But there are other possible interpretations. Pharisees would not have needed to immerse in the morning unless they had had sex or become impure through other means. The morning bathers seem to have immersed every morning regardless of the circumstances.[217]

The concept of *tebul yom* made it possible for the woman who had given birth (the *yoledet*) to lead a normal life after the initial 7 or 14 days, in spite of a total period of 40 or 80 days.[218] Although biblical legislation is not explicit about it, because of the analogy with menstruation, the *yoledet* immersed after the initial period, and was thence considered to be in an intermediate state. According to the *Mishnah*, she could eat second tithe and separate *terumah*, but not touch it after having separated it.[219] Sanders regards this as strong evidence against the view that food was generally eaten in purity, since such an impure person was even allowed to handle *terumah*. Since he does not, however, consider her status as a *tebulat yom*, his argument carries little weight.[220]

While Neusner in the 1970s seemed to regard the concept of *tebul yom* as a post-70 development, connected to the idea of degrees of impurity, which also should be regarded as fairly late,[221] I think there are convincing reasons for claiming that the basic idea of *tebul yom* was current during the Second Temple period, not least in view of the evidence from Qumran, verifying some mishnaic

---

only as a *tebul yom*, is a point of conflict between Pharisees and Sadducees in rabbinic texts. *mPar* 3:7; cf. 5:4; *tPar* 3:8.

[215] J. Baumgarten 1980, 159. "Without this leniency, defined by the rabbinic category of *tebul yom*, the widespread observance of purity and the maintenance of normal marital life would have been utterly irreconcilable." (158).

[216] Sanders 1990, 150; 1992, 440.

[217] Harrington 1993, 270. In addition, the dispute with the morning bathers concerns immersion before *saying prayers*, not before eating.

[218] Cf. Lev 12.

[219] Harrington 1993, 268. *mNid* 10:6–7; *mTY* 4:1–2.

[220] Sanders 1990, 197f.

[221] Neusner 1974–1977, 22: 148. Cf. 22: 62, 160ff. Note that the text of 4QMMT was not made available before the 1990s.

presuppositions.[222] Purification in general and immersion in particular cannot, however, be discussed without turning to the question of removes or degrees of impurity. What does the rabbinic system of degrees of impurity look like, and did it exist at least in principle before the fall of the Second Temple? What was the status of a *tebul yom* in the time of Jesus?

Degrees of impurity and contamination chains

Several scholars have developed charts for illustrating chains of contamination and degrees of impurity within different systems: the biblical, the sectarian at Qumran, and the rabbinic.[223] All such charts are constructions, based on textual evidence of different kinds, and sometimes in part on conjecture, but for many purposes helpful. The simplified charts in Chapter I (Figs. 1 and 2) describe how contamination was conceived of in the biblical and rabbinic systems respectively. All major sources of impurity share the same basic condition as corpse-contaminated persons and objects, thus being subject to a seven-day period of purification. They contaminate other persons and objects with a lighter, one-day impurity (except in the case of intercourse, which transfers a seven-day impurity), basically through touch, but in certain cases through overhang or pressure (*midras*). In the case of someone with a bodily discharge (*zab, zabah, niddah, yoledet*) exercising pressure (on objects used for lying, sitting or leaning), impurity can be transferred to persons and objects at a further remove.[224]

In the rabbinic tradition, the biblical customs were systematized, defined, developed and ordered, but mishnaic discussions have different points of departure for their chains of impurity: a system is at times outlined with a view to sequences of contact, based on the contaminating *power* of that which imparts impurity; at other times it is outlined with a view to various levels of sanctification, based on the *capacity* to receive contamination, i.e. susceptibility. This results in a certain opacity in many rabbinic passages, as is evident from the detailed and complicated discussions in *mToh* 2.[225]

---

[222] This is questioned by Grabbe 1997, 91ff, but his arguments are too weak even to convince himself fully (93). Cf. Schiffman 1994.

[223] David P. Wright 1987; Milgrom 1991; Harrington 1993.

[224] I.e. the chair of a *zabah* is impure for seven days and transmits a one-day impurity to other persons or objects.

[225] Neusner 1974–1977, 22: 160ff. Booth discusses the rabbinic distinction between impure (טמא) and unfit (פסול), explaining that an item is rendered impure if defiled by a subject possessing an impurity of at least two degrees higher than the lowest possible degree of the recipient, but only becomes unfit or invalid when defiled by a subject only one degree higher, in which case it cannot transmit impurity (Booth 1986, 128f). This is confusing, however, since it might be misunderstood to mean that a person unclean in the first remove (degree) could not defile ordinary food, but only *terumah* or *qodoshim*. The word "unfit" is used, however, for different types of food (*hullin, terumah, qodoshim*) at their lowest possible degree of susceptibility, i.e. *terumah* cannot be contaminated at a fourth remove; contamination stops at the third,

Fig. 3 is a more detailed illustration of the rabbinic system than Fig. 2, but still much simplified, and similarly taking both approaches into account, although basically construed from the notion of degrees of susceptibility. Within this system, immersion is thought to remove one "layer" of impurity, thus lessening the degree or remove by one. A person who during the day had come into contact with a "father of impurity," maybe inadvertently, or who had sexual intercourse or a seminal emission at night, would be impure in the first degree, and thus contaminate food and liquid, in the second degree. But after immersion, according to the concept of *tebul yom*, that person could handle ordinary food even before sunset (although not *terumah* or *qodoshim*).

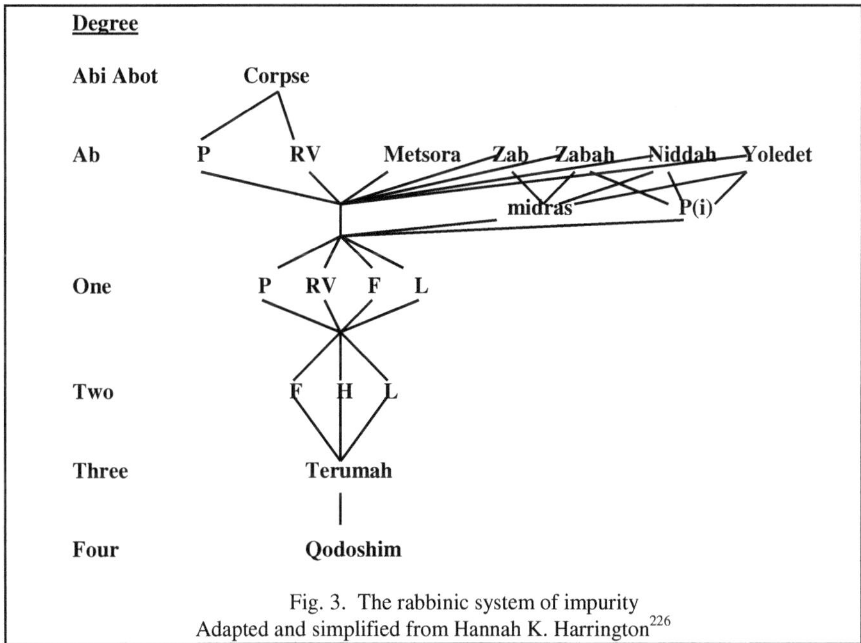

Fig. 3. The rabbinic system of impurity
Adapted and simplified from Hannah K. Harrington[226]

---

at which it is called "unfit." It may, however, contaminate items which are susceptible to further degrees of impurity. It should be noted that modern writers rarely use this terminological distinction.

[226] Harrington 1993, 149, 203, 240, 245. Abi Abot=Father of fathers; Ab=Father [of impurity]; P=Person; RV=Rinsable vessel; Metsora="Leper": Zab=Male discharger; Zabah=Female discharger; Niddah=Menstruant; Yoledet=Parturient; F=Food; H=Hands; L=Liquid; Terumah=Priestly rations; Qodoshim=Sacrificial food; (i)=intercourse; Midras refers here to objects for sitting or lying, which have been subjected to pressure, i.e. the greater weight of any of the four dischargers in the figure above has affected the object. Earthenware is not subject to *midras* impurity, but should for all other purposes be included in the category of RV. The special case of the saddle is not included.

When reading different mishnaic texts, however, the system does not appear as clear-cut as in the figure above. This has given rise to several interpretations. Consider the following (*mHag* 2:7):

> The clothing of ordinary folk [*ammei ha-arets*] is in the status of *midras* uncleanness[227] for abstainers [*perushim*]. The clothing of abstainers is in the status of *midras* uncleanness for those who eat heave offering [*terumah*]. The clothing of those who eat heave offering is in the status of *midras* uncleanness for those who eat Holy Things [*qodoshim*]. The clothing of those who eat Holy Things is in the status of *midras* uncleanness for those engaged in the preparation of purification water.[228]

Sanders claims this text in support of his view that many people were not very careful about purity. Pharisees, says Sanders, were more careful about avoiding impurity than the *am ha-arets*, while they were less careful than priests.[229] I believe that this passage, rather than measuring how careful people were, is intended to lay out ascending degrees of purity. However, the passage, together with its context (*mHag* 2:5–7), shows, especially when compared to other attempts at defining a system of degrees, as that in *mToh* 2:2–7, that a clear and unambiguous system is not fixed in the *Mishnah*, but rather emerges as a result of the discussions of the Tannaim. Neusner is of the opinion that the notion of removes, i.e. degrees of impurity, was first raised at Yavneh, and developed after 70 CE.[230] The various and conflicting points of departure found in mishnaic discussions suggest that a clear and elaborate system of degrees, such as in the chart above, was never fully developed during the Second Temple period. But the use of *miqvaot*, the concept of *tebul yom*, as well as the function of immersion among the Qumran sectarians, give reason for believing that *some* notion of levels of impurity existed during the first century, and was being discussed, although interpretations differed. Neusner himself points at chains of contamination in *mOhal* 1:1–3, which are verified by Aqiba, and thus cannot be later than the Yavnean period, possibly predating 70 CE.[231]

It is thus reasonable to presuppose some differentiation between different levels of impurity during the time of Jesus, while hesitating to rely on a full-fledged rabbinic system. This complicates the matter of hand-washing. According to Fig. 3 above, a person who immersed would have had access to food and drink without restrictions. The crux is the status of hands. If immersion

---

[227] I.e. contact requires immersion and waiting until the evening.

[228] Tr. J. Neusner, but without his explanatory glosses. Present explanatory glosses are mine.

[229] Sanders 1990, 205f.

[230] Neusner 1974–1977, 22: 160ff. The discussion between R. Eliezer and R. Joshua in *mToh* 2:2, based on the contaminating power, as compared with the sayings ascribed to R. Eleazar in 2:7, based on the notion of susceptibility, is taken as evidence for a post-70 development of degrees. Cf. Hübner 1986 [1973], 162f.

[231] Neusner 1974–1977, 22: 125. The organizing principle in *mOhal* 1:1–3 seems different from other chains of impurity, not really originating with either of the two notions (see previous note). Supported by Yavnean verification (Aqiba), I would regard it as a primitive tradition.

removed first-degree impurity, why should hands be washed before eating *hullin*? It seems as if this would be necessary only in the case of handling *terumah*. If people immersed, why would they need to wash their hands? And if they did not immerse regularly, of what use could hand-washing be, when the whole person suffered from first-degree impurity?[232]

Liquids, stone vessels, and the impurity of hands

In the mishnaic system, which presupposes regular immersions, hands are seen as susceptible to impurity separately from the rest of the body. There are, however, differences of opinion as to the degree. According to R. Aqiba, hands can be impure in the first degree, but according to the standard view, hands can be impure only in the second degree.[233] A possible explanation for hands defiling *hullin* can be found in the special status of liquids in the rabbinic purity system. Liquids were especially susceptible to impurity, which explains the extra probational periods concerning liquids for entering a *haburah* as well as the Qumran community.[234] In *mToh* 2:6–7, that which has second degree impurity, e.g. *hullin*, is said to render *terumah* unfit, but unconsecrated liquid *unclean*![235] The paradox is stated in *mPar* 8:7, paralleled in *mToh* 8:7.

> Whatever spoils heave offering renders the liquid unclean, to be in the first [remove], to render something unclean at one [further] remove and to render [heave offering] unfit at one [still further, namely, a third] remove. (except for a *tebul-yom*.) Lo, this one [food] says [to liquid], The things which made you unclean could not have made me unclean, but you made me unclean.

The passage explains that *terumah*, which would not have become impure (second degree) but only unfit (third degree) by e.g. *hullin* or hands of second-degree impurity, could become impure by liquid, contaminated by such *hullin* or hands, since liquid always receives first-degree impurity.[236] This means, that

[232] Sanders thinks that most people immersed infrequently, maybe once a month (1990, 228). Booth, after having shown a possible context for hand-washing (see below about liquids), retreats and ends up with a similar position: regular immersions were unrealistic. Thus hand-washing was useless, since male Jews would routinely be impure because of sexual emissions. An ordinary Jew would, according to Booth, be surprised if questioned about hand-washing, since his body was unclean anyway. Hand-washing would be useful only for a *tebul yom*, and there is no reason that the Pharisees should have regarded Jesus' disciples as *tebulei yom* (Booth 1986, 185ff). Cf. *mHag* 2:5–6 which mentions immersion for the eating of *hullin*, *terumah*, and *qodoshim* respectively.

[233] *mYad* 3:1–2. Hands should logically not be able to acquire first-degree impurity separately, since such impurity would affect the person as a whole! This is further evidence for the system not being fully harmonized until a later date. Aqiba is elsewhere expressing opinions which do not suit a neat chart or system. See above, and n.231.

[234] *tDem* 2:11–12; 1QS 6:16–22.

[235] For the distinction between unclean and unfit, see 78f, n.225.

[236] Cf. Neusner 1974–1977, 22: 161.

> if water was interposed between hands and solid *hullin*, its agency would render the *hullin* defilable by the hands: the hands, assumed second degree unless recently washed, would render the liquid first degree which, in turn, would render the *hullin* second degree.[237]

This would be the case when dipping bread in a common dish, or when moisture from the outside of a drinking cup was made unclean from some impurity of the cup's outside which was transferred via the person's hands to the food, or when moisture was made unclean from a person's hands of second degree, and transferred to the food, or to the drink. Some such view is probably behind the dispute in *mBer* 8:2 between the Houses of Hillel and Shammai about the order of mixing the cup and washing hands, the differing opinions being dependent on different views about the outside of cups.[238]

The following figure could illustrate the problem:

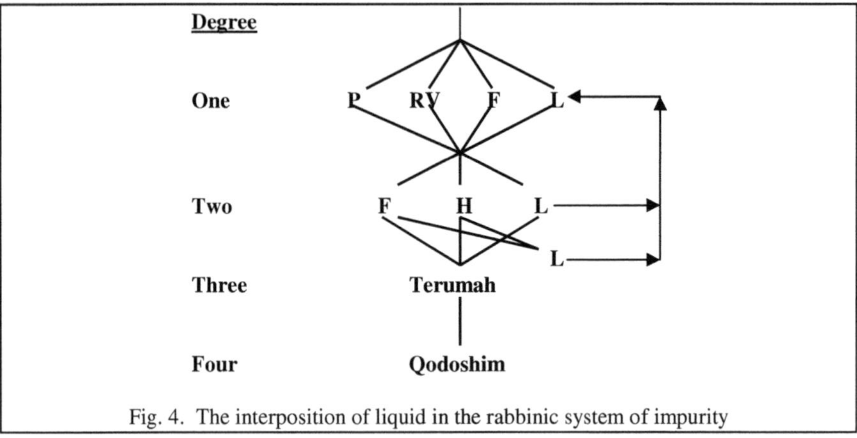

Fig. 4. The interposition of liquid in the rabbinic system of impurity

The problem involved here is not only that hands unclean in the second degree contaminate *terumah*, but that they might, via the interposition of liquid, render *hullin* unclean in the second degree. Since hands were suspected of receiving impurity very easily, they were in practice regarded as constantly unclean, and the washing of hands before eating would thus safeguard the purity of *hullin*.[239]

---

[237] Booth 1986, 184.

[238] Booth 1986, 183ff; Sanders 1990, 203f. See the explanation of *tBer* 6:2.

[239] Cf. Booth 1986, 172f. Booth goes to great lengths and appeals to diverse rabbinic evidence in attempting to prove that impurity of hands (*mZab* 5:12) belongs to the decrees passed in the upper room of Hananiah (*mShabb* 1:4), and that the Hananiah decrees should be dated around 51 CE, since they bear traces of conflicts with the Roman authorities, which would fit into the procuratorship of Cumanus. Booth interprets the Hananiah decree about hands as judging them to be more or less constantly unclean, unless recently washed, while an earlier decree of Hillel and Shammai, discussed in *bShabb* 14b, should have provided for the susceptibility of hands to *actual* defilement by a first-degree offspring of impurity. This earlier view should have gradually developed into the view reflected by the Hananiah decree (162–173). While I think Booth's

These are logical conclusions, based on mishnaic texts, but were such views and conditions current during the time of Jesus? As we have seen above, chains of contamination and degrees of impurity were being developed at the end of the Second Temple period, although they were more diverse and unspecific than the subsequent rabbinic system. I believe with Hübner that the idea of defilement of food by hands was current in Jesus' time, but in an undifferentiated form.[240] That does not necessarily mean a more lenient attitude, though. In the already mentioned saying ascribed to the early Tannaim Eliezer and Joshua (*mToh* 2:2), Joshua's statement that impure food of first and second degree imparts second-degree impurity to the eater, seems to presuppose an understanding of liquids, similar to what has been suggested above, while Eliezer's statement that the eater shares the same degree of impurity as the food, has different presuppositions and is in effect stricter.[241]

Liquids were definitely seen as problematic at the time of Jesus. In Qumran, wood and even stone were considered susceptible to impurity because of the "oil in them."[242] A clear example of liquids being discussed in Second Temple Judaism is found in 4QMMT:

> And concerning liquid streams: we are of the opinion that they are not pure, and that these streams do not act as a separative between impure and pure (liquids). For the liquid of streams and (that) of (the vessel) which receives them are alike, (being) a single liquid.[243]

Joseph Baumgarten points to the Pharisaic-Sadducean controversy in *mYad* 4:7:[244] "Say Sadducees: 'We complain against you, Pharisees. For you declare clean an unbroken stream of liquid.'" It seems as if the Qumran sectarians and the Sadduceans had a similar view on liquids as connectives, even when floating in an unbroken stream. The rabbinic position, however, was that a stream of pure liquid poured into an impure vessel did not transmit the impurity upwards.[245] While it is important to remember that the addressees of the polemi-

---

reconstruction is highly speculative and far too detailed in view of the scanty evidence, I find it reasonable to assume that hands were becoming an increasingly problematic issue in the expansionist current of the first century CE.

[240] Hübner 1986 [1973], 163.

[241] Eliezer's opinion seems to be based on the idea of connection; the eater is combined with the food. Joshua's opinion illustrates the interposing effect of liquids, The eater of food in the first degree is contaminated according to the system, and thus in the second remove (although strictly speaking this is possible for hands only in the fully developed Mishnaic system). The eater of food in the second degree, however, is contaminated by the liquid (saliva) interposing between the food and the eater. Since the liquid becomes unclean in the first remove, the eater receives a second-degree impurity. Cf. Neusner 1974–1977, 22:162.

[242] CD 12:15–17. Note the different view on stone as compared with the *Mishnah* (see below).

[243] 4QMMT B55–58, tr. Qimron and Strugnell, *DJD* 10, 53.

[244] J. Baumgarten 1980, 163–164.

[245] Except in case of thick liquid, like porridge, "because it shrinks backwards." *mMaksh* 5:9.

cal letter 4QMMT were not the Rabbis of the *Mishnah*,[246] they must have been some group belonging to the expansionist current of the Second Temple period, probably Pharisees. We have to allow for quite an advanced and detailed discussion between different groups about the role and function of liquids as transmitters of impurity, even before the first century CE.

This position is strengthened by the numerous finds of stone vessels, all over Palestine, from the Second Temple period. A stone vessel industry seems to have appeared during the second half of the first century BCE, and flourished during the first century CE, to diminish after the loss of the temple, and disappear completely after the Bar Kokhba revolt. Stone vessels were manufactured mainly around Jerusalem, but have been found in many places and were common in Jewish settlements, including Galilee.[247] A reason for using stone can be found in the *Mishnah*.[248] According to the Tannaim, stone vessels, together with unburned earthen vessels and cattle-dung vessels, were not susceptible to uncleanness.[249] The nature of the vessels found supports such an explanation. Stoppers/lids for pottery vessels, "measuring cups" containing an appropriate amount of water for ritual hand-washing, and household cups imitating other materials, all fit into the picture.[250] Large vessels have been found, probably used to store water for ritual washing of hands.[251]

In a thorough and detailed discussion about these stone vessels, mapping out all sites and findings, Roland Deines attempts an interpretation. He notes that stone vessels are taken into general use at the end of the first century BCE, i.e. simultaneously with the coming of Hillel. This would support the view of Hillel and Shammai as inaugurating a period of development of purity halakhah.[252] As we saw above, the *Damascus Document* suggests that the Qumran sectarians had a different view on the susceptibility of stone.[253] The general spread of stone vessels, however, supports Josephus' statements about people generally following Pharisaic customs, so that even the Sadducees had to adapt themselves to them.[254] Deines suggests that stone vessels may have been used for bringing *terumah* to the temple, and by Priests when giving the laity their share of sacrificial meat in the temple.[255] According to Deines there is no other way

[246] Cf. the critique of Elman 1996, 105–128.
[247] Magen 1994, 255f; Regev 2000, 229–234.
[248] *mKel* 2:1; *mOhal* 5:5; *mPar* 5:5; *mYad* 1:2.
[249] According to *mBes* 2:3, stone vessels could even be used for cleaning water by surface contact.
[250] Magen 1994, 248f.
[251] Magen 1994, 254. Cf. Jn 2:1–11.
[252] Deines 1993, 16ff. Cf. the rabbinic saying that "purity broke out in Israel." *tShabb* 1:14.
[253] CD 12:15–17.
[254] Deines 1993, 244f. Josephus, *Ant.* 13:298; 18:16f.
[255] Deines 1993, 243.

of interpreting these findings except as evidence for a wide-spread concern over purity of food, including ritual hand-washing.

> Darauf verweisen zum einen die Belege über die rituelle Reinigung der Hände, die überhaupt nur sinnvoll ist, wenn es solche Bemühungen gab, die priesterliche Reinheit auch bei profanen Mahlzeiten zu praktizieren. Neben den Texten ist hier auf die Meinung der Archäologen zu hören, nach denen ein Grossteil der Gefässe beim Ritus der Handwaschung Verwendung fand, d.h. die Gefässe sind es, die den eigentlichen Kommentar zu Stellen wie Mk 7,3 Lk 11,37 und Mt 15,1f liefern. Besonders die Form und das Fassungsvermögen der kleinen Massbecher („Sahnekännchen") unterstützen diese These.[256]

Vessels somewhat larger than these, fashioned as normal drinking cups, would, if used at meals, have eliminated the risk of hands becoming contaminated by liquid transferring impurity from the outside of the vessel. Deines suggests that plates, bowls and containers of stone might have been used by menstruating women and others in a state of impurity. Closed vessels could be used for especially susceptible foodstuffs, such as olives, and as a protection against small impure animals.[257] The stone vessels found give evidence to a high degree of consciousness about purity long before the fall of the temple. They also imply that the expansionist current in Second Temple Judaism actually provided practicable means for following an expanded *halakhah* without life becoming impossible or too expensive.[258] The stone vessels show, according to Deines,

> dass es in der jüdischen Bevölkerung vor 70 einen beträchtlichen Bevölkerungsanteil gab, der sich an die Reinheitsvorschriften im Zusammenhang mit Speiseaufbewahrung und -vorbereitung, sowohl was die Tempel- und Priesterabgaben als auch die eigenen Mahlzeiten betraf, gehalten hat. Und dazu gehörte offenbar auch die Reinigung der Hände...[259]

The combined evidence from archaeology, Qumran texts, and rabbinic sayings suggests that the impurity of hands was a well-known problem in Jesus' time, due to the susceptibility of liquids, and that the hand-washing conflict in Mk 7 is historically credible.

---

[256] Deines 1993, 245–246.

[257] Deines 1993, 245–246.

[258] See above, 71f, and 72, n.187. Stone vessels were fairly cheap compared to the glass and metal vessels of the upper classes. They were definitely not a matter of fashion among wealthy Jews. Magen 1994, 255f.

[259] Deines 1993, 272. Deines criticizes Sanders for following Neusner's method of verification and not taking anonymous Mishnayot like many of the key sayings in *mYad* 1–2, as well as *mHag* 2:5, into account, since they are not "verified" by Tannaim of the earliest generations. "Daraus aber den Schluß zu ziehen, daß sie erst lange nach 70 in Gebrauch kamen, ist unsinnig" (270). I do not agree, however, with Deines' conclusion, that the only explanation for hand-washing is an analogy to "Tempelspeisen" (274).

Summary: A case for purity as a wide-spread concern in Second Temple Judaism

While Jesus' adversaries cannot be restricted to the Pharisees only, his most important opponents in matters of law were found in the influential expansionist current, of which the Pharisees were a prominent part. The issue of impurity belongs in the context of Jesus' attitude to the Torah.

We have seen that the mapping out of the contemporary legal situation is difficult, but not impossible. In spite of the scarcity of contemporary legal texts, careful use of rabbinic texts, and comparisons with Qumran material and other Jewish works from the Second Temple period, as well as archaeological evidence, contribute to a fuller understanding of the contemporary legal situation.

Referring, although far too briefly, to the other major legal issue, the Sabbath, I have attempted to demonstrate that the method suggested for clarifying the legal situation in the Second Temple period is viable and contributes to the interpretation of certain gospel traditions. One major obstacle in interpreting Jesus' behaviour, however, is the polemical nature of the relevant traditions, as they are all shaped in the form of conflict stories. This applies to the Markan conflict story about hand-washing and defilement through food, too, which is usually focused upon when Jesus' attitude to impurity is discussed. The polemical function of the narrative in its present form has blurred the historical issues. In spite of this it is possible to make responsible reconstructions of Jesus' attitude as well as of contemporary legal conditions.

The traditions in Mk 7 have been interpreted in various ways. From the present discussions I find it reasonable that the saying in 7:15, albeit in an earlier form, closer to Mt 15:11 or *Gos.Thom.* 14, taken in a relative sense, could represent Jesus' answer to a question about hand-washing. Questions about what meat could be eaten—pork, idol meat, etc.—were not discussed in Jesus' context. Questions about the relationship between the law of God and human traditions, were probably not discussed by Jesus either, but at a pre-Markan stage in the early church.

Purity was definitely an issue in Second Temple Judaism, and questions of food and hands were discussed: how to handle *terumah* and *hullin* when impure; how to purify and when; how to regard the role of liquids as transmitters of impurity; how to deal with the possible defilement of hands; how to relate to others who were not as consistent about purity customs as oneself.[260]

---

[260] This general picture is supported by Sanders in his conclusions to the much-discussed essay repeatedly referred to above. In spite of what could be interpreted as a downplaying of evidence, Sanders claims that there was a concern for purity beyond the requirements of the law, with Pharisees and with others (1990, 246); the Pharisees furthermore made the extended rules observable and discouraged others from transgressing them; they wished others to conform to them (247); in some cases they held the extended laws to be biblical and wanted them kept gen-

During the Second Temple period, legal discussions were not as advanced, and halakhic development was not as detailed as in the *Mishnah*, *Tosefta* or *Talmudim*. But later materials can sometimes reflect early customs, and with the help of contemporary texts and archaeological evidence, a fairly balanced picture of the legal situation during the first century CE emerges. That is a picture of wide-spread concern for purity, although interpretations and degrees of consistency vary. I do not believe that immersion, purification of hands, attentiveness in matters of liquids and a careful handling of food, were concerns of a few *haberim* only. Such customs were part of a fairly influential expansionist current in Second Temple Judaism.

We do not know the exact circumstances or detailed regulations concerning such issues at the time of Jesus. But even if we do not know the first-century *rationale*, i.e. the current theoretical explanation for e.g. hand-washing or immersion, we have enough evidence to note that such practices or customs existed, and were not only *advocated* by the expansionist current, but were *made possible and practicable*. Even if we do not know the fine points of why and when and how such practices were carried out during the first century CE, we have enough evidence to conclude that a good part of the population considered it desirable and important to follow them.

How then should one explain the *haburot*? Does not the mere existence of such associations imply that the quest for purity was an interest of an extreme fringe movement only, and that most of the population never took much notice of the matter? I do not think so. The general population has never been the theological or legal experts in any society. Custom is followed by the majority without necessarily much thought being given to its *rationale*. But this means that most people, even when they regard adherence to tradition advisable, do not achieve total consistency. In the case of purity in first century-Judaism, many would have adhered to the rules and customs, but only the most well-informed and concerned would have been *consistent*. And in the case of purity, from a strict point of view, lack of consistency would threaten the whole system and make purity void. Thus there would be a need, among those for whom consistency was absolutely necessary in order to maintain purity, to co-operate in *haburot*.[261]

I do not think that the tradition about hand-washing in Mk 7 is based on a conflict between Jesus and a petty fringe extremist group. The "Pharisees and Scribes" questioning Jesus about his disciples' lack of observance may be imagined as *haberim* or not. In any case, their question touches on an important and

---

erally (247); their adherence to purity rules cut them off from the *am ha-arets* (248); in some cases they thought that their views should be obligatory on other people (249, 252); and although they are not to be fully identified with the *haberim*, they are very close to them, since like the *haberim*, Pharisees did not eat with *ammei ha-arets* (250).

[261] Cf. Westerholm 1978, 65.

substantial issue. At the core of the tradition in Mk 7 we find neither the limited question of hand-washing, nor the general classification of clean and unclean meat, but the basic issue of bodily impurity. And there was something in Jesus' behaviour towards this very serious issue that was disturbing. What must have been puzzling in a first-century Jewish context was this seemingly careless attitude from a person who was expected to be consistent and purposeful. Mk 7:15 has often been interpreted as Jesus advocating ethical purity *instead of* ritual. However, if a relative interpretation represents an answer of the historical Jesus to a question about hand-washing, it would rather imply a way of establishing *priorities*, which seems to be consistent with the findings in the brief section above on the Sabbath. I think this is part of the truth, albeit not a full answer. In order to explore this further, we will turn to other texts and a somewhat different approach.

Chapter IV
Jesus and defilement through contact: a neglected issue

IV.1 An alternative approach

Beginning with non-conflict traditions

When dealing with Jesus and purity, discussions have more often than not centred around questions of food, focusing on the traditions in Mark 7. We have seen that this enterprise is not without problems. I want to emphasize three of them.

The first relates to the search for Jesus' *ipsissima verba*. There has usually been an emphasis on determining whether or not particular sayings are authentic. The difficulties with such an approach and the problems with the necessary methods involved, have been discussed above in Chapter II. The uncertainty in linking the logion in Mk 7:15 with the hand-washing tradition in 7:1–5 has been noticed in the previous chapter. The second problem has to do with *Sitz im Leben*. Just as with the gospel traditions about Jesus and the Sabbath, the traditions in Mark 7 are placed within a context of conflict. We have seen that this context reflects discussions within the emerging church regarding the validity of distinctions between clean and unclean food, such as those based on Leviticus 11. We have further seen that it is highly unlikely that such distinctions were questioned by Jesus or his disciples during his lifetime. The third problem concerns the difficulty in assessing the legal situation of the first century CE, especially with regard to purity rules about hand-washing.

In spite of these problems, something can be said about the historical Jesus on the basis of Mark 7. However, this has very little to do with food laws in general, but rather with bodily impurity. The concepts of impurity which can be seen to underlie the hand-washing tradition are *basically* concerned with body, not with food *per se*. Thus I find the task of the present study justified, i.e. looking at Jesus and defilement through bodily contact.

In doing this, I will try to resolve the three problems just mentioned. I will, in the first place, examine traditions about Jesus' *actions*, not asking primarily for *ipsissima verba*, but looking for historically plausible traits which fit into a *Gesamtbild*. Secondly, I will take as my point of departure certain *non-conflict traditions*, in which purity is not a debated issue, and thus should not be expected to primarily reflect the interests of the early church. Thirdly, the focus is placed on sources of transmittable *bodily impurity*, as described in Lev 12–15 and Num 19. Such impurities are based directly on biblical legislation, which gives us a richer material and a longer background history for discussing their application during the first century CE, as compared with the very limited and extra-biblical case of hand-washing *halakhah*. A reliable assessment of Jesus' attitude to impurity should not be based on the narrow foundation of one specific and somewhat uncertain *halakhah*, but on a total picture of how he related to the major and basic forms of ritual impurity.

Hence I will take as my point of departure certain Markan non-conflict traditions, containing implicit purity problems which are not explicitly spelled out or exploited by the gospel writer (Mk 1:40–45; 5:25–34; 5:21–24, 35–43). These have evidently been subjected to redaction too, but they describe situations which contain what would have been purity issues in Jesus' Palestinian context, while not seeming to have been issues in the Markan church.

The traditions chosen illustrate the three main sources of impurity in Judaism at the time: the corpse, skin disease,[1] and bodily discharges.[2] In the following discussion I will examine these three concepts of impurity individually, looking at the relevant biblical legislation and asking how rules were interpreted and applied during the first century CE. Beginning with a particular non-conflict tradition, and supplementing it with other relevant gospel traditions, I seek to determine Jesus' attitude, and discuss how it fits into a first-century context.

This approach, however, is not without problems. The implicit character of the material can be explained in different ways. Sariola mentions two possibilities: Mark might not, as a Gentile Christian, have been aware of the implicit purity problems in his traditions. Conflicts about the Jewish law might have come to an end in Mark's context. Taken together, these suggestions could explain the apparent lack of awareness of purity problems both in traditional and redactional materials.[3] Westerholm points out that although this "makes it unlikely that the facts have been purposefully altered to suit some theological point ... the ... disinterest prompts the question if the tradition can be relied upon to report the matters regarding purity with the precision necessary if sound conclusions are to be drawn."[4] A redaction-critical discussion is thus required, although I do not aim at full redaction-critical analyses of the texts involved. The analyses should be sufficient, however, for discussing the purity issues involved.

---

[1] Usually called "leprosy" from the Greek λέπρα, used by the LXX to translate the Hebrew צָרַעַת, which denotes a number of rashes and skin diseases. Cf. below, 98f.

[2] All types of impurity are probably derived from these three categories. "[T]he entire complex of the priestly impurity rules is only a symbolic system. ... There are only three sources of actual impurity: the dead, genital fluxes, and a few skin diseases (ṣāraʿat)." (Milgrom 1994, 557).

[3] Sariola 1990, 241f. To conclude, however, as does Maccoby, that the absence of any mention of impurity or purification in a text would mean that such aspects are only imported by unaware exegetes, betrays too simplistic a view of textual traditions (Maccoby 1999, 162).

[4] Westerholm 1978, 68.

Another problem with this approach, which should be given a separate discussion, is the fact that the main traditions to be examined are miracle stories, and as such they are often considered to be cast into a certain mould. Thus we have to ask whether they transmit any "portraiture" or historical reminiscences of value, or whether all or most details belong to their form only, as standard motifs or themes.

Dealing with miracle stories

Healers or miracle-workers are known from history and were common in the contemporary world, in Hellenistic and Jewish environments alike.[5] Although magic (at least in certain forms) was surrounded with regulations and not officially accepted in Judaism, it seems to have been practised to some extent,[6] and healers are part of the heritage of the Hebrew Bible, and figure in rabbinic literature.[7]

In the gospels, Jesus is partly described as a miracle worker or a healer, but there is reason to believe that the purpose of these miracles in their literary context is theological rather than biographical. According to Bultmann, the miracles were told not as proofs of Jesus' character, but of his messianic authority or divine power. Thus, "even if some historical events underlie some miracles of healing, it is still true that their narrative form has been the work of the Tradition."[8]

The form critics distinguished miracle stories from apophthegms and paradigms because of their typical features. In identifying these accounts as "miracle stories," Bultmann noted their three-part structure: a problem, a miraculous act, a demonstration or acclamation. He also divided them into different categories: healings, exorcisms, raisings from the dead and nature miracles.[9] Since the aim of form criticism was to judge the function of a story from its form, the fact that miracle stories are never commented upon as a genre by writers from Antiquity, should pose a problem.[10] Wendy Cotter asks "how such subdivisions could be used to reconstruct first-century authorial intent when their 'form' and kinds were completely unattested formally anywhere in Greco-Roman evidence." It seems as if miracle stories cannot, against form critical preconceptions, be seen as necessarily and by definition without "portraiture,"

[5] For examples, see Weinreich 1909, 45–48; Blackburn 1991, 1ff, 13ff; Cotter 1999; Hruby 1977, 73–94; George 1977, 95–108; W. Kahl 1994, 56ff.

[6] Deut 18:9ff; Jeffers 1996; 7ff; 251f.

[7] W. Kahl 1994, 57f. Cf. the stories about Elijah and Elisha in 1Kgs 17; 2Kgs 4–5. For magic and miracles in Jewish literature and tradition, see references in Fiebig 1911, 9–75: Blackburn 1991, 130ff; Kollmann 1996, 118–173.

[8] Bultmann 1972 [1921], 219, 228.

[9] Bultmann 1972 [1921], 218–244; Cotter 1999, 2.

[10] Cotter 1999, 1.

focusing on the miraculous act *only*, since "[a]ny ancient author was free to tell the story his/her own way, turning it to whatever purpose might seem most attractive or advantageous."[11]

This is not to deny that miracle stories do exhibit typical features, regardless of origin and context. The structure of miracle stories has been carefully examined, and several surveys of themes and motifs are available from the past century.[12] Bultmann lists typical features, such as gravity of complaint (length of sickness, its dangerous character, ineffective treatment, etc.), difficulty of the healing, healing gesture, miracle-working word, withdrawal from public, and successful accomplishment.[13] His conclusion has been embraced by many scholars, that "the Hellenistic miracle stories offer such a wealth of parallels to the synoptic, particularly in style, as to create a prejudice in favour of supposing that the synoptic miracle stories grew up on Hellenistic ground."[14] At the same time, he poses a Palestinian origin for most of the Q material, as well as for certain Markan miracle stories containing Semitic formulations.[15]

The grounds for such a distinction have been questioned by scholars repeatedly, since it presupposes a distance between Palestine and the rest of the Hellenistic world, which does not seem to be historically warranted.[16] It is true that rabbinic writings present very few parallels to synoptic miracle stories, as compared with a wealth of Hellenistic material. But, as Kenzo Tagawa has pointed out,

> il faut compter sur le fait que dans les récits de miracles ce sont des milieux populaires qui s'expriment, tandis que les sectes juives (Pharisiens, Sadducéens, Esséniens, etc.) par lesquelles nous avons l'habitude de nous représenter le judaïsme du premier siècle représentent des milieux savants.[17]

Although intellectual circles were not without Hellenistic influence, the miracle stories reflect more a rural and popular environment. Tagawa talks about a Galileo-Hellenistic phenomenon.[18] While a Galilean origin for the miracle stories is disputed, a general Palestinian provenance does not necessarily gainsay

[11] Cotter 1999, 3.
[12] The basic study was done by Otto Weinreich in 1909, and is referred to by e.g. Bultmann 1972 [1921], 220f and Dibelius 1961 [1919], 51, n.1. Cf. Theissen 1983 [1972], 47ff, 81ff; Léon-Dufour 1977, 289ff; Cf W. Kahl's somewhat different structuralist analysis of "motifemes and their realizations" (1994, 62ff), and his critique of what he considers a confusion of terms in Theissen and others.
[13] Bultmann 1972 [1921], 220ff.
[14] Bultmann 1972 [1921], 240.
[15] Bultmann 1972 [1921], 240f.
[16] Légasse 1977, 116. Cf Hengel 1974 [1968], 103–108; Gerdmar 2001, 324–330.
[17] Tagawa 1966, 48.
[18] Tagawa 1966, 48. Cf. recent theories of Jesus as a Cynic healer.

the Hellenistic traits. Many miracle stories in Mark contain a mixture of traditional Jewish imagery and elements from a more Hellenistic world-view.[19]

An important reason for judging these stories as Hellenistic has been the interpretation, common since the emergence of the History of Religions School, of Jesus as a Hellenistic "divine man" (θεῖος ἀνήρ). This line of interpretation has been increasingly criticized during recent years. While the designation is true and convenient as a general characterization, no such title is used systematically, or applied to miracle-workers in general, throughout contemporary writings. There is also no such reflection about the personality of Jesus, or apologetic discussion in the Synoptic Gospels, as in the case of Apollonius of Tyana, who would otherwise provide the closest parallel.[20] Is it really plausible to argue that Mark has domesticated Hellenistic miracle-stories with an original θεῖος ἀνήρ character? The argument could be turned the other way. Mark could be seen as having used Palestinian traditions, sometimes even adding a θεῖος ἀνήρ touch to them.[21] Many traits attributed to Jesus and other features of the miracle stories have precedents in the Hebrew Bible or in intertestamental literature.[22]

There is thus no *intrinsic* need to deny the miracle traditions used by Mark a possible Palestinian provenance. Blackburn remarks that "one can hardly say *with confidence* that a given theme or motif originated in a more hellenized, Greek-speaking milieu."[23] It should, however, be pointed out that a Palestinian origin is not of itself a guarantee for the historical value of a tradition. Traditions are generally bearers of a theology, a certain image of Jesus, and the provenance or antiquity of a tradition is not equal to its historical value.[24] Legends sometimes evolve rapidly, even within the lifetime of a hero.[25]

Since almost *any* text could be seen as carrying an ideology, having parallels in contemporary literature and having a structure or form which is recognizable, there is no simple way of determining historical value. According to Theissen, primitive Christian miracle stories have an historical intention, but reproduce historical events in an intensified form.[26] I would argue that they cannot be disqualified for providing *any* historical clue just because they reflect an ideological bias or an ancient world-view; this would disqualify almost any text. Parallels usually cannot be adduced to posit *genetical* relationships. In the first

---

[19] Broadhead 1992b, 190.
[20] Tagawa 1966, 47; Légasse 1977, 116.
[21] Cf. Broadhead 1992b, 190.
[22] E.g. the Elijah and Elisha legends, and 1QapGen 20. Cf. below, 105f, 172–174.
[23] Blackburn 1991, 229. Blackburn argues that the narration of Jesus' miracles has an appropriate *Sitz im Leben* in the early Palestinian church, independent of the Gentile mission and a developing θεῖος ἀνήρ christology (240ff).
[24] Légasse 1977, 118; Blackburn 1991, 264.
[25] Examples provided by Hengel 1985, 11; Légasse 1977, 118, n.39.
[26] Theissen 1983 [1972], 276f.

place, much of Palestine was hellenized at the time of Jesus, and pagan cults were situated near and even within Palestine.[27] Furthermore, many of the basic miracle themes and motifs which are often considered "Hellenistic" can actually be found in different cultures and at different periods of time, far removed from the Hellenistic world of the first century.[28] Finally, arguments based on the form or structure of miracle stories are precarious. The three-part structure mentioned above (problem, miraculous act, demonstration/acclamation), which has been regarded as a particularly Hellenistic phenomenon, can hardly be avoided in a story about a miracle. Says Blackburn:

> the threefold pattern which characterizes and constitutes miracle stories is hardly an arbitrary pattern which one culture would have to learn from another, but is the logical and natural result when one narrates, in what might be described as a logico-chronological manner and in some detail, a miracle performed by one who has saved someone or something from disaster or at least some type of distress. This of course means that the discovery of 'the miracle story form' in the Gospels and in the wider pagan environment says nothing, in and of itself, about the dependence of one tradition upon another.[29]

If Blackburn's critique could be seen as lacking certain nuances,[30] based like most analyses of miracle stories upon initial form-critical categories, we find that a structuralist approach, such as that of Werner Kahl, while more "refined," could provide us with similar arguments. Employing a narrative schema (Greimas/Boers) with four phases—lack, preparedness, performance, and sanction (which is shared by non-miracle narratives as well)—he finds real differences between Jewish, pagan and Christian healing miracle stories in the *performance text*, but not with respect to their *morphology*.[31] Thus he states in his conclusion that the "structure of a miracle story is a trans-cultural and 'universally' uniform phenomenon," while their retelling in different contexts usually involves a refocalizing process.[32]

A final argument against the view that the form of miracle stories excludes them as possible bearers of historical data, could be added. As healers were quite common in the ancient world, and miracle stories told and transmitted, there is bound to be some correspondence between descriptions and actual be-

---

[27] Hengel 1974 [1968], 285f, 298; Blackburn 1991, 231, referring to McCasland 1939 and Duprez 1970, 63–79. Cf. Jacobs 2000.

[28] Blackburn (1991, 231f.) provides examples from *The Deeds of God in Ṛddipur* (Feldhaus 1984), a thirteenth-century document from the Mahānubhāva sect of western India. These deeds include healings of the lame and dumb, raisings of the dead, epiphanies, supernatural knowledge and various nature miracles.

[29] Blackburn 1991, 239f. Cf. his example from western India of the raising of a dead boy, which has a structure similar to that of several gospel stories (240, n.35).

[30] Cf. W. Kahl 1994, 229.

[31] W. Kahl 1994, 44ff, 216ff. Another author attempting a structural analysis of miracle stories is Funk 1978. But note Kahl's criticism of Funk for not going beyond a "formal" approach (W. Kahl 1994, 32ff.).

[32] W. Kahl 1994, 233f.

haviour. An analogy would be the realm of conversion today, in which stories of conversions usually follow the subcultural patterns of the religious environments in which they flourish, while they simultaneously inspire and influence the forms in which conversions are actually experienced. There is thus a mutual dependence between actual experience and its description. It is likewise reasonable to suppose that miracles were experienced according to those fairly stereotyped patterns by which they were described, and that healers actually behaved in ways and manners which were expected of them. Healings were thus described and experienced within a particular cultural context, and the context as such cannot be adduced as an argument against historical reminiscences adhering to the traditions.

If there is an historical background to Jesus' miracles at all, then it is unreasonable to suppose that all circumstances in the miracle stories are fictional.[33] I believe Gnilka is mistaken when, in dealing with Mark 5:21–43, he concludes that since the stories in their details correspond to existing structures and motifs, we must assume "dass beide Geschichten nicht konkrete Erinnerungen aufbewahrten, sondern die allgemeine Erinnerung an Jesu Wundertätigkeit konkretisierten. Wir gewinnen keinen Einblick in individuelle Wundergeschehnisse."[34] How would a general memory of Jesus as a healer be entertained and transmitted without any historically based details whatsoever? This does not mean that each and every miracle-story represents a particular historical memory, and even less that every detail mentioned has an historical basis. It simply means that it is reasonable to expect certain historical traits or features to adhere to the miracle traditions.

The purpose of this discussion, then, is neither to deny the miracle stories as a *genre* altogether, nor to blur the many and real parallels which exist between various miracle stories in the ancient world, but only to argue that gospel miracle traditions cannot be disqualified as historical sources, merely because of parallels in structure or subject matter. Each miracle tradition must rather be discussed separately.

Tracing historical reminiscences

In the end we are confronted with the question of separating tradition from redaction, which is possible only to a limited extent if some degree of certainty is desired. The most obvious difficulty in the non-conflict traditions chosen as a point of departure lies in the absence of extant Markan sources, but some conclusions can be drawn from comparisons to the way Matthew and Luke seem to

---

[33] This has nothing to do with the question of the historicity of miracles, i.e. how to regard "supernatural interventions" from a modern, scientific perspective. Such issues are neither part of my discussion, nor relevant to my study.

[34] Gnilka 1978, 219.

handle Markan material, as well as from general Markan tendences which can be observed throughout the gospel. This means that simple bridges and details belonging to the frame of a story generally should be possible to define with more certainty than the rest.

Gerd Theissen thus concludes that Mark probably handled his traditions in a way similar to that of Matthew and Luke, i.e. repeating motifs which heighten dramatic tension, as in 1:40ff, where the leper is spoken to sternly twice (41, 43), or in 5:21ff, where the public is excluded twice (37, 40). The encapsulation of one story within another, which is frequent in Mark, should also be regarded as a secondary development. In the case of 5:21–43, this is supported by arguments from grammar; the story about Jairus' daughter is told mainly in the present tense, while the story about the woman with a blood flow is dominated by past tenses. Theissen even notes that the four places where past tenses are used in the story about Jairus' daughter (21, 24, 37, 42f) are located at the beginning and end, and where the two stories join, i.e. where redactional influences are probable.[35]

Names of persons and places are usually regarded as belonging to the frame too, but constitute more of a problem. Bultmann noted how a novelistic interest grew with time. Lazarus, in the Johannine tradition, has a name, while in Luke the son of the widow in Nain is anonymous. The woman with a blood flow was later given the name Bernice/Veronica,[36] but the process can be observed already within the synoptic tradition, where the synagogue leader is named Jairus.[37] Similarly, Bultmann observed how indications of time and place are absent or scanty in most miracle stories, and thus should be seen as foreign to them.[38]

Theissen, however, does not agree with Bultmann about place-names. In discussing Mark 7:24f, 31f, and 8:22f, he concludes that no compelling ground for deleting place-names from tradition can be found, since they cannot be explained as the results of a coherent process of editing. These and other stories could not have begun with the phrase following the introductory link/bridge, in which a place is mentioned. Theissen admits that his suggestion is speculative, but as likely as others:[39]

> Mark seems to have been responsible for the form of the introductions, but to explain them as totally his creations is impossible. On the other hand, there does not have to be a sharp distinction between tradition and redaction. The miracle stories may have been introduced in the oral tradition by a 'title' which included the name of Jesus and (now and again) a reference to a place, something like τοῦτο ἐποίησεν ὁ Ἰησοῦς ἐν Καφαρναούμ. This traditional 'oral framework' would then have been integrated by Mark into

[35] Theissen 1983 [1972], 180ff.
[36] *Gospel of Nicodemus* (*Acts of Pilate*) 7. Schneemelcher 1991, 1:511.
[37] Bultmann 1972 [1921], 241.
[38] Bultmann 1972 [1921], 242.
[39] Theissen 1983 [1972], 126ff.

> the narrative to produce a coherent composition: within his gospel he would have 'reproduced' a traditional element afresh.[40]

After having made a comparison with the rabbinic introductory *mashal* formula, in which introductions were preserved, since story was simply followed by story, Theissen concludes that the

> constant two-element structure of the miracle stories can thus be explained as the result of a consistent transformation of the oral introduction into narrative. Those exegetes who delete the first element of Markan introductions to miracles are right to the extent that the story proper did not begin until the appearance of the suppliants; they are wrong to the extent that the oral framework antedated Mark. His work (or that of his possible predecessors) consisted in integrating this framework into the narrative. ... An analysis of the introductory motif shows that a sharp distinction between 'tradition' and 'redaction' is incorrect. The change is structural. The motif was moved from the level of commentary in the oral framework to the compositional level in the connected narrative; it no longer announces the narrative but has become part of it.[41]

We thus return to the observation that redaction and tradition are slippery concepts, blending with each other and notoriously difficult to separate.[42] This applies even to the framework of a miracle story, but especially to the body of a story. Broadhead points out that, apart from the lack of pre-Markan sources, "linguistic analysis shows that both the traditional material and the redactional material in the Gospel of Mark share a common pattern of language."[43]

We find ourselves constantly reminded of these problems. Just as there is no waterproof method to extract Jesus' *ipsissima verba*, there is none to distil the oldest layer of tradition, untouched by subsequent usage, from a Markan miracle story. Some separation of *previous* tradition from *subsequent* redaction can definitely be done, however; the question is what conclusions could be drawn. It is reasonable to expect historical reminiscences in the traditional material, but at what level? Theissen's suggestion is interesting and fits with the evidence discussed above: "the popular image of the historical kernel is misleading. It suggests that the kernel was transmitted. The truth is that the historical shell was transmitted."[44] As examples he discusses the Baptizer's preaching of repentance and Paul's teaching on justification and eschatology, which were made unrecognizable by "popular adaptation," as seen with Mark and Luke (e.g. Mk 6:17–29; Acts 13:38). Yet something of the content adheres to the shell and can be traced. Applied to the Jesus tradition, this means, according to Theissen, that while the eschatological context of the miracles is reduced in the gospel tradi-

[40] Theissen 1983 [1972], 128.
[41] Theissen 1983 [1972], 129.
[42] Cf. above, 30f.
[43] Broadhead 1992b, 188. The lack of sources means that the situation, according to Broadhead, is basically the same today as when Marxsen recognized the problem in 1956.
[44] Theissen 1983 [1972], 282.

tions, it can still be traced, through these very traditions, as their historical background.[45]

In the context of the present discussion, this means that it should be possible to trace the attitude of the historical Jesus through a number of non-conflict miracle stories, which do not primarily address the question of purity, but in their present form are adapted to transmit another type of message. Descriptions of Jesus associating with people usually considered unclean, touching and being touched, voluntarily entering the same room as a corpse, even touching it, are not without historical value just because they are used for reinforcing the picture of Jesus as a great miracle worker.

IV.2 Skin disease / "leprosy"

"Lepers" in gospel traditions

One of the main sources of impurity in Second Temple Judaism was, in the Hebrew Bible, called צָרַעַת.[46] The word was translated by the LXX as λέπρα, which became the term used by NT writers. The English translation "leprosy" is misleading, since it is our term for Hansen's disease, which does not suit many of the symptoms of צָרַעַת described in Lev 13. צָרַעַת rather denotes a number of skin rashes, not necessarily contagious. The term λέπρα is similarly used by Greek medical writers, as a generic term for scaly skin diseases.[47] Hansen's disease, however, seems to have been unknown in the Mediterranean area before the Hellenistic period, and was then described by the terms ἐλέφας or ἐλεφαντίασις.[48] This designation appeared, however, after the first Greek translations of the Hebrew Bible were made, and thus it is virtually impossible

[45] Theissen 1983 [1972], 282f.

[46] The word נֶגַע is sometimes used referring to צָרַעַת (61 times in Lev 13–14), usually in combination with צָרַעַת, i.e. נֶגַע צָרַעַת, but at times separately as well (Lev 13:22). In other places, נֶגַע is usually understood as having a broader reference, in view of the original meaning "blow," "affliction." צָרַעַת could be regarded as a specific designation of the general term נֶגַע. While there is no reason to regard these two words as denoting two separate diseases in Leviticus, the meaning is often ambiguous elsewhere. This applies to the DSS as well. A person afflicted by צָרַעַת is at times called צָרוּעַ (Lev 13:44) or מְצֹרָע (2Kgs 5: 1, 27) in the Hebrew Bible. In rabbinic literature מְצוֹרָע becomes standard. In Qumran literature the term מנוגע is often used.

[47] λέπειν = to peel. The idea of scaliness seems to be inherent in the Hebrew term צָרַעַת too. Hulse 1975, 92f; Milgrom 1991, 774f. This could include a number of diseases, especially *psoriasis* and *favus* (Hulse 1975, 96–100), and perhaps also *ichtyosis* (cf. Gånemo 2002, 14).

[48] Hulse 1975, 88; Wilkinson 1978, 158f; Browne 1989 [1985], 2. The term ἐλεφαντίασις refers to conditions in which the skin became thickened, probably including both Hansen's disease and *Bancroftian filariasis*. The earliest archaeological evidence (four leprous skulls from Dakhleh, Egypt) is dated to the 2nd century BCE (Browne 1989 [1985], 1).

to tell whether λέπρα in the gospel traditions, following LXX usage, could include Hansen's disease or not.[49] For convenience, however, I frequently use "leprosy" and "leper" when discussing biblical material, although with quotation marks.

"Leprosy" is mentioned in the New Testament only in gospel traditions about Jesus. The main tradition is Mk 1:40–45 (par. Mt 8:2–4; Lk 5:12–16), about a "leper" being healed by Jesus. In addition, Luke includes a somewhat similar tradition about ten "lepers" near a village between Samaria and Galilee (Lk 17:11–19). There are differing opinions on whether this tradition is secondary or independent. Except for these miracle-stories, "leprosy" is mentioned in four other gospel traditions. In the Matthean variant of Jesus' instructions to the disciples, they are charged: ἀσθενοῦντες θεραπεύετε, νεκροὺς ἐγείρετε, λεπροὺς καθαρίζετε, δαιμόνια ἐκβάλλετε (10:8). This could, however, easily be understood as a redactional summary of the types of miracles included in Jesus' activity in the preceding narrative (ch. 8–9), which the disciples now are expected to continue. Another mention is found in Lk 4:27, in which the Gentile "leper" Naaman is contrasted to the many Israelite "lepers" who were not healed. This could, especially in its context, be taken as a reflection of subsequent church polemics against unbelieving Jews, but the mention is interesting, since it belongs to a context which connects the miracles of Jesus with those of Elijah and Elisha. This is a perspective to which we will return, discussing the daughter of Jairus. Of more immediate interest is the Markan mentioning of Jesus' meal at the house of Simon the Leper (14:3; par. Mt 26:6), and the Q tradition mentioning "lepers" among those whom Jesus includes in his answer to the doubting Baptizer: τυφλοὶ ἀναβλέπουσιν, χωλοὶ περιπατοῦσιν, λεπροὶ καθαρίζονται, καὶ κωφοὶ ἀκούουσιν, νεκροὶ ἐγείρονται, πτωχοὶ εὐαγγελίζονται (Lk 7:22; par. Mt 11:5). The list reflects Isaianic expectations (cf. LXX Isa 29:18–19; 35:5–6); "lepers" are, however, nowhere mentioned in the texts from Isaiah, but added to the list. We cannot dismiss this list as a deduction from prophetic expectations only, just because it is a conflation of, or a loose allusion to, several texts. The mention of "lepers" is not necessitated by the Isaianic background, but rather seems to represent a fairly strong historical memory of "lepers" being included in the healing work and fellowship of Jesus.[50] While it is impossible to decide whether Simon the Leper was so called because he was actually a מְצוֹרָע or because he had *previously* been one, the epithet fits into a general picture of Jesus as having fellowship with "lepers."

[49] It likely did not. Wilkinson actually claims that leprosy as we know it today (Hansen's disease) cannot produce the necessary physical signs, the combination of which are necessary for the identification of צָרַעַת according to Leviticus (1977, 167f). It seems that λέπρα was first used to designate Hansen's disease in the 9th century CE (Hulse 1975, 89).

[50] Against Pesch 1970b, 36–44. The fragment 4Q521 2 2, which similarly combines various Isaianic expectations and which might reflect current Messianic expectations, neither mentions "lepers." Cf. below, 168f, 247, 327.

Such a picture could also be supported by the *Papyrus Egerton 2*, 1r, which will be discussed later.

The Markan non-conflict tradition

The primary synoptic tradition relating to Jesus and "leprosy" is Mk 1:40–45 (par. Mt 8:2-4/Lk 5:12-16):

> 40 καὶ ἔρχεται πρὸς αὐτὸν λεπρὸς παρακαλῶν αὐτὸν [καὶ γονυπετῶν][51] καὶ λέγων αὐτῷ ὅτι ἐὰν θέλῃς δύνασαί με καθαρίσαι. 41 καὶ σπλαγχνισθεὶς[52] ἐκτείνας τὴν χεῖρα αὐτοῦ ἥψατο καὶ λέγει αὐτῷ· θέλω, καθαρίσθητι· 42 καὶ εὐθὺς ἀπῆλθεν ἀπ' αὐτοῦ ἡ λέπρα, καὶ ἐκαθαρίσθη. 43 καὶ ἐμβριμησάμενος αὐτῷ εὐθὺς ἐξέβαλεν αὐτὸν 44 καὶ λέγει αὐτῷ· ὅρα μηδενὶ μηδὲν εἴπῃς, ἀλλὰ ὕπαγε σεαυτὸν δεῖξον τῷ ἱερεῖ καὶ προσένεγκε περὶ τοῦ καθαρισμοῦ σου ἃ προσέταξεν Μωϋσῆς, εἰς μαρτύριον αὐτοῖς. 45 ὁ δὲ ἐξελθὼν ἤρξατο κηρύσσειν πολλὰ καὶ διαφημίζειν τὸν λόγον, ὥστε μηκέτι αὐτὸν δύνασθαι φανερῶς εἰς πόλιν εἰσελθεῖν, ἀλλ' ἔξω ἐπ' ἐρήμοις τόποις ἦν· καὶ ἤρχοντο πρὸς αὐτὸν πάντοθεν.
>
> 40 And a leper came to him, called out to him and knelt before him and said: "If you want, you can make me pure." 41 And moved with compassion he stretched out his hand and touched him and said: "I want, be purified." 42 And immediately the "leprosy" departed from him and he was purified. 43 And rebuking him, he immediately sent him away 44 and said to him: "You must not say anything to anyone, but go away and show yourself to the priest and bring for your purification that which Moses commanded, as a witness to them." 45 But he went out and began to proclaim much and spread the word, so that it was no longer possible for him to enter a town openly, but he stayed outside in waste areas. And they came to him from everywhere.

Working backwards, the last verse is usually taken as a Markan addition, and because of the silencing command, most of vv 43–44 has often been seen as Markan redaction too, while vv 40–42 are regarded as traditional.[53] However, if the silencing command is not taken as intrinsic to a Markan messianic secret, it could just as well be seen as belonging to tradition.[54] Theissen regards such commands as elements of style in ancient miracle stories.[55]

There is a discrepancy between the command to silence and the man spreading the rumour, which could suggest redaction of an earlier, shorter form of the

---

[51] Codex Vaticanus (B) and Codex Bezae (D) do not include this phrase.

[52] D reads οργισθεις. This reading could be original for several reasons, one being the criterion of *lectio difficilior*. It is understandable if ὀργισθείς was changed to σπλαγχνισθείς, but not vice versa. Note that both Matthew and Luke have omitted the participle altogether, although both use σπλαγχνίζεσθαι for Jesus elsewhere. The matter is, however, complicated by a possible confusion of the Aramaic אתרחם (he was moved with compassion), with אתרעם (he was angry). Cf. Cave 1978–1979, 246; Wojciechowski 1989, 114f.

[53] Bultmann 1972 [1921], 212; Gnilka 1978, 90. Gnilka argues that since the command to be silent is connected to the sending away, v 43 ought to be redactional if v 44 is. Weiss, followed by Lohmeyer and Grundmann, considered the story a fusion of two parallel traditions with different endings (v 44b / vv 43–44a and 45). Cf. Boismard 1981, 283.

[54] Schweizer 1971 [1967], 57; Räisänen 1990, 148.

[55] Theissen 1983 [1972], 140ff.

story. The discrepancy seems, however, to be intended by Mark, and fits his general tendency of emphasizing how people spread the rumour about Jesus in spite of his prohibitions.[56] Attempts to explain the ὁ δὲ in v 45 as originally referring not to the "leper" but to Jesus,[57] must be considered unconvincing. In any case v 45 has no bearing on the question of Jesus' attitude to impurity.

It is otherwise with vv 43–44, which could be of importance for assessing Jesus' attitude to the law in general. It is a moot question whether εἰς μαρτύριον αὐτοῖς should be interpreted as a dative of advantage or disadvantage. Is the sacrifice of the "leper" seen as a positive witness *for* (gesture of evangelism, testimony to the healing, apologetic for Jesus' positive attitude to the law?), or as a negative witness *against* (condemnation of cultic practices, warning against judgement?) "them" (the priests/leaders/Jews)?[58] The answer ultimately depends on the overall interpretation of Mark's narrative and theology. Some think that Mark deliberately placed this story at the beginning of the gospel, before the conflict section in 2:1ff, to protect Jesus from the suspicion of pushing the law aside.[59] Others suggest that while the original story may have emphasized that Jesus did not want to question tradition and Torah, this could hardly have been in Mark's interest.[60] Mark does not otherwise particularly emphasize Jesus' concern for cultic piety. And a redactor, who elsewhere takes pains to justify Christian negligence of cultic practices, would hardly attribute to Jesus an instruction to follow a ritual precept.[61] It is more reasonable to view the injunction to be inspected by the priest and bring a sacrifice for cleansing, as part of tradition.[62] But what conclusions can be drawn from this? Jesus is seen as encouraging obedience to a prescribed purification ritual. This was necessary in order for the "leper" to be reintegrated in society. Such an injunction would be natural in a first-century Palestinian context. There are no necessary connotations. It is possible that the command has no place in a conscious literary strategy of Mark. It may be just one of those Jewish reminiscences which Mark has taken over from tradition fairly untouched, and thus has to explain to his

---

[56] Mk 5:43; 7:36. For a thorough discussion of different interpretations of the "Messianic Secret" in Mark, see Räisänen 1990.

[57] Cf. Kazmierski's discussion in 1992, 49f.

[58] For a discussion of possibilities and standpoints taken, see Broadhead 1992a, 257–265. A positive witness is understood by e.g. V. Taylor 1966, 190; Grundmann 1971, 52; Pesch 1976, 146; Derrett 1979a, 584. A negative witness is understood by e.g. Lohmeyer 1937, 47f. For a mixed view, positive in the traditional story but negative in Mark's macrotext, see Gnilka 1978, 91, 94.

[59] Schweizer 1971 [1967], 58; Loader 1997, 23.

[60] Räisänen 1990, 146.

[61] Broadhead 1992a, 257, 263; Wojciechowski 1989, 116.

[62] Cf. Sariola (1990, 68ff.), who regards all legal material traditional, even when there are contradictions. Mark is not really interested in the validity or meaning of the law, but consciously presents Jesus as sometimes keeping the law and at other times in conflict with it. The will of God can be according to or against Moses.

Gentile readers: ἃ προσέταξεν Μωϋσῆς.[63] It does give us a picture of Jesus as conforming to the Torah, but Loader's comment is valid, that "such detail is relatively incidental" and "[s]uch conformity to Torah was as natural as Jesus' attendance in the synagogue on the sabbath day."[64]

If the command to be examined by the priest and bring a sacrifice for purification is seen as belonging to tradition, it has consequences for the interpretation of Jesus' action in what is definitely part of tradition, the preceding vv 40–42. The command makes it implausible to interpret Jesus as exercising the priestly task of actually *declaring* the "leper" clean, as do several exegetes.[65] Although the terminology is one of cleansing (καθαρίσαι/ καθαρισθῆναι), it is apparently used here in the sense of healing.[66] Loader objects to the idea that Jesus' instructions for the man to act according to the legal provisions, would have been only a ploy to confront the priests. There are no evident signs of confrontation in the text. Jesus' gestures and words in v 41 should be seen as an act of healing, not as a priestly pronouncement.[67]

> In employing the word, καθαρίσθητι, Mark indicates both the healing and the effect. The effect must still be formally certified in accordance with the provisions of Torah and the man declared clean so that he can reenter the community.[68]

---

[63] This comment could well be redactional. Cf. Mark's redactional explanations of other Jewish practices (2:26 about the shewbread, 7:3f about washing) or Aramaic words (5:41 Talitha koum, 7:34 Effatha). Possibly, the whole phrase καὶ προσένεγκε περὶ τοῦ καθαρισμοῦ σου ἃ προσέταξεν Μωϋσῆς could be seen as redactional. If so, the εἰς μαρτύριον αὐτοῖς would refer directly to the man showing himself to the priest. Cf. Boismard 1981, 289. However, a comparison with the recent *P.Köln* 255 which fills into *P.Egerton* 2 and lacks εἰς μαρτύριον αὐτοῖς (cf. below, 124ff), suggests that this phrase rather than the ritual instructions is Markan redaction, reflecting his ideology: the healed man is understood as a witness to Jesus' miraculous powers. Cf. Lührmann 1987, 55; Marcus 2000, 207.

[64] Loader 1997, 23.

[65] The suggestion was first brought forward by Johannes Weiss and has been followed by some exegetes. Cf. Grundmann 1971, 51; Theissen 1983 [1972], 145f; Broadhead 1992b, 74; Cave 1978–1979, 246.

[66] Cf. Mt 10:8; Mt 11:5/Lk 7:22; and especially Lk 4:27, where Naaman's healing is described with καθαρισθῆναι. This use is quite natural; since the disease is defined as an impurity, the cure is conceived of as a cleansing. Cave's comment about the use of καθαρίζειν in Leviticus 13–14 not referring to healing at all (1978–1979, 246), is not as conclusive as one might think. Although terms of healing are used in Leviticus for the *cure* of "leprosy" (e.g. Lev 14:3, LXX: καὶ ἰδοὺ ἰᾶται ἡ ἁφὴ τῆς λέπρας ἀπὸ τοῦ λεπροῦ), there is a certain ambiguity in the terminology referring to *purity* and *purification* (e.g. Lev 13:37b, LXX: ὑγίακε τὸ θραῦσμα, καθαρός ἐστι, καὶ καθαριεῖ αὐτὸν ὁ ἱερεύς.). It seems as if a person is *deemed* clean on grounds of diagnosis rather than declaration (cf. 37a), and hence the priest *declares* that person clean. It is not difficult to imagine that if the *healed* state (not only the *declared* state) could be called "clean," the healing itself could be termed "cleansing," without thereby referring to the official priestly declaration.

[67] Loader 1997, 21ff; cf. V. Taylor 1966, 185.

[68] Loader 1997, 23.

Looking at the description of the healing itself, two questions come to the fore. One concerns the emotional language: Jesus is angered (ὀργισθείς, according to the reading of D),[69] and after healing the "leper" he treats him rather harshly (καὶ ἐμβριμησάμενος αὐτῷ εὐθὺς ἐξέβαλεν αὐτόν). Another, perhaps the crucial question, is whether the gestures of Jesus (ἐκτείνας τὴν χεῖρα αὐτοῦ ἥψατο) are to be seen as typical only of miracle stories in general, or as expressing something of the historical attitude of Jesus towards "lepers."

To interpret the emotional response of Jesus as evidence for an eye-witness tradition, as does Vincent Taylor, is not to take seriously the problems involved.[70] The language of anger and emotion demands explanation. Resorting to theories of misleading "literal" translations from the Aramaic, is usually risky.[71] Explanations are numerous.[72] Theories about Jesus being angry at the man for asking pronouncement from him instead of from a priest, can be dismissed in view of the discussion above.[73] Suggestions that Jesus is upset about the man breaking purity laws or social barriers are questionable; why does he then respond by touching or gripping the man?[74] Some suggest that Jesus is angry at demonic influence, evil, or sickness, and others interpret the anger as an internal commotion.[75] It seems less speculative to discuss the typical excitement of a miracle worker,[76] but evidence and parallels are indeed scanty.

It has been suggested that the emotional language reflects the exorcist character of an original tradition, or at least represents some kind of "spill-over" from adjacent exorcisms.[77] This is possible, but the issue is complicated. ἐμβριμᾶσθαι, which has the original meaning "to snort in," and with a dative "to rebuke,"[78] is not used in gospel traditions about exorcisms. The term is

[69] Nestle-Aland has σπλαγχνισθείς, but see above (100, n.52), for a discussion about ὀργισθείς being more original.
[70] V. Taylor 1966, 186.
[71] Cf. Wojciechowski 1989, who gives several suggestions. I generally have reservations about such theories. In this particular case, however (רחם / רעם, see above, 100, n.52), such a theory has some plausibility. It must however be coupled with speculations about oral transmission of Aramaic traditions (similarity in sound).
[72] For an overview, see Loader 1997, 19ff, notes 23–26.
[73] Cf. Cave 1978–1979, 249f.
[74] Against Loader 1997, 19ff, who does not regard such an argument as valid, but thinks that it "misses the crucial point and presumes that Jesus could not have had both reactions, one of anger and yet a willingness to cross the boundary, just as he did with the Syrophoenician woman…," (21, n.26). Kertelge (1970, 66f.) finds it improbable that Jesus is angry because of the "leper" approaching him against the law. The stretching out of the hand would then have to be interpreted as a parrying gesture, and the touching becomes awkward in the context.
[75] Sariola 1990, 66, n.86; Wojciechowski 1989, 116.
[76] "… the miracle-worker suffers because of the barrier between human distress, blindness, unbelief, and the realm of super-human salvation." Theissen 1983 [1972], 57–58. Cf. Pesch 1976, 144.
[77] Cf. Knox 1953, 8, n.1. Cf. below, 304, 332.
[78] Liddell-Scott[9], *s.v.* ἐμβριμάομαι.

used outside Mark in two other miracle stories: the healing of two blind men (Mt 9:30) and the raising of Lazarus (Jn 11:33, 38). In the first case, ἐμβριμᾶσθαι, just as in Mk 1:43, belongs to a silencing command. In the second case it describes Jesus' inner feelings at the death of a friend.[79] ἐκβάλλειν (throw out) on the other hand, is definitely an exorcist term, used frequently in synoptic exorcist stories. Except for this dominating use, the term is used by Mark about the expulsion of merchants in the temple (11:15), the tearing out of an eye (9:47), the spirit "throwing" Jesus out into the desert (1:12), and the dismissal of the crowd at the healing of Jairus' daughter (5:40).[80] ἐκβάλλειν is used with more variation in meaning, however, in the other Synoptic Gospels: take out (Mt 7:4; Lk 6:42), bring forth (Mt 12:35; 13:52; cf. the use of προσφέρειν in the corresponding Lukan parallel, Lk 6:45), excrete (Mt 15:17). Of special interest is the Q saying about the abundant harvest and lack of workers: δεήθητε οὖν τοῦ κυρίου τοῦ θερισμοῦ ὅπως ἐργάτας ἐκβάλῃ εἰς τὸν θερισμὸν αὐτοῦ (Lk 10:2; Mt 9:38). The meaning here of ἐκβάλλειν is apparently "to send out," almost equivalent to ἀποστέλλειν. The context of Mk 1:43 could justify a similar interpretation. The use of ἐκβάλλειν in this context is nevertheless conspicuous. Finally, ὀργή and ὀργίζεσθαι occur infrequently in the gospels. The terms are found in a couple of Matthean and Lukan parables, in Jesus' words of warning in the Sermont on the Mount, and in the preaching of the Baptizer. But there are no occurrences in exorcist stories, and only one in a miracle story (Mk 3:5), in addition to the uncertain reading of Mk 1:41. While every single item of the emotional language can be explained individually, the total impact makes exorcist connotations possible. The tradition could be seen as simply conveying Jesus' emotional involvment, a wish for secrecy, and a sending away of the cured "leper." It may, however, contain traces of a view of a certain relationship between impurity and possession.[81]

Jesus' gestures

What, then, can be said about the gestures of Jesus? In the gospels, Jesus is described as touching or gripping the hand of people in the context of healing: a "leper" (Mk 1:41 par), Peter's mother-in-law (Mk 1:31 par), the dead daughter

---

[79] If we look for a verb of reproach belonging to the sphere of exorcism, we must turn to ἐπιτιμᾶν, which is frequently used in the Synoptic Gospels by Jesus in relation to demons (Mk 1:25; Lk 4:35, 41), demon-possessed (Mk 9:25; Mt 17:18; Lk 9:42), the wind (Mk 4:39; Mt 8:26), fever (Lk 4:39), and when the disciples are prohibited from revealing his messianic identity (Mk 8:30; Mt 12:16; Lk 9:21). This verb is not used, however, in Mk 1:40–45. The argument of Cave (1978–1979, 247) that ἐμβριμᾶσθαι is always used in the LXX in the same sense as ὀργίζεσθαι or in association with ὀργή, carries little weight, since the verb is not used frequently, but only once (Dan 11:30), except for once in the versions of Aq, Sm and Al respectively.

[80] Note the motif of secrecy present in this last case.

[81] This relationship is discussed further in Chapter VII.

of Jairus (Mk 5:41 par), a deaf man (Mk 7:33), the blind (Mk 8:23; Mt 9:29; 20:34), the dumb and deaf boy (Mk 9:27); the bier of a dead person (Lk 7:14), the ear of a servant of the high priest (Lk 22:51).[82] In addition, there are several descriptions of people touching Jesus: the woman with a blood flow (Mk 5:27ff par), the woman anointing Jesus' feet in Simon's house (Lk 7:39), and the crowd, seeking healing (Mk 3:10; 6:56; Mt 14:36; Lk 6:19).[83]

It has long been claimed that healing by stretching out a hand and/or by touch is a common feature of many miracle stories. Weinreich gives numerous examples in his oft-cited *Antike Heilungswunder.*[84] Most texts, however, describe how gods, e.g. Asclepius, heal by touching a patient. This is confirmed by Gross, who claims, arguing against Behm's statement that healing through touch is wide-spread, that in Antiquity this is true only about the hands of gods. When it comes to human *Gottesfreunden*, healing through touch is very infrequent.[85] Blackburn gives a few examples of human miracle workers healing by touch: the mortal Asclepius, Pythagoras, Pyrrhus, Vespasian, Apollonius and Iarchas.[86] But he points out certain differences. In these stories, touch is not the primary means of healing, but it is accompanied by stroking, massaging, pressing the foot against the spleen, etc. Stories in which the patient takes the initiative to touch the healer are uncommon outside the gospels; non-intentional transfer of power through touch is not attributed to the healer in Hellenistic miracle-stories.[87]

The gestures of Jesus should also be seen against the background of miracle stories in the Hebrew Bible. The stories of Elijah and Elisha offer some interesting parallels. Both prophets are described as healing through bodily contact (1Kgs 17:21; 2Kgs 4:34; cf. Mk 5:35ff). Although these descriptions differ somewhat from the idea of stretching out a hand and touching, and although such descriptions are not common in the Hebrew Bible, they are no less similar to Jesus' healings by touch than most Hellenistic miracle stories. The nearest parallel from the Hebrew Bible is actually provided by the expectation of Naaman, which was not fulfilled: that Elisha should heal his "leprosy" by touching the affected skin. Hence, healing by touch was not foreign to Jewish tradition, which is further confirmed by a passage fairly close in time to the

[82] In some of these instances, the expression κρατήσας τῆς χειρός is used. The verb ἅπτεσθαι, in the context of healing, and with Jesus as its subject, is used in the story of the "leper" (Mk 1:41 par), in Matthew's variant of the healing of Peter's mother-in-law (Mt 8:41), in Mark's stories about healing deaf and blind men (Mk 7:33; Mk 8:22), and in Luke's stories about touching the bier of a dead person (Lk 7:14) and the ear of the servant (Lk 22:51).

[83] In most of the cases in which Jesus is touched, people are described as touching his garments or tassels.

[84] Weinreich 1909, 14–37. Cf also Gross 1985, 373ff, 377ff; Blackburn 1991, 24ff, 112–117.

[85] Gross 1985, 493. This had been noted earlier by Weinreich 1909, 45.

[86] Blackburn 1991, 114.

[87] Blackburn 1991, 114 ff.

gospels, from the *Genesis Apocryphon*, in which Abraham is described as healing Pharaoh by laying his hands upon the king's head.[88] Healing by touch can neither be dismissed as only a Hellenistic motif, nor be regarded as nothing but a typical trait of miracle stories.

As just mentioned, healing by touch is expected, but never occurs, in the story of the "leper" Naaman (2Kgs 5), which would otherwise provide a parallel from the Hebrew Bible to the tradition about Jesus and the "leper." Since there is no priestly influence on the Elijah/Elisha legends, they do not reflect any awareness of purity issues; no such conclusions can be drawn from the fact that Elisha does not heal through touch, although that is what Naaman expects. But the manner of healing could have served as a precedent for the Markan tradition.[89] It apparently did not.[90] Jesus is described as touching or gripping a "leper." In view of the discussion above, and the fact that several of the healing-by-touch traditions mentioned concern people generally considered unclean, it is reasonable to suggest that Jesus' gesture of touch and physical contact cannot be explained *only* as a motif of miracle stories in Antiquity, whether Jewish or Hellenistic, but should be seen as expressing an attitude, i.e. as part of a characterization.[91] From a structuralist analysis it has also been argued that the touch of Jesus actually occupies a central place in the first part (vv 40–42) of the story about the "leper,"[92] and thus ought to have been part of the pre-Markan tradition.[93]

While the explanation about the Mosaic law in v 44 shows that Mark was aware of Jewish conditions, his own value system is somewhat different, and he is not operating within a Jewish frame of reference. Hence, he gives no hints at possible historical-legal consequences of Jesus touching a "leper." That was, for him, not a relevant issue.[94] But details of the traditions which he conveys beg the question. They should be able to reveal something about Jesus' attitude to people in a state of impurity, such as "lepers."

In order to examine Jesus' attitude to "lepers" in detail, it is also necessary to discuss the legal status of "lepers" during the first century. Interpretation of Jesus' gestures will be uncertain, as long as contemporary legal practice is not

[88] 1QapGen 20:22, 29. Cf. Gross 1985, 493.

[89] This would have been quite natural, in view of the influence of the Elijah/Elisha legends on gospel traditions generally. Cf. resurrection miracles (Mk 5:21–24, 35–43; Lk 7:11–17; 1Kgs 17:17–24; 2Kgs 4:8–37) and multiplication miracles (Mk 6:30–43; 8: 1–10; 1Kgs 17:7–16; 2Kgs 4:1–7, 42–44). It has possibly influenced Luke's variant (Lk 17:11–19).

[90] Or possibly it did, i.e. the *expectations* of Naaman in the Elisha story influenced the Markan narrative. But this is rather far-fetched.

[91] Kertelge 1970, 64f.

[92] The centrality of Jesus' touch in Mk 1:40–42 is confirmed by the semiotic analysis of André Fossion 1980, 279–290.

[93] Cf. Wojciechowski 1989, 115ff.

[94] Cf. Loader 1997, 24.

established. The purity issues in Mk 1:40–45 are basically two, if rituals for cleansing are left aside. The first concerns the degree of isolation. Would "lepers" in Jesus' time be allowed to come close to, or have any fellowship with others? The second concerns bodily contact. Was touching or being touched by a "leper" seen as producing serious defilement, and was contact avoided? To examine these questions, it is necessary to turn to the biblical legislation concerning צָרַעַת.

Biblical legislation concerning "leprosy"

In commenting on the lack of knowledge among Christian scholars about Jewish laws or the extent to which they were developed at the time of Jesus, Sanders cites Mark 1:40–45, and claims that "here Jesus acts in general conformity with the law."[95] Dealing with the same text later, Sanders regards it as the clearest example of biblical purity laws in the synoptics, reflecting the knowledge and acceptance of Lev 13: "Jesus accepted the biblical laws relating to leprosy, including sacrifice for purification."[96] This is, however, too simplified a conclusion, when the complications in interpreting the laws of Lev 13–14 are taken into account.

Lev 13:1–46 contains numerous and elaborate descriptions of different types of "leprosy" (צָרַעַת), all aimed at diagnosis.[97] These should be seen as guidelines for the priest in determining whether a person should be declared clean or unclean. There are descriptions of symptoms which awake suspicion and necessitate examination by the priest. Certain symptoms occasion an immediate declaration of impurity; others result in a seven-day confinement, after which a second inspection is carried out. This time, certain symptoms cause a declaration of impurity, while others make the priest declare the person clean, or in some cases lead to a further seven-day period of isolation, after which the suspect is finally declared either clean or unclean.

At the end of this section, there are short instructions for the behaviour of a person declared impure because of "leprosy" (13:45–46). The "leper" should wear torn clothes, loosen the hair, cover his beard and shout: "Unclean, unclean!" A person with "leprosy" should live alone, outside the camp.

Lev 14:1–32 deals with the purification of a "leper," healed of the disease. When someone is healed of "leprosy," the priest examines the person outside the camp, and a ritual is carried out in three stages. The first stage takes place still outside the camp, with two birds, cedar wood, scarlet wool and hyssop, after which the person is declared clean. After washing his/her clothes, shaving

---

[95] Sanders 1990, 2.

[96] Sanders 1990, 91.

[97] The sections about "leprosy" on clothes and houses (Lev 13:47–59; 14:33–57), are left out in this discussion, except for possible influence on views of how "lepers" contaminated.

and immersing, the "leper" is said to be clean, and allowed into the camp, but must stay outside his/her tent for seven days. When a week has passed, the next stage takes place. After having washed his/her clothes, shaved and immersed a second time, the purifying "leper" is once more said to be clean. The last stage consists of three animal sacrifices (sin, guilt and burnt offerings) and a meal offering on the eighth day. The sacrifices are described in detail. Blood from the guilt offering (אָשָׁם) and oil from the meal offering (מִנְחָה) are smeared on the tip of the right ear, the right thumb and the right big toe of the healed "leper."

Several interesting observations are possible. The priest is not involved in any healing of the disease, but only in diagnosis aimed at defining and preventing the spread of *impurity*, as well as rituals for removing such impurity, once the "leper" is healed.[98] The text expresses an unspecified, but existing notion of degrees of impurity, since every stage in the purification ritual is said to result in the person becoming clean,[99] and even a long confinement occasions some sort of washing, normally seen as part of a purification procedure, although the person, according to the final diagnosis is said to be clean.[100] The purification rites are the most elaborate of those found in Leviticus, comparable only to those of the corpse-impure in Num 19, and in some ways even exceeding them.[101]

The "leper" seems, in one way, to be treated as the severest form of impurity bearer.[102] According to Milgrom, a crucial clue for understanding the place of "leprosy" in the impurity system, is the aspect of death, i.e. its bearer being treated like a corpse.[103] This is evident in the story about Miriam, who together with Aaron complained against Moses, and was struck with "leprosy." In pleading for her, Aaron likens her leprous state with death (כַּמֵּת). "Do not let her become like a dead,[104] whose flesh is half eaten, when it comes forth from its mother's womb" (Num 12:12). An implicit identification of "leprosy" with

---

[98] Cf. Maccoby 1999, 120. Maccoby points out that healing is the province of the prophet, as in the story of Elisha and Naaman.

[99] The three stages of purification are all seen to result in purity; they are commented upon with the same phrase: "and he will be clean" (וְטָהֵר), Lev 14:8, 9, 20.

[100] Cf. Milgrom 1991, 782f.

[101] In both cases there is a seven-day period of impurity, and cedar wood, scarlet wool and hyssop are involved in preparing the purifying water which is sprinkled. In the case of the corpse impure, the slaughter of the red cow is a very infrequent ceremony done separately, and its ashes are used continuously in purification rites for years to come, while in the case of the "leper," the bird ritual is repeated for every purification. In addition, the "leper," like the זָב, זָבָה and יוֹלֶדֶת, has to bring sacrifices. The number of sacrifices, however, exceeds those of other impurity bearers, and the final smearing of blood and oils has no counterpart.

[102] At least from the perspective of purification rituals. Cf. Milgrom 1991, 991. Maccoby, on the other hand, regards leper-impurity to be more severe than corpse-impurity only in respect of banishment from the camp (1999, 145).

[103] Milgrom 1991, 819.

[104] The LXX adds ὡσεὶ ἔκτρωμα.

death can be found in Job 18:13, where Job is described as one whose skin and limbs are eaten, and the disease is called "death's firstborn" (בְּכוֹר מָוֶת).[105] The association of the "leper" with death is found in Josephus, and further developed in rabbinic literature.[106]

It is clear that "leprosy" was taken seriously in biblical times. The "leper" was to dwell apart from others, outside the camp (Lev 13:46), interpreted as the city. This is the case with Miriam (Num 12), the four "lepers" outside of Jerusalem, discovering the Aramaean flight (2Kgs 7), as well as with king Uzziah (2Kgs 15:5; 2Chr 26:21), although in the latter case it is not clear whether the house of the king was within the city or not.[107] The exclusion of "lepers" is supported by Num 5:2–3 which, in addition to Leviticus, demands the exclusion of corpse-impure and people with discharges.

The exclusion of "lepers" in the Second Temple period

Exclusion of "lepers" in the Second Temple period is attested by Josephus.[108] In Qumran, Lev 13:45–46 was interpreted to mean that "lepers" should dwell apart from other impurity bearers as well; "unclean, unclean" was understood as unclean to the unclean, and impurity could be accumulated by contact between different types of impurity bearers (4Q274 1 1:1–4; 11Q19 [11QT] 46:16–18; 48:14–17). This can be compared with the rabbinic system, where touching lesser impurity does not add to one's own impurity, although the idea of keeping away from other impurity bearers could possibly be understood from certain sources.[109]

As seen from Josephus (*Ag.Ap.* 1:281) and implied in one gospel text (Lk 17:12), the "camp" in Leviticus seems to have been interpreted as "city," and probably even "village."[110] When examining rabbinic material, we find that this is a presupposition. A certain restrictive tendency appears, however. From *mKel* 1:7, it becomes clear that the exclusion of "lepers" concerns *walled* cities.

---

[105] Job is not explicitly said to be struck by צָרַעַת, but his boils (Job 2:7) could be classified as a form of "leprosy." Cf. Paschen 1970, 56; von Rad 1975 [1957], 274.

[106] Τοὺς δὲ λεπροὺς εἰς τὸ παντελὲς ἐξήλασε τῆς πόλεως μηδενὶ συνδιαιτωμένους καὶ νεκροῦ μηδὲν διαφέροντας, *Ant.* 3:264; *mKel* 1:4; *mNeg* 13:7, 11; *bNed* 64b (note the "overshadowing" similar to that of the corpse).

[107] In the story about Naaman (2Kgs 5), there is no mention of isolation, but since there is no hint of a priestly perspective in the Elijah-Elisha tradition, it is not strange that certain aspects of ritual purity are absent. Even within a cultic perspective, Naaman as a non-Jew would not have been constrained by ritual purity regulations.

[108] *Ant.* 3:264; *Ag.Ap.* 1:281. For the objection that Josephus deals with Mosaic legislation rather than contemporary practice, see the discussion about *Ag.Ap.* 1:281 below, 113f.

[109] E.g. *Sifra* to Lev 13:46 [Parashat Negaim Pereq 12]; *bArak* 16b. See Harrington 1993, 61–62, 80f, 209; Cf. Milgrom 1991, 805.

[110] μήτε μένειν ἐν πόλει μήτ' ἐν κώμῃ κατοικεῖν, *Ag.Ap.* 1:281; εἰσερχομένου αὐτοῦ εἴς τινα κώμην απήντησαν [αὐτῷ] δέκα λεπροὶ ἄνδρες, Lk 17:12.

In another context, a dwelling house in a walled city is defined as one in a city surrounded by walls from the time of Joshua ben Nun (*mArak* 9:6). Maccoby speculates about the exclusion of "lepers" being practised only when the Jubilee was observed, as is said to have been the case with certain other laws concerning walled cities, according to the *Talmud* (*bArak* 29a).[111] Such a discussion must, however, be put within a context. A development towards an increasing leniency can be observed in rabbinic literature. By defining signs of "leprosy" and areas of exclusion as narrowly as possible, the negative consequences for people were minimized, in view of the absence of means for purification, after the destruction of the Second Temple.[112] The *Mishnah*'s description of how to accommodate "lepers" in a synagogue, by means of a special partition, should also probably be seen as part of a later development (*mNeg* 13:12).[113] But during Second Temple times, the general attitude was more stringent.

This is confirmed by further evidence from Qumran. In the polemical discussion of 4QMMT we find the following:

> And also concerning lepers: we s[ay that] they should [not] enter the holy purity, but instead [reside outside the camp (GM: למחנה, Qimron: לבית, Bernstein: לעיר)], alone. [And] also it is written that from the moment he shaves and washes he should reside outside [his tent for seven] days. And it happens that when they are unclean, [lepers aproach] the holy purity, the house (לבית). And you know [...] and apart from him, shall bring [a sin-offering. And concerning him who acts offensively it is wri]tten that he is a slanderer and a blasphemer. [And further: when they have the uncleanness of leprosy] they should not eat any of the holy things until the sun sets on the eighth day.[114]

According to Schiffman, 4QMMT accuses its opponents of allowing "lepers" to touch pure food and enter the temple (interpreting בית as referring to the temple).[115] This is hardly credible. It would imply an extremely lax attitude, which is not attested elsewhere for that time-period.[116] The context seems to be the *mittaher* (מִטַּהֵר, i.e. purifying "leper"), who has shaved and washed, but must wait for seven days (or rather eight), before all purification rites are completed.[117] Such a person is, according to biblical and rabbinic law, allowed into

[111] Maccoby 1999, 146f. This suggestion seems too speculative, not supported by sufficient evidence. "This would mean that, in majority rabbinic opinion at least, there were no cities from which lepers were excluded from the beginning of the Second Temple period onwards." (147). Such a hypothesis goes against all other evidence.

[112] Harrington 1993, 198ff, 211ff.

[113] The rationale may have been that a synagogue did not count as a house, or possibly, that the partition counted as a separate house. In the previous paragraph (*mNeg* 13:11), the spread of impurity in a house where a "leper" entered is discussed. Although there are similarities with corpse-impurity in a "tent," leper-impurity was apparently considered weaker.

[114] 4QMMT B64–72, tr. *DSS*GM (= 67–75).

[115] Schiffman 1989, 248.

[116] Schiffman's own suggestion is that the accusation concerned some cases in which the authors and their opponents differed in opinion on whether or not a certain disease should be considered to be צָרַעַת. This is possible, but left without support.

[117] Cf. Qimron and Strugnell's explanatory gloss in *DJD* 10, 55.

the city, after the initial rituals on the first day, but not into his house (Lev 13:8; *mNeg* 14:2). According to the Qumran ideals for the temple city, stricter rules applied to Jerusalem than to ordinary cities. The Qumran sect extended the holiness of the temple to the temple city in its entirety.[118] Since they wanted to expel people from Jerusalem who otherwise were only prohibited from entering the temple[119], it is logical to think that they wished the *mittaher* to remain outside the temple city until the end of the purification period. The passage in its entirety can be interpreted according to its last phrase, as a concern to protect the purity of food.[120] But the polemical details can be discerned quite clearly. This is facilitated by an alternative reconstruction of Bernstein. Instead of reading the opinion of the Qumran sectarians as "we s[ay that] they should [not] enter the holy purity, but instead [reside outside the camp], alone," the purely conjectural למחנה[121] is exchanged for (the likewise conjectural) לעיר.[122] The polemical situation is thus clarified. The sectarians claim that purifying "lepers" should not be allowed access to pure food, and thus be kept outside of the temple city, until the end of their purification period. To support this they refer to Lev 13:8. For this reason they oppose the present practice, in which purifying "lepers" are allowed into the temple city, and thus risk contact with pure food.

Even if the details of this reconstruction are not accepted, it is clear that 4QMMT presupposes a common understanding, according to which "lepers" are *normally* excluded from their homes and cities. The discussion concerns the status of the *mittaher*, and probably, the special case of the temple city.

In view of this evidence, we must conclude that "lepers" were isolated during the first century CE, and not allowed into cities. This is in line with the treatment of "lepers" in neighbouring cultures.[123] It is uncertain whether they were allowed into smaller towns or villages, or precisely what rules applied to a *mittaher* during the period of purification. We may expect differences in opinion

---

[118] This tendency is demonstrated by García Martínez from the *Temple Scroll* (García Martínez and Trebolle Barrera 1995, 143ff): those impure because of sexual relations were traditionally excluded from the temple (*mKel* 1:8), but according to the *Temple Scroll* from the whole city (11Q19 [11QT] 45:11–12); similarly, hides of clean animals, slaughtered in other cities, were not accepted for making utensils for use in the temple city (11Q19 [11QT] 47:7–18).

[119] People with discharges, and semen pollution. 11Q19 [11QT] 46:16–18.

[120] Harrington 1993, 79, 81; cf. Bernstein 1996, 43.

[121] This conjecture, followed by García Martínez, is based on the fact that this phrase paraphrases Lev 14:8. Bernstein is, however, arguing against Qimron's reconstruction, לבית, which is unlikely. It is more reasonable to suppose that the authors of MMT either referred to the "camp" of Leviticus, or interpreted it explicitly by paraphrasing it as "city." In any case, "city" was to them the contemporary equivalent of "camp."

[122] Bernstein 1996, 43.

[123] The "leper" is, according to a Babylonian *kudurru* inscription, "[a]s a prisoner driven out of the gate of the city, forced to dwell outside its walls … so that its citizens do not approach him" (quoted in Milgrom 1991, 805).

and a variegated practice. It seems likely, however, that the rabbinic limiting definition of walled cities represents a post-70 development, and that "lepers" at the time of Jesus were supposed to keep out of ordinary towns and villages. They were regarded as bearers of a very serious form of impurity.

The contamination of "lepers"

It is surprising that nothing whatsoever is said about the contamination of the "leper" in the biblical material. Since "lepers" must be isolated and expelled from the community, it is only reasonable to conclude that by their continued presence, they would risk transmitting impurity to other persons and items, and in some way threaten the sanctuary. The absence of such discussions in Leviticus has been explained by isolation being taken for granted, and carried out completely; hence no contact with other people, and no contamination, should have been possible.[124] This explanation might be accepted, since expulsion and the lack of contamination rules both apply to "lepers," but not to other impurity bearers, at least not according to Leviticus. But in practical life, this absence of rules would not be satisfactory. And even if the expulsion of "lepers" had its origin in fears of demonic influence, certain ideas of how "lepers" contaminated must have been present at an early stage. Thus it is only natural that rules were deduced by analogy from the sections about leprous houses, and about other impurity bearers. A kind of "gap-filling" technique is used by rabbinic exegetes, as well as by modern interpreters, in reading Leviticus.[125]

In attempting to outline the contamination of a "leper" in biblical times, David P. Wright assumes "that an affected person polluted much like a *zāb*. Thus an infected person would pollute persons by contact and by spitting, requiring them to bathe and launder."[126] This is in agreement with rabbinic interpretation, where one becomes impure by touching a "leper" in the same way as if one touches a discharger (*zab, zabah, niddah* or *yoledet*).[127] Such a reconstruction is plausible.[128] In the rabbinic system, the "leper" is furthermore said to contaminate objects by sitting, lying or riding,[129] which in their turn can contaminate other persons or objects.[130] The rationale is probably that since "leprosy," because of isolation and purifying rules, is considered to result in a more serious form of impurity, the contamination possibilities of the discharger are added. But it is unlikely that such a chain of pollution should be ascribed to the

---

124 Maccoby 1999, 128.

125 Harrington 1993, 27. Cf. the method of Milgrom, in 1991, 1, and David P. Wright, in 1987.

126 David P. Wright 1987, 209–210.

127 *mZab* 5:6; cf. *tZab* 5:3.

128 Cf. Harrington 1993, 186, 188; Maccoby 1999, 122.

129 I.e. *midras*-impurity (מִדְרָס).

130 *mZab* 5:6.

biblical system, since this type of impurity (*midras*) in the biblical texts refers only to impurity bearers suffering from genital emissions.[131]

A special feature of the chain by which "lepers" transmit impurity is the idea of shade or "overhang," which is deduced from the rules about "leprous" houses (Lev 14:33–57). Before inspection, a suspected house should be emptied before it was shut up (v 36). The implicit presupposition is apparently that anything within the house would otherwise become impure. This is confirmed by the subsequent comment, that anyone who enters the shut house becomes unclean until the evening. Lying or eating within the house necessitates laundering of one's clothes (vv 46–47). There is an obvious similarity to the house with corpse-impurity,[132] but only a one-day impurity is incurred in the case of the "leprous" house. These biblical precepts, together with the instructions of Lev 14:8 that the *mittaher* must stay outside his/her tent during the purifying period, made the rabbis formulate the analogy: "A clean person who put his head and the greater part of his body inside an unclean house is made unclean. And an unclean person who put his head and the greater part of his body inside a clean house has made it unclean" (*mNeg* 13:8).[133]

If being under the same roof as a "leper" incurred impurity, how much more would physical contact? The ideas of both touch and overhang were seen as biblical precepts during the first century CE. This is attested by Josephus, in his argument against the claim of Manetho that Moses was a leprous priest:

> τοῖς γὰρ λεπρῶσιν ἀπείρηκε μήτε μένειν ἐν πόλει μήτ᾽ ἐν κώμῃ κατοικεῖν, ἀλλὰ μόνους περιπατεῖν κατεσχισμένους τὰ ἱμάτια, καὶ τὸν ἁψάμενον αὐτῶν ἢ ὁμωρόφιον γενόμενον οὐ καθαρὸν ἡγεῖται. καὶ μὴν κἂν θεραπευθῇ τὸ νόσημα καὶ τὴν αὑτοῦ φύσιν ἀπολάβῃ, προείρηκέν τινας ἁγνείας, καθαρμοὺς πεγαίων ὑδάτων λουτροῖς καὶ ξυρήσεις πάσης τῆς τριχός, πολλάς τε κελεύει καὶ παντοίας ἐπιτελέσαντα θυσίας τότε παρελθεῖν εἰς τὴν ἱερὰν πόλιν.[134]

It has been argued that Josephus does not describe contemporary practice, but speaks of the legislation of Leviticus or the ideal time of Moses. It should be noted, however, that neither the comment about spring water (πεγαίων ὑδάτων), nor the idea of the purifying "leper" not being allowed specifically into the temple city until sacrifices are made, i.e. until the eighth day, is present in the legislation of Leviticus. These positions seem to belong to Second Tem-

[131] Harrington 1993, 188; against David P. Wright 1987, 210.

[132] See below, 166.

[133] Harrington 1993, 186.

[134] *Ag.Ap.* 1:281–282. "In fact, he [Moses] forbids lepers either to stay in a town or to reside in a village; they must be solitary vagrants, with their clothes rent; anyone who touches or lives under the same roof with them he considers unclean. Moreover, even if the malady is cured and the victim returns to his normal condition, Moses prescribes certain rites of purification—to cleanse himself in a bath of spring-water and to cut off all his hair—and requires him to offer a numerous variety of sacrifices before entering the holy city."

ple times, and come close to those of the Qumran sectarians.[135] It is also interesting that Josephus specifies both towns and villages (μήτε μένειν ἐν πόλει μήτ' ἐν κώμῃ κατοικεῖν) as areas from which "lepers" were expelled. Such definitions are definitely interpretations of the biblical legislation, and it is reasonable to regard Josephus' statement about τὸν ἁψάμενον αὐτῶν ἢ ὁμωρόφιον γενόμενον, as reflecting a contemporary understanding of how the "leper" transferred impurity to others. It is necessary to conclude, with Maccoby, that the idea of enclosed-space-contamination, although probably post-biblical, must be pre-rabbinic, since it is taken for granted by Josephus as well as by the *Mishnah*, and treated as a biblical precept.[136]

While this idea of "overhang" does not exactly correspond to that of the corpse-impure, and does not operate in precisely the same way,[137] it may explain both the expulsion of the "leper" and the different purifying stages of the *mittaher*. It is the risk of contaminating people without their knowledge, possibly resulting in impurity being transferred to the temple or to sacred food, which prompts the isolation of the "leper."[138] The bird rite of the first day removes some of that risk. Would this mean that during the subsequent seven-day period the *mittaher* could contaminate only through touch?[139] If so, it does not fully explain why s/he is not allowed into his/her house.[140] I suspect that this level of systematizing the evidence cannot be assigned to the Second Temple period.[141]

---

[135] Spring water is mentioned for the bird rite (Lev 14:5), and used for the first-day sprinkling of a purifying "leper." But it is never stated as a requirement for first- or seventh-day ablutions in biblical legislation (cf. the rules for the *zab*, where spring water is required, Lev 15:13). Concerning exclusion of the purifying "leper," see the discussion above on 4QMMT, and entry into the temple city. The similarity between Josephus and the Qumran position is interesting in view of Josephus' positive attitude to the Essenes (e.g. *J.W.* 2:119–161; *Ant.* 18:18–22).

[136] Maccoby 1999, 143f. "... this very natural extension of biblical law arose in the Second Temple period and later became part of rabbinic law, too authoritative to be regarded as rabbinic, and therefore supported by a somewhat flimsy proof-text" (144).

[137] In rabbinic interpretation, a "leper" standing under a tree will contaminate a clean person passing by under its shade. As in the case of the "tent" of the corpse-impure, the "habitation" of the "leper" is defined by the ceiling. A clean person standing under a tree will not, however, be contaminated by a "leper" passing by, unless he stops (*mNeg* 13:7). Outside a "tent," corpse-impurity operates vertically only, but for an unlimited distance. "Leprosy"-impurity has no such contaminating effect outside a "habitation," but only by touching or carrying (except for a minority opinion, *tNeg* 7:3). Cf. the discussion of Maccoby 1999, 141–148.

[138] Milgrom 1991, 805f.

[139] This is the view of David P. Wright 1987, 213, and Harrington 1993, 208.

[140] This would fit into a logical system only if we assume that other impurity bearers with seven-day purifying periods had to live separately, which is suggested by some evidence, but gainsaid by other. See further discussion below, 147–150, 156–161, 187–189.

[141] Milgrom's reasoning about the two ablutions removing subsequent layers of impurity is logical, and supported by the repetition of וְטָהֵר in Lev 14:8–9. The first stage would remove air-borne impurity to the sanctuary, and, according to David P. Wright and Harrington, overhang impurity in the profane sphere. The second stage would (hypothetically) remove overhang impurity to the sanctuary, and touch impurity in the profane sphere. Milgrom 1991, 967; David P.

It belongs to the type of rabbinic discussions, found in e.g. *mKel* 1:1–4, where different types of impurities are sorted and classified into a hierarchical and coherent system. Discussions such as that of *mNeg* 13:11, about the height to which uncleannes reaches when a house is entered by a "leper," probably result from later developments as well.

According to Lev 13:45 a "leper" should cover his beard, i.e. upper lip or mouth. It is a moot question whether this should be seen as a sign of mourning, or whether it has to do with the risk of transferring impurity by way of breath.[142] The practice could be a survival from an early period, when "leprosy" was seen as the work of demons, which could damage others through the breath of the "leper."[143] In later rabbinic writings, we find the prohibition, however, of coming closer than four, or even a hundred cubits east of a "leper." The latter is said to apply when winds are blowing (*Lev.Rab.* 16:3).[144] This is in line with the requirement of 11Q19 [11QT] 46:16–18, that "lepers," dischargers and semen-impure should have their dwellings east of the temple city. As the prevailing winds came from the west, these considerations may have to do with the risk of contamination.[145] The opinion that a distance should be kept is confirmed by 4Q274 1 1:1–4. The "leper" is required to dwell apart from other impurity bearers, "at a distance of twelve cubits from the purity when he speaks to him; towards the northwest of any dwelling place shall he dwell at a distance of this measure."[146] The direction in this text is almost the opposite of that in the previous passages. This makes it unlikely that the idea of winds from the west carrying the contaminating breath of the "leper" would have been a general belief in Second Temple times. But the idea of keeping "lepers" at a distance is confirmed. Although this passage discusses the separation of different impurity bearers from each other, one of the underlying presuppositions is that a minimum distance should always be kept, even in personal communication with a "leper."[147]

Wright 1987, 213; Harrington 1993, 207f. I find it very difficult, however, to apply such a conscious systematization to the Second Temple period.

[142] According to *Sifra* to Lev 13:45 [Parashat Negaim Pereq 12] it is a sign of mourning. Other suggestions have been for the "leper" to make himself unrecognizable to spiritual powers around him (Milgrom 1991, 803).

[143] Maccoby 1999, 125.

[144] Cf. *yBBat* 2:9.

[145] Milgrom 1991, 804. According to Milgrom, this reflects a view of impurity as airborne, which in the Priestly system does not affect persons, unless they find themselves under the same roof. Contamination by breath is not incorporated into this system, but must, in the view of Milgrom, represent folk belief.

[146] 4Q274 1 1:1–2, tr. J. Baumgarten (1999a [*DJD* 35], 101). García Martínez's translation "North-east" must be a mistake, since the Hebrew is unambiguous (מערב צפון).

[147] J. Baumgarten (1999a [*DJD* 35], 101f) takes the passage as referring to the זָב, rather than to the מְצֹרָע (cf. Baumgarten 1995a, 1ff). His arguments are 1) the mention of bed and seat. He admits, however, that these terms are used metaphorically (bed of sorrow, seat of sighing); 2)

Physical contact and staying for some amount of time with a "leper" in the same house, was considered to render a person unclean in the first century CE. This much can be said with confidence. It should also be safe to conclude that the expansionist current in Second Temple Judaism did not approve of coming close to "lepers," but prescribed a certain distance in order to avoid contamination. We thus have to speak about an ostracism of "lepers," based on fear of contamination, during the Second Temple period. The cry of the "leper," "unclean, unclean," must be seen as a warning, in view of how much the "leper" was shunned, and how much contamination was feared. It should not be played down as a form of ritualized grief, although some rabbinic texts interpret it as a plea for empathy. Such texts are rather to be explained as reflecting a growing tendency to leniency in Talmudic times, which induce some rabbis to soften the harshness of ostracism.[148] Other rabbinic interpretations, however, stick to the natural interpretation of the cry as a warning to others to avoid contamination by the impurity of the "leper."[149]

"Leprosy" as punishment

The fact that "leprosy" was commonly regarded as a divine punishment contributed to the ostracism of the "leper." This is evidenced in the Hebrew Bible by the stories about Miriam, Gehazi and Uzziah (Num 12:9; 2Kgs 5:27; 2Chr 26:20–21), as well as the curse of David concerning the house of Joab (2Sam 3:29). The idea of "leprosy" as divine punishment is attested in ancient sources, from Mesopotamia to Greece,[150] and is found in diverse cultures throughout history.[151] According to Milgrom, it is seen as resulting from sins committed against the deity rather than against man, but at the same time it is usually a punishment for moral failings.[152] The moral aspect is elaborated on by the rab-

line 4b about a menstruant touching a זָב, suggests that the זָב is the one referred to in the preceding context. This argument does not seem valid to me, since the whole section mentions different impurity bearers touching other impurity bearers; 3) the sequence of subjects, זָב, נִדָּה and זָבָה, corresponds to the order in Lev 15. To me, the order rather supports the thesis that lines 1–4 should refer to the מְצֹרָע, since laws about "leprosy" (Lev 13–14) immediately precede those of Lev 15. Since the first four lines refer to the call of the "leper" (טמא טמא), and mention the term נגע (affliction/plague, although the word is partly reconstructed), which is used as a synonym to צָרַעַת, I find it difficult, indeed, to deny this passage as a reference to the "leper."

[148] Cf. *bNid* 66a. The cry is seen as expressing sorrow. Cf. Milgrom 1991, 804f.

[149] E.g. *bMQat* 5a; Maccoby 1999, 125.

[150] References in Milgrom 1991, 820f; among others the vassal treaty of Esarhaddon, a curse appended to the Code of Hammurabi, and Herodotus' descriptions of Persian conditions.

[151] Milgrom 1991, 821; cf. Douglas 1966, 130f, about the Nuer.

[152] Milgrom 1991, 821. Milgrom states that "except for the Bible, the attribution of scale disease to moral offences is not attested in the ancient Near East" (823). He supplies examples of "leprosy" as caused by moral offence from classical Greek literature, however.

bis, who link "leprosy" with a number of sins, especially gossiping.[153] Such a moralizing interpretation cannot, however, be seen as a post-70 development only.[154] Although "leprosy" neither in the Hebrew Bible, nor in rabbinic literature is *necessarily* interpreted as a punishment for sinful behaviour, the idea of it being a punishment for moral offences is dominant and often taken for granted in Second Temple Judaism. This is clear from several examples in the Qumran texts. In a Cave 4 fragment of the Damascus Document, the "leper" (ינגע בנגע צרעת) is mentioned in a catalogue of transgressors, in which no distinction is made between ritual and moral transgressions (4Q270 2 2:12).[155] Strengthening in front of a plague (נגע)[156] is set parallel to purification (!) from a multitude of sins (טהרתה מרוב עוון) in 1QH 9:32.[157] Baumgarten has pointed at the penitential tone of purification rituals in general, as is evidenced from 4Q512.[158] This is clear for "leprosy" specifically, as is seen from 4Q274 1 1:1: "He shall begin to lay his pl[ea]. He shall lie in a [b]ed of sorrow and reside in [a dwelling of] sighs."[159] The presupposition seems to be that the "leper" has sinned and must repent.[160] Refusal to repent is explicitly given as a rabbinic explanation for the ostracism of the "leper" (*tNeg* 6:7).[161] Says Harrington: "Thus, I conlude about the mĕṣōrāᶜ that only after being forgiven by God, as evidenced by healing, can the purification process begin."[162]

The Lukan tradition

Returning to the gospel traditions about Jesus and "lepers," we find that in the light of contemporary legal practices and discussions, they imply that Jesus at

[153] Milgrom 1991, 823; Maccoby 1999, 131. In *Lev. Rab.* 17:3 "leprosy" is associated with ten sins: idol worship, unchastity, bloodshed, desecration of the Name, blasphemy, robbing the public, usurping, pride, gossip and the evil eye. According to *bArak* 16a "leprosy" is due to gossip, shedding of blood, vain oaths, incest, arrogance, robbery and envy. Maccoby claims (1999, 120–121) that Lev 13 shows no trace of a moralistic approach, and that the moralizing of the rabbis is only aetiological, i.e. it concerns the cause of "leprosy" and does not judge its effect, "leprosy" itself, which is non-moral like all impurities. This distinction is somewhat strained, and has to do with Maccoby's overarching view of morality in relation to purity. See the discussion below in Chapter V.

[154] Against Beentjes 2000, 71f.

[155] J. Baumgarten 1990, 162.

[156] Regularly used for "leprosy." See above, 98, n.46.

[157] (Sukenik: 1:32). Harrington 1993, 82; Qimron 1991, 258. Hebrew text from Qimron 1991.

[158] J. Baumgarten 1990, 162; *DJD* 7: 262ff.

[159] Milgrom's translation, in 1995, 60. The Hebrew reads: יחל להפיל את תחנוׄנו משׁכב יג[ו]ן ישכ[ב ו]מׄושב אנחה ישב (*DJD* 35:100). I am not following J. Baumgarten's conjecture (1999a [*DJD* 35], 102) with an אל at the end of the preceding (non-extant) line, which would negate the first sentence, implying restrictions upon the recitations of prayers during the period of impurity.

[160] Milgrom 1991, 806; 1995, 61.

[161] Milgrom 1991, 806.

[162] Harrington 1993, 82.

times did not follow what was regarded as common behaviour. He was remembered as coming close to, touching and healing "lepers," possibly even visiting them.[163] The picture is confirmed by Markan traditions as well as by Q material (Mk 1:40–45 par; Mk 14:3/Mt 26:6; Mt 11:5/Lk 7:12).

We have seen that the expulsion and isolation of "lepers" was a general practice in Palestine during the first century CE.[164] This probably applied not only to walled cities, but to towns and villages as well. In view of all the evidence for "lepers" being excluded from towns, the phrasing of Luke's variant (καὶ ἐγένετο ἐν τῷ εἶναι αὐτὸν ἐν μιᾷ τῶν πόλεων καὶ ἰδοὺ ἀνὴρ πλήρης λέπρας, Lk 5:12) must be regarded as secondary, possibly due to a shallow knowledge of Palestinian conditions.[165] Lk 5:12 is, however, probably not intended to picture the "leper" *inside* the town; the incident is only said to have happened while Jesus was staying in one of the cities. This is part of Luke's scheme, which has been stated just before this incident, according to which Jesus leaves Capernaum to go on an evangelizing tour in the "other cities" (Lk 4:43). Hence this is part of Luke's frame, and is not a conscious attempt to place the "leper" inside a town.

The ostracism of "lepers" was real.[166] They were kept at a distance and their company was shunned. The behaviour ascribed to Jesus would have been objectionable, even if the impurity incurred was a "light" one, and could be dealt with by immersion.[167] There are no hints anywhere that Jesus should have immersed because of contamination from a source of impurity.[168]

The one tradition which does not immediately fit into this picture is Lk 17:11–19. The story about ten "lepers" at the outskirts of a village on the border of Samaria and Galilee is often regarded as a variant of Mk 1:40–45 par.[169]

---

[163] The difficulty in judging the status of Simon the Leper (Mk 14:3/Mt 26:6) has been mentioned above, 99. For further discussion about Jesus dwelling with "lepers," see below, 125.

[164] Cf. Sanders 1990, 158.

[165] On the other hand, the tradition in Lk 17:11–19 betrays a certain awareness of legal practice and isolation. (For a discussion of this text, see below.)

[166] The statement of Maccoby (1999, 125) to this effect may be true, but is phrased in a way that seems to aim at playing down the serious ostracism involved: "Indeed, there is no reason to conclude from the leper's exclusion that others were forbidden to talk to him or supply his needs, as long as such social contacts took place outside the camp (which means, in times later than the wanderings in the wilderness, outside the city). After all, even physical contact with a 'leper' caused only a one-day uncleanness to the person contacting him, and this could easily be removed by washing in the ritual pool. The requirement that the 'leper' should 'dwell alone' (13:46) means that he must not share living-quarters, or (as the rabbis interpret it) meals, with anyone except other 'lepers, but this does not preclude contacts necessary to his survival."

[167] Most impurities lasted one day, except for the "fathers." This is no argument for them not being avoided. Cf. Sanders 1990, 144f.

[168] Jn 13:10 possibly implies a ritual bath before the Passover meal. See below, 250–253.

[169] Bultmann 1972 [1921], 227, regards it as a heightened version of the tradition in Mk 1. The latter is also, however, taken over by Luke (Lk 5:12–16); Luke must accordingly have regarded them as separate. If not a variant, it belongs to Luke's special material.

A question prompted by the story is why the nine non-returning "lepers" are blamed by Jesus for actually carrying out his orders. This is explained by Luke's obvious interests. In the first place, the story is given a moralizing twist, in that the gratitude of the returning "leper" becomes an example of proper behaviour. Secondly, the authority of Jesus is confirmed by the "leper" returning to him before, or possibly instead of, turning to the official representatives of religion, and Jesus is seen as a supreme agent of God. The third and perhaps most important trait in the Lukan story is the emphasis on the man being a Samaritan (cf. 10:25–37), which is further underscored by Jesus' words: εἰ μὴ ὁ ἀλλογενὴς οὗτος;. Here it is a non-Jew who behaves in an exemplary way. This is important in Luke's ideology, and it adds emphasis to the final point, that Jesus proclaims salvation: ἡ πίστις σου σέσωκέν σε.[170] To Luke, salvation is more than healing, and it is given to Gentiles who by faith acknowledge the authority of Jesus and respond with pious gratitude.

While certain traits point at thorough Lukan redaction, others could be seen as contradictory. The "lepers" are pictured as meeting Jesus as he is about to enter a village. They stop at a distance and shout. This is, as we have seen, fully in accord with the legal situation of the time. "Lepers" living together in a group are attested in 2Kgs 7:3. Although these details might fit into any Hellenistic environment, they do reflect Palestinian conditions. If Lk 17:11–19 is to be seen as a Lukan, possibly more hellenized variant of the Markan tradition, a couple of questions must be answered. Why is Jesus not portrayed as touching the "lepers"? Avoiding it would suit Jewish circumstances, but why should Luke "de-hellenize" an earlier Markan tradition on such a point? And why would Luke de-emphasize the suddenness of the Markan miracle, by delaying the healing, or even making it happen gradually on the road?

We are thus left with an ambiguity in the evidence: on one hand the tradition is heavily influenced by Lukan ideology; on the other hand, it exhibits traits that fit into a Palestinian context. To treat it simply as a variant of the Markan tradition presents many difficulties. If independent, it adds little about Jesus' attitude to "leprosy," but it does confirm our picture of the legal situation in Palestine and the expected behaviour of "lepers" (exclusion from towns, keeping distance). It says nothing about the gestures of Jesus, however. Jesus just talks. His first statement: "Go and show yourselves to the priests" (v 14), is similar to his command in the Markan tradition, except for the plural (τοῖς ἱερεῦσιν)[171] and the lack of references to sacrifice. His second statement about

[170] For Lukan occurrences, see note 173 below.

[171] I. H. Marshall's explanation that the plural arises from the group of "lepers" being mixed (Samaritans and Jews), thus having to visit different priests, is somewhat strained (1978, 651). The plural is sometimes taken as an evidence of ignorance of Jewish circumstances and legal prescriptions, since Leviticus mentions one priest only (Lev 14:1f). I find it precarious, and somewhat literalistic, to draw such a conclusion on the basis of a plural form only. For further discussion, in comparison with *P. Egerton* 2, see below, 124.

gratitude and Gentiles (vv 17–18) has nothing to do with our discussion of "leprosy" and purity. The third statement (v 19) consists of two standard injunctions: ἀναστὰς πορεύου[172] and ἡ πίστις σου σέσωκέν σε,[173] which are found in various healing stories. They do not, however, address the question of purity. Jesus, in fact, does not act. Admittedly, nothing is said about Jesus touching the "lepers." But neither is anything said about hesitation on Jesus' part. The question of purity is not even implicit in the present form of this story; it has receded in favour of other interests.

Is it possible that Luke is consciously trying to present Jesus as law-abiding? This has been the thesis of some interpreters, who have seen evidence, for example, in Luke's omission of Mk 6:45–8:10, which contains the law-critical material of ch. 7.[174] While such omissions can be seen as reflecting the indifference to purity matters in Luke's Gentile environment, they could also be seen as conscious omissions. Bart Koet emphasizes the lack of travels into Gentile territory in Luke's narrative. He interprets this as avoidance of "Gentile impurity," which would have forced Jesus to undergo ritual purification before entering the temple.[175] As further arguments for his view, he discusses the purification rite in Lk 2:22–39, and the difference between Lk 17:11–19 and the Markan tradition.[176] It must, however, be questioned whether the issue of bodily purity is alive in Luke's context. In Lk 2:22–39, the temple visit is related to the law, but the rites are muddled up: the purification rite, required by the mother, is said to apply to both mother and child (τοῦ καθαρισμοῦ αὐτῶν), and is fused with the release of the first-born. Either Luke has a very shallow knowledge of Jewish law, or he simplifies and "hellenizes" ritual customs, in a manner remotely similar to Philo's, for the benefit of his readers. In any case, his aim seems to be to present Jesus as "law-abiding" in the *general* sense of a pious man. This makes it inadvisable to draw conclusions about Jesus' attitude to "leprosy," based primarily on the Lukan tradition in 17:11–19.

Papyrus Egerton 2

An interesting tradition, with certain affinities to Lk 17, was found in 1934 among a collection of papyri.[177] *Papyrus Egerton* 2 was published by Bell and Skeat (*Fragments of an unknown gospel*) the following year, and consisted of

---

[172] This wording is actually not standard, but the content is: ἔγειρε…καὶ περιπάτει (Mk 2:9/Mt 9:5/Lk 5:23/Jn 5:8), ἔγειρε…καὶ ὕπαγε (Mk 2:11), ἔγειρε καὶ…πορεύου (Lk 5:24).

[173] Mk 5:34/Mt 9:22/Lk 8:48; Mk 10:52/Lk 18:42; Lk 7:50; 17:19.

[174] Cf. Koet 2000, 104, with references (n. 38) to Banks, Esler and Pettem.

[175] Koet 2000, 104.

[176] Koet 2000, 101ff.

[177] *P. Egerton* 2 was acquired from a dealer, and thus its provenance is unknown. Some of the papyri which were bought simultaneously came, however, from Oxyrhynchus, which could be the probable origin of *P. Egerton* 2 as well (Bell and Skeat 1935a, i, 7).

three fragments. Two of these are fairly large, and although fragmentary, they contain four different pericopes. The first is "Johannine" in content, while the second and third are parallel to, and probably variants of, synoptic stories (healing of "leper" and paying tax). The fourth pericope, about a miracle on the bank of Jordan, is difficult to reconstruct and is not paralleled in any known gospel.

In 1978, a small scrap of papyrus was published as *Papyrus Köln* 255. This piece fits at the bottom of *P. Egerton* 2, frag. 1, and the two last lines of the latter partly go into the first lines of the former. The two fragments are obviously part of the same papyrus.

P. Egerton 2 was initially assigned a date around the middle of the second century, from paleographical considerations.[178] This meant that if the fragments were to be regarded as part of an unknown gospel, its composition must be still earlier. Since the impulse to write other gospels (except for the purpose of making special claims) diminished as the four gospels were gaining canonical status during the second century, and since the fragments contain no hints of heterodoxy, Bell and Skeat posed a date of origin between 80 and 120 CE.[179]

An apostrophe after the gamma in line 45 (Γ') of the Köln fragment has necessitated a revision of the dating of the papyrus. This trait is found in P. Bodmer too, and became common during the third century. It makes a dating of the fragments around the year 200 more likely,[180] but hardly affects the proposed date of composition. This is still one of the earliest Christian papyri.

Opinions have differed as to the value of this text. All pericopes contain both "Johannine" and "synoptic" traits. This has led to different hypotheses and conclusions. It has been regarded as a fragment of an independent gospel, partly dependent on common sources with the synoptic and Johannine traditions, or even providing a source for John. Others have judged it to be secondary and wholly dependent on the canonical gospels.[181] The blending of "Johannine" and "synoptic" traits is intriguing, and several studies of linguistic similarities have been made.[182]

Despite the Johannine content of the first pericope (cf. Jn 5:39; 9:29), it is linguistically closer to the synoptics; traits of Johannine theology are missing,

---

[178] Arguments against such an early dating (being a codex and not a roll, *nomina sacra* and contractions, diaeresis over initial ι and υ, regular omission of iota adscript) were discussed and dismissed; on all points, examples of early evidence can be found (Bell and Skeat, 1935a, 2ff).

[179] Bell and Skeat, 1935b.

[180] Gronewald 1987, 136f; the trait became common from the first decade of the third century CE, but isolated examples can be found from the very beginning and very end of the second century CE (Turner 1987 [1970], 11 and n.50).

[181] See Bell and Skeat, 1935b.

[182] In addition to the initial studies by Bell and Skeat, e.g. Jeremias 1936, 36–45; Dodd 1936, 56–92; Cerfaux 1936, 55–77; Mayeda 1946; Neirynck 1985, 153–160; Daniels 1991; Erlemann 1996. The attempt by David F. Wright 1985–1986 to resurrect the idea of identity with the *Gospel of Peter* is hardly convincing. For a comprehensive bibliography, see Willker 2001.

and the style of the story is more novelistic.[183] The third pericope is a variant of the synoptic tradition about paying tax (Mk 12:13–17 par), but is shot through with expressions recognized from John (Jn 3:2; 10:25). *P. Egerton* 2 might have had access to "Johannine" traditions, but cannot be dependent on John; it would require a cut-and-paste technique, making a mosaic out of extracts from John, still without achieving a distinct Johannine character. The text of *P. Egerton* 2 is rather coherent and the pericopes run smoothly.[184]

The second and third pericopes are variants of synoptic traditions, but "synoptic" language is found throughout the fragments. Focusing on the second pericope about the "leper," we find wordings similar to all Synoptic Gospels, but especially to Luke.[185] καὶ ἰδού is very frequent in Mt and Lk, but never in Mk and Jn; συνοδεύειν is used once in Acts 9:7; συνεσθίειν is found in Lk 15:2 and twice in Acts and Paul respectively; πανδοχεῖον is found only in Lk 10:34; καὶ αὐτός/αὐτῷ is used 40 times by Luke, as compared with Mk (4) and Jn (7); ἀφιστάναι is found only in Lk (4 times), Acts (6) and Paul (4), but never in the other gospels.[186] In spite of what appears to be Lukan language, this is no proof of dependence on Luke's gospel, because other differences are too great. It should rather be taken as proof of the author belonging to the Hellenistic world, writing for similar readers to those of Luke.[187]

Jeremias, followed by Schneemelcher, suggested that the author of *P. Egerton* 2 knew all of the canonical gospels, but reproduced traditions from memory, thus giving witness to the overlapping of oral and written tradition.[188] But, in the words of Bell and Skeat, "his memory must have been very vague to account for such discrepancies."[189] Koester's ironical remark is also apt: that if this were true, "*Papyrus Egerton 2* should be treated as a spectacularly early

---

[183] Mayeda points among other things to the use of ἀποκριθεὶς ... εἶπεν, common in the Synoptic tradition, rather than the Johannine ἀπεκρίθη ... καὶ εἶπεν; the simple ζωή, without the Johannine αἰώνιος, 26f; 71f.

[184] Bell and Skeat 1935a, 35; Mayeda 1946, 68ff; Koester 1980, 120f; Koester 1982 [1980], 2: 182f. Koester regards *P. Egerton* 2 as "an important testimony for the formation of controversy traditions that were later used and expanded in the Johannine discourses" (1982 [1980], 2: 183). Bell and Skeat think that *P. Egerton* 2 puts us in touch at first or second hand with one of John's sources (1935a, 38). Note also the much more nuanced ἄρξοντες in *P. Egerton* 2, line 6, as compared with John's generalizing Ἰουδαίοι. ἄρξοντες, partly reconstructed, is used in line 28–29 (=B&S 25–26) as well. This is evidence against *P. Egerton* 2 being dependent upon John, as Cerfaux (1936, 76) and Dodd (1936, 68, 75, 86, 89f) would like to have it.

[185] The issue has been discussed extensively between Neirynck and Boismard, but with some tendency, since their opposing interests have been to find confirmation for their respective theories of duality in Mark and something similar to the Griesbach hypothesis. See Boismard 1981, 283–291; 1990, 254–258; Neirynck 1985, 153–160; 1989, 161–167; 1990, 94–107.

[186] Mayeda 1946, 32f; 35; Neirynck 1985, 154. Mayeda (1946, 69) lists 15 words or expressions in the fragments, which occur only or most often in Luke.

[187] Mayeda 1946, 69.

[188] In Schneemelcher 1991, 1:96–97.

[189] Bell and Skeat 1935b.

witness for the four-gospel canon of the NT."[190] Attempts to account for a *genetical* relationship between this tradition and the canonical gospels are bound to be excessively speculative.[191] Attempts to explain *P. Egerton* 2 as dependent on the four canonical gospels are neither sufficient nor satisfactory. Whether it should be regarded as a "gospel" is partly a question of definition. The fragments contain only a limited amount of material. The pericopes are coherent in themselves, but the lack of a smooth transition to the story of the "leper" suggests that this was a collection of stories without a developed narrative framework, as in the synoptics.[192]

Turning to the second pericope in detail (Fragment 1r, lines 35–44; earlier numbering, B&S, lines 32–41[193]), we find that it is similar to Mk 1:40–45, although it deviates in several details, containing independent material, but also coming close to Lk 17:11–19. The transcribed text is given below, together with the reconstruction of Bell and Skeat, which is usually accepted:[194]

ⲔⲀ.[ ]ⲆⲞⲨⲖⲈⲠⲢⲞⲤⲠⲢⲞⲤⲈⲖⲐ̣[	καὶ ἰδοὺ λεπρὸς προσελθὼν αὐτῷ
ⲖⲈⲄⲈⲒ· ⲆⲒⲆⲀⲤⲔⲀⲖⲈⲒ̅Ⲏ̅ ⲖⲈ̣[	λέγει· διδάσκαλε Ἰη(σοῦ) λεπροῖς συν-
ⲞⲆⲈⲨⲰⲚⲔⲀⲒⲤⲨⲚⲈⲤⲐⲒⲰ[	οδεύων καὶ συνεσθίων αὐτοῖς
ⲈⲚⲦⲰⲠ.ⲚⲆⲞⲬⲈⲒⲰ ⲈⲖ[	ἐν τῷ πανδοχείῳ ἐλέπρησα
ⲔⲀⲒⲀⲨⲦⲞⲤⲈⲄⲰ· ⲈⲀ.[ ]ⲨⲚ̣[	καὶ αὐτὸς ἐγώ· ἐὰν οὖν σὺ θέλῃς
ⲔⲀⲐ̣ⲀⲢⲒⲌⲞⲘⲀⲒ· ⲞⲆⲎⲔ̅Ⲥ̣̅[	καθαρίζομαι· ὁ δὴ κ(ύριο)ς ἔφη αὐτῷ
Ⲑ̣Ⲉ̣Ⲗ̣[ ].ⲀⲐⲀⲢⲒⲤⲐⲎⲦⲒ· [	θέλω καθαρίσθητι· καὶ εὐθέως
]Ⲡ̣ⲈⲤⲦⲎⲀⲠⲀⲨⲦⲞⲨⲎⲖⲈⲠ̣[	ἀπέστη ἀπ᾽ αὐτοῦ ἡ λέπρα ὁ δὲ κ(ύριο)ς
]Ⲡ̣Ⲟ̣ⲢⲈ[	εἶπεν αὐτῷ πορευθεὶς ἐπίδει-
].ⲦⲞⲒ[	ξον σεαυτὸν τοῖς ἱερεῦσι[195]

[190] Koester 1980, 120.
[191] Cf. the attempts of Boismard, n.185 above.
[192] Mayeda (1946) denies that *P. Egerton* can be placed in the same genre as the canonical gospels. It is too novelistic, comes from a different world and the fragments are too short. The papyrus is rather to be seen as an example of private Christian literature (87ff). Mayeda justifies his scepticism with references to other papyrus finds, which had been enthusiastically proclaimed as remnants of unknown gospels (63). Some of these claims were, however, actually verified by the discovery of the Coptic *Gospel of Thomas*, soon after Mayeda's book appeared. This has made us aware of the fluid character of the genre, and weakens Mayeda's argument. Bell and Skeat's verdict from 1935 can still be regarded as true: "It is, in fact, indubitably a real Gospel," but the difficulty is deciding its relationship to other known traditions (1935a, 30).
[193] The later numbering (due to the discovery of *P. Köln* 255) is followed henceforth.
[194] Bell and Skeat, 1935a, 10f. ⲁ̣= uncertain, part of letter seen, or otherwise doubtful; . = trace of letter seen, but not enough to reconstruct it; [ ] = letter(s) missing. A "Coptic" font is used here to reproduce the papyrus text, since it best corresponds to the uncials of the papyrus.
[195] And lo, a "leper" approached him and said: "Teacher Jesus, travelling with 'lepers' and eating with them at the inn, I myself got 'leprosy' too. Thus if you wish, I am purified." The Lord said to him: "I wish, be purified." And at once the "leprosy" went away from him. But the Lord told him: "Go and show yourself to the priests." Cf. the photograph of the fragment above, 88.

In view of the discovery of another piece of this sheet, the last three lines must be slightly revised. *P. Köln* 255 *recto* reads (lines 42–48, with Gronewald's reconstruction):[196]

.Π̣[[197]	ἀπέστη ἀπ' αὐτου ἡ λέπρα· λέγει
ΔΕΑΥΤΩΟΙΗ[	δὲ αὐτῷ ὁ Ἰη(σοῦς)· πορευθεὶς σεαυ-
Τ̣ΟΝΕΠΙΔΕΙΞΟΝ[	τὸν ἐπίδειξον τοῖς ἱερεῦσιν
Κ̣ΑΙΑΝΕΝΕΓʼΚΟΝ[	καὶ ἀνένεγκον περὶ τοῦ κα-
[ ]ΑΡΙϹΜΟΥΩϹ̣[ΕΠ]Ε̣[[198]	θαρισμοῦ ὡς προ[σ]έταξεν Μω(ϋσῆς) καὶ
[ ]ΗΚΕΤΙΑ[ ]ΡΤΑΝΕ[	μηκέτι ἁμάρτανε[199]
]. . [	

There are several similarities with the synoptic tradition (Mark 1:40–45 par): the introduction (καὶ ἰδοὺ λεπρὸς προσελθὼν αὐτῷ) is almost identical to that of Matthew;[200] the story concerns one "leper," who comes to Jesus; and the answer of Jesus (θέλω καθαρίσθητι) is identical to the synoptics. The injunction to "bring for purification that which Moses commanded" is very similar to Mark, although the wording differs slightly. There are differences as compared with the synoptics as well: the "leper" of *P. Egerton* 2 shows no obeisance to Jesus; he calls him by name; Jesus is not described as stretching out his hand and touching him; there is no command of silence; and the inspection is to be made before the priests (the plural ἱερεῦσιν is necessary to reconstruct because of the article τοι[ς]). These deviations are in line with the tradition of the ten "lepers" in Lk 17:11–19.[201] In addition, the "leper" in *P. Egerton* 2 gives an explanation of the origin of his "leprosy," which is not paralleled elsewhere.

The leper's description of the origin of his disease has repeatedly been used as an argument for *P. Egerton* 2 being a secondary and fairly late tradition. The idea of travelling and eating with "lepers" at the inn does not suit Palestinian conditions. Likewise, the mention of priests in the plural (Leviticus uses singular), has been seen as evidence for the author's deficient knowledge of Jewish practices.[202] We must ask, however, whether in a Hellenistic environment people would freely associate with "lepers" and dine together with them at the inn? It is possible that ostracism of "lepers" was not as strong in certain rural areas as it was in the cities, but it is likely that not only Jewish readers would regard the

---

196 Gronewald 1987, 138, 140.

197 A trace of one of the vertical bars confirms the conjecture Π in line 42 (39) of *P. Egerton* 2.

198 The letters [ΕΠ] seem to have been corrected to ΠΡΟ (Gronewald 1987, 138).

199 … the "leprosy" went away from him. But Jesus said to him: "Go and show yourself to the priests and bring for purification that which Moses commanded, and sin no longer …"

200 "… but in the style of the Gospels there are only a limited number of ways of beginning an episode such as this, and the agreement may be accidental" (Bell and Skeat, 1935a, 19).

201 Mayeda 1946, 32f; 35f; Bell and Skeat, 1935a, 19; Neirynck 1985, 156.

202 Jeremias, in Schneemelcher 1991, 1: 97; Neirynck 1985, 154. The argument is also accepted by Koester, who takes it as evidence of continued development in oral and written transmission (1980, 122, n. 57).

idea of freely associating with such people as repulsive.[203] The problem can be partly solved by taking the participles συνοδεύων and συνεσθίων as referring to Jesus. This was suggested immediately after the text was published, but discarded as "improbable" by Bell and Skeat.[204] The judgment refers to their reconstructed reading and is based on grammar, since the participles ought to have an article (ὁ), if seen as attributes to Jesus. But when the text is reconstructed differently, the participles can more easily be seen as referring to Jesus, while "lepers" at the inn may be exchanged for tax-collectors. Such a reconstruction had been proposed by Schmidt in 1936. Lines 36–39 (33–36) read:

...διδασκαλε ιη λε[πρους ει εφ]	Lord Jesus, you are visiting "lepers"
οδευων και συνεσθιων [τελωναις]	and eating with tax-collectors
εν τω πανδοχειω ελ[εησον · ισος]	at the inn; have mercy.
και αυτος εγω · ...[205]	I myself am also the same [i.e. of that sort].

Schmidt's argument for his reading is that the reconstruction of Bell and Skeat

> ist sachlich nicht möglich, da λεπροι im πανδοχειον nicht geduldet werden; Wanderungen mit ihnen sind ebenso ausgeschlossen. Zudem ist die ganze Erklärung dafür, wie der Mann erkrankt ist, stilwidrig und gegen die Volksauffassung, die in der λεπρα eine Gottesstrafe sieht. Die Partizipien beziehen sich nicht auf den Kranken, sondern auf Jesus. Bekannt Jesu Heilungen von Aussätzigen, aber nicht Wanderungen mit ihnen; Aussätzige sind ausgestoßen oder im Hause verschlossen.[206]

Hence Schmidt conjectures λε[πρους ει εφ]οδευων, i.e. visit or approach[207] "lepers," since this fits with the picture of Jesus, who visits Simon the Leper (Mk 14:3; Mt 26:6). The "co-eating" is taken to refer to Jesus eating with tax-collectors; something which he is frequently accused of in the Synoptic Gospels.[208] The participles are not taken as attributes to "Teacher Jesus," but as belonging to an independent clause, with the main verb εἶ. Finally, by reconstructing ἐλέησον, the character of the leper's words are understood not as an

---

[203] While diseases and unfortunate conditions such as "leprosy" did not demand formal seclusion according to Greek popular belief, as did pollutions associated with birth, death and bloodguilt (which contaminated according to certain principles), they were nevertheless thought to "wipe off" on others, and association with such people was thus avoided (Parker 1983, 218ff). Cf. Josephus' dispute with Manetho and Chairemon about their claim that the Israelites were expelled from Egypt because of "leprosy" and other impure diseases. *Ag.Ap.* 1:233ff, 289ff. Cf. also above about Babylonian attitudes, 111, n. 123.

[204] Bell and Skeat 1935b.

[205] K. F. W. Schmidt 1936, 35. There are a few more letters in Schmidt's reconstruction as compared to that of Bell and Skeat, but there should be enough space for them, as a study of the papyrus fragment shows. For a comparison, line 33 (30) of Bell and Skeat's reconstruction would be just as long. A glance at the 1v and 2v fragments reveals that the right margin is very uneven, with much extra space.

[206] K. F. W. Schmidt 1936, 37.

[207] Liddell-Scott[9] 1940 and Lampe 1961, *s.v.* ἐφοδεύω.

[208] This is found in Markan tradition as well as in Q and in Lukan redaction: Mk 2:15, 16, par; Mt 11:19/Lk 7:34; Lk 15:2.

account of how he received the contagion, but as the humble supplication of someone asking for mercy.[209]

Schmidt's reconstruction was not accepted by Bell, who responded that it was not done on palaeographical grounds and hence could not be tested. This was certainly true, but the same applied to Bell's own text. Bell actually had no substantial counter-arguments, only that he was not convinced and did not believe in Schmidt's reconstruction.[210] These non-arguments were taken over by Mayeda, referring to Bell: Schmidt's reconstruction was not on palaeographical grounds, but only suppositions "auf Grund historischer Sachkritik," and they were not even accepted by Papyrologists (i.e. Bell?).[211]

The *P. Köln* fragment might give reason for a re-evaluation of Schmidt's proposal. Whether or not we accept Schmidt's reconstruction in its details, the point is that συν/εφοδεύων and συνεσθίων should be understood as referring to Jesus. We may take the participles as attributes (deficient grammar) or as belonging to an independent clause, but they give a description of Jesus which motivates the supplication of the "leper." The injunction μηκέτι ἁμάρτανε (elsewhere found in Jn 5:14; 8:11)[212] at the end of *P. Köln* 255, confirms that "leprosy" was generally considered as a punishment for sin, rather than a contagious disease contracted by association with other "lepers." It supports the idea of a penitential tone in the pericope, i.e. a reading in which the "leper" asks for mercy (ἐλέησον) from Jesus, because he is known to associate with outcasts and sinners. With such a reading, the supplication of the "leper" fits together with the resolution of the pericope (μηκέτι ἁμάρτανε), and renders it a coherent whole.[213]

---

[209] K. F. W. Schmidt 1936, 37; cf. Mk 10:47 par; Mt 15:22; 17:15. Cf. Erlemann 1996, 21.

[210] "Ich bekenne, daß sie mir sehr wenig überzeugend erscheinen. Ich bin nicht darauf aus, unsere Ergänzungen vorbehaltlos zu verteidigen. (Das ελ[επρησα] gefällt mir nicht sonderlich, und die Schwierigkeit betr. die Herberge gebe ich zu.) Aber an das ει εφοδευων kann ich nicht glauben, ebensowenig an das ισος και αυτος εγω und die Tatsache, daß es befremdlich ist, Aussätzige in einem Gasthaus zu finden, scheint mir kein genügender Grund für die Behauptung zu sein, daß der Autor unmöglich solches habe sagen können. Endlich hat ελεησον an allen von Schmidt angeführten Belegstellen einen Akkusativ bei sich." (Bell 1936, 73). Only the last objection is an argument, and it carries little weight, since several examples of ἐλέησον without an accusative can be found in contemporary texts. Cf. *Ant.* 9:64; Bar 3:2; *T.Job* 23:5.

[211] Mayeda 1946, 34.

[212] It cannot be claimed as a particularly Johannine trait, however, since Jn 7:53–8:11 for text-critical reasons (being omitted in early textual evidence; the earliest witness is D—Codex Bezae) cannot be original to the Gospel of John. It is usually considered as an independent tradition, with some relationship to the synoptics, which was incorporated into the Gospel of John at a later stage (possibly as late as the fifth century). The expression is relevant for a continued discussion about independent traditions, and *P. Egerton* 2's relationship to the canonical gospels, which cannot be pursued further within the scope of this study.

[213] This should not be seen as unwarranted "harmonizing," since both the surrounding pericopes give us reason to expect a smooth and coherent narrative. A different interpretation is suggested by Daniels, who thinks that the concluding comments rather reveal the Jewish character of *P.*

Jesus and "leprosy"

It is a plausible conclusion, based on the evidence reviewed, that Jesus associated with "lepers" and on occasion touched them. All available texts testify to the fact that during the Second Temple period "lepers" were considered as bearers of a highly contaminating impurity, and were thus avoided and expelled from towns and probably villages too. In addition, their impure state was often understood by people as a sort of divine punishment.

The Markan non-conflict tradition (Mk 1:40–45) about Jesus touching a leper must be interpreted in this context. It is the primary tradition giving evidence for Jesus' attitude and gestures. We have seen that the Lukan tradition (Lk 17:11–19) should not be used against such evidence, but it does attest to the fact that lepers were excluded from population centres.

The probably independent tradition in *P. Egerton* 2 must be used with caution, since it involves a fair amount of reconstruction, and its dating is not secure. I would claim, however, that the picture of Jesus as dealing with, and coming close to "lepers," in a way unacceptable to the legal interpretation which was wide-spread and influential in his time, is not gainsaid, but rather strengthened by this tradition.

Jesus was apparently remembered in Markan as well as Q and independent traditions as one who came into close contact with "lepers," included them in his healing work, visited them and even touched them. This cannot be regarded only as narrative embroidery or formal traits of miracle stories, not least in view of the common ostracism of "lepers" and impurity regulations in force during the first century CE. We must rather regard these references as reminiscences of historical memory, giving evidence of a behaviour which was not in line with the prevailing legal interpretation.

IV.3 Bodily discharges

The major dischargers

The second main source of impurity to be discussed is genital flux or bodily discharge. As in the case of "leprosy," the focus is on the contaminating power of the person suffering from the said condition, i.e. the impurity bearer. In the case of bodily discharges, however, a certain emphasis is put on the different

---

Egerton's community; the "leper's" former behaviour is not seen as compatible with purity laws, and thus Jesus must urge the man to observe the legal customs involved, and warn him not to sin again (Daniels 1990, 144, 148; cf. 264–274). These are far-reaching conclusions from a meagre base, however. The characterization of the community as "Jewish adherents of Jesus" (264) is mainly built upon this particular interpretation of the "leper" story, and without the traditional reconstruction of the text the somewhat circular chain of arguments falls apart.

types of discharges themselves, although to varying degrees, as will be seen from the discussion below.

Five different types of dischargers are discussed in the Hebrew Bible and early Judaism. Four of these are major impurity bearers, whose uncleanness or period of purification lasts for seven days; hence they are regarded as "fathers" of impurity in the rabbinic system. The fifth has to do with the emission of semen, accidentally or in the context of intercourse, which, according to biblical legislation, pollutes the male as well as items in contact with semen, and in case of intercourse, the woman, with a one-day uncleanness. Semen-impurity is not regarded as a "father,"[214] and will not be discussed independently, but only when necessary in reference to the other four types, which share many traits.

The four major dischargers are the *zab* (זָב: the man with an abnormal flux from his penis),[215] the *niddah* (נִדָּה: menstruating woman), the *zabah* (זָבָה: woman with a vaginal bleeding outside, or exceeding, the period of menstruation), and the *yoledet* (יוֹלֶדֶת: parturient, i.e. the woman who has recently given birth to a child).[216] The first three (as well as the semen-emitter) are treated together in Lev 15. The parturient is discussed in Lev 12, but the text makes it clear that her uncleanness during the first stage (seven or fourteen days) should be regarded as that of a menstruant.[217] Although male and female discharges are of a different nature, it is clear that the priestly redactor of Leviticus has attempted to place the four major dischargers at a similar level. The discharge itself is called זוֹב, both in the case of the flux of a *zab* and the blood of a *zabah* (Lev 15:2, 3, 25, 26). The menstruating woman is not introduced as דָּוָה or נִדָּה,[218] but as זָבָה (Lev 15:19).[219] And in the summary, the law is explicitly

---

[214] In the *Mishnah*, semen itself is regarded as a "father" of uncleanness, while the emitter of semen is in the first degree (*mZab* 5:10; Harrington 1993, 244f).

[215] This flux has recurrently been translated as gonorrhea, which is doubtful, indeed. The expressions used by Josephus are τοὺς περὶ τὴν γονὴν ῥεομένους (*Ant.* 3:261); γονορροίοις (*J.W.* 5:227); and γονορροϊκοῖς (*J.W.* 6:426). It is uncertain, however, whether the disease known to us as *Gonorrhoea virulenta* was in existence in Antiquity. Milgrom (1991, 907) argues against this, while Wright and Jones (1992, 205) refer to contrary opinions. They agree, however, on gonorrhea not being a suitable translation, since the urethral discharges referred to in Leviticus and rabbinic literature cannot be limited to that disease only.

[216] It should be stressed that the terms used here are technical terms in rabbinic Judaism, and do not always correspond to the terminology of Leviticus. Specific cases will be noted as they appear in the discussion.

[217] Seven in case of a boy; fourteen in case of a girl (Lev 12:2, 5). Note the way the first period is described (v 2: כִּימֵי נִדַּת דְּוֹתָהּ תִּטְמָא; v 5: כְּנִדָּתָהּ), in contrast to the second period (v 4: תֵּשֵׁב בִּדְמֵי טָהֳרָה; v 5: תֵּשֵׁב עַל־דְּמֵי טָהֳרָה). The natural interpretation is that during the seven and fourteen days respectively, the יוֹלֶדֶת is regarded in the same way as a menstruant.

[218] The word נִדָּה is used as a technical term for the menstruant in rabbinic literature (cf. the *Mishnah* tractate *Niddah*), but in the Hebrew Bible the meaning is ambiguous. The term is used for the menstruant's state of impurity (Lev 15:19, 20), often as an apposition in expressions like הַדָּוָה בְּנִדָּתָהּ (Lev 15:33) or אִשָּׁה נִדָּה (Ez 18:6). The latter use indicates the second meaning, which is "impurity" in general, or something abominable (Lev 20:21; 2Chr 29:5). The third

said to concern any זָב with a discharge, whether male or female (Lev 15:33).[220] Hence, the contamination potential of these four impurity bearers is usually considered the same in the rabbinic system.[221] At the same time, the Rabbis saw a certain hierarchy of impurity, where the *zabah* was regarded as the most impure of those with flows, followed by the *zab* and surpassed only by the "leper" and the corpse.[222] There is something logical in such a hierarchical order, since menstruation and post-natal bleedings are natural processes,[223] and by necessity recurring experiences, while non-seminal fluxes and excessive or irregular bleedings are usually due to pathological conditions. In this way, the *zabah* came to be regarded as the epitome of all those with discharges.

The bleeding woman and Markan sandwich construction

While there is no trace of any male dischargers in the New Testament, nor any discussion about menstruation, both the *zabah* and the *yoledet* figure in the Synoptic Gospels. The main tradition is the non-conflict story in Mk 5:25–34 par., about the bleeding woman who obtained healing by touching Jesus.

The story of the bleeding woman comes as an intercalation into the narrative about Jairus and his daughter. This is the case in Mk and the construction has been taken over by the other Synoptics. The encapsulation of one story within another is frequent in Mark, as noted by several exegetes.[224] In the previous discussion about miracle stories, some of Theissen's arguments for this encap-

---

meaning is somewhat of a paradox, probably stemming from the root meaning of the word ("separation" or "expulsion," referring to the flow of blood). In the context of the red cow rite, the purification water used for sprinkling is called מֵי נִדָּה (Num 19:9 etc.). This could be interpreted as "water for separating/turning away impurity." Cf. Milgrom and Wright 1986, 250–253. For a different interpretation of the red cow rite, see Maccoby 1999, 105–117, and the section below about corpse–impurity.

[219] Cf. Gerstenberger 1993, 186. The use of זָבָה for a menstruant here is notable, since it necessitates a clarification: "it happens that blood is exuding from her flesh during seven days." Such a circumscription is avoided in the summary of v 33, by simply calling the menstruant a דָּוָה בְּנִדָּתָהּ.

[220] וְהַזָּב אֶת־זוֹבוֹ לַזָּכָר וְלַנְּקֵבָה.

[221] *mZab* 5:1, 6, 10. The main exception is that female dischargers were seen as transmitting a seven-day impurity by intercourse, while the זָב was not. (Lev 15:24, 33; *mZab* 5:11; *Sifra* to Lev 15:24 [Parashat Zabim Pereq 7]; *Sifra* to Lev 15:25 [Parashat Zabim Pereq 8]; *bNid* 33a); Harrington 1993, 240.

[222] *mKel* 1:1–4; Harrington 1993, 37–38, 230.

[223] Harrington (1993, 225 f.) explains the apparent leniency in Lev 15:19 (one who touches a menstruant is not explicitly required to wash his clothes, as in the case of the זָב) with the normalcy of the situation.

[224] Cf. 6:7–13 and 30–32 separated by 14–29; 11:12–14 and 19–21 separated by 15–18; 14:1–2 and 10–11 separated by 3–9. See Nineham 1963, 112; Theissen 1983 [1972], 180ff; Hooker 1991, 17f. Nineham (1963, 156f) notes, however, that while Mark is fond of this technique, there is no precise parallel to this case, where an insertion divides another story into two so obviously interdependent halves.

sulation being a secondary development were noticed. The grammatical differences are evident. While the Jairus narrative is mainly in the present tense, the intercalation uses past tenses.[225] Linguistic differences are real, but should not be over-emphasized.[226] They provide evidence for the two stories originating and developing separately, but they cannot answer questions of when and why they were joined together.

According to a common opinion, the intercalation was made to create an interval between Jairus' statement and the death of his daughter, causing Jesus to come too late.[227] The necessity of an interval would have been caused by the Jairus story developing from a simple healing miracle to a resurrection narrative.[228] The explanation is not satisfactory, as has been pointed out by Trond S. Dokka. The need for a delay is not very great, and it could have been solved in various and different ways, as is exemplified by Matthew's version, in which the girl is dead from the very beginning, thus making the delay "redundant."[229]

We must thus look for other reasons for the sandwich construction. Although the death of Jairus' daughter does not necessitate a delay in the story, resulting in an intercalation, the stories are related to each other. The Jairus story, in its present form, is dependent upon the story of the bleeding woman, since it incorporates the crowd (Mk 5:21, 24), which is not necessary in the former story, but rather belongs to the latter (v 27, 30f), and seems to be forgotten when the Jairus story is resumed again (v 35ff).[230] Both stories contain similar themes, motifs and terms. Some of these, such as "twelve years" (v 25, 42) or "daughter" (v 23, 34, 35), have been repeatedly pointed out.[231] Monika Fander considers death in different forms (social and physical) as the main theme of both stories.[232] The most conspicuous motif holding the two narratives together is probably faith (πίστις, v 34; πίστευε, v 36). The faith of the bleeding woman "informs" the Jairus story, providing an example of faith

[225] Theissen 1983 [1972], 180ff; Gnilka 1978, 212, n.15; As already pointed out (see above, 96), Theissen even notes that the four places where past tenses are nevertheless used in the Jairus story (vv 21, 24, 37, 42f) are located at the beginning and end of the narrative, as well as where the two stories join, i.e. where redactional influences are probable.

[226] V. Taylor 1966, 289, comments that the language of vv 25–27 (the introduction to the story about the woman), is remarkable, as one of very few examples in the gospel of a longer Greek period, with several subordinated participles. Referring to Lohmeyer, he lists numerous differences of language between vv 21–24, 35–43 and 25–34. The Jairus story is said to contain no Hellenisms, no indirect speech, no periods and hardly a participle, but paratactic constructions, semitisms and an Aramaic phrase (293). While I agree that vv 25–27 are exceptional, there is, however, a good number of participles in the Jairus narrative too.

[227] Bultmann 1972 [1921], 214.

[228] Pesch 1976, 306, 312ff.

[229] Dokka 1992, 151–152.

[230] Bultmann 1972 [1921], 214; Gnilka 1978, 209; Kertelge 1970, 111.

[231] Kertelge 1970, 112; Loader 1997, 60.

[232] Fander 1992, 59. For Fander this means that belief in resurrection becomes the hermeneutical key to both stories (59–62).

which the latter is lacking, and creating expectations which lead to the climax when the daughter of Jairus is made alive.[233] Kertelge discusses similarities with the two preceding stories as well (4:35–41; 5:1–20), and regards them as a group of miracle stories, developing during a long period of time into a block, which was given an unusual climax by a pre-Markan redactor in the resurrection of the girl.[234] The sandwich construction would thus have a pre-Markan origin. Kuhn is more hesitant, but comes to the conclusion that even if a pre-Markan collection is difficult to prove, the different miracle stories at least share a similar *Sitz im Leben.*[235]

It is not possible to prove the sandwich construction to be pre-Markan. Loader argues for the intercalation being the work of Mark. It was done by someone with sensitivity to purity issues, but, since it resulted in an unclean Jesus (by contact with the woman), entering the house of a synagogue leader, the intercalator would not himself have paid attention to purity issues. This would speak for Mark.[236] While I do not find these arguments conclusive, I consider Mark responsible for the intercalation for other reasons. The technique of filling time lapses with similar insertions is, as pointed out by E. Schweizer, a typical trait of Mark (3:22–30; 6:14–29; 11:15–19).[237] While the need for a delay is not, as we have seen above, a sufficient explanation for the origin of the intercalation in 5:25–34, the technique is probably Markan, and is employed for thematic or theological reasons.

This means that the two stories probably did not originally belong together. Since I am not seeking primarily for Mark's literary and theological purposes, but looking for historical reminiscences, I will discuss the two traditions separately, and deal with the narrative of the bleeding woman without relating it to the Jairus story.[238]

---

[233] Cf. Kertelge 1970, 120.

[234] Kertelge 1970, 112–113.

[235] Kuhn 1971, 191ff, 210, 213. Kuhn discusses 6:32–52 in addition to the four stories already mentioned. According to Kuhn, these stories are marked by the *theios aner* idea and originated with Hellenistic Christians of Jewish background.

[236] Loader 1997, 61–62 and n. 118.

[237] Schweizer 1971 [1967], 116. Note that, in some cases, these intercalations are not taken over by Matthew or Luke. Mk 3:22–30 (Beelzebul) is paralleled in the other Synoptics, but they do not introduce a subsequent narrative in advance, as does Mark (3:31–35 is introduced by 3:21). This is even more evident in 11:15–19, which interrupts the story of the fig tree in Mark, but not in Matthew.

[238] The Jairus story will be focused upon in the section about corpse-impurity below. V. Taylor (1966, 289) takes the connecting link in v 35 ("while he yet spoke…") as an argument for the connection being not merely literary, but historical, since such links are fairly absent in Mark. If this were true, it would be necessary to discuss the two stories together, even in an historical investigation. Taylor's argument, besides not being valid as a conclusion from language, displays a somewhat *naive* understanding of the relationship between historical event and literary narrative.

A purity issue in the Markan tradition

The Markan textual tradition (Mk 5:25–34) is longer and more detailed than that of Luke and especially Matthew, who abbreviates considerably. Variants in the latter traditions will be discussed only when they could be of major importance for the questions under consideration.

> 25 καὶ γυνὴ οὖσα ἐν ῥύσει αἵματος δώδεκα ἔτη 26 καὶ πολλὰ παθοῦσα ὑπὸ πολλῶν ἰατρῶν καὶ δαπανήσασα τὰ παρ' αὐτῆς πάντα καὶ μηδὲν ὠφεληθεῖσα ἀλλὰ μᾶλλον εἰς τὸ χεῖρον ἐλθοῦσα, 27 ἀκούσασα περὶ τοῦ Ἰησοῦ, ἐλθοῦσα ἐν τῷ ὄχλῳ ὄπισθεν ἥψατο τοῦ ἱματίου αὐτοῦ· 28 ἔλεγεν γὰρ ὅτι ἐὰν ἅψωμαι κἂν τῶν ἱματίων αὐτοῦ σωθήσομαι. 29 καὶ εὐθὺς ἐξηράνθη ἡ πηγὴ τοῦ αἵματος αὐτῆς καὶ ἔγνω τῷ σώματι ὅτι ἴαται ἀπὸ τῆς μάστιγος. 30 καὶ εὐθὺς ὁ Ἰησοῦς ἐπιγνοὺς ἐν ἑαυτῷ τὴν ἐξ αὐτοῦ δύναμιν ἐξελθοῦσαν ἐπιστραφεὶς ἐν τῷ ὄχλῳ ἔλεγεν· τίς μου ἥψατο τῶν ἱματίων; 31 καὶ ἔλεγον αὐτῷ οἱ μαθηταὶ αὐτοῦ· βλέπεις τὸν ὄχλον συνθλίβοντά σε καὶ λέγεις· τίς μου ἥψατο; 32 καὶ περιεβλέπετο ἰδεῖν τὴν τοῦτο ποιήσασαν. 33 ἡ δὲ γυνὴ φοβηθεῖσα καὶ τρέμουσα, εἰδυῖα ὃ γέγονεν αὐτῇ, ἦλθεν καὶ προσέπεσεν αὐτῷ καὶ εἶπεν αὐτῷ πᾶσαν τὴν ἀλήθειαν. 34 ὁ δὲ εἶπεν αὐτῇ· θυγάτηρ, ἡ πίστις σου σέσωκέν σε· ὕπαγε εἰς εἰρήνην καὶ ἴσθι ὑγιὴς ἀπὸ τῆς μάστιγός σου.

> 25 And a woman who had been a blood discharger for twelve years 26 and had suffered a lot under many physicians and had spent all her means for no use, rather becoming worse—27 when she heard about Jesus she came in the crowd and touched his cloak from behind, 28 because she said that if I will touch even just his cloak I will be saved. 29 And immediately the source of her blood dried up, and she knew in her body that she was healed from the scourge. 30 And Jesus, who immediately felt in himself the power which had went out from him, turned around in the crowd and said: "Who touched my cloak?" 31 And his disciples said to him: "Look at the people pushing you, and you say: 'Who touched me?'" 32 And he looked around to see who had done it. 33 But the woman, who was fearing and trembling, knowing what had happened to her, came and fell down before him and told him the whole truth. 34 But he said to her: "Daughter, your faith has saved you. Go in peace and be well from your scourge."

Mark's intentions and awareness of legal issues have been extensively discussed.[239] In the present story about the bleeding woman, impurity is never mentioned explicitly. This is one of the reasons for some exegetes to doubt that purity is an issue here at all. Brigitte Kahl argues that the narrative does not employ the central terminology of clean and unclean, but rather uses terms of healing.[240] "Das, was die Frau zu ihrer Rettung braucht, ist nicht die Befreiung von der Tora, sondern die Befreiung vom Elend ihrer Krankheit—mindestens in der Darstellung des Markus."[241] It is true that the healing miracle is central for

[239] Loader 1997, 61–62; Sariola 1990, 239–261.
[240] B. Kahl 1996, 66.
[241] B. Kahl 1996, 67. Kahl reacts against the distortions which follow when the controversies of Jesus are not seen as intra-Jewish conflicts, but as principled denials of Jewish law, or Judaism. Compare Grundmann's interpretation (1971, 115, cf. 151f) that Jesus, in his manner of relating to the bleeding woman, demonstrated that the Jewish Law and purity thinking have come to an end, with Dewey's interpretation (1994, 471, 481) of an intra-Jewish conflict between a popular

Mark, and, as we have seen above, the context is one of faith and restoration ("resurrection"). In this process of healing, however, legal traditions about the separation of menstruants and persons with discharges seem to be disregarded. There is thus a purity issue inherent in the tradition, which had been recognized by early interpreters.[242] Their recognition cannot be explained by their anti-Jewish polemical context only, but, as will be shown below, an awareness of the purity issue is reflected in the textual tradition itself.

While healing is the central theme of the story, it is not really correct to claim, as does Kahl, that the "für Lev 12–15 eigentlich zentrale terminologische Bczug auf Rcinhcit/Unrcinhcit in Mk 5,2 ff mit kcincr Silbc auch nur angcdcutet wird."[243] The presence of words and expressions belonging to the key terminology of Lev 12 and 15 has been pointed out by several exegetes, and is

---

Jewish peasant movement and official leadership, resulting in a break with the system of purity, but not with Judaism (B. Kahl 1996, 65, n.15). Cf. Valtink (1996, 18): "seine Vorstellungen von Reinheit und Unreinheit werden in den meisten Jesusbüchern und exegetischen Kommentaren als äußerster Kontrast zum Judentum dargestellt und nicht als eine Möglichkeit *innerhalb* des pluralen und vielgestaltigen Judentums wahrgenommen." The traditional line of interpretation has, however, at times been taken over by feminist exegesis, recently criticized for anti-Jewish implications (Valtink 1996, 17; Fonrobert 1997, 124f). Fonrobert criticizes Selvidge (1990, 83) and others for "the persisting lack of understanding with which New Testament scholars reconstruct the presumed Jewish milieu of the story" (Fonrobert 1997, 124). She claims that "by passing a judgment on the suffering and oppression of the woman not only in this particular narrative, but by implication on Jewish traditions surrounding menstruation in general, and by making her the emblematic Jewish woman whom Jesus comes not only to heal but presumably also to liberate from the oppressive rituals of her culture, such hermeneutic approaches in New Testament scholarship also pass a judgment on Jewish women today, who choose to observe menstrual separation as a part of living their Jewishly-defined lives" (Fonrobert 1996, 125). The delicate discussion about anti-Jewish exegesis must not prevent thorough textual and historical investigations, however. It is necessary to keep the different levels of discussion apart. A claim that Jesus, by his behaviour, proclaims the end of Jewish purity legislation, may possibly be true on a literary level, but is hardly to be ascribed to the historical Jesus, on the evidence of this tradition. While Mark may intend his readers to see Jesus as giving up Jewish law (but cf. Loader 1997, 26, 28, 35–37), it is difficult to imagine the historical Jesus as consciously proclaiming Christian polemical theology through accidentally being touched by an unclean person.

[242] Dionysios of Alexandria, in his letter to Basilides, responds negatively to the latter's questions about menstruating women attending church and receiving the communion, by referring to the bleeding woman only touching the hem of Jesus' garment (*Dionysius to Basilides*, β'; cf. B. Kahl 1996, 62–63; Selvidge 1990, 17) The *Didascalia Apostolorum* (Syriac 26: 262; *versio Latinae* 62: =97v) argues against menstrual separation from prayer and communion by using the same story (Fonrobert 1997, 121–122; B. Kahl 1996, 62). Although the conclusions drawn are complete opposites, both of these interpretations assume that there is a purity issue in the story in Mk. The purity issue was recognized by Tertullian (*Marc.* 4:20; cf. Selvidge 1990, 20–21) and John Chrysostom (*Hom. Matt.* 31:1–2; Cf. B. Kahl 1996, 62, n.4). Although situated "within the framework of an Ekklesia-versus-Synagogue-dichotomy" (B. Kahl 1996, 78), such interpretations cannot automatically be discarded as anti-Jewish (B. Kahl 1996, 63, n.10).

[243] B. Kahl 1996, 66.

admitted by Kahl herself.[244] These are ῥύσει αἵματος (Mk 5:25), ἡ πηγὴ τοῦ αἵματος (v 29), and the repeated use of the verb ἅπτεσθαι (v 27, 28, 30, 31). ῥύσις αἵματος is not a normal expression for menstruation, used in Greek literature, but is paralleled by Lev 15:19, 25 LXX.[245] Likewise, πηγὴ τοῦ αἵματος is never used for vaginal bleeding, except in Lev 12:7 LXX (cf. 20:18).[246] The latter phrase caused Bultmann, who otherwise supposed a Hellenistic origin for most synoptic miracle stories, to consider a Palestinian origin for this story, because of true Semitisms.[247] These phrases show some kind of dependence on the language of Leviticus, and reveal an awareness of the purity issue involved in the story of the woman touching Jesus, at some stage in the tradition. There are no good reasons for questioning this relationship, as does Fonrobert, thinking that "this linguistic connection is not a necessary one,"[248] or suggesting that terminological connections are so small that they stay without importance, as does Sariola.[249] The emphasis in the Markan tradition on touch concurs with Lev 12 and 15. Touch is the principal means of transferring impurity in the case of people with genital discharges. The verb ἅπτεσθαι/נגע is repeated thoughout these two chapters.

The use of ἅπτεσθαι in the narrative of the bleeding woman can be interpreted as primarily a trait of Hellenistic miracle-stories. It seems as if the healing functions automatically, by some power which goes out from Jesus and stops the woman's bleeding.[250] But the motif of touching a miracle-worker must be discussed with discrimination. Stories in which the patient takes the initiative to touch the healer are uncommon outside the gospels, and in particular non-intentional transfer of power through touch is not attributed to healers in Hellenistic miracle-stories.[251] When the gospels are examined, it seems to be

---

[244] B. Kahl 1996, 66, especially n.20.

[245] The similarity of Mk 5:25 (καὶ γυνὴ οὖσα ἐν ῥύσει αἵματος) and Lev 15:19 (καὶ γυνὴ ἥτις ἂν ᾖ ῥέουσα αἵματι) as well as 15:25 (καὶ γυνὴ ἐὰν ῥέῃ ῥύσει αἵματος) is striking.

[246] Selvidge 1990, 48; Selvidge 1984; Gnilka 1978, 215; Sariola 1990, 70; Loader 1997, 61.

[247] Bultmann 1972 [1921], 240.

[248] Fonrobert 1997, 130. Fonrobert's criticism of Selvidge's method of counting words is justified. This applies especially to Selvidge's extended discussion of more or less irrelevant semantic similarities between Mark and Leviticus (1990, 49–51). Nevertheless, the presence in Markan tradition of the two phrases mentioned cannot possibly be explained by coincidence.

[249] Sariola 1990, 70. I agree, however, with Sariola about the danger of seeing too many allusions, and drawing exaggerated conclusions (71).

[250] Bultmann 1972 [1921], 219; Theissen 1983 [1972], 91f. Theissen discusses, but dismisses the idea of the story being a distortion of an original exorcism, reminiscent in the sequence: healing-trembling-falling down (cf. Thraede, 1969, 62), and in the term μάστιξ. He argues that the demonological sense is weakened in the NT, the story itself regards the emanation of power as therapeutic, and in the context (doctors etc.) the term δύναμις receives a therapeutic rather than a demonological slant. Theissen also dismisses the idea that touching Jesus was seen as a way of getting rid of a disease by passing it on (134; cf. Epidaurus 7 in Herzog 1931, 10–13, 133f).

[251] Blackburn 1991, 114ff.

Mark who generalizes this behaviour, as has been pointed out by Gnilka.[252] The generalizing comments in Mk 3:10 and 6:56 about people touching Jesus, or even his clothes, for healing, belong to typical bridge passages or summaries, which are not traditional, or at least heavily redacted by Mark.[253] In spite of what has at times been claimed about Mark's anti-magical stance,[254] these comments rather enhance a magical understanding of the miracle stories.[255] It is possible that the motif of touching in the pre-Markan tradition had less of a magical flavour than after subsequent Markan redaction. In view of the above-mentioned generalizing comments, it is possible to regard the ἱμάτιον of vv 27, 28 and 30, as Markan embroidery (note its absence in v 31), while the touching itself tightly belongs to the pre-Markan connection with Lev 15. This connection is thus reinforced by the frequent use of the verb ἅπτεσθαι in Mk 5.[256]

The difficulty lies in the fact that Mark never spells out this connection explicitly. The idea that in the pre-Markan tradition Jesus responded to the woman in anger, because she had defiled him,[257] is far too speculative.[258] Less so, but still unverifiable, are suggestions that the fear of the woman (v 33) is caused by her knowledge of having defiled Jesus.[259] On the textual level, her fear is explained by her knowledge of having been healed, and there are no hints that it was caused by knowledge of any transgression.[260] Since Mark uses purity terminology in other contexts (Mark 1 and 7), clearly denying certain purity practices, B. Kahl argues that he sees no purity issue in the story of the bleeding woman.[261] This is not plausible, however, when the texts are compared. In Mk 7, purity terminology is explicit, and consciously used by Mark in redactional comments, such as 7:3–4, 19. The reference to Mk 1 is doubtful, however, since, as pointed out above, the terminology (καθαρίσαι/ καθαρισθῆναι) is

---

252 Gnilka 1978, 215.

253 The first of these is taken over by Luke (Lk 6:19) and the second by Matthew (Mt 14:36).

254 Cf. T. J. Weeden's study (1971) and the interpretations which followed it. For a discussion, see Räisänen 1990, 62–68.

255 Cf. Gnilka 1978, 213, who understands the reflective clause in v 28 as a Markan attempt to make what happens more understandable. He likewise considers the disciples' comment about the crowd (v 31) redactional. While this may well be so, his suggestion, that the purpose of this redaction is to hinder a magical understanding of miracle, is to be doubted in view of the generalizing comments in 3:10 and 6:56.

256 If Gnilka is right about Markan redaction (see previous note), ἅπτεσθαι is traditional in v 27 and 30 only. This does not weaken the connection to Lev 15, however. There is no reason to regard all references to touching as redactional.

257 Loader 1997, 61, n.118. Cf. the discussion above (103) about Jesus' response to the "leper" in Mk 1:41.

258 Sariola 1990, 70.

259 Such a notion could be implied in the words (excluded in Matthew's parallel) about the woman telling Jesus πᾶσαν τὴν ἀλήθειαν (Mk 5:33).

260 Sariola 1990, 71. Fonrobert (1997, 132f, especially n.30) stresses that fear in the gospel of Mark is always the reaction when the significance of Jesus is recognized.

261 B. Kahl 1996, 66, mentions Mk 7 as well as 1:40ff.

apparently used here in the sense of healing.[262] Just as in the present case, the touching is not commented upon, and no purity practice is explicitly denied, as in Mk 7. But in 1:44, most of which probably belongs to tradition, Jesus commands the "leper" to show himself to the priest and offer the required sacrifices, in accordance with legal prescriptions.

There is thus an awareness of the purity issue in 1:40–45 on the pre-Markan level which, in view of the awareness shown by Mark in ch.7, must have been visible to him as a redactor. Yet he does not bring the purity issue out explicitly. In the narrative of the "leper," he is aware of the idea of purity, but does not address the bodily aspect, only the issue of cultic re-integration. Mark is aware of questions of purity, but does not exploit them, when his chief aim is elsewhere. Applied to the present text, this means that even if the terminological links to Leviticus belong to tradition, Mark could be aware of the purity issue involved. His reason for not exploiting the theme of purity could be, as Loader suggests, that menstruants in his context were no longer considered unclean. Thus the only issue for Mark is healing. In contrast to some other instances, the need to explain Jewish practices would have been absent here, since "some foreboding in relation to menstruant women was probably also present among the cultures to which Mark's hearers belonged, though less severe."[263]

We have found that purity is an issue in the narrative of the bleeding woman, although not central, or even explicit, at a literary level. In the present form of the story, the issue of purity is implicit only. It could have been explicit at a pre-Markan stage; it is even probable that it was, at *some* pre-Markan stage, otherwise it would hardly have adhered to the narrative. While the development of the textual tradition is beyond reconstruction, we cannot avoid the implications on an historical level. Jesus was remembered as coming into contact with people impure from bodily discharges.

Dischargers in Lukan traditions?

As in the case of the leper, there is some additional Lukan material of interest. It is well-known that women figure more frequently in Luke's gospel than in the other Synoptics, although opinions differ as to how this should be interpreted. In most of these Lukan narratives there are not even implicit purity issues.[264]

---

[262] For a discussion, see above, 102.

[263] Loader 1997, 61. Cf. Pliny the elder, *Nat.* 7: 63–66. This reasoning, applied to Mk 7, would account for the explanations about ablutions and immersions in 7:3–4, as practices which would not have been well-known to the readers of Mark. Applied to Mk 1:40–45, it would account for the explanation about the purification offering (v 44), as a lesser known practice, while the impure state of the "leper" is left unmentioned, since "lepers" were more or less isolated and abhorred among the cultures to which Mark's hearers or readers belonged, as well.

[264] Women are described as followers of Jesus (Lk 23:27, 49) who had been healed from evil spirits and diseases (8:2). What type of disease is not hinted at, however. While the woman in

The only Lukan tradition which is explicit about discharge and impurity is 2:22ff. Here we have an example of the *yoledet* bringing the prescribed purification offerings, according to Lev 12. But, as already mentioned, the rites of purification and release of the first-born (Ex 13) are muddled, and Luke's interest seems to be in describing the parents of Jesus as generally pious and law-abiding,[265] and possibly, implying that Jesus was consecrated to God.[266] Regardless of how Luke's attitude to the law in general or purity in particular should be interpreted, this tradition does not provide any clues as to the attitude of the historical Jesus to people with discharges.

Possibly, there is an implicit purity issue in the Lukan variant of the woman who anointed Jesus (Lk 7:36–50, par. Mk 14:3–9/Mt 26:6–13/Jn 12:1–8). There are several differences between Mark and Matthew on one hand and Luke on the other, which suggest that Luke had access to a separate tradition. Luke does not, like the others, place the incident immediately before the Last Supper, but during the healing and teaching mission of Jesus, in the first part of the gospel. He does not call Simon, the host, a "leper," but a Pharisee. The woman anoints Jesus' feet, not his head, and she is explicitly called a sinner. The issue for discontent in Luke is not, as in the other gospels, the waste of money, but the character of the woman, and the one embarrassed by this is the Pharisee, not some unspecified people (Mk) or the disciples (Mt).[267] What makes Luke's variant interesting for our purpose is the comment about the inner talk of the Pharisee: "If this man were a prophet, he should have known who and of what sort is this woman who touches him, that she is a sinner" (v 39). While the following narrative concentrates on sin and forgiveness, the embarassment of the Pharisee is apparently caused by the impropriety of the woman touching Jesus (ἅπτεται αὐτοῦ). As we have already seen, touching is a recurring feature in many of the traditions in which purity seems to be an issue, and it is central in the discussion about the contaminating power of persons unclean with bodily

Lk 8 (parallel to Mk 5) suffered from a blood flow, another woman in Lk 13 had a bent back. It could be argued that Luke's mentioning of women following Jesus has more in common with the apocryphal Acta literature.

265 See above, 120. In biblical and rabbinic tradition, the child is not sharing the impurity of the mother. It would be possible to argue that Luke could reflect a deviant practice, similar to that of the Falashas, or of Sakta, the Dosithean (a minority Samaritan opinion), according to which the baby's uncleanness was the same as the mother's (cf. Bóid 1989, 327). If so, this would testify to a deviant first-century *halakhah* of some influence. While such a view is attested in some Near Eastern texts, I find this interpretation highly unlikely and far too speculative, as long as no contemporary Jewish evidence for such a view is adduced.

266 Cf. I. H. Marshall 1978, 117.

267 In addition, Luke's narrative includes a dialogue between Jesus and Simon. The Johannine parallel (Jn 12) mostly follows Mark, although the setting is quite different (Bethany, the house of Lazarus), the woman is identified as Mary, and the feet of Jesus (as in Luke), not his head, are anointed. Some suggest that these traditions are independent from the beginning, e.g. I. H. Marshall 1978, 304–310; Brown 1966, 1: 449–452; Dodd 1963, 162–173.

discharges, as will be further explored below. We can thus suspect that purity is an issue in the underlying traditional material, and that Luke is aware of this,[268] although he does not exploit it, but gives the narrative a moral interpretation.[269]

In any case, there are no hints in the Lukan text as to the source of the woman's possible impurity. Any such discussion will amount to mere speculation. Menstruation or child-birth is out of the question, since these sources of impurity would never impart to anyone the epithet "sinner." The woman could possibly be taken as a *zabah*, since that state was at times seen as a result of indecent behaviour, or as divine punishment.[270] Or she could be regarded as a sinner by some Pharisees, because she did not follow the purity *halakhah* of the expansionist current in general.[271] The traditional interpretation of the narrative, which simply regarded the woman as immoral, is not necessitated by the text, but depends more on an overall interpretation of Luke's gospel.[272] While some purity issue is implied in this tradition, and even suggested by some of its terminology, no attempt to define it will suffice as a basis for building an argument. For this we will have to rely primarily on the non-conflict tradition in Mk 5. It is clear, however, that in Lk 7 Jesus is pictured as ignoring a Pharisaic opinion about the impropriety of physical contact between pious men and certain women, defending a behaviour which is contrary to Pharisaic expectations.

Interpreting the purity issue: biblical legislation

Even if Lev 15 is established as an intertext of Mk 5:25–34, and even if it is accepted that the historical Jesus came into contact with people with flows, this does not by itself interpret the nature of such contact, nor the degree of contamination. The argument that since the woman was healed instantly, there was actually no contamination,[273] cannot be accepted, since the instancy, the εὐθύς, belongs to a literary level, and is a Markan trait. On an historical level, we cannot claim that the actions or contacts of Jesus would have been seen as not in-

---

[268] The Pharisee is described in the introduction as inviting Jesus ἵνα φάγῃ μετ' αὐτοῦ. Jesus is described as εἰσελθὼν εἰς τὸν οἶκον τοῦ Φαρισαίου (7:36). In view of the discussion in Chapter III.2 above about Pharisees and *haburot*, hand-washing and commensality, these phrases could be taken to imply that the Pharisee regarded Jesus as trustworthy in matters of purity. The incident with the woman touching Jesus would then prove the Pharisee's expectation to be false, and risk defiling not only Jesus, but the food and drink.

[269] The two perspectives are not mutually exclusive, although the simplified equation, exemplified by I. H. Marshall (1978, 309: "a sinful, and therefore unclean, woman") is too common and certainly false. A general discussion about the relationship between purity and morality is postponed, however, to Chapter V.

[270] Cf. the view of dischargers in Qumran, implied by some 4Q fragments and late rabbinic material discussed below, 209f, 218.

[271] Such an interpretation would be vigorously disputed by E.P. Sanders, and several other exegetes (cf. Sanders 1985, 174–188), but see the discussion in Chapter V below.

[272] Cf. Caird 1963, 114, for a traditional interpretation.

[273] B. Kahl 1996, 66–67.

volving defilement, because the unclean people involved were instantly healed. On the other hand, we cannot claim that Jesus abrogated impurity laws simply by accepting the touch of a bleeding woman.[274] However, if we find Jesus' actions or contacts incompatible with the legal interpretation of his day, we can claim that they involved defilement serious enough for some to question his attitude to purity regulations.

Some scholars argue that neither according to the Priestly writings, nor according to mishnaic law, did the woman commit any transgression, or pass on any defilement, by touching Jesus.[275] Such claims, even if they were true, would not solve the problem, however, of the legal situation *at the end of the Second Temple period*, against which Jesus' behaviour must be interpreted. Thus it is necessary to review the evidence, beginning with the biblical legislation.

The background of biblical legislation concerning bodily discharges has been much discussed. A worldwide fear of menstrual blood as a repository of demonic forces has resulted in various forms of isolation, attested both in ancient texts and in more recent anthropological studies. The loss of vaginal blood or semen was regarded as a diminution of life and represented destruction and death.[276]

There are obvious discrepancies in the rules from Lev 15 concerning different types of genital dischargers. While they are given a similar form, there are important differences in many details. The person who touches a *zab* must launder, wash, and is unclean until the evening (v 7). The person touching a menstruant, however, is just said to become unclean until the evening (v 19), and nothing whatsoever is said about the person touching a *zabah*. Similarly, the *zab* is said to contaminate people and vessels by touch, unless he has washed his hands (vv 11–12). Nothing, however, is said about female dischargers contaminating by touch. The *zab* is given a more elaborate treatment: he contaminates by spitting (v 8), and everything upon which he sits when riding is contaminated (v 9). When it comes to purification rituals, the *zab* is required to launder his clothes and wash on the seventh day, as well as bring a sacrifice on

[274] Cf. the discussion of Fonrobert 1997, 135f. On a literary level, however, Fonrobert is wrong in claiming that "the attempt to read this story as abrogation of biblical traditions concerning menstruation and irregular discharges of blood remains unsuccessful," since, as she herself shows, this was one early reading, attested in the *Didascalia*.

[275] Fonrobert 1997, 133; Maccoby 1999, 162f.

[276] Milgrom 1991, 766–767. While monotheism made the demons recede into the background in Israel, the demonic, according to Milgrom, continued to reside in man. Cf. Maccoby, who does not find the life-diminishing aspect of discharges enough to substantiate a theory that requires that all life-diminishing disharges defile. As an example, he points out that the blood of a wounded person is not a source of impurity (Maccoby 1999, 31). Maccoby suggests that it is a matter of the whole cycle of mortality, life and death, that is expressed by impurity, and excluded from that which is holy (Maccoby 1999, 49–50).

the eighth (vv 13ff). Nothing is said about the menstruant, and the *zabah* is to wait for seven days and then bring a sacrifice (vv 28ff). When it comes to the *yoledet* in Lev 12, her impurity in the first stage (one or two weeks) is likened to that of a menstruant (v 2, 5). Nevertheless, during her second stage impurity (another 33 or 66 days) she is not allowed to touch anything holy or enter the sanctuary (v 4), and the period should be terminated by a sacrifice (vv 6ff). Nothing is said about washing or laundering.

How are we to explain these discrepancies? They could either be exploited, or the various rules could be read in a systemic way. Fonrobert takes the differences at face value, concluding that not only did the menstruant and the *zabah* not transmit impurity by touching, but the *zabah* could even be touched.[277] The opposite view is held by Trummer, who suggests that prohibitions for discharging women to touch clean people are absent because this was simply unthinkable.[278] Both standpoints are simplifications to be avoided. Gerstenberger suggests that the silence about several issues regarding women (i.e. spitting, touching, saddle) could be explained by a male view-point: women were not to spit, they were not to give men their hands, and they did not usually ride.[279] This may be so, but does not explain why instructions about touching vessels occur only in the regulations concerning the *zab*. As several interpreters point out, the discussions about female dischargers are made dependent on the previous basic regulations concerning the *zab*. The whole chapter should probably be read in a more systemic way. As the *zab* is first treated, the *niddah* and *zabah* incorporate certain traits of the former. This is clear from the attempts of the author to parallel the symptoms of the menstruant with those of the *zab*, which has lead to a somewhat clumsy construction in Lev 15:19 (וְאִשָּׁה כִּי־תִהְיֶה זָבָה דָּם יִהְיֶה זֹבָהּ בִּבְשָׂרָהּ) which parallels 15:2 (אִישׁ אִישׁ כִּי יִהְיֶה זָב מִבְּשָׂרוֹ זוֹבוֹ), in spite of specific terminology being available (v 33: הַדָּוָה בְּנִדָּתָהּ).[280] A systemic reading is encouraged by the fact that זָב is being used inclusively about both men and women in the concluding v 33 (הַזָּב אֶת־זוֹבוֹ לַזָּכָר וְלַנְּקֵבָה).[281]

If this is the case, Milgrom's suggestion that not only the *zab*, but all dischargers, are supposed to purify in spring water, like other seven-day impurity bearers (Lev 14:5–6, 50–52; Num 19:17), is probably true. While this is not

[277] Fonrobert 1997, 130–131.
[278] Trummer 1991, 112–113.
[279] Gerstenberger 1993, 187.
[280] Gerstenberger 1993, 186. It should be noted that זָבָה is the technical term in rabbinic Hebrew for a woman with long-term discharges of blood. In Lev 15, both זָבָה and דָּוָה are used for the menstruant, and the "rabbinic" זָבָה is referred to by the even more roundabout phrase אִשָּׁה כִּי־יָזוּב זוֹב דָּמָהּ יָמִים רַבִּים בְּלֹא עֶת־נִדָּתָהּ.
[281] Cf. Milgrom 1991, 948.

mentioned in the case of female dischargers, it is implied, since the regulations concerning the latter abbreviate those preceding, concerning the *zab*.[282]

What about the other differences in purification requirements for various dischargers? An important argument, developed by Wright and Milgrom, is that the expression יִטְמָא עַד־הָעָרֶב ("unclean until evening," e.g. in 15:19) always implied ablutions, i.e. washing the body. This can be deduced from several instances of parallel instructions, where the expression is used in one place with, and in another place without bathing being mentioned.[283] Assuming this to be the case, Harrington argues that since those who touch a menstruant are unclean until evening (15:19), i.e. must bathe, this must *a fortiori* apply to the menstruant herself.[284] Based on a similar logic, Wright suggests that the menstruant must launder her clothes too, as must those who touch her bed.[285]

The purification requirements of the *zabah* (15:28–30) mention only a sacrifice. If they are seen as an abbreviation of the requirements of the *zab*, laundering and bathing must be implicitly understood from v 13.[286] Sacrifices are, however, explicitly required only from the *yoledet*, the *zab* and the *zabah*, but not from the menstruant (12:6–8; 15:14–15, 29–30). Are we to harmonize from a systemic reading in this case too, or is the discrepancy intended? Perhaps there is a practical consideration: menstruants cannot be expected to afford sacrifices monthly.[287] Menstruation is in a way considered a slighter impurity than the others, since it is of shorter duration, and is not followed by a seven-day

---

[282] Milgrom 1991, 923–924, 934–935.

[283] Milgrom (1991, 919) mentions the following examples: "(1) Lev 11:40 states that one who eats the carcass of pure animals must 'launder his clothes and remain impure until evening.' A parallel passage states that whoever eats such carcasses must 'launder his clothes, *bathe in water*, and remain impure until evening' (17:15). (2) If washing of a *utensil* contaminated by a swarming creature is necessary (11:32), the same should be necessary for *people* who touch the swarming creature (11:31). (3) A priest who touches certain impurities 'becomes impure until evening' (22:6a). Lest there be any mistake, Scripture adds the explanation: 'He shall not eat of the holy things unless he has bathed his body in water' (v 6b). (4) Num 31:24 omits bathing, but Num 19:19 clearly requires it. (5) Bathing is lacking for the gatherer of the ashes of the Red Cow (Num 19:10), but is explicitly required for the priest and the burner who participated in this rite (vv 7, 8). (6) Ablution is often assumed and is thus omitted in the cases of the menstruant …, the parturient …, and the corpse-contaminated Nazirite (Num 6:9)." Cf. David P. Wright 1987, 185, n.38; Harrington 1993, 117–120.

[284] Harrington 1993, 228–229.

[285] David P. Wright 1987, 191, n.44.

[286] David P. Wright 1987, 193, especially n.47. It seems as if Wright assumes the same purification rites to apply also to the יֹלֶדֶת (195). Another explanation, taking into account the differences regarding sacrifices, will be discussed below.

[287] This is the argument of Milgrom (1991, 935). It could be argued that while child-birth is natural too, it does not occur so often; hence a sacrifice could be afforded. This is a questionable argument, however, since regular menstruation through the fertile period is a fairly recent phenomenon, dependent on modern family structures and birth control. See further discussion below, 160, n.369.

purification period. Menstruation itself could rather be seen as equivalent to the seven-day purification period of the other impurities.[288]

We have seen that a systemic reading of the biblical legislation seems natural in many cases, but is not always self-evident. Of crucial importance for evaluating the purity issue in the Markan tradition about the bleeding woman is the question of physical contact. In the case of a clean person touching a discharger, a systemic reading would mean that one is contaminated and has to purify in the same way after having touched a menstruant (15:19), as after having touched a *zab* (15:7), i.e. including laundering. Wright's argument is that since laundering is required from a person having touched something upon which a menstruant lies or sits, it must logically be required from someone directly touching her.[289] Against this, Milgrom argues that, although the phrase יִטְמָא עַד־הָעָרֶב implies bathing, it never includes laundering of clothes.[290] There is an apparent tension between v 19 and vv 21–22, which demand laundering from those touching the menstruant's bed and seat. The problem is made even worse when the *zabah* is considered. While both washing and laundering are demanded from the person touching her bed or seat (v 27), nothing is said about touching the *zabah* herself. This can be explained in different ways. Since the *zabah* is explicitly compared to the menstruant (vv 25–26) and since the menstruant is actually referred to as a *zabah* too, it could be argued that the same rules are assumed to apply, although some details are missing, due to abbreviation (i.e. touching her, touching items on her bed or seat, and intercourse). This is how the rules were interpreted and applied in Second Temple times, as will be seen below. Milgrom has suggested that the בָּם of v 27 should be read בָּהּ, as in two manuscripts.[291] This is supported by the LXX reading (αὐτῆς), and makes the verse read: "And everyone who touches *her* becomes unclean, and must launder his clothes and wash in water and is unclean until evening." If this reading is accepted, the rules about touching a *zabah* correspond to those

[288] If the requirement to bring a sacrifice is seen as a consequense of having polluted the sanctuary from afar (cf. Milgrom 1991, 999), the fact that this is not required from the menstruant (cf. Harrington 1993, 223) supports the idea that her impurity is in some aspects more akin to the seven-day purification period of other dischargers, rather than to the period of their actual discharge.

In rabbinic times, the seven days were *added* to the menstruation period. This is of a fairly late date, however, motivated by the difficulty in distinguishing different kinds of blood. Cf. Woolf 2000, 264ff; Maccoby 1999, 44–46; *bNid* 66a. Since it has been practised in Judaism until this day, some authors assume the addition of seven days as biblical or Second Temple practice. This is definitely untrue. One example of such an interpretation is Péter-Contesse 1993 (238), who discusses Lev 15 with no apparent knowledge of subsequent rabbinic developments.

[289] David P. Wright 1987, 189.

[290] Milgrom 1991, 935–936.

[291] Milgrom 1991, 943.

about touching a *zab* (v 7).[292] There is still a difference as compared to the menstruant, but this could be explained by menstruation being a natural and recurring process, limited in time, and thus not really considered to contaminate as seriously as the pathological discharges. Touching a *zab* or a *zabah* would thus require bathing and laundering, while touching a menstruant would require bathing only. This corresponds to the requirement for the former to bring a sacrifice, which does not apply to the menstruant, as previously noticed.[293]

If all the differences are taken at face value, without any "harmonizing" efforts, they could possibly be explained by differing origins. The priestly redactor(s) would then not have managed to combine the various regulations into a compatible system. While it is quite possible that rules concerning various dischargers have developed separately, there have been apparent efforts to shape the chapter into a coherent whole.[294] Even Lev 12, which is probably of separate origin, and inserted into the block somewhat later, is made to relate to Lev 15.[295] And since these rules were interpreted systemically during Second Temple times, it is likely that they were similarly, although not identically read in biblical times.

Further complications arrive when discussing the case of a person unclean with discharges touching a clean person, as in the Markan story of the bleeding woman. This is explicitly forbidden only in the case of the *zab*. He is said to contaminate clean persons and vessels by touching them without having first washed his hands (vv 11–12). It is reasonable to assume such contamination at least in the case of the *zabah* by analogy, and by implication from the fact that the *zabah* contaminates persons via her bed or seat.[296]

---

[292] Rules about not touching the bed and seat of the זָבָה must then be inferred from those about the menstruant. Cf. Milgrom 1991, 943.

[293] Cf. Milgrom 1991, 943.

[294] Cf. the roundabout way, discussed above, of describing the menstruant, in order to make her correspond to the זָב.

[295] Cf. Elliger 1966, 157.

[296] David P. Wright 1987, 193. Such an argument should apply to the menstruant as well, but is not discussed in Wright's text. The assumption appears, however, in his chart on p. 190.

Harrington is hesitant, however. "Perhaps these rules regarding the zāb's touch may be assumed for the zābâ and the menstruant as well, but one cannot be sure" (Harrington 1993, 224). It is somewhat unclear whether "these rules" in Harrington's statement refers to the rule about the *zab* contaminating by touch, or the exception when he has washed his hands. Does Harrington's hesitance concern the possibility of female dischargers contaminating by touch at all, or is that assumed and the hesitance concerns whether hand-washing allows female dischargers to touch without contaminating, as in the case of the *zab*? Milgrom discusses only the menstruant in this context, possibly including the *zabah*. He regards as an "inescapable" conclusion that "the menstruant may touch," but qualifies this in passing: "As long as she is scrupulous about rinsing her hands…" (Milgrom 1991, 953). This would imply the same rules as in the case of the *zab*, (cf. Milgrom's previous statement that the cases of the menstruant and of the *zabah* "abbreviate their contamination rules because they are derivable from the *zāb*,"1991, 924), but elsewhere Milgrom discusses the menstruant, concluding that "there is no prohibition barring

A question which is neither discussed explicitly by rabbinic authorities, nor extensively by modern commentators, concerns the definition of touch. The regulations about touching a *zab* (v 7) talk about his "flesh" (הַנֹּגֵעַ בִּבְשַׂר הַזָּב). This expression could be interpreted as his genitals,[297] but this is unlikely.[298] It rather refers to his body in general. This probably includes his clothes as well, since clothing could be regarded as an extension of a person's body. That "flesh" should not be taken literally can be argued from the parallel passage about the menstruant (v19) in which the object of touch is simply "her,"[299] Milgrom does not accept this explanation, but thinks that direct contact with the body of the discharging person is intended in both cases.[300] Wright conveys another line of argument, however, which makes use of an analogy with the bed. Since the clothing of the *zab* is in constant contact with his body, it is like the bed upon which he sits. Touching the clothes of a *zab* would thus incur the same impurity as touching his bed, requiring both laundering and bathing, as well as waiting until evening. The effect would be the same as that of touching the body of the *zab*.[301] We will return to this discussion about the definition of touch, since it is relevant to the interpretation of the Markan tradition about the bleeding woman touching the clothes of Jesus.

Excursus 1: Explaining discrepancies

a) By the impurity of discharges

While, as will be seen below, touching or being touched by any of the four main genital dischargers was later seen as equivalent, it is possible that the discrepancies between different sets of rules in Lev 15 reflect earlier differences. In addition to the attempts above to explain the somewhat lenient rules concerning the menstruant, it is possible to explain some other discrepancies, including those about the touch of the unclean person, by positing a *distinction between the genital discharger and the discharge itself.* The widespread fear of and disgust for genital discharges, and in particular menstrual blood, is widely attested in Antiquity.[302] It is reasonable to suggest that the impurity of people with discharges is derived from the fluids themselves. The remnants of such thinking can be observed in Samaritan *halakhah*,[303] where a person who

---

the menstruant from touching anyone. This can only mean that in fact her hands do not transmit impurity" (Milgrom 1991, 936).

[297] Cf. the translation of Elliger 1966, 191.

[298] Wenham 1979, 219. David P. Wright (1987, 183, n.34) points out that when the זָב is required in v 13 to wash his flesh in fresh water, it is clearly a matter of his whole body.

[299] David P. Wright 1987, 182f, n.34.

[300] Milgrom 1991, 914, 935.

[301] David P. Wright 1987, 183, n.34. For this argument Wright refers to Morgan W Tanner.

[302] Milgrom (1991, 763ff) gives numerous examples from ancient Egypt, Babylonia, Persia, pre-Islamic Arabia, the Hittites, Greece, etc. Ancient ideas about the danger of coming into contact with menstrual blood are attested by Pliny, *Nat.* 7:64: "Contact with it turns new wine sour, crops touched by it become barren, grafts die, seeds in gardens are dried up, the fruit of trees falls off, … even bronze and iron are at once seized by rust." A clear example of strong feelings against menstrual blood in Judaism is found in Ez 36:17.

[303] Samaritan texts are relatively late, from around 1000 CE and onwards, but represent one Israelite halakhic tradition based on an interpretion of the Torah.

comes into direct contact with a menstruant's blood (not only through intercourse, but through touching) is made unclean for seven days, just like the menstruant herself. Likewise, the menstruant has to wash off the first menstrual blood before the count of seven days can start, otherwise it will keep on re-contaminating her. Certain Samaritan rules concerning the *zab* similarly imply that the discharge itself is considered to be the contaminating agent. The idea of impurity being transmitted by the actual flux or blood seems to be strong.[304]

A similar view at the root of the legislation of Leviticus would explain several traits in Lev 15. It is likely that direct contact with the discharge is contemplated by the text. As underwear was not worn in biblical times,[305] anything situated underneath a *zab*, not only items used for sitting or riding, would run the risk of becoming contaminated by his discharge.[306] This could explain the wording of 15:10, where everything which has been situated *underneath* the *zab* is said to contaminate (כֹּל אֲשֶׁר יִהְיֶה תַחְתָּיו). This is added to the general rules about not coming into contact with the bed or seat of any discharger (15:4–6, 20–23, 26–27). While it could be argued that the specific rule in v 10 was applicable by analogy to all dischargers, another possible explanation is that this further elaboration would be needed only for the *zab*, since drops of his discharge which had happened to fall upon something situated underneath him, would not be detectable in the same way as blood.

The fear of contact with the discharge itself could also explain the prescription in v 11, which requires that the *zab* rinses his hands before touching anything. Since men touch their genitals when urinating, the hands of the *zab* must always be regarded as contaminating, unless recently washed, since they could transfer the unclean substance.[307] This would not apply to female dischargers, and could explain the lack of similar prescriptions for them.

When it comes to the contamination of objects for sitting and lying, the explicit rules are similar for both men and women (Lev 15:4–6, 20–23, 26–27). Due to the pressure of the body and the length of the time of contact, these objects could be suspected of contamination by unclean fluids, perhaps through the clothes of the discharging person. These rules were probably originally based on a fear of coming into contact with the unclean fluids themselves. The idea of pressure, however, subsequently developed into the concept of *midras* impurity, which eventually was not dependent on any kind of physical contact.

---

[304] *Kitâb aṭ-Ṭubâkh* [6–15] in Bóid 1989, 141; *Kitâb al-Kâfi* XI [84–89] in Bóid 1989, 150f; *Kitâb al-Kâfi* XIII [13–18] in Bóid 1989, 154; Cf Boid's comments, 199–204, 210, 218f, 236f,. In Samaritan law, the first menstrual blood is called *nidda*, contaminating for seven days, while the subsequent bleeding is called *daba*, and contaminates only for one day (*Kitâb al-Kâfi* XI [84–89], in Boid 1989, 141). It is also interesting to note that the left hand with which the woman washes off the *nidda* blood seems to be treated as being at the same level of uncleanness as the *nidda* blood itself for the whole week, even if there is no longer any blood on it (Marginal note IV in a manuscript of the *Kitâb al-Kâfi*, in Boid 1989, 196, 289). Concerning the *zab*, the Samaritan *Book of Insight* (*Kitâb aṭ-Ṭubâkh*) [103–106] considers an animal used for riding by a *zab* unclean, with the capacity for contaminating other people. This is explained by Boid (145, 218f) from the possibility of the animal having got some of the discharge on itself. Similarly, the *Ṭubâkh* considers the ground on which the *zab* has been standing as contaminating [103]. The most likely explanation according to Boid (218) is that the author is thinking of the possibility of some of the discharge having dripped onto the ground.

[305] For the sake of decency, underwear was compulsory for officiating priests (Ex 28:42f), but this was apparently an exception.

[306] Milgrom 1991, 911. Cf. Samaritan regulations about cleansing the ground which might have absorbed some moisture from a discharging person, with fire: *Kitâb al-Kâfi* XII [22–34] in Bóid 1989, 155f. Cf. Boid's comments, 246ff, 303. This would also apply to any ground on which a woman had walked before having washed off the *nidda* blood (247).

[307] Milgrom 1991, 911.

If a distinction between the impurity of the discharging person and the discharge itself is assumed as underlying the regulations of Lev 15, some of the discrepancies could thus be explained.

b) By the exclusion of women from the cult

Before turning to the question of isolation of people with discharges, we must discuss a different attempt to explain at least some of the discrepancies in the text of Lev 15. Judith Romner Wegner has offered an interpretation based on purity being necessary to perform cultic acts, according to the priestly system. The purifying *zab* is to launder his clothes and bathe after having waited for seven days (v 13) while the *zabah* is required to wait only seven days (v 28). Wegner does not accept Milgrom's explanation that laundering and bathing are implied, but understands this discrepancy to reflect differences in cultic status. Women are seldom involved in sacrifices, and when they are, as in the case of the purifying *yoledet* or *zabah* (Lev 12:6; 15:29), they *bring* (הֵבִיא) their offering to the priest, in contrast to the *zab* (15:14), who comes "before the LORD" (לִפְנֵי יְהוָה) and *gives* (נָתַן) the sacrificial animals to the priest. According to Wegner, laundering and bathing were necessary only for performing cultic rituals "before the LORD," which women did not do. For the same reason, nothing is said in v 33 about women lying with unclean men, only about men lying with unclean women, since such defilement disqualified them from cultic activities, while women were never qualified to begin with.[308] Wegner's analysis should be seriously considered. It does explain certain discrepancies in the text. It is safe to say that the regulations are structured and worded from a male perspective. In spite of this, Wegner's explanation does not account for all inconsistencies discussed above. It may be accepted as one among many partial and possible explanations. Wegner may be right that the "exclusion of women embodied a fundamental aspect of P's worldview."[309] If this is so, it also suggests that other views were in existence, both at the time of Leviticus' final redaction, and during earlier periods. According to Lev 15:18 both the man and the woman had to bathe after intercourse, and wait for evening before becoming clean. In Lev 12:4, the *yoledet* is prohibited from coming to the sanctuary, which suggests that she would regularly do so otherwise. Another trace of a different view, and of a possible priestly redaction, can be seen in 1Sam 1:9, where Hannah is praying for a child. According to the MT, she comes "after she had eaten in Shiloh and after she had drunk."[310] The LXX, however, does not read "after she had drunk," but καὶ κατέστη ἐνώπιον κυρίου (LXX 1Kgdms 1:9). The text would then read: "after a sacrificial meal in Shilo, Hannah appeared before the LORD." This reading is probably more original than that of the MT,[311] but has been redacted, possibly out of interests such as those which Wegner discusses. The variant has survived in the Greek translation, however, implying that women were not consistently excluded from the cult, and not throughout the biblical period.[312] While some differences between the traditions in Lev 15 may well be due to the interests of the redactors, there are discrepancies which have little to do with women's participation in the cult, but rather reflect early conceptions. In Second Temple times, the regulations

---

[308] Wegner 1998, 81–90. Wegner admits one exception which would allow women to come "before the LORD," namely the suspected adulteress (Num 5:16). She regards this as the exception that proves the rule, and emphasizes that even in this case the woman is not an active participant in a cultic act, but rather a passive object.

[309] Wegner 1998, 90.

[310] אַחֲרֵי אָכְלָה בְשִׁלֹה וְאַחֲרֵי שָׁתֹה. It should be noted that אָכְלָה is here treated as the main verb (3 sg. f.) which is complemented by an absolute infinitive (שָׁתֹה). When the text is reconstructed with the help of the LXX, אָכְלָה is taken as a noun ([sacrificial] meal).

[311] This reading is followed by e.g. *The Jerusalem Bible* (1971), and the Swedish *Bibel 2000.*

[312] Sander's statement that "at the time of Leviticus women did not actually enter the temple" (1990, 143), is too generalized.

concerning people with discharges, were not read with a view to cultic differences between men and women, but prescriptions were systematized and made applicable to all or most dischargers by the help of analogy.[313]

Expulsion or isolation of dischargers during the biblical period

In the previous section about "leprosy," we have seen that the relevant legislation (Lev 13–14) was concerned with diagnosis and purification, but not with contamination. This was explained from the fact that "lepers" were isolated and expelled from society. The legislation in Lev 15 about discharges contains no signs of expulsion, but detailed discussions about contamination. This suggests that people suffering from discharges were living within their communities. In no other way can we explain regulations concerning the transmission of impurity even via their beds and seats, and the purifying rites required from people being thus contaminated, or the instruction for the *zab* to wash his hands before touching anyone. All the rules seem to presuppose that clean people are constantly at the risk of coming into contact with discharging persons, directly or indirectly, and when this happens, appropriate purification rites must be carried out. Nothing is said about permission to enter the camp after initial purification, as in the case of the "leper" (Lev 14:8), which again suggests that people suffering from discharges were present in their towns and villages throughout their period of impurity.[314]

There is a separate tradition, however, found in Num 5:2–3, according to which neither "lepers" nor corpse impure, nor genital dischargers may remain in their communities:

> Order the children of Israel to send away from the camp every leper and every zab and every corpse-impure. Male or female, you shall send away; outside of the camp you shall send them; and they shall not defile their camp, where I live in their midst.

Opinions differ as to how this tradition should be regarded. Wright sees it as a law reflecting conditions of the wilderness camp, which could be regarded as

> a hybrid cross of a regular community and a war camp. It is well known from non-Priestly material that a war camp was under stricter conditions of purity than the normal community. ... God moves throughout the camp so that he might grant victory to the soldiers. The camp must be holy for God's presence to continue there.[315]

As an historical explanation of the presence of conflicting traditions, this does not suffice. Which practice was adhered to and when? Milgrom suggests that this tradition stems from a different textual layer: either P_2 or H.[316] It is impos-

---

[313] Examples from Qumran and rabbinic literature will be given below.
[314] Cf. David P. Wright 1987, 173.
[315] David P. Wright 1987, 171.
[316] Milgrom regards much of the P source as fairly early, reflecting the cult in Shiloh. The P_1 strand reflects the settled, urbanized Israelite society, and includes e.g. Lev 15. The P_2 strand contains older material, e.g. laws of the wilderness camp. The H source is later, dated to the end

sible to say whether the tradition of P_1 (Lev 15), which contained genital dischargers within the community, succeeded or was contemporaneous with the stricter tradition of Num 5. Expulsion from the community is, in any case, to be seen as an ancient idea, clearly evidenced in ancient Babylonian and Persian texts.[317] Milgrom thinks that P_1 "initiates the long historic process whereby the power of impurity is progressively reduced."[318] He explains this process with the demonic background of the concept of impurity, and the idea of airborne impurity, which threatened the sanctuary from afar. The idea of airborne impurity would have made it necessary to expel all severe impurity bearers, i.e. those suffering a seven-day impurity and required to bring a *hattat* sacrifice.[319] The concept of airborne impurity could not remain as the demonic idea vanished with time, and was finally eliminated in rabbinic Judaism. Hence all but the "leper" were allowed to remain at home.[320]

Milgrom's reconstruction, especially the theory about airborne impurity, has been criticized.[321] There is a missing link in the reasoning. If the requirement to bring a sacrifice indicates that the discharging person has defiled the *sanctuary*, although without having been in direct contact with it, why does this sacrifice (Lev 15:14, 29) belong to the rites necessary for purifying the *person*? The wording in Lev 15:31 "And you shall separate the children of Israel from their impurity, so that they shall not die in their impurity by their contamination of my tabernacle which is in their midst," does not necessitate pollution from afar, but בְּטַמְּאָם could be translated "when (if) they contaminate," rather than "by their contamination."[322] The issue is thus contamination by direct contact or entrance, as is clear from Lev 12:4, where it is stated explicitly: "She must not touch anything holy and not enter the sanctuary until the end of the days of cleansing."[323]

of the eighth century, and is dependent on and incorporates P material (Milgrom 1991, 998f; cf 3–35, 61–63; Milgrom 2000a, 1319–1367).

[317] Milgrom 1991, 763, quoting Gudea, Statue B IV.4: "the woman in labor I caused to go forth from the city." Cf. the relative isolation of menstruants in Zoroastrian religion (Boyce 1975, 307f).

[318] Milgrom 1991, 999.

[319] Milgrom 1991, 999. Cf. Harrington 1993, 223, who accepts Milgrom's theory. Cf. the rabbinic explanation that *zabim* were banished from the camp only after the tabernacle had been built; *Num.Rab.* 7:1; *Lev.Rab.* 18:4 in Neusner 1973a, 97.

[320] Milgrom 1991, 999.

[321] Milgrom's theory on airborne impurity and *hattat* as a purification offering, necessary to cleanse the sanctuary from contamination from afar, has been seriously questioned, most recently by Maccoby (1999), who deals with it in two consecutive chapters (165–192). The idea is not present in rabbinic interpretation, and there is no evidence for it in intertestamental or Qumran literature (184f).

[322] Maccoby 1999, 172f.

[323] Cf. Maccoby 1999, 170.

Maccoby suggests an alternative historical reconstruction, which takes the interpretation of the "camp" as its point of departure.

> If, according to one strand of P, the whole camp is a holy area from which impurity must be excluded, then there may be good reasons for requiring speedy purification without introducing any notion of aerial contamination of the Tabernacle from a distance.[324]

This is, according to Maccoby, reflected in an older stratum of P, in which prohibitions to defile the sanctuary referred to the whole camp, which was regarded as the outer grounds of the sanctuary. Those with major impurities were expelled, while those with minor impurities remained in the camp, but, because of its holiness, had to seek early purification. At the next stage, holiness was reduced in the camp and restricted to the sanctuary and its surroundings.[325] As a result, all impurity bearers except "lepers" were allowed within the camp, but could not enter the sanctuary. They had to seek early purification, to avoid defiling others who might enter the sanctuary. Finally, in rabbinic interpretation, three camps with ascending degrees of holiness were defined, corresponding to different parts of Jerusalem.[326]

These are attempts at generalized descriptions of a long historical process. When it comes to details, there are discrepancies. It seems that even according to the stricter legislation of Num 5, neither the menstruant nor the *yoledet* is expelled from the community,[327] in spite of the fact that the *yoledet* belongs to those required to bring a *hattat* sacrifice. This is probably due to the normality of their conditions.[328] Furthermore, unnatural discharges as well as "leprosy" were often regarded as signs of divine punishment.[329] It is probably wise to avoid any ideas about straight lines of historical development. Suffice it to state that divergent traditions are present already in the text of the Pentateuch, stemming from different sources, and apparently representing different practices. Milgrom himself discusses whether the two traditions of Lev 15 and Num 5

---

[324] Maccoby 1999, 185.

[325] This very much corresponds to Milgrom's idea, 1991, 316f.

[326] Maccoby 1999, 186f. Note the interpretation of the Qumran sect, where the whole of Jerusalem was seen as a holy area, with effects similar to those of Num 5:2–3. Cf. the discussion below, 157f, 187ff.

[327] Arguments from etymology, such as נִדָּה having the root meaning to cast out, or exclude, are of little value in reconstructing actual practice. In any case the root meaning is probably connected to the flow of blood ("expulsion," spattering), not the exclusion of the menstruant. Cf. Fonrobert 1997, 124, n.11.

[328] Cf. Milgrom 1991, 995. As we have already seen above, the menstruant was not required to bring a sacrifice, and her condition of impurity differs somewhat from the others, since her seven days were counted from the beginning of her bleeding, i.e. during the period of bleeding itself. The יוֹלֶדֶת was, during the first period, expressly likened to the menstruant, and her first seven or fourteen days were likewise counted not from the end of a period of bleeding, but during bleeding itself. At the end of the second period, however, she had to bring a *hattat* sacrifice, which, according to Milgrom's theory, would imply that she had defiled the sanctuary from afar.

[329] 2Sam 3:29. As for the attitude to "leprosy," see above, 116f.

should be seen as diachronically or synchronically related.[330] What can be said with some certainty is that, in addition to the main legal tradition concerning discharges (Lev 15), there are clear traces of a stricter tradition within the Torah itself (Num 5). Such a practice of exclusion could be older than that of Lev 15, as attested by texts from neighbouring cultures. It could also represent a later redaction or revision at a time of cultic reformation, possibly reviving a more ancient law.[331] The ambiguous texts were actually exploited by later interpreters in times of legal dissension. The two traditions represent what Milgrom and others have called a "minimalist" and a "maximalist" stance, which can be traced throughout the history of early Judaism.[332] As will be pointed out repeatedly, what I have previously called an expansionist current is not only an early phenomenon, but belongs to the Second Temple period as well.[333]

In the present case, however, we can consider an intermediate option. While expulsion of genital dischargers was not the general practice in biblical times, some kind of isolation could be considered. This is proposed for menstruants by Wright and Jones,[334] but doubted by both Maccoby[335] and Milgrom.[336] There are simply no indications, even less any clear evidence in biblical texts.[337] Such is only to be found in extra-biblical material for the Second Temple period.

Equalization and strictness in the Second Temple period

There is evidence for an "equalizing" tendency during the Second Temple period. The contamination potential and purification rituals of different genital dischargers were harmonized, since the regulations were interpreted systemically. While the mishnaic order of Purities begins with a hierarchical ordering of different types of sources of impurity (*mKel* 1:1–4), the differences between the contamination power of the major genital discharges are minimized, and for practical purposes they are equalized. This is clear from the tractates *Niddah*

---

330 Milgrom 1991, 998f. While allowing for simultaneous traditions, Milgrom seems to suggest a continuous development from the time of P_1. "Slowly, then, almost imperceptibly, airborne impurity was progressively eliminated: all impurity bearers, with the exception of the *mĕṣōrā‘*, were allowed to remain at home" (999). It is difficult to imagine how the integration of genital dischargers could have taken place slowly or imperceptibly, which must have been the case if it was dependent upon the vanishing of the concept of airborne impurity.

331 Cf. Harrington 1993, 227, especially n.6.

332 Harrington 1993, 227; Milgrom 1990, 85–89.

333 This seems to be the view of Milgrom as well (1990, 85–89), in spite of the formulations in 1991, 999.

334 Wright and Jones 1992, 205.

335 Maccoby 1999, 33ff.

336 Milgrom 1991, 952f.

337 Examples of menstruant women in the Hebrew Bible are found in narratives of non-priestly character: Gen 31:35; 2Sam 11:4.

and *Zabim*. Both begin with discussions attributed to Shammai and Hillel or their houses, about how to count days.[338] Much of *Niddah* is dedicated to questions of counting days and periods, and defining different types of blood. *Zabim* begins with a discussion between the houses of whether the *zab* should be likened to the *zabah* or to the seminal discharger (*mZab* 1:1). While the questions raised from a plain reading of Leviticus concern whether the contamination and purification of the *zabah* should be supplemented by the more specific instructions for the *zab*, the questions discussed in these mishnaic tractates belong to another level. Says Neusner,

> The secondary and derivative character of these inquiries [i.e. inquiries undertaken by the Houses before 70 CE, reflected in *mZab*] strongly suggests that the work on Zabim began before the Houses, that is, before the first decades of the first century A.D., just as is the case for Niddah. The exegetical work on the modes of the transfer of uncleanness of the Zab, moreover, was certainly complete before 70...[339]

Most of the "discrepancies" discussed above had probably been equalized by the first century CE. This is clear from the discussion in *mNid* 4:3:

> The blood of a woman who has not immersed after childbirth -
> The House of Shammai say, "It is like her spit and her urine."
> And the House of Hillel say, "It imparts uncleanness wet and dry."

While bathing is not explicitly prescribed for the *yoledet* in Lev 12, it is shown to be taken for granted in a discussion ascribed to the Houses. That the menstruant immerses in a *miqveh* at the end of her period is so self-evident that the fact itself is seldom mentioned in the *Mishnah*. When it is, it is taken for granted.[340] As for the *zabah*, her immersion was also taken for granted. She is regarded as being slightly more unclean than the *zab*, because she could render a man unclean for seven days by intercourse. For all other practical purposes, she is included in some of the legislation concerning the *zab*, separately identified only at times.[341] Immersion was widely practised during the first century CE, as evidenced by the frequent findings of *miqvaot*.[342] There are no reasons to doubt that this practice included all severe impurity bearers, men and women, at the end of the Second Temple period.

---

[338] *mNid* 1:1; *mZab* 1:1.

[339] Neusner 1974–1977, 18: 3.

[340] *mMiqv* 8:1; *mMiqv* 8:5: "A menstruating woman who placed coins in her mouth and went down and immersed is clean on account of her uncleanness [as a menstruant], but she is unclean because of her spit. If she put her hair in her mouth, closed her hand, pressed her lips together—it is as if she did not immerse." The main idea here probably concerns recontamination via the saliva (i.e. liquid). That the menstruant is required to immerse is self-evident in rabbinic Judaism, and the *miqveh* survived in post-temple times only for the sake of menstruants (Maccoby 1999, 43). It is the only Jewish purification rite which has survived until our time. (Ibid., 41f). Cf. Sanders 1990, 143.

[341] *mKel* 1:4; *mZab* 5:6.

[342] Cf. section III.2 above.

The contamination potential of different genital dischargers is, according to *mZab* 5:6, the same:

> He who touches the *Zab* and the *Zabah* and the menstruating woman and the woman after childbirth and the *mesora*, a bed or a chair [that any of these have lain or sat upon] imparts uncleanness at two removes and renders [heave offering] unfit at one further remove. [If] he separated, he imparts uncleanness at one remove and renders unfit at one further remove. All the same are the one who touches and the one who shifts, and all the same are the one who carries and the one who is carried.[343]

The fine points discussed above, concerning the possible difference in biblical times between touching or being touched by different impurity bearers, would not be relevant for the Rabbis. The anonymous saying in *mZab* 5:1 is clear:

> He who touches the *Zab*, or whom the *Zab* touches,
> he who moves the *Zab*, or whom the *Zab* moves
> imparts uncleanness to food and drink and utensils which may be cleaned through rinsing when [he is in] contact but not when he carries.

A similar equalizing tendency seems to be found in the material from Qumran. While it is not clear whether the rinsing of hands to prevent contamination applied only to the *zab*, or to other dischargers as well,[344] we find that all dischargers are basically considered to contaminate in the same way. In 4Q274, fragment 1, already discussed in the section about "leprosy," different impurity bearers, at their purifying stage of seven days, are instructed not to touch other impure people, thus incurring an added impurity.

4. ... And a woman who has a flow of blood, during the seven days she shall not touch a *zab*, nor any vessel [w]hich the *zab* touched or laid
5. upon or sat upon. And if she did touch, she shall wash her clothes and bathe, and afterwards she may eat. She shall with all her effort not mingle (with others) during her seven
6. days so as not to contaminate the ca[m]ps of the sanct[ities of] Israel; also, she is not to touch any woman with a blood [fl]ow lasting man[y] days.

---

[343] Cf. Harrington 1993, 230f. This passage is misunderstood by Sanders (1990, 208f), who doubts that "the Pharisees operated by this principle." This would have meant that they "sought to avoid sitting on things which had been sat on by people who had touched a zav, so that they could handle food from which the offerings had not yet been separated." The idea is that a person, while in contact with a זָב, him/herself functions as a "father of impurity," contaminating rinsable vessels, food and liquid in the first degree, hence hands, food and liquid in the second degree and *terumah* in the third degree. Such a person, although in contact with a זָב, does *not* contaminate other people or clay vessels. This is clear from *mZab* 5:1. When no longer in contact, the person who has touched the זָב, is unclean in the first degree, and contaminates only hands, food and liquid in the second (liquid in the first degree, according to *mZab* 5:1. See above, 81ff, for a discussion about liquid), and *terumah* in the third degree (cf. the similar reasoning about touching discharges; *mZab* 5:7, 8, 10). Cf. Harrington 1993, 230f, 240.

[344] 4Q277 1 2: 10–11: "And anyone touched by [a man who has] a flux [ ] [and whose] hand[s were not] r[in]sed in water becomes [unclean]" (tr. J.Baumgarten, *DJD* 35, 116). While the text is heavily damaged and reconstructed, the key words flux, hands and water appear.

7. And one who is counting (seven days,) whether male or female, shall not tou[ch one who has an unclea]n [flux] or a menstruating woman in her uncleanliness, unless she was purified of her [unclean]liness; for the blood of
8. menstruation is like the flux and the one touching it. And when [a man has] an emiss[ion] of semen his touch is defiling. A [man who tou]ches any person from among
9. these impure ones during the seven days of [his] purifi[cation shall no]t eat, just as if he had been defiled by [a human cor]pse; [and he must b]athe and wash (his clothes) afterwar[ds][345]

The underlying premise must be that impure persons contaminate not only pure, but also purifying people.[346] Those purifying hence had to be instructed to avoid other impurity bearers, especially those with the same type of impurity as themselves whom they, probably, had been associating with, during expulsion or quarantine.[347] These restrictions evidently applied to clean persons as well, otherwise they could not be applied to purifying or impure people. A menstruant is not to touch a *zab* or a *zabah* alike.[348] No (purifying) person should touch any *zab* or any menstruant. It is implied that different impurity bearers are equalized as to their contamination, by the fact that different types of discharges are put on the same level. Finally, touching a genital discharger is compared with corpse-defilement.[349] If we follow Baumgarten's reconstruction and inter-

---

[345] 4Q274 1 1: 4–9. Tr. J.Baumgarten, *DJD* 35, 101.

[346] That even impure people could be further contaminated is possibly implied by the preceding lines about the "leper." Cf. line 3: "Anyone of the unclean [wh]o [touches] him shall bathe in water and wash his clothes and afterwards he may eat; for this is as said, 'Unclean, unclean!'" As pointed out above (109), this could be taken to mean that impurity was accumulated by contact between different types of impurity bearers, which explains why they should be quarantined in separate areas (11Q19 [11QT] 46:16–18; 48:14–17), which is different from the rabbinic system, in which touching lesser impurity does not add to one's own impurity. The reconstruction of line 3 is very uncertain, however, and it is possible that the sectarians, like the rabbis, worried only about touching higher degrees of impurity. The gist of 4Q274 concerns *purifying* dischargers, who are warned not to come into contact with other *dischargers* who were still in their original uncleanness.

[347] See below for a discussion about expulsion or quarantine. It is not clear, however, whether the purifying persons are thought to be within or without the "camp."

[348] It was noted above that nothing is said explicitly about touching or being touched by a זָבָה in Lev 15. The comment that she should not mingle (תתערב), is difficult to interpret. Qimron suggests that it refers to intercourse (cf. J. Baumgarten 1999a [*DJD* 35], 102, n.2), but this is unlikely. (Cf. Milgrom's evidence for the term belonging to a ritual context in all Qumran occurrences except for one doubtful attestation; Milgrom 1995, 63). It is not clear whether the mingling is thought to be with impure or clean people.

[349] I follow the reconstruction of J. Baumgarten in *DJD* 35, 100–101, which reads בשבעת ימי טה̊[רתו א]ל יוכל (during the seven days of [his] purifi[cation shall no]t eat), rather than that of Milgrom 1995, 59f), which reads טה̊[רתם], (during the seven days of [their] purif[ication…). According to Milgrom's reading, the impure persons are the purifying people previously mentioned, which makes the text switch to speak about pure people touching purifying persons. This leads to problems in understanding the text. Milgrom furthermore follows Milik's restoration of line 8: ואם [תצא ממנו ש]כבת הזרע מגעו יטמא (and if he has an emission of semen, his touch transmits impurity), which makes the text say that the purifying man defiles by touch, when he has emitted semen. The implication, as Milgrom points out, is

pretation,[350] the last line (9) can be taken as summarizing the preceding rulings, thus referring to any of the previously mentioned purifying persons, male or female (line 7: אם זכר ואם נקבה). Bathing and washing (clothes) is a common requirement for all, regardless of the type of impurity bearer who has been touched. The equalizing tendency is further underscored when the translation of García Martínez is followed in lines 7–8:

> ... for behold, the blood of menstruation is considered like a discharge [for] him who touches it. And whoever [has an em]ission of semen contaminates through contact.[351]

The point seems to be that since discharges and menstrual blood are equally impure, contact with a menstruant should be avoided to the same extent as contact with a *zab*. And, adds the text, this applies to the semen-emitter as well. If the whole passage is not to be taken as a jumbled hotch-potch of unconnected instructions, the underlying premise must be understood: no distinction is being made between touching or being touched; all types of purifying persons are to avoid physical contact with any kind of impurity bearer, since they contaminate in basically the same way.

Equalization and leniency in rabbinic interpretation

In rabbinic interpretation, we can detect a wish to limit contamination, especially with regard to persons. Objects underneath one with a flow, which could contaminate further persons, were limited to items used for sitting and lying. Since these were subjected to pressure, this became the crucial factor in what

---

that the touch of the purifying man is not defiling, unless he has had a semen emission, which is strangely more lenient than Scripture (66–67). Baumgarten's reconstruction (*DJD* 35, 101ff) is more natural and removes the problem. By reading מאיש instead of ממנו, the semen-emitter is not the purifying man, but any man: "And when [a man has] an emiss[ion] of semen his touch is defiling" (Baumgarten 1994, 277). (That the semen-emitter is introduced separately could be explained by the fact that he was not expelled from the ordinary city, since his impurity was not regarded as serious as that of other genital dischargers. See the discussion below about 11Q19 [11QT] 46:16–18 and 48:14–17.) This fits the general tenor of the passage better, since the point is to warn purifying persons about contracting added impurity. When this point is borne in mind, the end of line 7 should not be misinterpreted as a concession. Milgrom's restoration of lines 8 and 9 has led Harrington (1993, 85–86) to misunderstand the whole passage. She understands line 7 to mean that purifying persons can actually touch a menstruant when she is clean (i.e. they can touch a clean person), without contaminating her. Accepting Milgrom's translation of lines 8 and 9, she concludes that "the Scrolls distinguish between one who touches the purifying person and one whom the purifying person touches: the former is made impure, the latter is not" (86). She admits that the difference is difficult to explain. No explanation is needed, however, since another reconstruction and interpretation is more reasonable. The text is not concerned about such differences, but with warning purifying persons about contracting further impurity.

[350] Cf. the discussion in the previous note.

[351] *DSSSE*. García Martínez reconstructs יחשב נוגע בו rather than J. Baumgarten's ואשר נוגע בו, which improves syntax and meaning considerably.

was called *midras* impurity. All other items (possible to immerse in a *miqveh*), came to be subject to the rabbinic concept of *maddaf* impurity, which was a kind of "overshadowing," which did not contaminate persons.[352] According to Neusner, these two types of uncleanness were contrasted with each other by a kind of logical reasoning.[353] As the concept of *midras* was taken for granted in discussions attributed to the Houses,[354] it may have originated before 70 CE. Neusner even conceives of its origins before the turn of the first century, and regards the idea of *maddaf* just as old, since it is correlated with *midras*.[355] This is possible, but difficult to prove. Since these concepts are not crucial to the arguments of the present study, they will not be further examined here, but it should be noted that they had the effect of limiting the transfer of impurity from genital dischargers to other persons.

The tendency not only to define, but to limit impurity, is strengthened in the period after the destruction of the temple, when purification became more difficult. An example is found in *mZab* 2:2, where seven possible "excuses" for a discharge are mentioned, which could be used to avoid being confirmed as a *zab*. These have to do with what he had eaten, drunk or carried, whether he had jumped or been ill, and what he had seen or fantasized. In the discussion, R. Aqiba appears with the most lenient of all suggestions:

> R. Aqiba says, "Even if he had eaten any sort of food, whether bad or good, or drunk any sort of liquid."
> They said to him, "Henceforth, there will be no *Zabim*."
> He said to them, "Responsibility for *Zabim* is not yours!"

A similar discussion is found in *mNid* 8:1–3. A woman who sees a bloodstain "blames it on any thing on which she can blame it" to avoid the *zabah* status. If she killed a louse, she may blame it on it. According to R. Hanina b. Antigonos, she may blame it on the louse even if she did not kill it. And R. Aqiba appears here too:

> One woman came before R. Aqiba. She said to him, "I have seen a bloodstain."
> He said to her, "Perhaps there was a wound on you?"
> She said to him, "Yes, but it has healed."
> He said to her, "Perhaps it can open and bleed?"
> She said to him, "Yes."
> And R. Aqiba declared her clean.
> His disciples did he see staring at one another. He said to them, "Why is this matter hard in your eyes? For the sages stated the rule not to produce a strict ruling but to produce a

[352] Harrington 1993, 239–253; Maccoby 1999, 50–53; Neusner 1974–1977, 22: 55, 63–71.

[353] On the basis of Lev 15:10, Neusner presents the underlying reasoning thus (1974–1977, 22: 69): "(1) What is unclean beneath the Zab is not unclean above him. (2) Then: What is not unclean beneath the Zab *is* unclean above him. Objects not used for sitting and lying, food and drink (2) are unclean above, because they (1) are clean below, the Zab. Thus: Objects used for sitting and lying are clean above, because they are unclean below, the Zab."

[354] E.g. *mKel* 20:2; 26:6; *mNid* 10:8.

[355] Neusner 1974–1977, 22: 55, 71.

lenient ruling, as it is said, *And if a woman have an issue and her issue in her flesh be blood* (Lev. 15:19)—blood and not a stain."

Nothing similar to this can be found in Qumran. *Zab* impurity is associated with death, and the *zab* is listed in a catalogue of transgressors.[356] While rabbinic *halakhah* waives his symptoms on grounds of erotic fantasizing, without moralizing, some Qumran fragments associate the *zab* with sinful thoughts.[357]

Since an equalizing tendency can be traced in both rabbinic and Qumran material, it is reasonable to consider this a trait of the Second Temple Period. The *zab* and the *zabah* must have been generally considered to contaminate by physical contact, and required to purify by bathing, washing of clothes and sacrifice. This probably applied to the menstruant and the *yoledet* as well, although the menstruant is never required to sacrifice and the *yoledet* is not discussed in Qumran literature. The tendency towards leniency, found in some rabbinic materials, gained in strength after the destruction of the temple, but probably had roots in the preceding period. The relative strictness in Qumran, and the negative evaluation of the *zab* displayed there, could imply that a strict attitude to genital dischargers was still fairly common at the end of the Second Temple period. To evaluate such a proposal, it is necessary to discuss whether people with discharges were expelled or isolated during the first century CE.

Exclusion and isolation at the time of Jesus

According to Josephus in *Ant.* 3:261, people suffering from discharges were banished from the city by Moses:

> Ἀπήλασε δὲ τῆς πόλεως καὶ τοὺς λέπρᾳ τὰ σώματα κακωθέντας καὶ τοὺς περὶ τὴν γονὴν ῥεομένους· καὶ τὰς γυναῖκας δ᾽ αἷς ἡ τῶν κατὰ φύσιν ἔκκρισις ἐπίοι μετέστησε πρὸς ἡμέραν ἑβδόμην, μεθ᾽ ἣν ὡς ἤδη καθαραῖς ἐνδημεῖν ἐφίησιν.[358]

Josephus' descriptions of purity rules are sometimes played down as ideal, or as reflecting the time of Moses, rather than his own.[359] We have already seen that such a reasoning with regard to *Ag.Ap.* 1:281–282 is to be doubted. This is the case here as well. The description neither agrees with Lev 15, nor with Num 5 in every detail. It is much more likely that it represents first-century practice. According to Josephus, "lepers" and dischargers were expelled (ἀπήλασε δὲ)

[356] 4Q274 1 1:8–9; 4Q278: 7; 4Q270 2 2; cf. J. Baumgarten 1999a [*DJD* 35], 84–87.

[357] 4Q266 6 1:15; 4Q272 1 2:4. It should be noted, however, that there are signs in later rabbinic literature that dischargers were associated with sinful behaviour. In *Num. Rab.* 7:10 discharge is associated with immorality, and in *Num. Rab.* 7:1 and *Lev. Rab.* 18:4 (cf. Neusner 1973a), discharge is explicitly said to result from the crime of calf-worship.

[358] "He banished from the city alike those whose bodies were afflicted with leprosy and those with contagious disease [genital discharges]. Women too, when beset by their natural secretions, he secluded until the seventh day, after which they were permitted, as now pure, to return to society."

[359] Maccoby 1999, 36; Sanders 1990, 160.

from the city. Thus far, his description is in accord with Num 5. But the dischargers expelled must be interpreted as the *zab* and the *zabah*. Menstruants, however, seem to have been isolated (μετέστησε). This interpretation is supported by another passage in *J.W.* 5:227: "γονορροίοις μὲν δὴ καὶ λεπροῖς ἡ πόλις ὅλη, τὸ δ' ἱερὸν γυναικῶν ἐμμήνοις ἀπεκέκλειστο,"[360] and fits with a comment in *Ag.Ap.* 2:103 (only preserved in Latin): "In exteriorem itaque ingredi licebat omnibus etiam alienigenis; mulieres tantummodo menstruatae transire prohibebantur."[361]

The passage from *Antiquities* about the seclusion of menstruants is followed by a comparison with corpse-impure people: "ὁμοίως δὲ καὶ τοῖς κηδεύσασι νεκρὸν μετὰ τοσαύτας ἡμέρας νόμιμον τὸ ἐνδημεῖν."[362] The most natural reading is that the corpse-impure are compared to menstruants, in that they must submit to some kind of quarantine or restrictions. This is, however, not according to Num 5, which requires that they be expelled from the "camp" altogether. Thus we find good reasons for taking Josephus' accounts as reflections of first-century purity practices, rather than ideal scenes or attempts to reconstruct biblical practice.

It is apparent that Josephus interprets "the camp" of Num 5:1–4 as "the city" of his own time, and that, at least in *J.W.* 5:227, it is a matter of the temple city. It is reasonable to assume that this is the case in *Ant.* 3:261 too, as the singular form of "city" is used. What other evidence is there for genital dischargers being excluded from Jerusalem during Second Temple times?

According to the *Temple Scroll* (11Q19 46:16–18), severe impurity bearers should be excluded from the temple city: "You shall make three places, to the East of the city, separate from each other, to which shall come the lepers and those afflicted with a discharge and the men who have an emission of semen." The context is one of increasing the purity of the temple, which includes a trench, 100 cubits wide (!), to separate the temple from the city. Apparently these rules reflect a dissatisfaction with the way the contemporary temple authorities guarded the holiness of the sanctuary. In rabbinic *halakhah* (*mKel* 1:6–9) we find a description of spheres of ascending holiness. They are, the land of Israel, the cities surrounded by a wall, within the wall of Jerusalem, the Temple Mount, the rampart, the three courts of the temple, the area between the porch and the altar, and finally the sanctuary, with the Holy of Holies. As for the Temple Mount it was ruled (1:8): "The Temple mount is more holy than it. For

---

360 "Persons afflicted with gonorrhoea or leprosy were excluded from the city altogether; the temple was closed to women during their menstruation..." Thackeray's translation does not emphasize the μὲν ... δέ structure of the Greek text. While dischargers and "lepers" were excluded from the city, menstruants were excluded only from the temple.

361 "The outer court was open to all, foreigners included; women during their impurity were alone refused admission." (LCL).

362 "A like rule applies to those who have paid the last rites to the dead: after the same number of days they may rejoin their fellows." *Ant.* 3:262.

Zabim, and *Zabot*, menstruating women, and those that have given birth do not enter there." The rabbinic and the sectarian standpoints actually agree more than is apparent at first sight; they both exclude genital dischargers from an area close to the temple. The difference is that the sectarians moved the dischargers one zone further out, at least in their wishes. The Temple Mount actually comprised a good part of Jerusalem. The sectarians in Qumran wanted to make a clear demarcation between the temple and the city, and expel dischargers from Jerusalem altogether. Only after the seven days of purification could a former discharger enter the temple city again.[363] We must expect that there were actually real and serious dissensions at the end of the Second Temple period, about whether or not genital dischargers should be allowed in Jerusalem. An expansionist viewpoint could find support in Num 5 for banishing dischargers altogether, and according to Josephus they seem to have had the upper hand, at least at times, and at least in the case of the *zab* and the *zabah*.

When we turn to the status of genital dischargers in other cities, things become more difficult. *mKel* 1:7–8 implies that they were allowed within the city, while "lepers" were expelled. The sectarians, however, were of a different opinion. According to 11Q19 [11QT] 48:14–17, dischargers were somehow to be isolated as well.

ובכול עיר ועיר תעשו מקומות למנוגעים בצרעת ובנגע ובנתק
אשר לוא יבואו לעריכמה וטמאום
וגם לזבים ולנשים בהיותמה בנדת טמאתמה ובלדתמה
אשר לוא יטמאו בתוכם בנדת טמאתם

> And in every city you shall make places for those contaminated with leprosy, and with sores and with scabies
> so that they do not enter your cities and defile them;
> and also for those who have a flux and for women when they are in their menstrual impurity and after giving birth,
> so that they do not defile in their midst with their menstrual impurity.

Careful attention should be paid to the construction of this passage, and its relationship to 11Q19 [11QT] 46:16–18. Whereas three categories of impurity bearers were to be excluded from the temple city, only two are mentioned in the context of the ordinary city. The semen-emitter, who in Qumran was considered to be unclean for three days, is not mentioned here. He was to be expelled from the temple city, in analogy with the soldiers of the Deuteronomic war camp (Deut 23:10).[364] In the ordinary city, he could remain, probably, as Milgrom has pointed out, due to an extra ablution required on the first day. For

---

[363] 11Q19 [11QT] 45:15–17: "Every man who purifies himself from his discharge shall count for himself seven days for his purification. And he shall wash on the seventh day his clothes and bathe his body completely in living water. Afterwards he shall enter the city of the temple."

[364] Harrington 1993, 91. The three-day impurity of semen-emitters was explained by Yadin (1983 [1977], 1: 285–288) as modelled after the encampment at Mt. Sinai, where the Israelites were to refrain from sexual activities for three days (Ex 19:10–15). Cf. Milgrom 1989, 174f.

entrance into the temple city, which was considered more holy, this first-day ablution was not enough.[365] The two categories not allowed in ordinary cities are "lepers" and genital dischargers. "Lepers" are definitely understood to be isolated *outside* the city, in spite of the preposition ב in בכול עיר, since the purpose of their isolation is explicitly to prevent them from *entering the cities* (אשר לוא יבואו לעריכמה וטמאום). The dischargers were to be treated in a similar way (גם ל־), and the purpose of their isolation was to prevent them from *defiling in their midst* (אשר לוא יטמאו בתוכם). The dischargers are defined as זבים (assumed to include both male and female dischargers), menstruants and parturients. נדת טמאתם can be understood generally as "defilement of their impurity," thus referring to the dischargers as a group, rather than to the menstruants only.[366] According to the most natural reading, all genital dischargers (except semen-emitters) are supposed to be isolated *outside* the cities. This is to be taken as an ideal, and it is impossible to judge whether this was actually applied anywhere during the Second Temple period. The 4Q274 fragment discussed above, with its detailed casuistry, suggests that this might actually have been the case, but it is difficult to believe that such a practice could have been common, except in the society/ies of the sectarians. Since the Qumran (visionary) rulings about the Temple city moved impurity "one step back," as compared with rabbinic *halakhah*, we should expect something similar when it comes to ordinary cities. We cannot be sure what this meant in detail. According to Josephus, dischargers (τοὺς περὶ τὴν γονὴν ῥεομένους, i.e. זָבִם) were expelled from Jerusalem, while menstruants were isolated within the city. For other cities we should expect diverging practices, depending on the degree of influence from expansionist ideals. It is reasonable to think that all genital dischargers were allowed in ordinary cities, but kept in some sort of isolation or, in the most lenient cases, surrounded by certain restrictions. We should thus expect the menstruant, and even more the *zabah*, to have been restricted, and probably kept in some sort of seclusion.

Sanders has questioned that menstruants were isolated, doubting that even priests in general tried to avoid contracting impurity from their wives. He argues mainly from practical reasons, claiming that adherence to such rules was possible only for Josephus and his class.[367] We must note, however,

> the virtually uniform practice of exotic and sectarian Jewish communities, particularly in regard to the quarantine imposed on parturients and menstruants. They comprise the following: Arabians..., Kurdistanis..., Samaritans and Karaites..., Falashas..., the sect reflected in *Baraita De masseket Niddah*..., and the sectaries of Qumran.[368]

---

[365] Milgrom 1991, 968–971. Cf. below, 187f.

[366] For the ambiguous use of נִדָּה, see above, 128f, n.218. The construction of the text makes it likely that "lepers" are depicted as separated from dischargers, but that all dischargers (except semen-emitters) were to be isolated together in one place.

[367] Sanders 1990, 160, 233.

[368] Milgrom 1991, 765, referring to Kister and Kister, Rivlin, Eshkoli, Epstein and Horowitz.

Practical considerations were apparently no hindrance.[369] While the *Baraita De masseket Niddah* is a late document from Gaonic times, advocating restrictions which are refuted by the *Babylonian Talmud*,[370] the strict rules of several sectarian communities may reflect earlier Palestinian conditions. *mNid* 7:4 mentions a house for impure [women], בֵּית הַטְּמֵאוֹת, which was apparently misinterpreted by the *Tosefta* as a place for ablutions, i.e. a *miqveh*, since the practice had ceased.[371] Even without separate houses or rooms, it is likely that *some sort of* quarantine was practised not only by the Qumran sectarians, but also among other expansionists during the end of the Second Temple period. Sanders exaggerates in claiming that keeping purity rules literally in a house where a menstruant was living should have made people starve.[372] Immersion, the concept of *tebul yom* and the use of stone vessels,[373] made a high level of purity possible, even in a home where a genital discharger lived.[374] The evidence of *Pss.Sol.* 8:12 and CD 5:6–7, mentioned by Sanders, in which expansionists accuse the priests of bringing menstrual blood into the sanctuary, or lying with a menstruant, is to be explained either as polemical blackmailing, or as reflecting dissensions about how to count days.[375] To take such accusations literally would imply a laxity unknown in any other sources. We must accept that quarantine-like restrictions were common for genital dischargers during the first century CE. It is also probable that the *zab* and the *zabah* were excluded from

369 It must be emphasized that menstruation was not as common in ancient times as in modern. Sanders falls victim of what he accuses others of, namely lack of imagination and a sense of what is practically possible. Quarantine rules would not upset every household one week a month (cf. Sanders 1990, 160f). Most women were pregnant or breast-feeding during the major part of their fertile period (Milgrom 1991, 953; Wenham 1979, 223–4).

370 E.g. a menstruant is forbidden to do much of the normal household work, and her husbund must not greet her or look at her. According to *bKetub* 61a, she may do all types of household work, except filling her husband's cup of wine, making his bed and washing him. Cf. Milgrom 1991, 949.

371 *tNid* 6:15 (בית המרחץ). The reading בית הטמאות (i.e. house of the impure [women]) is found in the best manuscripts (Kaufmann and Parma), and should be read בֵּית הַטְּמֵאוֹת, as in Codex Kaufmann (Parma is unvowelized here), rather than the common בֵּית הַטְּמְאוֹת (i.e. house of impurities), understood as a deficient reading for הַטּוּמְאוֹת (cf. the bT, ed. princ. Venezia 1520–1523, which reads הטומאת; Barslai 1980, 178). Harrington (1993, 271) opts for the reading of codex Kaufmann, but argues that even if the *Mishnah* read בֵּית הַטְּמְאוֹת, the expression would in any case refer to a place for segregating impure persons. The context is one of impure women, since the Samaritans are accused of burying their abortions in this place. This shows, furthermore, that the *Tosefta* has misinterpreted the matter, since the idea of burying abortions in a *miqveh* is somewhat odd. Sanders (1990, 156) accepts the interpretation of the *Tosefta*, but reads the expression as a public "women's bathhouse," rather than a *miqveh,* and thus explains the context differently. The idea of burying abortions in or around a public bathhouse is quite unlikely, however, even as anti-Samaritan propaganda.

372 Sanders 1990, 149.

373 Cf. above, 74–78, 84f..

374 Cf. J. Baumgarten's criticism of Sanders in *DJD* 35, 80.

375 Sanders 1990, 42 (8.14 is a misprint for 8.12); cf. 213.

Jerusalem, and that their presence in other towns was at least questioned by the expansionist current.

The bleeding woman and contamination by touch

From the discussion above, we find that several traits in Mk 5:25–34 are plausible. A *zabah* in a Jewish town during the first century CE might have been allowed to move about, but if so, she was surrounded by certain restrictions. There was probably some discrepancy between the actual behaviour of a *zabah* and that which was expected by the expansionist current. The action of the woman in Mark's narrative, would not, in any case, be acceptable.

It is possible, however, to see a crux in the fact that the woman is said to have touched Jesus' cloak (ἱμάτιον) and not his body. In Matthew and Luke, the object of touch is even said to be the fringe or tassel of the cloak (τοῦ κρασπέδου τοῦ ἱματίου αὐτοῦ). This is one of the instances in which Matthew and Luke agree against Mark in a way which is embarrassing for the two-source hypothesis. The agreement on this variant is easily explained from Mark, however, since the exact phrase (τοῦ κρασπέδου τοῦ ἱματίου αὐτοῦ) is used somewhat later, in the redactional summary in Mk 6:56. There is no evidence at all for the conclusion of Koet, that Jesus according to Matthew and Luke becomes impure to a lesser degree than in Mark, since the woman is said to touch only the *edge* of his cloak.[376] The effect of this variant is, just as in Mk 6:56, to emphasize the power of Jesus and enhance the magical flavour.

There is an uncertainty, however, about how defilement via clothes was thought to function, and the issue is strangely enough addressed directly neither by rabbinic texts, nor by modern commentators, except for a few remarks.[377] The silence of the former can be explained by some matters taken for granted, but that would give more reason for the latter to discuss it. As seen above, Milgrom and Wright differ in their interpretations of the biblical text (Lev 15:7), Milgrom taking "flesh" literally, while Wright considers clothes as an extension of a person's body.[378] The discussion concerns the case of a clean person touching the clothes of a *zab*. The reverse situation (i.e. a discharging person touching the clothes of a clean person) is never discussed.

We have seen that regulations concerning bodily discharges were "equalized" in the period of the Second Temple, so that touching or being touched was regarded all the same. When it comes to the touching of clothes, however, simple equalizing can be questioned and the issue must be discussed. In this case, our only source of information is rabbinic material.

---

[376] Koet 2000, 100.
[377] See above, 144. Cf. Harrington's comment in a discussion, in Sawyer 1996, 274.
[378] Milgrom 1991, 914, 935; David P. Wright 1987, 182f, n.34. Cf. above, 144.

It should be noted that clothes in the mishnaic system were regarded as rinsable vessels, thus subject to first-degree impurity.[379] Clothes touched by a discharger, or by a person in contact with a discharger, would contaminate food, liquid[380] and hands in the second degree. The clothes of the discharging person, would be unclean at least in the first degree, and contaminate food, liquid and hands. The least we can say is that, according to the rabbinic system, a clean person who touches the clothes of a discharger will have the hands contaminated in the second degree, and the discharger who touches a clean person's clothes will contaminate them in the first degree, thus contaminating the clean person's hands in the second degree. In the mishnaic system, however, it seems to be presupposed that clothes are subject to *midras* impurity, since they are used for sitting and lying.[381] The clothes of a discharging person would thus function as a "father," and contaminate people by contact in the first degree. The suggestion of Wright, that the clothes of a discharger are regarded unclean like a bed, because of pressure, thus contaminating like the body itself, would be true for the rabbinic system, even if its validity during the biblical period could be doubted.[382]

This is, however, a somewhat theoretical exercise, and there are reasons to think that even a discharger touching the clothes of a clean person would be seen as transmitting something like a first-degree impurity during the Second Temple period. Although a basic notion of removes seems to have been present, we should not expect a fixed and complete mishnaic system of degrees during the first century CE. Even Neusner, who otherwise sees most of the system of degrees as developing after 70 CE, regards the effect of the *zab* on clothing an exception.[383] The formulation of *mZab* 3:1 might reveal an underlying assumption:

> The *Zab* and the clean person who sat in a ship or on a raft,
> or who rode [together] on a beast,
> even though their clothes do not touch—
> lo, these are unclean with *midras* uncleanness.

---

[379] Cf. *mZab* 5:1. A person in contact with a discharger is defined as one who "imparts uncleanness to clothes," i.e. he is temporarily, through contact with the discharger, functioning as a "father," contaminating vessels, food and liquid in the first degree. "After he separates...," however, "he does not impart uncleanness to clothes."

[380] But because of the susceptibility of liquids, they would always become unclean in the first degree anyway.

[381] Harrington 1993, 242.

[382] David P. Wright 1987, 182f, n.34; cf. Neusner 1974–1977, 18: 179. Cf. *mOha* 1:5. For analogous reasonings in the *Mishnah*, cf. *mKel* 19:5. A bed unclean with a particular type of uncleanness contaminates a bed girth, which is wrapped around it, with the same degree of uncleanness, as long as it is in contact. As soon as it is removed, however, the bed girth's uncleanness becomes one degree less.

[383] Neusner 1974–1977, 22: 189f.

The third line above seems to imply that *ordinarily,* people were considered to be touching each other *if their clothes were in contact*. Arguments against such a view could possibly be taken from the *Sifra*, where the "flesh" of Lev 15:7 is thus explained:

> *The flesh of the Zab*, and not the excrement which is on him, and not the entangled hair which is on him, and not the chains, and not the finger-rings and not the ear-rings, even though they do not stick out [but are imbedded in the flesh]. Or might [I think that] I should encompass the hair and the fingernails? Scripture says, *It is unclean.*[384]

Hair and fingernails are apparently regarded as connected to the body, thus sharing the impurity of the person.[385] Chains or rings are not. The "flesh" of the *zab* is emphasized, but nothing is said explicitly of his clothes. We have seen, however, that the clothes of a discharger could be seen to share the same degree of impurity as the person, due to *midras*. This would not apply to jewellery or other "excrements," since they were not used for sitting or lying.

Another discussion in the *Tosefta* may be relevant. The assumption is that the *zab* transmits impurity even if he moves only part of a clean person, while a clean person will not acquire impurity unless he moves the greater part of a *zab*.[386]

ציציתו של טמא על גבי טהור טהור
ציציתו של טהות על גבי טמא טמא

> [If] the hair of the unclean person is on the clean person, he is clean.
> [If] the hair of the clean person is on the unclean person, he is unclean.[387]

The passage continues with a discussion about the hair of one person being on the hair of another. What is interesting for our purpose is the interpretation of hair (צִיצִית) as "fringe" or tassels.[388] Since צִיצִית is actually used as a technical term for fringes or tassels, traditionally worn on the outer garment,[389] the passage from the *Tosefta* could be interpreted to mean that even the fringe of a clean person's garment, coming into contact with a genital discharger, would be sufficient for the clean to become contaminated by the unclean, while the reverse would not be the case, i.e. a clean person would not become contaminated by merely touching the fringe of an unclean person's clothes.[390] The argument

[384] Transl. in Neusner 1974–1977, 18: 108.
[385] Cf. *Sifra* to Lev 15:7 [Parashat Zabim Pereq 3]; cf. *tZab* 5:2.
[386] Neusner 1974–1977, 18: 84.
[387] *tZab* 4:3, tr. Neusner 1974–1977, 18:84 (explanatory glosses excluded).
[388] The interpretation of R. Elia Wilna (Rengstorf 1960–1967:3, 200, n. 28). Cf. Neusner 1974–1977, 18: 84, with support from Lieberman 1999 [1939], 129f.
[389] This use of the term is attested already in the biblical period. Cf. Num 15:48, the classical passage appealed to for this practice. The ambiguous meaning is present in Aramaic too.
[390] The underlying rabbinic logic of the role of movement and weight in transferring impurity will not be discussed here. Cf. Neusner 1974–1977, 18:84f; Rengstorf 1960–1967:3, 200f; Liebermann 1999 [1939], 129f.

would thus refer to accidental contacts via clothes. This is a much more likely issue for rabbinic discussion than the idea of contact via hair.

While this interpretation is reasonable, we would have to regard conclusions from a few rabbinic texts for our Markan tradition as somewhat speculative. It seems, however, that the idea of impurity being conveyed by physical contact via the clothes was presupposed in Tannaitic times. Since we find an increasing tendency in rabbinic legislation to leniency, especially restricting the transmission of impurity to persons,[391] as well as an increasing development of the concept of degrees, we should expect a simpler and undifferentiated idea of contamination via clothes to have been present at the end of the Second Temple period. We cannot argue from the mishnaic system that the physical contact described in Mk 5:25–34 was of little or no significance, resulting in only a minor defilement. The Markan tradition rather attests to the state of development of impurity laws.

Jesus and discharges

We have found that purity was an issue in the Markan tradition about Jesus and the bleeding woman (although not exploited at the level of final redaction), and that Jesus was remembered as coming into contact with people impure from bodily discharges. We have furthermore seen that a *zabah* would normally have been subject to serious restrictions, even in ordinary towns, outside of Jerusalem, at least in areas where expansionist norms dominated. The reactions of Jesus towards the *zabah* in the Markan tradition, as well as to the woman with a probable but unidentified impurity in the Lukan tradition, signal an attitude which does not worry about the defilement. While the exact mechanisms of contamination in Mk 5:25–34 remain somewhat uncertain, the most plausible suggestion is that dischargers at this time were considered to convey impurity by touch, via the clothes. All attempts to downplay or deny the transfer of impurity have been unconvincing. It is difficult to avoid the conclusion that Jesus' relative indifference to impurity from genital discharges was inherent in early tradition.

IV.4 The corpse

The nature of corpse-impurity

The corpse is the third main source of impurity to be discussed. It was regarded as the "father of fathers of impurity"[392] in the rabbinic system, since it con-

---

[391] Cf. above, 154–156.

[392] אֲבִי אָבוֹת הַטּוּמְאָה.

taminated persons and vessels with a seven-day impurity, not only by touch, but even by overshadowing. Corpse-impure persons or vessels were thus themselves regarded as "fathers," in one sense on a par with "lepers" and genital dischargers.[393] In another sense, however, corpse-impurity should rather be likened to menstrual impurity, since both are temporary states, and the counting of days begins as soon as the impurity is acquired, or at least after a first-day initial ablution.[394] The relevance of this observation will be explored further below.[395]

It is possible to see an analogy between the way the corpse functions towards persons and things, and the way genital discharges can be thought to have contaminated. As seen in the previous section, the independent contaminating power of the discharges themselves, explicitly attested in Samaritan *halakhah*, is probably to be assumed behind some biblical texts.[396] This explains what could otherwise be regarded as an anomaly, i.e. that an item beneath a discharger (i.e. seat, bed, clothes) is contaminated with a seven-day impurity and thus itself becomes a "father" of impurity, just like the discharging person. Both items and persons could be seen as equal, however, in that they are similarly contaminated by contact with flux or blood, and thus the discharge itself functions as a "father of fathers," in relation to genital dischargers and their beds and seats. This would then be analogous to the contaminating function of the corpse, which renders persons and vessels unclean as "fathers" of impurity (i.e. being unclean for seven days, rendering other persons and vessels unclean for one day). Such a comparative explanation is perhaps somewhat anachronistic, since "father" is a rabbinic concept, and flux or blood no longer has this independent effect in the rabbinic system. Only the corpse remains as the most serious source of impurity.

Biblical legislation about corpse-impurity is found not in Leviticus, but in Numbers (Num 5:1–4; 19:11–22; 31:19–24). The main passage in Num 19 is centred on the red cow rite (19:2–10), and the focus is on the mode of purifica-

[393] *mKel* 1:1–4. The corpse itself is called simply מֵת, both in biblical Hebrew and in rabbinic literature. To make it clear beyond doubt what is meant, Num 19:13 defines מֵת with a circumscription: נֶפֶשׁ הָאָדָם אֲשֶׁר־יָמוּת. The technical term for corpse-impurity in the *Mishnah* is טְמֵא מֵת (e.g. *mKel* 1:1).

[394] For a discussion of the evidence for a first-day ablution at the end of the Second Temple period, see below, 185–189. (Cf. 11Q19 [11QT] 49:16–21; *Spec.Laws* 3:206). Cf. the Samaritan view about the necessity to wash off the initial menstrual blood before the counting of days could begin. See above, Excursus 1a, 144–146.

[395] It seems as if corpse-impurity during the Second Temple period was, *in practice*, treated as a somewhat milder type of impurity, like menstruation, and that corpse-impure people, like menstruants, were not generally expelled from cities, not even from Jerusalem, in contrast to the *zab* and the *zabah*. See above, 156–161, and below, 187–189. This leniency could be explained by both menstruation and death being natural and necessary parts of the life-cycle. Neither menstruants nor the corpse-impure are required to offer a sacrifice after their seven-day period of impurity. Cf. Milgrom 1981, 70ff, esp. n.25.

[396] See above, 144–146.

tion (19:17–22). The insertion of this legislation in Numbers, rather than in Leviticus, could point to a different development or a later origin than the types of impurity discussed in Lev 12–15.[397] At first sight the rules are quite straightforward. Touching a corpse renders a person impure for seven days (19:11). The same applies to the person touching a human bone or a grave (19:16). Within the tent where the corpse is lying, a seven-day impurity is transferred to people and open vessels with no physical contact, i.e. by their mere presence within the same enclosed space as the dead body (19:14–15). Failure to purify is seen as a severe matter; the neglecting person is to be expelled from Israel / the congregation (וְנִכְרְתָה הַנֶּפֶשׁ הַהִוא מִיִּשְׂרָאֵל / מִתּוֹךְ הַקָּהָל; 19:13, 20).[398]

The seemingly plain text gave occasion for numerous later discussions and definitions, and even during biblical times different practices concerning corpse-impurity can be traced. Some of these variations will be dealt with below, but some are of little importance in investigating the attitude of Jesus, and will be passed over briefly. It is clear, however, that the "tent" (אֹהֶל) of Num 19:14 was generally interpreted as "house." This is apparent from the text of the *Temple Scroll* (11Q19 [11QT] 49:5–19), in which the biblical legislation is partly paraphrased, and "tent" exchanged for בית, as well as from the LXX, where it is consistently translated with οἰκία.[399] The rabbinic discussions in the mishnaic tractate *Ohalot* take the equation of "tent" with "house" for granted.[400] Without going into a discussion about which types of overhang were defined as "tents" and by whom, or how corpse-impurity was thought to exude from openings of a certain size, or could be hindered by particular barriers or cavities, we can initially work from the understanding that any person touching a corpse or being present in the same room as a dead body, was regarded as contaminated with a seven-day impurity. The same applied to anyone who had come into contact with a human bone or a grave, i.e. walked across a burial field. This was true in general throughout the Second Temple period; not just for certain groups at particular times. Further evidence will be discussed below, but the initial understanding suffices for surveying the Jesus tradition. Was Jesus remembered as incurring corpse-impurity by coming into contact with, or being present in the same room, as dead bodies? What traces of such behaviour can be found, and what conclusions can be drawn? Was corpse-impurity actually regarded as something that *ought* to be avoided?

---

[397] Milgrom 1981, 70ff; Milgrom 1990b, 43. B. Levine 1993, 102–106, argues that all legal material in Numbers has been adapted and modulated by the priestly school, which worked over a long period of time. Some of the essential content of P should be seen as of early postexilic provenance, expressing postexilic institutions.

[398] For a discussion about the *karet* penalty, see Milgrom 1990b, 405–408.

[399] In Num 19:18 (LXX) οἶκος is used.

[400] It is clear from e.g. *mOha* 3:7 that "tent" was understood by the Rabbis as an enclosed space in principle. This, and numerous other passages in *Ohalot*, explicitly discuss houses.

A purity issue in resurrection stories?

Several gospel narratives report the raising of dead people, but some hardly come into consideration when discussing corpse-impurity. The story of Lazarus in Jn 11:1–44 has certain affinities with the raising of the daughter of Jairus in Mk 5, in that some standard motifs recur:[401] the delay of the miracle-worker[402] and death being described as a "sleep,"[403] as well as the injunction to believe,[404] and the resistance from the crowd.[405] In the Johannine story, however, Jesus neither enters the grave, nor does he touch the dead body. His behaviour is rather lofty and authoritative. It would be a serious mistake to "invert" the argument, claiming that Jesus hence is pictured as respecting purity regulations by not coming into contact with the corpse. The narrative has a strong christological intent, and neither explicit nor implicit purity connotations are to be found.

Likewise, there is no purity issue in the Lukan stories about resurrections in Acts 9:36–43 and 20:8–12. Here the narrative context is outside Jewish lands. These stories belong to Luke's portrayal of Peter and Paul as true apostles, repeating the miracles of Jesus. Both narratives are stereotyped, containing standard ingredients (the complaining crowd, the public expelled, prayer, the healer embracing the deceased person).

When discussing Jesus' attitude to corpse-impurity, there are only two resurrection stories of importance: Lk 7:11–17 (the widow in Nain) and Mk 5:21–24, 35–43 with parallels (the daughter of Jairus). Before discussing these traditions in detail, however, a key question must be addressed. Are dead people present in gospel traditions, simply because they are needed for resurrection miracles, which are literary constructions only? Did the historical Jesus deal with dead people at all? If these traditions rest on pure fiction, or if they are original healing stories which later developed into resurrection stories, they could be dismissed in a discussion of Jesus' attitude to corpse-impurity. No purity issue would be present, since the narrative corpses were necessary only to produce resurrections. In discussions of resurrection stories, it has been pointed out that scholars have seen historical reminiscences behind healing miracles rather than behind nature miracles and resurrections. Discussions have been biased because of modern ideas about what is rationally possible. Such restrictions did not necessarily trouble the ancient mind, and cannot be regarded as a valid criterion for sorting out historical traces.[406] I do not discuss whether Jesus *actually* raised dead people or not. My question is whether he claimed to do it and/or

---

[401] Cf. Marcus 2000, 361f.

[402] Jn 11:6; but not so evident in Mk 5:35, see the discussion above, 130.

[403] καθεύδειν is used by Mark (5:39), while John uses κοιμᾶσθαι (11:11f).

[404] Mk 5:36; Jn 11:25ff. In John, faith is a matter of believing in the identity of Jesus as Christ and Son of God, while the focus in Mark is on believing in the power of the miracle-worker.

[405] Mk 5:40; in John the "resistance" is weaker, rather doubtful hesitance, Jn 11:37, 39.

[406] Cf. Pesch 1970b, 142.

whether people thought he did. If this was the case, he must have come into contact with people considered dead, i.e. corpses.

Jesus was apparently remembered as raising dead people. The injunction of Jesus to the disciples in Mt 10:8 (heal the sick, raise the dead, cleanse the "lepers," exorcize demons) is probably redactional. Matthew seems to shape the description of the disciples' mission to form a parallel to the previously narrated works of Jesus, and it cannot be treated as evidence for Jesus' activities. The section about Jesus' answer to the questions of the Baptizer (Mt 11:2–19/Lk 7:18–35), apparently from the Q source, contains material of greater importance. In responding to the doubting Baptizer, Jesus gives a list of miracles supposed to verify his identity (Mt 11:5/Lk 7:22):

> τυφλοὶ ἀναβλέπουσιν, χωλοὶ περιπατοῦσιν, λεπροὶ καθαρίζονται καὶ κωφοὶ ἀκούουσιν, νεκροὶ ἐγείρονται, πτωχοὶ εὐαγγελίζονται[407]
>
> Blind see again, lame walk, lepers are cleansed and deaf hear, dead are raised, poor are told good news.

There is no need to discuss the possibility of *ipsissima verba*. It is enough to regard these words as early Palestinian Christian testimony. As already pointed out, this is an allusion to texts from Isaiah (Isa 29:18–19; 35:5–6; and possibly 61:1). We have already seen that the "leper" was missing in the Isaianic material. This is also the case with the raising of dead people. An obvious explanation would be that, by adding "lepers" and dead to the Isaianic list, the author achieved a better match between the historical memories of Jesus and messianic expectations inspired by Isaiah. It is possible, however, that the description in Q does not go back directly to Isaiah, but to "primeval prophetic images of the Messianic age."[408] This idea is supported by a Qumran fragment of a messianic text (4Q521), which, in the context of the Messiah, includes poor, prisoners, blind, and dead among those whom the Lord will benefit.

> For the Lord will consider the pious, and call the righteous by name, and his spirit will hover upon the poor, and he will renew the faithful with his strength. For he will honour the pious upon the throne of an eternal kingdom, freeing prisoners, giving sight to the blind, straightening out the twis[ted.] … And the Lord will perform marvellous acts such as have not existed, just as he sa[id,] [for] he will heal the badly wounded and will make the dead live, he will proclaim good news to the poor …[409]

The text seems to allude to the same Isaianic passages as those mentioned above. The spirit which will hover upon the poor (ועל ענוים רוחו תרחף) is possibly reminiscent of Isa 61:1, and the dead made alive (ומתים יחיה) might allude to Isa 26:19 (יִחְיוּ מֵתֶיךָ). The list could thus correspond to some "standard" expectations for the messianic age. While the Q tradition in Mt 11:5/Lk

[407] Lk 7:22.
[408] Jeremias 1972 [1947], 116.
[409] 4Q521 (Messianic Apocalypse) 2 2:5–8, 11–12.

7:22 cannot be used as a simple list of *ipsissima facta* about the historical Jesus,[410] it is reasonable to expect some correspondence with historical memories. The list in the Q tradition is probably shaped by messianic ideals from Scripture and/or from apocalyptic interpretations, but it is independently formed, without imitating any known formula. The general healing and teaching activities of Jesus are commonly accepted as having an historical basis. There is no reason to doubt that he came into contact with dead people as well, in the course of his healing activity, just because raising the dead has eschatological and christological (messianic) connotations. Such hyper-critical conclusions would disqualify most of the Jesus tradition, since it is all permeated by christological intent in its present form. As will be seen below, there is at least one resurrection miracle narrative in which an underlying concern with concrete realities can be traced in spite of the christological and theological overlay.

The Markan tradition about Jairus' daughter

The most important gospel tradition for discussing Jesus' attitude to corpse-impurity is Mk 5:21–24, 35–43 par. Since the intercalation (vv 25–34) has been dealt with above, the present tradition is discussed as one unit.

> 21 καὶ διαπεράσαντος τοῦ Ἰησοῦ [ἐν τῷ πλοίῳ] πάλιν εἰς τὸ πέραν συνήχθη ὄχλος πολὺς ἐπ' αὐτόν, καὶ ἦν παρὰ τὴν θάλασσαν. 22 Καὶ ἔρχεται εἷς τῶν ἀρχισυναγώγων, ὀνόματι Ἰά□ρος, καὶ ἰδὼν αὐτὸν πίπτει πρὸς τοὺς πόδας αὐτοῦ
> 23 καὶ παρακαλεῖ αὐτὸν πολλὰ λέγων ὅτι τὸ θυγάτριόν μου ἐσχάτως ἔχει, ἵνα ἐλθὼν ἐπιθῇς τὰς χεῖρας αὐτῇ, ἵνα σωθῇ καὶ ζήσῃ. 24 καὶ ἀπῆλθεν μετ' αὐτοῦ. καὶ ἠκολούθει αὐτῷ ὄχλος πολὺς καὶ συνέθλιβον αὐτόν. ... 35 Ἔτι αὐτοῦ λαλοῦντος ἔρχονται ἀπὸ τοῦ ἀρχισυναγώγου λέγοντες ὅτι ἡ θυγάτηρ σου ἀπέθανεν· τί ἔτι σκύλλεις τὸν διδάσκαλον; 36 ὁ δὲ Ἰησοῦς παρακούσας τὸν λόγον λαλούμενον λέγει τῷ ἀρχισυναγώγῳ· μὴ φοβοῦ, μόνον πίστευε. 37 καὶ οὐκ ἀφῆκεν οὐδένα μετ' αὐτοῦ συνακολουθῆσαι εἰ μὴ τὸν Πέτρον καὶ Ἰάκωβον καὶ Ἰωάννην τὸν ἀδελφὸν Ἰακώβου. 38 καὶ ἔρχονται εἰς τὸν οἶκον τοῦ ἀρχισυναγώγου, καὶ θεωρεῖ θόρυβον καὶ κλαίοντας καὶ ἀλαλάζοντας πολλά,
> 39 καὶ εἰσελθὼν λέγει αὐτοῖς· τί θορυβεῖσθε καὶ κλαίετε; τὸ παιδίον οὐκ ἀπέθανεν ἀλλὰ καθεύδει. 40 καὶ κατεγέλων αὐτοῦ. αὐτὸς δὲ ἐκβαλὼν πάντας παραλαμβάνει τὸν πατέρα τοῦ παιδίου καὶ τὴν μητέρα καὶ τοὺς μετ' αὐτοῦ καὶ εἰσπορεύεται ὅπου ἦν τὸ παιδίον. 41 καὶ κρατήσας τῆς χειρὸς τοῦ παιδίου λέγει αὐτῇ· ταλιθα κουμ, ὅ ἐστιν μεθερμενευόμενον· τὸ κοράσιον, σοὶ λέγω, ἔγειρε.
> 42 καὶ εὐθὺς ἀνέστη τὸ κοράσιον καὶ περιεπάτει· ἦν γὰρ ἐτῶν δώδεκα. καὶ ἐξέστησαν [εὐθὺς] ἐκστάσει μεγάλῃ. 43 καὶ διεστείλατο αὐτοῖς πολλὰ ἵνα μηδεὶς γνοῖ τοῦτο, καὶ εἶπεν δοθῆναι αὐτῇ φαγεῖν.

> 21 And when Jesus had returned to the other shore in the boat, a great crowd gathered around him and he was by the lake. 22 And one of the synagogue leaders, named Jairus, came, and when he saw him he fell before his feet 23 and beseeched him much: "My little daughter is dying. Come and lay your hands on her so that she is saved and will live.
> 24 And he went with him, and a great crowd followed him and pushed him. ... 35 While he was still speaking they came from the synagogue leader and said: "Your daughter is

[410] Cf. Pesch 1970b, 43f.

> dead. You should no longer disturb the teacher." 36 But when Jesus overheard what was spoken he said to the synagogue leader: "Do not fear, just believe." 37 And he allowed no-one to come with him, except for Peter, James, and John, the brother of James. 38 And they came to the house of the synagogue leader, and he saw an uproar and many crying and wailing people, 39 and he went in and said to them: "Why do you shout and cry? The child is not dead, but sleeps. 40 And they laughed at him. But he threw everyone out and took with him the child's father and mother and those with him and went in where the child was. 41 And taking the child's hand, he said to her: "Talitha koum" (which in translation means: "Little girl, I tell you, rise"). 42 And immediately the little girl got up and walked. She was twelve years old. And they were at once exceedingly astonished. 43 And he commanded them strongly not to make this known to anyone, and he told them to give her to eat.

There are a couple of text-critical problems in the Markan text which should be mentioned: the name "Jairus" in v 22 and the Aramaic words "Talitha koum" in v 41. Since Jairus is not mentioned by name in Codex D, several scholars since the time of Bultmann have suggested that it was introduced into Mark secondarily, from the Lukan tradition. The presupposition is that early traditions do not contain names of people and places.[411] The arguments for this view are not strong, however. Codex D deviates at several other points as well in the context, and differs elsewhere on names.[412] "Talitha koum" means literally "Lamb, stand up," and the variant reading "Talitha koumi" represents the old Palestinian form of an Aramaic imperative.[413] Codex D has a variant reading here as well, which is an apparent corruption.[414]

Looking for traces of Markan redaction, the most obvious detail is probably the mention of the three disciples, Peter, James and John. The disciples are certainly inserted by Mark, since they play no role in this story, but are prominent in Mark's overall narrative (cf. 9:2; 14:33). There is a tension between the singling out of these three and the vague reference to "those with him" (τοὺς μετ᾽ αὐτοῦ) in v 40.[415]

The Aramaic "Talitha koum" has often been regarded as an example of *rhesis barbarike*, i.e. "foreign language," strange and secret words of power, thus exemplifying a motif from Hellenistic miracle stories.[416] This could certainly be the case had the words been uncomprehensible and left untranslated. In this case, however, the words are translated, and in an original setting (i.e. in an Aramaic-speaking context) they would have been perfectly understandable. While the motif of secret words might explain why the phrase was retained in a

---

[411] Bultmann 1972 [1921], 215. Cf. V. Taylor 1966, 287, who considers Jairus an early scribal addition.

[412] Pesch 1970a, 252–256.

[413] Hooker 1991, 150; Gnilka 1978, 218, note 44.

[414] ραββι θαβιτα, which is meaningless, but could be a corruption from ραβιθα (via some dittography), meaning little girl. W reads (ταβιθα) under the influence of Acts 9:36.

[415] Cf. Gnilka 1978, 210.

[416] Cf. Theissen 1983 [1972], 149; Marcus 2000, 363. The expression is used by Lucian of Samosata (*The Lover of Lies*, 9), about healers using unintelligible words (ῥῆσις βαρβαρική).

Greek account, "Talitha koum" does not function as a secret spell. These words should be considered as belonging to pre-Markan tradition.[417]

The concluding verses (42–43), describing the acclamation and wonder of the onlookers, are not necessarily to be seen as Markan redaction either. While an unbroken command to silence is usually connected with the secret of Jesus' identity,[418] it should be noted that secrecy commands in miracle stories do not explicitly refer to Jesus' identity. This points to such commands as belonging to early tradition in miracle stories, and Mark is responsible for transferring such commands to other genres.[419] The command to silence thus has a christological function in the present form and context of the story, but probably not in the underlying tradition. The tension between the command to silence and the crowd present outside the house is not necessarily a sign of redaction, but can just as well be seen as an example of the sometimes illogical structure which is considered a typical trait of oral style and unprepared narrative.[420]

To solve this tension, and to remove difficulties about the order, Theissen has suggested that vv 42 and 43 be reversed. This would make the Aramaic words "Talitha koum" occasion a command to silence, thus connecting the command with the "magical words." After this, the girl is given something to eat, which makes her rise and walk, thus connecting her embetterment with the intake of food.[421] As we have seen above, however, it is very uncertain that the Aramaic phrase was originally conceived of as *rhesis barbarike*. In the present form of the story there may be such notions, but then it is difficult to see why the order was changed. We would then have to hypothesize an intermediate form of the tradition, with a strong magical notion, which Mark wished to remove. Theissen admits that his reversal of order is hypothetical. To give it an explanation would require even more speculation.

There has been a tendency to regard this story, as well as other stories of resurrections, as originally ordinary healing traditions which developed into the raising of a dead person.[422] Others have suggested that an earlier form of the narrative of the Capernaum officer has later developed into a resurrection story.[423] Such speculations are without foundation,[424] and are probably to be understood against the background of rationalistic criticism. It is not reasonable, however, that the interpreter's need for a rationally acceptable historical explanation becomes the basis of theories of narrative development. On the histori-

---

[417] Cf. Hooker 1991, 150; Gnilka 1978, 211.

[418] Cf. Räisänen 1990, 166, 168. According to Räisänen, the disclosure of this miracle would reveal too much about Jesus as the conqueror of death.

[419] Theissen 1983 [1972], 150f.

[420] Theissen 1983 [1972], 193.

[421] Theissen 1983 [1972], 149f.

[422] Cf. Pesch 1976, 296, 312–314.

[423] Kertelge 1970, 113.

[424] Gnilka 1978, 212.

cal level, suggestions have been made that the girl actually was in a comatose state. The comment about the girl sleeping (v 39) has been used to support such a theory, but sleeping is a common metaphor for death. Such speculation is to be seen in the ancient parallels about Apollonius and Asclepiades, to be discussed below. While such suggestions are possible and even plausible for giving a rational explanation to the contents of a story which is deemed to be basically historical, they are out of place in this context. The girl is considered dead by Mark, as well as by the different figures in the story world. If there are historical traces transmitted by the Markan tradition, they are not memories of the historical Jesus handling people in coma, but rather resuscitating people considered to be dead.

Against the idea of the growth of an original healing story stand the clear parallels with the Elijah and Elisha tradition (1Kgs 17:17–24; 2Kgs 4:18–37). Both deal with the raising of a dead child. It is obvious that the tradition of the Hebrew Bible has influenced the form of the present story.[425]

As seen in the previous section, the story of the bleeding woman is fitted into the present narrative with the help of the key concept "faith" (vv 34, 36: πίστις, πίστευε). It is reasonable to regard the words of Jesus in v 36b as Markan redaction: "do not fear, only believe" (μὴ φοβοῦ, μόνον πίστευε). By the intercalation, Mark gives emphasis to faith, and thus connects faith and resurrection in the Jairus story, to the effect that the raising of the girl prefigures the resurrection of Jesus, in which faith is likewise needed. The theme of faith surrounds the Gospel of Mark, as it is introduced by the preaching of Jesus (Mk 1:15), and implicitly called for at the abrupt end of the gospel. The women at the grave are frightened by the sight of the young man, but encouraged not to fear (16:6: μὴ ἐκθαμβεῖσθε). In spite of this, the women react with silence, since they were afraid (16:8: ἐφοβοῦντο γάρ). This amounts to a challenge to the hearer/reader to respond more appropriately. A good pattern or example of such an appropriate response has been delivered already in the previous narrative, by the bleeding woman and by Jairus. Since their faith resulted in new life, and confirmed the identity and power of Jesus, even his power over death, the reader should not fear, but believe in Jesus' own resurrection, and thereby in his identity and power, which would ensure a new life for the believer as well.

Such is the sermon inherent in Mark's structure and redaction. We have seen that Mark has given the narrative a christological and theological intent by his redaction, but also by utilizing traditional material in his overall structure. Under this ideological overlay we look for traces of the concrete, historical world. What we find are memories of Jesus entering the house of a dead person, and touching a corpse, in the course of his healing mission. These traits point to an

---

[425] Kertelge 1970, 117f.

implicit purity problem, which is ignored by Mark, but must have been discernible in the underlying tradition, in a Jewish first-century context.[426]

Against this there are two possible arguments, both seizing upon the *similarities* with the resurrection miracles of Elijah and Elisha (1Kgs 17:17–24; 2Kgs 4:18–37). One would point out that no purity issue is implied in these stories, and claim that the regulations of the Torah could not apply to these kinds of circumstances (i.e. resuscitating dead people), because of their exceptional nature.[427] It would be surprising, however, to find any issue of corpse-impurity in popular tales from the time of the First Temple, for which the legal development of rules for corpse contamination is fairly unknown. Judaism was accustomed to a heritage of narratives which at times came in conflict with legal traditions (cf. the incestuous behaviour of Reuben in Gen 35:22 and Judah in Gen 38).[428] In the case of a first-century narrative in a Jewish context about a first-century person entering the house of a dead and touching a corpse, the purity issue would be obvious.[429]

The second argument would claim that entering the house and touching the corpse are literary motifs only, borrowed from the Hebrew Bible, and thus lack any value as historical traces. In our search for traces of the concrete, we find only another ideological layer, exhibiting a christological variant: Jesus as the prophet in the tradition of, or even outdoing, Elijah and Elisha.

While some influence is certain, there are actually no signs of direct literary dependence.[430] The allusions to the Elijah and Elisha traditions probably have a christological intent. But this is hardly sufficient to claim that the narrative of Jairus' daughter has been construed only from these stories, with no historical memories behind it. Jewish tradition in general, and the Hebrew (or LXX) Bible in particular, belonged to the natural frame of reference, within which any early account about Jesus would have been shaped. In such an environment, stories about someone considered a prophet and miracle-worker, could hardly have avoided being influenced by the ancient religious and national heritage, especially not if the person involved was remembered as having on some occasion made a dead individual come alive.

While the case cannot be settled conclusively, there is reason to assume historical traces of a purity issue under the christological overlay. We noted earlier

---

[426] Cf. Sariola 1990, 71f.

[427] Banks 1975, 105.

[428] Incidents such as these were apparently embarrassing, since incest would incur the death penalty according to the law. Cf. the elaborate discussions of these two cases in *Jub.* 33 and 41, to the effect that no exception to the death penalty should be made with appeal to Reuben or Judah.

[429] This is *not* to imply that incurring corpse-impurity should be any *violation* of law. Loader's suggestion (1997, 61, n. 118) that the comment that the girl was sleeping actually removes the purity issue, rests on taking a metaphor literally.

[430] Gnilka 1978, 212.

that Mark was probably using a notion of secrecy already existing in pre-Markan tradition for his own christological construction. Similarly, it can be argued that a pre-Markan tradition used historical memories about Jesus entering the house of a dead person and touching a corpse, for constructing a narrative with another christological slant, which aimed at presenting Jesus as a successor to the early Israelite prophets of the Hebrew Bible. At an early stage, however, and in a Palestinian setting, the purity problem inherent in the tradition must have been discernible. The emphasis in v 40 on Jesus entering the very place where the dead child lay (καὶ εἰσπορεύεται ὅπου ἦν τὸ παιδίον)[431] hardly serves any christological purpose. It must belong to a pre-Markan stage. This is supported by a synoptic comparison. Matthew reduces the emphasis by briefly mentioning the entrance using a participle (εἰσελθών, Mt 9:25), and omitting not only the father and mother, but also "those with him," mentioned by Mark. It is likely that the purity issue would have been recognizable in Matthew's context, but was played down so as not to detract attention from the christological message. Luke's redaction, on the other hand, would have made the purity problem even worse, had its setting been Palestinian, since it not only specifically mentions the "chief disciples" Peter, John and James as those entering the house together with Jesus and the parents (Lk 8:51), but also pictures a crowd of mourning people (πάντες) as being within the house at the same time (8:52). No purity issue is alive to Luke's readers, however, and no notice is taken of the notion, but the narrative is adapted to Hellenistic conditions. While Luke seems ignorant of the purity issue and Matthew consciously plays it down, Mark is seen to retain it, although it is overruled by christological concerns. At an earlier, pre-Markan stage, however, purity must have been an issue, discernible and alive, in this tradition.

The widow's son in Lukan tradition

While the resurrection miracle in Mk 5 is performed in private (5:40), probably in similarity with the miracles of Elijah and Elisha (1Kgs 17:19; 2Kgs 4:33), the special Lukan tradition about the widow's son in Nain (Lk 7:11–17)[432] portrays Jesus as raising a boy in public. The setting is different: the miracle worker meets a funeral procession and, overcome with passion, draws close to the bier and restores the dead person to life. Such traits have been understood as signs of a Hellenistic type of miraculous resuscitation, and evidence that the Lukan

---

[431] Manuscripts A and C supply ανακειμενον.

[432] While surrounded by Q material, this tradition is usually seen as stemming from the special Lukan source, because of its many Lukanisms. The reason for Luke inserting the narrative at this point is obvious. Since he, unlike Matthew, does not include the story of Jairus until after the questions from and answers to the Baptizer (Lk 7:18–23), where Jesus is reported to raise the dead, he needs a resurrection story to corroborate these claims. Cf. Bovon 1989, 355f, esp. n. 1.

tradition is secondary.[433] A closer examination reveals that the Hellenistic parallels are real but few. Apart from an inscription from Epidauros about the god Asclepios meeting a sick person carried on a stretcher,[434] there are two possible parallels to the Lukan story. One is a tradition about the first-century BCE physician Asclepiades meeting a funeral procession and discovering that the man to be buried is not actually dead.[435] The other parallel, which is closer, comes from Philostratus' account of the first-century CE miracle worker Apollonius of Tyana.

> A girl had died just in the hour of her marriage, and the bridegroom was following her bier lamenting as was natural his marriage left unfulfilled, and the whole of Rome was mourning with him, for the maiden belonged to a consular family. Apollonius then witnessing their grief, said: "Put down the bier, for I will stay the tears that you are shedding for this maiden." And withal he asked what was her name. The crowd accordingly thought that he was about to deliver such an oration as is commonly delivered as much to grace the funeral as to stir up lamentation; but he did nothing of the kind, but merely touching her and whispering in secret some spell over her, at once woke up the maiden from her seeming death; and the girl spoke out loud, and returned to her father's house, just as Alcestis did when she was brought back to life by Hercules.[436]

Philostratus continues discussing whether the girl was really dead or only seemingly so. Such hesitance is never found in the gospel tradition.

Meeting a funeral procession could be seen as a motif, belonging to the common traits of miracle stories in Antiquity. This is only natural, however, since funeral processions should have been common and normal experiences for inhabitants in any village or town.[437] As for the other parallels between the above-mentioned stories, they are not as evident. The motif of the seemingly dead person who is saved in the last minute from being buried alive, is found in modern times too, but is not present in the Lukan tradition. The Apollonius story, which provides the only real parallel, was given its present form more than a century after the Lukan narrative, although Apollonius himself belonged to the first century. Philostratus' sources and their value have been much debated,[438] and it is by no means evident in which direction influence (if any) should be imagined between Luke and Philostratus' source.[439] The Lukan tradi-

---

[433] Cf. Bultmann 1972 [1921], 215.

[434] *IG* 4, 952:26–35. Cf. Weinreich 1909, 172. The sick person had not received any healing dream while in the temple, but met the god on the way home.

[435] This tradition is preserved in two sources from the second century CE; one elaborate and legendary in style, (Apuleius, *Florida* 19), the other a passing comment by Celsus (*On Medicine* 2.6.15–18), which introduces a discussion about medicine as a conjectural art.

[436] Philostratus, *Vit.Apoll.*, 4:45.

[437] Funeral processions were frequent and common experiences. This is clear from texts discussing risks and obligations, such as those mentioned below (*Ag.Ap.* 2:205; *mOha* 5:1; 11:4–5).

[438] See the *Forschungsbericht* in Koskenniemi 1994, 18–36.

[439] Fitzmyer 1981, 657; Cotter 1999, 43. Several scholars think that Philostratus simply invented his "source." Cf. Palm 1976, 13–17; Bowie 1978, 1663–1667; Kee 1983, 256–265. Meier (1994, 578–581) suggests that Philostratus could have borrowed some gospel miracle

tion is furthermore seen to contain many Semitic elements and several allusions to the Elijah tradition. The verbs are usually in parataxis, joined by καί, and there are several instances of redundant pronouns. Many details coincide with the legend about Elijah in Zarephath (1Kgs 17:7–24): the prophet comes to the city gate, he meets a widow, restores her son to life and gives him back to his mother.[440] In the last instance there is almost complete verbal agreement between 1Kgs (LXX: 3 Kgdms) 17:23 and Lk 7:15 (καὶ ἔδωκεν αὐτὸν/αὐτὸ τῇ μητρὶ αὐτοῦ). There is simply not evidence enough to claim that the Lukan tradition is shaped on a particularly Hellenistic type of miraculous resuscitation.

As for the purity issue, Lk 7 is not explicit. According to Josephus, not only the relatives, but also those who passed by (πᾶσι δὲ τοῖς παριοῦσι), were expected to join the funeral procession.[441] Thus far, the behaviour of the Lukan Jesus could be regarded as normal. It is clear, however, that Josephus distinguishes between the two groups; the relatives undertake the burial (τὰ μὲν περὶ τὴν κηδείαν τοῖς οἰκειοτάτοις ἐπιτελεῖν) while by-passers join the procession and take part in mourning (πᾶσι δὲ τοῖς παριοῦσι καὶ προσελθεῖν καὶ συναποδύρασθαι), and only the former (καὶ τὸν οἶκον καὶ τοὺς ἐνοικοῦντας) are required to purify. The latter must then be assumed not to have contracted corpse-impurity. Although the *Mishnah* contains rabbinic discussions about when and how persons and items could be contaminated when a corpse was carried past the house in a funeral procession (*mOha* 5:1; 11:4–5), the issue for discussion is how to apply the principle of overshadowing. Overshadowing, together with touching, transmitted corpse-impurity. Merely to join a funeral procession did not of itself make a person unclean.

According to the Lukan narrative, however, Jesus does not join the procession, but touches the bier. In the rabbinic system, the bier would count as a rinsable vessel, transmitting a seven-day impurity, just like the body (*mOha* 1:1–3).[442] This probably applied in Second Temple times too. The extended chain of corpse-contamination which is reflected in *mOha* 1 must have been developed by the time of Aqiba (early second century CE).[443] It is unlikely that the

traditions. Koskenniemi (1994, 203–206) argues that Philostratus could have known Christian miracle traditions in oral, but not in literary forms.

[440] Fitzmyer 1981, 656, 659; C. F. Evans 1990, 346.

[441] *Ag.Ap.* 2:205.

[442] The susceptibility of the bed is taken for granted e.g. in the discussions of *mKel* 18–19. Cf. Harrington 1993, 149.

[443] This chain is exceptional for corpse-impurity, as compared with other types of impurity, since "vessels" contaminated by a corpse, may transfer their seven-day impurity to other vessels or persons. Even persons contaminated from a corpse or from a vessel, may transfer their seven-day impurity to vessels. (The latter transference is not recognized by the *Palestinian Talmud*, *yNaz* 7:4. Cf. Harrington 1993, 149.) In *mOha* 1:3, R. Aqiba (late first and early second century CE) is pictured as commenting upon these possible chains of contamination. It is reasonable to suppose that something of the sort should have been present already during Second Temple times. Cf. Neusner 1974–1977, 22:125.

origins of such a complicated chain do not go back in time. Unfortunately, the Qumran texts do not help us much on this matter. One passage in the *Temple Scroll* might provide a clue, however, as for an expansionist presupposition. A pregnant woman, whose child dies in her womb, is considered as unclean as a corpse while the child is within her (11Q19 [11QT] 50:10–18).[444] This is most easily explained by the idea of being in continuous contact with the source of impurity, which has been mentioned above in the section about discharges.[445] I would suggest that an analogous idea about corpse-impurity and continuous contact is the natural presupposition behind this ruling in the *Temple Scroll.* This means that during the time of Jesus, the bier of a dead person, being in constant contact with the corpse, would most probably have been seen as contaminating people who touched it with a seven-day impurity.

In its present form, and for the readers of Luke, the narrative of the widow's son carries no purity connotations. While the historical value of the tradition behind the Lukan narrative could be questioned, it cannot, as we have seen, be regarded as a Lukan construction, based on Hellenistic motifs alone. If the tradition behind the present narrative has a Palestinian origin,[446] it is likely that purity was at least an implicit issue, which Luke then ignored or/and deemed irrelevant for his readers.

The impurity of graves and Jesus' attitude

The fear of contamination from dead bodies was common in Antiquity not only in Judaism, as is seen from the idea of *contagio funesta*, attested in several Roman sources,[447] or corpse-contamination in Zoroastrianism.[448] Early evidence from ancient Babylonia shows that dust around a grave was considered polluting, and contact with it required a seven-day purification period.[449]

In the biblical material we find traces of some ambiguity. While according to *Numbers* (19:16), mere contact with a grave is considered as defiling as

---

444 This is in contrast to later rabbinic rulings (*mHul* 4:3). Cf. Harrington 1993, 75.

445 Such an idea concerning people with discharges is found in explicit form in *mZab* 5:6, and in relation to corpse-impurity in the *Babylonian Talmud* (*bAZ* 37b, *bNaz* 42b).

446 Arguments against Lukan invention, but in favour of a Palestinian origin are: 1) Nain is mentioned nowhere else in contemporary sources, but excavations have shown that it was a walled town (and thus had a gate); 2) the Greek text shows possible signs of a Semitic substratum; 3) Luke buttresses the unspecific "a great prophet" (pre-Lukan tradition) with the first instance in his third-person narrative of the christologically significant *kyrios*; 4) Luke's tendency to avoid doublets speaks against him having included another resurrection miracle (in addition to that of Jairus' daughter), had it not belonged to what he considered to be authoritative sources. Meier 1994, 795ff.

447 Wagenvoort 1947, 133f, referring among others to Virgil (*Aen.* 2:539; 3:227; 6:150), Cicero (*Rab.Perd.* 11) and Pliny the younger (*Ep.* 4, 11, 9).

448 Boyce 1975, 300–306.

449 Milgrom 1990b, 160, 162. In Egypt, all forms of decay fell into the category of impurity, except for the corpse. Tombs had the same holy status as cult centres. Milgrom 1991, 768.

touching a corpse, the kings of Jerusalem were regularly buried "in the city of David," according to the books of *Kings* and *Chronicles*.[450] The burial places of kings from the time of Manasseh and onwards are phrased differently, but seem to refer to places within Jerusalem as well.[451] This fact, together with the vehement protest of Ezekiel against such a practice (Ez 43:7–9) could be interpreted as evidence for corpse-contamination, at least via graves, being a fairly late development.[452] Archaeological evidence, however, may point in a different direction. During the First Temple period, ordinary people were buried outside the city wall on the western hill, and when the city expanded from the time of Hezekiah and onwards, these tombs were emptied, evidently to remove corpses from what would become part of the city.[453] This does not prove the case, but might imply that avoidance of grave-impurity, at least in some basic form, was already present during the First Temple period. It is uncertain, however, to what extent the rules about contamination in Num 19 were in effect during this time. In the case of burial of kings and at times priests and prophets, considerations of honour or reverence may have carried more weight than aspects of purity.[454] The stricter view, represented by Ezekiel, probably came to dominate during the Second Temple period. The *Temple Scroll* states what should be seen as a general Israelite norm, rather than a sectarian rule:

> And you shall not do as the gentiles do: they bury their dead in every place, they even bury them in the middle of their houses; instead you shall keep places apart within your land where you shall bury your dead. Among four cities you shall establish a place in which to bury.[455]

While opinions were divided among post-70 rabbis as to whether exceptions should be made for the graves of kings and prophets, the general rule was that graves within a distance of 50 cubits from a city limit should be cleared.[456] The

---

[450] This includes kings from David (1Kgs 2:10) to Ahaz (2Kgs 16:20). For a full list of references and a detailed discussion, cf. David P. Wright 1987, 117ff, esp. 118, notes 11 and 12.

[451] 2Chr 32:33; 2Kgs 21:18/2Chr 33:20; 2Kgs 21:26; 2Kgs 23:30/2Chr 35:24. Cf. Wright 1987, 119.

[452] Cf. Weill 1920, 40–45. B. Levine (1993, 105f) considers the rituals of Num 19 to be predicated on Ez 43. The legislation in Num 19 would then institutionalize an exilic or post-exilic concept of corpse-impurity.

[453] Broshi 1974; David P. Wright 1987, 120ff. References to burials, such as those in Judg 10:2; 1Sam 25:1; 2Sam 2:32 or 2Sam 21:14, do not necessarily mean that people were buried *within* towns, but rather in the area of a particular town. Cf. Wright 1987, 117, n. 9.

[454] The priest Jehoiada was buried with the kings, according to 2Chr 24:16. In the legend about the dead man revived by contact with Elisha's bones (2Kgs 13:20–21), there is no issue of impurity, but the bones of the holy man make the dead person come to life again. According to Ex 13:19, the Israelites carried the bones of Joseph with them through the desert.

[455] 11Q19 [11QT] 48:11–14.

[456] *tBBat* 1:11 (Cf. *mBBat* 2:9). R. Aqiba represents a dissenting voice, holding on to a view similar to the explicit view of Ezekiel and the implicit view of the *Temple Scroll*, according to which no exceptions were to be made. The impurity of graves is further discussed by the rabbis in *mOha* 16–18. Although the requirement of the *Temple Scroll* for separate burial grounds

general fear of contracting corpse-impurity from graves is attested for the Second Temple period by the well-known case of Tiberias, reported by Josephus. This Galilean town was built as a new capital by Herod Antipas in 19 CE at the western shore of the lake of Galilee, but on a burial site, which led most Jews to avoid it; hence the city remained predominantly Hellenistic. According to Josephus, Herod Antipas even had to force people to settle there, and give them houses and land, because the settlement was considered to be against Jewish law, i.e. the law of corpse-impurity (*Ant.* 18:36–38). Josephus' statement that such settlers were unclean for seven days, according to the law (μιαροὺς δὲ ἐπὶ ἑπτὰ ἡμέρας εἶναι τοὺς οἰκήτορας ἀγορεύει ἡμῖν τὸ νόμιμον),[457] probably reflects a general Jewish attitude to corpse-impurity in his time. To walk over a grave resulted in the same impurity as touching a corpse, and this was seen as a serious matter, by all means to be avoided.

This general attitude is reflected in gospel traditions. According to Lk 11:44 (par Mt 23:27), Jesus addresses the Pharisees:

> Οὐαὶ ὑμῖν, ὅτι ἐστὲ ὡς τὰ μνημεῖα τὰ ἄδηλα, καὶ οἱ ἄνθρωποι [οἱ] περιπατοῦντες ἐπάνω οὐκ οἴδασιν.
>
> Woe unto you, since you are like unmarked graves, and the people who walk over them do not know it.

The saying comes from the Q source. In the Matthean variant, the emphasis is not on the graves being invisible, but white-washed, which is interpreted as hypocritical behaviour in the subsequent sentence (Mt 23:28). The material is thus shaped to suit Matthew's general polemic against scribes and Pharisees. The Lukan wording should be taken as more original.[458] The literary context is one of purity since the saying is preceded by one dealing with cleansing the outside or inside of vessels. The context of purity is further underscored in Luke, where these sayings are prefaced with a table scene, in which a Pharisee reacts to Jesus' negligence of proper ablutions before the meal.

Lk 11:44 could be taken to represent Jesus as acknowledging rules for corpse-impurity, while not accepting Pharisaic purity practice. This seems possible at first sight, but even if it were the case, these words would not tell us to what degree he adhered to corpse-impurity rules or how important they were to him, in relation to other issues. They would only show that he was a Second

---

might not have been reflected in *general* contemporary practice (the Tannaim seem not to have required particular burial areas as long as graves were marked, cf. *mMQat* 1:2; Schiffman 1990, 137), the distance of at least fifty cubits seems to have been generally observed. This fits with the distance between the main cemetery at Qumran and the settlement, which is estimated at 30–40 metres (Hachlili 2000, 125).

[457] *Ant.* 18:38.

[458] Luz 1997, 340f. A possible exception is Matthew's κεκονιαμένοις, which Luke may have substituted with ἄδηλα, to avoid explaining to his Gentile readers the Jewish practice of white-washing graves before Passover, to prevent pilgrims from contracting impurity unintentionally. Cf. Fitzmeyer 1985, 949; Bovon 1996, 231, n.68.

Temple Jew, who worked with the general concepts of his culture and time. The case of Tiberias was more than well-known, and it would be only natural for a Galilean Jew to allude to it.

Tiberias is not mentioned explicitly by any New Testament writing, however.[459] At a distance of less than 30 kilometers from Nazareth and about half that distance from Capernaum, across the lake, Jesus ought to have visited it. The absence of any such mention has at times been explained as indicating that Jesus avoided Tiberias for reasons of purity. Such an argument from silence is hazardous, to say the least. There is likewise no mention of Jesus visiting Sepphoris, the other Galilean Hellenistic town. Only a few places are mentioned in the gospel narratives, which should not be read as itineraries. It is possible that Jesus avoided these towns, and kept to Jewish villages and people of his own kind.[460] But no conclusions regarding Jesus' observance of corpse-impurity rules can be made on such a basis.[461] The most plausible explanation for Jesus' avoidance of these towns is the fate of his predecessor, John the Baptizer, who was imprisoned and executed by Herod Antipas.[462]

Impurity of graves is an issue in the story of the demoniac, in Mk 5:1–20 (par Mt 8:28–34; Lk 8:26–39). We will return to this narrative in Chapter VII, to discuss Jesus as an exorcist. For the present purpose, we should note the link between the unclean graves, the unclean spirits and the unclean swine. Although not explicit, there is definitely a connection on the narrative level. Furthermore, the incident seems to take place on Gentile (unclean?) territory. Loader conjectures that as a pre-Markan Christian Jewish story, it was composed in a community in which Jewish purity values were still in operation, and thus reflects an image of Jesus as sharing these values. In relation to the Gentile mission it would still operate with strongly Jewish assumptions, indicating that Jesus effectively exorcized Gentile land.[463] Says Loader:

> The pre-Markan tradition behind 5:1–20 preserves an image of Jesus which assumes he lives by Torah and that he shares the value of the Jewish community in relation to Gentile uncleanness. In such an isolated anecdote there would have been no need to address Jesus' subsequent purification upon returning from Gentile land. It would have been assumed.[464]

---

[459] Except for the Gospel of John where "the lake of Tiberias" is used as an alternative name for the lake of Galilee (Jn 6:1, 23; 21:1).

[460] Cf. Sanders 1990, 40f.

[461] If such an argument from silence should be allowed to carry any weight, it would only confirm how seriously corpse-impurity was regarded, and thus accentuate the discrepancy between a general attitude and the specific behaviour of Jesus, implied in the traditions.

[462] Mk 6:17ff; Josephus *Ant.* 18:116–119. Cf. Fredriksen 2000, 165. Several gospel traditions support the idea that Antipas was aware of Jesus, and that Jesus was regarded as a threat to him. Cf. Mk 3:6; 6:14–16; Lk 13:31–33.

[463] Loader 1997, 59f, n. 107.

[464] Loader 1997, 60, n. 107.

These conclusions are not self-evident, however. Whether of Jewish or Christian origin, the story seems at some stage to have made a point against Roman occupation, perhaps being a satire on Roman military presence. The unclean spirit(s), named *Legion* (a Latin military term), beg Jesus not to be sent out of the country (ἵνα μὴ αὐτὰ ἀποστείλῃ ἔξω τῆς χώρας, Mk 5:10), but rather wish to enter (εἰσέλθωμεν) the swine (τοὺς χοίρους). The term χοίρος was sometimes used for female genitalia.[465] Military occupation has often been metaphorically associated with, and literally accompanied by, rape. The narrative also contains several other terms capable of military interpretation.[466] The story could be seen as associating the occupying Romans with demonic powers, defeated in the encounter with Jesus.[467]

This much can be said about the narrative level. On an historical level, we can neither conclude that Jesus intended to overthrow the Romans, nor that he was an enthusiastic adherent of purity regulations. Discussing Mk 7, we found no reason to believe that Jesus rejected the food laws of Lev 11. This does not imply, however, that he readily embraced all regulations about purity of food. Similarly, the fact that Jesus was a Second Temple Jew, living with the general concepts of his culture, does not prove that he cherished the dominant idea of corpse-impurity. If the narrative in Mk 5:1–20 contains historical reminiscences,[468] it should be noted that Jesus is pictured as present in a grave area. As will be seen in Chapter VII, there is a probable relationship between Jesus' exorcisms and his attitude to bodily impurity, but rather in the way that the exorcisms could explain his lack of regard for rules of bodily impurity. The attitude of the historical Jesus to Jewish views on Gentile impurity can hardly be decided from this tradition. Loader's conclusion that Jesus' subsequent purification upon returning from Gentile land was assumed by the Jewish-Christian pre-Markan tradition rests on weak evidence, mainly arguments from silence, and must be seriously questioned.

Was corpse-contamination avoided?

Ed Sanders has argued that contracting corpse-impurity was "on the whole, *positively good*, or at least so much a part of nature as to raise no possible objection."[469] While "positively desirable," he points out that it was "a transgression to bring any impurity into the presence of what is holy."[470] At the same

---

465 Aristophanes *Ach.* 773f. Cf. Marcus 2000, 345, 351f. In addition, the boar was the emblem of the Roman legion in Palestine, as well as a symbol of Esau, and later Rome, in Jewish tradition (Marcus 2000, 351).

466 E.g. πέμπειν, ἐπιτρέπειν, ὡρμᾶν. Cf. Derrett 1979b.

467 Cf. Loader 1997, 59f, n. 107.

468 Cf. Meier's evaluation of historical reminiscences in this tradition (1994, 650–656).

469 Sanders 1990, 142.

470 Sanders 1990, 146.

time he affirms that corpse-impurity was taken very seriously not only by Pharisees, but by people in general.[471]

A problematic trait in Sanders' interpretation is his claim that the Pharisees did not avoid biblical corpse-impurity, but only their own extensions.[472] He claims that "*the accidental sources of the impurity which they wished to avoid they had first to create.* … Instead of avoiding corpse-impurity as defined by the Bible, they extended it and then avoided some of the extensions."[473] And further: "The extremely careful definition of where corpse-impurity is and is not probably encouraged caution."[474] This is an example of what Hannah Harrington criticizes as "a sort of backwards logic where the rules create the need for avoidance."[475] The dichotomy between biblical and extended corpse-impurity is strained. Sanders discusses biblical corpse-impurity as if it were a matter of contact with dead bodies only. He argues that Pharisees did tend and mourn for their dead.[476] There is no reason to question this. Taking care of one's dead is a religious duty in all cultures, and likewise in Judaism. Restrictions applied to priests, who were allowed to become corpse-contaminated only in the case of near relatives, and the High Priest and nazir, who were forbidden to contract corpse-impurity even in such cases.[477] But biblical corpse-impurity includes much more than tending one's dead. It includes coming into contact with any corpse (Num 19:11), or entering the same tent (house) as a corpse (19:14), as well as coming into contact with vessels or persons which have been present in such a house (19:15, 22). It furthermore includes touching human bone or a grave (19:16). This takes care of two of Sanders' four examples of Pharisaic extensions of corpse-impurity, namely walking over graves and the idea of overshadowing.[478] The former is explicitly mentioned in Num 19:16, and the latter is inherent in the law about the tent (19:14). The other two examples mentioned by Sanders (escape through holes; impure entrances and intention),

---

[471] Sanders' overall aim to picture the Pharisees as pious and humane emphasizing that they did not try to live like priests, at times makes it difficult to follow his discussion. This might give the reader the feeling that Sanders is trying to downplay the seriousness of corpse-impurity (Sanders 1990, 232).

[472] Sanders 1990, 34.

[473] Sanders 1990, 191f. Cf. 232: "they vastly expanded the domain of corpse-impurity and then tried to avoid becoming impure according to the new rules. … what they avoided they had first to create."

[474] Sanders 1990, 187.

[475] Harrington 1993, 169.

[476] Sanders 1990, 34.

[477] Lev 21:1–4, 10–12; *mNaz* 7:1. The rabbinic passage furthermore discusses a possible exception: a neglected corpse. According to R. Eliezer, even a High Priest ought to care for a neglected corpse, but not a Nazir. The majority opinion, however, is exactly the opposite. Cf. Maccoby 1999, 27, who describes Eliezer's opinion as the general rule, without acknowledging the divergencies in the discussion.

[478] Sanders 1990, 186.

are shown by Harrington to be the result of systemic reading rather than mere innovation.[479]

The net result is that most of what Pharisees, and Jews in general avoided (corpses, graves, corpse-impure vessels and food, overshadowing) could be labelled "biblical impurity." To tend and mourn for one's dead was surely "positively good," but there is no evidence that corpse-impurity was regarded as something "desirable" in any other case but this exception. The mishnaic elaborations on overshadowing, and other minute discussions about corpse-impurity in the tractate *Ohalot*, should be interpreted as evidence that it was considered a serious matter generally. Even if we should expect that the fine points were not adhered to by the unscrupulous, and that much of the development is of a post-70 date, the general presupposition is that corpse-impurity is serious and should be avoided at all costs. During the time of the Second Temple it was important to know how it was contracted, so that proper purification could be undertaken.

Sanders admits that people generally considered purity to be good for its own sake and avoided contracting corpse-impurity unnecessarily.[480] But he interprets Josephus' comment in *Ag.Ap.* 2:205, that all who pass by a burial procession must join and share in the mourning,[481] as evidence for a general custom, a "pious duty of becoming corpse-impure."[482] The argument rests on a mishnaic passage (*mOha* 18:4), mentioning a field of mourners (שְׂדֵה בוֹכִין), which is taken as a field next to the graveyard where the priests and their families "presumably mourned" in order to avoid contracting corpse-impurity.[483] This is taken by Sanders to imply that all others mourned within the graveyard and thus contracted corpse-impurity.[484] Josephus does not suggest this, however, since he goes on to mention the subsequent purification of the house and its inhabitants (καθαίρειν δὲ καὶ τὸν οἶκον καὶ τοὺς ἐνοικοῦντας ἀπὸ κήδους). Nothing is said about the passers-by, and there is no reason to think that they were considered to have become corpse-contaminated by showing the gesture of sympathy briefly sketched by Josephus.[485] We should assume that people generally avoided becoming overshadowed, or entering grave areas or houses with corpses, unless they had some relationship to the deceased person.

Sanders' argument that even a *haber* did not avoid corpse-impurity similarly rests on a questionable interpretation of *mDem* 2:3. Says Sanders: "In the middle of the second century R. Judah proposed that Associates should not contract

---

[479] Harrington 1993, 153–159.
[480] Sanders 1990, 188.
[481] "πᾶσι δὲ τοῖς παριοῦσι καὶ προσελθεῖν καὶ συναποδύρασθαι." Cf. above, 176.
[482] Sanders 1990, 187.
[483] Sanders 1990, 193.
[484] Sanders 1990, 187.
[485] Against Sanders 1990, 159, who suggests that since Josephus says nothing about keeping the impure relatives separate from those joining the procession, this implies that they became corpse-contaminated.

corpse-impurity, but he was overruled."[486] R. Judah actually adds four diverse rules for a *haber* to the four initially mentioned, which all deal with how a *haber* and an *am ha-arets* relate to each other in exchanging agricultural products and hospitality. The majority rule does not deny R. Judah's points,[487] but deems them out of context (לֹא בָאוּ אֵלּוּ לַכְּלָל). They simply did not belong to the topic discussed.[488] Alternatively, the discussion could be understood as implicitly referring to the duty to bury dead relatives, and thus contracting corpse-impurity. This was compulsory for laity; only priests were exempted, and *haberim* did not differ from that rule. Harrington suggests that R. Judah's dissension is to be understood against this background, and the wish to avoid corpse-impurity in an age when no purification rite was available.[489] Even in this case, however, the majority rule would not be a sign of disregard for corpse-impurity.

The general avoidance of corpse-impurity is implied by another mishnaic tradition, discussed by Sanders. According to the discussion between the houses in *mEdu* 1:14, Shammaites, and subsequently Hillelites, after being convinced, would not eat food protected from corpse-impurity in a clay vessel of an *am ha-arets*, although it was deemed fit for the *am ha-arets*. This was not on the grounds of corpse-impurity, however.[490] As for corpse-contamination, food kept in a clay vessel is protected for the *am ha-arets* according to the same rules as for the houses, but the latter cannot accept the initial status of the vessel belonging to the *am ha-arets* because of differing practices relating to other types of impurity. The *am ha-arets* is not, however, suspected of being lax in matters of corpse-impurity. The whole discussion assumes that Pharisees and ordinary people agree about rules for corpse-impurity and avoid it.

---

[486] Sanders 1990, 34.

[487] These points are: 1) not raise small cattle; 2) not be profuse in making vows; 3) not contract corpse-impurity; 4) minister in the study house. To be consistent, Sanders would have to argue for none of these points being relevant to a *haber*.

[488] כְּלָל is sometimes used almost as a technical term, meaning "rule" or "general principle." It can at times be translated as "generalization," "inclusion" or "comprehension under a class." There is thus a notion of classification involved. The Hebrew could theoretically be taken to mean that R. Judah's additional rules were not considered applicable to a *haber* at all, but this does not convince. The explanatory gloss supplied with the translation of Richard S. Sarason, is even more unconvincing: "These [rules] do not enter the category [under discussion, viz., they do not deal with matters of cleanness]." Judah's additional rules (see the previous note) definitely have to do with purity; in the case of corpse-impurity it is explicitly stated. What distinguishes the initial four rules from Judah's supplementation, however, is that the former all deal with the relationship between a *haber* and an *am ha-arets*, while the latter address general and diverse issues, and hence cannot be subsumed under the same heading as the former. They have nothing to do with agriculture, even less with tithing, which is the context of the order of *Zeraim* and the tractate of *Demai*.

[489] Harrington 1993, 178f.

[490] Cf. Sanders 1990, 188ff.

Purification and the first-day ablution

While purification from corpse-impurity was necessary before entering the temple, there is ample evidence that some sort of purification was carried out generally, far from the temple and regardless of any coming pilgrimage. As has been pointed out earlier, the frequency of *miqvaot* in sites all over Palestine confirms the general picture of people immersing in order to remove all types of impurities, without directly relating this to the temple cult. In the case of corpse-impurity, the purification process included sprinkling with water mixed with ashes of the red cow, on the third and seventh day (Num 19:12). It is uncertain to what extent these ashes were available outside of Jerusalem, especially in the Diaspora.[491] This may explain why many pilgrims coming to Jerusalem for Passover were considered corpse-impure. Philo gives evidence for the idea of pilgrims arriving one week early, in order to be sprinkled on the third and seventh day (*Spec.Laws* 1:261). After a final immersion, the purifying person could enter the temple, in accordance with the law.[492] This would agree with the comment in Jn 11:55, that at Passover people from the countryside went to Jerusalem in advance, in order to purify (καὶ ἀνέβησαν πολλοὶ εἰς Ἱεροσόλυμα ἐκ τῆς χώρας πρὸ τοῦ πάσχα ἵνα ἁγνίσωσιν ἑαυτούς).

We do not know whether a seven-day purification period within Jerusalem was compulsory for *all* pilgrims as a safety measure, but even if this was the case, it would not imply that corpse-impurity was of no concern except before temple visits. Philo, in another passage (*Spec.Laws* 3:205–206), gives testimony to the fact that Jews in his environment sprinkled and washed to become clean after having touched a corpse (οἴεται δεῖν μὴ εὐθὺς εἶναι καθαρούς, μέχρις ἂν περιρρανάμενοι καὶ ἀπολουσάμενοι καθαρθῶσιν), and those who had entered a house in which anyone had died must bathe and wash their clothes before touching anything (προστάττει μηδενὸς ἅπτεσθαι, μέχρις ἂν ἀπολούσωνται καὶ τὰς ἐσθῆτας αἷς ἀμπίσχοντο προσαποπλύναντες). While not having access to the red cow rite, Diaspora Jews took corpse-impurity seriously and underwent a purification ceremony immediately, accord-

---

[491] It should be noted, however, that the red cow rite was the only purification ritual that was not connected with the temple cult, and that the sprinkling of water with ashes was not specifically required to be done by a priest.

[492] Josephus reflects in a passing comment the same waiting period, mentioning a portent which happened "at the time when the people were assembling for the feast of unleavened bread, on the eighth of the month Xanthicus" (*J.W.* 6:290). Sanders points out (1992, 134f.) that Josephus simply equates the Macedonian month Xanthicus with Nisan. Since Passover began on the 14th of Nisan, Josephus' comment seems to imply that people came one week early. There is no need to discuss another system of time reckoning, since Josephus elsewhere places Passover on the 14th of Xanthicus. The fact that Josephus, like most people, at times does not distinguish Passover (14th of Nisan) from the subsequent feast of unleavened bread (15th of Nisan and a week ahead), should not be allowed to confuse the discussion. For a detailed discussion and further references, see Sanders 1992, 132–135, 511 notes 39 and 46.

ing to the basic pattern, and in line with the legislation of Num 19, which prescribed the *karet* penalty for those who neglected to purify themselves after having become corpse-contaminated. Philo's comments furthermore imply that the later rabbinic restriction visible in *mKel* 15:1, which limited susceptibility to utensils formed as receptacles,[493] was unknown to him, since in the case of a house with a corpse, "all vessels and articles of furniture, and anything else that happens to be inside, practically everything" was regarded as unclean.[494]

According to Philo, the domestic rite made a person "fully clean," although it did not suffice for entering the temple (εἰς μέντοι τὸ ἱερὸν οὐδὲ τοῖς σφόδρα καθαροῖς ἐφῆκεν εἰσιέναι ἐντὸς ἡμερῶν ἑπτά).[495] We should probably expect a similar situation in Galilee and Judaea outside of Jerusalem. Whether or not ashes of the red cow were available in the country, people would have purified themselves immediately after corpse-contamination, even if an extra purification was required in Jerusalem before a temple visit.

There is some evidence for an initial first-day ablution being practised generally at the end of the Second Temple period, in addition to the prescribed sprinklings at the third and seventh day, and the final immersion. While not prescribed by the legislation in Num 19, it can be deduced from Philo's statement referred to above (*Spec.Laws* 3:205–206), as well as from certain Qumran passages. It is explicitly prescribed in the *Temple Scroll* (11Q19 [11QT] 49:16–21):

> And the man: everyone who was in the house and everyone who come to the house shall bathe in water and wash his clothes the first day (והאדם כול אשר היה בבית וכול אשר בא אל הבית ירחץ במים ויכבס בגדיו ביום הראישון). And on the third day they shall sprinkle over them the waters of purification, and they shall bathe and wash their clothes and the utensils which are in the house. *Blank* And on the seventh day they shall sprinkle a second time, and they shall bathe and wash their clothes and their utensils. And they shall be clean by the evening from the dead person, so that they can approach all their pure things.[496]

A first-day ablution also seems to be assumed in Tobit 2:9.[497] The presence of *miqvaot* in Judaean cemeteries of the Second Temple period also seems to confirm that this practice was not a merely sectarian one, but fairly common, both

---

493 כְּלֵי עֵץ כְּלֵי עוֹר כְּלֵי עֶצֶם כְּלֵי זְכוֹכִית פְּשׁוּטֵיהֶן טְהוֹרִין וּמְקַבְּלֵיהֶן טְמֵאִין *mKel* 15:1.

494 σκεύη δὲ καὶ ἔπιπλα καὶ ὅσα ἄλλα ἔνδον εἶναι συμβέβηκε πάνθ' ὡς ἔπος... *Spec.Laws* 3:206. Cf. Harrington 1993, 42, 174, n.66.

495 *Spec.Laws* 3:205.

496 Cf. 11Q19 [11QT] 50:13–16 and 1QM 14:2–3. Further traces of this practice are found in *4Q Ritual of Purification A* (4Q414 frag. 2 col. 2+frag. 3:1–2): "and you will puri[fy] him according to [your] ho[ly] laws [...] for the first, the third and the se[venth...]" (ותטה]ר [בו לחוקי קודש]כה [... לראשון [ו]לשלישי ולש[ביעי ...]).

497 After having buried a dead man, Tobit washes himself in the evening, before entering the courtyard: καὶ αὐτῇ τῇ νυκτὶ ἐλουσάμην καὶ εἰσῆλθον εἰς τὴν αὐλήν μου (text of C. Sinaiticus). Cf. the detailed discussion about the different Greek, Hebrew and Aramaic versions and possible halakhic interpretations in Boid 1989, 321f, n.220.

inside and outside Palestine, although not according to Pharisaic *halakhah*.[498] It should also be noted that the practice of a first-day ablution not only in the case of menstruant women,[499] but also in the case of corpse-contaminated persons, is attested in certain Samaritan texts, where a corpse-impure person is called *nâṭir* (i.e. one who has to be careful) until having immersed a first time. This immersion is necessary to start the seven-day count.[500]

In the Samaritan tradition of Kâfi, a first-day ablution is necessary, since the *nâṭir* will otherwise contaminate like the corpse itself. This is not the case in the texts we are studying from the Second Temple period. Milgrom has suggested that the initial ablution removed a degree of impurity, making it possible for the corpse-contaminated person to stay within ordinary cities. According to Num 5:2–3 (cf. 31:19), corpse-impure persons should stay out of the camp for seven days, until purification is complete. The discrepancy between this tradition, other traditions and actual practice has been discussed extensively in the previous sections about "leprosy" and discharges and will not be reiterated. While a purifying "leper" is allowed to enter the camp after an initial purification (Lev 14:8), there are no traces in Num 19 of the corpse-impure being expelled from or re-admitted to the camp. It is rather the red cow rite that is to take place outside. The corpse-impure is sprinkled together with the contaminated tent and vessels inside the camp (Num 19:17–18).[501] The stricter ruling may have been older or later, but diverging opinions or practices may also have existed side by side. To some, a strict position could have been mitigated by a first-day ablution.[502]

In the *Temple Scroll,* rules differ for the temple city (Jerusalem) and the ordinary city.[503] According to 11Q19 [11QT] 46:16–18, "lepers" and dischargers should be expelled from Jerusalem. The different wording of 11Q19 [11QT] 48:14–17, relating to ordinary cities, has been discussed in detail above. While the most natural reading leads to the conclusion that both "lepers" and dischargers were to be kept out of ordinary cities too, it is possible to read the passage in line with Josephus' statement in *Ant.* 3:261. In that case, 11Q19 [11QT] 48:14–17 would correspond with Second Temple practice as confirmed by Josephus: "lepers" were banished so that they should not enter the cities (אשר לוא יבואו לעריכמה) while dischargers were in some way isolated or restricted, so as not to transmit their impurity within the city (אשר לוא יטמאו בתוכם).

[498] E. Eshel 1999, 138f; Netzer 1982, 115f. A first-day ablution could possibly seen as a priestly tradition originating in early Second Temple times (cf. Ez 44:26).

[499] In Samaritan texts, the initial menstrual blood re-contaminates the woman with a seven-day impurity until washed off. Counting could begin only after an initial washing. See above, 145.

[500] *Kitâb al-Kâfi* III [43]; XIII [11–13], in Boid 1989, 153f. Cf. Boid's comments, 242f; 324.

[501] David P. Wright 1985, 215, n.7; Milgrom 1981, 71; Cf. Milgrom 1990b, 442f.

[502] Cf. Ez 46:26–27, which could be interpreted to mean that a priest could remain in Jerusalem, because of a first-day ablution, but not enter the temple area until seven days had passed.

[503] For details, see above, 157–159.

What then about the corpse-impure? The continued discussion in the *Temple Scroll* about corpse-impurity in ordinary cities (11Q19 [11QT] 50) nowhere hints that anyone should be expelled. The presence of corpse-contaminated persons and items within the city is rather taken for granted. A possible explanation for this "leniency" could be the practice of a first-day ablution, removing a layer of impurity.[504] Since the temple city was considered more holy than other cities, it would be logical to assume that corpse-impure persons were to be kept out of Jerusalem altogether, according to the *Temple Scroll*. This is not said in the extant text. Milgrom claims that this was nevertheless the case, and suggests that the corpse-impure were mentioned right after the "lepers," dischargers and semen-emitters (11Q19 [11QT] 46:18), at the non-extant top of the following column (47).[505] This is speculative and based on the combined arguments of silence and logic.[506] I would rather leave the question open. As for actual practice, the case is complicated by the fact that different groups had different interpretations of what area the temple city actually consisted of, and the difference between the camp of the Levites and that of Israel.[507]

The *Temple Scroll*, although not a sectarian document, nevertheless reflects somewhat utopian ideals. To some degree it seems to correspond to expansionist interpretations, and some of its prescriptions probably reflect the practice of some segments of Second Temple Jewish society. The question of how corpse-impurity was dealt with in Jerusalem is difficult to resolve. In cities generally, it is reasonable to conclude from the evidence presented above that, while corpse-impurity was taken very seriously by most groups of Jews, the widespread practice of a first-day ablution made it possible for people to remain in their societies during the seven-day purification period, even in expansionist environments. This meant that the most serious form of impurity was in a way mitigated, so as to be treated on the same level as other types of impurities. The arrangement is understandable, because corpse-impurity was partly unavoidable as death is a part of daily life. There is no evidence, however, that this "leni-

---

504 This is the thesis of Milgrom 1978, 512–518. J. Baumgarten's interpretation of טמאתו הרישונה in 4Q514 as referring to the initial impurity of a person who has not yet undergone a first ablution, supports Milgrom's idea (Baumgarten 1992, 205; Cf. E. Eshel 1999, 138). In the case of 4Q514, the argument would be that an initial ablution makes it possible for a purifying person to partake of food before the seven-day period is finished. In the case of the *Temple Scroll* passages discussed above, the point is that an initial ablution would make it possible for a corpse-impure person to remain in the city. In both cases the possibility depends on the notion of removing a layer of impurity by this ablution.

505 Milgrom 1978, 515, n.44.

506 The semen-emitter is expelled from the temple city (11Q19 [11QT] 46:18) but not mentioned in the rules for the ordinary city. Dischargers are likewise expelled from the temple city (46:18) but could possibly be seen as only quarantined in ordinary cities (48:15–17). Since corpse-impure people were apparently allowed to stay in ordinary cities (50), one would at least expect some sort of restriction for the temple city.

507 Cf. Harrington 1993, 57f.

ency" should have lessened the contamination potential or otherwise affected the seven-day impurity of the corpse-contaminated person. The presence of corpse-impure people within the cities of Israel was the normal case during the Second Temple period, provided for in the legislation of Num 19. In view of expansionist currents, being influenced by stricter "wilderness camp" or "temple city" traditions, this arrangement could nevertheless continue, thanks to the idea of an initial ablution, as well as careful adherence to purity *halakhah*. Expansionists had to live with corpse-impurity as well.

The good Samaritan and a presumptive corpse

In addition to the stories discussed above about Jesus raising dead people, the issue of corpse-impurity has been detected in the parable about the good Samaritan (Lk 10:25–37). The priest and the Levite are both represented as avoiding the half-dead (ἡμιθανῆ) traveller, by passing by on the other side of the road (ἀντιπαρῆλθεν). This has been interpreted as a result of legal concerns; the man was seemingly dead and both of them wanted to avoid becoming corpse-contaminated.[508] Svartvik has pointed at a problem with such a line of interpretation: Jewish law is seen as the cause of merciless behaviour.[509] An anti-Jewish connotation is not, however, necessarily attached to the question of purity. This is clear from Billerbeck, who denies a purity issue in the text, but nevertheless focuses on the heartlessness of the priest.[510] Whether the parable is read as having an anti-halakhic or anti-clerical stance, the interpreter can always add an anti-Jewish flavour.[511]

The Lukan context raises questions as to the sources of the passage. The lawyer's question (Lk 10:25–28), which introduces the story of the Samaritan (vv 29–35) has synoptic parallels (Mt 22:34–40/Mk 12:28–34). Luke's version is, however, adapted to his own variant of the likewise synoptic tradition about the "rich young man" (Mk 10:17/Mt 19:16/Lk 18:18).[512] Compared with the Markan version (Mk 12:28–34), Luke makes similar omissions as does Matthew. The similarities with Matthew are, however, not consistent enough to

[508] Mann 1915–1916; Derrett 1964, 24–28. Jeremias 1972 [1947], 203ff, mentions the idea, but regards it as uncertain. Some exegetes almost ignore the purity issue (Bovon 1996, 79–99), while others take it more or less for granted (cf. Caird 1963, 148; Fitzmyer 1985, 883). Billerbeck (SB 2: 183) discarded it, since the parable was about helping a living person, and his judgement was accepted by, among others, I. H. Marshall (1978, 448). The idea should not be dismissed too easily, however, without taking into account a possible history of textual development. The purity issue has been argued recently by Bauckham 1998.

[509] Svartvik 2000, 5; especially the examples in n.12.

[510] SB 2: 183.

[511] Whether this is done already by Luke is a question which will not be discussed here, since our primary interest concerns earlier levels.

[512] This is evident in the initial question of the man, which in both cases in Luke is identical: τί ποιήσας ζωὴν αἰώνιον κληρονομήσω;

ensure a common origin from a partly overlapping Q source. To the Lukan variant of the ruler's question is appended the actual story about the Samaritan, which belongs to Luke's special material, and begins with a further question: "who is my neighbour?" The story does not answer the question directly, but rather inverts it, by giving an example of how to be a neighbour to somebody else.

The somewhat awkward joining of question and narrative has been taken as a sign of Lukan redaction.[513] But the opposite case could also be argued. Since the story does not directly answer the question, Luke would not have joined them were they not found as a unit before.[514] The latter line of reasoning seems, however, somewhat strained. Joining a question with a parable or exemplary narrative, and turning a question or statement upside-down, seems to be a trait of Luke's style.[515]

If Luke is seen as responsible for the redaction, he could be suspected of having created the story himself. This is unlikely, however, in view of the apparent discrepancies between question and story.[516] In style and vocabulary, the story has at times been regarded as "exceptional even in Luke,"[517] but this is somewhat exaggerated. The quality of language is high, just as in other major passages stemming from what is considered as Luke's special source.[518] Luke probably found the story of the "good Samaritan" in written form and joined it, with necessary adaptations, to the lawyer's question.

The possible purity issue in the story is not made explicit, and would probably not have been recognized by Luke's readers. While the story must have reached Luke in a "Hellenistic" form (i.e. written in good Greek), arguments from source and style of language are not decisive for the questions about the background or origin of the narrative. We have to turn to the content as well. An examination reveals a number of details which fit into a Palestinian-Jewish context. The dangers of the road between Jerusalem and Jericho are historically known.[519] Banditry was an increasing phenomenon during the first century CE.[520] The careful wording (καταβαίνειν is used for going *down* from Jerusalem to Jericho) betrays an awareness of geographical conditions. The identities

---

[513] Cf. Fitzmyer 1985 882f.

[514] Cf. I. H. Marshall 1978, 445f. This line of thought is not convincing, and is necessary only if one presupposes that the present application of the story must have belonged to its original form.

[515] Cf. the narrative about Simon, the Pharisee, the woman who anointed Jesus' feet, and the parable about the two debtors in Lk 7:36–50. The silent question of the Pharisee is not exactly what is answered by the parable. Furthermore, the point of the parable is that forgiveness creates love, while the application amounts to love causing forgiveness.

[516] C. F. Evans 1990, 467.

[517] C. F. Evans 1990, 467.

[518] Bovon 1996, 84, especially n.10.

[519] Bovon 1996, 89, with references to Strabo (16.2.41) and Josephus (*J.W.* 4:474).

[520] Cf. Freyne 1988b.

of the role figures in the story (priest, Levite, Samaritan) are not necessary for the general point of compassion and neighbourly love which the narrative serves in its Lukan setting, but gain more detailed relevance in a Palestinian-Jewish setting, with its particular social and ethno-religious tensions. While signs of "Palestinian provenance" are uncertain as criteria of "authenticity," such signs do give clues as to the context and function of a tradition.

In a Palestinian-Jewish setting, this narrative of the "good Samaritan," even in its present form, cannot have failed to address the question of purity.[521] There are three possible objections to such a claim. The most important counter-argument deals with the fact that the traveller is described as "half-dead" (ἡμιθανῆ, v 30). He is thus not a corpse yet. The fact that he is not "actually" dead, however, has no bearing upon our issue as such. What is important is that within the story world, he is perceived as dead, or possibly dead, by some of the other characters, i.e. the priest and the Levite. While this is not explicitly said, it must be understood as belonging to the implicit suppositions of the hearers.[522]

A second argument against a purity issue in the text, that only priests but not Levites were to avoid corpse-impurity according to biblical law, is formally correct.[523] But Levites were to join the priests, and may well have appropriated the same rules for themselves. During the period of the Second Temple, their status increased, and they were assigned priestly functions.[524]

A third argument would emphasize that the priest and Levite were on their way *from* Jerusalem (v 31, κατέβαινεν), and thus would not need to worry about contracting impurity, since it would not hinder them in their temple service.[525] This argument has no validity, however, in view of what we have seen above about how seriously corpse-impurity was treated. It was generally avoided, and some sort of purification was undertaken, regardless of whether or not a temple visit was at hand. Furthermore, priests were not allowed to contract corpse impurity except in case of close relatives (Lev 21:1–4), and the biblical prohibitions were general, not conditioned by temple service.

Excursus 2: ἡμιθανής as seemingly dead

The term ἡμιθανής is a *hapax* in the NT and an unusual term in any Greek writing.[526] It is at times used for persons who are pictured as far from unconscious.[527] In the Hellenistic Jewish

[521] Bauckham 1998, 477–480.
[522] For an extended discussion of the use of the term ἡμιθανής, see Excursus 2 below.
[523] Maccoby 1999, 150f.
[524] Cf. Lev 21:1–3; Num 18:2–4; Neh 10:37–38. Sanders 1990, 41f. Cf. Milgrom 1978, 501–506; Fitzmyer 1985, 883, 887, n.32.
[525] While κατέβαινεν is used about the priest only, it could be inferred that the Levite travelled in the same direction.
[526] ἡμιθανής first in Dionysius of Halicarnassus (10:7); Diodoros of Sicily (12.62.5); and Strabo (2.3.4) instead of the classical ἡμιθνής. Cf. Liddell-Scott[9] 1940, *s.v.* ἡμιθανής.

romance *Joseph and Aseneth*, however, the term is used with the meaning of "almost dead." In an attempt to kidnap Aseneth, Pharaoh's son is hindered by Benjamin, who throws a stone which strikes his left temple, leaving him seriously wounded. "And Pharaoh's son fell down from his horse on the ground, being half dead" (ἡμιθανὴς τυγχάνων).[528] The wounded prince is pictured as seemingly dead or unconscious, since only later in the narrative does he move.[529]

Levi attempts to save his life, but Pharaoh's son dies on the third day. The description of Levi's action, however, contains several motifs, also found in the parable of the "good Samaritan."

> And Levi raised Pharaoh's son from the ground and washed the blood off his face and tied a bandage to his wound, and put him upon his horse, and conducted him to his father Pharaoh, and described to him all these things.[530]

Literary dependence in either direction is to be doubted, since (except for ἡμιθανὴς in the earlier passage) verbal similarities are almost non-existent. Similarities in motifs, however, are striking: taking care of and bandaging the wounds of a half-dead person, lifting him onto an animal, and transporting him to another place.

While the date and provenance of *Joseph and Aseneth* have been difficult to determine, some date between 100 BCE and the Second Jewish War (132–135 CE) is probable. Egypt is often suggested as the place of origin, but an underlying Semitic original from Palestine or Syria is possible.[531] The writing probably elaborates on a Jewish popular tale from the end of the Second Temple period. It may well have been known in some form by a Palestinian narrator of the parable of the "good Samaritan." Although it is Levi who acts in an appropriate way in *Joseph and Aseneth*, it is not one of his descendents, but a Samaritan, in the gospel parable.

As we have seen above, there are signs of a Palestinian origin for the Lukan tradition. What was conspicuous in a first-century Palestinian environment about Levites and priests, was their obligation for a higher degree of purity than ordinary people. As will be seen below, the question of how to balance the requirement for purity with the responsibility to the dead, with regard to such categories of people of whom a higher degree of purity was required, was a contemporary and relevant issue. A parable addressing such a dilemma would fit into a first-century context, and give a plausible and a somewhat defensible explanation for the behaviour of the priest and the Levite in the narrative. Without a purity issue in the story of the "good Samaritan," this tradition would represent a position of crude anti-clericalism, or an unsubtle Christian polemic against Jewish leaders. Such an attitude could possibly be credible on part of the gospel writer, but it is to be doubted for the earlier underlying Palestinian tradition. The idea of the man being seemingly dead, and purity being the issue, is superior for explaining the function and relevance of the Lukan parable in an earlier Palestinian context. While the story would not be seen from a purity perspective in Luke's Hellenistic context, this would be natural in a Palestinian environment. *Joseph and Aseneth* shows us that other popular tales were told at the time, in which

---

[527] Cf. 4Macc 4:11.

[528] *Jos.Asen.* 27:3. This is the reading of most Greek manuscripts. Burchard 1983, 714, n. 3.

[529] *Jos.Asen.* 29:1 "And Pharaoh's son rose from the ground and sat up and spat blood from his mouth…" That ἡμιθανής was understood as seemingly dead is clear from several early translations of this work. The influential Latin manuscript tradition (L1) reads "quasi mortuum," and the Armenian version reads "ew elew nman meṙeloy" (and was like a dead). Cf. Burchard 1983, 714, n. 3.

[530] *Jos.Asen.* 29:5. Καὶ ἀνέστησε Λευὶς τὸν υἱὸν Φαραὼ καὶ ἀπένιψε τὸ αἷμα ἐκ τοῦ προσώπου αὐτοῦ καὶ ἔδησε τελαμῶνα εἰς τὸ τραῦμα αὐτοῦ καὶ ἐπέθηκεν αὐτὸν ἐπὶ τὸν ἵππον αὐτοῦ καὶ ἐκόμισεν αὐτὸν πρὸς τὸν πατέρα αὐτοῦ. Καὶ δηγήσαντο αὐτῷ Λευὶς ἅπαντα τὰ παρακολουθήσαντα.

[531] Burchard 1985, 181, 187.

attempts were made to rescue an unconscious or seemingly dead person, and when such a tale was put into Greek writing, ἡμιθανής was deemed a suitable term to use.

Priestly purity and priority

It has been questioned whether the situation pictured in the story of the good Samaritan is realistic, since there were exceptions in the legal tradition for extreme cases. Maccoby claims that even a priest is "not only permitted, but obliged, to lay aside his purity" in such a situation, and that the duty to give a corpse a decent burial "far transcends ritual purity considerations."[532] Referring to *mNaz* 7:1, Maccoby argues that even a High Priest was obliged to contract corpse-impurity if he found a corpse by the road (מֵת מִצְוָה).[533] This is not self-evident, however, as a statement about historical conditions during the first century CE. The mishnaic passage is structured as a discussion between R. Eliezer and the sages. After an initial statement, confirming the general rule that neither a high priest nor a *nazir* should contract corpse-impurity except in the case of close relatives, there is a discussion about the case of a neglected corpse by the road. R. Eliezer argues for a high priest rather than a *nazir* contracting corpse-impurity, while the sages argue the opposite.

> [If] they were going along the way and found a neglected corpse -
> R. Eliezer says, "Let a high priest contract corpse uncleanness, but let a Nazir not contract corpse uncleanness."
> And sages say, "Let a Nazir contract corpse uncleanness, but let a high priest not contract corpse uncleanness."
> Said to them R. Eliezer, "Let a priest contract corpse uncleanness, for he does not have to bring an offering on account of his uncleanness. But let a Nazir not contract corpse uncleanness, for he does have to bring an offering on account of his uncleanness."
> They said to him, "Let a Nazir contract corpse uncleanness, for his sanctification is not a permanent sanctification, but let a priest not contract corpse uncleanness, for his sanctification is a permanent sanctification."[534]

Eliezer's argument is primarily economic, while the sages reason in theological terms. This mishnaic passage gives evidence for the general rule, and for an amount of discussion. We cannot from this, however, draw definite conclusions as to the legal situation during the Second Temple period, and this rabbinic passage can hardly be used as an argument against the presence of a purity issue in the narrative of the "good Samaritan." The opposite should rather be the case. The appropriate action of a priest finding a corpse by the road was apparently not self-evident, but was discussed by the Tannaim in the period following

---

[532] Maccoby 1999, 150f. Cf. Derrett 1964, 27.

[533] Maccoby 1999, 27. Cf. Svartvik 2000, 5 n.13. For a discussion on the מֵת מִצְוָה, see Mann 1915–1916, 417ff. Cf. *bNaz* 47b, 48a–b.

[534] *mNaz* 7:1.

Yavneh.[535] These are all reasons to believe that the question would have been raised some decades earlier. When the parable of the "good Samaritan" is seen in such a context, it becomes an implicit but pointed comment on the debate.[536]

The discussion in *mNaz* 7:1 is interesting, since it gives evidence of different opinions, and the possibility of different types of behaviour. Arguments such as respect for the dead or compassionate behaviour are not explicitly appealed to in the rabbinic text as overruling purity concerns, although the presupposition is that extraordinary conditions must be treated extraordinarily. A rabbinic anecdote from the *Tosefta*, with several parallels, might also be relevant to our investigation. The context is the daily clearing of ashes from the altar.[537]

> M'ŚH Š: *There were two who got there at the same time, running up the ramp. One shoved the other,*[538] within the four cubits [of the altar]. The other then took out a knife and stabbed him in the heart. R. Ṣadoq came and stood on the steps of the porch and said, "Hear me, o brethren of the House of Israel! Lo, Scripture says, *If in the land which the Lord your God gives you to possess, any one is found slain, lying in the open country, and it is not known who killed him, then your elders and your judges shall come forth, and they shall measure the distance to the cities which are around him that is slain* (Deut. 21:1–2). Come and let us measure to find out for what area it is appropriate to bring the calf—for the Sanctuary, or for the courts!" All of them moaned after his speech. And afterward the father of the youngster came to them, saying, "O brethren of ours! I am your atonement. His [my] son is still writhing, so the knife has not yet been made unclean." This teaches you that the uncleanness of a knife is more grieveous to Israelites than murder. And so it says, *Moreover Manasseh shed much innocent blood, till he had filled Jerusalem from one end to the other* (II Kings 21:16). On this basis they have said, "Because of the sin of murder the Presence of God was raised up, and the sanctuary was made unclean."[539]

---

[535] The discussion in *mNaz* 7:1 is attributed to R. Eliezer (b. Hyrcanus), a second generation Tanna.

[536] Cf. Bauckham 1998, 480–485, 489.

[537] In *mYoma* 2:1–4, which forms an appendix, commenting on *mYoma* 1:8 (cf. Neusner 1981–1983, 3:76), it is stated that whowever reached the altar first was allowed to take up the ashes. However, because of an incident, the court decided that the right to clear off the ashes should be distributed by lot only. The incident is found in the example story in *mYoma* 2:2: Two priests got to the altar simultaneously, and one pushed the other so that he fell and broke his foot or leg. In *Tosefta*'s variant (*tYoma* 1:12), which is also found in *Sifre* to Num 35:34 (161), the quarrel is a matter of outright murder, and occasions a problem of purity. The narrative ends with a comment on the departure of the *Shekinah* and the sanctuary made unclean. In the *Babylonian Talmud*, however, this end note is missing. Instead there is a discussion on how to reconcile the two traditions (broken leg and murder). Which incident took place before the other? If the broken leg, the ensuing rule should have prevented the later incident of murder. If the murder, why was no rule about lots issued at once, but only after the less serious incident with a broken leg? The case is solved by regarding the murder as the first incident, but considered so exceptional that no rule was issued (*bYoma* 23a).

[538] This far the *Tosefta* follows *mYoma* 2:2.

[539] *tYoma* 1:12. Tr. Neusner 1981–1983, 3:77.

The critical note, which is even more transparent in the variant of the *Palestinian Talmud*,[540] should be registered. The comment about the uncleanness of the knife being more important than murder is probably a gloss, expressing a redactor's judgment on what was perceived as earlier conditions.[541] It seems as if the attitude displayed in the example story was deemed unsuitable, because it implied priorities which were considered as false. We should thus take the comments around this tradition as evidence for an inner-Jewish critical discussion about priorities, and the somewhat relative value of purity in comparison to matters of life and death. Later rabbinic generations expressed elsewhere the idea that the emphasis on purity during the late Second Temple period was disproportionally high.[542] While this opinion should not be accepted without reservations, the material discussed above (*mNaz* 7:1; *tYoma* 1:12) reveals that questions about priority and the relative value of purity were open to debate, and related to earlier conditions. This is not to claim that "ritual rigidity" dominated the Second Temple period, but only to give evidence for the existence of a discursive context in which the story of the "good Samaritan" would fit very well.

It could perhaps be argued that *mNaz* 7:1 presupposes that the מֵת מִצְוָה (the obligation to defile oneself in the case of a neglected corpse) applied to *both* a High Priest *and* a *nazir*, and that the discussion concerns only cases where there was a choice between the two.[543] If this is so, the discrepancy between this attitude of the Tannaim and that which is implicitly criticized in *tYoma* 1:12 becomes more visible. Although the earlier tendency of simply ascribing Tannaitic material to the Pharisees should be treated with suspicion, the suggestion of Jacob Mann, that the parable of the "good Samaritan" contained an attack on Sadducean positions, should be seriously considered. As Mann points out, the מֵת מִצְוָה went against the explicit commands of biblical law (Lev 21:1ff, 11ff; Num 6:7), and rabbinic attempts at exegetical justification were never very successful, and would not have been readily accepted by Sadducees during the Second Temple period.[544] A strict view on corpse-impurity in regard to a priest or a *nazir* may be regarded as a Sadducean position. This would fit the Lukan narrative, since priests and Levites were usually identified with the Sadducees. A critical view on legal priority and an anti-clerical stance could thus be seen to coincide in the story. Whether first-century Pharisees would

---

540 "Dies (lehrt), daß ihnen Unreinheit schwerer wog als Blutvergießen—zu (ihrer) Schande" (*yYoma* 2:2, *ÜTY* II/4, 49). The last word (לגנאי in Ed. princ. Venedig, לגניי in MS Leiden) is missing in Neusner's translation.

541 Cf. Kuhn's comment in his translation of *Sifre* to Num 35:34 (2.9: 687, n.54).

542 "Purity broke out in Israel" (פרצה טהרה בישראל), *tShabb* 1:14; cf. *bShabb* 13a; *yShabb* 1:3.

543 Cf. Mann 1915–1916, 418.

544 Mann 1915–1916, 418f. Cf. *Sifra* to Lev 21:1 [Parashat Emor Parashah 1]; *bNaz* 47b, 48a–b; *bZeb* 100a. Bauckham 1998, 482, n.13, doubts Mann's arguments.

generally applaud the legal stance implicit in the narrative of the "good Samaritan" is another question. We do not know to what extent the מֵת מִצְוָה was an accepted interpretation among Pharisees at the end of the Second Temple period. If any clue should be taken from *mNaz* 7:1, it would be that opinions were divided.

Hence the narrative in Lk 10:30–35 can easily be seen to address first-century purity concerns. It cannot, however, serve as proof for Jesus disregarding purity laws. Nor does its implicit view on the relative value of purity over against other concerns represent a unique position within contemporary Judaism. However, the priorities advocated were not uncontroversial, but in direct conflict with some Jewish opinions. The story of the "good Samaritan" thus represents an early voice, criticizing certain Jewish authorities for setting false priorities in their application of corpse-impurity rules. There is no reason why the gist of the story should not go back to Jesus.

Jesus and corpse-impurity

As defilement from corpses was a general idea in Antiquity, not only among Jews but in all neighbouring cultures, there is no reason to imagine that Jesus operated without this concept, or ignored it totally. Several gospel traditions reveal a seemingly indiffent attitude, however, especially when seen against the fact that corpse-impurity was generally avoided not only in view of temple visits.

The Lukan tradition about the widow's son in Nain (Lk 7:11–17) involves corpse-contamination, but there is some uncertainty concerning the degree of impurity contracted in the interaction. This ambiguity is not present in the Markan narrative about Jairus and his daughter (Mk 5:21–24, 35–43). Here Jesus enters both the house and the very room in which the corpse is lying, and he touches the corpse directly. With the biblical legislation (Num 19) about corpse-impurity in mind, it would be evident to any reader or listener with a Jewish background that Jesus, by his action, incurred a seven-day impurity.

A "lenient" attitude is further underscored by the Lukan tradition of the good Samaritan (Lk 10:30–35). In this narrative we find similarities with later rabbinic discussions about the priority between the obligation towards the dead and the demand for purity, but Jesus seems to have gone further, and at an earlier time. We also find differences, however, since the rabbis at least formally defended the מֵת מִצְוָה by exegesis. We should assume that practical considerations were important for both Jesus and later rabbis, so that rules about corpse-impurity in certain cases were deemed as having less priority than other issues. However, Jesus' unqualified way of setting other priorities in an area, in which biblical legislation was clear, and at a time when strictness dominated, must have evoked opposition.

Summary: A case for Jesus' attitude as seemingly indifferent

Throughout this chapter I have argued that the early Jesus tradition contained remnants of purity issues. These must be acknowledged, in spite of the fact that they are more or less implicit in the present form of the narratives. Working from non-conflict traditions about Jesus' actions rather than conflict stories and sayings of Jesus as the primary point of departure, I have tried to give evidence for an attitude to impurity which cannot have passed unnoticed in a Jewish environment at the end of the Second Temple period.

Although the Markan traditions which have set the agenda are miracle stories, this does not disqualify them as possible bearers of historical remains. We have seen that the various motifs and details of these narratives, as well as Jesus' gestures, cannot be dismissed merely as typical traits of Hellenistic miracle stories. While most traditions in their present form reflect subsequent christological concerns, it is possible, with a moderate use of redaction criticism, to identify historically plausible details and circumstances which had no prominent function in the ideological construct of the gospel redactors, but must have been conspicuous in a Jewish environment from a purity perspective.

Discussing the main sources of impurity, "leprosy," genital discharges and the corpse, I have attempted to show that the end of the Second Temple period saw an increase in expansionist interpretation and practice. Early Jesus tradition retained the memory of Jesus acting in ways which must have been considered unacceptable in contexts where expansionist ideals were influential.[545]

I have argued that the exclusion of "lepers" from ordinary towns, including isolation and avoidance of physical contact, is attested by unanimous contemporary sources, while Jesus is remembered in various independent traditions as having associated with "lepers," visiting them and touching them.

On the issue of genital discharges, contemporary practice is more difficult to assess, but we have seen that some type of isolation of "permanent" dischargers and menstruants seems to be warranted by the sources, as well as by material remains, such as stone vessels. Jesus' attitude to this type of impurity is not as clearly spelled out in the relevant traditions, as for the cases of "leprosy" or corpse-impurity. The problem of contamination in the Markan tradition of the bleeding woman is, however, the particular purity issue in the gospels which is most clearly recognized in the early church. In view of contemporary halakhic discussions, the interaction between Jesus and the discharging woman involved contamination, and certain Lukan traditions may also retain traces of similar contamination.

[545] The details will not be repeated here, since they are summarized under the headings Jesus and "leprosy"/discharges/corpse-impurity, respectively (See above, 127, 164 and 196).

The case of corpse-impurity is more clear-cut. Corpse-impurity was generally avoided, not only in view of temple visits. Narrative traditions retain a memory of Jesus coming into contact with corpses in a way which would have rendered him corpse-impure, with no hint of subsequent purification. Other traditions reveal an awareness of the issue, and fit into contemporary discussions about halakhic interpretation, where questions about priority come into focus.

In spite of their relative disinterest in the issues involved, the available sources retain memories of Jesus as not conforming to, or being in tension with, the expansionist purity ideals, which were influential on the contemporary scene. While this could possibly be seen as an early effort belonging to that movement for leniency in interpretation, which becomes apparent with later generations of rabbis, we find little evidence that Jesus, like the rabbis, should have justified his position with sufficient exegesis.[546] Other explanations must be sought for Jesus' position.

As I concluded in the previous chapter, it is highly implausible that Jesus was directly opposed to, or attempting to do away with, Jewish law and tradition. It is clear that he operated within a cultural and religious context, to which the purity paradigm belonged. Within such a paradigm, however, the behaviour of which we find traces in tradition would easily have been understood as reflecting a careless or indifferent attitude. An increasing demand for consistency was, as we have seen, a driving force behind much expansion and intensification of purity *halakhah*. In such an environment, Jesus' attitude should have evoked protest. A charge of carelessness or indifference is also in accord with various accusations, found in the Jesus tradition.[547] To say that Jesus was indifferent to purity, however, is to take an interpretative leap which is not fully substantiated. Jesus' attitude was apparently understood as *seemingly* indifferent in his contemporary context. It is uncertain whether anyone who lived within a society imbued with such a purity paradigm could be *genuinely* so. Interpretation of Jesus' attitude must be carried out within the framework of contemporary society and culture, and using conceptions inherent in the purity paradigm itself. An attempt at such interpretation becomes the task of subsequent chapters.

---

[546] The parable of the "good Samaritan" could be seen as part of a halakhic dialogue, but it contains no exegetical justification in a rabbinic sense. The arguments in Mk 7:6–8 and 9–13 function as exegetical arguments in the final form of the gospel, but their original context is problematic. Cf. above, 63f.

[547] Cf. Mk 2:18; 7:5; 14:4f; Mt 9:11/Lk 5:30; Mt 11:19/Lk 7:34; Mt 9:3; 17:24; Lk 15:2; 19:7.

PART THREE:

EXPLANATORY MODELS

Chapter V
Purity and morality

In Part Two we saw traces in early Jesus traditions of an attitude to impurity which must have caused problems for the influential expansionist current in Second Temple Judaism. Jesus was remembered for setting questionable priorities in an area where biblical legislation was clear, at a time when interpretation and implementation was strict, and without defending his position with acceptable exegesis. This begs some explanation.

In Part Three of this study, three possible explanatory models will be discussed. They are neither to be seen as giving a complete picture, nor as mutually exclusive models. They are rather intended as partial and possible explanations, and in my own view plausible as well, since they agree with textual evidence on one hand, and with the religious as well as the social context in first-century Palestine on the other.

The first suggestion, to be explored in the present chapter, is that Jesus viewed purity primarily from a moral perspective. The idea is by no means new and fits well with subsequent Christian "spiritualizing" of the idea, which is evident already in many New Testament letters.[1] While such a view was taken for granted in the past, it is being increasingly questioned today by scholars viewing Jesus in a first-century Palestinian Jewish context. To what extent was there a moral aspect to purity in Second Temple Judaism?

The issue is complicated and misunderstandings abound. While purity is basically a cultic or ritual concept, purity language is used in the Hebrew Bible with reference to sinful behaviour. Opinions differ as to how this should be interpreted, however. Is defilement from sin to be regarded as a metaphor only, or should it, at least at times, be seen as something concrete and literal, affecting the body of the sinner as well? Or could defilement from sin even be taken as something "literal" without affecting the body of the sinner with a transferable contagion (like the impurities of Lev 12–15), or even without affecting the body of the sinner at all, but having other concrete effects? Is defilement from sin a marginal, an important, or perhaps a dominant idea in ancient Judaism? To what extent are the different conceptions of impurity blended or kept apart, and how did this vary between various groups and in different periods of time?

Some of these questions are discussed in great detail by Jonathan Klawans.[2] His thesis is that "moral impurity" is not a metaphor, but should be seen as a

[1] E.g. Rom 1:24; Gal 5:19; 2Cor 7:1; Heb 9:13–14.

[2] Klawans 1997a and 2000 (the latter is a revised version of his 1997 dissertation). For a review of scholarship on sin and impurity, see Klawans 2000, 3–20.

separate category from (bodily) "ritual impurity." While opinions differed in ancient Judaism as to how the relationship between moral and ritual impurity should be understood, it is only in the sectarian writings from Qumran that the two ideas are almost completely integrated, and merge into a single concept of defilement. The Tannaim on the other hand "compartmentalized" the two, and discussed almost exclusively ritual impurity.[3]

While not all of Klawans' discussion is relevant to my own investigation, several of his major questions are, and I will repeatedly refer to his analyses. Klawans suggests that John's baptism was thought to remove moral impurity, and that Jesus is best understood as giving priority to moral over ritual purity.[4] While I agree with many of his results, I am not convinced about the terminology and the categories used (literal-metaphorical, ritual-moral), which leads to some reservations about his schematization of the differing opinions in conflict during the time of Jesus. This will become clear in the subsequent discussion.

When considering whether Jesus gave priority to a type of purity other than that which has been discussed in previous chapters, we will turn to traditions about inner and outer impurity. It is notable that relevant material can be found both in Q and Thomas traditions as well as in Mark. It is necessary to deal with purifications too, and to discuss not only the immersions carried out by John the Baptizer, but also the possible evidence for Jesus administering, endorsing and/or opposing purification rites. Hence certain Johannine material, as well as an Oxyrhynchus papyrus, will be analyzed.

V.1 Immorality and bodily defilement in ancient Judaism

Sin and impurity

New Testament scholars have too often confused sin and impurity, if not equated the two altogether. This is largely a faulty interpretation, as has been vigorously argued for long by Sanders and others.[5] The plea has not gone unheeded, to the effect that some have clearly distinguished the two, and even denied any connection whatsoever.[6] Among scholars of ancient Judaism, confusion has been more rare, but many have ignored, and some almost denied, an ethical aspect to purity in ancient Judaism, except for the Qumran sect, which is often seen as a special case. Neusner is definitely overstating the case:

---

[3] Klawans 2000, 67–117. "Compartmentalization" is Klawans' characterization of the Tannaitic attempt to "separate the conception of ritual impurity from the conception of sin."
[4] Klawans 2000. 138–150.
[5] Sanders 1985, 182–185. Cf. Klawans 2000, 12, 137f, 144f, who criticizes Malina, Neyrey, Rhoads and Borg to this effect.
[6] Cf. Fredriksen 2000, 67f.

> … representing uncleanness as sin and a sign of wickedness for this Judaism is simply an error. … We emphasize this point because the Judaism we consider here contrasts its uses of the theme of purity with the ways in which some of the important statements of nascent Christianity treat the same topic. In the case at hand, the representation of uncleanness as a mark of sin or wickedness which requires eschatological purification through baptism constitutes Christianity's reading of uncleanness. … the representation of uncleanness as a matter of sin formed a systemic statement of that Christianity, not a response to or a use of a fact of "Judaism." E.P. Sanders, in *Jesus and Judaism,* by contrast stresses that uncleanness in some instances in and of itself is a sin. In the Judaism put forth by the Pentateuch and the Mishnah, that is simply false. Accordingly, Sanders errs when he reads uncleanness as a moral category. It is worth dwelling on the case, because the error in the reading of this Judaism is commonplace because of the theology of cleanness as moral put forth by Christianity, and because Sanders's mistake is therefore routinely made in interpreting the meaning of the sources of uncleanness under consideration in this chapter.[7]

Neusner's attack on Sanders is somewhat misleading since Sanders has been one of the foremost advocates for *not* equating sin and impurity. What Sanders *has* claimed is that according to biblical legislation there are instances when impurity could amount to sin, when it is not dealt with properly.[8] Sanders and Neusner are, however, talking about different Judaisms. Sanders is (assumingly) describing a first-century "common Judaism," while Neusner is discussing the priestly legislation of the Hebrew Bible as interpreted by the Tannaim of the *Mishnah.*[9] Neusner actually admits that other types of Judaism, e.g. the "Essene Judaism of Qumran" and that of John the Baptizer, correspond more to Sanders' description, but this is not the case with "the Judaism represented, as to its initial statement, by the Mishnah."[10]

Neusner's position seems ambiguous when his classic and much earlier work is taken into account. In the second chapter of *The Idea of Purity in Ancient Judaism*, he describes how the concept of purity was transformed into a metaphor for that which is good, right and holy, throughout the writings of the Hebrew Bible.[11] He contrasts the priestly writings, in which purity is a cultic affair, with the prophetic and sapiential writings, in which it is applied to ethics outside the cult. And he finds "a remarkable correspondence."[12]

---

[7] Neusner 1994, 57–58.

[8] Sanders 1985, 183f. Sanders' position is that the term "sinners" in the gospels refers to notorious sinners, traitors and the like, not to impure people in general. Sanders argues that impurity was not sinful in general, but only a hindrance for entering the temple area. Exceptions were a few transgressions of purity laws (e.g. eating blood) which were regarded as inherently sinful. A person who intentionally ignored the purity laws would furthermore be regarded as a sinner, not because of impurity, but because of disobedience to the law. Sanders 1985, 177–188.

[9] This is clear from the quotation above: "In the Judaism put forth by the Pentateuch and the Mishnah" (cf. the repetition of "*this Judaism*"), as well as from the general context.

[10] Neusner 1994, 59.

[11] Neusner 1973a, 7–31.

[12] Neusner 1973a, 24.

> [T]he interpretation of the purity-laws contains virtually all of the motifs important in the use of purity as a moral or other sort of metaphor. One therefore cannot distinguish legal from non-legal views of the matter; the one represents in the context of the concrete cultic ritual what the other describes in the setting of ethics, morality, or theology.[13]

Neusner seems to find a common origin for the different types of purity in the idea of guilt, which is often, but not necessarily, a matter of ethics. The connection can be seen in the legal terminology used about impure people. A *yoledet* is required to bring a sin-offering (*hattat*), a "leper" brings a guilt-offering as well (*asham*), and the water used for purifying the Levites is called "sin-water" (מֵי חַטָּאת).[14] From this Neusner concludes:

> It is possible that the notion of "an ethical offense, a sin" evolved from the general class of "acts that make you unfit for the holy community." So these traces of "ethical" terminology in purity law may be not late contaminations, but fossils from an earlier time when all offenses produced impurity, and all impurities were offenses.[15]

Neusner further points out that the largest number of sources in which purity is discussed derive from priestly writers, and that priestly authorities have taken over, for the temple only, almost all legal material and symbols associated with purity. The sources are thus biased, and we cannot regard purity as primarily a cultic concern, but rather as originating with ideas about that which is loathsome, giving rise to rules which were observed regardless of the cult.[16]

A natural suggestion, based on Neusner's discussion, would be that impurity came to refer to several diverse phenomena which were experienced as loathsome or offensive, whether because of certain types of (un-)ethical behaviour or because of certain natural or pathological physical processes, or because of taboos or aversions to eating certain types of animals.[17] Such a loose model could actually account for all three types of impurity which are found in the Hebrew Bible, and in the priestly legislation. Impurity terminology (טָמֵא) is used in the following contexts: 1) The classification of animals into clean and unclean, i.e. edible and non-edible (Lev 11). This legislation gives no sanctions in case of transgression, nor does it envisage any means of purification, but assumes that

---

[13] Neusner 1973a, 24.

[14] Lev 12:6, 8; 14:12, 19; Num 8:7. Neusner (1973a, 25) actually makes a mismatch, ascribing a guilt-offering to the *yoledet* (which is false) and a sin-offering to the "leper" (which is correct, although it is the guilt-offering which is particular to the "leper." In addition, the *zab* and the *zabah* are required to offer a sin-offering (Lev 15:15, 30). The translation of חַטָּאת and אָשָׁם with ethical terms is questioned by many scholars; cf. below, 211–214.

[15] Neusner 1973a, 25.

[16] Neusner 1973a, 29f; "We must keep in mind the deliberate bias introduced by the biblical priests and the accidental distortion resulting from the limited sample of evidence. While purity is essential to the religious system of Israel, its larger implications are exceedingly difficult to determine." Neusner 1973a, 31.

[17] Without discussing diverse anthropological theories about the origin of concepts of impurity, it can be observed that there is often a high degree of coincidence between what is regarded as unclean and common ideas about what is repulsive.

the rules are always followed. 2) The system of bodily transferable impurity (Lev 12–15; Num 19), discussed in the previous parts of this study. This legislation provides both sanctions and purification rites, and descriptions about how impurity is transferred as well as instructions on how to avoid contamination, since it assumes that people at times become impure, either by necessity or accident. 3) Laws concerning grave sins which were regarded as polluting: certain sexual sins and idolatry, particularly child sacrifice (Lev 18–20), as well as murder (Num 35). Sexual sins and child sacrifice render the persons involved impure (Lev 18:24)[18] All three grave sins are seen as making mainly the land (Lev 18:25), and in the case of child sacrifice even the temple (Lev 20:3) impure, with the result that the land will vomit the people out, i.e. exile them. No purification is envisaged, but in the case of murder the land can be atoned for only by vengeance (Num 35:33).

Such a reconstruction leads to a model of different trajectories developing and interacting throughout ancient Judaism.[19] We will see below how this idea can be further pursued and compared with Klawans' model.

Excursus 3: Impurity as a metaphor

While most scholars regard the use of impurity language for sinful behaviour as figurative or metaphorical,[20] Jonathan Klawans has argued that in many cases this use is to be taken literally. The cases in question are principally the three "heinous" sins of the *Holiness Code* (Lev 17–26), which pollute the land (sexual sins, idolatry and bloodshed).[21] He argues that these acts do not make sinners *ritually* impure with a contagious but impermanent impurity, which can be dealt with by certain purification rites. It is nevertheless a question of *real* impurity, in the sense of degradation or desecration, which is not metaphorical. This is not a way of calling something

[18] However, nothing is stated about how this impurity manifests itself.

[19] Neusner stops short of discussing interacting trajectories, just like some other scholars of ancient Judaism, in order to affirm the non-ethical aspects of impurity as the genuine or original, or even better view. Neusner claims that "the terms 'pure' and 'impure' *originally* had no ethical value" (Neusner 1973a, 11; italics supplied). The metaphorical developments are valued as "superficial and homiletical" because they do not exploit the *details* of the purity laws (Neusner 1973a, 15; cf. 31). The Qumran sectarians are said to have added nothing new to the ideology of purity, while the Christians "*reverted* to the prophetic and sapiential contrast between ethical and cultic purity, but developed nothing in the already-available interpretative legacy." "Only with rabbinic Judaism" comes original development (Neusner 1973a, 31; italics supplied). The idea that only the *Mishnah* interprets the Pentateuch correctly is found in Hyam Maccoby too. We find with Maccoby a similar combination of priestly legislation and rabbinic interpretation, as well as a similar distinction between ritual and morality (Maccoby 1999, 195, 204), which is said to be valid for *all* Judaism. Commenting on the limitations of the common anthropological approach for interpreting Leviticus, Maccoby states that it "fails to appreciate fully the level of consciousness, differentiating between ritual and morality, that is characteristic of Judaism at *all* periods" (Maccoby 1999, 205; italics supplied). Such a view would have to regard the obvious blending of impurity and sin at Qumran as very uncharacteristic of Judaism.

[20] Cf. Ringgren 1982; André 1982. Cf. Klawans 2000, 32.

[21] Klawans 2000, 26–31.

sinful, but people and land are actually seen as physically defiled.[22] He presents two main arguments. Just as in the case of the bodily impurities of Lev 12–15, this type of impurity is about "perceived effects that result from actual processes," although the effects are different in each case. It is thus a matter of "two analogous *perceptions of contagion*, each of which brings about effects of legal and social consequence."[23] The second argument has to do with the nature of metaphorical language. Since Klawans defines it in opposition to literal usage, it must involve a degree of transference, and thus must be regarded as secondary to a prior, literal usage.[24] Klawans points out, however, that the usage of purity terminology in moral contexts appears in texts (*Holiness Code*, Deuteronomy, the Deuteronomistic history and prophetic texts) that are often regarded as *earlier* than the priestly traditions which are evidence for the "primary" usage of impurity language. Thus "[w]e simply cannot know which usage came first."[25]

Klawans has been criticized by, among others, Maccoby, who argues that the defilement of the Land is an image, which conceives of the Land as a large animal which suffers nausea at the accumulation of grave sins, to the point of vomiting out its inhabitants. Says Maccoby:

> To literalize the metaphor is to reduce the moral disgust: as if to say, 'The reason why you must avoid these sins is because the Land has a delicate digestion.' It is precisely when a person is overwhelmed by moral disapproval that he is likely to use metaphors based on physical disgust.[26]

While Maccoby's criticism is somewhat exaggerated,[27] it nevertheless seems as if Klawans has fallen into the common trap of confusing literal with real. While he notes that none of the scholars discussing a metaphorical use of impurity clearly defines the terminology, Klawans does not himself attempt a full definition either. At one point he actually suggests that the best course might be to drop such terms from the discussion altogether.[28] I agree with this suggestion, and regret that he does not follow it. As far as I understand, Klawans wants to show that impurity as a result of immoral actions was conceived of as real and factual, albeit somewhat different when compared with bodily impurity.[29] The categories of "literal" and "metaphorical" are not ontological, however; they say nothing about the *reality* of the referent, but they are linguistic classifiers, i.e. tools for distinguishing different types of language.[30] With this in mind, their relevancy for analyzing the concept of purity must be questioned.

There is neither room nor need for a discussion about metaphor theories in this study. For historical purposes it is sufficient to point out that, although the concept of metaphor is both ancient and Mediterranean (Plato and Aristotle), it is not a Hebrew category.[31] The categories of "literal" and "metaphorical" are imposed on these texts by us. They do not quite fit. They do

---

[22] Klawans 2000, 32–34; against David P. Wright 1992, 743.

[23] Klawans 2000, 34.

[24] Klawans 2000, 33.

[25] Klawans 2000, 35, referring to Hos 5:3; 6:10; Jer 2 and 3; Deut 21:23; 24:1–4, 1Kgs 14:24; 2Kgs 16:3 (in addition to material from the Holiness Code, e.g. Lev 18–20). See below, 213–216, about the significance of the dating of P and H for the discussion about a moral trajectory.

[26] Maccoby 1999, 201.

[27] Klawans' observation that with bloodshed and perhaps sexual sins as well, the ground is more or less physically defiled, could be seen as a possible defense (Klawans 2000, 35, 175, n. 86). Klawans talks about "a real, physical process or event" which has a perceived effect, and that Lev 18:24–30 "should be taken literally" (Klawans 1997a, 63, 64).

[28] Klawans 2000, 32f.

[29] Klawans 1997b, 5f.

[30] Cf. Caird 1980, 131–133, 193f.

[31] The term μεταφορά is found only once in the Greek translation of the Hebrew Bible, in Theodotion's translation of Hos 8:13, and then with a different meaning.

not help us to answer how ancient Jews conceived of the relationship between sin and impurity. This is shown by comparing the (relatively few) usages of impurity language which Klawans admits are truly metaphorical, with the others. It is difficult, for example, to understand why impurity in Ps 106:34–41 or Ez 36:16–18; 22–25 should be read more literally than in Isa 1:15–17; 64:4–5 or Ps 51:4–5, 9 (where it is metaphorical according to Klawans).[32] Or is it only because the former texts explicitly refer to some of the capital sins of the *Holiness Code*?

Logically we would expect impurity to refer primarily to a condition in which an item has been physically besmirched with some sort of dirt or other objectionable substance. As seen in the previous chapter, this seems to have been one basic conception underlying much of the legislation in Lev 12–15. A person was conceived of as impure when sullied by menstrual blood, certain skin rashes or some sort of quasi-physical substance believed to ooze from a corpse. When the defiling "substance" was somehow removed, the person could become clean. In certain circumstances, however, impurity remained for some time, despite the removal of the "substance." Contamination was not dependent on any substance being transferred, although the risk of transferring an impure substance might have been behind the origin of some of the rules concerning dischargers.[33] We thus see that there is an element of secondary use or transference already with first- and second-degree impurities.[34] When impurity is used to describe the effect on the sanctuary or the land of immoral actions, it is in a transferred sense as well, but where to draw the line between literal and metaphorical is not obvious.[35] As pointed out by Kittay,

> an expression is not metaphorical in an absolute sense. It is metaphorical only relative to a given conceptual organization in which certain categorizations capture similarities and differences taken to be salient for that language community.[36]

This means that something which originated as a metaphor might at another time and in another context be conceived of as literal, and vice versa. Hence the distinction between literal and metaphorical must be relativized.[37]

As there is an element of transferred meaning in several of the impurities of Lev 12–15, as well as traces of actual physical defilement in certain passages about defiling sins, it will not be possible either to equate literal with ritual impurity and metaphorical with moral impurity, or to claim that all or most impurities are to be taken in a strictly literal sense. While Klawans is to be believed that ancient Jews did not generally confuse the system of bodily impurity (Lev 12–15) and that of defiling immorality (*Holiness Code*), this was not due to their application of categories such as literal and metaphorical, but because of the clearcut instructions about conse-

---

[32] Klawans 2000, 28f, 30f, 35f.

[33] Lev 15:11, 21–23. For details, see above, 144–146.

[34] Cf. Klawans' comment: "I certainly cannot understand why the defilement of the land by blood spilled upon it ought to be a metaphor, while the defilement of a person who merely enters a tent in which there lies a corpse is real" (1997a, 63). Apart from the confusion of metaphysics with linguistics, there is a valid point in the argument. The conclusion in my mind, however, ought to be that the categories of "literal" and "metaphorical" must be left out of this type of investigation.

[35] Cf. Stolz's examples of visual and ritual elements. The gesture of washing hands before performing a rite means more than to remove dirty particles. It has actually a metaphorical dimension (Stoltz 1999, 214).

[36] Kittay 1987, 19.

[37] Kittay 1987, 20. Kittay gives as an example of a metaphorized literal expression Homer's phrase "the rosy-fingered dawn," which could have been conceived of as literal by ancient Greeks, believing that dawn was a human-like goddess. As an example of the opposite—a literalized metaphor—Kittay suggests "wave" as applied to sound, which was originally metaphorical, but now considered as literally describing the properties of sound.

quences and purifications which differed between the two systems. This applies to the third system as well, that of clean and unclean foods (Lev 11). This impurity system is neither obviously metaphorical, nor moral, but the consequences and purifications spelled out for bodily impurity (Lev 12–15) did not apply to the distinction between clean and unclean foods. Ancient Jews thus did not confuse the systems, in spite of the same impurity terminology being used. A certain overlap between the systems is detectable, however, and will be discussed below, since it is relevant for the relationship between purity and morality.

Ritual and moral in biblical legislation

Jonathan Klawans points out that the connection between impurity and sin in Judaism has been largely ignored or downplayed. He finds much evidence for immoral behaviour being regarded as defiling, but nevertheless considers the two concepts of ritual and moral impurity to have been kept apart prior to the Qumran sectarian writings.[38]

The distinction between ritual and moral aspects in ancient religious texts and traditions is problematic, however. It is not used by the texts in question. Klawans agrees to this, and notes some of the problems involved, but opts for the terminology for lack of better options.[39] As with the categories literal-metaphorical (Excursus 3 above), "ritual" and "moral" are ours, not theirs. The results of Klawans' investigation, that bodily impurity is generally free of ethical connotations and that the defiling power of immoral actions does not generally occasion bodily contagion and purifications, except in the Qumran sect, are basically correct, but we should hesitate before equating this distinction with our categories "ritual" and "moral" impurity.

The problem of how to relate ritual and moral to the priestly purity legislation and its continued practice and interpretation in ancient Judaism, could be expressed as two questions: 1) Was sin, i.e. immoral behaviour, regarded as defiling? 2) Was bodily impurity regarded as sinful?

As for the first question, Klawans has shown beyond doubt that at least some immoral actions were regarded as defiling. This applies primarily to the three grave sins from the *Holiness Code* mentioned above, and is evidenced not only in the Pentateuch, but in both pre-exilic prophetic writings and exilic and post-exilic literature.[40] In intertestamental literature, including pre-sectarian Qumran literature (11Q19 [11QT] and CD), we see a certain development in which a few more sins are included as causing defilement. This is due, however to a process of "homogenization," where certain sins are incorporated into the cate-

---

[38] Klawans 1997, 20.

[39] Klawans 2000, 22.

[40] Klawans 2000, 26–36, 43–46. Klawans gives evidence from the Pentateuch (e.g. Lev 18:24–30; 19:30: 20:1–3; Num 35:33–34), from pre-exilic prophetic writings (e.g. Hos 5:3; 6:10; Jer 2:23; 7:30), and from exilic and post-exilic literature (e.g. Ez 5:11; 22:1–4; 36:16–18, 22–25; Ezra 9:10–12; Ps 106:34–41).

gory by analogy and intertextual exegesis.[41] Only in the sectarian texts from Qumran are sin and impurity more or less identified. Impurity language is used for sin in general, and the terms נדה and תועבה are not used as before in a restricted sense, but applied to all sorts of immoral behaviour.[42] Sin is dealt with by purification, and immoral actions are paralleled by "impure abominations."[43] Both sinful outsiders and insiders are regarded as ritually defiling, and "repentance from sin and purification from defilement have become mutually dependent."[44]

This basic line of development is not disturbed, even when Klawans' distinction between metaphorical and literal moral impurity is no longer upheld. While forms from the root טהר in the Hebrew Bible are at times used to describe the morally upright person in general, i.e. one who is acceptable in God's eyes (Ps 51:12; Prov 20:9; Job 4:16), forms from the roots טמא and נדה are, when referring to sinful behaviour, usually used in contexts in which specific sexual sins, idolatry or bloodshed are in focus (e.g. Isa 64:5; Jer 2:7; Ez 36:17; Zech 13:1; Ps 106:34–39).[45] Exceptions are few, but Isa 6:5 must be men-

---

[41] Klawans 2000, 46–60. The term "homogenization" is Milgrom's. Klawans shows with a row of examples (*Jub.* 4:22; 7:21–22, 33; 16:5; 21:19; 22:16–20; 30:13–15) that even in the book of *Jubilees*, all defiling sins can be assigned to one of the three serious sins from the *Holiness Code*. The only possible exception would be the last reference (47). Turning to the pre- or protosectarian *Temple Scroll*, however, Klawans finds that bribery is seen as defiling as well (11Q19 [11QT] 51:11–15; bribes defile the house [ומטמא הבית] probably referring to the temple). This was due to an intertextual exegesis, in which bribery was classified as a type of deceit (11Q19 [11QT] 51:13), and, since deceit in Deut 25:13–16 was referred to as an "abomination" (תּוֹעֵבָה), and such are defiling (Lev 18), bribery must cause impurity as well. Klawans' argument that the *Damascus Document* expands the category of sexual sins defiling the sanctuary (not only the land, as in Lev), is problematic, due to the fact that many of his examples can rather be explained as expansions of the idea of *bodily* defilement from sexual relations. This also applies to examples from *T.Levi* and *Pss.Sol.* texts.

[42] Klawans 2000, 75–79; see especially 1QS 4:10, 17. This is not yet so clear in early sectarian texts, such as 1QpHab or 4QMMT (68–75). It should be noted, however, that greed and theft seem to be included among the defiling sins (1QpHab 8:8–13; 12:6–9).

[43] 1QH 19:10–11 (Sukenik column 11:10–11): "For the sake of your glory, you have purified man from offence (טהרתה אנוש מפשע), so that he can make himself holy for you from every impure abominations (מכול תועבות נדה) and guilt of unfaithfulness (ואשמת מעל)". Klawans interprets this as impurity language being used for sinfulness in general, but it can also be taken as parallelism, where impurity and guilt of unfaithfulness are put on a par. In the latter case this becomes an even clearer example of how immorality and impurity are treated together as sin (פשע), and remedied by purification (טהר).

[44] Klawans 2000, 79–88. Quote from p 85. Cf. 1QS 3:4–9; 5:13–14; 6:24–25; 8:16–18; 4Q512 29–32: 8–10; 4Q274 1 1:1–4). For a different interpretation of these and other related texts, suggesting that the association of sin and impurity in Qumran was primarily evocative rather than halakhic, see Himmelfarb 2001.

[45] This could even be argued for some instances in which the verb טָהֵר occurs in a moral context (e.g. Jer 33:8; Ps 51:3–12). While sexual relations in general led to only a one-day bodily defilement (Lev 15:18), and were not discussed in the *Holiness Code* in connection with defilement of the land, it could be argued that the sexual relationship between David and Bathsheba,

tioned, where both the prophet and the people are said to have impure lips (טְמֵא־שְׂפָתַיִם). Such usage, together with the use of purity terminology for describing the morally upright person, suggests that the overlap between the conceptions of bodily impurity and defiling sins had the potential to expand in a way which is indicated in some intertestamental literature, and becomes obvious in sectarian Qumran material.

The second question is more difficult to deal with. As mentioned above, the answer of many scholars of ancient Judaism is that bodily impurity was not generally regarded as sinful. There are inconsistencies and discrepancies in biblical legislation, however, which complicate the picture. Three such examples will be discussed.

In the first place, impurity is often associated with something loathsome. This is explicit in the systems of clean and unclean foods (Lev 11:11, 13, 20, 23, 41) and defiling sins (Lev 18:23, 24–30; 20:12–14, 22–23). But it is also implicit in texts concerning bodily impurity. Many of the impurities in Lev 12–15 stem from decomposition, abnormal discharges and skin diseases. The disgust felt towards "leprosy" is expressed in the narrative of Miriam's punishment (Num 12), in which she is likened to a half-rotten, still-born foetus. The idea of something loathsome thus links bodily impurity and certain immoral actions.

The narrative of Miriam is part of a second argument as well. Several of the bodily impurities were associated with disease, and disease was often seen as divine punishment. Different degrees of restriction and/or isolation hardly mitigated such experiences. Both motifs are visible in the narrative of Miriam, in which her impure condition is interpreted as a punishment from God, and causes a seven-day isolation (Num 12:9–15). The period of isolation is interpreted as a punishment of shame (v.14: תִכָּלֵם שִׁבְעַת יָמִים), like that when having been spat in the face by one's father. Other oft-quoted traditions which testify to impurity-producing diseases being regarded as punishments include David's curse on Joab's house (2Sam 3:29): "May the house of Joab never lack a discharger (זָב) or a "leper" (מְצֹרָע)," as well as the narrative about king Uzziah, who was struck with "leprosy" after having attempted to burn incense in the temple (2Chr 26:16–21). While the idea that divine punishment could lead to certain impure conditions is not tantamount to impurity being sinful, this line of thought nevertheless establishes another link between some impurities and sin.

A third point will be given a lengthy treatment in the excursus below, although it requires an even more extensive discussion than is possible here. It has to do with the sacrifices involved in various purification rituals. While purification rituals in Lev 12–15 differ, the *hattat* (חַטָּאת) sacrifice is present in

---

referred to in Ps 51, was tantamount to one of the three grave sins, since she was not yet clean from her menstruation (2Sam 11:4; cf. Lev 18:19, 24–25).

all cases of defilement, except for semen emissions and menstruation.[46] This sacrifice is traditionally translated as "sin-offering," which implies that there are moral connotations to all those cases which require such sacrifices. While the translation is somewhat misleading, purification-offering being a better alternative, this sacrifice is prescribed in cases where something objectionable to God must be removed, whether impurities or moral offence. The terminology does not equate sin with impurity, but suggests another link.

Since links have been established, we have to ask to what extent concepts were kept apart. When the same or similar terminology is being used for different phenomena, this probably reveals something about the thinking of the people using that language. When the same or similar rites are prescribed for different phenomena, we must ask how the people performing those rites regarded the relationship between those phenomena. It is hardly reasonable to pose a chasm between impurity and immoral action. They were never equated but they were seen as having some things in common. They were both, to varying degrees, regarded as objectionable to God, and for some reasons threatening to the sanctuary.[47] They were associated with human feelings of aversion or disgust. The terminology and ritual prescriptions of biblical legislation reveal that our clear-cut categories of ritual and moral cannot be applied to ancient thought without modification.

This is further underscored when the three "systems" of impurity, mentioned above, are scrutinized. They all overlap to some degree. This ought not to have caused any confusion as to which rules and which rites were applicable in different cases, since that was explicitly spelled out in each case respectively. But classification was not done according to our systematics. Lev 11 about clean and unclean animals, i.e. edible and non-edible meat, transmutes into a discussion about animal carcasses and their defilement by contact (v 24ff). The issue of eating is still present, and ends the section (v 41, 47), but the emphasis has shifted to a type of impurity which is transferred in the same way, and requires the same type of purifications, as do the bodily impurities of Lev 12–15. Within the system of bodily impurity (Lev 12–15; Num 19) there is little which deviates, but the isolation of the "leper" (Lev 13:45–46, and possibly that of the *zab* and the corpse-impure, if Num 5 is taken into account), must have been to some degree stigmatizing, which is evidenced by the view of discharges and "leprosy" mentioned above (i.e. Miriam's punishment, etc.). There is thus at least a hint for a moral connotation. Finally, the system of defiling immorality in the *Holiness Code* (Lev 18; 20) overlaps with the other two systems, including the pro-

---

[46] The purification from corpse impurity (Num 19) is not discussed here. No sacrifice is involved in that purification rite, but only sprinklings and immersions. The purification-water requires ashes from the red cow, however, which is explicitly called a *hattat* (Num 19:9). For a discussion about the red cow sacrifice as a possible *hattat*, see Milgrom 1983, 85–95.

[47] See Excursus 4 below.

hibition of sex during menstruation[48] (Lev 18:19; 20:18; cf. 15:24) in the midst of discussions about serious sexual sins, and a reference to the distinction between clean and unclean food (Lev 20:25; cf. 11:46–47). We must admit either that this material is unsystematic, or that it does not operate according to the categories we try to apply.

Excursus 4: The חַטָּאת sacrifice

The translation "sin-offering" for the *hattat* has been questioned by several scholars, notably by Milgrom, who considers it false on contextual, morphological and etymological grounds. Milgrom's suggestion of "purification-offering" has been widely accepted.[49] The *hattat* sacrifice is often referred to in contexts with no relationship to immoral acts, such as Nazirite vows of abstinence or installing a new altar (Num 6; Lev 8).[50] Milgrom argues that the object of the *hattat* sacrifice is never the offerer, but the sanctuary and sancta, on which blood is sprinkled.[51] He reconstructs a system of graduated purification-offerings according to the graded power of impurity to contaminate from afar, where inadvertent individual sins contaminate the altar, inadvertent communal sins contaminate the Holy, and advertent sins penetrate into the Most Holy Place, which is purified only once a year at the Day of Atonement (Lev 16).[52]

Milgrom's views of contamination from afar as well as the graded purification-offering have been both lauded and criticized. The most problematic part is perhaps the claim that the *hattat* sacrifice has no role whatsoever in removing human sin. The individual sinner is rather forgiven by repentance, a feeling of remorse (אָשֵׁם), while the purification-offering only removes the resulting defilement of the sanctuary and its sancta.[53] Milgrom claims that in the context of the

---

[48] Note the condemnation, in 4Q266 6 2:2, of the man who sleeps with a menstruant: "the sin of impurity is upon him" ([ע]וון נדה עלו). While the first letter is reconstructed, the reading is fairly certain. 4Q266 belongs to an "expanded" version of the *Damascus Document* and is dated no later than the middle of the first century BCE (*DJD* 18: 28, 30).

[49] Milgrom 1971a. Cf. Anderson 1992a, 879f. Milgrom's arguments in short run as follows: The חַטָּאת is prescribed for a range of persons and objects which cannot possibly have sinned. The noun derives from the pi'el form of the verb, which does not mean "to sin" but "to cleanse, expurgate, decontaminate." The function of the מֵי חַטָּאת in Num 8:7 is purifying only. For a full description of Milgrom's view, see the collection of articles in Milgrom 1983, or the slightly revised material in his Leviticus commentary (1991, 253–292).

[50] Anderson 1992a, 879.

[51] Milgrom 1983, 76f. Milgrom appeals to *mShebu* 1:4f. as support. An important part of Milgrom's argument rests on the use of prepositions used with כִּפֶּר, which leads him to conclude that the effect of the purification-offering is not directly on people, but on behalf of people. For a criticism of arguing from the "slippery" use of prepositions in Hebrew, see Maccoby 1999, 177f, and below.

[52] Milgrom 1983, 77–79.

[53] Milgrom 1991, 254ff. Thus Milgrom translates אָשֵׁם in Lev 4:27–28; 5:2–5, 17, 23 and Num 5:6–7 as "feels guilt." It is this feeling of guilt which atones for the actual sin, while the forgiveness (Lev 4:20, 26, 31) obtained by the חַטָּאת sacrifice is not for the moral transgression, but for the resulting defilement of the sanctuary. Hence the purification-offering is freed from all moral connotations. Milgrom 1976a, 7–12; Milgrom 1983, 47–66; Anderson 1992a, 880. For a thorough critique of Milgrom's assertion that the *hattat* sacrifice purifies *only* the sanctuary, see Zohar 1988, 609–618. Zohar, referring to Lev 17:11 as well as Gen 9:4–6, discusses the nature of blood as נֶפֶשׁ, not detergent, which becomes a means for transferring the contamination of impurity or sin from the offerer through the laying of hands on the animal, to the altar.

purification-offering, *kipper* (כִּפֶּר) never means "expiate" but always "purge." This fits with the terminology used about the *hattat* sacrifice in contexts of bodily impurity (Lev 12:8; 14:20), where the priest performs the purgation rite, and the individual becomes pure (וְכִפֶּר עָלֶיהָ הַכֹּהֵן וְטָהֵרָה / וְכִפֶּר עָלָיו הַכֹּהֵן וְטָהֵר). In the context of inadvertent sins, however (Lev 4:1–5:13), the result of the priest performing the purgation rite is described as forgiveness (Lev 4:20, 26, 31, 35; 5:10, 13). The same phrase is used, except for וְנִסְלַח ל־ replacing וְטָהֵר. While Milgrom states that "the impure person needs purification and the sinner needs forgiveness," he is forced by his translation of כִּפֶּר to claim that the offence which is forgiven is not the original one (which is expiated by a feeling of remorse), but the resulting additional sin of indirectly causing defilement to the sanctuary.[54]

This interpretation is somewhat strained. The claim, based on the use of prepositions, that only the sanctuary and sancta are objects for purgation at the *hattat* sacrifice, has been challenged by others.[55] It seems that we must ascribe the words *hattat* (חַטָּאת) and *kipper* (כִּפֶּר) a wider and more complicated range of possible interpretations. While "purification-offering" and "purge" belong within this range, concepts such as inauguration and atonement must also be taken into account.[56]

The *hattat* sacrifice is referred to in texts outside the Pentateuch as well.[57] In the Chronicler's narrative of the reforms of Hezekiah, supposedly stemming from priestly circles, we find *hattat* sacrifices in the context of the temple's purification (2Chr 29:21, 24). It is important to note, however, that the purification of the Sanctuary itself is described in the previous section (29:1–19), consisting of removing every impure item. This process is explicitly called a sanctification and a purification.[58] In the subsequent description of the sacrifices, however, the *hattat* sacrifices are said to be offered for (עַל־) the kingdom, the sanctuary and the Judaeans (v 21), or more generally for all Israelites (v 24: לְכַפֵּר עַל־כָּל־יִשְׂרָאֵל). We see how Milgrom's fine point that the *hattat* sacrifice effects the purging of the sanctuary *on behalf of* people, breaks down here, since both sanctuary and people alike are juxtaposed and pictured as objects of these

---

Zohar's model must wrestle with "the paradox whereby bringing the most contaminated part of the animal (its blood) into contact with the most holy sites in the sanctuary could be perceived as attaining atonement or as purging the sanctuary itself" (613). His solutions that either God by his omnipotence annihilates the contamination essence on contact, or its residues are heaped up at the altar to be removed to Azazel once a year, are not entirely satisfactory, but rather a result of his wish to detach the notion of a manipulative blood-ritual from the *hattat* sacrifice. His criticism of Milgrom's model is apt, however: the *hattat* animal must be regarded as deriving its contamination from the offerer, not from the sanctuary; hence there is an element of transference of and dissociation from contamination in the sacrificial act itself. This is strengthened by etymological arguments, according to which the basic meaning of חטא ought to be "replace/displace/transfer."

[54] Milgrom 1991, 255f.

[55] Maccoby 1999, 175–179. Maccoby points out that the preposition בעד, which according to Milgrom can be used only for persons, meaning "on behalf of," is actually used about the sins themselves in Ex 32:30. The verb כפר can even be used without an object (bring atonement) as in 2Sam 21:3. Maccoby warns against basing arguments on the uncertain use of prepositions, and cites an exemple: וְכִפֶּר עָלָיו can in theory be translated "he shall cleanse it," "he shall cleanse him," or even "he shall cleanse [absolute] by means of it."

[56] Cf. Maccoby 1999, 179–181. Cf. also A. Marx's interpretation of the *hattat* as a "sacrifice of separation," discussed in Milgrom 1991, 289–292.

[57] Milgrom discusses the following texts: Ezra 8:35; 2Chr 29:21–24; Hos 4:8; 2Kgs 12:17; Ps 40:7; Jer 17:1. Milgrom 1991, 284–288.

[58] 2Chr 29:17–18 (טהר, קדש).

sacrifices.[59] It is evident that this sacrifice must be interpreted in a wider sense than purifying only the temple and its sancta. While this is one of the effects of the *hattat* sacrifice, it is not the only one. It should be remembered that not only the goat which is offered for the purification of the sanctuary and altar on the Day of Atonement (Lev 16:15–19), but also the goat for Azazel carrying the sins of the people, is called a *hattat* (Lev 16:5).[60]

The case is further complicated by a comparison with the *asham* (אָשָׁם) sacrifice (Lev 5:14–26). The traditional translation is "guilt offering," but "reparation offering" has been proposed as more relevant. The sacrifice itself is very different from the *hattat*, but its context and effect are similar. Some suggest that the distinction between the meaning of the two sacrifices was no longer understood by P, while others suggest a distinction to the effect that the *hattat* deals with impurity, while the *asham* deals with profanation of sacred items.[61] This does not cover all cases, however, since neither the "leper" nor the man who rapes a betrothed slave girl can be said to have violated *sancta*, and yet have to bring an *asham* (Lev 14:12; 19:21).[62]

A reasonable suggestion for the *hattat* would be that it serves to remove something objectionable to God, whether impurities or guilt. This is not the same as equating bodily impurities with sin, but certain objectionable states and certain objectionable acts were apparently thought to have similar effects, and thus required the same type of sacrifice.

It has been questioned whether the cultic legislation of P contained any ethical elements at all. Israel Knohl argues that "the interpenetration of ethical and cultic considerations" comes only with the later "Holiness School." Knohl argues that the ethical outlook of P is universalistic and taken for granted, but the revelation to Moses, associated with the divine name, signifies the establishment of the cultic system, which does not deal with ethical issues. This leads Knohl to an interpretation in which the phrase "sins against any of the Lord's commandments" (תֶּחֱטָא אַחַת מִכָּל־מִצְוֹת יְהוָה ...) refers only to *cultic* imperatives (Lev 4:2; 5:17).[63] Milgrom, on the other hand, argues that "the Lord's commands" must include ethical requirements as well.[64] Part of the argument is focused on the use of the term עָוֹן, which according to Milgrom is used in P with an ethical import in a number of contexts (Lev 5:1, 17; Num 5:15, 31; 30:16). Knohl denies this, however, arguing that in every instance the primary transgression is against God rather than against other humans, and thus the cultic, sacral component dominates.[65] The argument aims at interpreting the Day of Atonement rite (Lev 16), which could be seen as dealing with defilement caused by cultic *and* ethical transgressions, or as a cultic concern *only*. While it is obvious that the H source has a much stronger emphasis on human relations (see below), the sharp distinction between ritual and ethical must be regarded as somewhat anachronistic.[66] Even Milgrom, while arguing that both cultic and ethical transgressions can cause defilement to the

---

[59] It seems strained to claim that the preposition על with non-human objects signifies that the object itself is purged, while the same preposition with a person as object must be translated "on behalf of." Cf. Milgrom 1983, 76; Maccoby 1999, 177–179.

[60] For a discussion of different types of *hattat*, see B. Levine 1974, 101–114; Milgrom 1976b. A discussion about the Day of Atonement *hattat* falls outside the scope of this study.

[61] Anderson 1992a, 880f; Milgrom 1976a, 127. Milgrom's definition is that "the *asham* expiates for sancta *desecration*, the *hattat* for sancta *contamination*."

[62] Anderson 1992a, 881.

[63] Knohl 1995, 225-230; quote from 229.

[64] Milgrom 1991, 24. Milgrom uses comparative material from Mesopotamian texts as arguments for the presence of ethical elements in the cultic legislation of P.

[65] Milgrom 1991, 25; Knohl 1995, 227ff.

[66] Discussing comparative Near Eastern material, Milgrom refers to the conclusion of Lambert (1959, 194), that "there was no distinction such as we tend to make between morally right and ritually proper. The god was just as angry with the eating of ritually impure food as with oppressing the widow and orphan." (quoted in Milgrom 1991, 24).

sacred, separates the two more than necessary. It seems unavoidable that the *hattat* sacrifice as well as the Day of Atonement ritual establish another link between bodily impurity and at least certain types of human transgressions, whether or not these actions are defined as belonging to the realm of ethics.[67]

A moral trajectory

We have found links in biblical legislation between bodily impurity and certain types of immoral actions. We have also seen that our categories of literal *versus* metaphorical and ritual *versus* moral cannot be strictly applied to the material without forcing it into categories which do not belong to its origin. At the same time, differences in emphasis between different strands are evident, and tendencies seem to develop with time.

While the P source in the Pentateuch has traditionally been regarded as the latest strand, there is a growing tendency today to regard the *Holiness Code* (Lev 17–26) as later.[68] Knohl has provided detailed arguments on both legal and linguistic grounds for what he calls a *Holiness Source*, which grows out of, and has edited, the Priestly Torah. This source contains more than the *Holiness Code*, and is responsible for editing the Torah. Both sources are seen as processes, in part overlapping, and extending through several centuries. Knohl sees H as expanding the concept of holiness and integrating ethical and cult considerations, while P restricts holiness to the cultic sphere.[69]

Knohl's reconstruction is well argued,[70] but I question the description of the P legislation as devoid of ethical elements. Purity terminology referring to sin-

[67] This is partly a matter of defining ethics. Knohl's interpretation and use, where the legislation of P is not defined as ethical since it does not focus on human relations, seems too narrow.

[68] Milgrom 1991, 13–35; 2000a, 1319–1367.

[69] Knohl 1995, 200ff, 229. On the last point Milgrom disagrees, since he claims that ethical issues are involved in the defilement of the sanctuary and the Day of Atonement ritual. Cf. the discussion above (Excursus 4) and Milgrom 1991, 21–26; 2000b, 2440–2446. Both agree, however, on the relationship between H and P (although Milgrom dates both earlier than does Knohl), and hold H responsible for extending the sphere of God's holiness to encompass the whole land of Israel. Cf. Milgrom 1991, 44; 2000a, 1397–1400.

[70] In his historical reconstruction, Knohl suggests that P, with its concentration on its own inner world, the cult, has its roots in the beginning of Solomon's temple (1995, 226). H grew out of priestly circles in response to idolatrous practices, Molech worship, social injustice and prophetic criticism. Knohl argues for the reign of Ahaz as a plausible period of origin. The second half of the eighth century is the period of classical prophecy (Amos, Hosea, Isaiah, Micah). Despite a growing criticism of society and religion, the P tradition was not able to respond adequately, because of its division between morality and cult. The "Holiness School" represents a change in direction within priestly circles, which influenced the reforms during the reign of Hezekiah at the end of the century (204–216; this is the period when the northern kingdom falls and refugees, including priests from the north flood into Jerusalem. Knohl associates laws about the relationship between Levites and priests with an influx of priestly refugees from the Northern kingdom, 209–212). Thus we find in H an emphasis on justice and honesty (Lev 19) and ideas about social reform (the Jubilee, Lev 25). The concept of holiness is changed and enlarged, i.e. given a moral content and applied to all Israel and the whole land. Idolatry is con-

ful behaviour is found in texts that could be earlier than priestly traditions referring to bodily impurity. We cannot be sure which use is the earlier on the basis of textual evidence and reconstructions of tradition-history. Rather than speak of ritual and moral impurity (Klawans) or about a separation between the cultic and ethical until the emergence of the "Holiness School" (Knohl), I would suggest that we speak about a moral trajectory within the idea of purity in Judaism.

This is not to be understood as "moral impurity." The expression is problematic and somewhat contradictory, since it suggests a type of impurity which is not ritual. As far as I understand it, impurity is a ritual concept, and there is a ritual element in all types of impurity, unless the term is fully spiritualized.[71] When we speak of a moral trajectory, this does not mean that the defilement involved should itself be defined as moral, but that there are some moral aspects to various types of impurity, or that certain types of immoral actions are thought to cause some types of defilement.

A moral trajectory, through the history of the concept of impurity in ancient Judaism, can be traced at different levels and in most materials.[72] It is prevalent in H, but traces can be found in P as well, as argued above. And as impurity language is used frequently to condemn the sins of the people, it is difficult to believe that the strong denouncement of prophets like Ezekiel would neither reflect nor effect a negative view, at least in some circles, on impurity in general, including the system of bodily defilement. When the idolatrous deeds of the people are likened to the bleedings of a menstruant (כְּטֻמְאַת הַנִּדָּה),[73] we cannot expect that bodily impurity, which is objectionable in the context of the cult, would be regarded as completely neutral when outside it. The development demonstrated by Klawans, which culminates in the sectarian writings from Qumran (1QS; 1QH), in which sinners are seen as defiling through bodily contact and bodily impurity is regarded as sinful, must be understood against this

---

demned and the cult centralized. Priestly separatism is abandoned and popular beliefs and practices integrated (216–224). Knohl finds the H tradition continuing through the exile, being responsible for the final redaction of the Pentateuch at the beginning of the Persian period (226).

[71] This is possibly the case in some NT writings, such as the letters. Klawans' use of "moral impurity" is problematic. An example of this is his treatment of Deut 21:22–23 (in the version of 11Q19 [11QT] 64:10–13) about those hanged on a tree, who must be buried the same day, lest the land be defiled. Klawans calls this moral defilement of the land. There is, however nothing immoral according to the Torah in hanging a criminal, so it is not a matter of bloodshed. The problem is possibly the immorality of the criminal, but that ought to be taken care of by hanging. The problem is rather the dead body, and thus there is a similarity with corpse-impurity rules. The only reason for calling this moral impurity is that the resulting defilement of the land fits Klawans' scheme.

[72] Rules about clean and unclean meat are left out of the discussion. Except for their rationale, their interpretation is never much developed or problematized during the Second Temple period, nor in rabbinic thought. They become, of course, of great importance in politico-religous conflicts during Hellenistic rule, but remain a self-evident part of Jewish identity.

[73] Ez 36:17.

background.[74] The "compartmentalization" which is so evident in rabbinic literature[75] could likewise be seen as a reaction to a tendency toward "homogenization," which is so evident in Qumran, and which in the end might risk confusing the different impurity legislations, and render it difficult for ordinary people to keep them in detail.[76]

Klawans' suggestion that the Pharisees at the end of the Second Temple period had already "compartmentalized" sinful actions and bodily defilement to the extent that appears in Tannaitic literature, must be doubted, however.[77] It is more reasonable to assume a diversified situation. "Compartmentalization" ought rather to have been a likely attitude of the Sadducees, as inheritors of the priestly tradition. We should remember that the Tannaim were not heirs of the first-century Pharisees only, but other traditions were also incorporated in the emerging rabbinic movement after 70 CE.[78] The Qumran sectarians seem to have shared priestly perspectives with the Sadducees, and expansionist concerns with the Pharisees. Knohl suggests that the *halakhah* of Qumran and the Sadducees preserves the hard core of the cultic conception of the P tradition, while the popular heritage of the H tradition found its way mainly through the circle of Ezra into the *haburot* of the Pharisees. He points out, however, that some of Qumran's positions must be seen as more in line with the H tradition.[79] While

---

[74] Klawans 2000, 75–91. The identification of bodily impurity and defiling immoral actions is seen in five ways, according to Klawans (75): 1) all sins are regarded as impurities; 2) outsiders are assumed to be impure; 3) insiders who sin are defiling; 4) initiation involves both repentance and purification; 5) ritual purification of insiders includes repentance (see the discussion above and notes 40–45 for examples and references). It is interesting to note a somewhat similar and contemporary tendency in the Egyptian *Papyrus Jumilhac* 12: 16–21 (18, *Les interdictions*), from the second century BCE (Vandier 1962, 123f). This text lists cardinal religious offences without attempting to distinguish between purity and morality, but classifying all as "abominations of God," which is a common expression for cultic taboos. The purity rules in this text seem to have applied to the population at large, not only to priests. (R. Meyer 1999, 49ff.)

[75] The "compartmentalization" of the rabbis is discussed at length in Klawans 2000, 92–117. Since Klawans sees two very distinct conceptions of defilement, integrated only in the literature of the Qumran sectarians, the effect is that the rabbis are pictured as very close to the view of impurity in the Hebrew Bible (1997, 205f). The "compartmentalization" is obvious by the fact that the *Mishnah* discusses bodily impurity and purification in page after page, without any moral connotations, but in a very "neutral" voice. There are exceptions, however, some of which will be noted below. And as soon as we turn outside the *Mishnah* we find contrary evidence. One of the clearest examples, although late, is found in Midrash on Psalms (*Midrash Tehillim*) 51:2, in which it is stated that "every man who commits a transgression is as unclean as though he had touched a dead body and must be purified with hyssop." Braude 1959, 1: 472.

[76] Cf. already CD, where column 12 shows an example of how instructions about separation of clean from unclean combines rules about unclean meat with rules about bodily impurities, including corpse-impurity, within the same short section.

[77] Klawans 2000, 150. Klawans admits that "[t]he evidence for this claim, admittedly, is not as strong as I would like."

[78] Cf. Stemberger 1995 [1991], 140–147.

[79] Knohl 1995, 224.

such a broad outline needs further substantiation, it fits into a common idea of the relationship between the different sects at the end of the Second Temple period. I would suggest that the Pharisees at the time of Jesus did not "compartmentalize" sin and bodily defilement to the extent evidenced in the *Mishnah*. Although they should not be ascribed the views of the Qumran sectarians either, they must have related to them. I suggest that although they did not equate bodily impurity and sin, they saw some possible links.

The evidence for this is not conclusive, but there are three lines of argument which should be considered. First, we ought to regard as reasonable that the integrated view of the Qumran sectarians developed within a context and during a period of time. Although early sectarian texts give clear evidence only of bribery, greed and theft being regarded as defiling sins, in addition to the "three serious," it is reasonable to suppose an analogous development with regard to other immoral behaviours. It is also likely that other expansionists at the end of the Second Temple period saw links between sinful behaviour and defilement.

Second, we must note that in spite of his strong case for rabbinic "compartmentalization," Klawans mentions a few examples which could be regarded as remains of a moral trajectory. A "leper" who was affected several times is included among a number of "multiple transgressors" who have to bring only a single offering (*mKer* 2:3).[80] In the case of "leprosy" on a wall dividing two houses, both owners have to tear it down, and work on it. "On this basis have they said, 'Woe to an evil person. Woe to his neighbor'" (*mNeg* 12:6). It seems as if the person in whose house the plague appeared is considered to be wicked (רָשָׁע). And *tNeg*6:7 clearly states that "plagues come only because of gossip, and leprosy comes only to those who are arrogant."[81] This is continued by a list of locations for afflictions, all followed by the injunction to repent. Klawans downplays this tradition, pointing out that it is the only one in the *Tosefta* to this effect, that the crucial statements are put in the mouth of an examining priest, not a named rabbi, and that the Tannaim are forced to admit that "leprosy" can come about because of slander, since this is confirmed in Scripture by the stories of Miriam and Uzziah.[82] Klawans' examples could, however, be used as support for the continued presence of popular views, i.e. evidence for a moral trajectory, which is still making itself heard, in spite of an "orthodox" mainline

[80] This passage is admittedly complicated as a piece of support, since the context is about offerings, and the offerings involved vary. (In this particular case it is probably a *hattat*, but the term used is the general קָרְבָּן, which includes different types of sacrifices.) The term עֲבֵירוֹת (sins, transgressions) is used, however, as an umbrella term for one who raped a slave-girl repeatedly, a *nazir* who became unclean several times, one who suspected his wife of repeated adultery, and a "leper" who was afflicted several times. Moral terminology is thus used for bodily impurities.

[81] שאין הנגעים באין אלא על לשון הרע ואין הצרעת באה אלא על גסי הרוח (Rengstorf 1967). Tr. in Neusner 1974–1977, 6:235. Cf. the association of guilt and skin disease in Southeast Asia (Browne 1989 [1985], 3).

[82] Klawans 2000, 100f.

attitude taking form in the *Mishnah*. While Klawans and, to a certain extent, Neusner point at an expansion in the Amoraic period of the idea that impurities result from sins,[83] the development at Qumran suggests that bodily impurities and sinful behaviour were linked much earlier. Later rabbinic material could attest to earlier views. *Sifre* to Num 5:3 ascribes to R.Yose the Galilean (early second century) the idea that before the people fell into sin there were no dischargers or "lepers" among them.[84] Lists of sins which cause "leprosy" are found in *bArak* 16a, being further elaborated on in *Lev.Rab.* 17:3. Although these lists represent later elaborations, the general idea that certain types of impurity come from sin seems to belong to the earliest stage of rabbinic interpretation.[85] It is notable that Klawans omits any discussion about dischargers (except for menstruants). Although not as conspicuous as in the case of "leprosy," the idea of discharges as punishments for sin appears in a few texts too.[86] According to Neusner,

> [t]he Rabbinic movement began with the assertion, first appearing in the second century, that specific sins stand behind particular forms of uncleanness. That assertion, while an extraordinary innovation when compared to antecedent opinions, came in the context of biblical thought, which had seen purity as a metaphor for righteousness, impurity for sinfulness. It represented the making concrete of what until then had been an abstract and undeveloped assertion. Once the concrete assignment of particular sins to specific uncleannesses had entered the rabbinic system, the process of conserving and repeating that idea began.[87]

Neusner may be right about the general path of development. But taking the moral trajectory traced above into consideration, and especially its development at the end of the Second Temple period as attested in Qumran, we must regard some sort of link between bodily impurity and sin as a necessary condition for the subsequent rabbinic development, present already before 70 CE.

The third argument centres on the Greek translation of a Hebrew term. As argued above, the use of identical terms for different things, not only testifies to the conceptualization of the people using those terms, but also influenced subsequent development of thought. Not only is purity language used in the Hebrew Bible both for bodily defilement and sinful actions, but the *hattat* sacrifice is prescribed in the case of both impurity and moral transgression.[88] In spite of the modern translation "purification offering" and attempts to explain this sacrifice totally outside the ethical realm, it remains that the LXX consistently translated the *hattat* with ἁμαρτία, which definitely is an ethical term. This reflects

---

[83] Klawans 2000, 102ff; Neusner 1973a, 78.
[84] *Sifre Numeri*, Parashat Naso 1; Börner-Klein 1997, 7.
[85] Neusner 1973a, 87, 90, 99f.
[86] *Sifre Numeri*, Parashat Naso 1; *Num.Rab.* 7:1, 10; *Lev.Rab.* 18:4. The evidence of *Num.Rab.* 7:10 is perhaps doubtful, since it is rather an allegory (Neusner 1973a, 81, 96–97, 100, 102).
[87] Neusner 1973a, 106.
[88] Cf. above, 212ff.

how the translators interpreted the concept, and it must also have influenced people's ideas and way of thinking. The LXX testifies to the presence of a moral trajectory, which it must have strengthened by its continued influence, at least in diaspora Judaism.

We have to conclude that, in spite of much uncertainty, there are traces of a moral trajectory. If we want to reconstruct the situation during the first century CE, we must suppose that the relationship between bodily defilement and immoral actions was discussed between different groups, but that "compartmentalization" or integration was not the very dividing line. We rather must make room for ideas of *some* sort of interaction or link between sin and bodily impurity both in popular belief and among Essenes as well as among Pharisees. We have too little evidence to speculate any further, but as to the general outline, a diverse and complicated situation must be assumed for the time of Jesus.

Alternative categories: inner and outer

I have used the idea of a moral trajectory to trace the interaction between the concepts of impurity and sin through ancient Judaism and draw some general conclusions about the situation among Jewish groups at the end of the Second Temple period. The ideas we have found are very diverse, however, such as considering sinners as impure or sins as causing impurity, regarding certain states of bodily impurity as caused by sinful behaviour, or as direct punishment for sin, thinking about impurities and sin in similar categories, seeing both as loathsome, requiring the same type of sacrificial atonement, and using the same terminology for both. All these ideas are not part of a coherent whole.

Using the idea of a moral trajectory makes it easier to see a more diversified development than was possible with the clear-cut but insufficient and somewhat anachronistic opposites "literal-metaphorical" and "ritual-moral." I have still used the idea of morality, which is our concept, not theirs, although what we call morality was definitely part of ancient Jewish thinking, if not articulated in our way. But if we are looking for concepts which figure in the period of the Second Temple, we should perhaps discuss purity in categories of "inner" and "outer." These are not identical with ritual and moral, although they might seem so in our eyes. Nor are they totally analogous to the Greek distinction between body and soul, although this is a common misunderstanding.[89]

---

[89] A Greek view of purity of the soul is found in Plato (*Leg.* 715e): ἀκάθαρτος γὰρ τὴν ψυχὴν ὅ γε κακός ("For the wicked man is unclean of soul"), or in the inscription over the entrance of the Ascleipos sanctuary at Epidauros: ἁγνεία δ'ἐστὶ φρονεῖν ὅσια ("Purity is to think pious things"), which Porphyry uses as an argument, discussing purity of body and wickedness of the soul (*Abst.* 2:19). Stroumsa 1999, 415; cf. Burkert, 1977, 132 and Parker 1983, 281ff, 322–325, for similar examples. Cf. *Phaedo* 65d–69d. After the manuscript was finished, an article by Risto Uro (2000) came to my attention, which basically supports my interpretations of Philo, Q, and *Gos. Thom.* below (220, 223–228). I have included references in the footnotes.

Such is the interpretation of Klawans, discussing Philo's distinction between purity of body and soul. Philo states that the law requires of the person bringing a sacrifice that he should be pure in body and soul:

> Βούλεται τὸν ἀνάγοντα θυσίας ὁ νόμος καθαρὸν εἶναι σῶμα καὶ ψυχήν, ψυχὴν μὲν ἀπό τε τῶν παθῶν καὶ νοσημάτων καὶ ἀρρωστημάτων καὶ κακιῶν τῶν ἔν τε λόγοις καὶ πράξεσι, τὸ δὲ σῶμα ἀφ' ὧν ἔθος αὐτῷ μιαίνεσθαι. κάθαρσιν δ' ἐπενόησεν ἑκατέρῳ τὴν προσήκουσαν, ψυχῇ μὲν διὰ τῶν πρὸς τὰς θυσίας εὐτρεπιζομένων ζῴων, σώματι δὲ διὰ λουτρῶν καὶ περιρραντηρίων, περὶ ὧν μικρὸν ὕστερον ἐροῦμεν· ἄξιον γὰρ τῷ κρείττονι καὶ ἡγεμονικωτέρῳ τῶν ἐν ἡμῖν, ψυχῇ, καὶ τὰ τῶν λόγων ἀπονεῖμαι πρεσβεῖα.
>
> The law would have such a person pure in body and soul, the soul purged of its passions and distempers and infirmities and every viciousness of word and deed, the body of the defilements which commonly beset it. For each it devised the purification which befitted it. For the soul it used the animals which the worshipper is providing for sacrifice, for the body sprinklings and ablutions of which we will speak a little later. For precedence in speech as well as elsewhere must be given to the higher and more dominant element in ourselves, the soul.[90]

Philo speaks of two types of purifications, sacrifice for evil thoughts and actions of the soul and water rituals for bodily defilements, but to Klawans this is a clear-cut example of the distinction between ritual and moral impurity.[91] It comes close, but is not identical. Philo makes the Greek distinction between body and soul. But note that both body and soul are purified by ritual purifications, either sacrifice or water rites. If the legislation of Leviticus really intended to convey the idea that sin was atoned for by repentance, and the *hattat* sacrifice purified only the sanctuary from the resulting ritual defilement, Philo seems not to have grasped it. But in one sense he has gone much further. Although both purifications are ritual, he interprets them as *symbols* of repentance and self-knowledge.[92] The analogy Philo makes is not basically between ritual and moral purification, but between ritual purifications (of both bodily impurities and sinful thoughts and acts) on the one hand, and their deeper allegorical meaning (religious insight and reformation) on the other. The distinction between body and soul comes close to our popular western anthropology, but should not be forced onto Hebrew Jewish tradition. What Philo formulates is perhaps a Greek Jewish way of expressing that which in Hebrew Jewish tradition would be described as "inside" and "outside."[93]

Hebrew anthropology was corporeal indeed, and all types of feelings and human capacities were associated with concrete parts of the body.[94] The heart

---

[90] Philo, *Spec.Laws* 1:257–258.

[91] Klawans 2000, 64ff.

[92] Philo, *Spec.Laws* 1:259–266. Note that both are interpreted allegorically. Cf. Uro 2000.

[93] It is true that something like a dualistic anthropology can be seen in later rabbinic literature (e.g. *bNid* 31a). This is not a dominating trait, however, but experienced as problematic, as seen in some attempts at harmonization (*bSanh* 91a–b). Cf. Ruzer 1999, 374f.

[94] Cf. Wolff 1974 [1973], 10–79.

(לֵב) was seen as the seat of human will, and the interior (קֶרֶב—literally midst or entrails) of man's body (בָּשָׂר) was considered the source of human action, while the soul (נֶפֶשׁ) expressed the integrated human being, and the spirit (רוּחַ) stood for the life-giving element, the animating force. What we call morality was not seen as residing in the soul, but in the body. This is clearly seen in two classical passages from the Hebrew Bible (Ps 51:12 and Ez 36:25–27):

לֵב טָהוֹר בְּרָא־לִי אֱלֹהִים וְרוּחַ נָכוֹן חַדֵּשׁ בְּקִרְבִּי

Create in me, God, a pure heart, and restore a steadfast spirit in my interior (belly, intestines)

וְזָרַקְתִּי עֲלֵיכֶם מַיִם טְהוֹרִים וּטְהַרְתֶּם מִכֹּל טֻמְאוֹתֵיכֶם וּמִכָּל־גִּלּוּלֵיכֶם אֲטַהֵר אֶתְכֶם׃ וְנָתַתִּי לָכֶם לֵב חָדָשׁ וְרוּחַ חֲדָשָׁה אֶתֵּן בְּקִרְבְּכֶם וַהֲסִרֹתִי אֶת־לֵב הָאֶבֶן מִבְּשַׂרְכֶם וְנָתַתִּי לָכֶם לֵב בָּשָׂר׃ וְאֶת־רוּחִי אֶתֵּן בְּקִרְבְּכֶם וְעָשִׂיתִי אֵת אֲשֶׁר־בְּחֻקַּי תֵּלֵכוּ וּמִשְׁפָּטַי תִּשְׁמְרוּ וַעֲשִׂיתֶם

And I will sprinkle pure water on you, and you will be purified from all your abominations, and from all your idols shall I cleanse you. And I will give to you a new heart and a new spirit shall I put in your interior and I shall remove the heart of stone from your flesh and I shall give to you a heart of flesh. And my spirit shall I put in your interior and I shall make you walk in my statutes and guard and do my judgments.

A pure or new heart signifies an undivided will to do what is right. In the passage from Ezekiel, it is furthermore evident that this heart (will) is situated in the "flesh," and that it must be conceived of as made of flesh (i.e. corporeal, human) in order to be sensitive and responsive. It is also evident in both passages that righteous action demands a new or steadfast spirit, which is located in the very midst of the body. The same type of thinking is expressed in a text from Qumran, to be further discussed later. In an eschatological passage from the *Community Rule* we read:

ואז יברר אל באמתו כול מעשי גבר יזקק לו מבני איש להתם כול רוח עולה מתכמי בשרו ולטהרו ברוח קודש מכול עלילות רשעה

Then God will refine, with his truth, all man's deeds, and will purify for himself the structure of man, ripping out all spirit of injustice from the innermost part of his flesh, and cleansing him with the spirit of holiness from every wicked deeds.[95]

The object for purification is the structure (מבני) of man, and the cause of man's sinful deeds is the spirit of injustice which dwells in the innermost part of man's body (מתכמי בשרו), and thus must be replaced.

With this very corporeal anthropology, the "inside" of man becomes of utmost importance as the seat of human will and action. The innermost part of the body is seen as the seat of good and evil, the seat of purity and impurity. "Morality" is located in the body, and purification from evil thougts and acts is in a sense perceived as a purification of the innermost parts of the body.[96]

[95] 1QS 4:20–21.

[96] Lack of attention to Hebrew anthropology at times leads interpreters astray. This can be seen in the interpretation of 1QS 3:6–9, which contrasts those who enter or renew the covenant of God with those who refuse. "For it is by the spirit of the true counsel of God that are atoned the

When such thinking is translated into Greek, changes occur, but to various degrees. In the LXX, Hebrew categories often prevail.[97] In Josephus, and especially in Philo, we find a much more dualistic Greek anthropology. The "inside" of man is equated with the soul (ψυχή), and is thus contrasted with the body. This development is crucial when discussing how a Christian spiritualized concept of purity evolved in the early church. When discussing Jesus' attitude to purity, however, Hebrew anthropology is a more suitable point of departure. When we turn to the Jesus tradition, the concepts of inner and outer, inside and outside, suggest themselves as plausible and contemporary categories. They are frequently used in the gospels. And they are probably more suitable for discussing the relationship between sin and impurity in Second Temple Palestinian Judaism, than "soul and body" or "moral and ritual."

V.2 Jesus: inner and outer impurity

Traditions and sources

A contrast between inner and outer impurity or purification is found in many strands of the Jesus tradition. Relevant material is found in Mark (Mk 7:14–23), Q (Mt 23:25–28/Lk 11:39, 40, 44), the *Gospel of Thomas* (14, 89) and *Papyrus Oxyrhynchus* 840. In the case of Thomas, the independence of the traditions can be questioned. *P.Oxy.* 840 has at times been regarded as a fairly late Hellenistic legend with no historical value. There are good reasons, however, for a different evalutation, and the evidence will be discussed below.

In most of the traditions just mentioned, the explicit or implicit context is one of purification. This is interesting, not least in view of the claims, made by some exegetes, about Jesus as regularly practising purificatory rites. Such claims could range from the simple presupposition that Jesus, like any pilgrim, underwent the prescribed immersions before festivals, to the idea that he advo-

---

paths of man, all his iniquities, so that he can look at the light of life. And it is by the holy spirit of the community, in its truth, that he is cleansed of all his iniquities. And by the spirit of uprightness and of humility his sin is atoned. And by the compliance of his soul with all the laws of God his flesh is cleansed by being sprinkled with cleansing waters and being made holy with the waters of repentance." The last of these four sentences has been interpreted as bodily purification in contrast to the earlier part, which is taken to refer to sinful actions, to be cleansed by repentance and reformation. The conclusion is drawn that repentance must precede ritual purification (Thiering 1980, 266–277; J. Baumgarten 1999b, 209). The context implies, however, only that no purifications or atonements will purify an unrepentant sinner. Speculative ideas about double purification rites in a certain order result from reading נפש in a Greek sense, thus contrasting soul with body, as in Philo (*Spec.Laws* 1:257–258) or Josephus (*Ant.* 18:117).

[97] A corporeal anthropology should often be assumed in other Jewish Greek writings as well, such as many New Testament books. The LXX translation varies at times. קֶרֶב in the Ezekiel passage is translated ἐν ὑμῖν, while more literally as ἔγκατα (intestines) in Ps 51 (LXX Ps 50).

cated an elaborate programme for purification.[98] A possible stance is to deny that contact with impure people caused Jesus or his surroundings any problem, since he must be supposed to have undergone purification rites (i.e. bathed in a *miqveh*) as soon as the opportunity arose.[99] The traditions about inner and outer purification point in a slightly different direction, however.

Inner and outer impurity in Q and the *Gospel of Thomas*

In the Q passage where inner and outer impurity are contrasted (Mt 23:25–28/Lk 11:39, 40, 44), Jesus is accusing the Pharisees. Because of the polemical character of this tradition, and the divergences between Matthew and Luke, any discussion about tradition and redaction is bound to be complicated. Not all details, however, are relevant to the main discussion in this chapter.

Matthew's version (23:25–28) is the more structured of the two:

> 25 Οὐαὶ ὑμῖν, γραμματεῖς καί Φαρισαῖοι ὑποκριταί, ὅτι καθαρίζετε τὸ ἔξωθεν τοῦ ποτηρίου καὶ τῆς παροψίδος, ἔσωθεν δὲ γέμουσιν ἐξ ἁρπαγῆς καὶ ἀκρασίας.
> 26 Φαρισαῖε τυφλέ, καθάριζον πρῶτον τὸ ἐντὸς τοῦ ποτηρίου, ἵνα γένηται καὶ τὸ ἐκτὸς αὐτοῦ καθαρόν.
> 27 Οὐαὶ ὑμῖν, γραμματεῖς καί Φαρισαῖοι ὑποκριταί, ὅτι παρομοιάζετε τάφοις κεκονιαμένοις, οἵτινες ἔξωθεν μὲν φαίνονται ὡραῖοι, ἔσωθεν δὲ γέμουσιν ὀστέων νεκρῶν καὶ πάσης ἀκαθαρσίας. 28 οὕτως καὶ ὑμεῖς ἔξωθεν μὲν φαίνεσθε τοῖς ἀνθρώποις δίκαιοι, ἔσωθεν δέ ἐστε μεστοὶ ὑποκρίσεως καὶ ἀνομίας.

> 25 Woe unto you, scribes and Pharisees, hypocrites, since you purify the outside of the cup and the bowl, while inside they are full of greed and intemperance. 26 Blind Pharisee, purify first the inside of the cup, so that also its outside may become pure.
> 27 Woe unto you, scribes and Pharisees, hypocrites, since you closely resemble whitewashed graves, which look handsome on the outside, while inside they are full of bones of the dead and every impurity. 28 Likewise you too appear righteous on the outside to the people, while inside you are full of hypocrisy and lawlessness.

Previously, Matthew has followed Mark up to Mk 12:37a, where he considerably expands Mark's short warning for the scribes (Mk 12: 37b–40; Mt 23:1–12). This serves as an introduction to seven harsh woes against scribes and Pharisees (Mt 23:13–36), among which we find the Q tradition above as woe numbers five and six. These two, together with Matthew's woe number four (about tithing herbs), are found in Luke as well, although in another context. Luke also has a woe against seeking the best seats in the synagogues and wishing to be greeted in public, not found in Matthew, probably because a similar criticism is included in the introductory material (23:6) which Matthew has taken over from Mark 12:39. Luke's version is as follows (11:39b–44):

> 39b νῦν ὑμεῖς οἱ Φαρισαῖοι τὸ ἔξωθεν τοῦ ποτηρίου καὶ τοῦ πίνακος καθαρίζετε, τὸ δὲ ἔσωθεν ὑμῶν γέμει ἁρπαγῆς καὶ πονηρίας. 40 ἄφρονες, οὐχ ὁ ποιήσας τὸ

[98] Fredriksen 2000, 198, 200, 205f; Cf. Chilton 1994, although Jesus' purity programme in Chilton's version seems to contain very little of conventional purification rites.
[99] Cf. Loader 1997, 59f, n. 107.

ἔξωθεν καὶ τὸ ἔσωθεν ἐποίησεν; 41 πλὴν τὰ ἐνόντα δότε ἐλεημοσύνην, καὶ ἰδοὺ πάντα καθαρὰ ὑμῖν ἐστιν. 42 ἀλλὰ οὐαὶ ὑμῖν τοῖς Φαρισαίοις, ὅτι ἀποδεκατοῦτε τὸ ἡδύοσμον καὶ τὸ πήγανον καὶ πᾶν λάχανον καὶ παρέρχεσθε τὴν κρίσιν καὶ τὴν ἀγάπην τοῦ θεοῦ· ταῦτα δὲ ἔδει ποιῆσαι κἀκεῖνα μὴ παρεῖναι. 43 Οὐαὶ ὑμῖν τοῖς Φαρισαίοις, ὅτι ἀγαπᾶτε τὴν πρωτοκαθεδρίαν ἐν ταῖς συναγωγαῖς καὶ τοὺς ἀσπασμοὺς ἐν ταῖς ἀγοραῖς. 44 Οὐαὶ ὑμῖν, ὅτι ἐστὲ ὡς τὰ μνημεῖα τὰ ἄδηλα, καὶ οἱ ἄνθρωποι [οἱ] περιπατοῦντες ἐπάνω οὐκ οἴδασιν.

39b Now you Pharisees, you purify the outside of the cup and the plate, but your inside is full of greed and evil. 40 Fools, did not he who made the outside also make the inside? 41 Rather give the contents as alms, and lo, all is clean to you. 42 But woe unto you Pharisees, since you tithe mint and rue and every vegetable, and overlook justice and the love of God. You should have done this without neglecting the other. 43 Woe unto you Pharisees, since you love the first seat in the synagogues and the greetings in the squares. 44 Woe unto you, since you are like unmarked graves, and the people who walk over them do not know it.

The matter is further complicated, however, because Luke continues in vv 46–52 with three more woes against the lawyers (νομικοί).[100] The first of these woes finds its correspondence in Matthew's introduction (23:1–12) which expands Mark 12:37b–40. The second corresponds to Matthew's last woe, and Luke's third woe against the lawyers is found as Matthew's first. It seems thus as if the core of all Matthew's seven woes come from the Q tradition.

For several reasons it is likely that Matthew is responsible for more redactional changes than Luke.[101] Some details can easily be explained by the fact that Matthew inserts this whole section (ch. 23) as an expansion of Mark 12:37b–40. This is the case with the change of νομικοί to γραμματεῖς, as well as the absence of the woe against seatings and greetings. Other differences can be explained by Matthew's bias against Jewish leaders. There is no wish to differentiate between Pharisees and scribes, because all criticism is seen as relating to Matthew's contemporary Jewish adversaries. The epithet ὑποκριταί is certainly found in Luke too, twice for the people (Lk 6:42; 12:56 - Q) and once for a synagogue leader (Lk 13:15 - L?), but never for Pharisees.[102] The use of ὑποκριταί for Pharisees does not come from the Q tradition, but from Mark 7:6, and the context of handwashing. Matthew has multiplied the abusive expression, especially in Ch. 23.

We now turn our attention to the details of the relevant verses, beginning with the saying about vessels. It is reasonable to conclude that the gist of Mt 23:25/Lk 11:39 comes from Q. There is a statement about the Pharisees, that they cleanse (καθαρίζετε) the outside of the cup and bowl/plate (τὸ ἔξωθεν

---

[100] Lk 11 46–52.

[101] Cf. Bovon 1996, 221ff.

[102] The noun ὑπόκρισις is used for the leaven of the Pharisees, in Lk 12:1, which seems to parallel Mk 8:14–15/Mt 16:5–6. Only Luke uses the term, however. The verb ὑποκρίνεσθαι is used by Luke in 20:20, likewise parallel to Mark and Matthew (Mk 12:13/Mt 22:16). Again only Luke uses this term.

τοῦ ποτηρίου καὶ τῆς παροψίδος/τοῦ πίνακος). This is contrasted to the inside (ἔσωθεν) which is full (γέμουσιν/γέμει) of greed and evil (ἁρπαγῆς καὶ ἀκρασίας/πονηρίας). In Matthew the inside refers to the vessels just mentioned, while the reference in Luke is the Pharisees (τὸ δὲ ἔσωθεν ὑμῶν).[103] In both versions, however, a comparison is intended between the purification of the outside of vessels, and the inside of people. This *simile* would be perfectly understandable if relating to the common opinion at the end of the Second Temple period, that certain vessels, when properly sealed, protect their contents from becoming contaminated by various sources of impurity, requiring only the vessel itself to be sprinkled or purified in a *miqveh*, after which the contents can be consumed as intact and pure.[104] In this text, however, open vessels are mentioned. We could, of course, speculate that this is due to later confusion, and that the saying originally concerned closed vessels. There are other possible interpretations, however. Discussions about the relationship between the purity of the inside and outside of cups are found in the *Mishnah* and ascribed to the Houses of Hillel and Shammai. Although the exact practice behind the saying is difficult to retrieve, there is no reason to doubt that it refers to a first-century custom.[105] The comparison is made on two levels. Since the contents of a vessel cannot be improved by purification of its outside, the impure "inside" of a greedy person does not benefit from outer purifications, i.e. immersions of the body.

Things become more difficult when we look at the continuation of the saying, where Luke and Matthew differ. It is reasonable to regard Mt 23:26 as redaction, since the image of the "blind Pharisee" fits Matthew's bias. What about Luke's continuation (ἄφρονες, οὐχ ὁ ποιήσας τὸ ἔξωθεν καὶ τὸ ἔσωθεν ἐποίησεν)? Is Lk 11:40, with its appeal to creation, to be regarded as part of an original Q source or Luke's own redaction?[106] While the phrase could be regarded as breaking the theme of greed and alms-giving (vv 39, 41), it is paralleled in *Gos.Thom.* 89:

> ⲡⲉϫⲉ ⲓ̅ⲥ̅ ϫⲉ ⲉⲧⲃⲉ ⲟⲩ ⲧⲉⲧⲛ̅ⲉⲓⲱⲉ ⲙ̅ⲡⲥⲁ ⲛⲃⲟⲗ ⲙ̅ⲡⲡⲟⲧⲏⲣⲓⲟⲛ ⲧⲉⲧⲛ̅ⲣ̅ⲛⲟⲉⲓ ⲁⲛ ϫⲉ ⲡⲉⲛⲧⲁϩⲧⲁⲙⲓⲟ ⲙ̅ⲡⲥⲁ ⲛϩⲟⲩⲛ ⲛ̅ⲧⲟϥ ⲟⲛ ⲡⲉⲛⲧⲁϥⲧⲁⲙⲓⲟ ⲙ̅ⲡⲥⲁ ⲛⲃⲟⲗ
>
> Jesus said: Why do you wash the outside (**ⲃⲟⲗ**) of the cup? Do you not understand that the one who created the inside (**ϩⲟⲩⲛ**) also created the outside (**ⲃⲟⲗ**)?

---

[103] ὑμῶν may well be redactional, however. Luz 1997, 335.

[104] Lev 11:32; 15:12; Num 19:15, 18. Various items were purified by immersion and even water could be purified in a *miqveh*. This is assumed in *mMiq* 10:1–6. In the case of overshadowing by a corpse, closed vessels protected the contents and were purified by sprinkling (cf. *mEdu* 1:14). Cf. David P. Wright 1987, 96f, 198; Sanders 1990, 185–190, 227; 1992, 228f.

[105] *mBer* 8:2; cf. above (67–72). Cf. Neusner 1974–1977, 3:355–384; Maccoby 1982.

[106] The idea of ποιεῖν referring to cleansing is unlikely, and the production of cups is used as a metaphor for creation in Acts (cf. Uro 2000). A somewhat similar appeal to creation is found in Jesus' answer to the Pharisees in Mt 19:4/Mk 10:6. However, this saying has no parallel in Lk.

In contrast to the Lukan version, the order outside-inside is reversed, and introduced by a direct question. This suggests that *Gos.Thom.* 89 is not directly dependent on Luke, but that the reference to God as creator of both inside and outside could perhaps be taken as belonging to tradition.[107]

The following phrase (Lk 11:41), "rather give the contents as alms, and lo, all is clean to you," seems at first sight obscure. It reveals, however, that v 39 is understood quite literally; the food and drink of the Pharisees are viewed as expressions of greed or injustice, more in need of being distributed to the poor than being externally purified. The idea thus suits the theme of greed and is coherent with v 39b. Hence v 41 can be seen as part of tradition as well.[108] In view of the prophetic custom of condemning greed, and the development attested in Jewish literature according to which greed was included among the serious defiling sins, the whole saying about vessels in Lk 11:39–41 ought to be regarded as traditional, coming from the Q source.[109]

The saying about graves (Mt 23:27–28/Lk 11:44) has already been discussed in the previous chapter.[110] In this case too, there are arguments for Luke's wording being more original. It is much shorter than Matthew's variant, and the latter is easily explained by Matthew's bias.[111] Matthew's variant is given a structure parallel to the previous saying. The contrast between the outside and the inside of the adversaries is taken from the previous saying and elaborated on, in order to emphasize the blatant hypocrisy. The Lukan variant has no mention of outside and inside here, and the purity issue is only implicit, although readily understood, if not by Luke's readers, surely by readers or listeners in an early Palestinian setting. The saying about graves could thus be seen as coming from early tradition too. Its point is not the outright hypocrisy of Jesus' adversaries, as in Matthew, but the relationship between inner and outer impurity, although the terms ἔσωθεν and ἔξωθεν are not used in the Lukan version.

Comparing the wider literary contexts of Matthew and Luke, it is obvious that Matthew has redacted and expanded Markan material and Q sayings into a coherent speech, which suits his own bias. The context for the material about inner and outer impurity is thus a polemical speech, i.e. a literary construction. Although Luke has a bias as well, and his woes are also a literary construction, it is interesting to note that they are situated at a meal (Lk 11:37–39a):

---

[107] The order is transposed in some early manuscripts (e.g. P^{45}). Cf. Uro 2000 about the possible independence of *Thomas'* version.

[108] Against Luz 1997, 335.

[109] ἐλεημοσύνη is a Lukan favourite (cf. 12:33 and 7 times in Acts), but this is not a decisive argument against a Q origin, since the term is found in Mt 6:1–4, which has no correspondence in Lk, as well as in *Gos.Thom.* 6 and 14. Thus there is no need to regard it as Lukan redaction.

[110] For a discussion about grave impurity, see above, 177–181.

[111] In Matthew, this saying follows right after that about vessels. Both are similarly constructed; scribes and Pharisees are combined. The contrast between outside and inside is parallel to the previous saying and is further developed in v 28. Cf. Luz 1997, 340; Bovon 1996, 231, n.67.

37 Ἐν δὲ τῷ λαλῆσαι ἐρωτᾷ αὐτὸν Φαρισαῖος ὅπως ἀριστήσῃ παρ' αὐτῷ· εἰσελθὼν δὲ ἀνέπεσεν. 38 ὁ δὲ Φαρισαῖος ἰδὼν ἐθαύμασεν ὅτι οὐ πρῶτον ἐβαπτίσθη πρὸ τοῦ ἀρίστου. 39a εἶπεν δὲ ὁ κύριος πρὸς αὐτόν·

37 While he was speaking, a Pharisee asked him to dine with him [i.e. at his place], and he went in and laid down [i.e. at the table]. 38 But the Pharisee saw this and was surprised that he did not first immerse before the dinner. 39a But the Lord said to him:

Luke could of course have invented this setting, in order to give the woes a framework. In view of the frequency of table scenes and recent studies of the *symposion* genre and Luke's literary style,[112] the suggestion is plausible. The syntax (infinitives and participles) suggests some Lukan redaction.[113] Nevertheless the saying about vessels makes sense in such a context.[114] Historically, Jesus' practice of "commensality" is fairly well attested.[115] And the picture of Jesus as relating not only to more dubious parts of the population but also to Pharisees and other religious leaders is more plausible than the polemical picture of Matthew, in which Jesus' relationship to the Jewish leadership is almost exclusively one of confrontation and conflict. Although v 37a (ἐν δὲ τῷ λαλῆσαι) is definitely a Lukan bridge,[116] connecting the woes to the previous section, the Pharisee's reaction to Jesus not purifying (v 38) could well represent the introduction of an original Q apophthegm. As we will see below, the usual context for traditions in which inner and outer impurity are discussed is bodily purification (Mk 7; Lk 11; *P.Oxy.* 840),[117] although that was not the most likely conflict issue in the environments of the redactors of these texts. Hence this context is best explained as part of early tradition.

The exception is found in the *Gospel of Thomas*, in which sayings are rarely provided with situational contexts, usually due to the lack of a narrative framework (cf. logion 89 quoted above). The concepts of "outer" and "inner" are found in two additional sayings, of which logion 22 does not refer to purity, but discusses the union of divisions or opposites (two into one, inner and outer, male and female) as a condition for entering the kingdom. In logion 14, however, inner and outer impurity are discussed, and the saying itself combines the themes of mission (cf. Lk 10:8–9a) and impurity (cf. Mt 15:11):

---

[112] Steele 1984; Dennis E. Smith 1987. For an overview of the *Symposion* in general, see Murray 1990.

[113] But cf. the linguistic arguments of Jeremias for the Pharisee's invitation belonging to pre-Lukan tradition (1980, 205f).

[114] Cf. Uro 2000.

[115] Mt 11:19/Lk 7:34; Mk 2:17; Lk 7:36; 11:37. Cf. Bolyki 1998.

[116] Cf. Jeremias 1980, 205.

[117] Even if Luke's hand is visible in several table-scenes, it is reasonable to suppose that some basic traits of table-scenes belonged to the traditional material used by Luke, which he developed further (cf. Dennis E. Smith 1987, 616). We cannot dismiss the table setting too lightly as Lukan invention in this case, where it contains a context (purification) for a saying about inner and/or outer impurity, which is present in several sources (Cf. Mk 7:1–2, 5, 15–23; *P.Oxy.* 840; see below for further discussion).

> **ⲁⲩⲱ ⲉⲧⲉⲧⲛ̄ϣⲁⲛⲃⲱⲕ ⲉϩⲟⲩⲛ ⲉⲕⲁϩ ⲛⲓⲙ ⲁⲩⲱ ⲛ̄ⲧⲉⲧⲙ̄ⲙⲟⲟϣⲉ ϩⲛ̄ ⲛ̄ⲭⲱⲣⲁ ⲉⲩϣⲁⲣ̄ⲡⲁⲣⲁⲇⲉⲭⲉ ⲙ̄ⲙⲱⲧⲛ̄ ⲡⲉⲧⲟⲩⲛⲁⲕⲁⲁϥ ϩⲁⲣⲱⲧⲛ̄ ⲟⲩⲟⲙϥ̄ ⲛⲉⲧϣⲱⲛⲉ ⲛ̄ϩⲏⲧⲟⲩ ⲉⲣⲓⲑⲉⲣⲁⲡⲉⲩⲉ ⲙ̄ⲙⲟⲟⲩ ⲡⲉⲧⲛⲁⲃⲱⲕ ⲅⲁⲣ ⲉϩⲟⲩⲛ ϩⲛ̄ ⲧⲉⲧⲛ̄ⲧⲁⲡⲣⲟ ϥⲛⲁϫⲱϩⲙ̄ ⲧⲏⲩⲧⲛ̄ ⲁⲛ ⲁⲗⲗⲁ ⲡⲉⲧⲛ̄ⲛⲏⲩ ⲉⲃⲟⲗ ϩⲛ̄ ⲧⲉⲧⲛ̄ⲧⲁⲡⲣⲟ ⲛ̄ⲧⲟϥ ⲡⲉⲧⲛⲁϫⲁϩⲙ̄ ⲧⲏⲩⲧⲛ̄**
>
> And if you should go into (**ⲃⲱⲕ ⲉϩⲟⲩⲛ**) any land and walk in the country, if they receive you, eat that which they will set before you, heal the sick among them. For that which goes into (**ⲃⲱⲕ ⲅⲁⲣ ⲉϩⲟⲩⲛ**) your mouth will not defile you. But it is that which comes out of (**ⲉⲃⲟⲗ**) your mouth which will defile you.

This combination suggests that mission was seen as a theological justification for neglecting Jewish food laws in parts of the early church.[118] We should hesitate, however, before suggesting itinerant missionary activities of Jesus and his disciples as the *historical* context in which to place sayings about inner and outer impurity. The link seems to be theological and literary, perhaps only literary.[119] As a candidate for an historical context, bodily purification is better attested and has more arguments in its favour.

Mark 7 revisited

From the perspective of inner and outer impurity, we will now return to Mark 7. In Chapter III, the central saying of Mk 7:15 was examined, and a relative reading was advocated.[120] The idea of Dunn, that the wording of Mt 15:11 and *Gos.Thom.* 14 would represent a more original form of the saying, was found tempting, but clear signs of Matthean editing of Mark make it less likely that both Thomas and Matthew drew on a similar independent tradition.[121] Although we cannot exlude the possibility of traces of an alternative, weaker, and perhaps earlier rendering in Mk 7:18b and 20,[122] this is part of Mark's "in-house" section, which is his typical way of expounding meaning and relevance to his contemporary audience, and in any case the difference is not that great. This does not mean, however, that what we suggest to be an underlying dialectical negation, comparing the defiling force of that which goes in with that which comes out, is attested in one source only. Such a conclusion would be a gross simplification, limiting historical enquiry to searching the surface of the

---

118 Cf. Svartvik 2000, 153ff. Cf. the speculative reconstruction of Crossan 1991, 332–348.

119 On a textual level, the combination of a mission saying and a purity saying in the *Gospel of Thomas* is due to literary rather than theological motifs. Note that both sayings begin with the same catchwords: "go into" (**ⲃⲱⲕ ⲉϩⲟⲩⲛ**). The combination of the two sayings can thus be regarded as literary only, possibly a mnemonic device already at an oral stage. Although there is no extant Greek fragment for this logion, the catchword connection would apply similarly to a corresponding εἰσέρχεσθαι εἰς.

120 I.e. "A man is not so much defiled by that which enters him from outside as he is by that which comes from within." Cf. above, 66.

121 Uro 1998, 23–26; cf. Dunn 1990, 37–60.

122 Dunn 1990, 44; cf. above, 66f.

Greek text. As we have seen above, it is exactly this type of opposition of inside and outside that we find both in Q and *Thomas*.

In addition to Mk 7:15 with parallels, I have thus argued for evidence in different textual traditions (Q, Thomas, *P. Oxy.* 840) that some uses of the categories "inside" and "outside" for impurity go back to Jesus himself. Postponing a discussion of *P. Oxy.* 840 for the moment, I suggest that it is very likely that "inner" and "outer" were categories available during the time of Jesus, and that he actually used them discussing impurity.

The most likely historical context for such discussions was something similar to that provided by Luke (11:37 41), i.e. disagreements about bodily purifications, rather than the missionary context of the *Gospel of Thomas*, which is secondary. This strengthens the case for the saying in Mk 7:15 as originally having nothing to do with food laws, but providing an answer to discussions about bodily purifications, such as that represented in Mk 7:1–2, 5.[123] The difference between the settings of Mk 7 and Lk 11 should be noticed, however. In Mk, the disciples of Jesus are accused of not undertaking proper purifications before eating, i.e. hand-washing. In Lk Jesus himself is questioned and the issue is immersion. In principle, however, the context is the same. The very intent of Mk 7 in its present form as an argument for freedom from food laws in the church, suggests that the disciples are depicted as representing Markan Christians. While questioning the behaviour of a rabbi's disciples might be a way of discussing his teaching, it is likely that Jesus was directly criticized for his own behaviour as well, just as in the Lukan (Q) tradition. Another difference concerns the type of purification expected by expansionists before meals. In view of the problems in reconstructing first-century halakhic practices, it is difficult to judge whether Mk (hand-washing) or Lk (immersion) is more original. It is possible, however, that practices varied between different groups and according to different circumstances. Jesus was probably criticized for laxity in regard to both of these purification rites.

A relative interpretation of Mk 7:15, supposing an underlying dialectical negation, is supported by the Q sayings about the inner and outer impurity of vessels (Lk 11:39–41) and graves (Lk 11:44). Giving priority to Luke's version, as argued above, the Q saying contrasts the inside and outside of human beings, arguing for the need for each to be in accord with the other. Inner purity is defined as justice or compassion, which is given relative importance over against bodily purifications. Justice or compassion results in full purity, which is not possible when outer, bodily purifications are combined with inner greed.[123a]

The reference to God as creator of both outside and inside in Q (Lk 11:40) and Thomas (logion 89) has no direct correspondence in Mark 7, but there is a possible trace of at least a similar thought to be found in the discussion about

[123] Cf. above, 63, 65, 67, 86, 88, where this conclusion is drawn on other grounds.

[123a] Cf. the juxtaposition of δικαιοσύνη and "καθαροὶ τῇ καρδίᾳ" in the beatitudes (Mt 5:6,8).

traditions of men and the law of God (Mk 7:6–13). Behind this discussion we might find ideas about the divine intention, which can also be seen behind arguments from creation, as is more evident in the question about marriage (Mk 10:6ff/Mt 19:4ff). Without attempting to reconstruct the historical context of Mk 7:15 in any detail, it is nevertheless reasonable to suggest that ideas about the divine intention with legal prescriptions was also a factor behind Jesus' stance in questions of purity. This fits into the historical context as well, since divine intention was taken into account in contemporary discussions.[124]

Finally, the notorious phrase in Mk 7:19c may even be reconsidered. The expression πάντα καθαρά in Lk 11:41 reminds us not only of Mk 7:19 but even more of Rom 14:20. The Markan comment (καθαρίζων πάντα τὰ βρώματα) is usually regarded as redaction. This is obvious, since through the participle construction it is not even phrased as a saying but as a comment. Paul's expression (πάντα μὲν καθαρά), however, is used in a discussion which could hint at the possibility of the phrase somehow deriving from the Jesus tradition (cf. v 14: οἶδα καὶ πέπεισμαι ἐν κυρίῳ Ἰησοῦ ὅτι οὐδὲν κοινὸν δι' ἑαυτοῦ).[125] If any saying about "everything is clean" could be imagined as originating with Jesus himself, a context similar to that in Luke 11:37–41 is the most likely one. In this context the phrase gains a relative sense as an argument for justice (inner purity) as more important than immersion (outer purity), and the point of the saying fits well into a purity discussion during the first century CE. There is no need to argue for this expression originating with Jesus. But the possibility exists, in view of Lk 11:41, and the phrase makes sense as part of a discussion about bodily purifications. Such a context could explain the presence of the expression in different strands of tradition, while at the same time it could explain the comparative lack of *wirkungsgeschichte*, since the expression was part of a saying which originally had nothing to do with food laws. Only at a later stage was its potential as an argument in a new context realized and utilized. But its origin must be sought in the context of bodily purifications and Jesus' attitude to inner and outer aspects of impurity.

On the basis of the different traditions discussed so far, it is reasonable to suggest that Jesus (and hence his disciples) were criticized for not always washing or immersing before a meal, in a way expected by the expansionist current during the first century CE. It is also reasonable to suggest that Jesus did dis-

---

[124] The question of divine intention seems to be explicit or implicit in several discussions about the *rationale* for various laws. Cf. *Let.Aris.* 139, 142, 147, 150ff; Philo in *Spec.Laws* 1:257–266; *bNid* 31b.

[125] Usually both Mk 7:19 and Rom 14:20 are regarded as having no connection with the Jesus tradition. Cf. Räisänen 1986, 209–218; Svartvik 2000, 115f. Mk 7:19c is definitely a redactional comment. But the question I raise concerns the possible background. As used in the present Markan context, the comment represents the ideas of the early church. But it may have a pre-history in the Jesus tradition, although not in a radical sense and not relating to food laws. Cf. Dunn 1990, 37–60.

cuss purity and impurity with other religious leaders, using categories of "inside" and "outside," making comparisons between vessels and people. These two suggestions are interconnected, since discussions about principles and criticism of practices belonged together. It seems as if Jesus justified his apparently negligent behaviour by contrasting inner and outer purity in a manner reminiscent of earlier Jewish prophets

It remains to define the meaning of outer-inner arguments further. When interpreted in a relative sense, they would mean that inner purity (i.e. justice) has priority over outer purity (i.e. bodily purifications such as immersions). This would mean that outer purity is of no value without inner purity. Is such an attitude possible, without downplaying outer impurity at least to some degree? The Q saying in Mt 23:23/Lk 11:42 about tithing suggests that Jesus advocated no break even with such voluntary and supererogatory obligations (tithing minor herbs) as were not required by the Torah. This might on the other hand reveal an original conciliatory setting for such discussions and arguments. Jesus did not require Pharisees or other expansionists to abstain from their extensive legal interpretation and adherence, as long as "weightier matters" were not neglected. It does not mean that Jesus and his followers lived according to the same degree of observance in matters of tithing or purity. If so, he would not have been criticized, but would only have issued criticism himself. It seems clear that Jesus considered inner purification to be achieved by compassion and justice only, and not by bodily purification rites at all. But what was his attitude to outer purification? Did he observe only the minimum of purification rites prescribed in the Torah? Or does the material suggest that he considered bodily purification rites unimportant or even unnecessary? It is impossible to pursue this question further without seeking Jesus' relationship to his "predecessor" John the Baptizer, and his application of John's particular immersions as a purification rite.

V.3 John and Jesus: inner and outer purification

John the Baptizer

The quest for the "historical John" has produced much literature, although not as much as the quest for the historical Jesus.[126] It is commonly accepted by scholars that the image of John the Baptizer in the gospels must be regarded as to a large extent shaped by Christian theology. At the same time, it is acknowledged that the different ways in which gospel writers handle the embarrassment

[126] Recent important contributions are Webb 1991, J. E. Taylor 1997, and J. P. Meier's monograph-sized section (more than 200 pages) on John and Jesus in his second volume of *A Marginal Jew* (Meier 1994), which contains a voluminous bibliography up to 1992 (63f).

associated with the Baptizer provide the strongest evidence for the historicity of the man, and reveal certain basic facts about him and his movement. One of these is the baptism of Jesus by John, which is usually considered as an historical fact, since it evidently embarrassed the early Christians to the degree that all gospels found differing strategies to downplay or neutralize the implications. These range from theological explanations (Jesus did not need baptism to gain forgiveness for sins, Mt 3:14–15) to literary constructions (John's imprisonment is narrated before the baptism of Jesus, and John is not mentioned as the agent, Lk 3:19–20, 21f; cf. Jn 1:29–34). There is no attempt, however, to deny the Baptizer an important role in the history of Jesus, but only to give a "correct" interpretation. This suggests both that the Baptizer was an important figure for the emerging Christian movement, and that Jesus' relationship to, or dependence on him, belonged to the bedrock facts of early Christian tradition. The survival of the Baptizer's movement into the time of the early church and beyond also made impossible any attempt to deny this.[127]

The precise interpretation of John's baptism and Jesus' relationship to John is much disputed, however. The questions are numerous, and there is no room to deal with them in the present study except in a cursory way. The most important questions for this study concern the baptismal rite as a purification ritual. Did John administer this rite himself, and was it a one-time ritual or a repeated one? What connections are reasonable to suggest between the Baptizer and other Jewish groups, the Essenes in particular, and especially the Qumran sectarians? How did John's baptism relate to repentance, forgiveness, bodily purification and the temple cult? Such questions will be pursued presently, while questions about Jesus' relationship to John and his baptismal activity will be dealt with in the subsequent section.

The available sources for assessing the teaching and baptizing activity of John consist mainly of Q material (Mt 3:7–12 / Lk 3:7–18 and Mt 11:2–19 / Lk 7:18–35),[128] the short Markan tradition introducing that gospel (Mk 1:1–8 paralleled in Mt 3:1–6 / Lk 3:1–6) and a passage from Josephus (*Ant.* 18:116–119). The Markan tradition places the baptizing activity of John in the desert (ἐν τῇ

---

[127] Cf. Acts 18:25; 19:1–6; Joseph Thomas 1935, 89–139.

[128] The latter text is important for the discussion of Jesus' relationship to the Baptizer, and will be dealt with in the subsequent section. This is the case with certain Johannine traditions as well. In the Lukan version of the former text (Lk 3:7–18), the middle part (10–14, John as a moral preacher) has no parallel in Matthew. Meier discusses the arguments for and against this being part of Q tradition (1994, 41f, 61f), suggesting that "there is no convincing reason why Matthew, an evangelist intent on moral catechesis, should have omitted this moral sermon from his Gospel" (42). I think there is. In Mt, the Baptizer's judgmental sermon is aimed at Matthew's usual target, i.e. the Jewish leaders. In Lk, on the other hand, it is aimed at the people, and conditions for their conversion are thus spelled out (vv 10–14). Mt does not conceive of any conversion of the Jewish leaders and omits the ethical instructions. If John's baptism is to be understood in a context of covenant renewal and repentance (cf. the discussion about Josephus and Qumran below), vv 10–14 are necessary for understanding his denouncements.

ἐρήμῳ) or rather "wilderness" at the river Jordan, and describes him in the manner of a Hebrew prophet.[129] He is proclaiming "a baptism of repentance for/unto/with a view to the forgiveness of sins" (βάπτισμα μετανοίας εἰς ἄφεσιν ἁμαρτιῶν).[130] The first block of Q-material portrays John as a fiery eschatological prophet, demanding righteous behaviour in view of the coming judgment and destruction. This apocalyptic note is totally missing in Josephus' account. In a passage about the reason for the destruction of Herod Antipas' army by the Nabatean king Aretas, Josephus recounts a popular explanation, which turns into a digression on the nature of John's baptism:

> Τισὶ δὲ τῶν Ἰουδαίων ἐδόκει ὀλωλέναι τὸν Ἡρώδου στρατὸν ὑπὸ τοῦ θεοῦ καὶ μάλα δικαίως τιννυμένου κατὰ ποινὴν Ἰωάννου τοῦ ἐπικαλουμένου βαπτιστοῦ. κτείνει γὰρ δὴ τοῦτον Ἡρώδης ἀγαθὸν ἄνδρα καὶ τοῖς Ἰουδαίοις κελεύοντα ἀρετὴν ἐπασκοῦσιν καὶ τὰ πρὸς ἀλλήλους δικαιοσύνῃ καὶ πρὸς τὸν θεὸν εὐσεβείᾳ χρωμένοις βαπτισμῷ συνιέναι· οὕτω γὰρ δὴ καὶ τὴν βάπτισιν ἀποδεκτὴν αὐτῷ φανεῖσθαι μὴ ἐπί τινων ἁμαρτάδων παραιτήσει χρωμένων, ἀλλ' ἐφ' ἁγνείᾳ τοῦ σώματος, ἅτε δὴ καὶ τῆς ψυχῆς δικαιοσύνῃ προεκκεκαθαρμένης.
>
> But to some of the Jews the destruction of Herod's army seemed to be divine vengeance, and certainly a just vengeance, for his treatment of John, surnamed the Baptist. For Herod had put him to death, though he was a good man and had exhorted the Jews to lead righteous lives, to practise justice towards their fellows and piety toward God, and so doing to join in baptism. In his view this was a necessary preliminary if baptism was to be acceptable to God. They must not employ it to gain pardon for whatever sins they committed, but as a consecration of the body implying that the soul was already thoroughly cleansed by right behaviour.[131]

Josephus' description seems to contradict the Markan idea that associates John's baptism with forgiveness. Which picture should be given precedence?

David Flusser opts for Josephus' interpretation. He claims that it is almost identical with the Essene theology of baptism, as found in texts from Qumran.

> The Essenes, and John following them, adopted the idea that immersion purified the body; but they believed that a person's body was defiled not only through contact with objects which were ritually unclean, but also through sin. When someone sinned his body was defiled, and therefore a man who had not repented before his immersion would

[129] The interpretation of ἔρημος is disputed. Mt adds τῆς Ἰουδαίας, which would imply the land towards the Dead Sea (cf. Qumran), but this does not fit with the river Jordan and the abundance of water. Lk corrects Mk in stating not that the Baptizer appeared in the desert, but that the word of God came to him in that location (Lk 3:2). The description of John's clothes (and food?) imply a similarity with Elijah (1Kgs 17:2–6; 2Kgs 1:8).

[130] The expression has been much discussed. Cf. Meier 1994, 53–56. It is adopted by Luke (3:3), but not by Matthew. The reason could be that Matthew avoids to associate forgiveness of sins with the Baptizer, but only with Jesus, and specifically with his death (cf. Mt 26:28).

The concrete content of the Baptizer's proclamation according to Mk concerns the "coming one" (1:7–8). These verses seem to overlap somewhat with the Q tradition, since they recur in Mt and Lk at the end of the subsequent Q block (Mt 3:11 / Lk 3:16), but in a slightly different version, and integrated with the Q material. Cf. also the Johannine version in Jn 1:26–27). For further discussion, see below, 246f.

[131] *Ant.* 18:116–117.

> not become pure. While the immersion might purify the body, the body would immediately be defiled again through the person's sin.[132]

This explanation of the reason for repentance being a necessary prerequisite for purification (i.e. to avoid re-contamination of the body) is not made explicit in the sources, and must be regarded as speculative. Flusser affirms the Qumran understanding discussed above, however, where sinful behaviour is associated with bodily impurity. He regards the idea that baptism in itself purified from sin as a mistaken concept, against which John fought. By uncritically accepting Josephus' interpretation, Flusser simplifies the issue. If "repentance purified a man from sin, and water only purified the body,"[133] then it is difficult to explain why the Baptizer should administer a separate water-rite, to effect something which could otherwise be taken care of by regular immersions in a *miqveh*. We must at least ascribe to John's baptism an additional function which goes beyond that of mere bodily purification.

The Markan expression (βάπτισμα μετανοίας εἰς ἄφεσιν ἁμαρτιῶν) has been thought to reflect later Christian baptismal theology. Meier gives several arguments for the converse, however. The NT never applies the full Markan phrase to Christian baptism,[134] and the vocabulary of repentance and forgiveness of sins is not connected with baptism in Paul's letters or in Johannine literature. Furthermore, it would be strange for Christians at a later stage to attribute to John's baptism the power of forgiveness, were this not necessitated by tradition. We find that Matthew actually omits the phrase, probably because of embarrassment. Associating John's baptism with forgiveness of sins would not only give increased weight to the claims of rival baptizing movements, but would also cause embarrassment for a christology which viewed Jesus as sinless.[135] Hence the association of baptism and forgiveness must belong to early traditions about the Baptizer.

Josephus' description of the Baptizer must be evaluated in view of his tendency to downplay eschatological and messianic ideas. This is evident in his account of the Essenes, and easily explained by the historical context in which he writes.[136] Josephus instead emphasizes the ethical part of John's message, and thereby supports the picture given in Lk 3:10–14.[137] Both Luke and Josephus thus seem to agree that ethical action or re-orientation was necessary for

---

[132] Flusser 1987, 46.
[133] Flusser 1987, 46.
[134] Meier admits that Acts 2:38 comes close. Repentance is missing here, however. Cf. the claim of Stegemann (1998, 219) that "one of the principal meanings of Christian communal baptism was the forgiveness of sins (1 Cor. 6:11; Rom. 3:25; 6:1–23; etc.)." None of the texts referred to explicitly state what is claimed.
[135] Meier 1994, 53f. Cf. Matthew's variant of the Q material in Mt 3:11: Ἐγὼ μὲν ὑμᾶς βαπτίζω ἐν ὕδατι εἰς μετάνοιαν.
[136] Cf. Meier 1994, 60f.
[137] Cf. Meier 1994, 61f.

baptism. This is implicit in the Markan expression βάπτισμα μετανοίας as well. Repentance and baptism are linked together in all sources dealing with the Baptizer, except for the Gospel of John. Josephus' outright denial of forgiveness having anything to do with John's baptism seems to be directed against some sort of "misunderstanding." It is as if baptism and forgiveness were possibly associated in the minds of his readers, and this is incompatible with his view of the Baptizer as a righteous moral preacher.[138] Since Josephus uses the Greek dichotomy between soul and body to explain the difference between moral purity and ablutions of the body to his Greek-speaking readers, this is a necessary result.[139] The forgiveness associated with John's baptism must be understood in an eschatological perspective, however. Change of mind and action, together with a rite of immersion, are deemed necessary in view of the coming judgment, in order not to be destroyed together with the chaff by the "coming one." Without this eschatological perspective, which Josephus shuns, the forgiveness associated with John's baptism cannot be understood.

The Baptizer and Qumran

The relationship between the Baptizer and Essenes in general, or the Qumran sectarians in particular, has been discussed at length since the discovery of the Dead Sea Scrolls. The similarities are far too many to be ignored. John is reported to have appeared in a geographical area close to Qumran. Prophecy, especially the book of Isaiah, seems to have played an important role both in Qumran and in traditions about the Baptizer.[140] In both cases we find a need for an abundance of water, due to a "concern for eschatological purification by means of ritual cleansing in living water."[141] Other similarities can be seen in the apocalyptic outlook and an ascetic and probably celibate life-style.[142]

Attempts to downplay these similarities are seldom successful. Stegemann argues that the only thing John and the Essenes had in common was the ritual use of water for immersion, which was a common practice in contemporary Judaism at large. The interpretation of Isa 40:3 is said to have led John and the Essenes to different regions; the geographical proximity had no significance; the eschatology of John was imminent, while that of the Essenes was not, since the end was expected several decades ahead in time.[143] Stegemann finds only dif-

---

[138] Josephus' reservations concerning baptism effecting forgiveness are similar to those of the Qumran sectarians concerning purifications. In both cases it is emphasized that the ritual is of no use without a repentant mind. Cf. 1QS 3:1–12.

[139] Concerning Josephus' "Hellenized" description of John, see Webb 1991, 166f., 187ff., 195.

[140] Dunn 1994. Note the interpretation of Isa 40:3 in Mk 1:2–3 par; 1QS 8:13–16; 9:19–21. Cf. Charlesworth 1997.

[141] Charlesworth 1999, 357.

[142] Charlesworth 1999, 358.

[143] Stegemann 1998 [1993], 222ff.

ferences.[144] John's baptism was always administered by himself and had a sacramental significance. It was carried out in one place only as a one-time event, which sealed the execution of a conversion and guaranteed the forgiveness of sins in the coming judgment. There was no probationary period and those baptized did not become members of an organization.[145]

While some of these differences are true, they do not detract from the similarities, which make a closer comparison necessary. The one-time character of John's baptism is never explicitly stated, but inferred from the fact that he administered the rite himself, and that people came from far away in order to undergo baptism.[146] In view of the eschatological context with expectations of an imminent judgement, it is furthermore unlikely that people were supposed to undergo this rite repeatedly. It was associated with salvation from the coming wrath.[147] The eschatological perspective in Qumran should not be downplayed, however, but must be seen as the background for Essene initiation, which involved repentance, confession, immersion and covenant renewal. The role of Isa 40 in eschatological interpretation as well as the geographical proximity between the Baptizer and Qumran must be seriously considered.

The Essene practice of regular immersions before communal meals and after contact with outsiders or even junior members, is described by Josephus (*J.W.* 2:129, 150), together with communal ownership (*J.W.* 2:122, *Ant.* 18:20), hierarchical structures (*J.W.* 2:134, 140, 150), different grades of membership and periods of probation (*J.W.* 2:137–142, 150).[148] The overall picture fits with that of the *Damascus Document* and the *Community Rule*. The frequent use of immersion is supported by archeological findings of *miqvaot* and water-conduits.[149] While the general practice among Essenes of immersing before meals and after bodily contamination is assumed and implied in various Qumran fragments, the use of immersion for the annual ritual of initiation and/or covenant renewal must be deduced from the *Community Rule*. Here we find evidence for immersions within a covenant community and associated with confession and repentance, anticipating an eschatological restoration.[150] Since the

---

[144] Cf. J. E. Taylor (1997, 15–48) who denies almost any connection between John and Qumran.
[145] Stegemann 1998 [1993], 221f. Cf. Meier 1994, 50f, who mentions similar differences.
[146] Meier 1994, 52. Jeremias (1971, 51) argued on linguistic grounds (hypothetical Aramaic retranslation, referral to variant readings etc.) that people baptized themselves under the supervision of John, but his arguments are refuted by Meier 1994, 94, n.155.
[147] Meier 1994, 51.
[148] Apart from the lengthy description in *J.W.* 2:119–161, Josephus provides an abbreviated version in *Ant.* 18:18–22. Philo's description of the Essenes (*Good Person* 75–91) is on the whole compatible with that of Josephus, although he only indicates ritual purification by the phrase τὴν παρ' ὅλον τὸν βίον συνεχῆ καὶ ἐπάλληλον ἁγνείαν (84).
[149] Schiffman 1995, 40–42. Cf. the speculative ideas of Cook 1996 about Qumran being a purification centre for the Jerusalem branch of the Essenes.
[150] 1QS 1:13–20; 3:4–9; 5:13–14; 11:14–15. For an analysis of the relevant passages, see Excursus 5 below.

communal meal was in focus, immersion must have been part of any initiation and annual covenant renewal, although there is no clear evidence for a *special* rite of immersion on this occasion.

Some interesting comparisons can be made between Qumran and John the Baptizer. Both practised immersions which were associated with confession and repentance. Both offered a covenant renewal which required a change of mind and action. Both rejected those who did not show signs of genuine repentance. Both are placed in an eschatological context in which covenant renewal and purification rites must be seen in view of the coming judgment, destruction and spiritual cleansing. In both cases the water rites involved achieve, together with confession and repentance, an atonement which could be described as a kind of anticipatory forgiveness.[151]

John the Baptizer must definitely be seen in relation to many of the ideas and much of the theology reflected by Qumran documents such as the *Community Rule*. Whether he was acquainted with the Qumran sectarians, a former member,[152] or just influenced by general Essene ideas, is not of crucial importance. In any case we find that the picture of the Baptizer which can be reconstructed from the Synoptic Gospels fits quite well into a first-century Jewish Palestinian context, and that the description offered by Josephus should not be accepted without reservations, since Josephus adapted it to his Hellenistic readers and avoided the original eschatological setting.

The difference between the Baptizer and Qumran or Essene immersion must not be sought in eschatological ideas of repentance and forgiveness, but in the availability of the immersion rite, and its singular character. The singular character must be inferred from the fact that John himself administered the rite. It was this very fact that provided the epithet "baptizer" (βαπτιστῆς) for him.[153]

The availability of the rite is perhaps the most important distinction between the Baptizer and the Qumran community. In Qumran, immersions, and hence participation in the community meals of the group, were available only for those who entered the community through a long period of probation and promised to follow the authority and legal interpretation of the sect.[154] This was not possi-

[151] Cf. the list of similarities provided in Pfann 1999, 347. I have reservations, however, concerning Pfann's dichotomy between soul and body, as well as concerning his detailed reconstruction of the candidate confessing past sins as part of the initiation rite, and his idea that John's baptism initiated a life-long practice of immersions, all requiring repentance.

[152] Cf. the speculative thesis in Charlesworth 1999, 360–375, that John was in the process of entering the Qumran community, but left it a few months before his initiation, because he could not say his "Amen" to the community's curses of all outsiders. The idea is sympathetic but totally unsubstantiated. It stems from the observation, however, that John's message and mission addressed everybody (even Gentiles?, cf. the Roman soldiers in Lk 3:14), although to a large extent moving within the same symbolic world as the Qumran community.

[153] The epithet is neither comprehensible nor relevant unless John himself administered a rite of immersion which was regarded as the very centre of his mission. Cf. Meier 1994, 51.

[154] Cf. CD 15:12–15; 1QS 5, especially 5:13.

ble unless one severed previous social ties and adapted one's way of life considerably. The Baptizer offered eschatological forgiveness through a rite of baptism to all types of people who showed repentance of mind and action. This repentance did not involve adherence to a particular halakhic interpretation, however, but concerned ethical matters, based on social justice. Those baptized seem to have returned home to live ordinary lives, in anticipation of the judgment, but not as initiates into a new sect. John's "disciples" did not include all those who were baptized by him, but rather a small number of followers.

We do not know how the Baptizer conceived of further purifications. A passing comment in Jn 3:25 about a couple of the Baptizer's disciples discussing purifications with some "Jews" implies that they did not practise regular immersions, but no case can be built upon such slight evidence. At most we can surmise that differences in practice existed. A few more details imply a lesser concern with bodily purifications, however. In the first place, the ethical aspect totally dominates all traditions about the Baptizer.[155] Secondly, the transformation of immersion into *the* rite of covenant renewal suggests that it acquired something of a lasting validity. Thirdly, the baptism of John was administered to different groups of people with different standards of purity. In view of this it does not seem likely that John and his movement advocated a certain purification practice for everybody. Finally, John's baptism could be seen as a protest against the religious establishment. Webb has suggested that it "provided an alternative to the temple's sacrificial system as a means of forgiveness,"[156] and that those baptized "were no doubt aware that, in receiving forgiveness of sins through a repentance-baptism, they were bypassing or eliminating the temple rite."[157] Although the Qumran community was critical to the present temple authorities and interpreted its legal obedience as some kind of atonement,[158] we should not draw too hasty conclusions about John's baptism as a substitute for temple sacrifices. While it must be regarded as a popular challenge to the religious authorities, this extraordinary form of covenant renewal does not necessarily contradict the ordinary means of obtaining forgiveness under normal circumstances. My immediate concern, however, is not the temple cult, but purification rites. And with John's ethical emphasis in mind, baptism could be seen as a popular alternative to the regular and repeated immersions practised by the many expansionists, emphasizing the moral or inner aspects of purification over the outer.

---

[155] Even Josephus uses no distinct purification language (προεκκεκαθαρμένης) for the body but for the soul. The body is more generally said to be consecrated (ἐφ' ἁγνείᾳ) by John's baptism.

[156] Webb 1991, 203.

[157] Webb 1991, 205.

[158] Cf. 1QS 8:5–10; 9:3–6; 4Q174 1–2 1:2–7. C. A. Evans 1992, 246–250. In 4Q174, line 7, מעשי תורה could possibly be read as מעשי תודה (cf. *DSSSE*). Allegro has no note on the problem, however, and the ר is admittedly faint, but fully visible in Plate XIX (*DJD* 5). תורה is the most probable reading, not least in view of 4QMMT C27 (מקצת מעשי התורה).

In comparing the immersions at Qumran with John's baptism, Webb suggests that "both are understood to cleanse the person from uncleanness caused by moral contagion."[159] The difficulty with the idea of "moral impurity" has already been discussed. In Qumran we should perhaps rather speak of a combination or even blending of inner and outer impurity. The inside and outside of man are cleansed alike by water rites, accompanied by confession, true repentance and a humble mind (1QS 3:4–9). In John's baptism, the ritual immersion of the body which he administered concerned inner impurity only.[160] Although the sources could be suspected of neglecting to mention outer purification because of their bias and the perspective of their intended readers, the fact that no mention is ever made of such impurities as were normally taken care of by immersions must be taken seriously. This makes John's baptism stand out from every other known purification practice of the time.[161]

Excursus 5: Immersion and covenant renewal in the *Community Rule*

The *Community Rule* (1QS) gives instructions for entrance into and life within a renewed covenant, necessitated by evil times, wicked deeds, calendar perversions and legal misinterpretation.

ולוא לצעוד בכול אחד מכול דברי אל בקציהם ולוא לקדם עתיהם ולוא
להתאחר מכול מועדיהם ולוא לסור מחוקי אמתו ללכת ימין ושמאול וכול
הבאים בסרך היחד יעבורו בברית {א}לפני אל לעשות ככול אשר צוה ולוא
לשוב מאחרו מכול פחד ואימה ומצרף נסוים בממשלת בליעל ובעוברם
בברית יהיו הכוהנים והלויים מברכים את אל ישועות ואת כול מעשי אמתו
וכול העוברים בברית אומרים אחריהם אמן אמן

> They shall not stray from any one of all God's orders concerning their appointed times; they shall not advance their appointed times nor shall they retard any one of their feasts. They shall not veer from his reliable precepts in order to go either to the right or to the left. And all those who enter in the Rule of the Community shall establish a covenant before God in order to carry out all that he commanded and in order not to stray from following him out of any fear, dread, or testing (that might occur) during the dominion of Belial. When they enter the covenant, the priests and the levites shall bless the God of victories and all the works of his faithfulness and all those who enter the covenant shall repeat after them: "Amen, Amen."[162]

The dating of the *Community Rule* has been discussed since its discovery.[163] The cave 1 manuscript is usually dated at approximately 100 BCE, but for one of the cave 4 manuscripts, dates up to fifty years later *or* earlier have been suggested.[164] In any case, several of the cave 4 frag-

[159] Webb 1991, 212. Cf. the critique of J. E. Taylor 1997, 79f.

[160] J. E. Taylor 1997, 88ff denies this possibility in arguing against Webb. The argument depends on the claim that "metaphor and actuality" were never confused (90).

[161] There is no room for discussing Jewish proselyte baptism here. In any case there is little evidence for it during the Second Temple period. Cf. Meier 1994, 51f, 93f, n.153.

[162] 1QS 1:13–20.

[163] For a bibliography on the dating of the manuscripts, see Metso 1999, 308, n.5. For a discussion about the dating of the textual traditions, see Metso 1997a 144ff and 1997b 146ff.

[164] I.e. 4Q259 [4QS^{e}]. Metso (1997a, 145, n.12) mentions the datings of Milik (150–100 BCE) and Cross (50–25 BCE). Cf. Stegemann 1998 [1993], 108.

ments represent earlier variants of the *Community Rule*. The existence of contradictory rules in 1QS has been noticed before, and several suggestions have been made.[165] In her study of the textual development of the *Community Rule*, Sarianna Metso shows that the earliest version of this collection neither included the first four columns, nor the final hymn (columns 10–11), but must have been a shorter version of columns 5–9.[166] Just as with legal materials of the Hebrew Bible and the *Mishnah*, developments in practice seem to have influenced the text, causing revisions and additions, while older materials were retained, resulting in certain discrepancies.[167]

The short version confirms the suspicion that the *Community Rule* originally applied to Essenes living in diverse places, before the establishment of Qumran.[168] This makes sense of the reference to "all their places of residence" (כול מגוריהם) and the idea of meeting other people, in 1QS 6:2.[169] While serving as an argument for a certain pattern of initiation and covenant renewal being a trait of the Essene movement in general, the complicated textual history of the *Community Rule* renders impossible any simplified reconstruction of ceremonies, based on a linear reading of 1QS. Hence detailed reconstructions of the different stages of a covenant renewal ceremony, such as those of Stephen Pfann or Barbara Thiering, must be questioned.[170]

Stephen Pfann's attempt to reconstruct such a ceremony follows the order of the text of 1QS in its present form. This may be possible to a certain point, as the first columns probably reflect a yearly covenant renewal/initiation ceremony as practised in Qumran. Pfann lists a blessing of God and his work (1QS 1:18–20), the priests recounting God's mighty works (1QS 1:21–22), the Levites recounting the sins of Israel (1QS 1:22–23), confession of sin (1QS 1:24–2:1), blessings (1QS 2:1–4) and curses (1QS 2:4–18).[171] The next step is dubious, however, when Pfann interprets the continuation of the text as an annual census and entry ceremony, immediately following the preceding features.[172] The continuation in 1QS 2:19ff. ("They shall act in this way year after year, all the days of Belial's dominion") seems to recapitulate the ceremony, but from a hierarchical angle (order and rank). It is not at all clear that this describes a subsequent entry ceremony. Although the use of the term עבר probably implies a "crossing over" into the covenant,[173] it is not evident that this rite followed the previous curses, nor is a special initiatory immersion necessitated by the subsequent passage (2:25–3:12). Pfann assumes this, however, and adds two more stages to the ceremony: confession of commitment and further testing. The former is supported by 1QS 3:13–4:26, which is an instruction about the two ways or two spirits.[174] This section is often regarded as an "appendix in the form of a literarily independent didactic piece."[175] The latter is deduced from 1QS 6:17–23, which according to theories of textual development belongs to an earlier version of the rule. But Pfann disregards the textual history of the *Community Rule* in his reconstruction.

---

165 Metso discusses those of Jerome Murphy-O'Connor, Philip Davies and E. P. Sanders respectively. Metso 1999, 309ff.

166 Metso 1997b, 107–110, 143–149, 153f.

167 Metso 1999, 312ff. This is clear from scribal additions by a second copyist in col 7–8 of 1QS. Metso 1997a, 146.

168 The settlement is usually dated to ca. 100 BCE. Cf. Stegemann 1998 [1993], 51f.

169 Metso 1999, 311, n.12.

170 Pfann 1999; Thiering 1980.

171 Pfann 1999, 344.

172 Pfann 1999, 345.

173 Pfann 1999, 341f. The term is used for the entrance of the priests, the Levites and the people respectively (1QS 2:19–21). While עבר is here used by itself, it corresponds to the expression לעבור בברית, found in 1QS 1:16, 18, 20, 24 and 2:10. Cf. Webb 1991, 142, who admits the possibility but rather thinks that entrance into the meeting place is referred to.

174 Pfann 1999, 345.

175 Stegemann 1998 [1993], 107.

Looking at the crucial section 1QS 2:19–3:12, we find that the account of the order of entrance into the covenant (initiation and/or annual renewal) turns into an exposition about the person who refuses to enter (1QS 2:25–26):

וכול המואס לבוא [בברית א]ל ללכת בשרירות לבו לוא [יעבור בי]חד אמתו

> And anyone who declines to enter [the covenant of Go]d in order to walk in the stubbornness of his heart shall not [enter the Com]munity of his truth

The reason given is that he does not have the power to fully convert (שוב) his life (1QS 3:1). Hence he must not enter the community, since no atonements or purifications will cleanse him. This is the context for what is usually deemed the most important passage implying an initiatory baptism (1QS 3:4–9). The first part reads (3:4–6):

לוא יזכה בכפורים ולוא יטהר במי נדה ולוא יתקדש בימים ונהרות ולוא
יטהר בכול מי רחץ טמא טמא יהיה כול יומי מואסו במשפטי אל לבלתי
התיסר ביחד עצתו

> He will not become clean by the acts of atonement, nor shall he be purified by the cleansing waters, nor shall he be made holy by seas or rivers, nor shall he be purified by all the water of ablution. Defiled, defiled shall he be all the days he spurns the decrees of God, without allowing himself to be taught by the Community of his counsel.

The point is that no acts of atonement (כפורים), no purification water (מי נדה),[176] no natural or running water (מים ונהרות) and no immersions (מי רחץ) will purify such a person, if repentance is absent. This is further explained in the subsequent lines (3:6–9):

כיא ברוח עצת אמת אל דרכי איש יכופרו כול עוונותו להביט באור החיים
וברוח קדושה ליחד באמתו יטהר מכול עוונותו וברוח יושר וענו{ת}ה תכופר
חטתו ובענות נפשו לכול חוקי אל יטהר בשרו להזות במי נדה ולהתקדש במי
דוכי

> For it is by the spirit of the true counsel of God that are atoned the paths of man, all his iniquities, so that he can look at the light of life. And it is by the holy spirit of the community, in its truth, that he is cleansed of all his iniquities. And by the spirit of uprightness and of humility his sin is atoned. And by the compliance of his soul with all the laws of God his flesh is cleansed by being sprinkled with cleansing waters and being made holy with the waters of repentance.

A detailed analysis of these lines has been supplied by Webb.[177] The four lemmas are similarly structured, with כפר and טהר alternating as main verbs. The lemmas apparently parallel each other, although they give different nuances. The spirit is the agent in all but the last sentence. Atonement and purification seem to be used as alternative expressions with regard to sin. Purification concerns both sins (עוונות) and the body (בשר). The attempt of Thiering to trace two types of cleansing rites in this text, one for inner sin and the other for outer sin, both connected with initiation, is far too speculative.[178] The passage emphasizes the impossibility of practising holiness and being part of the covenant outside of the community, as well as the necessity of submitting to the authority and interpretation of the community for purity.[179]

---

[176] I.e. water mixed with ashes from a red heifer for purification of corpse impurity. Cf. Webb 1991, 144ff.

[177] Webb 1991, 146–152.

[178] Thiering 1980.

[179] Webb 1991, 149.

Possibly, the מי דוכי could be taken as referring to a particular immersion of initiation or covenant renewal, which should be done in a spirit of humility and repentance.[180] This is very speculative, however, since there is no explicit mention of a special immersion anywhere in the text. We have to agree with Webb that

> [w]ith respect to immersions in this passage, the issue is not their use or non-use. That an immersion was to be used is taken for granted. Rather, at issue is the question, what is required for an immersion to be effective in cleansing the candidate? The answer given is that, because the person has been defiled by his/her iniquities, efficacious cleansing requires the immersion to be accompanied by spiritual virtues. The appropriate spiritual virtues are those which indicate a commitment to obey the community's sectarian interpretation of the Torah.[181]

Similar conclusions must be drawn from another passage in 1QS in which the mention of water could be relevant.[182] In column 5, which is probably the introduction of an older version of the *Community Rule*, we find an emphasis on the voluntary nature of the community (המתנדבים)[183] and the necessary segregation (הבדל)[184] from others. This is the context for a statement about men of injustice (1QS 5:13–14).

אל יבוא במים לגעת בטהרת אנשי הקודש כיא לוא יטהרו כי אם שבו מרעתם
כיא טמא בכול עוברי דברו

> He should not go into the waters to share in the pure food of the men of holiness, for one is not cleansed unless one turns away from ones wickedness, for he is unclean among all the transgressors of his word.

The passage could be seen as redactional, referring to a person who, as in 1QS 2:25–3:6, is judged to be insufficiently sincere and therefore must not be initiated or renew his commitment.[185] But it could also be taken to refer to non-members who would like to bridge the separation and join in immersions in order to be able to dine with members. According to the text, such solutions must not be sought, however, since segregation is total and supported by Scripture.[186]

We find that there is no clear evidence in the *Community Rule* for a *special* rite of immersion occupying the central place in a ritual of initiation or covenant renewal. Since the culmination of the long period of probation was admittance into the community and the sharing of the pure food and drink, the passage above (1QS 5:13–14) is evidence for immersions before meals.[187] Immersion simply must have been part of any initiation or covenant renewal.[188] But we do not have evidence to claim that this immersion was considered *different* from the numerous subse-

---

[180] Cf. the humble attitude of the community member, displayed in the concluding hymn: "However, I belong to evil humankind, to the assembly of unfaithful flesh; my failings, my iniquities, my sins, {...} with the depravities of my heart, belong to the assembly of worms and of those who walk in darkness" (1QS 11:9–10).

[181] Webb 1991, 150.

[182] מי נדה is mentioned in 1QS 4:21 as well, but only in a *simile*, as an analogy to the eschatological spiritual purification. For a discussion of the passage, see above, 221f.

[183] 1QS 5:1, 6, 8, 10, 22.

[184] 1QS 5:1, 10. Cf. the subsequent argument based on Scripture about not associating but remaining at a distance, in 1QS 5:14ff.

[185] Knibb 1987, 111.

[186] Webb 1991, 154.

[187] Thus verifying that the statements of Josephus (*J.W.* 2:129–130) are correct and confirming that immersions before meals are taken for granted throughout the sectarian literature.

[188] Cf. Webb 1991, 155; J. E. Taylor 1997, 81.

quent immersions which a member must undergo. In fact, *every* immersion seems to have been associated with repentance, as evidence such as 4Q274, 4Q414 and 4Q512 suggests. This is in accord with the general association of sin and impurity which is so clearly exhibited at the end of the final hymn in 1QS. Humble penitance characterizes 1QS 11:9–15. The section concludes (1QS 11:14–15):

> he will judge me in the justice of his truth, and in his plentiful goodness always atone for all my sins; in his justice he will cleanse me from the uncleanness of the human being and from the sin of the sons of man, so that I can give God thanks for his justice and The Highest for his majesty.

Although immersion is not explicitly mentioned, purification is associated with forgiveness in a context of repentance. While the reference in the hymn may be to an eschatological, spiritual purification, the present means of purification, necessary for admittance into the covenant community and participation in its communal meals, is water. In the eschatological context, which is obvious in the final hymn (1QS 10–11) and in the section about the two spirits (1QS 3:13–4:26), the present purification in water serves, however, as a *simile* for God's future act of spiritual purification. It is thus possible to trace a notion of anticipation in the immersion rites of the community.

As we have seen above, the textual history of the *Community Rule* makes it impossible to assign certain sections to certain stages of development or periods of history. But since the present copy of 1QS is dated as early as the foundation of the Qumran settlement, the prehistory of the text attests to general ideas and practices that were common in a broader, probably Essene movement at an even earlier date.[189] We must conclude that some practice of water purifications (immersions) within a covenant community, associated with confession and humble repentance, and in anticipation of divine restoration in the future, has roots well into the second century BCE.

Jesus and baptism in gospel traditions

It is beyond doubt that Jesus was baptized by John, since this caused embarrassment for the early church. For the question of purity, however, it is not the christological implications which are important, but rather the question of Jesus' dependence on the Baptizer. Did Jesus become a disciple of the Baptizer? His baptism could imply that, but most of the people baptized by John seem to have returned to their homes to live ordinary lives. That John did have disciples, however, is attested by several strands of gospel tradition,[190] and there are reasons for believing that Jesus initially was one of them.

The Markan reference to Jesus spending a period of time in the wilderness (Mk 1:12f.) places him in the same area as John. While this reference receives a mythical note in Mark, and is given a "midrashic" treatment in Q, it may go back to an historical memory of Jesus spending some time, like John or possibly together with John, in the wilderness. While this is admittedly speculative, the idea of Jesus as a disciple of the Baptizer is supported by a few passing remarks

---

[189] For a discussion of the *Sitz im Leben* of the *Community Rule*, see Metso 1999. For recent discussions of the Essene hypothesis, see VanderKam 1994, 71–98 and Boccaccini 1998.

[190] Mark (Mk 2:18, par. Mt 9:14/Lk 5:33; Mk 6:29, par. Mt 14:12); Q (Mt 11:2/Lk 7:18); John (Jn 1:35; 3:25; 4:1); Acts 19:1ff.

in the Gospel of John. In spite of this gospel's highly stylized narrative of Jesus' baptism, in which the Baptizer is made a witness rather than an agent, and in spite of the aim of portraying the first disciples of Jesus as choosing to follow him because the Baptizer had declared him as his successor, the notion remains that not only his first disciples, but Jesus himself, originally belonged to the circle around the Baptizer (Jn 1:29–39). Another hint is found in Jn 3:22–26, in which Jesus and his disciples are pictured as conducting a baptizing mission in Judaea, parallel to that of John. The passage introduces another testimony from the Baptizer about the superiority and identity of Jesus. In this introduction, however, John's disciples report to him about the doings of Jesus with the phrase: (v. 26): "Rabbi, he who was together with you on the other side of Jordan..." (ῥαββί, ὃς ἦν μετὰ σοῦ πέραν τοῦ Ἰορδάνου...). While the wording is put in the mouth of John's disciples by a redactor or an earlier tradition, it reveals a consciousness at some stage about Jesus staying with the Baptizer for a period of time.[191] The idea of Jesus as a disciple of John, conducting a parallel baptizing mission, makes sense as a background to his conflicts with Judaean authorities as well as to the belief of the people/Herod that the powers of the executed John were manifest in Jesus' actions (Mk 6:14–16, par. Mt 14:1–2/Lk 9:7–9).

The picture of Jesus as a baptizer is a very likely one, especially in view of the fact that a redactor of the Fourth Gospel felt compelled to deny it. After the christological passage based on the testimony of John the Baptizer, and introduced by the account of Jesus and John baptizing simultaneously (Jn 3:22–36), the narrative continues (Jn 4:1–3):

> When Jesus realized that the Pharisees had heard that Jesus was making and baptizing more disciples than John—and yet it was not Jesus himself who baptized but his disciples—he left Judaea and went away back to Galilee.

This sudden and surprising contradiction, not only of the clause into which it is interpolated, but also of statements in the previous context (3:22), is regarded by almost every scholar as a redactor's comment.[192] Meier suggests a possible reason for the denial. Since the giving of the Spirit is so prominent in the Fourth Gospel, but associated with Jesus' death and resurrection, and since Christian baptism was seen as conferring the spirit, the final redactor solved a theological dilemma by introducing a modification: Jesus did not himself baptize.[193] In doing this, however, he confirmed the picture of a baptizing Jesus as belonging to early tradition.

---

[191] For a discussion about historical data in the Fourth Gospel and clues to Jesus as a disciple of John, cf. Meier 1994, 116–130.

[192] Cf. Dodd 1953, 311, n.3; Brown 1966, 1: 164; Culpepper 1983, 193.

[193] Meier 1994, 196, n. 75; cf. J. E. Taylor 1997, 297f, who suggests that subsequent Christian interpretation of baptism made it difficult to explain Jesus' immersing activity. D. M. Smith (1996, 227) thinks the comment intends to harmonize the Johannine account with the Synoptics.

It is thus possible to regard Jesus as an administrator of a physical purification rite. In view of what has been said above about John the Baptizer, however, the baptism administered by Jesus should likewise be seen not as a purification from such bodily transferable impurities as were caused by i.e. discharges or contact with a corpse, but as an inner purification accompanied by repentance, a covenant renewal in view of the coming judgment. Since most of the clues for Jesus as a baptizer are found in contexts in which John figures, the baptism which Jesus administered cannot be interpreted apart from that of John. It must be regarded as bearing a similar eschatological connotation.

The lack of any mention of Jesus' baptizing activity in the rest of the Gospel of John or in the Synoptic Gospels is all the more remarkable.[194] We could certainly speculate about possible theological reasons, such as that suggested by Meier for Jn 4:2, or a reluctance in the early church to picture Jesus as a follower and imitator of John. Perhaps the gospel writers wanted to reserve the rite of baptism for later Christian use.[195] But in spite of such speculations, it nevertheless remains to explain why no trace of any baptismal activity has survived in the synoptic material, although the themes of repentance and judgment occur repeatedly. In view of the eschatological setting of Jesus' activity and teaching in the Synoptic tradition, we should expect some trace of a baptismal activity, had Jesus been engaged in such.

This makes imperative the question: did Jesus at some point stop baptizing? It has been suggested that baptizing belonged only to the initial phase of his mission. This is the idea of Paul Hollenbach, who argues that Jesus drastically changed his mind at some point. This "conversion" led him to drop significant ritual actions such as fasting and prayer, as well as rejecting John's ascetic lifestyle. The cause, according to Hollenbach, would have been Jesus' discovery of his powers of healing and exorcism, which led him to modify his eschatology. Baptism became irrelevant, since healing occurs now, showing that God is already visiting his people.[196]

Hollenbach's reconstruction has been criticized for being anachronistic, for claiming knowledge about Jesus' inner life, and for mixing and rearranging synoptic and Johannine material without warrant, in an act of "uncritical harmonization."[197] The suggestion that Jesus suddenly realized unexpected powers of healing is speculative indeed. The popular idea of Jesus as a John *redivivus*

---

[194] The only possible implication of Jesus baptizing someone, except for the references in Jn 1–4, is the so-called *Secret Gospel of Mark*. Apart from the extremely uncertain evaluation of that fragment, the statement in III(2r):6–7 that after six days "Jesus commissioned" the young man (καὶ μεθ' ἡμέρας ἕξ ἐπέταξεν αὐτῷ ὁ ἰησοῦς) could be interpreted in various ways. Cf. Morton Smith 1973, 115, 167–188, 452; Schneemelcher 1991, 106ff.

[195] Cf. the suggestions of J. E. Taylor 1997, 297f, who assumes that Jesus, like John, immersed people to remove outer impurity, for which the Gentile Church would have felt little sympathy.

[196] Hollenbach 1982.

[197] Cf. Meier 1994, 125.

because of his powers, actually suggests that the Baptizer might have been a miracle worker too.[198]

The idea of different phases in Jesus' mission is nevertheless plausible and is not unique to Hollenbach.[199] While the positions that Jesus continued to baptize and that he stopped baptizing both rest in a sense on arguments from silence, I regard the latter as the more probable. A strong burden of proof lies upon those who wish to claim that baptism belonged to the latter part of Jesus' ministry, even as a prominent feature.[200] The absence of hints throughout the Jesus tradition about Jesus baptizing, except for the Johannine passing remarks belonging to the context of the Baptizer, must not be disregarded.

While it is quite certain that Jesus began with John, evidence shows that he differed from the Baptizer too. This is apparent not only from the popular comparison that the Baptizer was an ascetic and Jesus a glutton and drunkard (Mt 11:18–19/Lk 7:33–34), but by the Baptizer's questions about Jesus' identity (Mt 11:2–6/Lk 7:18–23):

> But when John heard in the prison[201] about the works of Christ, he sent and asked him through his disciples: "Are you the coming one (ὁ ἐρχόμενος) or should we wait for another?" Jesus answered them: "Go and tell John what you hear and see: blind see again and lame walk, lepers are cleansed and deaf hear, dead are raised and poor are told good news. Blessed is the one who is not offended because of me.[202]

The question in focus in this Q-saying is the identity of the "coming one" (ὁ ἐρχόμενος). This is the expression used in the previous Q-material about the Baptizer for the figure coming after him (Mt 3:11).[203] There is an apparent discrepancy, however, between the answer of Jesus and the picture given in Mt 3/Lk 3. John is described in Q as expecting a coming executor of judgment. Jesus' answer is not compatible with the eschatological judgment, separating wheat from chaff and burning the latter, for which John's baptism was thought to function as a protection.[204]

We have seen that both John and the Qumran community saw their missions in the light of Isa 40:3.[205] The context was eschatological, in view of God's coming judgment. In the *Community Rule* the preparation of a way in the wilderness was interpreted as the study of the Torah, which came to expression in a segregated life in obedience to the regulations of the community. For the Baptizer, the preparation was interpreted as conversion to righteous living and social justice, expressed by baptism. In both cases, however, the judgment of God

---

198 Cf. Mk 6:14–16, par. Mt 14:1–2/Lk 9:7–9.
199 Cf. B. Meyer 1992.
200 Against Meier 1994, 127.
201 The reference to the prison is not found in Luke.
202 Mt 11:2–6
203 Cf. Uro 1996, 95ff.
204 Cf. Kloppenborg Verbin 2000, 122ff.
205 1QS 8:12ff; 9:19ff.

was expected to follow. In the *Community Rule* this seems to have included a spiritual purification of the inside of man by God himself (1QS 4:20f.). John seems to have expected a human figure, the "coming one," as God's agent for this task (Mt 3:11/Lk 3:16).[206]

Views about the judgment, divine agents and the function and identity of the Messiah(s) differed and developed during the Second Temple period. A fragment from a Messianic Apocalypse found in Qumran reveals one description, based on prophetic expectations mainly from Isaiah.

> [for the heav]ens and the earth will listen to his anointed one, [and all] that is in them will not turn away from the precepts of the holy ones. Strengthen yourselves, you who are seeking the Lord, in his service! *Blank* Will you not in this encounter the Lord, all those who hope in their heart? For the Lord will consider the pious, and call the righteous by name, and his spirit will hover upon the poor, and he will renew the faithful with his strength. For he will honour the pious upon the throne of an eternal kingdom, freeing prisoners, giving sight to the blind, straightening out the twis[ted.] And for[e]ver shall I cling to [those who] hope, and in his mercy [...] and the fru[it of ...] ... not be delayed. And the Lord will perform marvellous acts such as have not existed, just as he sa[id,] [for] he will heal the badly wounded and will make the dead live, he will proclaim good news to the poor and [...] ... [...] he will lead the [...] and enrich the hungry. [...] and all [...][207]

There are apparent similarities with Jesus' answer to John. This is probably due to common messianic expectations, based on a combined reading of various Isaianic passages.[208] However, this was neither the only contemporary messianic characterization, nor necessarily the dominating one.[209]

The question of Jesus' self-consciousness is an old problem, subject to severe methodological limitations, and cannot be discussed in all its detail within the scope of this study. Suffice it to point out that there is nothing intrinsically impossible with a first-century Jew indentifying himself with a messianic figure.[210] The eschatological consciousness of people such as the Teacher of Righteousness or John the Baptizer must have encouraged others to look for and even identify themselves as messianic agents. The prime reasons for questioning Jesus' messianic self-consciousness have been the so-called "Messianic secret," and the idea that messianic identification must be part of an emerging christology in the early church. As Räisänen has shown, the "Messianic secret" must be regarded as largely a Markan literary construct. At the same time, the

---

206 The suggestion that this expression could refer to God does not make sense in view of John's statement about not being worthy enough to untie his sandals.

207 4Q521 2 2:1–14.

208 Isa 29:18–19; 35:5–6; 61:1. Cf the discussion in the previous chapter, 99, 168.

209 For a study of various messianic paradigms at the end of the Second Temple period, see Collins 1995.

210 Josephus mentions several revolutionary figures which could be understood as messianic pretenders (e.g. *Ant.* 18:85ff; 20:97f, 169ff; *J.W.* 2:261ff, 433ff; cf. *J.W.* 6:312ff.) Cf. Collins 1995, 195–214.

origins of the secrecy theme are very complicated.[211] During the period of Roman dominance, any sensible Jew with messianic aspiration would have been careful and hesitant in his claims. "Messianic" and "christological" language could, however, be used about human beings during the Second Temple era, without necessarily deifying them.[212]

It makes good sense to suggest that Jesus saw a messianic role for himself through a process in which the eschatological kingdom was already being realized through healings and community building. Such ideas were not without precedent, but differed somewhat from the Baptizer's expectations and mission. Hollenbach may be right that Jesus underwent a change which was associated with his eschatology and healings. Although I am inclined to see less of a break and more of a continuity with the Baptizer, there is nevertheless a change, which ought to have to do with Jesus' self-consciousness. While this is inaccessible for historical research, the discrepancy between the Baptizer's expectations and Jesus' actions is visible. This suggests an eschatological view and possibly a messianic self-consciousness, which renders baptism as an anticipatory act of repentance and covenant renewal secondary, if not redundant. The reasons for the lack of references to Jesus as a baptizer may simply be that baptism was not part of, or at least no important constituent in his independent ministry. In the end time, purification of the innermost part of man was expected to be accomplished by the spirit.

Jesus and purification rites

We have seen that except for a few passing remarks at the beginning of the Gospel of John, there are no references in the available sources to Jesus baptizing other people. The situation is similar when we look for evidence that Jesus should have purified himself by immersion. There is no mention of any such purifications in the Synoptic Gospels. In this case too, the only possible references are found in the Gospel of John. To be sure, purity language is used in Jesus' farewell discourse, but this is hardly relevant in a search for historical traces of Jesus' practice.[213] Of more relevance, however, is a passing remark in Jn 11:55: "The passover of the Jews was close at hand, and many went up to Jerusalem from the countryside for the passover, in order to purify themselves."

[211] Räisänen 1990.

[212] Collins 1995, 154–172.

[213] Jn 15:2–3: "Every branch in me which does not bear fruit he takes away, and every one which bears fruit he prunes/cleanses (καθαίρει) so that it should bear more fruit. You are already pruned/clean (καθαροί) through the word which I have spoken to you." On the level of Johannine theology and/or final redaction, the relationship between this passage and others, such as Jn 13:1–20 (to be discussed below), is interesting. The nature and complicated tradition history of the farewell discourse, however, renders this spiritualized use of purity language of little use as a clue to Jesus' attitude to purification practices.

The comment refers to the practice of pilgrims arriving in Jerusalem one week in advance, to go through the purification ritual necessary for removing corpse impurity. The ritual included sprinklings and immersions on the third and seventh (and possibly first[214]) day. The practice is confirmed both by Philo and Josephus,[215] and supported by the large number of immersion pools found in Jerusalem and close to the temple.[216] It was necessary for taking part in the Passover meal.[217]

Since entry into the temple required purity, it is reasonable to suppose that Jesus and his disciples immersed on such occasions like other people. At the same time interpretation and practice varied between different groups. At the important festivals, however, we should probably expect that all pilgrims followed the custom of purifying a week in advance, although the huge amount of people and the varying standards of purity made a high degree of tolerance necessary.[218] While the Fourth Gospel pictures Jesus as coming to Jerusalem only five days before his last Passover,[219] the Synoptic accounts seem to suppose that he arrived together with other Galilean pilgrims.[220] Any conclusions as to Jesus' purification practice must be drawn by inference.

Paula Fredriksen draws far-reaching conclusions about Jesus' practice of purification by appealing to such inferences. Jesus must have purified since he partook of the Passover meal. Since he came before the feast together with other pilgrims, the purpose was purification.[221] His instruction about reconciliation before bringing gifts to the altar (Mt 5:23–24) presupposes purification too, since it was required before entering the temple. Says Fredriksen:

> Why would Matthew's audience presuppose that Matthew's believer who worships at the Temple's altar would disregard the biblical laws of purity (which would require his having immersed before entering the area), while observing what they were linked to, the laws of offerings? More likely, Matthew's original ancient audience would suppose that this worshiper would have prepared properly to approach the altar; and that, therefore, is what they would have heard the evangelist's Jesus saying, too.[222]

---

[214] 11Q19 [11QT] 49:16–21; *Spec.Laws* 3:205–206.

[215] *Spec.Laws* 1:261; *J.W.* 6:290. Cf. the discussion above, 185–189, about this practice and the immersions involved.

[216] Sanders 1990, 214–227, 355 n.28; 1992, 222–230. Cf. above, 53f, 74f; below, 259, 281.

[217] Cf. Jn 18:28.

[218] Cf. Fredriksen 2000, 67.

[219] Jn 12:1, 12. For the suggestion that Bethany and Bethphage were included in the "suburbs" where pilgrims could lodge and yet be counted as being in Jerusalem, see Jeremias 1958 [1923], I: 68–70; cf. *mMen* 11:2. Even if this were the case, Jn 12:1 would suggest that Jesus came too late for the seven day purification period. This could, however, be seen as part of a Johannine tendency to portray Jesus as opposing purity laws (cf. Jn 2:1–11).

[220] Mt 21:1–11; Mark 11:1–11; Lk 19:28–40.

[221] Fredriksen 2000, 205f.

[222] Fredriksen 2000, 205. Fredriksen also refers to Jesus' instructions to the leper about purification offerings in Mk 1:40–44 (203f). Cf. above, 101f.

The purpose is to show that no problem was involved in Jesus becoming impure, since we must presuppose that he underwent regular purifications.[223]

While we must presuppose that Jesus was a Jew and lived like a Jew, the question is not that easily solved. As will be further discussed in the following chapter, Judaism was diverse at the end of the Second Temple period. And as we have seen above, the evidence for Jesus initially practising baptism is no proof for an interest in purification of bodily transferable contagion.

Fredriksen suggests that although her argument is based on silence, "the loudness of this silence in this instance gives the measure of our own *un*familiarity with and distance from the ancient world."[224] The silence about Jesus administering baptism is a strong argument for his giving up this rite, since baptism was a very *special* trait, associated with the message and mission of the specific person administering it. In the case of immersion, where we deal with a *general* practice, just like sacrifice or dietary restrictions, it is precarious to interpret the silence as non-observance. Nevertheless Fredriksen's conclusions to the opposite are too far-reaching. There are almost no hints that Jesus took any interest in purification practices. Since practices varied to a greater degree than in the case of sacrifices or food restrictions, we cannot be certain. It is likely that Jesus purified, like most or all other people, at large festivals. I do not suggest that he gave up the practice altogether. But we know nothing about whether he purified on other occasions. Sayings about reconciliation and sacrifices cannot be adduced as arguments. There is simply no evidence.

A possible passage of interest is the foot-washing tradition in Jn 13:1–20. It is not possible to account for the complicated redactional and theological development of this tradition.[225] We will look only for possible traces of the historical Jesus which could shed some light on his purification practice.

While vv 1–3 to a large extent consist of redactional material, introducing the whole section (Jn 13–17),[226] vv 4–5 convey the concrete narrative, to which dialogue and exposition is appended in the typical Johannine manner. Since Bultmann, it has been recognized that this narrative is given two different explanations, one in the dialogue with Simon Peter (vv 6–10: symbolic action), the other in Jesus' exposition (vv 12–17: example of service). Both can follow vv 4–5 independently.[227] They do not fully agree, since v 7 (γνώσῃ δὲ μετὰ ταῦτα) refers to the time of Jesus' death, resurrection and ascension, when the disciples will understand the full meaning of his action, while v 12 (γινώσκετε τί πεποίηκα ὑμῖν;) introduces an instant and different explanation. In vv 6–10a the foot-washing is interpreted as a sign of Jesus' death, later to be inter-

---

[223] Fredriksen 2000, 200.
[224] Fredriksen 2000, 206.
[225] For such discussions, see J. C. Thomas 1991 and Segovia 1982.
[226] Segovia 1982, 38–42.
[227] Bultmann 1971, 461f.

preted sacramentally, while vv 12–17 suggest that it is to be seen as an example to repeat.[228] The first explanation fits well into the Johannine pattern in which an act of Jesus is interpreted as "sign," to be understood after his death. The second explanation is immediately understood, but its tendency (discipleship and imitation) parallels that of 1John, and may well be ascribed to a final redactor.[229] This fits with the idea that foot-washing was actually practised within the Johannine community at some point.[230] Thus vv 4–10a would represent the earlier tradition.[231] It reads:

> 4 ἐγείρεται ἐκ τοῦ δείπνου καὶ τίθησιν τὰ ἱμάτια καὶ λαβὼν λέντιον διέζωσεν ἑαυτόν· 5 εἶτα βάλλει ὕδωρ εἰς τὸν νιπτῆρα καὶ ἤρξατο νίπτειν τοὺς πόδας τῶν μαθητῶν καὶ ἐκμάσσειν τῷ λεντίῳ ᾧ ἦν διεζωσμένος. 6 ἔρχεται οὖν πρὸς Σίμωνα Πέτρον· λέγει αὐτῷ· κύριε, σύ μου νίπτεις τοὺς πόδας; 7 ἀπεκρίθη Ἰησοῦς καὶ εἶπεν αὐτῷ· ὃ ἐγὼ ποιῶ σὺ οὐκ οἶδας ἄρτι, γνώσῃ δὲ μετὰ ταῦτα. 8 λέγει αὐτῷ Πέτρος· οὐ μὴ νίψῃς μου τοὺς πόδας εἰς τὸν αἰῶνα. ἀπεκρίθη Ἰησοῦς αὐτῷ· ἐὰν μὴ νίψω σε, οὐκ ἔχεις μέρος μετ' ἐμοῦ. 9 λέγει αὐτῷ Σίμων Πέτρος· κύριε, μὴ τοὺς πόδας μου μόνον ἀλλὰ καὶ τὰς χεῖρας καὶ τὴν κεφαλήν. 10 λέγει αὐτῷ ὁ Ἰησοῦς· ὁ λελουμένος οὐκ ἔχει χρείαν εἰ μὴ τοὺς πόδας νίψασθαι, ἀλλ' ἔστιν καθαρὸς ὅλος·
>
> 4 He stood up from the meal and took off the cloak and, taking a towel, tied it around his waist. 5 Then he poured water in the basin and began to wash the feet of the disciples, and to wipe them with the towel which was tied around. 6 He came to Simon Peter who said to him: "Lord, are you going to wash my feet?" 7 Jesus answered and said to him: "What I do, you cannot realize now, but you will understand afterwards." 8 Peter said to him: "Never in eternity will you wash my feet!" Jesus answered him: "If I do not wash you, you will have no part with me." 9 Simon Peter said to him: "Lord, not only my feet, but my hands and head, too." 10 Jesus said to him: "One who has bathed has no need to wash anything except the feet, since he is clean all over."

Two questions must be asked from this tradition. The first is whether it represents an historical memory of Jesus washing his disciples' feet. If so, the nature of such a washing needs to be examined. This leads to the second question, which concerns the final saying in the Johannine dialogue. If it represents an attitude of Jesus to immersion and foot-washing, it might indicate something about his practice of purification.

It is characteristic of the Gospel of John to elaborate on narrative material, which is at times parallel to synoptic traditions.[232] The view that the author is dependent on the Synoptics only and has created all other materials himself is

---

[228] Segovia 1982, 36.

[229] Segovia 1982, 42–48. Segovia notes that the tendency of vv 12–17 is found elsewhere in the gospel of John only in 13:34–35 and 15:1–17, i.e. in other parts of the farewell discourse, and in texts which are often regarded as secondary as well.

[230] Cf. the speculative theory of H. Weiss 1979. His basic idea is credible, however, and would explain the preservation of the tradition (4–10) as well as the added explanation (12–17).

[231] A similar opinion is held by Brown 1970, 562.

[232] Cf. Jn 6:1–13. For a discussion of the relationship between synoptic traditions and Johannine redaction, see Dunderberg 1994.

not tenable, however. It is more likely that other narratives which are taken as points of departure for dialogues and expositions come from tradition, too, although the sources are unknown to us. On three occasions in the gospel it is stated that the disciples believed or understood later, after Jesus' resurrection. The first case (Jn 2:22) refers to a saying about tearing down and building up a temple, paralleled in Mark and Matthew.[233] The second case (Jn 12:16) refers to Jesus' entry into Jerusalem, which is found in all three synoptics.[234] In Jn 13:7 we find the third statement, associated with the foot-washing tradition, which has no extant parallel. It is likely, as Richard Bauckham notes, that

> in chap. 13, as in the other two cases, John sees, with post-resurrection hindsight, a deeper significance in a feature of the traditions of Jesus' words and deeds, rather than creating an event to which he attributes such significance.[235]

Since sayings of Jesus about the greatest being a servant are found in several variants and sources, but without any verbal similarities with the Johannine tradition in question,[236] Bauckham suggests that the foot-washing narrative in Jn 13 is created neither to replace such sayings, nor to provide a setting for such sayings, but does represent an historical memory of an action of Jesus.[237]

While the dialogue with Peter is a Johannine construction, with its typical misunderstandings through which the reader is guided towards the real meaning of Jesus' words and actions, the logion in v 10 could possibly refer to some concrete and historical purificatory practice. The textual tradition is uncertain, however, with a short reading omitting the phrase εἰ μὴ τοὺς πόδας.[238] While some scholars prefer the short reading,[239] the majority opt for the long reading because of its better attestation[240] and because it makes more sense. "One who has bathed has no need to wash, but is clean all over" seems a strange answer when the issue is over the need for foot-washing. The possibility exists, however, that the short reading represents an early traditional saying, into which εἰ μὴ τοὺς πόδας was inserted, to make it fit in the dialogue.

The complicated tradition history of these verses cannot be disentangled with any certainty at all. But supposing that the saying in v 10 has some historical background, what might it refer to? ὁ λελουμένος may be understood as a ref-

---

[233] Mk 14:58/Mt 26:61.

[234] Mk 11:1–10/Mt 21:1–9/Lk 19:28–40.

[235] Bauckham 1999, 420.

[236] Except for the term δοῦλος in Jn 13:16. This verse, together with 13:20, are separate Amen-sayings which do have parallels in the synoptics, but not in contexts about the greatest being a servant. Cf. Bauckham 1999, 424f.

[237] Bauckham 1999, 420–425.

[238] The phrase is omitted by ℵ, vgst, Tertullian and Origen^{com}. Cf. J. C. Thomas 1991, 19ff. The variants are actually numerous, but only two differ substantially and are worth considering.

[239] Grossouw 1966, 130; Boismard 1964. Brown 1970, 552 hesitates.

[240] B, C*, W, Ψ, arm, Origen^{txt}, Augustine. Other variants of the long reading are furthermore attested by P^{66}, P^{75}, A, D, and a number of versions. Cf. J. C. Thomas 1991, 19ff.

erence to one who has been baptized. "One who has bathed has no need to wash, but is clean all over" could then be taken as a rejection of any further purification rituals, subsequent to (John's) baptism. If we opt for the long reading, the foot-washing could be interpreted as representing some additional purification rite. This is possible when the tradition is read in its Johannine eschatological context,[241] in which Jesus is being prepared for and prepares his disciples for witness unto death, leading to glorification.[242] John's baptism was an eschatological immersion in view of the coming crisis, God's judgment. Those already baptized need not repeat the rite of eschatological cleansing, but nevertheless cannot meet their own coming martyrdom without entering the same state of eschatological preparation and sanctification as does Jesus.[243] Although most of this belongs to the level of Johannine theology, it is possible to suggest an historical trace of foot-washing as a means for eschatological protection in retrospect of John's baptism, and in view of the coming crisis and evil end.[244]

Another possibility is that "one who has bathed" refers to the pilgrim who has undergone the paschal immersion(s) included in the purification ritual before major feasts (Jn 11:55). The verb λούειν usually translates the Hebrew רָחַץ and is normally used for immersing the body. νίπτειν on the other hand is more common for washing in general. Jesus would then have suggested foot-washing as a complementary purification ritual, not to baptism, but to the paschal immersion(s), either as a preparation before the meal or in view of the coming temple visit. While foot-washing was a common practice in Antiquity, the evidence for it as a purification ritual is scanty. A few sources suggest that the temple should not be entered with dusty or unwashed feet. An injunction to this effect is found in the *Mishnah* as well as in the *Tosefta*:

לא יכנס [אדם] להר הבית ... ובאבק[ו] שעל רגליו

> No [man] must enter the mountain of the house (i.e. the Temple Mount) … with dust on his feet.[245]

---

[241] An eschatological note is perhaps to be found in Jesus' words to Peter (v 8): "If I do not wash you, you will have no part with me (οὐκ ἔχεις μέρος μετ' ἐμοῦ)." As pointed out by several commentators (e.g. Brown 1970, 565f; Manns 1981, 166ff), the word μέρος indicates a share in the heavenly world (this Greek term is used in the LXX to translate חֵלֶק, the heritage of Israel, which came to receive an after-worldly connotation). This would make foot-washing of crucial importance, but seems to fit ill with the long reading, according to which foot-washing must be understood as subordinate and secondary to washing (Cf. Barrett 1978, 441f). The short reading is of no help, however, since it would make foot-washing unnecessary altogether.

[242] Note that Mary anoints Jesus feet as a preparation for his coming death (Jn 12:1–8), and Jesus prepares his disciples in the Farewell Discourse for their eschatological *martyrion*.

[243] Foot-washing could actually symbolize necessary preparation. An example is found in Philo's use of the expression "with unwashed feet" in *QG* 4:60. Cf. J. C. Thomas 1991, 34.

[244] Jesus may have expected a violent death in a martyr tradition; cf. Charlesworth 1988, 139–145; Theissen and Merz 1998 [1996], 429f.

[245] *mBer* 9:5; *tBer* 7:19; אדם is missing in the *Mishnah*, as well as the ו.

This might imply that foot-washing was presupposed before temple visits.[246] Such a view may be supported by Philo, who seems to quote a general saying, in support of his interpretation of certain sacrificial details, stating that "one should not enter with unwashed feet on the pavement of the temple of God."[247] While the rabbinic passage concerns every worshipper, the clear statement from Philo may refer to instructions for priests. As for officiating priests, the washing of hands *and* feet were part of their purification,[248] but for ordinary people, we have to admit that evidence is uncertain, both with regard to meals and visits to the temple.[249] Although *P. Oxy.* 840, to be discussed further below, suggests that foot-washing was actually required for entering the temple precincts, we find no rabbinic legal discussions about ritual foot-washing for laity which are even remotely similar to those about hand-washing.[250] While immersion for the sake of purity was assumed for any Jew visiting the inner court,[251] it is possible

---

[246] Cf. the possible "footbaths" discovered in Jerusalem. Avigad 1984 [1980], 84, 86. Cf. *mYad* 4:1.

[247] Philo *QE* 1:2 (preserved in an Armenian version only). LCL.

[248] Ex 30:18–21; Philo, *Moses* 2:138. Cf. the discussions in the *Mishnah* tractate *Yoma* about the High Priest's immersions and washings of hands and feet on the day of Atonement. The High Priest was said to immerse five times and wash hands and feet ten times that day (*mYoma* 3:3, 4, 6; 4:5; 7:3, 4). There is a requirement (for priests?) to wash hands and feet after urination (*mYoma* 3:2). In a discussion about different spheres of holiness, foot-washing is deemed necessary for entering the Sanctuary itself (i.e. the shrine), although R.Yose considers it necessary for entering the area between the porch and the altar as well (*mKel* 1:9). In view of the ten washings of the High Priest, however, it could be that every new task or every entrance into a higher sphere of holiness, was accompanied by a new washing of hands and feet. *mTam* 1:4 and 2:1 suggest that such washings preceded all tasks which involved the use of sacred utensils. Note that the rabbinic term for this washing is קדש (cf. the use of ἁγνίζειν in Jn 11:55, and in Josephus, see below, n.251). It was performed in the bronze laver (Ex 30:18) situated "between the porch and the altar, towards the south" (*mMid* 3:6). Foot-washing in this cultic context is never discussed separately, but as a priestly combined ritual of sanctifying hands and feet.

[249] In view of archaeological findings, a statement in the Cairo Geniza (cf. Runesson 2001b, 124f), and a gloss in the bT (cf. Bar-Ilan 1991) it is possible that foot-washing before synagogue prayer developed in the diaspora at an early date, perhaps in imitation of temple practice.

[250] For discussions about hand-washing as a purification rite, cf. the *Mishnah* tractate *Yadayim*.

[251] Cf. the discussion above about the necessity of removing corpse-impurity in time before the large festivals. The removal of impurity, i.e. immersion, before entering the court of Israel is presupposed in *mKel* 1:8. But it seems as if immersion was *always* required for *any* visit to the inner court. In *mYoma* 3:3 it is stated that "a person does not enter the courtyard for the service, even if he is clean, unless he immerses" (אֵין אָדָם נִכְנַס לַעֲזָרָה לָעֲבוֹדָה אֲפִלּוּ טָהוֹר עַד שֶׁהוּא טוֹבֵל). While the context is one of priestly service, the saying seems to be general, referring to any visitor in the court assigned for worship, i.e., the inner court, of which the "Israelites' court" constituted a part. This is how the saying is understood in the Palestinian *Talmud*, which concludes that immersion is needed for any visitor to the inner court, whether taking part in worship or not (*yYoma* 3:3; cf. Marmorstein 1914). Even if this understanding was not universal, it must have been a fairly common opinion that an extra immersion was necessary for entrance into the inner court, even for people who had recently undergone the necessary rituals for removing some impurity. A trace of different opinions on this matter is found in *tNeg* 8:9, where it is discussed whether a purifying leper bringing his sacrifice needs an extra immersion in addition to that of the preceding day, belonging to the purification ritual. The

that foot-washing was assumed too. The evidence never associated such foot-washing for laity with purity though, but it should rather be understood as an act of cleanliness and preparation.

It must be remembered that foot-washing was a dire necessity in the ancient world, regardless of religion or ethnicity.[252] The saying "one who has bathed has no need to wash anything except the feet" must be regarded as quite natural, in any Mediterranean context in Antiquity. If taken concretely, however, in the context of a Passover feast in Jerusalem, it is reasonable to see a reference to immersion. The simplest interpretation of the saying might be that of Kieffer: one who has immersed for purity in view of the feast, has no need to wash off material dirt before the meal, except for the feet, which always get dirty.[253]

The most plausible context for a saying about foot-washing and immersion would be that of an approaching temple visit. Although foot-washing for laity was not formally regarded as a purification rite, it would have been a sign of preparation and respect. Immersion, on the other hand, was requested of every visitor to the court of Israelites, regardless of whether he had immersed the day before and was formally pure. This seems to have been the general rule, although there were possibly deviant opinions. The saying suggests an attitude which did not consider special immersion necessary, but regarded either John's baptism or the general paschal immersion sufficient. Jesus probably rejected the requirement for special immersion in order to enter the inner court. This is consonant with *P.Oxy.* 840, although there is a discrepancy with regard to the attitude to foot-washing, as will be seen below.

We have seen that while interpretation of the Johannine foot-washing tradition is notoriously difficult, the idea of foot-washing representing an historical purification ritual is hardly convincing. There is simply no concrete evidence for Jesus advocating any extra purification ritual or exhibiting any special interest in purification. There would be implicit evidence, however, that Jesus and his disciples did immerse when attending important festivals, like all other pilgrims. This is not equal to regular immersions after contact with different types of impurity bearers. There are rather signs of Jesus being more lax than the majority about purifications even at temple visits. The motivation attached to some such signs is the idea about inner purification, to which we must return.

---

majority opinion, however, is that an extra immersion is compulsory. The same understanding is presupposed by Josephus (e.g. *J.W.* 5:227; *Ag.Ap.* 2:104). This becomes clear from Josephus' use of ἁγνίζειν, ἁγνεύεσθαι and ἁγνεία in reference to purification by immersion. For an extensive discussion of evidence from Josephus, as well as rabbinic texts supporting the idea of immersion being necessary for any visit to the inner court, cf. Büchler 1908, 332–335.

[252] Cf. J. C. Thomas 1991, 31–35, 44–46.

[253] Kieffer 1998, 217–223. If the foot-washing is seen as no more than a removal of physical dirt, it might be argued, however, that the bath with which it is contrasted ought to be an ordinary bath, since immersion in a *miqveh* was not a matter of hygiene.

P.Oxy. 840 and inner purification

To conclude this chapter, an extra-canonical tradition will be examined, which presents Jesus as both neglecting requirements for bodily purification rituals and discussing purity and purification in terms of inside and outside. *Papyrus Oxyrhynchus 840* was found in 1905 and consists of a single vellum leaf with writing on both sides and one corner missing. The handwriting points to a fourth-century date.[254] The main part of the fragment (39 of 45 lines) contains a narrative about Jesus and his disciples visiting the temple and walking in the inner court,[255] without having undergone the required immersion. This results in a discussion with a chief priest.

καὶ παραλαβὼν αὐτοὺς
εἰσήγαγεν εἰς αὐτὸ τὸ ἁγνευτήριον καὶ
περιεπάτει ἐν τῷ ἱερῷ. καὶ προσε[λ]-
θὼν Φαρισαῖός τις ἀρχιερεὺς Λευ[εὶς?]
τὸ ὄνομα συνέτυχεν αὐτοῖς καὶ ε[ἶπεν]
τῷ σω(τῆ)ρι, τίς ἐπέτρεψέν σοι πατ[εῖν
τοῦτο τὸ ἁγνευτήριον καὶ ἰδεῖν [ταῦ-
τα τὰ ἅγια σκεύη μήτε λουσα[μ]έν[ῳ] μ[ή-
τε μὴν τῶν μαθητῶν σου τοὺς π[όδας βα-
πτισθέντων; ἀλλὰ μεμολυ[μμένος
ἐπάτησας τοῦτο τὸ ἱερὸν τ[όπον ὄν-
τα καθαρόν, ὃν οὐδεὶς ἄ[λλος εἰ μὴ
λουσάμενος καὶ ἀλλά[ξας τὰ ἐνδύματα πατεῖ, οὐδὲ ὁ[ρᾶν τολμᾷ ταῦτα
τὰ ἅγια σκεύη. καὶ σ[τὰς εὐθέως ὁ σω(τὴ)ρ
σ[ὺν τ]οῖς μαθηταῖ[ς ἀπεκρίθη αὐτῷ,
σὺ οὖν ἐνταῦθα ὢν ἐν τῷ ἱερῷ καθα-
ρεύεις; λέγει αὐτῷ ἐκεῖνος, καθαρεύω· ἐλουσάμην γὰρ ἐν τῇ λίμνῃ τοῦ Δ(αυεὶ)δ καὶ δι᾽ ἑτέρας κλίμακος κατελθὼν δι᾽ ἑτέρας
ἀ[ν]ῆλθον, καὶ λευκὰ ἐνδύματα ἐνε-
δυσάμην καὶ καθαρά, καὶ τότε ἦλθον
καὶ προσέβλεψα τούτοις τοῖς ἁγίοις
σκεύεσιν. ὁ σω(τὴ)ρ πρὸς αὐτὸν ἀπο-
[κρι]θεὶς εἶπεν, οὐαί, τυφλοὶ μὴ ὁρῶν-
τ[ε]ς· σὺ ἐλούσω τούτοις τοῖς χεομένοις
ὕ[δ]ασιν ἐν οἷς κύνες καὶ χοῖροι βέβλην-
[ται] νυκτὸς καὶ ἡμέρας, καὶ νιψάμε-
[ν]ος τὸ ἐκτὸς δέρμα ἐσμήξω, ὅπερ
[κα]ὶ αἱ πόρναι καὶ α[ἱ] αὐλητρίδες μυρί-

[254] Grenfell and Hunt 1908a, 1.

[255] The term ἁγνευτήριον (lines 8 and 13) is a bit odd. It is not used anywhere else in connection with the temple, and Grenfell and Hunt suggest from the context that it refers to the part of the inner court which was allowed for male Israelites (1908, 8). Büchler's suggestion about one of the chambers of washing (1908, 339f.) is more speculative, but it cannot be too lightly dismissed in view of Josephus' use of terms from the same stem (ἁγνός, ἁγνίζειν) for ritual immersion (Büchler 1908, 332–335).

[ζ]ου[σιν κ]αὶ λούουσιν καὶ σμήχουσι
[καὶ κ]αλλωπίζουσι πρὸς ἐπιθυμί-
[αν τ]ῶν ἀν(θρώπ)ων· ἔνδοθεν δὲ ἐκεῖ-
[ναι πεπλ]ήρω<ν>ται σκορπίων καὶ
[πάσης κα]κίας. ἐγὼ δὲ καὶ οἱ
[μαθηταί μου] οὓς λέγεις μὴ βεβα-
[πτίσθαι βεβά]μμεθα ἐν ὕδασι ζω-
[ῆς αἰωνίου τοῖ]ς ἐλθοῦσιν ἀπὸ . . [.]
[. . . . . ἀλ]λὰ οὐαὶ [τ]οῖς [. . .].[256]

The narrative has been variously assessed. The original editors claimed that it was full of inaccuracies concerning the temple and its regulations.

> So great indeed are the divergences between this account and the extant and no doubt well informed authorities with regard to the topography and ritual of the Temple that it is hardly possible to avoid the conclusion that much of the local colour is due to the imagination of the author, who was aiming chiefly at dramatic effect, and was not really well acquainted with the Temple. But if the inaccuracy of the fragment in this important respect is admitted, the historical character of the whole episode breaks down, and it is probably to be regarded as an apocryphal elaboration of Matt. xv. 1–20 and Mark vii. 1–23. In these circumstances the gospel to which the fragment belongs can hardly have been composed before the middle of the second century.[257]

A similar judgment is repeated by Booth:

> In view of the difficulties in this Fragment, and the surprising ferocity of Jesus' polemic against the cult, we are inclined, on balance, to regard the passage as the product of a Hellenistic, strongly anti-Jewish church, and we prefer not to rely on it for our present purpose.[258]

Booth definitely overstates the case, however, since there is no polemic against the cult as such, nor are there any explicit anti-Jewish statements. What we find is a characterization of Jesus as one who does not conform to certain Pharisaic

---

[256] "And he took them and brought them into the very place of purification, and was walking in the temple. And a certain Pharisee, a chief priest, whose name was Levi (?), met them and said to the Saviour: 'Who allowed you to walk in this place of purification and to see these holy vessels, when you have not washed nor yet have your disciples bathed their feet? But defiled you have walked in this temple, which is a pure place, in which no-one else walks, without having washed and changed clothes, neither dares to look at these holy vessels.' And the Saviour at once stood still with his disciples and answered him: 'Are you then, being here in the temple, clean?' He said to him: 'I am clean, for I washed in the pool of David, and having descended by one staircase I ascended by another, and I put on white and clean garments, and then I came and looked at these holy vessels.' The Saviour answered and said to him: 'Woe you blind, who do not see. You have washed in these running waters in which dogs and swine have thrown themselves night and day, and you have washed and wiped the outer skin, which also the prostitutes and the flute-girls anoint and wash and wipe and beautify for the lust of men; but within these are full of scorpions and all wickedness. But I and my disciples, who you say have not bathed, have been dipped in the waters of eternal life which come from … But woe to the…'" Translation adapted from Grenfell and Hunt 1908a, 7f.

[257] Grenfell and Hunt 1908a, 3–4.

[258] Booth 1986, 213.

requirements of bodily purification, with his actions motivated by a discussion of outer and inner purity.

Very early on the skepticism of Grenfell and Hunt was gainsaid by other scholars. Many of the details have been shown to reflect conditions of the Second Temple accurately. We know of no high priest with the name of Levi, but the reading is uncertain,[259] and the expression τις ἀρχιερεὺς probably designates one of the chief priests, rather than *the* High Priest.[260] The possibility for laity to view the "holy vessels" is disputed, but several suggestions have been offered, based on rabbinic material. The expression could refer to temple treasures which were kept in store rooms adjoining the wall of the inner court,[261] or to vessels of the shrine which were taken out and immersed the day after great festivals.[262] The simplest solution, however, would be to interpret the ἅγια σκεύη as the tools and vessels used in the court of priests for daily services. These were seen by any visitor to the court of Israelites. We have already found that an extra immersion was required before entering the inner court.[263] To walk in the court of Israelites and to see the holy vessels are construed as parallels; they are two sides of the same unacceptable action, namely to enter into the inner court without having immersed.

The requirement of foot-washing has also been discussed above.[264] To separate the priest's criticism of the disciples from his criticism of Jesus, as Büchler does, is unnatural.[265] We must take these two elements as parallels, too, constituting a criticism of Jesus *and* his disciples for not conforming to purity requirements. It is disputed whether a change of clothes was included in the requirements not only for priests, but also for laity. This is the view of

[259] Jeremias 1947, 99f. Only three letters are visible. The first could be Λ or A. The second is E or O. The third is possibly Y, I or K. Levi is the most probable reading, however, and it may well be merely a narrative construction.

[260] Jeremias 1947, 100; 1958, IIB 33–40. This makes the statement that the priest was a Pharisee possible, too. Although this seems part of the anti-Pharisaic tendency of the text (cf. the woes of lines 31 and 45, reminiscent of the woes of Q (Mt 23 and Lk 11), there were priests belonging to the Pharisaic party.

[261] Jeremias 1947, 100f.

[262] Büchler 1908, 337ff; Marmorstein 1914f, 337. Cf. D. Schwartz 1986, who speculates about an exhibition of temple utensils before the crowds of pilgrims as a result of Pharisaic pressure for popularization of the temple cult.

[263] Cf. above, 254, n.251.

[264] Cf. above, 252–255.

[265] Büchler 1908, 340f. Büchler suggests that Jesus was in the inner court, while the disciples remained outside. Hence they should only have needed to wash their feet, while Jesus should have immersed. But this is an unlikely interpretation, since the possible evidence for foot-washing (cf. above, 253f) suggests that it was required for visiting the temple area generally.

Note that the whole issue of foot-washing in *P. Oxy.* 840 is built on a reconstruction which is plausible yet uncertain. The phrase τοὺς π[όδας βα]πτισθέντων is partly reconstructed. Possible, although less likely alternatives are πήχυντα or πέπλους. The case is complicated by the fact that neither the final ς in τοὺς, nor the π in πόδας are fully visible.

Büchler,[266] while most deny it. Jeremias suggests that the καί in λουσάμενος καὶ ἀλλά[ξας τὰ ἐνδύ]ματα should be understood in a Semitic sense as "respectively," thus making immersion refer to laity and change of clothes to the priests.[267] Here, too, the simplest interpretation is to take the two as parallel, acknowledging that immersion was usually associated with a change of clothes, since the old clothes were washed as part of the purification rite.[268]

The pool of David has never been located. This is hardly a valid objection against the narrative, however. At least two suggestions have been made: part of the Bethesda baths or a *miqveh* within the court of priests. In both cases Jesus' description of the water could apply (τούτοις τοῖς χεομένοις ὕ[δ]ασιν), since Bethesda could be interpreted as "place of running waters" and the water for the temple came from streams via an aqueduct.[269] If the water came from without, Jesus' ironic comments about dogs and swine could be explained, since the water passed many villages on its way to Jerusalem. It is probably better, however, to regard these words as an implicit *simile*, just as the subsequent phrase. Harlots do not become pure by washing and anointing their outer skin, and dogs and swine are not purified by jumping into water.[270] ἐν οἷς does not necessarily refer to the very pool, but to the type of water in principle,[271] which does not cleanse from inner impurity. The implicit charge is thus that the priest's immersion does not purify from wickedness or injustice (κακία).[272]

An important detail is the reference to two stairs (δι' ἑτέρας κλίμακος κατελθὼν δι' ἑτέρας ἀ[ν]ῆλθον). This was first deemed to be merely the imagination of the author,[273] but numerous findings in Jerusalem and elsewhere have revealed *miqvaot* both with divided staircases and double entrances, which ensured that the purified person was not recontaminated on his/her way up.[274] It seems as if Büchler's 1908 statement is still apt: "In no detail is the writer of the fragment ignorant of the law or guilty of gross error."[275] The tradition in *P.Oxy.*

[266] Büchler 1908, 336f.

[267] Jeremias 1963, 55f. Jeremias' earlier suggestion (1947, 102f.) that the change of clothes would refer to the required removal of stick, sandals and girdle, before ascending the Temple Mount, is unnecessarily speculative.

[268] Cf. Gen 35:2; Ex 19:10; Lev 14:9; 15:6, 8, 11, 13, 21, 22, 27.

[269] Büchler 1908, 344; Jeremias 1947, 103f; 1963, 56; Sanders 1992, 118.

[270] βέβληνʹ[ται] must not be taken in the passive sense but in the middle; hence I translate: "have thrown themselves," (i.e. "jumped") rather than Grenfell and Hunt's "have been cast."

[271] Hence the objections of Grenfell and Hunt that it is incredible that dogs and swine were cast into the pool of David are based on an unnecessarily literal reading.

[272] This removes the need to discuss whether swine were reared in Jewish territory. Cf. Büchler 1908, 344, who argues for the possibility from the existence of a prohibition in *bSota* 49b.

[273] Grenfell and Hunt 1908a, 3.

[274] Sanders 1990, 217f; 1992, 225; Reich 1980 [not viewed]; 1981, 52; 1984; Netzer 1982, 116f. Recontamination was probably thought to occur through accidental contact with impure people on their way down into the *miqveh*. For a different explanation cf. Büchler 1908, 343.

[275] Büchler 1908, 345. Cf. *mSheq* 8:2.

840 reveals an acquintance with the Second Temple and its purification practices. While the conclusion that "we have here more original materials than are to be found in the Synoptics"[276] is somewhat exaggerated, the narrative is nevertheless useful as evidence for the attitude of Jesus. Although there are a few signs of a fairly late date (mainly the use of σωτήρ as a title for Jesus in lines 12 and 30),[277] there are no substantial arguments against dating this tradition to the end of the first century CE, which would render it as ancient as several of the canonical NT writings.

Thus we must treat this tradition as another piece of evidence retaining the memory of Jesus as displaying a controversial attitude to purity, which was motivated by giving more weight to inner purity than to outer purification. We have here another example of inner impurity defined as moral and social evil (ἔνδοθεν δὲ ἐκεῖ[ναι πεπλ]ήρω<ν>ται σκορπίων καὶ [πάσης κα]κίας), for which bodily purification of the outer skin (νιψάμε[ν]ος τὸ εκτὸς δέρμα) is of no effect.

There is a possible discrepancy between the Johannine foot-washing narrative and the tradition in *P.Oxy.* 840, if the former is interpreted as expressing an opinion that foot-washing is sufficient for entering the temple, while the latter suggests that Jesus' disciples neglected that, too. We should not attempt a harmonization, however, and I certainly do not suggest that *P.Oxy.* 840 be treated as an historical report. What I do claim is that this tradition hands down a memory of Jesus as neglecting certain required purification rituals, and that this negligence was perceived as a conscious position. The motivation associated with Jesus for such an attitude was, according to *P.Oxy.* 840, a criticism of outer purification as being incapable of removing inner impurity, interpreted as wickedness, i.e. moral evil and social injustice. To achieve this, some other type of "water" was needed.[278] This inner purification was deemed of higher importance than immersions and foot-washings as preparations for a temple visit. Such an attitude and motivation are in accord with the picture of Jesus that we have found in almost every other strand of the Jesus tradition.

What is different in this text as compared with others discussed in this chapter is the location in the temple. In no other tradition do we find this location for a discussion between Jesus and his opponents about purity and moral, inside and outside. There is a similarity with most of the other traditions, however, in that sayings about inner and outer purity are placed in contexts in which there are conflicting ideas about proper purification practices.

---

[276] Büchler 1908, 346.

[277] To this the "Johannine" expression ὕδασι ζω[ῆς αἰωνίου] could be added. Note however that most of the phrase is reconstructed. Other reconstructions are possible, e.g. ὕδασι ζῶ[σι τοῦ πν]ς (i.e. contraction for πνεύματος).

[278] The reconstruction "waters of eternal life" suggests a spiritual source of purification for which water serves as a metaphor. We may guess that it comes from God (θεοῦ), which in a contracted form would fit into the remainder of the missing line.

Summary: A case for Jesus as part of a moral trajectory in Judaism

We have found traces of a moral trajectory throughout the history of purity in Jewish texts from both the First and the Second Temple periods. The use of purity language in contexts of moral evil and social injustice cannot simply be described as metaphorical or secondary in relation to a ritual or primary use. Although different parts of the purity system were generally not blended or confused, there are usually ritual and bodily aspects to ethical and social action in Hebrew thinking.

The moral trajectory, so prominent with some of the biblical prophets, finds somewhat diverse expressions in the Qumran community, the mission of John the Baptizer and the activities of Jesus. The discussions about the relative weight of inner purity *versus* outer purity, evidenced in different strands of the Jesus tradition, fit well into a Second Temple context. Although later rabbinic theology "compartmentalized" the two, such a dichotomy between inside and outside should not be ascribed to first-century Pharisees. The evidence shows, however, that Jesus emphasized inner purity over outer purifications to the degree that he was considered as downplaying the latter.

Throughout the texts discussed in this chapter, I have found evidence that Jesus displayed what was perceived as a lax attitude to bodily purification. This does not mean that he denied concepts of bodily impurity altogether, or refused to take part in basic and general purification practices, such as immersion in preparation of great festivals. But it seems as if he did not practise immersion regularly after having contracted impurity from contact with different impurity bearers or before every visit to the temple.

The practice of baptism cannot be equated with repeated immersions for the sake of purity, and it is likely that Jesus left this practice behind during his independent ministry. Portrayals of Jesus as concerned with alternative rites of outer purification are not plausible.

The motivation ascribed to Jesus in the different sources for his seemingly lax attitude, all centre on the same idea, that inner purity is more important than outer purity. This is in line with the old prophetic heritage, but amounts to a downplaying of outer purification rituals, since these are not perceived as having any effect on moral evil and social injustice. In this Jesus seems to have gone further than many of his Jewish contemporaries, not only in his verbal criticism, but in his actual disregard for practices which others would regard as crucial. In their eyes he carried relativization to the point of neglect.

While such an attitude and action could probably have been tolerated on the part of common people in the periphery, Jesus appeared as a religious teacher and related to other religious leaders. In this context he apparently approached the limit of what was tolerable. We must ask what room there was in contemporary Judaism for such a position. In order to explain Jesus' attitude to purity further, it is necessary to look more closely at the diversity within Second Temple Judaism, and not primarily at the influential "sects" or parties, where we find much of the expansionist current, but at rural and peripheral expressions of Judaism as well. The fact of Jesus' background in Galilee is well attested, but almost no details are known. In the following chapter I will discuss what role this background might have played for Jesus' position on purity.

Chapter VI
Purity and diversity

I have suggested that Jesus' attitude to impurity can be explained by a moral trajectory, which can be traced in both priestly and prophetic traditions from the time of the First Temple and onwards. This explanation is necessary, but neither complete nor sufficient. In the present chapter I will follow another train of thought, looking at diversity in Second Temple Judaism, and what such diversity might have meant for Jesus' views on purity.

Some differences between the various sects or parties have been discussed through the previous chapters. Such differences are important for reconstructing the development of purity laws, but they do not seem to be crucial for understanding Jesus' particular stance. In this chapter, more weight is given to regional and social aspects. There are northern literary traditions of some interest, but do we have evidence for deviating northern halakhic traditions as well? What role did Jesus' Galilean background play? And how do we explain his attitude in view of the dominating great tradition?

VI.1 Common Judaisms

Generalizing tendencies and the necessity to differentiate

It has long been recognized that Second Temple Judaism was not monolithic, but the degree of diversity has been variously evaluated. Should we talk about Judaism or Judaisms?[1] It could be argued that descriptions and evidence of the many divergent views on numerous matters reflect the perspectives of insiders only, while outsiders would have readily identified Judaism as a coherent and unified system.[2]

In one sense it is appropriate to use an umbrella term like "Common Judaism" for all or most varieties of Judaism during the Second Temple period. The foremost advocate for such an idea is probably Ed Sanders. This Judaism was defined as "covenantal nomism" in *Paul and Palestinian Judaism*,[3] and Sanders has subsequently developed the idea in *Judaism: Practice and Belief*.[4] Such a Common Judaism is usually defined by certain obvious identity markers, such

---

[1] Cohen 1990, 55–73; cf. the article "Judaism" in Neusner and Green 1999, 346–350, esp. 346.
[2] Cf. Cohen 1994, 3–12.
[3] Sanders 1977, 419–428.
[4] Sanders 1992.

as the centrality of the temple and the Torah, monotheism and a basic covenant theology, including the practice of circumcision, the Sabbath and purity rules. While interpretations varied, at times extensively, these characteristics made Jews different from others and accounted for a certain sense of separation.[5]

The emphasis on a single, unified Judaism may be understood from a number of motives, some of them theological, whether Jewish or Christian.[6] In the case of Sanders this is probably part of his battle against anti-Jewish tendencies in traditional exegesis where disagreement between different factions is one standard component. There is a risk, however, of generalizing to the point of meaninglessness; if Judaism was thus "common" and no more, we have learned very little, and explained very little. This is an important part of Jacob Neusner's at times vehement criticism of Sanders. Although his criticism is excessive, Neusner highlights important problems, when diversity is not given its due place. We must be careful not to ascribe to Second Temple Judaism in general everything which is presupposed in a given contemporary text. And prescriptions and presuppositions from texts of different origins do not easily combine to make up a common theology.[7]

It is thus necessary to differentiate. We could speak about "Judaisms," not in the sense of separate religions, but to indicate that diversity must be taken into proper account.[8] Without giving due regard to differences within Judaism, it is impossible to provide satisfactory explanations for the many practices and conflicts encountered when studying the end of the Second Temple period.

Jesus and the major parties

What does diversity mean for explaining Jesus' attitude to purity rules? Assertions that there was room for all of Jesus' actions and sayings within contemporary Jewish discussion must be verified.[9] General references to diversity, coupled with the idea that there was always some group or fraction which would agree with Jesus' position in a given case, are not sufficient.

As we have already seen in previous chapters, purity rules were interpreted differently by different groups. Diverging opinions concern matters such as the susceptibility of oil, the contaminating power of liquids, the purity of the *tebul*

---

[5] Cohen 1994, 9–12; Cf. Sanders' summaries in 1992, 47f, 241, 278.

[6] Both Jews and Christians may reflect the dream of a unified origin, from which an (unfortunate?) diversity or lack of conformity has evolved. It is necessary to posit a unified Judaism if something like a single Christianity should be seen as evolving from it. Cf. Neusner's criticism of such a view, 1993b, xxii. There is no room for pursuing this discussion within the scope of this study, however.

[7] Neusner 1993b, xxi–xlviii.

[8] For a thorough review of the "Judaisms hypothesis" and a criticism of Neusner's interpretation, see Pasto 1999, 336–464.

[9] Klausner 1925, 275f; 363–368; Flusser 1987, 21–25; Vermes 1993, especially 11–45; 1996, 108–122.

yom, the extent of and restrictions within relative spheres of holiness around the temple, the degree of isolation of serious impurity bearers, etc.[10] By examining such matters in detail, we can at times reconstruct dividing lines, but even when these are shown to be precarious, it is often possible at least to define underlying presuppositions shared by many.

This has been done above in some cases, for example concerning the widespread use of stone vessels, the exclusion of lepers, or the balancing of the requirement for avoiding corpse impurity with that of burying the dead.[11] In such cases it is at times possible to provide a relief to the Jesus tradition, which often confirms that its content actually fits into the historical context, since it touches matters that were contemporary issues. This is the case especially with some of the logia, such as those about inner and outer purity, or certain parables. Here we find traces of commonly shared presuppositions, against which Jesus could be seen as provocative, but still within the limits of contemporary discussion.

However, in some traditions, especially in the narrative non-conflict traditions focused upon in this study, we have found traces of a behaviour and an attitude which clash with known practices and attitudes of the major groups: Sadducees, Essenes and Pharisees. There are instances in which we must conclude that Jesus shared the presuppositions of neither group.

An analysis of detailed differences between purity practices of different groups does not always help in tracing and explaining the stance of Jesus. While the Essenes (at least those in Qumran) were opposed to the present order in the Jerusalem temple, they shared a priestly perspective with the Sadducees. The agreement in part between Qumran and Sadducean *halakhah* has been addressed above, and can be deduced from a comparison of Qumran and Tannaitic material. This can be contrasted with Pharisaic rulings. On the other hand, Pharisees and Essenes could both be seen as representing an expansionist tendency, which proceeded from certain common assumptions, but with different aims and interpretations. While Jesus could possibly be seen as taking a Sadducean point of view in some cases,[12] he is usually deemed to have been closer to the Pharisees than to other contemporary groups. At times he has been understood as representing Shammaite views, but more often those of Hillel.[13] When it comes to issues of purity, however, such classifications are not very meaningful. There is no obvious correspondence between Jesus' stance on purity and that of any one particular group or faction. At times there is a basic difference between Jesus' standpoint and those of the major parties. This does

[10] Cf. above, ch. III–IV. Stemberger 1995, 73–88. Several of these points are listed in 4QMMT.
[11] Cf. above, 84f, 109–112, 189–196.
[12] I.e. rejecting the "traditions of the fathers," in favour of the scriptural command only, as in Mk 7:8, and possibly in Mk 10:2–9. Cf. the warning against the Pharisees in Mk 8:15. But these examples could be understood as expressions of Christian polemics.
[13] Fornberg 1989, 94ff.

not necessarily mean that Jesus' stance was less Jewish, however, especially if the views of the major groups did not always represent the views of the majority of the people.

The influence of the major groups

The degree of influence which the major groups exercised on the population at large has been variously judged. The parties seem to have been fairly small, consisting of a few thousand Essenes and Pharisees.[14] For the Sadducees we have no exact number, except that they were few,[15] which seems credible, since they consisted chiefly of aristocrats.

We must ask, however, what the numbers represent, and how they relate to the general influence of the different groups within society. Are we talking about "practising members," adherents or sympathizers? Do the numbers represent the number of leaders, scribes and scholars? The numbers as such tell us very little about actual influence.

The identification and description of the different groups are well-known and notoriously recurring problems among scholars today. One main problem is the bias of Josephus, who provides much of the source material. Josephus' ambiguous descriptions of the Pharisees have been discussed at length,[16] and attemps to explain the discrepancies as due to poorly harmonized sources are not convincing.[17] Nor is the suggestion of a change of attitude between *War* and *Antiquities* sufficient.[18] While it would seem that Josephus claims to be a Pharisee himself, Steve Mason's explanation of the crucial passage is rather convincing.[19] Josephus' statement that at the age of 19 he began to govern his life according to the Pharisees (ἠρξάμην [τε] πολιτεύεσθαι τῇ Φαρισαίων αἱρέσει κατακολουθῶν)[20] should be taken simply as a pragmatic decision to adapt to Pharisaic custom as part of his public career, but has nothing to do with

---

[14] We have estimates from Josephus (more than 4000 Essenes, *Ant.* 18:20; more than 6000 Pharisees, *Ant.* 17:42), and from Philo (more than 4000 Essenes, *Good Person* 75). There is no good reason for disbelieving these numbers as rough approximations, since both estimates of the Essenes concur, and it would be difficult to see why or how the bias of the respective authors should have influenced their calculations.

[15] *Ant.* 18:17.

[16] See the survey of previous research by Mason 1991, 18–39. Cf. Stemberger 1995, 5–20; Meier 2001, 301–305.

[17] D. Schwartz 1983.

[18] E.g. Cohen 1979, 144–151, 237f. Cf. Neusner 1987, whose contrast between *Jewish War* and *Antiquities* is considered unconvincing by Stemberger 1995, 13 n.7. Neusner's statement that in *Antiquities* "[t]he mass slaughter of *War* in which the Pharisees killed anyone they wanted, is shaded into a mild persecution," (1987, 288) is hardly warranted by a comparison between *J.W.* 1:113f and *Ant.* 13:410ff. Cf. Feldman's comment (1987, 50) that the Pharisees of *Antiquities* are no less "depicted as evil geniuses who are ruthless in cutting down their opponents."

[19] Mason 1991, 342–356.

[20] *Life* 12.

joining a party.[21] Josephus' sympathies seem to be with the Essenes, of whom he writes only positive things and at length, while Pharisees are often, and Sadducees always, criticized.[22]

Such a reading of Josephus makes reconstruction a bit easier. Although his descriptions of the three groups are intended to make them look like Greek philosophical schools, we can gain some reliable information from them. The Essenes are described as living all through the country, as being bound by strict rules, especially on purity, and as having severe entrance requirements and rules for expulsion.[23] They are thus described as a somewhat closed community, which fits into the description of their relationship to the temple cult:

> εἰς δὲ τὸ ἱερὸν ἀναθήματα στέλλοντες θυσίας ἐπιτελοῦσιν διαφορότητι ἁγνειῶν, ἃς νομίζοιεν, καὶ δι' αὐτὸ εἰργόμενοι τοῦ κοινοῦ τεμενίσματος ἐφ' αὑτῶν τὰς θυσίας ἐπιτελοῦσιν.[24]
>
> They send votive offerings to the temple, but perform their sacrifices employing a different ritual of purification. For this reason they are barred from those precincts of the temple that are frequented by all the people and perform their rites by themselves.

The Qumran sectarians could be fitted into this picture if they are regarded as an extreme variety of Essenes.[25] There is a variant reading in the passage quoted above, where ἐπιτελοῦσιν is negated,[26] to the effect that the Essenes are said *not* to sacrifice in the temple. This is congruent with Philo's remark about the Essenes not sacrificing animals but sanctifying their minds (οὐ ζῷα καταθύοντες, ἀλλ' ἱεροπρεπεῖς τὰς ἑαυτῶν διανοίας κατασκευάζειν ἀξιοῦντες).[27] But even without this variant, Josephus depicts the Essenes as distancing themselves from the general cultic practices of ordinary people. The total rejection of the temple service as evidenced in certain sectarian writings from Qumran is only a sharpened version of this attitude. Such a stance could evoke respect and hold some attraction, but should not be expected to have had much influence on the general public.

The priests, on the other hand, ought to have had much more influence on the people at large, not because of their (mostly) Sadducean affiliation, but since they bore the main responsibility for the public cult. Josephus describes the Sadducees as rude (ἀγριώτερον) to their own and ungentle (ἀπηνεῖς) to others.[28] This could possibly reflect such aristocratic manners as usually widen the gap between common people and their leaders.[29]

---

[21] Stemberger 1995, 5–7. Meier (2001, 302f) argues that Josephus is simply lying in *Life* 12.
[22] Cf. Baumbach 1989; Mason 1991, 372–375.
[23] *J.W.* 2:119–161.
[24] *Ant.* 18:19.
[25] Josephus mentions different types of Essenes, celibate and non-celibate: *J.W.* 2:160–161.
[26] οὐκ ἐπιτελοῦσι (Epitome); non celebrant (Latin version).
[27] *Good Person* 75.
[28] *J.W.* 2:166.
[29] Cf. Sanders 1992, 318 for arguments about Sadducees consisting mostly of aristocratic priests.

Josephus asserts that the Sadducees were forced to make concessions to the Pharisees, because the latter were very influential with the common people.[30] This has been denied by several scholars, and judged as reflecting post-temple times or Josephus' bias towards the Pharisees.[31] As we have already seen, Josephus' attitude to the Pharisees was ambiguous, and he is critical of the influence of the Pharisees, even in his late works. There is no reason for him to describe them as influential if this was not the actual case. While his description in *Antiquities* could be suspected of reflecting post-temple conditions, it should be noted that this work covers the period *before* the war.[32] Josephus himself regards his description of the parties as dealing with ancient philosophies,[33] and the relevant wording seems to refer to cultic practices, of which at least some must have belonged to the time before 70 CE.[34] This is congruent with several indications in rabbinic literature about the influence of Pharisaic practice before the fall of the temple.[35]

The important question, however, is how to *interpret* the influence of the Pharisees. As pointed out by Qimron and Strugnell, in their discussion about 4QMMT, it was not dogma, but *halakhah* which produced serious schisms in Second Temple Judaism.[36] It was probably in the area of *halakhah* that the Pharisees were most influential with the people, as compared with Sadducees or Essenes. This is a reasonable conclusion from the passages in Josephus, as well

---

[30] καὶ δι' αὐτὰ τοῖς τε δήμοις πιθανώτατοι τυγχάνουσιν καὶ ὁπόσα θεῖα εὐχῶν τε ἔχεται καὶ ἱερῶν ποιήσεως ἐξηγήσει τῇ ἐκείνων τυγχάνουσιν πρασσόμεθα. ("Because of these views they are, as a matter of fact, extremely influential among the townsfolk; and all prayers and sacred rites of divine worship are performed according to their exposition.") ... ἀκουσίως μὲν καὶ κατ' ἀνάγκας, προσχωροῦσι δ'οὖν οἷς ὁ Φαρισαῖος λέγει διὰ τὸ μὴ ἄλλως ἀνεκτοὺς γενέσθαι τοῖς πλήθεσιν. ("though they [the Sadducees] submit unwillingly and perforce, yet submit they do to the formulas of the Pharisees, since otherwise the masses would not tolerate them.") *Ant.* 18:15, 17. Cf. the numerous instances where Josephus mentions the power and influence of the Pharisees, e.g. *J.W.* 1:110–112; *Ant.* 13:288; 298.

[31] Cf. Neusner 1987; Sanders 1992, 488ff.

[32] *Ant.* 20:259f.

[33] *Ant.* 18:11.

[34] *Ant.* 18:15. ὁπόσα θεῖα εὐχῶν τε ἔχεται καὶ ἱερῶν ποιήσεως ἐξηγήσει τῇ ἐκείνων τυγχάνουσιν πρασσόμενα.

[35] Cf. Comments in *bNid* 33b about menstruation rules and *bYoma* 19b about incense. Although the former does not necessarily apply to pre-70 times, the latter certainly does. This is the case with the discussions about the status of the High Priest on the Day of Atonement (*tebul yom* or not) and the use of young boys in the red cow rite as well, where rabbinic sources claim that Pharisaic practice was followed (*mPar* 3:2–4, 7). In the case of the red cow rite, the use of young boys is presupposed in Christian polemics (*Barn.* 8:1) and explicitly opposed in Qumran texts (4Q277 1 2:7; cf. 4Q271 2 1:13; cf. J. Baumgarten 1995b), which attests to the preponderance of Pharisaic practice at the end of the Second Temple period. Likewise, the emphatic statement in 4QMMT that all who engage in the red cow rite must be pure at sunset (i.e. against the Pharisaic concept of *tebul yom*) is best interpreted as evidence for the dominance of Pharisaic *halakhah* (4QMMT B13–16; cf. Schiffman 1994, 287–290).

[36] Qimron and Strugnell 1994, 175f. Cf. Deines 1997, 549f. and n.69; Meier 2001, 322, 339.

as from the rabbinic texts just mentioned. In the gospels, too, the influence of the Pharisees comes to the fore, less in matters of dogma than in matters of *halakhah*.[37] This is quite natural, since practice is usually more important to common people than abstract theology.

There are good reasons why Pharisaic practice was more attractive than other varieties. It was expansionist, yet relatively practical. It was separationist, yet relatively inclusive. As the foremost example of an expansionist tendency in exegesis and halakhic development, Pharisaic practice could be seen as a type of "pietist" intensive spirituality. Pharisees seem to have been regarded with respect, as serious practitioners of Judaism. This applied to the Essenes as well, but in contrast to them, the Pharisees realized their programme within society, and made the conduct of daily life according to a higher degree of holiness possible, if not always easy. There was thus a certain amount of separation involved, but not basically *from* other Jewish groups, but rather from impurity and from Gentiles. Such separation could strengthen a sense of identity among people identifying or sympathizing with this attitude, as long as they were not themselves excluded by it. Compared with other major parties, the Pharisees were a popular lay movement, with relatively more influence.[38]

Expansionists and common people

To say that the Pharisees were influential with the common people is not tantamount, however, to saying that most people were actually Pharisees or lived according to Pharisaic rules. As we have seen in previous chapters, there are several instances in which Pharisaic practices on sabbath and purity observance were adapted to and made more practical for ordinary people as compared with Essene or Sadducean *halakhah*.[39] In addition, certain traditions about Pharisaic practices imply that the Pharisees aimed, if not at a "democratization" of the cult, at least at a higher degree of popular participation or involvement.[40] Statements to the effect that most of the people favoured the Pharisees rather than other parties, are indeed plausible. This means that many would support the Pharisees ideologically, and were ready to follow their practice to the extent that was possible or practical, but without feeling obliged to do so in every detail, or attempting to be as consistent. Such a suggestion, however, requires further corroboration.

An ambiguous relationship involving contact, mutual dependance, separation and contempt between the religious (expansionist) elite and the common people, is evidenced by the numerous passages in rabbinic literature discussing the

---

[37] Cf. Mk 2:18, 23f; 7:1f; 10:2f; Lk 7:39; 14:3; 15:2.
[38] Cf. Deines 1997, 534–555; Meier 2001, 297f.
[39] Cf. above, 55f about sabbath *halakhah* and 74f, 84f about purity rules.
[40] Cf. the idea about the Pharisees making the temple vessels available for the people to view on festivals; D. Schwartz 1986.

am ha-arets. The identity of the "people of the land" has been given various interpretations.[41]

Traditional Christian interpretation in the past uncritically adduced rabbinic statements to posit a far-reaching antagonism between the Pharisees and the common people. The Pharisees' hatred and exclusion of the *ammei ha-arets* were painted as a contrast to Jesus' accepting attitude. The methodological failure of such a reconstruction was made evident by Adolf Büchler a century ago, but he overstated his case by claiming that the concept of *am ha-arets* belonged to the Ushan period (135–200 CE), and was applied to priestly descendants who had moved to Galilee after the two wars, and had ceased to observe Levitical purity and tithing laws.[42]

Büchler's limitations have proved untenable. Oppenheimer has shown that the concept of "people of the land" can trace its development to the beginning of the Hellenistic period, and that the Rabbis applied it to people who either did not scrupulously observe certain purity and tithing rules (*ammei ha-arets le-mitsvot*) or who were ignorant of or did not study the Torah (*ammei ha-arets le-torah*). It did not define a certain class of people, however, but could be applied to rural farmers and urban craftsmen alike.[43]

In the literature reflecting rabbinic viewpoints of the Ushan period, the expression *ammei ha-arets* seems to refer to common people in general. The relationship between the sages and the *ammei ha-arets* testifies to the initial exclusivity of the rabbinic movement as well as to its continuous development. A fair amount of antagonism during the second century is evident. It should be noted, however, that the evidence for outright hatred between rabbis and the common people is found mostly in the *Babylonian Talmud*. Whether this is to be understood as reflecting the inventiveness and hardships of Babylonian Rabbis,[44] or as expressing the true feelings of the Rabbis in the Ushan period,[45] a change of attitude can be seen from the early Amoraic period onwards. This could be explained by a change in the social position of rabbinic leaders, as well as the need for closer relations with the common people.[46] The development coincides with a general decline in observance of purity and tithing rules during the third century.

While the distinction between *ammei ha-arets le-mitsvot* and *ammei ha-arets le-torah* is somewhat artificial,[47] the latter refers to the situation evolving after the fall of the temple, when Torah study gained further significance as a substi-

[41] Cf. the survey in Oppenheimer 1977, 1–10.
[42] Büchler 1968 [1906].
[43] Oppenheimer 1977, 10–22.
[44] The view of Cohen 1992, 166. Cohen claims that the Rabbis looked at the *ammei ha-arets* with "disdain, yes, but not hatred" (1992, 173).
[45] Oppenheimer 1977, 172–188.
[46] Oppenheimer 1977, 188–195.
[47] The two terms probably refer to the same social stratum. Cf. Oppenheimer 1977, 170.

tute for the temple service, while the former refers to practices intimately connected with the temple and cult, i.e. tithes and purity rules. It should be noted that there is little or no evidence in the Tannaitic discussions about the *ammei ha-arets* and purity, of any hatred or sharp antagonism. What we find are rules about how to relate to an *am ha-arets*, without incurring impurity. It is clear from several traditions that the *ammei ha-arets* were considered reliable in certain matters of purity, while in others they were not. This did not mean that they were unobservant, but that they did not attain the same level of purity as did Pharisees, sages or *haberim*.[48]

Ordinarily in rabbinic texts, common people were not suspected of wilfully contaminating things, but rather of ignorance or possibly laxity. This position is not unanimously agreed upon.[49] The basic attitude, however, seems to have been one of coping with the problems caused by differing standards of purity. Seemingly lenient rules about social intercourse with common people could be argued for "in the interest of peace."[50] In view of the development of purity rules, such leniency should perhaps be assigned to the post-70 period.

Traditions about leniency at the three great pilgrim festivals are most likely of ancient date, however, although there is no *explicit* evidence for the *ammei ha-arets* being regarded as pure during festivals, before the *Babylonian Talmud*. Certain statements in *mHag* 3:6–8 seem to presuppose such a view, however, perhaps implying that this was a kind of "concession," since there are differing opinions about whether items which had come into contact with common people during the festival would remain pure afterwards, or needed purification.[51]

---

[48] Detailed discussions of various passages, such as *Let.Aris.* 106; *tSanh* 3:4; *mHag* 2:7; *mEd* 1:14; *mToh* 8:2; *tToh* 9:1; *mToh* 7:1–2; *tHag* 3:19, 22, are found in Oppenheimer 1977, 83–96.

[49] *mToh* 7:1–2. R. Simeon has a deviating opinion in *tToh* 8:1. Cf. Oppenheimer 1977, 90f.

[50] *mGit* 5:9.

[51] "He who opens up a jug of wine or broke into dough [to sell them] for the needs of the festival—R. Judah says, 'He finishes [selling them after the festival].' And sages say, 'He does not finish [selling them after the festival].' After the festival was over, they undertook the purification of the Temple court. ... How do they undertake the purification of the Temple court? They immerse the utensils which were in the Sanctuary..." (*mHag* 3:7–8). Cf. the interpretation of Oppenheimer 1977, 93–95. According to Oppenheimer, the discussion concerns the continued purity of wine or dough, which had come into contact with *ammei ha-arets* during the festival when their impurity was waived. The sages' position would mean that after the festival, remaining dough and wine should be regarded as contaminated, just as temple utensils, which were immersed. The latter may have been a Pharisaic requirement, since *tHag* 3:35 pictures the Sadducees as mocking the Pharisees for immersing the menorah. But the idea of purification because "the vessels were rendered impure retrospectively" (Oppenheimer 1977, 160) seems a bit awkward, and is necessitated only by the idea of temporary abolishment of impurity. Opinions apparently differed, and the simplest explanation would be that some regarded all pilgrims as pure by virtue of their special purification (i.e. 7 days in advance, from corpse-impurity; for details and evidence, cf. above, 185), while others, among them Pharisees, did not regard all pilgrims as being in a sufficient state of purity. Such diverging views would be reflected in *mHag* 3:7–8 and *tHag* 3:35.

Rather than thinking in terms of concessions, we may explain this leniency by the fact that everyone was more conscientious about purity in view of a temple visit, and all people were required to undergo a special purification rite. This would be officially accepted as sufficient, while some expansionists did not agree.

We thus find signs of an ambiguous attitude on the part of some of the expansionists toward the common people, going back to the time when the temple was still standing. Pharisees were known on the one hand for their attempt to bring cultic involvment and legal adherence closer to the common people. On the other hand they had to distance themselves to some extent, especially those belonging to *haburot*,[52] in the interest of purity and tithing rules. This resulted in barriers between them and the common people, although not necessarily based on social class, as in the case of the Sadducees. There are no clear signs of hatred or sharp antagonism between Pharisees and common people before the fall of the temple, however.

The resulting picture is coherent. The relationship between Pharisees and common people was characterized by mutual ambivalence. The Pharisees probably had the support of the majority of the common people, although there were tensions. Most people looked at Pharisaic piety as an ideal, which was aspired to but not consistently adhered to. The Pharisees offered an intensified everyday religion for the whole people, and while this was recognized, the intensive variety was not embraced in all its detail by the majority of the people.[53]

Jesus and the common people

It is tempting to identify Jesus' attitude to impurity with the viewpoint of the common people. After the Jewishness of Jesus came to the fore in scholarly research, there has been a tendency to regard conflicts between Jesus and the Pharisees as minor differences in interpretation. Jesus is thought not to have accepted (parts of) the *halakhah* of (some of) the Pharisees. He is supposed to have shared this attitude with most of the people, however, and hence this would not have been much of a problem, except for the Pharisees, who expected him to follow stricter practices, since he appeared as a religious teacher.[54] In matters of purity, Jesus would simply have followed the practice of most people, but not Pharisaic *halakhah* in particular.

Such a picture is too simplified, however. The idea of the common people not following Pharisaic ideals at all is unconvincing. We have seen through previous chapters that many people at the end of the Second Temple period were influenced by expansionist concerns. Archeological findings, such as the

---

[52] Cf. above, 46ff, 87f.

[53] Cf. Deines 1997, 546ff.

[54] E.g. Sanders 1985, 245–269.

numerous and wide-spread occurrence of stone vessels and *miqvaot*, are evidence for expansionist purity *halakhah* being influential far beyond the limits of the Pharisaic group itself.[55]

Jesus, however, did not share those expansionist concerns. We have seen in the previous chapters that his actions and attitude stood in contrast to the contemporary tendency to increase the sphere of purity. Since this tendency involved not only Essenes and Pharisees, but many of the ordinary people, it is not possible to claim that Jesus represented the viewpoint of the *ammei ha-arets* or the common people, without further qualification.[56] While it could be argued that Jesus reflected a kind of popular common sense towards halakhic rules, both in his defence of Sabbath healings and in his contacts with impure people, this does not mean that he represented the collective views of the general population who did not belong to any of the influential parties. It could be argued that he represented the viewpoint of those segments of the people who would not, or could not, take part in the wide-spread concern to increase purity in society. But in narrowing the case in this way, we are no longer speaking of the common people in general. To find out whether Jesus represented any particular segment of society, we must look at social and regional aspects as well.

VI.2 Social and regional differences

Great and little tradition

In spite of their popular appeal and character as a lay movement, the Pharisees must be viewed as representatives of great tradition. The concepts of "great" and "little tradition" were developed by cultural anthropologists, notably by Robert Redfield, in the 1950s.[57] A great tradition is usually characterized as "a *learned* and *literate* tradition, preserving and developing the dominant systems of thought and value of a civilization."[58] It is usually associated with the ruling elite, located in population centres, i.e. urban areas, and has left its imprint in written documents. Little traditions, on the other hand, are popular, rural, often village-based and illiterate.[59]

The two are related and are mutually dependent. Little traditions borrow from a common great tradition traits which are popularized and given various

---

[55] Cf. above, 74–78, 84f.

[56] The concept of *ammei ha-arets* went through a number of changes in nuance, and its precise definition in various strata of the Hebrew Bible is a bone of contention. At times it represents the common people at large. But since it gains a specific meaning in rabbinic literature, it seems best to avoid using it except when such literature is discussed.

[57] Redfield 1956, 70ff. Cf. Singer 1972; Redfield and Singer 1956 [1954].

[58] Singer 1972, 55.

[59] Redfield 1956, 70ff; Redfield and Singer 1956 [1954].

local forms, at the same time as a great tradition continually transforms, develops and integrates expressions of little traditions.[60] "Great and little tradition can be thought of as two currents of thought and action, distinguishable, yet ever flowing into and out of each other."[61] Much in little tradition can actually be seen as originating in an earlier great tradition, going back to orthodoxies of earlier times. And much in great traditions has its roots in and emerges from folk culture.[62]

This constant and mutual relationship leads to an ambiguous interaction involving both attachment and tension. From this perspective the Pharisees' ambivalent stance towards the common people, as well as the latter's support of the Pharisees in spite of not following them in all aspects, become intelligible indeed. The Pharisees' attraction for the common people can be explained by this model, as is evident from Scott's observation: "To the extent that elite culture represents an idealized and more elaborate formulation of folk culture, it also becomes an object of admiration if not aspiration."[63] Similar examples are found in various cultures. The suggestion that people could identify with the Pharisees without adhering to all of their *halakhah*, fits this pattern.

Little tradition sometimes finds expression in profanations or symbolic reversals, which are often intent on equality.[64] Several recent reconstructions of the historical Jesus are open in this direction.[65] Some of his actions in general, and his attitude in particular, could be interpreted according to this line of thought. Even the Pharisees' "popularization" of official custom and cultic traditions could be seen as a cautious expression of this phenomenon in relation to the Sadducees, while Jesus' temple "cleansing" and neglect of purity *halakhah* could be seen as more obvious manifestations of popular self-assertion.

Little tradition is usually associated with oral tradition and local customs, containing more elements of syncretism as compared with great tradition.[66] This makes it difficult to map out little tradition, however. Historical reconstructions are usually centred on written records, which are great tradition documents.[67] In the present case of purity practices, the available records, such as biblical material, Josephus or Mishna, all reflect great tradition in various ways. This does not completely exclude them as possible sources for little tradition, however. Since, as we have seen above, great and little tradition interrelate continuously, documents of the former may reveal something of the latter,

---

[60] Scott 1977, 8.
[61] Redfield 1956, 72.
[62] Scott 1977, 12f; Singer 1972, 55.
[63] Scott 1977, 13.
[64] Scott 1977, 29ff, 224ff.
[65] Cf. Crossan 1991; Horsley 1987.
[66] Scott 1977, 22, 26.
[67] Cf. Scott 1977, 240f.

since they adapt and incorporate parts of it to a certain extent. Thus it may be fruitful to look at some traditions in the Hebrew Bible from this perspective.

Popular traditions

Among the traditions of apparently non-priestly origin which concern impurity, there is some material which is interesting for tracing popular conceptions. In this context, the idea of land being polluted through the shedding of blood may be mentioned.[68] We have seen in the previous chapter that this idea does not easily fit into the cultic system of impurity, although it may be related to the concept of corpse impurity. The ancient and popular origin of this idea becomes evident when the Deuteronomic tradition about how to deal with a murder by an unknown perpetrator is studied (Deut 21:1–9). The animal rite prescribed for atonement or purification (כפר) on such occasions has archaic traits and seems to have the intent of breaking an otherwise unavoidable and threatening chain of cause and effect.[69] It evidently had no cultic connection, and the priests in v 5 are clearly a redactional insertion, since their function is never defined, and the rite could be carried out just as well without them.[70] The prayer in v 8 likewise represents a later re-interpretation of the rite with the intent of making it conform to cultic practices which regard God as an actor in the process of purification.[71] The tradition reveals an early practice, however, based on a more "automatic" view of cause and effect, which fits into the conception of impurity as a demonic threat, to be pursued further in Chapter VII.

One can also find traces of a popular concept of impurity with no specific connection to the cult in some of the narrative material. This possibility has already been mentioned in Chapter IV, and some of the relevant material has been discussed. It seems that the popular attitude towards leprosy and genital discharges was one of loathing, and that this was associated with impurity. David curses the house of Joab with the words: "may there never be wanting a discharger (זָב) or a "leper" (מְצֹרָע)."[72] Both of these categories figure in a number of stories, which do not imply any connection with the cult. Leprosy figures in the story of Naaman and Elisha, which will be discussed further be-

[68] This conception has been discussed in Chapter V above. For references, see 204ff.

[69] Paschen 1970, 39.

[70] Cf. the bird rite in Lev 14 where the priest seems to carry out all details of the rite according to Lev and *mNeg*, while the *Tosefta* and the *Sifra* reserve only certain acts for the priest. This might reflect a tendency in the *Mishnah* (already in the *Torah*) to make invisible the pagan roots of originally independent ceremonies by integrating them into the priestly system, while the *Tosefta* and the *Sifra* were less sensitive to pagan overtones. Cf. J. Schwartz 2000, 209, 218f.

[71] Cf. Paschen 1970, 39: "Diese Überlieferung vermischt—wie so oft in Deut—uraltes mit relativ jungem Gut und prägt das Frühere im Sinne der späteren Auffassung um."

[72] 2 Sam 3:29.

low. Impurity associated with genital discharges in a broad sense[73] is found in the story of David and Bathsheba.[74] The terminology used for purification after intercourse (מִתְקַדֶּשֶׁת) is different, however, from that of priestly legal material (טָהֵר).[75] In the narrative of David at the court of Saul, David is absent from the New Moon Festival, and Saul believes the reason is that he has become temporarily unclean.[76] The expression מִקְרֶה הוּא probably implies nocturnal pollution (cf. Deut 23:11), but the unusual expression for impurity (בִּלְתִּי טָהוֹר instead of the usual טָמֵא) deviates from priestly terminology.[77]

There is no cultic setting to these narratives, and the non-priestly material on purity shows no connection to the temple. It is a bit fragile, however, to serve as a basis for discussing official purity *halakhah* as compared with popular practice, i.e. great versus little tradition. The nature of the texts discussed above is non-legal, and hence they do not provide any details which could be compared to the legislative material in Leviticus. But they nevertheless attest to a non-cultic strand, a popular concept of purity, probably with fewer details and possibly with demonic traits. In spite of this material being incorporated into a corpus redacted from priestly interests, i.e. adapted to great tradition, we are still able to hear the voice of little tradition.

Northern literary traditions

In traditional pentateuchal source criticism, material from the so-called Elohist has been seen as stemming from the northern kingdom. In addition, the nucleus of the Deuteronomic tradition has often been regarded as of northern origin. Today there is an increasing awareness of the limitations and weaknesses of such simplified (or at times complicated!) models.[78]

It is nevertheless obvious that traditions of various origins have been incorporated into the common literature of the Hebrew Bible. The Elijah and Elisha cycles in 1–2 Kings contain legendary material from the northern kingdom and combine elements from popular religion as well as official tradition.[79] The most interesting part for the present purpose is the narrative about the Aramean

---

73 While nocturnal pollution or sexual intercourse does not constitute a *zab* or a *zabah* in a legal sense, the fact that all of these cases are discussed together in Lev 15 reveals an underlying view of the impurity of genital fluids in general.

74 2 Sam 11:2–27.

75 Paschen 1970, 35.

76 1 Sam 20:26.

77 Paschen 1970, 31f.

78 See Clements 1989, 79–83 for positions on Deuteronomy and the northern kingdom.

79 Freyne 2000, 19. Overholt 1996 finds shamanistic features in the two cycles, which he regards as an integral part of Israelite religion during the period of the monarchy. The essays in Coote 1992 (Todd 1992; Hill 1992; Rentería 1992; Bergen 1992) all relate the Elijah and Elisha literature to the social realities in Israel during the ninth century BCE. For a combined form and literary critical study of these legends, especially the Elisha cycle, cf. Rofé 1988.

leper Naaman.[80] The conception of purity in this narrative is far from that of priestly legislation. The leper Naaman appears before the king of Israel, and later before the prophet Elisha. While Elisha sends only a messenger to Naaman, there is nothing in the narrative to indicate that this is due to fear of contamination through contact. There is rather the notion that the miracle is enhanced by being performed at a distance. There are no traces of any of the cultic practices associated with leprosy in the priestly legislation of Lev 13–14. In Leviticus, the leper is not healed but, in a case where symptoms have disappeared, is *declared* clean by a priest, in connection with a bird rite. After this he must wait for a week, at the beginning and end of which he immerses.[81] Contrary to this, Naaman is purified in the sense of being healed through bathing in the Jordan river. The offerings mentioned in this legend are not those prescribed in Leviticus, but promises of future sacrifices to Jahve on Naaman's return to Aram. None of the restrictive legal practices is hinted at. The legend belongs to another world of thought. Leprosy is implicitly regarded as an impurity, since its bearer is in need of cleansing (טהר),[82] but the disease is not treated as a legal or cultic purity issue.

It seems as if this narrative was incorporated into the official Hebrew Scriptures with few adaptations. There is an obvious discrepancy between the treatment of leprosy as well as the view on sacrifices here as compared with the great tradition of Jerusalem. The Naaman legend is evidence for the existence of attitudes to leprosy which were less strict and regulated than those implied by priestly legislation. As it was incorporated into a growing corpus of Scripture, however, it did not provide a standard for dealing with leprosy, but that was done by the official priestly legislation.

Did traditions such as this survive and play a continuous role in the north even during Second Temple times, independently of their incorporation into the Hebrew Scriptures, and without being subordinated to priestly legislation? If so, we could think of Jesus as representing northern attitudes to impurity, a little tradition, with ancient roots. This is possible, but the possibility depends to some extent on how the history of the north is reconstructed.

The Galilean population

There are basically two different theories about the population of the north in general and Galilee in particular, one emphasizing continuity and the other discontinuity with the ancient Israelites of the northern kingdom.[83] According to one influential view, the Galilean peasantry remained more or less undisturbed

[80] 2 Kings 5.
[81] For details, see above, 107f.
[82] 2 Kings 5:10, 12, 13, 14.
[83] Extreme and tendentious positions (cf. Grundmann 1940, 175, 196–200: Jesus was no Jew since Galilee was largely settled by non-Semites) are not taken into consideration at all.

by the Assyrian campaigns and conquests at the end of the eighth century BCE. At the fall of Samaria, only a small number of the ruling elite was taken captive and replaced by a new governing non-Israelite elite, which was never integrated with the peasantry, but developed their own version of the Torah. Later, this elite resettled in Shechem and built the Gerizim temple.[84]

This meant that much of the peasant population in the north remained, and that the impact of the Assyrian conquest was minimal, especially in Galilee, where only administrative officers were replaced by Assyrian ones, while the Israelite village communities were left fairly free to continue following their ancient customs.[85] Such is the view of Richard Horsley, who concludes that "during second-temple times most inhabitants of Galilee were descendants of the northern Israelite peasantry."[86]

This reconstruction is complicated by archaeological evidence for a thorough depopulation of lower Galilee following the Assyrian campaign of 733/732 BCE. According to Zvi Gal, the theory of a remaining Israelite peasantry becoming the core of the Jewish population in Galilee during Second Temple times is difficult to maintain in view of the scarcity of settlements during the Persian period. "Whatever had not been destroyed by the wars was removed or laid waste by the exiles, and the region was not occupied during the seventh and sixth centuries B.C.E."[87] Many Galilean villages were first established in the middle of the sixth century BCE as agricultural hinterland to Phoenician-Persian settlements along the coastal plain.[88] The idea of a continuous Israelite village culture throughout the seventh and sixth centuries BCE is difficult to maintain.[89]

In upper Galilee we find an area sparsely populated until Hasmonean times. Settlements in all of Galilee increased considerably, however, between the Hellenistic and Roman periods.[90] This points at an "aggressive Jewish colonisation of the Galilee by the Hasmoneans in line with what we know from Josephus of their approach at Samaria and Scythopolis"[91] and could possibly be concomitant with an enforced Judaization of the previous population.[92]

[84] Alt 1953, 409ff, 455, n.1 (the material comes from *Palästinajahrbuch des Deutschen evangelischen Instituts für Altertumswissenschaft des Heiligen Landes in Jerusalem*, between 1937 and 1940); Horsley 1995, 25–29. This reconstruction is based on the biblical account in 2 Kings 15:29; 17:23 and Assyrian annals. Cf Freyne 2000, 116.
[85] Horsley 1995, 28.
[86] Horsley 1995, 40.
[87] Gal 1992, 108.
[88] Gal 1992, 109.
[89] Reed 2000, 28–34.
[90] Freyne 2000, 67f; Aviam 1993, 453f.
[91] Freyne 2000, 68. Coin finds suggest that several settlements were Hasmonean foundations.
[92] Freyne 2000, 177; cf. Reed 2000, 34–43.

There are certain observable differences between lower Galilee on the one hand and upper Galilee and Golan on the other. Although archeological findings have shown that the latter area was not as isolated as has sometimes been supposed,[93] there are real differences. According to Eric Meyers, architectural decorations in public buildings display fewer animal and human forms, and Greek epigraphic remains are almost unknown in upper Galilee. Furthermore, Hellenistic urban installations such as aqueducts, baths, large statues, temples and theatres are rarely found. This is the case in the Golan as well.[94] In lower Galilee, on the other hand, all of these elements are found frequently, especially in urban population centres. It is an issue how extensively Greek was being used, but it may possibly have been used as the everyday language by many Jews in Tiberias and Sepphoris, as well as in the region around the lake. In any case there is a difference as compared to upper Galilee and the Golan, where Aramaic or possibly Hebrew was entirely dominating.[95]

It would seem that upper Galilee and the Golan display typical conservative Jewish traits.[96] These can hardly be explained as the result of an old Israelite heritage. The proximity of Golan to the district of Batanaea may not be without significance, where Herod the Great settled a number of Babylonian Jews, creating a buffer zone. According to Josephus, these settlers were "devoted to the ancestral customs of the Jews" (οἷς τὰ Ἰουδαίων θεραπεύεται πάτρια).[97] Freyne speculates that the Batanaean Jews may have influenced the ethos of the Galileans.[98]

We have to ask, however, whether a conservative ethos was peculiar only to upper Galilee and the Golan. While lower Galilee was more Hellenized and urbanized,[99] and differed from upper Galilee in some respects, it could be argued that the conservative ethos was basically the same. Most of the characteristics of Galilean society in urban centres could be interpreted as a cultural veneer only.[100] Postponing for a moment a discussion about the effects of Hellenization and urbanization on Galilean Judaism, we must examine material and literary evidence for the type of Judaism which was prevalent in first-century Galilee.

---

[93] This is clear from findings such as ceramics, Tyrian coinage, jewelry and glass, which indicate trading relations. Meyers 1997, 58.

[94] Meyers 1997, 58f.

[95] Cf. Freyne 1998 [1980], 139ff; Meyers 1985, 125–128; Edwards 1992, 69ff; Horsley 1995, 247–250.

[96] Meyers 1985, 125ff.

[97] *Ant.* 17:23–28.

[98] Freyne 1998 [1980], 318f.

[99] Upper Galilee actually had no proper cities, hence this area could later in Byzantine times be designated τετρακωμία (Goodman 1983, 248, n.119). Lower Galilee had several towns, although they were generally not organized as Hellenistic *poleis*. A general discussion about urban-rural relationships will be postponed until the subsequent section.

[100] Meyers 1997, 58.

What type of Judaism?

What type of Judaism did Jesus grow up with, and what attitudes to impurity prevailed? From the previous discussion we realize that no simple answers can be found by reconstructing the history of Galilee. While there are literary traditions indicating Israelite views on purity, less attached to the Jerusalem temple cult, it is difficult to decide, through the turmoil of history, the extent to which such practices were transmitted to Galileans of post-Hasmonean times. It is risky to lean on old Israelite origins for advancing a view of special Galilean practices. This does not mean that the idea should be totally discarded. Galilee had mixed origins, and some heritage from its Israelite past could have survived. This is not sufficient, however, to ascertain the nature of Galilean Judaism during the first century CE.

When archaeological evidence is taken into consideration, the idea of a syncretistic ethos with lenient practices is difficult to maintain. Although most of the evidence from Galilean sites is later than the first century CE, and although most first-century evidence is disturbed by later building activities, some conclusions can be drawn, not least on the basis that pre-industrial material culture changes very slowly and over a long period.[101]

Of most interest for our quest are material remains belonging to the private sphere, since this is where local and ethnic culture is best discovered.[102] While public buildings, town plans and infrastructure may reflect the dominant Hellenistic culture, the deep-rooted indigenous ethos is revealed by what is less spectacular. One example is the arrangement in most Galilean synagogues, where a row of columns was placed between the benches against the wall and the central worship space, in imitation of the Jerusalem temple construction. Although most synagogue remains are fairly late, this applies to the more ancient remains in Gamla, Qiryat Sefer, and possibly Capernaum as well.[103]

Of direct interest for the question of purity are the numerous *miqvaot* found both in public places and in private houses in Sepphoris as well as in other Galilean population centres, of which several belong to the early Roman period.[104] A strict practice of burial outside the city is evidenced in Sepphoris.[105] Numerous finds of stone vessels all over Galilee, including "measuring-cups" for handwashing, testify to the broad spread of those expansionist concerns regarding purity, which are usually associated with the Pharisees, but not to be as-

[101] Groh 1997, 32ff.

[102] Reed 2000, 43–53.

[103] Cf. ancient Judaean synagogue remains in Qumran, Jericho and Herodium. Strange 1997, 43f; Runesson 2001a, 174–185. It seems that several of the *miqvaot* adjacent to early synagogues appeared in conjunction with settlements of the Zealots." Runesson 2001a, 178.

[104] Sanders 1990, 214–227; 1992, 222–229; Hoglund and Meyers 1996, 39f.

[105] Meyers 1992, 325.

cribed to them exclusively.[106] It is interesting to note, however, that the *miqvaot* of Sepphoris do not have an adjacent reservoir (*otsar*), and furthermore lack facilities separating those coming up from those going down. Especially the former trait is associated with rabbinic (and presumably Pharisaic) requirements. This has raised some doubt as to whether the pools at Sepphoris are *miqvaot* at all,[107] but there is no reason to assume halakhic unity.[108] Some early *miqvaot* from Gamla, Ceresin etc. have storage pools attached to them.[109] All this points to a Torah-true population in Galilee, with expansionist traits, although many did not observe the details of Pharisaic *halakhah*.

The suggestion of a separate Galilean *halakhah* is not far-fetched, but difficult to prove. For a separate Samaritan *halakhah* we have literary evidence, but it is late,[110] and we cannot know for certain what it looked like at the end of the Second Temple period. Certain indications for a Galilean *halakhah* may be read from the *Mishnah* and the *Tosefta*, but they are not conclusive. Even avoiding later Amoraic deductions found in the *Talmud*, it is difficult to judge the extent to which the relevant passages reflect first-century concerns.[111]

There are numerous references to differences in weights and measures between Galilee and Judaea, as well as different practices concerning the eve of Passover and the Day of Atonement.[112] These must be deemed as fairly minor local deviations, however. If anything, the Galilean practice of not working at all during the day before Passover must be seen as a conservative trait.[113]

---

[106] Strange 1997, 43f. For a discussion about *miqvaot* and stone vessels, see above, 74f, 84f.

[107] H. Eshel 1997, 131ff. The assumption that the people of Sepphoris "were observants of Jewish Law as stated in the *Mishnah*" and thus could not have used these pools as *miqvaot* is not convincing, since it supposes an unprecedented degree of halakhic uniformity.

[108] Cf. the discussion above, 75.

[109] Reich 1981; Netzer 1982; Sanders 1990, 217f; H. Eshel 1997, 133, n.14.

[110] Samaritan halakhic texts are, in their present form, probably from the eleventh century CE and later; extant manuscripts are still later. Cf. Bóid 1989, 21–47.

[111] We also have to exclude a number of references to the behaviour of people in Galilee generally from the Ushan period, when the rabbinic movement was based in Galilee. Unless statements about Galilean practice are contrasted with practice elsewhere, they give us no clues for a possible Galilean *halakhah*. This is one of the problems of some of the references listed in Oppenheimer 1977, 200–217.

The ahistorical nature of rabbinic material in general always makes its use for historical reconstruction problematic. On this ground Neusner (1982, 65–70) accused Freyne (1998 [1980]) of being too credulous, which caused Freyne to withdraw from, or balance, parts of his earlier discussion about Galileans and the Torah (1988a, 213–218). I would argue, however, that the predominantly Tannaitic material to be discussed immediately below has some relevance for first-century conditions for the following reasons: 1) differences in weights and measures, as well as in marriage laws, are deeply rooted in local culture, and do not change overnight. Second-century discussions about Galilean deviations in these areas attest to earlier practices. 2) references to tithing practices, closely associated with the temple cult, must be suspected of going back to Second Temple times.

[112] E.g. *mKet* 5:9; *mHul* 5:3; 11:2; *mTer* 10:8; *mPes* 4:5. Freyne 1998 [1980], 317.

[113] Cf. Schiffman 1992b, 153 ff.

Another difference concerned marriage laws, where Galilean custom differed to the effect that the virginity of the bride was not controlled as rigidly. This may possibly be seen as a sign of laxity, but could just as well imply that the moral standards of the Judaeans were generally more lax; hence they applied more rigid rules.[114]

Rules relating to tithing are of more direct interest. An oft-quoted example comes from *mNed* 2:4:

> Vows which are not spelled out are subject to a more stringent rule, and [vows] which are spelled out are subject to a more lenient rule. ...
>
> "[If he said], 'Lo, it is to me like heave offering,'
> "if he vowed that it was like heave offering of the chamber [of the Temple], it is binding.
> "And if it was like that of the treshing floor, it is not binding.
> "And if it was without further specification, it is binding," the words of R. Meir.
> R. Judah says, "A statement referring without specification to heave offering made in Judah is binding. But in Galilee, it is not binding.
> "For the men of Galilee are not familiar with heave offering belonging to the chamber.
> "Statements that something is devoted, without further specification, in Judah are not binding, and in Galilee they are binding.
> "For the Galileans are not familiar with things devoted to the priests."

This passage has been taken to mean that Galileans were considered ignorant about the heave offering (*terumah*) and the consecration offering (*herem*[115], i.e. "something devoted"). The discussion concerns the validity of vows, which depends on how they are specified. The point is that when a vow is not specified, it is taken in the strictest sense. Heave offering is thus taken to mean that of the chamber, i.e. the half shekel offering to the fund for daily sacrifices, which was disputed by certain groups. In Galilee, however, far from Jerusalem, an unspecified reference to heave offering would be intended and understood in its plain sense, i.e. the compulsory priestly portion.[116] Since a vow ("this will be as forbidden to me as x") was considered valid only if it referred to "some object usually permitted but now consecrated," a reference to heave offering in Judaea would be valid, while in Galilee it would not. The inverse situation applied to vows referring to consecration offerings, which in Judaea would be taken as referring to portions consecrated for the priests, which were always forbidden, and hence such vows were invalid. In Galilee, however, they would be intended as referring to offerings for temple repair, which were voluntary offerings, and hence such vows would be binding.[117] The passage provides

[114] *mKet* 1:5; 4:12; *mYeb* 4:10. Schiffman 1992b, 145–148.

[115] Heb. חֵרֶם.

[116] Freyne 1998 [1980], 278–281.

[117] Cf. Schiffman 1992b, 148–151. Note, however, that Schiffman seems to confuse the second issue (consecration offerings) by arguing for such vows *not* being valid in Galilee, contrary to the text of the *Mishnah* (Ibid., 149).

evidence for different definitions of terms in Judaea and Galilee, but not necessarily for laxity or ignorance. Says Schiffman:

> Some have taken this mishnah to indicate that the Galileans did not contribute to the sanctuary or give portions to the priests. Nothing could be farther from the truth. The discussion concerns the meaning of the terms *terumah* and *ḥerem* in the various regions of Palestine.[118]

The discussion should not be reduced to a matter of definitions, however, as the text does not unreservedly attest to Galilean interest in priestly offerings. It implies Galilean loyalty to the ancient practice of *terumah*,[119] as well as a willingness to contribute to the temple with voluntary gifts, but it could also suggest a certain resistance to, or lack of recognition of, the more recent half-shekel temple tax. In view of the centralized tithing system during the Second Temple period,[120] and its development and diversification,[121] it is a plausible suggestion that many Galileans supported their local priests with heave offerings and tithes, and showed their loyalty to the temple by occasional voluntary gifts, but grumbled about extended tithes and the half-shekel temple tax.[122] Resistance to payment of multiple layers of tithes may be deduced from Josephus' comments about the coercive methods used in collecting them.[123]

Other signs of resistance have been suggested in the report of Johanan ben Zakkai's complaint about the unwillingness of people to pay the half-shekel offering,[124] and in the letter which Gamaliel and the elders are said to have dictated to Johanan, the scribe, with the purpose of reminding the people of Galilee to bring tithes from their harvest of olives.[125] In what could possibly be a variant of the letter, the complaint is more evident and the Galileans are asked to hurry and bring their tithes in order not to hinder the confession.[126] While this

---

[118] Schiffman 1992b, 150.

[119] The *terumah* is problematic as a category, but rabbinic treatment assumes that this small token gift to the priests (between one fortieth and one sixtieth) was not questioned but given by all people. Cf. the mishnaic tractate *Terumot* and Sanders 1992, 155.

[120] Cf. already Malaki and Nehemiah; Horsley 1995, 141.

[121] I.e. second tithe, poor tithe, rules for the distribution of tithes different years, etc. The legislations of Leviticus, Numbers and Deuteronomy were actually combined into a system in which fourteen tithes were paid in every seven years (cf. Tobit 1:6–8 and *Ant.* 4:240), mitigated by the rabbis into twelve tithes. For a comprehensive description of tithes, first-fruits and heave offerings during the Second Temple period, see Sanders 1992, 146–157. Cf. the rabbinic discussions in the mishnaic tractates *Terumot, Maaserot* and *Maaser Sheni.*

[122] Note the concept of *demai* (i.e. agricultural produce which may not have been properly tithed) which evolved among the Rabbis, because they knew that some people paid only the priests' part of the first tithe, but not the Levites'. Cf. Sanders 1992, 429–431; *tMSheni* 3:15.

[123] *Ant.* 20:181, 206–207.

[124] *Mek.* Ex 19:1 (Bahodesh 1); Freyne 1998 [1980] 280).

[125] *tSanh* 2:6; cf. *ySanh* 1:2; *bSanh* 11b.

[126] *Midrash Tannaim* to Deut 26:13, in Hoffmann 1909, 176. Here the letter is said to be written by Simeon ben Gamaliel and Johanan ben Zakkai. It is reasonable to take this as a variant,

variant is fairly late, and the texts could be variously judged,[127] the tradition of some such letter is well established, and does at least imply a resistance to or some discrepancy between Galilean practice and what seems to be Pharisaic tithing *halakhah*. While this could be explained as a result of the distance to Jerusalem, it is more satisfactory to suggest that local customs differed.

It should be noted that in spite of the extortionist methods being used at times by the Jerusalem priesthood, Josephus pictures the Galileans in general as willing to support him and other priests with their tithes.[128] This fits the picture which appears from the discussion of evidence above, however, where the Galileans are viewed as hesitant to certain innovations, such as the half-shekel offering and not always applying the details of Pharisaic tithing or purity *halakhah*, but contributing with tithes and other gifts at least to the priests, observing purity rules to an increasing degree, and being loyal to the temple. Galilean Judaism probably had as many traits in common with the Sadducees as with the Pharisees, but it should rather be called traditional or conservative.[129]

Whether this amounts to a "Galilean *halakhah*" is a matter of definition. There is no clear evidence of a well-defined deviating legal tradition, with its own representatives, as in the case of Samaritan *halakhah*. There are no explicit signs of a deviating purity *halakhah*. There are no signs of deviations based on particular Galilean synchretistic tendencies. Certain differences might go back to northern traditions, but there is little evidence to support this. Galilean Judaism at the end of the Second Temple period was oriented towards Jerusalem.[130] This is further underscored by the practice of pilgrimage at the three major feasts. While the extent of Galilean participation has been questioned, there is ample evidence for large-scale pilgrimage to Jerusalem.[131]

---

although Freyne seems to be arguing (1998 [1980], 282, 285f, 302f, n.73) for the two letters as representing separate historical events.

[127] Cf. Freyne's somewhat speculative reconstruction (1998 [1980], 282–286), in which he suggests that this is evidence for Galileans following priestly or Sadducean custom rather than Pharisaic. Schiffman (1992b, 153) interprets the tradition (without taking the variant into consideration) not as a complaint, but as simple evidence for the observance of the Galileans. Horsley mentions the letters (1995, 143), but notes that they may reflect later polemics, and is careful not to claim them as reflecting historical events.

[128] *Life* 63, 80. While this is part of Josephus' apologetics, the passages attest to a general practice among Galileans to pay tithes to priests.

[129] Such a reconstruction fits with *mKet* 4:12 in which Galileans are said to have phrased their marriage contract as the Jerusalemites, in contrast to the Judaeans. The Galilean-Jerusalemite version seems more traditional-conservative, taking lifelong responsibility for a widow, while the Judaean version is more "liberal," making it possible for heirs to pay off the widow's marriage contract. The Judaean version could possibly be a Pharisaic invention, while the Galilean stance is better characterized as traditional-conservative rather than according to party-lines.

[130] Cf. Sanders 2002; Reed 2000, 43–55.

[131] Safrai 1981, 45–65, 93–97. Cf. Horsley 1995, 144ff, who claims that "Galileans would have come only by the hundreds" (145). Horsley dismisses evidence from Lk 2:41–51 as a reflection

The Galilean orientation towards Jerusalem may seem strange in view of the distance and the increasing influence of Hellenistic cities in the area. Moreover, the influence of Jerusalem in Galilee cannot be described simplistically as either priestly authority or Pharisaic dominance. In matters of purity and other issues pertaining to the cult, we find signs of an increasing commitment, but they are not unambiguous. To gain a further understanding of Jesus' Galilean background, we should also examine the effects of Galilean "urbanization" and the relationship between centre and periphery.

VI.3 Centre and periphery

Urbanization and Hellenization

Recently, the "urbanization" of Galilee has attracted growing interest. This is partly due to excavations at Sepphoris, which have highlighted the central role of this town from the end of the Second Temple period onwards, but also to the boom of excavations all over Galilee, which has brought to light a network of trading routes, and a "market economy" in which smaller villages and towns specialized in pottery or fish industry, and traded their goods all over the area.

The idea of Lower Galilee as urbanized, coupled with an increasing awareness of the problematic dichotomy between Jewish and Hellenistic geographical areas, have produced reconstructions of Galilean society as largely Hellenized, Greek-speaking, synchretistic, oriented towards the large cities, and with popular Cynic influences even down to village level.[132]

As we have already seen from the previous section, there are too many signs for a conservative Jewish ethos for this picture to be plausible. Material remains in the private or semi-private sphere attest to a Torah-true population. Widespread trading patterns do not necessarily imply profound cultural adaptation. External patterns and characteristics of the ruling power may be appropriated and adapted, while remaining a thin cultural veneer.[133] In Galilee, as in many other places, a local and ethnic culture continued to exist fairly undisturbed within a larger Hellenistic framework.

The urbanization of Galilee must not be exaggerated. While there were several Hellenistic cities (*poleis*) along the Mediterranean coast and in the area of Decapolis, Galilee had only two proper cities: Sepphoris and Tiberias. These contained many of the attributes of Hellenistic cities, such as theatres and baths,

---

of a Lukan agenda rather than Galilean practices (146). For a more nuanced discussion of figures, although no estimate of Galilean pilgrims is given, cf. Sanders 1992, 125–128.

132 Mack 1988; 1993; Crossan 1991. Cf. the reservations of Aune 1997.

133 As a prime example of this, the total rebuilding of the Jerusalem temple in Hellenistic style by Herod must be mentioned. Cf. Horsley 1995, 321, n.31.

but were nevertheless predominantly Jewish. There seem to have been no pagan temples or large public statues in Sepphoris as in other Hellenistic cities.[134] Neither Sepphoris nor Tiberias was a typical πόλις, but functioned as administrative centres for Galilee.[135] There are signs of tension, however, between these cities and the rest of the province, which will be explored below.

As for the rest of Galilee, centres of population such as Magdala (Tarichaeae), Capernaum or Bethsaida were not organized as Hellenistic *poleis*, and their somewhat intermediate status can be understood from the varying terminology used by different sources. In the gospels, Capernaum and even Nazareth are called cities (πόλις).[136] The distinction between city and village seems at first quite straightforward as in the Matthean juxtaposition of the two terms (τὰς πόλεις πάσας καὶ τὰς κώμας; πόλιν ἢ κώμην). The Lukan "to every city and place" (εἰς πᾶσαν πόλιν καὶ τόπον) and especially the strange Markan compound κωμοπόλεις suggest that there might have been a differentiation between settlements which is not expressed by the use of two Greek terms only.[137] This suspicion is supported by the more varied terminology in Jewish sources. Galilean towns were not "real" cities in the Greek sense.[138] The byzantine designation of Upper Galilee as a τετρακωμία,[139] suggests that in this part of the region there were no cities at all, but only four major population centres.

The question of urbanization is partly one of definition. If defined as the spread of Hellenistic *poleis*, we can distinguish two periods of urbanization: one during the Ptolemaic/Seleucid period when a number of cities were established around Galilee, and a Herodian, interior phase, involving Sepphoris and Tiberias. If a number of lesser Galilean towns are taken into consideration, however, we must reckon with another, perhaps more important period of "urbanization," i.e. the Hasmonean expansion in the late second and early first century BCE. If so, then Galilean urbanization is as much a question of its Judaization as of its Hellenization.[140]

---

[134] Freyne 2000, 69; Horsley 1995, 167; Sanders 2002, 6f.

[135] Cf. Horsley 1995, 163–174; Sanders 2002, 24, n.52. Sanders lists arguments for not regarding Sepphoris and Tiberias as πόλεις.

[136] Mk 1:33; Lk 1:26; 4:31.

[137] Mt 9:35; 10:11; Lk 11:1; Mk 1:38. Cf. the discrepancies between various gospels and Josephus. Mk calls Bethsaida a κώμη (Mk 8:23), while Mt and Lk call it a πόλις (Mt 11:20; Lk 9:10). Josephus says it was raised by Philip from the status of a village to a city (*Ant.* 18:28). Capernaum is called a city by the gospels (Mt 4:13 + 9:1; Mk 1:21+33; Lk 4:31), but a village according to Josephus (*Life* 403). Freyne 1998 [1980], 146, n.11.

[138] Cf..Freyne 1998 [1980], 103f; 146, n.10, 11; 2000, 60, 64. Rabbinic sources use several terms: כרך, עיר, and כפר (*kerakh, 'ir,* and *kefar*), as well as variations. Cf. Horsley 1995, 191f; Goodman 1983, 27–40.

[139] Goodman 1983, 248, n.119.

[140] Freyne 2000, 60, 67f; cf. Reed 2000, 39–43.

Town and country

The relationship between town and country in Galilee is a much disputed issue, which also has received new impetus from recent excavations. Basically the same evidence is interpreted in opposite ways, however. Signs of extended trade, mentioned above, as well as the short distances in the area, have made some scholars overestimate the degree of interaction between town and country. Richard Horsley has warned against projecting later ideas of urban-rural relationships onto first-century Galilee. He finds an example of this in Eric Meyers' description of Sepphoris as a place where "[p]eople from the surrounding area probably also flocked ... either to attend the theater or to hawk their wares."[141] This is to project a modern market economy onto first-century Galilee:

> Rather than assume the modern market-economy model and then "discover" data in our literary and archaeological sources that illustrate it for ancient Galilee, it would make more historical sense to reason dialectically back and forth between an economic model derived from studies of traditional agrarian societies and the literary and other evidence available for ancient Galilee.[142]

In traditional agrarian society, the productivity of the land is crucial, and urban aristocracies are dependent on its surplus. Systems for extracting such a surplus could be more or less exploitative.[143] While small-scale industry, such as pottery and fish processing flourished, and traders marketed these goods all over the region, people in general did not run to the cities for entertainment. Agricultural surplus was often paid as tithes and taxes, and collected at village level rather than sold in town.[144]

Landowning patterns in first century Galilee are difficult to ascertain, but it seems that the Jewish ideal of small, private holdings was compromised already at an early time, perhaps during the Persian period. There is evidence in the *Zenon papyri* from the Ptolemaic period for royal land, as well as gifts of land to veterans in Palestine, including Galilee. In Beth Anath there were apparently villagers who both leased and owned property. There seems to have been a mixture of large estates with different types of workers and tenants, and small private holdings, and this pattern was not significantly changed during Hasmonean rule. Much of the royal land passed through the Hasmoneans to the Herodians. Far-reaching changes in landowning patterns can be traced from the time of Herod the Great, who settled thousands of veterans in the Great Plain and in former Samaria, as well as Babylonian Jews in the Transjordan, giving

---

141 Meyers 1992, 333.

142 Horsley 1995, 203.

143 Cf. Horsley 1995, 207ff.

144 Horsley 1995, 179f. Josephus' reference to imperial corn (τὸν Καίσαρος σῖτον) in *Life* 71, which was stored in Upper Galilee, implies that Galilean agricultural surplus, like that of Egypt and Syria, was sent to Rome to alleviate the lack of corn in Italy. Freyne 2000, 96f.

away land alottments.[145] Herod's and later Antipas' building activities demanded resources which had to be gained through taxation and income from the land.[146]

Although archaeological surveys of settlement patterns cannot help us to distinguish private land from lease holdings, evidence from other parts of the Roman empire suggests that the two co-existed.[147] The pattern of absentee landlords is attested by Josephus as well as by several gospel parables. The latter also attest to the problem of debts and the presence of displaced day labourers.[148] This seems to have been an increasing tendency during the first century, which came to a climax at the time of the revolt in 66 CE.[149]

While the Galilean cities are nowhere said to have had their own territory (χώρα),[150] i.e. they did not own the surrounding land with its villages and peasants, as a Hellenistic *polis* generally did, they must nevertheless have been supported by agricultural produce from the vicinity. This was not done through trading and market exchange on equal terms only, but through some sort of land-owning as well, including rent and taxation. The citizens of Tiberias were given land by Antipas, and if this is not to be understood as an integration of the immediate surroundings, it could only mean that Tiberian citizens owned land allotments elsewhere.[151] This fits the picture of country estates with absentee landlords already mentioned.

While ownership was certainly mixed, there are signs of tension between the rural population and citizens of the towns, due to unequal conditions and exploitation. Although this is denied by some,[152] tension seems to have developed into outright hatred at the time of the first revolt. Josephus, who writes about the "Galileans" in terms of the Galilean country people,[153] describes their hatred of the citizens of Sepphoris and Tiberias, as well as a couple of other towns.[154]

---

[145] Freyne 1998 [1980], 156–166.

[146] Horsley 1995, 177f.: "Considering that the only economic base of Antipas's tetrarchy was the 'surplus' agricultural product of the Galilean and Perean villagers and townspeople, his massive building projects would have required intensified exploitation of that base."

[147] Freyne 2000, 98f.

[148] *Life* 33; Mk 12:1–12 par; Mt 18:23–24/Lk 7:41; Mt 24:45–57/Lk 12:42–46; Lk 16:1–6. Cf. Freyne 1998 [1980], 165.

[149] Cf. Goodman 1982; Freyne 2000, 193ff, 205.

[150] Josephus never talks about the χώρα of the Galilean cities, except in *Life* 155, where the Tiberian citizens are said to have asked the king to protect their territory (χώρα). Here the term should be taken to refer to their surrounding areas, rather than to a particular city territory.

[151] Freyne 2000, 195; Horsley 1995, 171, 177. Galilee was not divided into the territory of Tiberias and Sepphoris until the reign of Hadrian (Freyne 1998 [1980], 90; Horsley 1995, 214f).

[152] E.g. Meyers 1997, 61: "Theories that suggest that urban centres exploit the surrounding countryside are to be soundly rejected on the basis of archaeological evidence alone." The evidence referred to, however, is the usual: small local industry and trade (pottery, fish-processing), monetary transactions (coins), etc. This can be interpreted in different ways.

[153] Freyne 2000, 30–35.

[154] *Life* 375, 384.

In spite of Josephus' overstatements and bias, this reflects not only, or mainly an enmity due to the pro-Roman stance of these cities,[155] but must be explained in other ways. The revolutionary and anti-Roman spirit of Galilee has been generally exaggerated, and was clearly manifested only in the revolt. In the end, however, the revolt resulted in very little activity and hence very little damage to Galilee, and the only towns which actually resisted the Romans in 67 CE were Gamla and Jotapata.[156] The tensions between the Galilean rural population and Sepphoris and Tiberias must be explained by inner Galilean factors.

Hence an increasing exploitation of the countryside, leading to indebtedness and poverty, is plausible as a partial explanation for the revolt.[157] Tensions were to a large extent internal, and these conditions must have been developing over a long period of time. We find in the gospel parables signs of the beginning of such a development already at the time of Antipas.[158] This means that Jesus' activities must partly be seen against a background of growing tensions. These tensions were to some extent both social and religious, and the two aspects cannot always be separated. The fact that the antagonism of rural Galileans toward their own administrative centres never found an equivalent in their attitude to Jerusalem, in spite of that city's economic and legal claims, asserted by its aristocracy, shows that a simplified view of the tensions between town and country is not possible.

---

[155] Freyne 2000, 35–44.

[156] Rappaport 1992, 95–102; Freyne 2000, 35–40.

[157] Goodman 1982.

[158] While anti-Roman feelings and revolutionary attitudes should not be exaggerated, the opposite tendency should also be avoided, i.e. downplaying tension and protest. Andrew Overman (1997, 67–73) attempts to downplay peasant opposition to taxes and exploitation by referring to a French study about peasant revolts in early modern France (Bercé 1990 [1986]; not Brece, as in Overman's misspelling). With the help of analogy Overman utilizes, in an almost revisionist way, this historical study to claim that most stories about taxes and oppression, as well as rebellions and protests were given mythical proportions, which served the function of creating some sort of balance. While it is certain that Josephus' picture of the revolt is exaggerated and biased, we cannot dismiss the evidence for a social situation full of tensions, by looking for analogies with a (likewise biased?) interpretation of seventeenth century France. The type of quotations Overman takes from Bercé are revealing, since they almost ridicule any uprising: "Sometimes the resistance took the form of a dozen people slamming their doors in the face of a bailiff." "Risings which broke out in cities threw up a number of ringleaders. Previously unknown leaders rose to prominence in the course of the secret discussions which took place in shops and taverns and the seditious meetings which were held in broad daylight in the open space afforded by a churchyard or the public square. ... When the rising seemed about to collapse in the face of general apathy and fear of government reprisals, a core of diehards would also emerge from the ranks of the population to make an unexpected last-ditch stand ... desperation drove them to the suicidal tactics of setting the town on fire and lynching the magistrates ... They clung to the legends which circulated in the world of tax resistance, and preferred to die rather than to lose a traditional freedom, or submit to an *gabelle*." Quotes from Bercé 1990 [1986], 197, 276. (The quotes in Overman 1997, 70–72, are slightly inaccurate).

Sepphoris or Jerusalem? Orthogenetic and heterogenetic cities

Several ideas about the historical Jesus have been based on reconstructions of tensions between town and country. The Galilean situation at the end of the Second Temple period, however, cannot be reduced to a simple urban-rural conflict. The best attempt at a nuanced picture has been provided by Sean Freyne.[159]

Freyne applies to the Galilean situation the distinction between orthogenetic and heterogenetic cities, developed by Redfield and Singer in the 1950s.[160] In their article "The Cultural Role of Cities," Redfield and Singer describe orthogenetic cities as those which "carry forward, develop, elaborate a long-established local culture or civilization. These are cities that convert the folk culture into its civilized dimension." In heterogenetic cities, on the other hand, "the prevailing relationships of people and the prevailing common understanding have to do with the technical not the moral order, with administrative regulation, business and technical convenience," and/or "these cities are populated by people of diverse cultural origins removed from the indigenous seats of their cultures."[161] This is then

> the distinction between the *carrying forward into systematic and reflective dimensions an old culture* and the *creating of original modes of thought that have authority beyond or in conflict with old cultures and civilizations.*[162]

This does not mean that orthogenetic cities are static, or that a particular city has only one of these roles. It can be both, although at a certain stage or point in time one of the two functions predominates. The same event or phenomenon may appear differently to different groups, however. For our purpose the interesting question is: how did the Galilean Hellenistic cities (Sepphoris and Tiberias) appear to common Galilean Jews in comparison to Jerusalem?

Applying this discussion to Galilee, Freyne examines different aspects of orthogenetic and heterogenetic cities, to find that Jerusalem fits the description of the former, while the Greek and Herodian cities of Galilee fit the description of the latter. Using evidence mainly from Josephus and the gospels, Freyne looks at dominant social types, the relationship with the countryside, economic patterns and social unity. In Jerusalem the dominant types were literati who fashioned great tradition. The relationship between the countryside and Jerusalem was based on common loyalty to a shared world-view, where the common people accepted myths of the past as recreated by the literati. Inequality was partly accepted as necessary or divinely ordained, and unity was achieved by consensus. In the Galilean cities, on the other hand, the dominant social types were

---

[159] Freyne 1992 and 1997b, revised and reprinted in Freyne 2000, 45–72.
[160] Redfield and Singer 1956 [1954].
[161] Redfield and Singer 1956 [1954], 168f.
[162] Redfield and Singer 1956 [1954], 169.

businessmen, bureaucrats, officials, military and tax collectors. In spite of mistrust at the cultural level, and conflicting myths, relationships between these cities and the country were pragmatic. Economic exploitation resulted in tensions, however, and undisguised dissent was understood as rebellion. Unity was maintained by force.[163]

The application of this model to the Galilean cities supports the observations made above and makes the mix of seemingly contradictory factors intelligible: trade and interaction between country and city, resentment and tension but not to the point of revolution, dependence and exploitation, the creation of new social types[164] (tax collectors, dispossessed day labourers etc.), and the continued loyalty of the countryside to Jerusalem and the shared myths, even if every religious tax was not necessarily accepted. The tensions between Galileans and their cities as well as their loyalty to Jerusalem is thus confirmed and to some extent explained. Says Freyne,

> ... there appears to be a converging picture from the literary sources of ongoing tensions between town and country in first-century Galilee, not because such hostility was inevitable, but because the Herodian foundations of Galilee represented alien values as far as 'country' Jews were concerned, that is, the Jewish population of the Galilee living in towns and villages, whose loyalties to Jerusalem and the symbolic world represented by its cult-centre were sufficiently intact, despite the distance, social and physical that separated them from that centre.[165]

The idea of "alien values" may be further pursued. Freyne suggests that Jesus avoided Sepphoris and Tiberias because he rejected certain of their values.[166] This is hard to prove, and ignores the simple fact that he was wanted by Antipas as the most apparent reason for avoiding these cities. Apart from this, the clash of values resulting from these Herodian cities must be seen as an important factor in explaining a Galilean-based Jewish movement or renewal programme in the 20s or 30s of the first century CE. While other Hellenistic cities in the area had an ethos even more foreign to Galilean Jews in general, and were perceived as "gentile enclaves in a Jewish hinterland," Sepphoris and Tiberias introduced into the midst of Galilee values which clashed with tradition, but which nevertheless were embraced by a number of Jews.[167]

Discussing the economic aspects of this clash of values, Freyne suggests that Jesus' attitude to wealth and possessions may be seen in the light of ancient legal traditions not being able to counteract or challenge the new types of inequalities which resulted from Herodian-Roman rule. The poor man's tithe and other traditional redistributing systems had no real effect on the structurally

[163] Freyne 2000, 45–58; cf. especially the table, 47.
[164] Cf. Redfield and Singer 1956 [1954], 174 on the effects of secondary patterns of urbanization.
[165] Freyne 2000, 71f.
[166] Freyne 2000, 71, 111.
[167] Freyne 2000, 62.

conditioned development in Galilee.[168] Loyalty to Jerusalem had little effect on impoverishment and extortion. In this context, Jesus and his movement offered a modified value system which purportedly would bring about more of a change.

Is there a possible analogy to the issue of purity? A discussion must be fairly speculative, but should nevertheless be attempted.

Beyond great and little tradition

We have seen that a simplified attempt to explain Jesus' attitude to purity as representing Galilean rural little tradition as distinct from Jerusalem urban great tradition is not really possible. The historical situation was much more complex. We have found Galilean practice to have been more conservative or traditional at times than that of Jerusalem, at least that of the Pharisees. In addition, the relationship of Galilean rural people to heterogenetic and orthogenetic cities must be taken into account.

The ethos of the Hellenistic cities must have been a problem for a traditional practice of purity. This should have included the Herodian Galilean centres at the time of Jesus as well, in spite of their predominiantly Jewish population, as is seen from the difficulty in populating Tiberias.

The most influential interpreters of the Jerusalem great tradition, the Pharisees, probably made life within the Galilean cities easier through their legal interpretations, at the same time as they developed purity *halakhah* and made rules more detailed.

It should be remembered that Galilean local tradition, although conservative, was not identical to the Jerusalem great tradition, certainly not to expansionist interpretations of it, but must rather be identified as a simpler, less detailed, traditional variant.[169] The common people in Galilee at the end of the Second Temple period were thus caught between two forces: the laxer standards of the cities and the increasing demands of the expansionist retainers of the Jerusalem tradition. As in the case of economy and injustice, great tradition, here as interpreted by Jerusalem representatives, did not provide satisfactory answers to particular local questions and needs. While the threat of the cities to the purity of the people could be met by higher standards and more detailed rules, as well as by a number of innovations and diversified interpretations, this was not a viable way for most of the Galileans from village and country.

If Galileans were generally conservative, they wished to be loyal, but at what cost? The influence of the heterogenetic cities could be counteracted, but with

[168] Freyne 2000, 56.

[169] Note Josephus' accusations of John of Gischala (*J.W.* 7:264) for violating purity regulations. Theissen and Merz suggest that this might only mean that he followed a different Galilean practice (Theissen and Merz 1998, 178).

what economic and social consequences? At a time when expansionists were developing associations (*haburot*) for coping with the threats of contamination and preserving a high degree of purity in loyalty to their interpretation of the Torah, others, as loyal to basically the same ancestral traditions, found no adequate solution to the problem. Many common people living within the village economies of Galilee could neither afford nor accept expansionist solutions that would affect social relationships and the tight-knit pattern of the extended family which were as much part of ancestral tradition as well.

This is a possible picture in which Jesus and his attitude to impurity can be situated. It might represent a way out of the dilemma in which many of the common people were caught. To some it looked much like laxity, however, while it was in fact based on an attitude of loyalty to ancestral religion.

Jesus and Pharisees in Galilee

The sketch outlined above is admittedly speculative, but it does fit into a broader picture of the Jesus movement and the Pharisees both struggling for influence in first-century Galilee. This picture is sometimes regarded as a polemical construction of the gospel writers at the end of the first century, reflecting the power struggle between the emerging Christian and rabbinic movements. We have seen above, however, that there is good evidence for the Pharisees being the most influential group with the common people in the first half of the first century CE, and that evidence from Galilee suggest definite inroads there too, although not necessarily dominance.

There is as usual the problem of assessing second-century rabbinic evidence. Although the Rabbis are not to be identified with the Pharisees, the fact that the Rabbis had certain problems in establishing themselves in Galilee after the second revolt suggests that this region did not experience Pharisaic domination a century earlier. Rabbinic traditions about Johanan ben Zakkai's stay in Galilean Arav suggest that Pharisaic authority was far from generally accepted.[170] The famous saying ascribed to Johanan: "Galilee, Galilee! You hate the Torah. Your end will be to be besieged"[171] has been questioned repeatedly as legendary.[172] The fact that it seems to be paralleled in the Fourth Gospel ("This

[170] *yShabb* 16:8; *mShabb* 16:7; 22:3. According to the Palestinian *Talmud*, only two cases were brought to Johanan during his stay in Arav. Since the comment in *yShabb* 16:8 is based on the existence of the two comments in the *Mishnah*, it cannot be taken as representing an historical memory of the exact number of cases referred to Johanan during his Galilean soujourn. But nor should it be seen as a rabbinic precedent for contemporary problems in Galilee only. Had the Galileans of Second Temple times been known as following Pharisaic *halakhah* in general, this would have been appealed to in later polemical conflicts.

[171] *yShabb* 16:8. This is the traditional translation of the Hebrew: גליל גליל שנאת התורה סופך לעשות במסיקין. Cf. Neusner's translation: "You will end up working for tax farmers."

[172] Cf. Neusner 1970, 133f; 1982, 67; Freyne 1998 [1980], 315.

crowd which does not know the law is accursed"),[173] could be taken merely as reflecting views on popular lack of observance at the end of the first century. The Johannine saying, however, is associated with a discussion about whether Galilee could possibly qualify for producing a prophet,[174] and must be regarded as independent evidence for a suspicious attitude from the Jerusalem retainer class towards the Galilean people at large. In spite of Neusner's criticism, based on the ahistorical nature of rabbinic literature,[175] and in spite of the tendency of the Fourth Gospel, I think that this type of short statement can make a fairly good claim for having some sort of socio-historical background, however exploited in later polemics.

Examples of Pharisaic representatives sent from Jerusalem to Galilee, without being obviously successful, are found both in Josephus and the gospels. The group of four men, including three Pharisees, sent to depose Josephus, did not have much authority with most of the Galileans.[176] Mark mentions scribes coming from Jerusalem (Mk 3:22; 7:1). While such statements have been ridiculed, as if Jerusalem would send spies to Galilee for the purpose of watching Jesus,[177] the Markan text speaks only of the origin of the scribes. While they are not explicitly said to be Pharisees,[178] the presence in Galilee of scribal retainers from Jerusalem, such as Johanan in Arav, is confirmed. As representatives of the great tradition they attempted to gain influence. Not all were Pharisees, but many of them were, and expansionist viewpoints were probably held by a majority. They were influential, but apparently did not have the same degree of authority in Galilee as in Judaea.[179] The Pharisees were supposedly the more successful, but did not have the same influence in the Galilean countryside as in some indigenous towns around the lake. Jesus, on the other hand, seems to have been more influential in rural areas than in certain of the towns. The woes of Jesus against Chorazin, Bethsaida and Capernaum may attest to this.[180]

Jesus and the Pharisees would thus have been competing for influence, although sharp antagonism should not be presupposed, as is indicated by Lukan evidence of friendly interaction.[181] The greater attraction of Jesus in the eyes of

---

[173] Jn 7:49.
[174] Jn 7:41, 52.
[175] Neusner 1982, 67f.
[176] *Life* 197ff; For a discussion of the evidence, see Freyne 1988a, 206ff.
[177] Sanders 1985, 265.
[178] In 7:1 they are coupled with the Pharisees. For a discussion about the relationship between scribes and Pharisees, as well as references to gospel passages mentioning them in conjunction, cf. above, 44ff.
[179] Cf. the discussion above, 280f, about the distribution of archeological evidence for purity practices, and signs of non-Pharisaic practice.
[180] Mt 11:20–24/Lk 10:13–15. Cf. Freyne 1988a, 211.
[181] Cf. Lk 7:36ff; 11:37; 14:1. Historically, Luke's indications of friendly interaction must be taken as more plausible than Matthew's picture of implacable antagonism. The latter is rather

the country people could be explained in several ways. Looking at his attitude to purity, there are three points to be made in this respect.

In the first place, Jesus' attitude to impurity posed no problem for social interaction, as is evident in the issue of table fellowship. While Pharisees did not necessarily take recourse to associations (*haburot*), they were particular about their eating company. Jesus was apparently accepted as an eating partner by some Pharisees,[182] while his own habits of eating and interaction were criticized.[183] Restrictions concerning table fellowship could be more easily motivated in towns with some population mix, and would be easier to uphold in an urban environment than in rural villages. In the countryside, social relation ships were tightly knit and based on the extended family. Practices which could obstruct those relationships and complicate interaction would not readily be embraced. This applies not only to table fellowship, but to contamination by contact as well. The continuous development of rules for corpse impurity, discharges and "leprosy" by expansionist retainers of great tradition would have rendered social interaction at the village level more difficult. Jesus' attitude to impurity made it possible to regard oneself as faithful to ancestral religion, without following the Pharisees or other retainers of the Jerusalem tradition.[184]

The second point is related to the first. As we have seen, Galileans at large did not follow any particular school or party, but represented a general conservative traditionalism. Their halakhic attitude was thus determined not by which school people followed, but by tradition and pragmatism. A trace of this is found in the logia about domestic animals falling into a well or a pit on the Sabbath.[185] While such issues were discussed by the different groups,[186] Jesus' stance is pragmatic and typical of little tradition, appealing to the common sense and judgment of the listeners. Galilean villagers in general could hardly afford to lose an animal because of strict legal interpretations. The case of purity *halakhah* is not as obvious, but similar conditions would apply. Interpretations which could result in foodstuff being discarded would have had no appeal to those of small means. While risks could be reduced by frequent use of stone vessels and *miqvaot*, we do not know for certain how widespread those practices were in small villages, since archeological evidence is recovered mostly from towns. However that may be, Jesus' attitude to impurity must have held some attraction for townspeople and countrypeople alike, since it confirmed the practice of little tradition of interpreting rules pragmatically, according to cir-

reflecting later controversies between Jews and Christians. A certain mixture of interaction and conflict should be regarded as historical.

[182] Lk 7:36; 11:37; 14:1.

[183] Mk 2:16; Lk 15:2.

[184] Cf. discussions about Jesus' table fellowship or open "commensality," e.g. Crossan 1991, 341–344. Cf. Bolyki 1998, 225ff, 228f.

[185] Lk 13:15; 14:5; Mt 12:11.

[186] For a comment on the interpretation of the passages involved, see above, 58f.

cumstances. The interpretation of the Pharisees, while aiming at practicability, faithfulness and care, would have been difficult for the poorer parts of the mainly rural population to follow in full. Again, Jesus' attitude to impurity made it possible to remain faithful without adjusting to expansionist concerns.

Thirdly, in contrast to the retainers of the Jerusalem tradition, Jesus exhibited traits of religious leadership, more akin to those of a "man of deed." The prime examples of such a figure which have been discussed are Honi, the circle-drawer (first century BCE) and Hanina ben Dosa (first century CE), both mentioned in rabbinic literature.[187] Geza Vermes has developed the idea of a northern type of charismatic "holy man" tradition, modelled on Elijah and Elisha, into which Jesus would fit, together with Honi and Hanina.[188] The idea has been taken up by other scholars, although with modifications.[189] Vermes identifies the "holy man" with the *hasid* of rabbinic literature, and describes him as a "man of deed" (אִישׁ מַעֲשֶׂה) known for his prayers, by which he could effect miracles, rather than as a teacher of law. Vermes' theory has a number of weak spots, which will be further examined when Jesus' activity as an itinerant exorcist is discussed in the next chapter.[190] While there are grounds for questioning Vermes' Galilean miracle-working *hasid* as being too simplified a reconstruction,[191] there are similarities between Jesus and Hanina, as "men of deed," whose popular type of piety and authority would have been attractive to rural Galileans, with their loyalty to Jerusalem and the temple, although not necessarily to Pharisaic *halakhah*. Discussing Hanina, Freyne says:

> In these circumstances of what may justifiably be described as a 'pilgrimage religion', the Pharisaic movement that was designed to bridge the gap between the temple and the everyday, but particularly adapted to meet the needs of townspeople rather than the rural population, was likely to have little appeal in rural Galilee. Consequently, the 'man of deed' had a definite religious function of bringing the power and presence associated with the temple into the lives and needs of country people.[192]

---

[187] *mTaan* 3:8; cf. *Ant.* 14:22–24; *mBer* 5:5; *bBer* 34b; *yBer* 5:5. Cf. the studies of Green 1979 about Honi, and Vermes 1972 and 1973a about Hanina.

[188] Vermes 1972, 1973a, 1973b.

[189] Borg 1984, 230–237.

[190] Cf. below, 318–320.

[191] Note that Honi is nowhere explicitly located in Galilee, although Vermes finds some possible evidence for associating him with the north (1973b, 72). This is very speculative, however. Hanina, on the other hand, is explicitly located in Galilean Arav (*yBer* 4:1), and associated with Johanan ben Zakkai (*bBer* 34b). For a careful discussion of the evidence, see Freyne 2000, 132–159. Freyne points out that the designation of Hanina as a *hasid* occurs only twice, and both references are late, while as a "man of deed" he is differentiated from the *hasidim* (*mSota* 9:15). Neither magical elements nor indifference to legal or ritual matters fit into a conventional picture of hasidic piety. Freyne shows that the transformation of Hanina into a *hasid* is part of his "rabbinization" whereby he is claimed by orthodoxy. Hanina is further not characterized as a Galilean in the earliest traditions, which weakens the claim for placing him in Galilee (Crossan 1991, 157; Meier 1994, 588). For a more elaborate discussion, see below, 318–320.

[192] Freyne 2000, 154.

This is the context of Jesus as well, and the analysis explains the popular reaction to Jesus as described by Mark: "They were astonished by his teaching, because he was teaching them as one having power (ὡς ἐξουσίαν ἔχων) and not as the scribes."[193] The miracle-working activity of Jesus in a Galilean setting functioned in a way subsequently not accepted by the rabbis,[194] namely as authorization of his teaching and as legitimatization of his behaviour. Jesus' attitude to impurity was thus corroborated by his authority as a "man of deed."

Summary: A case for Jesus' attitude as a reaction to a Galilean dilemma on purity

The present discussion about purity and diversity has probably provided more questions than answers. It has become clear, however, that Jesus' attitude to impurity did not represent that of any of the known major groups within Second Temple Judaism. Although the positions of the different groups (Essenes, Sadducees and Pharisees) can be fairly well defined at least on a few issues, this is of little help in the attempt to further define Jesus' stance.

A possible alternative would be to identify Jesus' attitude with the position of the common people. This is too general a suggestion, however, which must be narrowed and qualified. Using rabbinic statements about the *ammei ha-arets* for determining the status and legal observance of the common people during the first century CE is problematic. Expansionist concerns were influential among large segments of the population during the end of the Second Temple period.

There are good reasons for accepting the picture found in Josephus and in many gospel traditions of the Pharisees as the more influential of the contemporary parties, without claiming that they ran everything or had superceded the aristocratic and cultic leadership which was mainly Sadducean. The Pharisees were thus influential with the common people, who often looked upon them as a religious ideal and supported them rather than the other parties ideologically, but followed their *halakhah* to various, limited extents only, and at times not at all. The latter seems to have applied especially to common people in Galilee. The relationship between the Pharisees and the common people was ambivalent, characterized by a mixture of respect, acceptance, tension and at times contempt.

---

[193] Mk 1:22. In Mark's mind, the power of Jesus' teaching is immediately associated with his exorcisms (1:27): "A new teaching with power, and he commands the impure spirits, and they obey him" (διδαχὴ καινὴ κατ' ἐξουσίαν· καὶ τοῖς πνεύμασι τοῖς ἀκαθάρτοις ἐπιτάσσει, καὶ ὑπακούουσιν αὐτῷ). This association will be discussed in the subsequent chapter.

[194] *bBMes* 59b; Cf. Vermes 1973b, 81f.

The tensions may be understood, at least in part, as those between a great (official, urban, literate) and a little (popular, rural, oral) tradition. However, signs of little tradition are, due to its nature, difficult to recover. Attempts to find remains of northern Israelite traditions in the Hebrew Scriptures in order to explain Galilean attitudes to purity have yielded some results, although limited, which suggest a popular concept of impurity, rather non-cultic, possibly with demonic traits, and with fewer details than that of official Second Temple Judaism. It is difficult, however, to assess what significance the presence of such traditions should be given in explaining regional conditions, i.e. a Galilean attitude to impurity in particular. The uncertainties regarding the circumstances and the background of the Jewish population in Galilee make any conclusions based on the purported heritage of the Galilean people hazardous.

Archaeological and literary evidence suggests that the Galileans during the first century CE were fairly traditional and conservative, and that Pharisaic influence was not overwhelming, although the Pharisees seem to have made inroads in some of the towns. Attempts to suggest the existence of a separate Galilean *halakhah* have been largely frustrated. There is some evidence, however, for the Galileans being somewhat resistant to the payment of certain religious tithes and taxes which could be considered as recent (Pharisaic) innovations, while remaining loyal to the temple and supporting their local priests.

Galilean loyalty to Jerusalem may be explained by that city's orthogenetic function. The "urbanization" of Galilee during the Hasmonean period must be regarded largely as part of the Judaization of the province. Tensions between the mainly rural population and urban Hellenistic culture is seen above all in the relationship between the countryside and the Herodian cities of Sepphoris and Tiberias. These cities had a heterogenetic function, bringing elements of foreign culture into the heartland of Galilee. Changes of land-owning patterns and increasing indebtedness, dispossession and poverty, contributed to these tensions.

The rural population of Galilee at the end of the Second Temple period could be described as caught between two forces. The influence of the heterogenetic cities was experienced as a threat to ancient values and social structures, and represented an oppressive element. The (mainly) Pharisaic retainers of the Jerusalem tradition represented the common myth and the ethnic and religious identity. Despite the general loyalty of Galileans towards Jerusalem, however, the course of action suggested by expansionist retainers of great tradition did not meet the needs and problems of the Galilean general population. In spite of their ambitions, the Pharisees' halakhic development, with increasing demands in areas such as tithing and purity, did not provide a satisfactory solution for many who wished to remain faithful to ancestral religion, but complicated social interaction and economic relationships further.

Jesus' attitude to purity might be interpreted in view of this Galilean dilemma. It provided a way out for segments of the population, which explains Jesus' relative success in rural Galilee, as compared to the Pharisees. Jesus' attitude made it possible to regard oneself as remaining faithful to ancestral religion without compromising table fellowship or other types of social interaction, especially important at the village level. His attitude was more in line with the pragmatism of little tradition, and did not entail economic losses for the poor. His authority as a charismatic religious leader and "man of deed" was more readily recognized and accepted in a Galilean context, than that of the halakhic teachers and scribal retainers of Jerusalem tradition.

This last point has to do with his reputation as healer and exorcist. Since impurity language is sometimes used for Jesus' exorcist activity, a separate chapter must be devoted to the possible connections between this activity and his attitude to impurity.

Chapter VII
Impurity and demonic threat

What connections are there between Jesus' exorcist activity and his attitude to impurity? The very fact that demons in the Jesus tradition are frequently called "impure spirits" (τὰ πνεύματα τὰ ἀκάθαρτα), and that this expression is found in both Mark and Q,[1] makes the exorcisms of Jesus interesting in an attempt to explain his attitude to bodily impurity.

This link has, however, been dealt with by only a few exegetes. In a recent article, Bruce Chilton proposes an interpretation of Jesus' exorcisms based on a dynamic view of purity. Jesus' purity is not affected by encountering the severest impurities, but rather destroys them.[2] The idea was suggested a decade earlier by Klaus Berger, in a discussion about Jesus and early Christians as a new sort of Pharisees. Berger talks about an offensive purity/holiness, which functions in the same way as impurity, but is stronger, and thus conquers it. If Jesus saw himself as a bearer of such a purity, this would explain his contacts with impure people, and provide a background for his exorcisms, which caused conflicts with the Pharisees. This reversal of power relationships is the missing link between Jesus' eschatological message and charismatic deeds.[3]

The perspective is challenging, but left uncorroborated at large.[4] In order to suggest links between Jesus' exorcisms and his contacts with impure people, we must show that there was a demonic aspect to impurity in his contemporary cultural and religious context. While it is generally acknowledged that demon-belief and apotropaic practices lie at the roots of impurity concepts, the extent to which demonic traits survived in Jewish monotheistic religion is a matter of dispute. Since Jesus' attitude could be interpreted in line with little tradition

---

[1] The expression "impure spirit" in the singular or the plural is used predominantly by Mark (1:23, 26, 27; 3:11, 30; 5:2, 8, 13; 6:7; 7:25; 9:25), while Matthew has adopted only one of these instances (10:1), giving preference to "spirit" or "demon." Luke shows a similar tendency, although he has taken over a few more instances of the expression (4:36; 6:18; 8:29; 9:42; cf. the compound πνεῦμα δαιμονίου ἀκαθάρτου in 4:33, and the alternating use in 9:37–43). It may not be appropriate to speak of a tendency in Luke, however, since he uses the expression "impure spirit" in Acts 5:16 and 8:7. In addition to the instances originating with Mark, Matthew and Luke both retain τὸ ἀκάθαρτον πνεῦμα in the Q tradition about the returning spirit (Mt 12:43–45/Lk 11:24–26), in spite of the tendency of at least Matthew to substitute this expression for others.

[2] Chilton 1999, 234. Chilton regards purity and kingdom as intimately connected. Cf. 1996, 80f, 85f, 94f, 98ff, 112f.

[3] Berger 1988, 240–247.

[4] Chilton supplies very little evidence and seems to be unaware of Berger. Berger's evidence comes to a large extent from NT letters and later Christian literature.

and popular religion, as I suggested in the previous chapter, I find it necessary to discuss whether demonic and perhaps "non-cultic" aspects of impurity survived or resurged in Second Temple Judaism. If this was the case, it might be possible to understand Jesus' attitude to impurity in the context of his exorcisms as part of his eschatological message.

While Jesus' exorcist activity is often affirmed and interpreted eschatologically, this is by no means self-evident. I thus find it necessary to examine briefly the most prominent traditions, narratives and logia which deal with Jesus as an exorcist, placing the question of exorcism within the broader context of disease and healing miracles in Antiquity.[5] I will also discuss various interpretations of Jesus' exorcisms, suggested by scholarly reconstructions. How do exorcisms fit in with pictures of Jesus as an itinerant prophet, a Jewish Cynic or a Galilean *hasid*? What role do they play in relation to Jesus' message about the kingdom?

From this it will be possible to move forward, and suggest a relationship between Jesus' exorcisms and his attitude to impurity.

VII.1 Demonology and impurity

Demons in ancient Israel

Belief in demons and demon-possession is widely attested in the ancient world, including Palestine. No qualitative distinction was made between demons and gods, neither in the East nor in Greece, but demons were usually thought to have less power. They were often divided into classes, associated with the underworld, and pictured as living in dark, dry or desert places, or near graves. They were usually seen as being more active at night than during the day.[6]

Demons were very much part of reality for most people, and many ritual practices and magical methods were developed for protection against, and expulsion of evil spirits. Evidence for this can be found from earliest times in Mesopotamia, and can be traced in various incantation texts and apotropaic rites from the Near East and the Hellenistic sphere of influence.[7]

The demonology of the ancient world permeated Jewish culture as well, in spite of the fact that demon belief, magic and sorcery were discouraged or suppressed as part of monotheistic development. Magical practices are usually condemned in priestly literature stemming from the First Temple period or the

[5] The aim is not to deal with miracle stories as such, however. This has been done to a limited degree in Chapter IV, 91–95.
[6] Hillers, Rabinowitz and Scholem 1971, 1522.
[7] Fridrichsen 1929, 299f. Evidence can be found in e.g. Weber 1906; Thompson 1908; Weinreich 1909; *PGM* (Preisendanz, Betz); Böcher 1970; Thraede 1969; Cunningham 1997; Naveh and Shaked 1993; cf. Penney and Wise 1994, 649; 4Q560.

exile.[8] Vestiges of magical ideas and exorcist rites, such as the the bird rite for "lepers," the scapegoat, the red cow rite, the paschal sacrifice, or even circumcision, were, however, adapted and incorporated into the official purity legislation and sacrificial system.[9]

The mere existence, however, of warnings and vestiges in the normative texts of Judaism suggests that demon belief, with its ensuing magic and exorcist rites, did survive and continued to be practised as part of popular culture and spirituality. Israel was no isolated enclave, in spite of its monotheism, and suggestions that even popular religion was purged of demonic vestiges are implausible.[10] While demonology in pre-exilic and exilic Israel was "low" and not very developed in comparison with the post-exilic period, it is hardly correct to claim that it had never been suppressed, but "was simply not, in any meaningful sense, there."[11] Demonology was suppressed, demonic rites had been transformed, but various demonic individuals or classes of demons are nevertheless reflected in the Hebrew Bible;[12] in addition to evil spirits (רוּחַ רָעָה)[13] we find demons (שֵׁדִים),[14] goat demons (שָׂעִיר),[15] Lilith (לִילִית)[16] Azazel (עֲזָאזֵל),[17] Death (מָוֶת),[18] and the Destroyer (מַשְׁחִית).[19]

It is true, however, that there is not yet any systematic demonology or hierarchy of demons evident in the Hebrew Bible. Demonology developed considerably in the post-exilic period, probably due to Persian influence.[20] This is evident in literature from the Second Temple period, such as *1 Enoch*, *Jubilees*, and the *Community Rule*, which provide an etiology of demons and subordinate the demons to the authority of Belial (Satan), thus integrating them into a Jewish world-view.[21] Several Qumran fragments give evidence for a more devel-

---

[8] Ex 22:17; Lev 20:27; Num 23:23; Dt 18:9–14; Ez 13:17–23. Cf. Thraede 1969, 56f; Kollmann 1996, 118f.

[9] Lev 14:4–7; Lev 16; Num 19; Ex 12; Kaufmann 1960 [1937–1948], 101–115. The exception is the rite of the heifer whose neck is broken (Deut 21:1–9), which is not incorporated into the cultic system; the priests are barely squeezed into the tradition, but they remain mere spectators. Examples of what are often considered as apotropaic details or rites within the sacrificial cult are bells on the High Priest's robe, altar horns, incense, the smearing of doorposts, blue colour, phylacteries. Cf. Hillers, Rabinowitz and Scholem 1971, 1524.

[10] Cf. Kaufmann 1960 [1937–1948], 313f.

[11] Alexander 1999, 351.

[12] Cf. Annen 1976a, 139; Hillers, Rabinowitz and Scholem 1971, 1523f.

[13] Judg 9:23; 1Sam 16:14–16, 23; 18:10; 19:9.

[14] Deut 32:17; Ps 106:37.

[15] Lev 17:7; 2Chr 11:15; Isa 13:21; 34:14.

[16] Isa 34:14.

[17] Lev 16:8, 10, 26.

[18] Isa 28:15, 18; Jer 9:20. Cf. Mot, the Canaanite underworld god.

[19] Ex 12:23; 2Sam 24:15–17; 1Chr 21:14–17. For more suggestions, like Plague, Pestilence, Terror, Arrow, or Destruction, see Hillers, Rabinowitz and Scholem 1971, 1524.

[20] Annen 1976a, 139; Alexander 1999, 351.

[21] Cf. Alexander 1999, 337–347.

oped classification of demons, explicitly listing them, as in 4Q510: "all the spirits of the ravaging angels and the bastard spirits, demons, Lilith, owls and [jackals ...] and those who strike unexpectedly."[22] Another list, although fairly damaged, is found in the incantation formula 4Q560:

> "the midwife, the chastisement of girls. Evil visitor ... [...] [...who] enters the flesh, the male penetrator and the female penetrator [...] ... iniquity and guilt; fever and chills, and heat of the heart [...] in sleep, he who crushes the male and she who passes through the female, those who dig [...w]icked [...]"[23]

The lists are somewhat vague and the demonic world of Qumran is not as developed as that of later Jewish, Christian or pagan magical texts.[24] They nevertheless represent an advance as compared with what is found in the Hebrew Bible, and they are evidence for a fairly developed demonology being part of the Jewish world-view at the end of the Second Temple period.

Healing and exorcism

Demons in Antiquity were among other things thought to cause sickness, and were sometimes given the names of various diseases, such as Fever or Headache.[25] That this was the case in Second Temple Judaism as well is evident from 4Q560, in which Fever and Chills are personified as demonic beings.

Demons were also thought to possess people. This was a well-known phenomenon in Jesus' environment.[26] Some scholars want to uphold a clear distinction between demon possession and diseases.[27] Possession is seen as caused by demons entering a person's body and taking over his/her personality, and thus had to be treated by exorcism. Disease is often seen as caused by demons too, but the effect is in some sense external; the demon is not considered to inhabit the sick person, and sick people are thus at times healed but not exorcized.

The distinction seems neat and simple, but in reality the categories are somewhat overlapping. This is seen in Josephus, in the passage about Solomon's wisdom (*Ant.* 8:45), in which he seemingly mixes exorcist and therapeu-

---

[22] 4Q510 1 5–6 (כול רוחי מלאכי חבל ורוחות ממזרים שדאים לילית אחים ו[ציים ...] והפוגעים פתע פתאום); cf. 4Q511 10 1–2. In 4Q511 1 6 we find the Destroyer (משחית) and evil spirits (רוחי רשע).

[23] 4Q560 1 1:2–6 (וילדתה מרדות ילדן פקד באיש ש[...] [...דין] עלל בבשרא לחלחיא דכרא וחלחלית נקבתא [...]רא עואן ופשע אשא ועריה ואשת לבב [...]ה בשנא פרך דכר ופכית נקבתא מחתורי). For a slightly different reconstruction and translation, in which Fever, Chills and Chest Pain are taken as proper names of demons, see Penney and Wise 1994, 631ff. Another list of demons apparently preceded the extant fragment 11Q11 2. No details are yet available about 4Q230 and 4Q231 (4Q Catalogue of spirits a and b).

[24] Cf. *T.Sol.*; *bBer* 6a; *bPes* 110a–112b. Cf. Hillers, Rabinowitz and Scholem 1971, 1526ff.

[25] Hillers, Rabinowitz and Scholem 1971, 1522.

[26] Cf. Josephus' on Eleazar, the *Babylonian Talmud* on R.Simeon ben Yose and Philostratus on Apollonius of Tyana, as well as gospel references to Jewish exorcists. See below, 310, 323f.

[27] Cf. Theissen 1983 [1974], 85–94.

tic language. Even if the text is read so as to speak separately about illnesses (τὰ νοσήματα) and possessions (οἱ ἐνδούμενοι τὰ δαιμόνια), illnesses are relieved by incantations (ἐπῳδάς), which suggest healing methods closely related to exorcism. Similarly, in the Jesus tradition, diseases are sometimes described in language close to that of possession,[28] and exorcist language is used in healing.[29] This is congruent with the evidence of 4Q560, in which demons are named according to specific diseases and conceived of as entering the body, after which something like an exorcist formula follows, apparently for the purpose of curing the disease in question.[30] "With regard to the Gospels," say Penney and Wise, "this incantation poses the question whether 'exorcism' and 'healing' were truly distinguished in the minds of the evangelists."[31]

The problem could be exemplified by one of the traditions central to the present study, Mk 1:40–45, in which the phrase καὶ ἐμβριμησάμενος αὐτῷ εὐθὺς ἐξέβαλεν αὐτὸν could be seen as a vestige of an exorcism, referring to the impure spirit causing leprosy, rather than to the "leper," meaning "and rebuking him, he cast him out immediately."[32] The term ἐμβριμησάμενος would then have a similar function and meaning here to ἐπετίμησεν in the preceding exorcism narrative (1:25).[33] The underlying presupposition is a view in which "leprosy" would have been regarded as caused by demonic powers, possibly even as a type of possession. The story of Pharaoh being afflicted by a "purulent" or possibly "peeling" spirit in the *Genesis Apocryphon* might suggest some type of skin disorder.[34]

This possibility is strengthened by the regulations for "lepers" found in the 4Q versions of the *Damascus Document*, in which a spirit is involved in producing the symptoms of "leprosy" by entering the body and taking hold of the artery.[35] The passages are admittedly obscure, but do fit the idea of leprosy as having some sort of demonic cause, which is suggested by the prescribed bird rite.[36] It is not always possible to separate disease fully from possession or impurity.[37]

---

[28] E.g. Lk 13:11: "γυνὴ πνεῦμα ἔχουσα ἀσθενείας."
[29] Cf the use of ἐπιτιμᾶν not only in exorcist stories but also in Mk 4:39 and Lk 4:39. Cf. Kee 1967–1968.
[30] The text of 4Q560 1 1 is quoted above. There is a trace of an exorcist formula in column 2: "And I, O spirit, adjure [...] I enchant you, O spirit, (ואנה רוח מומה [...] אומיתך רוחא).
[31] Penney and Wise 1994, 650.
[32] For a more extensive discussion about the terminology, see above, 103f.
[33] Cf. Kee's suggestion that ἐμβριμᾶσθαι, just like ἐπιτιμᾶν, can function as a Greek equivalent of the Hebrew גער. Kee 1967–68, 238, n.2.
[34] The spirit is characterized as רוח שחלניא (1QapGen 20:26). Cf. Klutz 1999, 157.
[35] 4Q266 6 1:5–7; 4Q269 7 1–3; 4Q272 1 1:1–3.
[36] Cf. suggestions by Maccoby 1999, 125. The bird rite is further discussed below, 307.
[37] Cf. Mt 10:7–8, where healing, purification and exorcism are listed together with proclamation of the kingdom.

Impurity and exorcism in the Israelite cult

Turning from disease to impurity, we must ask whether there is a similar relationship to demon possession. While impurity is not equal to possession, and purification not equal to exorcism, could it be that at least in certain cases or contexts impurity was conceived of as caused by demons, and dealt with in manners reminiscent of exorcism? This is very likely, as will be seen below.

Most scholars agree that the Israelite cult contained a number of pagan vestiges, i.e. traits of rituals with an original magic or apotropaic function, often associated with the fear of demons. The most important of these vestiges, which have, or may have, significance for the question of impurity, are the bird rite for "lepers," the scapegoat, the red cow rite, and the calf whose neck is broken.[38] There seems to be some basic agreement, too, that these vestiges were to some degree neutralized and transformed by Israelite monotheism. Opinions differ, however, about the extent of this process. This is to some degree a sensitive issue, because it touches the nerve of Israelite faith. A prominent example is provided by Yehezkel Kaufmann, who gives numerous examples of pagan vestiges, aimed at protection or warding off demonic threat, including the system of impurity.[39] Even the *hattat* offering was originally

> not a propitiatory offering to the deity, but an exorcising sacrifice directed toward the domain of evil and impurity. The connection of the *ḥaṭṭāth* with various sorts of maladies suggests also that in prebiblical times it had a role in priestly therapeusis, like Babylonian therapeutic sacrifices.[40]

According to Kaufmann, "[t]he magical elements … were most difficult to refashion," and Israel's cult "retained magical features, so deeply rooted as to defy extirpation." Nevertheless he claims at the same time that "[a]ll was reformed and brought into harmony with the new idea. The cult laws of the Bible have no mythological or magic background." "In contrast to the pagan conception impurity is in itself not a source of danger; its divine-demonic roots have been totally destroyed."[41]

These statements are somewhat contradictory, and although most would agree with Kaufmann that Israelite monotheism thoroughly transformed rituals with a pagan background, the amazing amount of magic and apotropaic demonic vestiges that can be found in spite of heavy monotheistic redaction of the

---

[38] These rites are all performed outside the temple and the camp. Cf. Maccoby 1999, 83ff, who suggests that while these outside rites have something anomalous and primitive about them, only those which resulted in impurity for the participants (i.e. the red cow rite and the scapegoat) had demonic origins, while the rite of the calf whose neck is broken did not. The idea is implausible, however, since the bird rite breaks the pattern; it does not render those who administer it unclean, but it shares the exorcistic traits of the scapegoat and the red cow rite.

[39] Kaufmann 1960 [1937–1948], 104ff, mentions among other things, the scapegoat, the ban on the sinew of the thigh vein, prohibited foods, the paschal blood on doorposts and circumcision.

[40] Kaufmann 1960 [1937–1948], 113.

[41] Kaufmann 1960 [1937–1948], 102, 103.

texts should suggest a considerable degree of survival. In his somewhat apologetic attempt to show the uniqueness of Israelite religion, Kaufmann actually provides much evidence for demonic vestiges.

Baruch Levine discusses a number of such vestiges, but comes to quite a different conclusion: there was no prohibition against therapeutic magic in Israelite religion, but we find rather an "interplay of magical, ritual, legal and administrative factors operative in the cultic institutions of ancient Israel."[42] Levine regrets that "there has been a tendency to minimize the extent of active magical components in the public cult of Israel as portrayed in the priestly sources of the Bible," and continues:

> To us it is clear that the distinctive objectives of magical activity and those of the cult, proper, converged in pursuit of the common end of eliminating destructive or demonic forces identified as the sources of impurity, and viewed as the matrix of sinfulness and offense to the deity.[43]

Milgrom seems to take a middle position, claiming that "the world of demons is abolished" in priestly theology, but "Israel's battle against demonic beliefs was not won in one stroke ... it was a gradual process."[44] Milgrom sees evidence for this in the progressive reduction of contagious impurity as well as holiness through different strata. I am not fully convinced of this evolutionary outline, but think that we should rather look for different co-existing trajectories.[45] It is reasonable to suggest that demonic and non-cultic aspects of impurity did survive and live on, partly in official and priestly circles, but mainly in popular tradition and practice.

One piece of evidence for such an interpretation is the Qumran fragment 4Q274, which implies the view that an existing impurity is increased by contact with other impurities greater in strength. Milgrom suggests that this reveals a dynamic (and, taken together with the fact that the forces of Belial are ascribed impurity, even a demonic) concept of impurity, in which impurity was held to be autonomous and dangerous.[46] While such views could be seen as (re)emerging, beginning with the period of Persian influence, I would suggest that they had survived, although to various degrees, throughout the First Temple period both in official and popular tradition.[47] This explains the retention of certain rites with exorcistic traits.

---

[42] B. Levine 1974, 91.

[43] B. Levine 1974, 55f.

[44] Milgrom 1995, 43, 44.

[45] Cf. Milgrom's explanation of Ez 44:19 and 46:20 which do not follow the evolutionary pattern according to which the contagious power of sancta should have been reduced: "Clearly, this ... was not accepted by all Priestly schools." (Milgrom 1991, 45).

[46] Milgrom 1995, 66. This is in contrast to the rabbinic non-dynamic view.

[47] If P has a ritual pollution based on a limited concept of sanctuary holiness, and H has a non-ritualistic pollution based on a dynamic concept of holiness for all Israel (cf. Milgrom 1991, 48f), perhaps H's view of purity may be seen as based on an earlier non-cultic (demonic) understanding. P has limited and de-demonized an earlier view of impurity, because of monotheism,

One such example is the bird rite prescribed for the purification of "lepers" and "leprous" buildings in Lev 14: 1–7, 49–53. The rite is performed by a priest, but the introduction in v 4 (וְצִוָּה הַכֹּהֵן וְלָקַח לַמִּטַּהֵר) might indicate that the priest has been added to a tradition that originally had none.[48] Except for the priest, the rite is not adapted to the cult at all, but represents earlier pagan practice. The red wool and cedar wood, known from Mesopotamian purification rites, are used to sprinkle the blood of the slaughtered bird, mixed with water, on the patient, in order to reverse the death process. This is in contrast to sacrificial blood, which was sprinkled only on items. The living bird, which is also dipped in the red water, carries the impurity away. It must be wild, lest it return and bring the impurity back.[49] Suggesting that the rite was originally accompanied by incantations, Milgrom states:

> The Priestly tradition, as we now see, has incorporated an older exorcistic rite, and though it serves no practical function at all—the patient has already been healed and the residual impurity is eliminated by the subsequent ablutions ...—it stands as the indispensable beginning of an eight-day purificatory rite, because the people, not the priests, have demanded it. ... it was retained not because Israel's priests wanted it but probably because the people at large demanded it, practiced it, and would not have tolerated its deletion. For them this rite of exorcism was indispensable.[50]

Another example with similar details is the red cow rite (Num 19) in which a red cow is burnt outside the camp, again together with red wool, cedar wood and hyssop. The ashes are collected and mixed with water, to be used for sprinkling corpse impure people. It is clear from the biblical text that the priest's role is minimal and symbolic. He is supposed to supervise the slaughter and burning, but not take part in it himself (19:3, 5).[51] He should also sprinkle some of the blood in the direction of the sanctuary and throw the accessories on the fire. The red cow rite, however, is said to be a *hattat* sacrifice, in contrast to the bird rite, which was not considered a sacrifice until the time of the *Babylonian Talmud*.[52] Milgrom has shown how the red cow rite has been transformed into a *hattat* from having been a rite of exorcism, analogous to Mesopotamian rituals. It is treated like a burnt *hattat*, defiling its handlers but purifying its recipients. There are some anomalies, however. The ashes are sprinkled primarily on

---

and H widened the concept, taking up an earlier trajectory, but retaining monotheism. On a popular level the demonic traits survived and remained all the time.

[48] It should be noted that while the *Mishnah* (*mNeg* 14) seemingly takes for granted that the priest performs the whole ceremony, the *Tosefta* and the *Sifra* both restrict the role of the priest (*tNeg* 8:5; *Sifra* to Lev 14:2–4 [Sifra Parashat Mesora Parashah 1]. For a discussion, see J. Schwartz 2000, 218f.

[49] Milgrom 1991, 832–839.

[50] Milgrom 1991, 837–838.

[51] The priestly supervising is explained by Milgrom (1981, 65f) from the need to prevent the ritual from slipping "back into pagan moorings."

[52] *bArak* 15b. See J. Schwartz 2000, 217f.

persons, as in the case of the bird rite. The priest's sprinkling of some blood *in the direction of* the Sanctuary seems a somewhat forced adaption to the *hattat.*[53]

The non-priestly or non-sacrificial character of the red cow rite is seen in the fact that during the Second Temple period minors were used in preparing the ashes and for sprinkling,[54] something that was opposed by the Qumran sectarians, who considered the whole red cow rite a priestly matter, effecting expiation (כפרה).[55] This implies that as late as at the end of the Second Temple period, the red cow rite had not been fully incorporated into the sacrificial system. The demonic association is acknowledged in rabbinic literature, in a discussion attributed to Yohanan ben Zakkai, and the rabbinic uneasiness with this idea is apparent.[56]

The anomalies in the bird rite and the red cow rite suggest a background in which "leprosy" and corpse impurity were considered dangerous, independently of the sacrificial cult, and the result of demonic hostilities, perhaps even as forms of possession, requiring various exorcistic riddance rites. Another cow rite (the calf whose neck is broken, Deut 21:1–9) might originally have been associated with corpse impurity too. This rite is totally independent of the cult, and the sudden mention of the priests (v 5), together with a defence for their participation, although they are given no role whatsoever in the subsequent description, suggest that this is a matter of redactional insertion at a fairly late stage.[57] The rite itself is used in case of bloodshed when the perpetrator is unknown. The elders of the nearest town should take a calf to a ravine and break its neck, wash their hands over it, assure their innocence and pray for expiation, that no blood-guilt should rest on them.[58]

The scapegoat ritual (Lev 16), however, is much more integrated into the cultic system, in spite of clear signs of pagan origins. The similarity of this rite with the bird rite for the purification of "lepers" is evident: one of a pair of animals is slaughtered for the purification of the people, and the impurities are transferred to the other animal which is chased away into uninhabited areas not to return. Removing communal impurity by transferring it to an animal wich is dispatched or killed was common in ancient religions. The scapegoat rite has

---

[53] Milgrom 1981.

[54] *mPar* 3:2–4; *Barn.* 8:1.

[55] 4Q276, 4Q277. J. Baumgarten 1995b.

[56] *Pesiq. Rab Kah.* 4:7. The passage is discussed below, 312.

[57] "And the priests shall approach, the sons of Levi, because the LORD, your God, has chosen them to serve him and to bless in the name of the LORD, and according to their command shall be every dispute and all violence" (Deut 21:5).

[58] Cf. above, 215, n.71, about the possible connection between bloodshed, corpse impurity and defilement of the land. Milgrom 1971b suggests that the pollution of the land caused by bloodshed is transferred to an uncultivated area. For a different view see Maccoby 1999, 92f. Maccoby thinks that the purpose of the rite is to free the locality from guilt, not from impurity. This presupposes a sharp distinction between the two, however.

been incorporated into the Day of Atonement ritual with its sacrifices of a bull and a ram, but it is explicitly and openly revealed as having to do with demons; the living goat is chased away to the desert-demon Azazel (Lev 16:8, 26).[59] The person who chases the goat away becomes unclean in the process, which might be explained as an effect of his transaction with the demon Azazel.[60]

Both goats are called *hattat*,[61] although the goat for Azazel is no sacrifice. It might be so called because of its function, to remove sin, but it is more likely that the designation is part of the incorporation of a pagan rite into the Israelite sacrificial system.[62] The statement in Lev 16:10 that "the scapegoat shall be stationed alive before the LORD to perform expiation upon it" seems to give the scapegoat a prominent place in the atonement process. It is possible, however that the phrase לְכַפֵּר עָלָיו is best explained as an interpolation or as a result of this incorporation.[63] The tensions in the text reveal that originally the scapegoat was not a sacrifice either to God or Azazel, nor did it originally eliminate the sins of the people, but instead it was a vehicle for transporting demonic impurities to where they belonged, i.e. to the desert and its demon, analogous to the bird rite for "lepers."[64]

Traces of exorcizing impurity are not only found in non-sacrificial rites. Kaufmann suggests that even the *hattat* sacrifice itself was originally "not a propitiatory offering to the deity, but an exorcising sacrifice directed toward the domain of evil and impurity."[65] This is in line with the translation of *hattat* as

---

[59] Azazel should be identified as a demon. Cf. *1Enoch* 10:4–5. The *Temple Scroll* read Azazel (עזאזל) as עזזאל (11Q19 [11QT] 26:13), i.e. "fierce god." For a discussion about the name and evidence of a demonic referent, see Milgrom 1991, 1020f. Cf. Maccoby 1999, 85ff.

[60] Maccoby 1999, 85. This would also apply to the red cow rite, and imply a demonic background. The idea is plausible. From this we cannot conclude, however, that the other outside rites, i.e. the bird rite and the calf whose neck is broken, did not share that background, just because their participants were not rendered unclean. Why should we expect the same vestige to have survived in all of these rites?

[61] Lev 16:5, 9, 10.

[62] Milgrom 1991, 1018.

[63] Kiuchi thinks that the Azazel goat ritual is the "climax of the Israelite system of atonement ceremonies." Kiuchi 1987, 164. If this were so, the rite should have been more thoroughly transformed and adapted to the priestly sacrificial system. The rabbinic uneasiness with the rite, and the prophetic and rabbinic emphasis on repentance as that which really atones, suggest that the scapegoat was not the climax, but a vestige. Cf. Maccoby 1999, 89f.

The interpretation of the phrase לְכַפֵּר עָלָיו is disputed. B. Levine translates "to perform rites of expiation besides it" (B. Levine 1974, 80), while Milgrom argues for "to perform expiation upon it" (Milgrom 1991, 1023). Different translations depend on how the verb כפר is understood together with various prepositions. For different interpretations cf. B. Levine 1974, 56–77; Maccoby 1999, 175–179. Cf. above, 212f. This is a detailed and technical discussion which cannot be entered into here. Regardless of the exact interpretation, the difficulty of interpreting expiation in relation to the scapegoat suggests that it has been accommodated into a system where it originally did not fit.

[64] Cf. Milgrom 1991, 1023f, 1044.

[65] Kaufmann 1960 [1937–1948], 113.

"purification offering," and the observation that the *hattat* is prescribed as part of the purification ritual for almost all cases of defilement.[66] Likewise the verb *kipper* (the *piel* form כִּפֶּר), which came to denote expiation in general, seems to have developed from an original meaning of "purification" as a concrete rubbing off of dangerous impurity.[67] It seems that "expiation" had its roots in apotropaic practices, using blood for the protection not only of worshippers, but of the deity and his surroundings, from demonic threat.[68]

Impurity and demons in Second Temple Judaism

We have seen that numerous vestiges of purificatory and apotropaic rites remained even within the official cultic texts and practices of ancient Israel. Among these, there are rites dealing with "leprosy" and corpse impurity, which have exorcistic traits, implying that these impurities were regarded as caused by demonic powers, which must be somehow driven away and prevented from returning. It is reasonable to suggest that such beliefs and attitudes survived in little tradition, even during periods of suppression by official religion.

During the Second Temple period, demonology developed, and demon-belief and possessions are well attested in Jewish sources.[69] The development continued to the extent that Jewish spells and divine names or attributes were frequently used by pagan miracle workers in the Hellenistic world.[70]

Examples of outright possession and exorcism are not as numerous as references to demon-belief in general, but suffice to establish that this was part of a Jewish first-century context. While texts about Apollonius of Tyana or R.Simeon ben Yose come from the third and perhaps fourth century CE, both text and content in Josephus' story about the exorcist Eleazar come from the first century.[71] The presence of Jewish exorcists during this period is also attested by Mark (Mk 9:38–40/Lk 9:49–50), Q (Mt 12:27/Lk 11:19) and Acts (Acts 19:13–16).[72]

In view of the increase in demonology and exorcistic practice evidenced during the Second Temple period, it is likely that demonic associations were part of

---

[66] Cf. above, 211–214.

[67] Milgrom 1991, 1079–1084; cf. B. Levine 1974, 56–63.

[68] Cf. B. Levine 1974, 73f.

[69] 1Sam 16:14–23; Tob 3:7–17; 6–8; 1QapGen 20; 4Q242; 4Q510; 4Q511; 4Q560; *Ant.* 6:166–169; 8:45–48. For a thorough discussion of these and other textual evidence, see Trunk 1994, 242–318. Later texts, such as rabbinic material concerning Hanina ben Dosa as well as the *Testament of Solomon*, are discussed below. Examples of exorcism from the so-called *New Testament Apocrypha*, such as the *Acts of Peter* or the *Acts of Andrew*, will not be discussed at all, because of their late date and special tendency. They possibly reflect conditions of neither their own time, nor that of the apostles. For a consideration, see Twelftree 1993, 19ff.

[70] *PGM* 1:297–347; 4:1496–1595; 5:96–172; 12:264. Cf. Trunk 1994, 391–410.

[71] Philostratus *Vit.Apoll.* 4:20. *bMeil* 17b. *Ant.* 8:45–48.

[72] Cf. Trunk 1994, 298–374, for a discussion of Hellenistic and rabbinic exorcist stories.

popular attitudes to certain types of impurity. Jesus' exorcisms not only fit well into the environment, but their interpretation as battles against impurity becomes the more plausible when some contemporary texts are taken into account. While no explicit impurity connotations can be found in Josephus' account of the exorcist Eleazar,[73] certain Qumran fragments attest a conceptual link between possession, disease and impurity, as well as sin.

The "blending" of disease and impurity in certain Qumran texts has already been noted.[74] The demonic aspect is evident in 11Q5 19:13–16:[75]

סלחה y h w h לחטאתי וטהרני מעווני רוח אמונה ודעת חונני אל אתקלה
בעויה אל תשלט בי שטן ורוח טמאה מכאוב ויצר רע אל ירשו בעצמי

> Forgive my sin, YHWH, and cleanse me from my iniquity. Bestow upon me a spirit of faith and knowledge. Let me not stumble in trangression. Let not Satan rule over me, nor an evil [impure] spirit; let neither pain nor evil purpose take possession of my bones.

Obviously, physical disease, moral weakness and impurity are paralleled and seen to be caused by demonic powers, i.e. impure spirits.[76] Says Menahem Kister:

> The lack of discrimination between the "spiritual" dominion of evil spirits (with the result of committing sins) and bodily disease in this passage is not surprising when considered against the background of demonology and magic, as noted above; the combination of the belief that illness is the result of sin and that it is caused by demons contributes to the equation of sin with demons.[77]

From this perspective, Kister argues that conversion could be understood in exorcist terms. Those outside the sect were seen as possessed by evil sprits, while those inside were protected, as in the following text from the *War Scroll*:

ורוחי [ח]בלו גערתה ממ[נו ובהתרשע אנ]שי ממשלתו שמ̄תה נפש פדותכה

> You have chased away from [us] his spirits of [de]struction, [when the m]en of his dominion [acted wickedly] you protected the soul of your redeemed ones.[78]

If joining the sect, i.e. conversion or salvation, was understood as a kind of exorcism, several texts could be seen to fit into such a conception. Kister suggests that this is the *Sitz im Leben* for the fragments of 4Q 510–511 and 4Q444.[79] A similar frame of reference is found in early Christianity too, as outsiders were

---

[73] *Ant.* 8:45–48; see below, 323f.
[74] Cf. 4Q560; 4Q266 6; 4Q269 7; 4Q272. Se above, 302–304.
[75] The text belongs to a fragment of Psalms, mostly based on canonical Psalms, but in part extracanonical. Flusser assigns the text to the type or genre of "Jewish 'apotropaic' prayers" (Flusser 1966, 201, 203, 205).
[76] Cf. 11Q5 24:11–13. Kister 1999, 170. Note רוח טמאה in spite of García Martínez's translation "evil spirit."
[77] Kister 1999, 170.
[78] 1QM 14:10.
[79] Kister 1999, 172–176. 4Q 510–511 have been referred to above, 303 and n.22. They consist of hymnic material of apotropaic character. 4Q444 has the character of confession or incantation.

considered impure and belonging to demons,[80] and baptism acquired the character of exorcism.[81] At the same time, the Christian water rite, like the ablutions of the Qumran sectarians, was perceived as a method of purification.[82] The link between demons and impurity seems to be present below the surface, even when it is not made explicitly.

This link *is* made explicit in the admittedly late tradition about Yohanan ben Zakkai and the gentile discussing the red cow rite.

> A heathen questioned Rabban Yohanan ben Zakkai, saying: The things you Jews do appear to be a kind of sorcery. A heifer is brought, it is burned, is pounded into ash, and its ash is gathered up. Then when one of you gets defiled by contact with a corpse, two or three drops of the ash mixed with water are sprinkled upon him, and he is told, "Your are cleansed!" Rabban Johanan asked the heathen: "Has the spirit of madness ever possessed you?" He replied: "No." "Have you ever seen a man whom the spirit of madness has possessed?" The heathen replied: "Yes." "And what do you do for such a man?" "Roots are brought, the smoke of their burning is made to rise about him, and water is sprinkled upon him until the spirit of madness flees." Rabban Yoḥanan then said: "Do not your ears hear what your mouth is saying? It is the same with a man who is defiled by contact with a corpse—he, too, is possessed by a spirit, the spirit of uncleanness, and, [as of madness], Scripture says: *I will cause [false] prophets as well as the spirit of uncleanness to flee from the land*' (Zech. 13:2).[83]

The story continues with the astonishment of Yohanan's disciples at the answer, which causes Yohanan to explain that neither impurity nor purification have any intrinsic power, but are dependent only on the decree of God. This is interesting in itself, but for our purpose the link between impurity and demon possession is crucial. While the tradition does not *argue* for an equation, it attests to such a link being natural to common people at the time and within the context in which the tradition originated and/or was transmitted. We must conclude that impurity and demon possession were closely associated in popular tradition, and, whether or not it was accepted by the Rabbis, purification was conceived of as a kind of exorcism.

It was previously suggested that corpse impurity as well as "leprosy" had been, in popular understanding, associated with demonic powers since ancient times. While the rabbinic tradition about Yohanan is fairly late, the Qumran fragments suggesting that "leprosy" was caused by a demon moving in the arteries[84] come from the Second Temple period. There is reason to think that the link between impurity and demon possession was common in Jesus' day. This causes Todd Klutz to question the dominant definition of demon possession:

---

[80] 1Cor 7:14. In *Barn.* 16:7, the heart of the unbeliever is described as a "house of demons" (οἶκος δαιμονίων). Cf. Gal 4:3. Kister 1999, 176.
[81] E.g. *Acts Paul* [*Acts of Paul and Thecla*] 25; *Ps.-Clem. Rec.* 4:17; Tertullian, *Bapt.* 9. Cf. Kister 1999, 177f; Cf. Böcher 1972, 170–180.
[82] E.g. Eph 5:26. For a discussion of Qumran water rites, see above, 235–243.
[83] *Pesiq. Rab Kah.* 4:7. (Braude and Kapstein 1975, 82.)
[84] 4Q266 6 1:5–13; 4Q269 7 1–8; 4Q272 1 1:1–8. Cf. above, 304.

> this intersection of demonology and impurity raises serious questions about what exactly the demonic afflictions were that Jesus healed. Among other things, it points toward some interesting alternatives to the massively problematic, but still widely accepted, hypothesis that the demoniacs healed by Jesus were seriously damaged psychotics, victims of multiple personality syndrome, or sufferers of comparably serious mental disorders. In view of the nexus between demons and impurity in the assumed cosmology, might not the clients healed by Jesus' exorcistic interventions be better understood as sufferers of common skin diseases and urogenital disorders. The clients suffered from ailments which in most cases would not have been physically debilitating in themselves. But, since they required their victims to be excluded from the cult and healthy society, they may well have nurtured the micro-social processes of demonization and deviance-labeling that ultimately create demoniacs.[85]

Klutz's suggestion is interesting, but difficult to prove. It opens up the possibility, however, that the various unspecific gospel references to possessed people, such as the dumb (and blind) man in Q (Mt 12:22/Lk 11:14) or Mary Magdalene (Lk 8:2), do not necessarily imply that these people were maniacs, but might relate to certain conditions involving impurity. Likewise, the injunction to expel demons in Jesus' commission to the disciples (Mt 10:8), is not necessarily to be interpreted as a separate category, but might be seen as including the preceding charges: to heal the sick, raise the dead and cleanse the "lepers." It seems as if exorcism and purification partly overlapped conceptually.

VII.2 Jesus as exorcist

Traditions about Jesus' exorcisms

Most scholars agree that Jesus did perform acts which were considered by his contemporaries as successful exorcisms.[86] This is based on the facts that exorcism is the most common single category in the miracle traditions ascribed to Jesus, that exorcisms are attested in multiple sources (Mark, Q, L, and M?), and that the words of Jesus and the narratives about his exorcisms are coherent.[87]

[85] Klutz 1999, 162.

[86] Cf. Pesch 1970b, 20f; Annen 1976b, 112–115. The picture is not coherent, however. Dunn (1988, 29ff) criticizes Sanders (1985, 133–141, 165ff) for paying too little attention to Jesus' reputation as an exorcist.

[87] There are six narrative traditions about Jesus' exorcisms in the Synoptic Gospels (depending on how one counts. The Fourth Gospel does not mention exorcisms at all; but cf. Broadhead 1995). These include four Markan traditions (Mk 1:21–28/Lk 4:31–37; Mk 5:1–20/Mt 8:28–34/Lk 8:26–39; Mk 7:24–30/Mt 15:21–28; Mk 9:14–29/Mt 17:14–21/Lk 9:37–43), one Q tradition (Mt 12:22–23/Lk 11:14), and one Matthean doublet (Mt 9:32–34). The most important logia are found in the "Beelzebul-controversy" (Mk 3:22–30/Mt 12:22–32/Lk 11:14–23), for which we must assume both a Markan and a Q source (for a detailed discussion, see Boring 1992). The logion in Lk 13:32 presumably comes from Luke's special source. Finally Jesus' exorcisms are mentioned in a number of summaries (Mk 1:32–34/Mt 8:16/Lk 4:40–41; Mk 3:7–12/Mt 4:24–25/Lk 6:17–19; Lk 7:21; Lk 8:1–3) which shows their importance in the minds of

The stories about Jesus' acts of exorcism have been widely regarded as creative compositions based on an historical generalized memory of Jesus as an exorcist, while the details of individual narratives are impossible to verify. If exorcism played such a prominent role in Jesus' activity, it is reasonable to suppose, however, that some individual narratives partly reflect historical circumstances.[88] Meier makes an attempt to evaluate the various narratives and proposes an historical background for the possessed boy (Mk 9:14–29 par), the reference to Mary Magdalene (Lk 8:2), and probably for the Gerasene demoniac as well (Mk 5:1–20 par). In addition, the stories about the demoniac in the Capernaum synagogue (Mk 1:23–28 par) and the mute demoniac in the Q tradition (Mt 12:22–23/Lk 11:14) may carry historical reminiscences.[89]

The criterion of embarrassment can be applied both to the general claim that Jesus was an exorcist and to individual traditions. Jesus was apparently accused by some of his adversaries of expelling demons with the help of the prince of demons (Mk 3:22 par), and such accusations were subsequently developed in rabbinic and pagan polemics into the idea of Jesus practising magic and sorcery.[90] There would have been no good reason to include such accusations in the gospels were they not deeply rooted in historical memory.

Similarly, a number of individual narratives contain embarrassing details, which are best explained as having some historical basis: the inability of the disciples to exorcize the possessed boy (Mk 9:18) and the previous exorcism of Mary Magdalene (Lk 8:2) who is subsequently portrayed as a witness to the resurrection. The dialogue between Jesus and the legion of spirits possessing the Gerasene demoniac (Mk 5:9–13) results in something like a concession, and could thus be interpreted as a sign of Jesus' limited power. It is less likely that such embarrassing details were invented off-hand by the church.[91]

The exorcism narratives constitute one of the traditional classes of miracle stories.[92] The historical problems related to the form of miracle stories have been dealt with above, and I have argued that parallels in structure or subject matter do not automatically disqualify miracle traditions as possible bearers of

---

the synoptic authors. Cf. Annen 1976b, 108–112; Meier 1994, 646–677. In addition to traditions about Jesus' own exorcisms, his disciples are pictured as being sent on a mission, in which exorcism seems to have had the prime of place (Mk 6:7/Mt 10:1, 7/Lk 9:1; Lk 10:17–20).

[88] Blackburn 1994, 365. Cf. Fuller 1963, 32; Perrin 1967, 136f; Pesch 1976, 125.

[89] Meier 1994, 646–661. According to Meier, the two latter stories may also be literary creations, based on Jesus' typical activity.

[90] Meier 1994, 406; a number of rabbinic and pagan texts are provided by Morton Smith 1981 [1978], 45–67, and Geller 1977.

[91] Another argument based on the criterion of embarrassment has to do with what Theissen and Merz call "the retreat of exorcisms." Exorcism narratives are not found in the Pauline, Johannine and Thomas traditions, since they could cause various types of difficulties in these contexts (Theissen and Merz 1998 [1996], 299). For a list of more evidence for the essential historicity of Jesus' exorcisms, see Aune 1980, 1525f.

[92] E.g. Bultmann 1972 [1921], 218–244, esp. 231–232.

historical memories.[93] In the case of exorcism stories specifically, Bultmann's traditional genre description must be questioned. It has even been suggested that the scheme of such a *Gattung* would of necessity force itself onto the Jesus tradition.[94] Annen has shown, however, that such a fixed scheme as is often presupposed, did not yet exist generally during the first century CE. While it is possible to speak of a literary genre of exorcisms *within* the New Testament (i.e. in the Synoptics and Acts), comparative material earlier than or contemporary with the New Testament is limited, and contains single elements, but nothing like the scheme of Bultmann. Something similar is found outside the New Testament in later texts, many of which are likely to be dependent on the New Testament to some degree. Hence it is questionable to adduce these texts against the historical value of the traditions about Jesus' exorcisms.[95]

The traditions of Jesus as an exorcist rest on firm historical ground, in the sense that Jesus was remembered as having liberated possessed people from impure spirits. As for the evaluation of the various narratives, each tradition must be discussed separately. This is not possible to do in full, but certain details and traditions relevant for a discussion about demons and impurity will be dealt with. While the present narratives reflect the theology of their redactors, clues for historical interpretation are at times to be found in the details of a tradition.[96]

To interpret Jesus' exorcisms, however, it is necessary to fit them into a more defined context. *Wanderradikalismus* is an obvious possibility.[97] There is much to support the idea that at least the core of the early Jesus movement (both before and after Easter) consisted of itinerant charismatic healers and prophets. Jesus is depicted in this way by all four canonical gospels, and he is said to have sent out his disciples on a similar mission.[98] The earliest Christian mission according to Acts and the letters could be interpreted in this manner,[99] and the pattern survived into the second century, as is clear from the Johannine letters and the *Didache*.[100]

It is not possible here to enter into the discussion about the relationship between wandering charismatics and local communities of members or sympa-

---

[93] Cf. above, 91–95.

[94] This is how Annen (1976b, 121) understands Fuller (1963, 33), although Fuller's claim is not as categorical as in the German version; he only claims that stories about Jesus' miraculous deeds would naturally fall into an existing pattern.

[95] Annen 1976a, 115–127; Annen 1976b, 120–124.

[96] Annen 1976a, 82.

[97] Theissen 1973, 245–271; 1978 [1977], 8–16.

[98] Apart from the commonplace that the basic Jesus narrative portrays him as (almost) constantly travelling, this is further corroborated by sayings, such as Mt 8:19–20/Lk 9:57–58 or Lk 13:32f. The sending out of the disciples is explicitly linked with Jesus' own wanderings in the Markan narrative tradition, Mk 6:6b–13, and implicitly in the Lukan joining of Lk 9:57–62 with 10:1ff.

[99] E.g. Acts 9:32, 38–39, 43; 10:23–24, 48; 11:27; 21:10. The so-called missionary journeys of Paul and others could be seen in this perspective as well. Cf. Theissen 1978, 9ff.

[100] 2Jn 10, 3Jn 5ff; *Didache* 11:3–6; 12; 13:1.

thizers.[101] The important thing for the present purpose is to note the prominent place given to exorcisms in the traditions about Jesus sending out his disciples. Exorcizing demons or impure spirits is mentioned as a prime reason, or even *the* reason for calling and sending disciples.[102] This makes it plausible that Jesus himself saw exorcism as one of his foremost tasks, along the lines of the Lukan saying in answer to Herod, that he would exorcize and heal for another two days, before moving on.[103] It seems as if exorcism and itinerancy belonged closely together. That connection has been given various interpretations, however.

A Jewish Cynic?

The picture of Jesus as an itinerant charismatic has for some scholars suggested similarities to the Cynic movement. In addition to the itinerant life-style, the apparent poverty of the early Jesus movement provides an analogy.[104] The discussion about Jesus as a kind of counter-cultural Jewish Cynic has focused on the sayings material, where some have seen similarities between various words of Jesus and Cynic sayings.[105] Burton Mack compares the core of various pronouncement stories of Jesus (*chreiai*) in Mark and L, and finds similarities with a number of anecdotes about Cynics such as Antisthenes and Diogenes. He furthermore gives examples of aphorisms and injunctions in the Q tradition, arguing that they are spelling out a programme which fits the popular profile of the Cynic in Antiquity.[106]

The Cynic hypothesis is tempting but rests on a number of questionable presuppositions. One of them is the thorough Hellenization and urbanization of a purportedly semi-pagan Galilee. This view depends to a large degree on interpretations of the Sepphoris excavations, of which Richard Batey's book *Jesus and the Forgotten City* is representative.[107] According to such a view, Jesus would have met Cynics in Sepphoris and become acquainted with their teaching and style. The idea of Sepphoris and to some extent Tiberias as Hellenistic and predominantly pagan cities, rests mainly on archaeological evidence later than the Second Temple period, and has been severely criticized.[108] The implausibility of such reconstructions should be evident from the discussion in the previous chapter about the Jewish character of Galilee and the rural base for Jesus' activities. This makes it more reasonable to suggest influence from Jewish popular and prophetic traditions as decisive for Jesus' mission.

---

[101] Cf. Theissen 1978, 17–23.
[102] Mk 3:15; 6:7, 13; Mt 10:1/Lk 9:1; Lk 10:17.
[103] Lk 13:32–33.
[104] Cf. Crossan 1991, 72–88.
[105] Cf. Vaage 1994.
[106] Mack 1997, 27–33.
[107] Batey 1991.
[108] Cf. Miller 1992; Sanders 1996; Freyne 2000, 171f, 190, 214f; Chancey 2001.

The second presupposition is based on the Q research of the last decades, which has led to elaborate theories about different strata in the Q source, as well as hypotheses about the development of the communities responsible for the various strata.[109] It is a highly speculative enterprise to build a theory of the social and religious development of the earliest Christian community on a redaction-critical reconstruction of different levels in a hypothetical document. The gist of this presupposition is that the earliest stratum of Q reflects the earliest available layer of the Jesus tradition, which proves to consist of a number of Cynic-like sayings.[110] The Cynic character would thus be more apparent in Q than in the canonical gospels as we now have them. In a study of the *Gospel of Thomas* and the Cynic Jesus, John Marshall shows that there is rather the opposite movement. Examining logia of Cynic-like practice, he concludes that while *Gos.Thom.*[111] attests to an early tradition of itinerant mission, both Q and Mark recognize similarities to the Cynics and seek to differentiate the Jesus movement from them. Likewise, comparing *chreia*-like logia,[112] Marshall finds that the synoptics rather than *Thomas* or Q move towards shaping sayings of Jesus in *chreia* form.[113] He concludes:

> In comparison with Cynic practice and Cynic literary forms, three findings emerge: there is an element of itinerancy and world rejection in the earliest Jesus traditions for which Cynicism may well provide a helpful context; there is a tendency within the synoptic branch of the Jesus traditions to "Cynicize" the literary forms in which Jesus' teaching emerges; and Q takes some care to differentiate the missionary practice of the Jesus movement from Cynic practice. Thus the historical Jesus is likely to have been somewhat less of a Cynic than he is portrayed in the synoptics.[114]

The third presupposition rests on a connection between Cynics and healing and/or exorcism. This connection is actually very weak.[115] The best example of a miracle-working *possible* Cynic is Apollonius of Tyana, who is never defined as one, although he has certain Cynic traits. This is not much on which to build a case, in view of the historical problems with the Apollonius traditions, mentioned previously, and the fact that Apollonius is not explicitly identified as a Cynic.[116] While itinerant miracle-workers were fairly common in the Hellenistic world, they were not identical to Cynic itinerant teachers.

---

[109] Kloppenborg 1987; Mack 1993, 73–102; Vaage 1994, 103–106.

[110] Vaage 1994, 1.

[111] Many have used *Gos.Thom.* "to validate the existence of Q by offering it as an extant example of a sayings tradition that makes no reference to the death of Jesus." (J. W. Marshall 1997, 43).

[112] For a description of the *chreiai*, see Kloppenborg 1987, 306–316; Humphries 1993, 123ff.

[113] J. W. Marshall 1997, 56–58.

[114] J. W. Marshall 1997, 59.

[115] Cf. Crossan 1991, 303–353, who suggests this connection implicitly, rather than explicitly, by his combination of themes and material in the chapter "Magic and Meal."

[116] For discussions about Apollonius, cf. Koskenniemi 1994; Meier 1994, 576–581; Kee 1983, 256–265; Cf. above, 175f.

It is clear that the case for a Cynic Jesus rests on unverified presuppositions. Although it seems a small step from an itinerant healer to a Cynic miracle worker, Crossan's designation of Jesus as a "peasant Jewish Cynic" suggests "an unattested hybrid unlikely to be recognized as such in first-century Galilee or Judea."[117] Marshall's conclusion is more to the point: "Although Cynicism provides a helpful comparative model for understanding itinerancy, the reason Jesus is not explicitly described as a Cynic in the first century is that he was probably not seen as one in the first century."[118]

A Galilean *hasid*?

Seeking a more Jewish context in which itinerancy and miracle-working could be combined, the idea of Geza Vermes about Jesus as a charismatic Galilean *hasid* suggests itself. The hypohesis was touched upon at the end of the last chapter, and some difficulties were briefly mentioned. In Vermes' reconstruction, Jesus is likened to Honi the circle-drawer (first century BCE), and Hanina ben Dosa (first century CE), both mentioned in rabbinic literature.[119] Honi is reported to have forced God to intervene with rain during a period of drought, by refusing to move outside a circle which he drew around himself.[120] Hanina is described as having healed through his prayers,[121] and is called a "man of deed" (אִישׁ מַעֲשֶׂה).[122]

Vermes builds his case for a Galilean *hasid* type (man of deed) on some similarities between these figures.[123] They were all miracle-workers. There are clear parallels between these figures and the northern traditions about Elijah and Elisha. It is possible to argue a Galilean connection for all three.[124] They were all in some sense regarded as sons of God.[125] Hanina and Jesus both healed, even at a distance, and says Vermes, "both Jesus and Hanina, and no doubt the Hasidim in general, showed a complete lack of interest in legal and ritual affairs and a corresponding exclusive concentration on moral questions."[126]

Despite the criticism levelled against Vermes by several scholars,[127] Hanina in particular remains an important point of comparison when evaluating Jesus' position in a Galilean context. Like Jesus, he is said to have healed at a dis-

---

[117] J. W. Marshall 1997, 60.
[118] J. W. Marshall 1997, 60.
[119] Vermes 1973b, 69–82. Cf. Green 1979 about Honi, and Vermes 1972 and 1973a about Hanina.
[120] *mTaan* 3:8; cf. *Ant.* 14:22–24.
[121] *mBer* 5:5; *bBer* 34b; *yBer* 5:5.
[122] *mSot* 9:15.
[123] Cf. the list given by Blackburn 1994, 376f.
[124] Vermes 1973b, 72f.
[125] Honi is likened to a son in *mTaan* 3:8. Hanina is called "my son" by God himself in *bTaan* 24b. Cf. Vermes 1973b, 206ff.
[126] Vermes 1973b, 77.
[127] Cf. Crossan 1992, 156ff; Meier 1994, 581–588; Blackburn 1994, 377ff; Freyne 2000, 132–159.

tance, had power over demons, renounced possessions, and possibly had been indifferent to questions of ritual.[128]

Vermes' argument falters on several points, however. The Galilean connection of Honi is purely conjectural, which is admitted by Vermes himself,[129] and the location of Hanina in Galilee is found only in late references.[130] Explicit or implicit designations of pious people as sons of God are found elsewhere in contemporary Judaism as well, rabbinic tradition included.[131]

The greatest difficulty with Vermes' hypothesis is the identification of these miracle-working figures with the rabbinic *hasidim*, especially since Vermes argues that the former did not show much interest in legal or ritual affairs. The primary traditions about *hasidim* point in a different direction, however, in which radicalism and zeal for the law was paramount.[132] The equation of charismatic miracle-workers with *hasidim* creates a Galilean hybrid type of rabbinic authority, which is nowhere explicitly attested. The "men of deed" and the *hasidim* even seem to be explicitly differentiated in the *Mishnah*.[133]

There is reason to believe that the ascribing of hasidic traits to Honi and Hanina is secondary. While all of the rabbinic material about these figures is extremely legendary, there is no reason to doubt their existence as miracle-workers. This was their prime identity in popular memory, and this is particularly the reason why the miraculous is toned down in late sources as a basis for their authority and legitimity; instead they are "rabbinized" and turned into teachers of law, since halakhic argument rather than miraculous gifts provided authority in the rabbinic movement.[134] The traditions about these popular miracle-workers were too strong to be ignored. In order to be contained within official tradition they were thus assigned the traits of rabbis or *hasidim*.

While the similarity between Jesus and Hanina as miracle-workers is evident, neither Hanina nor Honi is ever described as an exorcist. There is only a tradition in the *Babylonian Talmud* that Hanina encountered Agrath, the queen of demons, and restricted her activity.[135] Furthermore, neither of the two purported Galilean *hasidim* is explicitly portrayed as carrying out an itinerant mission.[136] While the charismatic "man of deed" is a useful leadership model for

---

[128] *bBer* 34b; *yBer* 5:5; *bPes* 112b; *bTaan* 24b, 25a. Vermes explains traditions about Hanina's legal observance (*yDem* 22a; *Abot R. Nat.* A8) as late legends with the intent of making him strict, although he was suspected of not following rabbinic *halakhah* (Vermes 1972, 45f).

[129] Vermes 1973b, 72.

[130] *yBer* 4:1; cf. *bBer* 34b where Hanina is associated with Johanan ben Zakkai, who had lived in Galilean Arav (*mShabb* 16:7; 22:3; *yShabb* 16:8. Cf. Blackburn 1994, 378.

[131] *mAb* 3:14; *yQid* 1:7; cf. Vermes 1973b, 195ff.

[132] Cf. Freyne 2000, 135.

[133] *mSot* 9:15. The interpretation of and relationship between these terms is notoriously difficult; cf. Freyne 2000. 133f; Green, 1979.

[134] Green 1979 (Honi) and Vermes 1973a (Hanina); Vermes 1973b, 81f.

[135] *bPes* 112b.

[136] Blackburn 1994, 379.

understanding Jesus' authority in a rural Galilean setting,[137] drawing on certain historical analogies with Honi and Hanina, it provides no real key for interpreting Jesus' activity as an itinerant exorcist, especially not when coupled with the rabbinic ideal of the *hasid*. There is simply not enough evidence for making this combined type into a distinct class.

It is notable that Vermes' reconstruction of Jesus as a charismatic *hasid* gives no room for the apocalyptic framework in which Jesus' exorcisms are usually interpreted.[138] As will be made clear below, an eschatological perspective is necessary for the traditions about Jesus as an exorcist to make sense, and it is precisely within such a perspective that the narrative traditions about exorcism and some of the logia about the kingdom converge.

A Solomonic magician?

The relationship between miracles and eschatology is not as straightforward as sometimes supposed, however. The fact that Jesus is described as a miracle-worker does not of itself automatically suggest an eschatological perspective. There are other possibilities which must be examined. It is possible to see Jesus within a general magical trend in the ancient world.

The Hebrew Bible exhibits an ambiguous attitude towards magical practices, condemning some while attesting the presence of others, at least in remnant forms.[139] Scholars exhibit a similar ambiguity towards the idea of magic in the Jesus tradition. Many hesitate to call Jesus a magician, and various attempts have been made to distinguish between miracle and magic. The problem is partly one of definition, in which magic is often considered to have a pejorative flavour, even when efforts are made to define the term neutrally.[140] Definitions have usually centred either on attitudes or on methods.[141] A view of miracles as something which could be effected almost automatically by coercive means,

---

[137] Cf. the discussion in the previous chapter, 296f.

[138] Aune 1980, 1539; Blackburn 1994, 379.

[139] The classical passage, prohibiting sorcery and various magical practices, is Deut 18:9–14. Note, however, that a clear and comprehensive prohibition is not found until the Deuteronomic layer. This should be compared to narratives such as that of Moses and Aaron competing with the Egyptian magicians (Ex 7:8–12), the golden boils (1Sam 6), or various divinatory practices (Ex 28:30; 1 Sam 28:6). For a thorough inventory of all types of magical practices and practitioners which can be traced in the literature of ancient Israel, see Jeffers 1996.

[140] For discussions about the definition and characterization of magic in the history of research, see Aune 1980, 1510–1516; Jeffers 1996, 1–16; Meier 1994, 560f, n. 26. Aune 1980 attempts to treat the term without any pejorative connotations, but note the objections raised by Blackburn (1994, 381f), due to the fact that the term or its equivalent has been used pejoratively since ancient times. Meier (1994, 539) points out that "examples of a positive sense of magic can be found, but such a view remained in a hopeless minority." For an attempt to distinguish between magic and miracle, while admitting the difficulties involved, see Kee 1986.

[141] Cf. Meier 1994, 541–551.

was disturbing already to ancient Jews, and caused some reworking of earlier traditions.[142]

The most consistent scholarly presentation of Jesus as a magician is given by Morton Smith, who draws far-reaching conclusions from extra-biblical hints and apologetic traits in the gospels. Smith thinks that Jesus was viewed by his contemporaries as a magician, exhibiting typical characteristics, such as compulsive traits of shamanic behaviour or possession (Mk 1:12; 3:21), neglect of law, and making supernatural claims ("son of God"). Magical details have been toned down or omitted in gospel redaction, but are still visible in certain exorcism stories (name of the demon in Mk 5) or in the eucharist, which was a magical rite and not a passover meal.[143] Smith's ideas have been only partly accepted.[144] Most scholars find both differences and similarities between Jesus' miracles and contemporary magic. It is difficult to draw a sharp line between magic and miracle, and magical traces are not absent from the Jesus tradition.[145]

The widespread practice of magic at the beginning of the common era is attested by the large number of Greek, Demotic and Coptic magical papyri, dating from the first to the sixth centuries CE, but at times preserving older materials.[146] Other evidence for magical practices are Aramaic, Syriac and Mandaic incantation bowls, most of them from around 600 CE, some a century or two earlier.[147] Jewish and Christian elements, as well as appeals to the name of Jesus, are found in the magical papyri as well as in bowl inscriptions.[148]

---

[142] Meier (1994, 591) mentions Josephus' insertion of a lengthy prayer by Moses before dividing the Red Sea with his staff (*Ant.* 2:324–338). Vermes, discussing the miracle stories about Hanina ben Dosa, notes R.Aha's derogatory comments (*yBer* 5:5; *bBQam* 50a) and the elaborations on the snake bite episode (*tBer* 3:20; *yBer* 5:1). Vermes 1972, 31–36; 1973a, 63.

[143] Morton Smith 1981 [1978], 140–147,

[144] Cf. Meier 1994, 538, 557f, n. 16.

[145] E.g. the bleeding woman touching Jesus' garment (Mk 5:25–34 par.), the deaf mute (Mk 7:31–37) and the blind man at Bethsaida (Mk 8:22–26) healed with the aid of spittle.

[146] *PGM* (Preisendanz; Betz).

[147] Magic bowls flourished in Mesopotamia and Iran between the fifth and the eighth centuries CE (Juusola 1999, 4). Incantation bowls are vessels which were possibly placed upside-down at the corners of a building to protect it from evil and entrap demons. They were inscribed mainly on the inside with magical texts in a spiral pattern. For texts, see Naveh and Shaked 1993, 113–143. Cf. Montgomery 1913. At least 500 such bowls are known, and almost all of them are late, except for two from Crete which date from the fifteenth century BCE. There are similar "non-bowl" inscriptions, however, from various Near Eastern locations, dated between the fifteenth and first centuries BCE. Duling 1975, 246, n.44. In addition, the language of the Aramaic incantation bowls has been shown to contain various archaic features (Juusola 1999, 245–254), which suggests a textual history older than the artefacts.

[148] Geller 1977; Aune 1980, 1547f; Morton Smith 1981 [1978], 63f; Kee 1986, 107–112. Most of the Aramaic bowls are written in Hebrew script, and are likely to be Jewish, but the language and script of the bowls do not necessarily reflect the religion of the scribe. "The fact that the bowls reflect the syncretic magic beliefs of popular religion common to Jewish, Christian, and Mandaic communities of the era makes it difficult for us to be absolutely sure of the origin of a given text." Juusola 1999, 2.

Most of this material is later than the Second Temple period. This also applies to rabbinic evidence, which comes mainly from the *Babylonian Talmud* and attests to the existence of magical practices, incantations and exorcisms within a Jewish context.[149] There is a general scepticism in rabbinic literature, however, towards practices which could be interpreted as magical in character. The function of miracles in rabbinic traditions becomes that of confirming the authority of an individual rabbi and his legal interpretation.[150] While the rabbinic evidence is scanty, the existence of these traces in spite of official scepticism suggests the presence of magical elements and miracle-workers back into the Second Temple period, partially suppressed in the sources.[151]

Firm textual evidence for magical practices within Second Temple Judaism is found since the fragments from Qumran cave 4 were made available. An incantation ritual, possibly an exorcism, is found, although fragmentary, in 4Q560, and has been quoted above.[152] This Aramaic text preserves, according to Penney and Wise, an apotropaic magic formula, within the broad tradition of amulets and incantation texts so common in the ancient Near East.[153]

In none of the texts just mentioned do we find any association between magic or miracle-working and eschatology. Miracles function to confirm the authority of the miracle-workers, they usually come about through magical practices, and they are not part of a larger framework or scheme.

When the exorcisms of Jesus are seen in the context of ancient Near Eastern magical practices, the title "Son of David" gains a further meaning. This title is primarily used by the Synoptics about Jesus in his capacity as a healer, which is evident in the Markan tradition of the healing of Bartimaios outside Jericho.[154] The traditional messianic interpretation of the title is not sufficient, however, especially since the Messiah is not explicitly portrayed as a healer in Jewish tradition.[155] To explain the Synoptic usage as the influence of an Hellenistic *theios aner* conception on the Davidic Messiah-figure is unnecessary, however.[156] There are Jewish precedents in the portrayal of David, and especially Solomon, as magicians.

In Matthew's version of the Q-material usually termed "the Beelzebul pericope," Jesus' identity as "Son of David" is suggested by the crowd in response to an exorcism (Mt 12:23). David himself is described in 1Sam 16:14–23 as playing the harp for Saul, who was periodically tormented by an evil spirit from

---

149 *bMeil* 17b; *bPes* 112b; *bQid* 29b; *bShabb* 67a.
150 Trunk 1994, 369–374; Kee 1986. 80–83.
151 Cf. the traditions about Honi and Hanina discussed above, 318–320.
152 See text and translation above, 303 and n.23.
153 Penney and Wise 1994, 649f.
154 Mk 10:47; cf. Mt 9:27; 12:23; 15:22; 20:30. Lövestam (1972–1973, 197) points out that even when the crowd give their tribute to Jesus, this is associated with healing (Mt 21:9, 14–15).
155 Burger 1970, 169. Note however 4Q521 2 2:1–14, which may be evidence of the opposite.
156 Burger 1970, 169.

God. The story is embellished by Josephus, who portrays David not as an outright exorcist, but as having power to charm away spirits.[157] Solomon, son of David, is described as a master magician and exorcist in various Jewish traditions. The idea is based on the comment in 1Kgs about the wisdom of Solomon, his proverbs and parables and songs, and his talking about plants and animals.[158] In Wis 7:15–22 he is said to know the position of heavenly bodies, the forces of spirits and the power of roots.[159]

It is in the context of the Beelzebul pericope, i.e. in a discussion about exorcism, that we find the only reference in the Jesus tradition to the wisdom of Solomon.[160] In late texts, such as the *Apocalypse of Adam* or the *Testament of Solomon*, Solomon is primarily associated with demons and exorcism. In the latter text one of the crucial artefacts ensuring Solomon's success is a ring with a seal.[161] References to Solomon's exorcisms and his seal-ring are found in a number of incantation bowl texts as well as in the *Talmud*.[162] While Christian influence on some of these texts is certain and cannot be excluded in the case of others,[163] they have precedents which belong to, or come close to, the Second Temple period. In describing Solomon, Josephus emphasizes his exorcisms:

> παρέσχε δ' αὐτῷ μαθεῖν ὁ θεὸς καὶ τὴν κατὰ τῶν δαιμόνων τέχνην εἰς ὠφέλειαν καὶ θεραπείαν τοῖς ἀνθρώποις· ἐπῳδάς τε συνταξάμενος αἷς παρηγορεῖται τὰ νοσήματα καὶ τρόπους ἐξορκώσεων κατέλιπεν, οἷς οἱ ἐνδούμενοι τὰ δαιμόνια ὡς μηκέτ' ἐπανελθεῖν ἐκδιώκουσι.[164]
>
> And God granted him knowledge of the art used against demons for the benefit and healing of men. He also composed incantations by which illnesses are relieved, and left behind forms of exorcisms with which those possessed by demons drive them out, never to return.

To exemplify the technique (τέχνη) that Solomon developed for exorcisms, Josephus tells about Eleazar, a Jew who exorcized people in the presence of Vespasian by a seal-ring with roots:

> καὶ αὕτη μέχρι νῦν παρ' ἡμῖν ἡ θεραπεία πλεῖστον ἰσχύει· ἱστόρησα γάρ τινα Ἐλεάζαρον τῶν ὁμοφύλων Οὐεσπασιανοῦ παρόντος καὶ τῶν υἱῶν αὐτοῦ καὶ χιλιάρχων καὶ ἄλλου στρατιωτικοῦ πλήθους τοὺς ὑπὸ τῶν δαιμονίων λαμβανομένους ἀπολύοντα τούτων. ὁ δὲ τρόπος τῆς θεραπείας τοιοῦτος ἦν· προσφέρων ταῖς ῥισὶ τοῦ δαιμονιζομένου τὸν δακτύλιον ἔχοντα ὑπὸ τῇ σφραγῖδι ῥίζαν ἐξ ὧν ὑπέδειξε Σολομὼν ἔπειτα ἐξεῖλκεν ὀσφρομένῳ διὰ τῶν μυκτήρων τὸ δαιμόνιον, καὶ πεσόντος εὐθὺς τἀνθρώπου μηκέτ' εἰς αὐτὸν ἐπανήξειν ὥρκου Σολομῶνός τε μεμνημένος καὶ τὰς ἐπῳδὰς ἃς συνέθηκεν ἐκεῖνος ἐπιλέγων. βουλόμενος δὲ

[157] "τίς ἐστιν ἐξᾴδειν δυνάμενος καὶ ψάλλειν ἐπὶ κινύρᾳ" *Ant.* 6:166.
[158] 1Kgs 4:29–34 (5:9–14 MT). As the Solomon tradition grew, a number of books were ascribed to him both within and outside the canon.
[159] Duling 1975, 237f. Duling reconstructs a trajectory of Solomon-as-exorcist, 248f.
[160] Mt 12:42/Lk 11:31. This is pointed out by Lövestam 1972–1973, 203.
[161] *Apoc.Adam* 7:13; *T.Sol.* 1:6–7.
[162] For references, see Duling 1975, 244f, 247 n.50. According to the *Talmud*, the seal-ring was inscribed with the Tetragrammaton (*bGit* 68a).
[163] Cf. Charlesworth 1995, 82.
[164] *Ant.* 8:45.

πεῖσαι καὶ παραστῆσαι τοῖς παρατυγχάνουσιν ὁ Ἐλεάζαρος ὅτι ταύτην ἔχει τὴν ἰσχύν, ἐτίθει μικρὸν ἔμπροσθεν ἤτοι ποτήριον πλῆρες ὕδατος ἢ ποδόνιπτρον καὶ τῷ δαιμονίῳ προσέταττεν ἐξιόντι τἀνθρώπου ταῦτ᾽ ἀνατρέψαι καὶ παρασχεῖν ἐπιγνῶναι τοῖς ὁρῶσιν ὅτι καταλέλοιπε τὸν ἄνθρωπον.[165]

And this kind of cure is of very great power among us to this day, for I have seen a certain Eleazar, a countryman of mine, in the presence of Vespasian, his sons, tribunes and a number of other soldiers, free men possessed by demons, and this was the manner of the cure: he put to the nose of the possessed man a ring which had under its seal one of the roots prescribed by Solomon, and then, as the man smelled it, drew out the demon through his nostrils, and, when the man at once fell down, adjured the demon never to come back into him, speaking Solomon's name and reciting the incantations which he had composed. Then, wishing to convince the bystanders and prove to them that he had this power, Eleazar placed a cup or footbasin full of water a little way off and commanded the demon, as it went out of the man, to overturn it and make known to the spectators that he had left the man.

Josephus apparently saw Solomon's power over demons as the most important proof of his wisdom.[166]

This is the basic view underlying the apocryphal psalms from Qumran cave 11, of which some seem to have functioned as incantations against demons. In the heavily damaged second column we read: "Solomon, and he will invo[ke...] [...the spir]its and the demons, [...] [...] These are [the de]mons, and the Pri[nce of Animosi]ty [...w]ho [...] the aby[ss...]"[167]

It is thus possible that references to Jesus as the "Son of David" in the gospel traditions fall back on a popular understanding of Jesus as a Solomonic exorcist. If so, the designation need not have messianic connotations. Exorcist connotations, however, are not necessary, but only possible. As Charlesworth has pointed out, they come to the surface neither in the apocryphal passages celebrating Solomon, nor in the Psalms of Solomon.[168] A moderate suggestion would be that the designation "Son of David" facilitated the incorporation of notions of healing and exorcism into popular messianic expectations. As will be argued below, such notions actually did have their place in Jewish messianic tradition as well.

A messenger of the eschatological kingdom

While it is possible to look at magic and miracles outside an eschatological context, this is not likely in the case of Jesus. This applies especially to his exor-

[165] *Ant.* 8:46–48.

[166] Lövestam 1972–1973, 204, refers to Josephus' subsequent explanatory comment: γενομένου δὲ τούτου σαφὴς ἡ Σολομῶνος καθίστατο σύνεσις καὶ σοφία δι᾽ ἥν, ... (And when this was done, the understanding and wisdom of Solomon were clearly revealed, ...); *Ant.* 8:49a.

[167] 11Q11 2:2–5 ([...]ה שלומה ויקר[א ...] [... הרו]חות והשדים [...] [...] אלה [הש]דים ושׂ]ר המשט[מה [... א]שר [...]ל תהו[ם ...]ך).

[168] E.g. Sir 47:23; 2Macc 2:8–12; *1Esd* 1:1–4; *4Ezra* 10:46; *4Macc* 18:16; *Sib.Or.* 11:80–104. Charlesworth 1995, 82. Note that in *Pss.Sol.* 17:21–44 the Messiah is identified as the Son of David (v 21, 32), and his acts are described at length, but there is no mention of miracles at all.

cisms. The overall context for Jesus' activities, according to the Synoptic gospel traditions, is the kingdom of God. The expression occurs mainly on the lips of Jesus, but cannot be found in the Hebrew Bible and plays no large role in Paul's letters or the rest of the NT. It does not seem to have been a popular concept in early Christianity, which warrants the conclusion that the kingdom of God was central to Jesus himself.

The kingdom of God is primarily a Jewish apocalyptic concept, which is found, albeit sparsely, in Greek as well as in Hebrew literature from the Second Temple period.[169] The expression did exist but was not prominent.[170] It refers either to "God's decisive intervention in history and human experience," or to "the final state of the redeemed to which this intervention is designed to lead."[171] This is not entirely identical with the distinction between present and future aspects of the kingdom so often discussed by exegetes, since intervention at least can be interpreted in both a present and a future sense.[172]

The interpretation of Jesus' message about the kingdom of God has been a bone of contention for centuries, and the discussion cannot be entered into here.[173] Whether the kingdom is seen as future, present or realized, it is nigh impossible to disregard its strong eschatological flavour. This is especially apparent when it is associated with demons and exorcisms. In apocalyptic texts from the Second Temple period God's kingdom is mentioned in contexts of a battle between good and evil, or victory over Satan and demons. The hymn at the end of the *Testament of Moses* begins: "Then his kingdom will appear throughout his whole creation. Then the devil will have an end."[174] In the *War Scroll* the kingdom (מלכות) of God is mentioned in the context of the eschatological battle between the sons of light and the sons of darkness, and in one fragment of an incantation hymn from Qumran, all (demons?) are said to

---

[169] *Pss.Sol.* 17:3; *T.Mos.* 10:1; 1QM 6:6; 12:7; 1Q28b [1QSb] 4:25f; 5:21; 4Q510 1 4. The evidence from the *Sibylline Oracles* (*Sib.Or.* 3:46ff, 767) cannot be appealed to due to the uncertain dating. For a discussion of the evidence see Perrin 1963, 168–170, 178–181; Meier 1994, 253–270.

[170] The expression is found frequently in the Aramaic *Targum Jonathan* on the Prophets, which, although dated in its present form to around the fifth century CE, might contain material going back to Second Temple times. See *Tg.Isa.* 24:23; 31:4; 40:9; 52:7. Cf. Chilton 1984, 57–90. For a critical discussion, see Meier 1994, 262–265, 287, n.113.

[171] Perrin 1963, 184.

[172] Cf. Perrin 1963, 185. Caird defines the kingdom as "the final vindication of God's purposes in the reign of justice and peace" which is future, and "the redemptive sovereignty of God let loose into the world for the destruction of Satan and all his works" which Jesus regarded as present (1980, 12). Chilton suggests that the dichotomy is unnecessary when the kingdom is understood according to the Isaiah Targum as the saving self-revelation of God (Chilton 1984 [1979]). However, this must not be allowed to obscure the apparent eschatological character and context of the expression. Cf. Meier 1994, 264, 287, n.113.

[173] For a history of research, see Perrin 1963. For a thorough discussion of kingdom sayings and different interpretations, see Meier 1994, 289–506.

[174] *T.Mos.* 10:1.

"flee from the dwelling of the glory of his kingdom."[175] The effect of the glory of the kingdom on the evil powers is immediately described:

ואני משכיל משמיע הוד תפארתו לפחד ולבו[הל] כול רוחי מלאכי חבל
ורוחות ממזרים שדאים לילית אחים ו[ציים ...] והפוגעים פתע פתאום לתעות
רוח בינה ולהשם לבבם

> And I, a Sage, declare the splendour of his radiance in order to frighten and terr[ify] all the spirits of the ravaging angels and the bastard spirits, demons, Lilith, owls and [jackals ...] and those who strike unexpectedly to lead astray the spirit of knowledge, to make their hearts forlorn.[176]

Although this perspective is not the dominant one in Second Temple Judaism, its existence is proved in apocalyptic literature, and it cannot be regarded as unimportant. It provides a frame of reference for the saying of Jesus in Mt 12:28/Lk 11:20, in which Jesus defends himself against the criticism that he expels demons with the help of Beelzebul.

> εἰ δὲ ἐν πνεύματι(Mt)/δακτύλῳ(Lk) θεοῦ [ἐγὼ][177] ἐκβάλλω τὰ δαιμόνια, ἄρα ἔφθασεν ἐφ᾽ ὑμᾶς ἡ βασιλεία τοῦ θεοῦ.

> But if by the spirit(Mt)/finger(Lk) of God I cast out the demons, then the kingdom of God has come upon you.

There is reason to believe that the Lukan rendering "finger" rather than Matthew's "spirit" is the original reading in the Q source,[178] but this detail is unimportant for the present discussion. This saying has been much discussed among exegetes, and is usually considered to be a key for interpreting Jesus' exorcisms or even miracles in general.[179]

The common view, based on the three suppositions that this is a detached saying of Jesus which is authentic and shows that Jesus viewed his exorcisms as evidence for the presence of the kingdom, has been questioned by Sanders.[180] While the question of authenticity is partly one of definition,[181] Sanders may well be right that this saying belonged together with the previous one from the very beginning; it definitely did in Q.[182] But the hesitance towards Jesus re-

---

[175] 1QM 6:6; 12:7. 4Q510 1 3–4 (ויחפזו מהדר מע[וז] כבוד מלכותו; *DJD* 7:216: "ils prennent la fuite devant la majesté de la de[meure de] gloire de sa royauté.").
[176] 4Q510 1 4–6.
[177] ἐγώ is certain in Mt, while in Lk some important witnesses lack the pronoun.
[178] Spirit is a favourite word with Luke (which a quick glance in a concordance will reveal), and it seems strange that he should have replaced it here, had it occurred in the source he was using.
[179] Perrin 1963, 20, 42f, 59f, 170f; 1976, 63–67.
[180] Sanders 1985, 134.
[181] Sanders' arguments, which aim not to prove the saying to be inauthentic, but to emphasize the uncertainties, deal with all types of problems normally involved in any discussion about logia and authenticity (context, transmission, translation, grammar etc.). The problems involved in this saying are no more serious than in any other case, however, but belong to the standard premises by which exegetes generally work. Cf. Dunn 1988, 47f.
[182] The material in Mt 12/Lk 11 will be discussed more in detail in Excursus 6 below.

garding his exorcisms as evidence of the kingdom seems to be caused in part by an unnecessary polarization between the present and future perspectives, and in part by a similar polarization between the exorcisms of Jesus and those of others. It is not necessary to argue that Jesus regarded his own exorcisms in contrast to those of others as signs that the kingdom was fully present. The question is whether he saw his exorcisms as signs of the coming kingdom at all, regardless of how other exorcists were viewed or how ἔφθασεν is translated.

The idea of liberation from evil forces did belong to apocalyptic expectations of the end time. An expection that the evil spirit would be removed from the world can be traced in several texts.[183] The most explicit reference, in addition to *T.Mos.* 10:1 referred to above, is a passage in *T.Levi* where the eschatological priest is described as binding Satan:

> And he shall open the gates of paradise; he shall remove the sword that has threatened since Adam, and he will grant to the saints to eat of the tree of life. The spirit of holiness shall be upon them. And Beliar shall be bound by him. And he shall grant to his children the authority to trample on wicked spirits.[184]

This is a case of a messianic figure who is expected to have power over the demons, and the saying in Mt 12:28/Lk 11:20 fits into this frame of reference.

It could be argued that Jesus' exorcisms were mainly seen as healing miracles, and since no messianic figure was expected to be a miracle worker,[185] neither miracles nor exorcisms would have served as evidence or interpretation of the kingdom for the historical Jesus. The view that the Messiah was not expected to perform healing miracles is not entirely correct, however, as is evident from the second fragment of 4Q521, discussed in previous chapters.[186] Here God's Messiah (משיחו) is mentioned in a context in which he (the Lord or the Messiah?) will free prisoners, give sight to the blind, heal the badly wounded and make the dead live, as well as proclaim good news to the poor.[187] The items reflect various passages in Isaiah, and are basically the same as those found in Jesus' answer to the Baptizer in Mt 11:2–6/Lk 7:18–23.[188] The similarities suggest that these were, if not standard expectations, at least one possible contemporary framework. Jesus' miracles in general and his exorcisms in particular must be seen in the eschatological context of the kingdom.

---

[183] Cf. Aune 1980, 1533 n.117.

[184] *T.Levi* 18:10–12. Sanders thinks that this is not much evidence for "a view common in Judaism" that the Messiah was expected to overthrow the demonic world and demonstrate it by exorcisms (1985, 134f). My argument is not based on how common or detailed such a view was. There are precedents, however, which provide a context for the interpretation in Mt 12:28/Lk 11:20, and make it plausible.

[185] Cf. Hahn 1963, 262; Burger 1970, 169.

[186] See above, 168f, 247.

[187] 4Q521 2 2:1, 8, 12.

[188] Cf. above, 99, 168. Cf. also Luke's quotation of Isa 61:1 in Lk 4:18.

Excursus 6: A power struggle in the Beelzebul pericope

The exorcisms of Jesus are pictured as part of a power struggle about the kingdom. The key saying supporting this perspective (Mt 12:28/Lk 11:20) has already been discussed briefly, but its context, i.e. the so-called Beelzebul pericope, must be examined further. This pericope is a prime example of an overlap between Mark and Q and has been studied from that angle by several scholars.[189] Matthew and Luke both used Mark and Q, but Luke followed Q more closely, while Matthew conflated the Markan and Q forms to a greater degree.[190]

Since the overlap is fairly extensive and evident, attempts have been made to retrieve the contours of an underlying oral stage of tradition which might have been common to the two strands.[191] Instead of looking at this section as an expanded apophthegm it might be more fruitful to regard it as "a series of sayings of Jesus, sometimes of disparate origin, gathered in the oral tradition due to their thematic connection to a topic of importance to his followers."[192] The relevant material can be structured in the following way:[193]

1) An introductory healing account	Mt 12:22–23/Lk 11:14
2) An accusation	Mt 12:24/Mk 3:22/Lk 11:15–16
3) An answer in 3 parts (kingdom, house, Satan)[194]	Mt 12:25–26/Mk 3:23–26/Lk 11:17–18
4) An answer about "your sons"	Mt 12:27/Lk 11:19
5) An answer about the spirit/finger of God	Mt 12:28/Lk 11:20
6) A parable about the strong one[195]	Mt 12:29–30/Mk 3:27/Lk 11:21–23
7) A saying about sin against the spirit	Mt 12:31–32/Mk 3:28–30/Lk 12:10
8) A saying about the returning spirit	Mt 12:43–45/Lk 11:24–26

The material common to Mk and Q is easily extracted, even if the precise relationship is difficult to disentangle at times. It consists of (2), (3), (6) and (7).

Mark lacks an introductory healing account (1). However, this is due to the fact that he has sandwiched the Beelzebul pericope with references to the family of Jesus, and associated their worries about him being out of his mind with the accusations of the scribes that he was possessed. There is good reason for supposing that Matthew and Luke reflect an original short opening reference to an exorcism in an underlying common tradition.[196] While the introduction provides a context for the various sayings, and is one of several references to exorcisms, it does not contribute any particular information, and will not be discussed further.

The saying about sin against the spirit (7) at the end of the list above, is well integrated into the Markan text, and concludes this pericope, which begins with suspicions and accusations, with a warning. Matthew follows Mark here, while Luke has a similar saying in a different

---

[189] Mt 12:22–30/Mk 3:22–27/Lk 11:14–23. The sections about sin against the spirit (Mt 12:31–32/Mk 3:28–30/Lk 12:10) and the returning spirit (Mt 12:43–45/Lk 11:24–26) belong thematically to the same context, but were probably not part of an earlier underlying common tradition (see below). For a good example of a study of the overlap with Q, see Boring 1992.

[190] Boring 1992, 619.

[191] A "dominical discourse" or "oral cluster;" Sellew 1988.

[192] Sellew 1988, 98. For a different view, suggesting a written Aramaic source behind the versions of both Mark and Q, see Hultgren 1979, 100–106.

[193] Cf. Dunn 1988, 34; Sellew 1988, 100, 102; Guijarro 1999, 119ff.

[194] Apart from an introductory phrase Jesus' answer consists of two proverbial sayings about a divided kingdom and a house not standing, as well as a syllogistic conclusion about Satan divided and thus not standing. Cf. Sellew 1988, 100.

[195] Here I have not specified the Q saying "for or against me," which concludes the parable in Mt and Lk, but is found elsewhere in an exorcist context (Mk 9:40/Lk 9:50).

[196] Cf. Sellew 1988, 100f; Twelftree 1993, 101–104.

context, which suggests that it belonged to Q but was not part of the Beelzebul pericope there, and thus probably not part of a supposed underlying common tradition.

The saying about the returning spirit (8) belongs thematically to this group of material and is interesting because of the insight it gives into contemporary demonological ideas, but provides no direct information about Jesus' exorcisms. While it is immediately attached to the Beelzebul pericope in Luke, Matthew "inserts" the sign of Jonah before it, and in view of Matthew's tendency to gather material thematically it is unlikely that he would have detached this saying from an original setting following the Beelzebul pericope.[197]

The main problem concerns the answers (4) and (5). According to a theory of an underlying (oral) common tradition, these sayings would not be included, but introduced into the context by Q. The logical link between the tripartite answer (3) and the parable about the strong one (6) as in Mark 3:24–27 is difficult to see, however, and the Q version including (4) and (5) provides a transition, if not entirely smooth. Whether or not there was a common oral tradition underlying the Markan and Q versions, it might be wiser to discuss each relevant element separately, i.e. items (2) to (6).

As seen above, the accusations against Jesus are proof of the general historicity of his exorcisms. Mark's "scribes" are to be preferred as adversaries, rather than Matthew's conventional "Pharisees." In this section (2) Jesus is accused of driving out demons with the help of Beelzebul,[198] but also, in Mark's version, of being possessed himself. One method in contemporary exorcism was to use the power of stronger demons to drive out weaker.[199] The accusation is probably historical, but was suppressed by Q because it was embarrassing.

The discussion of which form of the tripartite answer about the divided kingdom (3) should be regarded as more original is not crucial. More important is the logic of the argument. Some have found it problematic. Marcus thinks there is a missing line of argument. If the parable of the divided kingdom should function as an argument that Jesus cannot expel demons with the help of Satan, the implicit acknowledgment must be that "Satan's kingdom has obviously not been laid waste, and is not about to fall."[200] There is supposed to be a discrepancy between this parable and the subsequent sayings in Q (5 and 6) which suggest that Satan's kingdom is on the point of collapse.[201] This is over-interpreting the argument, however, since the point of the argument is only to demonstrate the absurdity of the accusation. Jesus' argument simply means: if your accusation were true, there would be no demons to expel. If taken to its logical end, however, Marcus' line of reasoning would mean that it would be impossible to deny the accusation unless one approved the strength of Satan's rule.[202] The discrepancy between the traditions

---

[197] The case is complicated, since Matthew followed Mark and inserted sin against the spirit (7) after the parable about the strong one (6), and expanded it with other (predominantly Q) material, concluding it with a reference to the day of judgment. The day of judgment is the link to the subsequent pericope about the sign of Jonah, and the return of the spirit (8) which follows, ends on the same note (τῇ γενεᾷ ταύτῃ τῇ πονηρᾷ; Mt 12:45; cf. 12:39, 41, 42).

[198] This name refers to the Caananite sky god Baal Shamayin, symbolizing the leader of all demons. Cf. Sellew 1988, 104.

[199] Cf. Thraede 1969, 46; Böcher 1970, 161–169; Trunk 1994, 22, 48f, 51f.

[200] Marcus 1999, 249; cf. Lane 1974, 142f.

[201] C. F. Evans 1990, 491.

[202] Marcus goes to great lengths in discussing various alternative interpretations, but discards the most plausible one, which has the support of many scholars (which Marcus himself shows; Marcus 1999, 255f). According to this interpretation the argument is a kind of *reductio ad absurdum*, affirming that Satan simply cannot be that stupid. The polarization between a strong Satan in the parable about the divided kingdom and a paralyzed Satan in the parable about the strong one, is exaggerated (260). That Satan is strong does not mean that he is unharmed. Note that the parable of the divided kingdom is a response to criticism of Jesus' *exorcisms* which means

is hardly serious. The effect of Marcus' discussion, however, is to highlight the character of power struggle in the exorcisms of Jesus.

The two Q sayings (4 and 5) are joined together with εἰ δέ in their present context, but could well have been transmitted as separate units. The answer about "your sons" (4) has already been cited as evidence for the existence of other exorcists contemporary with Jesus.[203] Some have seen a discrepancy between Jesus' acknowledgment of other exorcists and the subsequent saying (5) in which exorcisms are seen as signs of the kingdom. The underlying presupposition is that Jesus would have regarded himself and his mission as unique. This is not self-evident, however, and the two traditions might not have belonged together originally anyway. Attempts to solve the purported discrepancy are hardly convincing.[204] This saying is an additional argument against the accusations of driving out demons with the help of Beelzebul, and has to do with Jesus' source of power, which he shares with other exorcists. It is congruent with the tolerant attitude suggested at the end of the Beelzebul pericope in its Q version, as well as elsewhere in Mark.[205] The subsequent saying (5) has already been dealt with in the previous section, and associated Jesus' exorcisms with the coming of the kingdom. There is a notion of at least relative, if not absolute, uniqueness in this claim. It is unnecessary, however, to read these two possibly unconnected sayings as if Jesus either must have regarded all types of exorcisms as equal signs of the kingdom, or must have denied the claims of other exorcists. The latter would even be stupid, since such an attitude would never be believed, as other exorcists actually operated. We must rather suppose that Jesus' success and/or methods made him stand out in comparison with others, something which is supported by the fact that his name was used by other exorcists.[206]

If we grant that Luke's "finger of God" in saying (5) is original ("But if by the finger of God I cast out the demons, then the kingdom of God has come upon you"), this may be an allusion to Ex 8:19, which is one of the few examples of the expression in the Hebrew Bible. After the third plague, the Egyptian magicians are no longer able to imitate the miracles of Moses and Aaron, but exclaim: "This is the finger of God." Behind the Egyptian magicians was Satan, according to contemporary Jewish interpretation,[207] and the saying may indicate a view of Jesus' exorcisms as part of a similar power struggle, with equal significance.[208]

---

that Satan is actually affected. The accusation is considered absurd and the parable can be used as an argument since the presence of satanic evil is taken for granted, but it is not used for proving the strength of Satan's kingdom. Marcus' own solution is a highly speculative hypothesis, saving both parables for the historical Jesus, but assigning them to different stages in Jesus' career, i.e. an early pre-baptismal stage, when he performed exorcisms without believing that he had overthrown Satan, and a later post-baptismal stage, when, after having had a vision of Satan's fall (Lk 10:18, cf. Marcus 1995), he concluded that Satan's dominion was being replaced by the dominion of God (Marcus 1999, 260–270). The idea is tantalizing, but impossible to prove. I have difficulties seeing the necessity of polarizing the supposed discrepancy.

[203] Cf. above, 310.

[204] Cf. Shirock 1992, who claims that "your sons" refers to Jesus' own disciples, referring to the interpretation of Hilary, Chrysostom, Jerome and Calvin. This would possibly mean that the parents of the disciples were among the accusers; cf. Guijarro 1999, 121.

[205] Mt 12:30/Lk 11:23; Mk 9:40/Lk 9:50; cf. Twelftree 1993, 107. For a discussion of the authenticity of the tradition about the "strange exorcist" cf. Twelftree 1993, 40–43; Meier 1994, 468f, n.72; Klutz 1999, 159.

[206] Mt 7:22; Mk 9:38/Lk 9:49; Acts 19:13. Cf. *PGM* 4:3019–3020.

[207] Belial, CD 5:18–19.

[208] Cf. Dunn 1988, 39f.

The character of power struggle is enhanced in the parable of the strong one (6), whose property is plundered (ἁρπάζειν) by another. This is possible through the previous binding (δεῖν) of the strong one. In the Matthean version which follows Mark, the parable reads:[209]

> ἢ πῶς δύναταί τις εἰσελθεῖν εἰς τὴν οἰκίαν τοῦ ἰσχυροῦ καὶ τὰ σκεύη αὐτοῦ ἁρπάσαι, ἐὰν μὴ πρῶτον δήσῃ τὸν ἰσχυρόν; καὶ τότε τὴν οἰκίαν αὐτοῦ διαρπάσει.
>
> Or how could anyone go into the house of the strong one and plunder his property unless he would bind the strong one first? Then he can plunder his house.[210]

The need to bind possessed people, who were too violent, is apparent from the story of the Gerasene demoniac (Mk 5:3–4), but in that case the binding was unsuccessful. The parable of the strong one suggests that Jesus is successful in binding Satan and plundering his property, i.e. liberating possessed people, and thus the kingdom takes the upper hand in the power struggle.

The cryptic saying of Jesus in Mt 11:12/Lk 16:16 should be considered in this perspective. The Matthean version reads:

> ἀπὸ δὲ τῶν ἡμερῶν Ἰωάννου τοῦ βαπτιστοῦ ἕως ἄρτι ἡ βασιλεία τῶν οὐρανῶν βιάζεται καὶ βιασταὶ ἁρπάζουσιν αὐτήν.
>
> From the days of John the Baptizer until now the kingdom of heaven suffers violence and the violent plunder it.[211]

The Matthean variant is in my opinion to be preferred in most respects, except for the usual substitution of "kingdom of heaven" for "kingdom of God," where Luke is more original.[212] The last words of the saying are not difficult to analyze one by one, but their meaning is notoriously difficult to determine. Luke's simplification is perfectly understandable, and thus secondary. According to Meier, one point is clear, though, that the kingdom "understood in this saying as the palpable, immanent manifestation of God's kingly rule in Israel's history, and more particularly in the ministry of Jesus, is suffering violent opposition."[213] Meier claims that such an idea is foreign to the Hebrew Bible, intertestamental literature or the rest of the NT.

It is possible to interpret the violent (βιασταί) in this saying as spiritual powers.[214] The saying could thus be read as referring to the conflict between Jesus and demons apparent in his exorcist activity. Of the four elaborate narratives about exorcisms, three describe the possessed persons as violent in their behaviour, and the power struggles involved in the exorcisms are

---

[209] Matthew uses the simple verb ἁρπάζειν once and the compound διαρπάζειν once, while Mark uses the compound in both cases. Luke's version here deviates on several points, which could be explained in two ways: either Luke is following Q or he rewrites Mark considerably. Since the latter is unusual, the former suggestion is preferable. The parable of the strong one is also found in *Gos.Thom.* 35, in a version close to Mark. Cf. Guijarro 1999, 121; Twelftree 1993, 111.

[210] Mt 12:29; cf. Mk 3:27. In Mark the first sentence is phrased not as a question, but as a statement.

[211] The Lukan variant is somewhat different: Ὁ νόμος καὶ οἱ προφῆται μέχρι Ἰωάννου· ἀπὸ τότε ἡ βασιλεία τοῦ θεοῦ εὐαγγελίζεται καὶ πᾶς εἰς αὐτὴν βιάζεται.

[212] Davies and Allison 1991, 253f. Meier is of a different opinion, arguing for the first half of Luke's version being more original ("The law and the prophets until John; from then on…" Meier 1994, 157ff. However, I believe that this division of time into distinct periods reflects Lukan salvation history rather than the historical Jesus or the Q source.

[213] Meier 1994, 403.

[214] Dibelius 1911, 24–26; Fridrichsen 1929, 306; Wilder 1950 [1939], 58. Cf. Kümmel 1953, 116, who leaves it open whether βιασταί refers to spiritual or human adversaries. The two could possibly be seen in combination; cf. Mk 8:33/Mt 16:23.

violent as well.[215] Plundering (ἁρπάζειν) would then refer to the struggle between the kingdom of God and the demons, just as in the parable of the strong one.

When interpreted through the sayings in the Beelzebul pericope, Jesus' exorcisms are seen as part of an eschatological power struggle between the kingdom of God and the demons of Satan. The idea of exorcisms as signs of the coming kingdom cannot be regarded merely as a post-Easter Christian interpretation of the tradition, as if Jesus would have regarded his exorcist activity as an indecisive power struggle. This should be clear from comparing the Markan exorcism narratives with the interpretations in the Beelzebul pericope. It is apparent that the various narratives serve a christological function in the Markan context, i.e. Mark interprets Jesus' exorcisms as signs, not primarily of the kingdom, but of Jesus' power and hence as evidence for his identity.[216] This is not the interpretation that comes out of the sayings material in the Beelzebul pericope, in which the emphasis is on the struggle about the kingdom.

This relative lack of christological claims at earlier stages of the traditions about Jesus' exorcisms is accompanied by an absence of miraculous detail, which further underscores the original significance of these narratives.

> They were not intended, as was the case with the hellenistic wonder-worker stories, to glorify the one who performed the act. They were told instead to identify his exorcism as an eschatological event which served to prepare God's creation for his coming rule.[217]

We can thus see an example here of the process pointed out by Bultmann, in which the focus on the message (kingdom of God) was shifted to the messenger (christology).[218] The interpretation of Jesus' exorcisms as signs of the kingdom was relevant in Jesus' own historical context, but became less so in the early church. It thus represents Jesus' own understanding and message.

Impurity and power struggle in the Jesus tradition

Since Jesus' exorcisms were seen by others and by himself as signs of the kingdom, it is possible to suggest that his attitude to impurity could be explained by his view of God's coming reign.

The overlap between impurity and possession, or between exorcism and purification, which has been demonstrated in ancient Israelite tradition as well as in Second Temple Judaism, is usually not apparent, however, in the gospel miracle stories involving impure people. In the narrative of the "leper" (Mk 1:40–45) we have seen that it is only hinted at.[219] This is only natural, since the purity issue is merely implicit, being secondary to Mark, and the miracle stories are given mainly a christological function. Hence it it necessary to look at other important gospel narratives about Jesus' exorcisms to see if other associations

---

[215] Cf. Mk 1:21–28; 5:1–20; 9:14–29. The exception is the healing of the daughter of the Syro-Phoenician woman (Mk 7:24–30) which is pictured as an exorcism at a distance; hence the condition of the daughter is never described.

[216] In Mk 1:21–28 the identity of Jesus is in focus, and the Messianic secrecy motif can be found. Jesus' identity is emphasized in 5:1–20 as well, and the result of the event is that the message about Jesus is spread throughout all Dekapolis. In 7:24–30 the power of Jesus is one of the motifs (healing at a distance), and 9:14–29 emphasizes Jesus' power to do anything.

[217] Kee 1967–1968, 245.

[218] Bultmann 1952 [1948], 33.

[219] Cf. above, 103f, and 304.

between demons and impurity can be found, apart from the observation that they are often called "impure spirits" (τὰ πνεύματα τὰ ἀκάθαρτα).

The story of the demoniac in the Capernaum synagogue (Mk 1:23–28 par) ends on a common Markan christological note: people ask themselves about Jesus' identity and authority.[220] Despite this, the narrative itself centres on the power struggle between Jesus and the demoniac. If there are historical reminiscences in this tradition—which Meier finds possible[221] and I regard as probable—they should be found in this power struggle. The power struggle is underscored by the demon's attempt to ward off Jesus by naming him, claiming knowledge of him and thus authority over him ("I know who you are, God's holy one"). The expression "God's holy one" (ὁ ἅγιος τοῦ θεοῦ) is rare indeed; except for the Lukan parallel, the only other occurrence in the NT is found in Jn 6:69, as part of Peter's confession. The title serves Mark's christological purpose, but is not his choice and hardly created by him.[222] The power struggle is further emphasized by the violence involved in the exorcism (καὶ σπαράξαν αὐτὸν τὸ πνεῦμα τὸ ἀκάθαρτον καὶ φωνῆσαν φωνῇ μεγάλῃ ἐξῆλθεν ἐξ αὐτοῦ).[223] It seems likely that Mark has inherited a tradition in which the focus was on the power struggle between unclean spirits and God's holy one, between demonic impurity and divine holiness, and that Jesus was pictured as overcoming the former by means of the latter. This struggle was at an early stage interpreted in an eschatological perspective.[224] Later, "the ultimate victory of Jesus was stressed more and more until it came to be seen as a manifestation of his authority"[225] which caused the aspect of struggle to fall into the background, and with it, the contrast between divine holiness and demonic impurity in early tradition was blurred.

In two other Markan exorcism stories we hardly find any purity connotations at all. Although the healing of the daughter of the Syro-Phoenician woman (Mk 7:24–30 par) is placed directly after the key passages about clean and unclean food, this must be regarded as Mark's redactional joining, reflecting his main interest in this context, i.e. the place and conditions for gentiles in the early church. The reason for this juxtaposition is certainly the relevance of the exorcism story for the gentile question. The possible impurity of gentiles is hardly

---

220 While the question of the crowd in Mk 1:27 is τί ἐστιν τοῦτο; the significance and function of this question is identical to the somewhat parallel reaction of the disciples when Jesus calms the storm in 4:41: τίς ἄρα οὗτός ἐστιν. In both cases the actions of Jesus evoke questions which point to the origin of his authority and the true identity of Jesus.

221 Meier 1994, 648–650.

222 There are no signs that the expression was ever a popular title in the early church.

223 Cf. Chilton 1999, 227f.

224 Note the words of the demoniac: "have you come to destroy us?" (ἦλθες ἀπολέσαι ἡμᾶς;), which seems a bit odd, since an exorcist normally attempted to bind (δεῖν) or torment (βασανίζειν) the demon (cf. Mk 5:7). Chilton 1999, 223 ff; Kee 1967–1968, 242ff.

225 Chilton 1999, 230.

implied by the narrative in its present form since, except for the introduction (7:25), the possessing spirit is called "demon" rather than "impure spirit."[226]

In the narrative of the possessed boy (Mk 9:14–29 par) the spirit is once called impure in passing (v.25) but not throughout the story, which seems to be well integrated with Mark's christological and soteriological aims, following the transfiguration narrative.[227] While the narrative exhibits clear signs of an eschatological power struggle (v.25: ἐπετίμησεν τῷ πνεύματι τῷ ἀκαθάρτῳ ... ἐγὼ ἐπιτάσσω σοι; v 26: καὶ κράξας καὶ πολλὰ σπαράξας ἐξῆλθεν· καὶ ἐγένετο ὡσεὶ νεκρός), it is difficult to trace any impurity connotations in it.

The opposite must be said of the story about the Gerasene demoniac (Mk 5:1–20 par), which bristles with such connotations. As was noted in Chapter IV, several sources of impurity are brought together in this narrative: unclean graves, unclean spirits, swine and probably gentile land as well. The story has been interpreted in different ways; on one level it alludes to the impurity of gentiles, while on another it seems to transmit subtle anti-Roman criticism.[228] The narrative might at some stage have served as a satire on Roman military presence. Possible allusions to Roman occupation and repression have been married with modern socio-psychological and anthropological theories for explaining mental illness and possession. Mental illness could be seen as originating with social tensions and colonial oppression. Drawing on a study by Fanon about mental illness during the Algerian war, Hollenbach argues for analogies with Roman Palestine. The oppressed "native" is said to develop a divided mind, demonizing the oppressor to the degree that disintegration of the personality lies close at hand. Mental illness can furthermore "be seen as a socially acceptable form of oblique protest against, or escape from, oppressions," since the organism chooses a lesser evil to avoid catastrophe, and it functions as an escape valve, helping the dominant classes to control oppressed groups.[229] Hollenbach suggests that the demoniac in Mk 5

> is able to "give the Romans the devil" by identifying their legions, probably the most visible Roman presence to him, with demons... However, he is able to do that only obliquely, through madness. It is likely that the tension between his hatred for his op-

---

[226] Note however Klutz's opposite judgment. He finds the impurity of the demon almost impossible to overlook. Although the juxtaposition is in line with Mark's theological aim, "the highly indirect manner in which the conceptual links are effected ... suggests that the demon-impurity connection probably had the status of common knowledge. As a widely shared belief, the link probably had already functioned for a considerable time as a semantic resource that could be adapted for a variety of rhetorical purposes." (Klutz 1999, 163).

[227] Cf. Sterling 1993, 485, who considers the driving force of this tradition in its Markan context to be discipleship rather than christology.

[228] Cf. above, 180f. Loader's suggestion (1997, 59f, n.107) that the story indicates a picture of Jesus as effectively exorcizing Gentile land, and that his subsequent purification when returning is taken for granted in the underlying pre-Markan tradition, must be doubted.

[229] Hollenbach 1981, 572–580. Quote from p. 575.

pressors and the necessity to repress this hatred in order to avoid dire recrimination drove him mad.[230]

Hollenbach's suggestions are challenging, but rest on very little evidence. The possible anti-Roman connotations in the narrative belong to the narrative level, and can hardly be utilized for building highly speculative hypotheses about why the Gerasene demoniac went mad. A certain confusion of levels is also present when Hollenbach concludes that Jesus was resisted because his exorcism brought the man's (and the neighbourhood's) hatred of the Romans into the open, transforming him from an "Uncle Tom" to a "John Brown," and because his exorcizing activity challenged the social system and its values, threatening the position of the Pharisees.[231] While Jesus' exorcisms partly aimed at, or at least resulted in, social restoration, we must beware of historicizing an uncertain anti-Roman narrative flavour with the help of psychological and anthropological speculation.

A different line of interpretation, with more evidence for it, understands the various pointers to impurity in the context of Gentile mission. This is the view of Annen, who has devoted a monograph to the narrative, and argues that all the elements of impurity (unclean spirits, graves and pigs) are allusions to traditional Jewish criticism of gentiles and their idolatry.[232] This is still on a narrative level, of course. Through painstaking and careful redaction criticism, Annen has suggested a reconstruction of a pre-Markan version of the story, which has much to commend it.[233] Some have claimed that the story is a composite, since the episode of the pigs is awkward and not necessary to the exorcism story itself.[234] The pigs could be seen as a secondary proof of Jesus' success, as the basin or statue in the stories of Eleazar or Apollonius.[235] This is unlikely, however, since the unclean spirits are said to enter into (εἰσῆλθον εἰς) the pigs, not to move them like objects to prove that they left the possessed person.[236] The pre-Markan version probably contained the episode of the pigs as well. They function as vehicles for the spirits on their way to their true element, the watery depths.[237]

---

[230] Hollenbach 1981, 581.

[231] Hollenbach 1981, 581ff. The interpretation of Guijarro (1999, 127f) is a bit more moderate, but similar: "The analogy of the situation in first-century Palestine with that of other societies in which demonic possession is frequent has been the clue to discovering that Jesus' exorcisms were perceived as threatening to the governing elite and their retainers. By casting out the demons and restoring people to society, Jesus threatened a social order in which demonic possession was an escape-valve." For a criticism of Hollenbach, see Davies 1995, 78–81.

[232] Cf. Isa 65. Annen 1976a, 133–184.

[233] Annen 1976a, 39–74. The reconstruction is found on p. 70. Cf. Ådna 1999, who accepts and builds his argument on Annen's reconstruction.

[234] Twelftree 1993, 74.

[235] Cf. *Ant.* 8:46–48; *Vit.Apoll.* 4:20.

[236] Twelftree 1993, 74f.

[237] Cf. Böcher 1970, 50–52, 195–201; Trunk 1994, 108–111.

Annen thinks that the *Sitz im Leben* for the pre-Markan version should be sought among early Jewish Christians, struggling around gentile mission. The narrative of the Gerasene demoniac became an argument for viewing Jesus as the saviour of Gentiles as well as of Israelites, liberating them from their "possession" and impurity.[238] The episode of the pigs is suited to support such an interpretation, since "by the time of the first century CE the pig had become the very symbol of paganism to be avoided at any price in the eyes of all Jews."[239] The episode was possibly joined to the narrative at this pre-Markan stage. This would explain the discrepancy between the geographical locality, the inland city of Gerasa, and the drowning of the pigs in the Sea of Galilee. While Gerasa is by far the best reading, the number of alternative readings, as well as the differing suggestions in the parallel accounts of Matthew and Luke, attest to the uneasiness felt by early scribes and redactors.[240] "Without the panicky pigs and their dip in the deep, the environs of Gerasa, a city some 33 miles southeast of the Sea of Galilee, create no problems for the story."[241]

Behind the narrative level we probably have an historical memory of Jesus having performed an exorcism near Gerasa. The geographical name is a *hapax* in the NT, and the mention of Decapolis in Mk 5:20 seems to be the earliest occurrence of the term in ancient literature. Such details are not likely to be made up of nothing.[242] While the narrative has a plausible *Sitz im Leben* in early Jewish Christianity, it must have made sense in some pre-Markan form, even before gentile mission took form, reflecting an early understanding of Jesus' exorcisms. The impure spirits and the burial ground probably belong to the earliest stage of the narrative. While the number of spirits/animals and the drowning in the sea looks like narrative embellishment, I find no compelling reason for excluding pigs altogether from early tradition.[243] With or without the pigs, however, impurity connotations are strong. We must ask about their meaning before coming to serve as symbols of gentile idolatry in a Christian missionary context.

As in several of the narratives discussed above, the power struggle between Jesus and the demon(s) is emphasized by the violence of the demoniac. In this case the motif is carried to the extreme; the man had often been bound by chains, which he always broke, and he was constantly hurting himself with stones (vv 4–5). The mutual attempt by Jesus and the demoniac to gain power over the opponent is conspicuous. The demon adjures Jesus by God (ὁρκίζω σε τὸν θεόν, v 7) and Jesus requires the demon to reveal his name (v 9).

---

[238] Annen 1976a, 187–190.
[239] Ådna 1999, 293.
[240] Annen 1976a, 201–206, Ådna 1999, 294ff; Meier 1994, 651f.
[241] Meier 1994, 651.
[242] Meier 1994, 653.
[243] For a different view, see Ådna 1999, 290–298.

Although the "theological usefulness" of the story for the early church is apparent (missiology, christology), the narrative with many of its details "cannot be explained as a mere reflection of [Christian] theology."[244] It rather suggests an eschatological power struggle, in which the exorcist overcomes and destroys demonic impurity. This may be understood as due to his pure and holy status (a dynamic type of purity), or to an inherent power or spiritual authority.[245]

Such a status or authority could be associated with the exorcistic methods used by Jesus, according to the gospel tradition. Certain differences between these methods and those described in contemporary literature have been noted by several scholars.[246] The suggestion that the exorcism traditions circulated among groups more interested in Jesus' exorcistic methods than in his message or person, is hardly credible, in view of the "relative absence of technical detail and practical advice" as compared with e.g. the Magical Papyri.[247] Jesus is never described as exorcizing by the use of elaborate spells, incantations, or mechanical devices such as roots, smoke or rings.[248] He is not portrayed as appealing to any authority or source of power. He is not even said to have laid his hands on possessed people, praying to God for deliverance, as did Abraham to Pharaoh in the *Genesis Apocryphon*.[249]

The picture of Jesus as exorcizing through only a simple command suggests a claim for some kind of spiritual authority, which explains why other exorcists were using his name as a source of power at a very early stage.[250] I would suggest that Jesus and his followers saw this power or authority, the "finger of God," as a sign of, or even, a result of the coming kingdom.[251] If Jesus understood his authority as the power of God's coming reign somehow being embodied in, or residing with himself, this would explain his somewhat different exorcizing practice, which did not rely upon precautionary measures and external techniques.

It could also explain his somewhat (in)different attitude to impurity, where little heed was given to protection from pollution, or acts of purification, in spite of the demonic threat that impurity represented. A possible reason for this would be the idea of an intrinsic authority, sufficient to overcome the unclean

---

[244] Chilton 1999, 229. Chilton is here discussing Mk 1:21–28, but the reasoning can be applied to the present narrative as well.

[245] Cf. Chilton 1999, 234.

[246] Dunn 1988, 41; Twelftree 1993, 157–165; Meier 1994, 406.

[247] Chilton 1999, 228.

[248] Cf. methods described by Josephus in his account of Eleazar (*Ant.* 8:46–48), or by the author of Tob 8:2–3, where smoke from the liver and gall of a fish is used to chase away a demon.

[249] 1QapGen 20:28–29.

[250] Cf. Klutz 1999, 159f, who argues that Jesus' name was already being used for exorcism during his life-time. Klutz's argument is based on the discrepancy between the very tolerant attitude ascribed to Jesus in Mk 9:38–39/Lk 9:49–50 and the contrasting situation in Acts 19:13–20.

[251] Lk 11:20. Cf. above, 326f, 330f.

spirits and the impurities involved. In view of God's coming reign, and the powers or authority associated with it, Jesus did not regard impurity in the form of contact-contagion as menacing enough to give it much attention.

Summary: A case for Jesus as overruling impurity with the kingdom

It is clear that the Synoptic Gospels' portrayal of Jesus as an exorcist goes back to historical experience. While the exorcism narratives in Mark can neither be taken at face value as historical records, nor be dismissed as wholesale creations according to a fixed genre, they do provide more than a generalized memory of Jesus' exorcistic activity. Certain details may provide clues for historical interpretation.

In an attempt to situate Jesus' exorcisms within a framework, the Cynic theory has been found wanting and the ideas of Jesus as a Galilean *hasid* or man of deed enlightening but insufficient. Jesus' exorcisms can be properly understood only within an eschatological context. They make most sense when interpreted within the framework of the coming kingdom of God, announced by Jesus. Without polarizing present and future aspects of the kingdom, it is possible to argue that Jesus' miracles in general and his exorcisms in particular were understood as power struggles, paving the way for, or signalling the coming of God's eschatological reign.

While the exorcism narratives serve a christological purpose in the Markan framework, their interpretation as eschatological power struggles is supported by the sayings material in and associated with the so-called Beelzebul pericope.

The connection between Jesus' exorcist activity and his attitude to purity is not only suggested by the terminology (impure spirits), but confirmed when the relationship between demons, disease and certain impurities are examined. We have seen that various diseases as well as "leprosy" and corpse impurity are associated with the activity of demons, in the Hebrew Bible as well as in texts from the Second Temple period. The demonic aspect of impurity is also evident in several rites belonging to the Israelite cult, and it is probably at the root of the purification offering (*hattat*) and cultic expiation (*kipper*). The association between possession and impurity can be found in texts from Qumran as well as in later Christian interpretation of baptism and in rabbinic material concerning the red cow rite.

Thus it becomes the more reasonable to interpret Jesus' power struggles with unclean spirits in an impurity framework. In the words of Klutz:

> There is thus a strong likelihood that Jesus, and many of his Jewish contemporaries, saw the demons of affliction as impure spirits. At least one implication can be confidently drawn about his exorcisms: they ought to be seen as, among other things, rituals of puri-

> fication which, symbolically and paradoxically, both assumed the validity of the demonology-impurity semiotic system and simultaneously flouted it.[252]

This points to a dynamic understanding of purity, in which the holy status of the exorcist is understood as overcoming demonic impurity. The proper context for such an understanding is the eschatological kingdom announced by Jesus, and the prerequisite for such an understanding would be that Jesus regarded himself as the bearer of some intrinsic authority, signalling, or resulting from the coming reign of God. The differences in Jesus' exorcistic method as compared with methods attested in other literature, support this idea.

Jesus' attitude to bodily impurity could be explained in part by this understanding of the coming kingdom, with its ensuing authority, the "finger of God," a power which he considered to be residing somehow within himself. Expressions such as "dynamic purity" or "offensive holiness" may not be warranted by the available evidence. Jesus' attitude should nevertheless be seen within the context of a power struggle, in which the force of bodily impurity was overruled by the power of the kingdom in a similar way to unclean spirits being overcome by exorcism. What was perceived by some as indifference may be seen as a paradoxical acceptance of the impurity concept, in which the power of the kingdom was understood as stronger than the threats associated with impurity, thus relativizing the need for conventional purification.

[252] Klutz 1999, 163.

PART FOUR:

CONCLUDING REFLECTIONS

Chapter VIII
Reconstruction and interpretation

How did Jesus relate to impurity? This is the basic question I have tried to answer throughout this study. Since fairly extensive summaries are available at the end of each chapter, there is no need to repeat conclusions in detail. In this final chapter I will rather try to relate my results to the ongoing quest for the historical Jesus and discuss my findings within a broader context. Reconstruction and interpretation are kept apart in the structure of this chapter, but the separation is in a sense forced, since the two progress in constant interaction, or feed upon each other in actual practice.[1] The structure is used for convenience, however, since the two concepts correspond to the two major parts of this study.

VIII.1 Reconstructing Jesus' attitude to impurity

Legal situation

Reconstructing the state of halakhic development at the end of the Second Temple period is difficult indeed. I have argued that it is possible, however, in certain areas and to a certain extent, through a balanced comparison of rabbinic, Christian, Hellenistic Jewish, intertestamental and Qumran sources. In addition, archaeological evidence contributes to the picture.

It has become clear that rabbinic texts, especially early Tannaitic material, do to some extent reflect conditions before 70 CE, but that the details of halakhic discussion and the general level of halakhic development were usually not as advanced at the end of the Second Temple period as at the time of the *Mishnah*. This is impossible to formulate as a general rule. In some cases, issues which were formerly regarded as late developments are now seen to belong to earlier times, but this does not always apply.

I suggest that this way of reasoning can be applied to other areas as well. The large amount of new Qumran fragments, especially from cave 4, will continue to provide material for assessing the legal situation and halakhic development at the end of the Second Temple period, against which Jesus' activities and teachings must be continuously interpreted.[2]

---

[1] Cf. the methodological discussion about the relationship between the interpretation of individual traditions and an historical *Gesamtbild* in Chapter II, 28–30, 35–37.

[2] This also applies to other issues, which are not strictly halakhic, where detailed comparison between recently available texts with standard sources may shed new light on Jewish practices and beliefs during the Second Temple period, thus influencing the study of the Jesus tradition.

In the area of purity, we have seen signs of an influential expansionist trend towards the end of the Second Temple period. This trend seems to have had the support of an increasing number of common people, who regarded it as an ideal, although they were not always consistent themselves in all matters of purity. There was a general aspiration, however, to a high level of purity, and closer adherence was encouraged. This entailed the general exclusion of "lepers" from towns, some type of isolation of dischargers, coupled with certain practical arrangments to limit the spread of impurity, strict rules for corpse-impurity, and regular purifications by frequent use of *miqvaot*, not only in view of temple visits, but in various circumstances and throughout the country.[3]

Historical evidence

When Jesus is placed in this context, his attitude to impurity may be evaluated. I have found evidence in various Jesus traditions for a behaviour which does not fit smoothly into the legal situation, but is somewhat disturbing from an expansionist point of view. This impression is further corroborated by sayings material, which reflect little concern for purity issues.

I have argued that the Jesus tradition retains historical memories of Jesus' actions, and that it is possible to reconstruct his behaviour in certain areas, at least to some extent. Such reconstruction involves the use of redaction criticism, and the search for hints and implicit pieces of information, which often do not correspond to the ideological interests or concerns of the final redactor/author or hearers/readers of a gospel. I have attempted to show that there are implicit purity issues in several narrative traditions, which must have been understood as such in a Palestinian environment, and that the presence of such issues in the final form of these traditions is best explained as remains from an earlier context and function. I suggest that this method is applicable in other areas as well, and is especially fruitful for narrative traditions.

Examining Jesus' attitude to impurity, we have seen that he was remembered for not conforming to the expansionist trend. Within the framework of his healing and exorcizing activities, he visited "lepers" and touched them, came into contact with women unclean through discharges, and touched corpses. It is also probable that he did not avoid grave-impurity and did not purify regularly by frequent immersions. We thus must acknowledge an apparent tension between Jesus' behaviour and contemporary aspirations and expectations.

---

[3] For detailed discussions, see above: the exclusion of "lepers," 109–112; stone vessels, 84f; isolation of dischargers, 147–150; general avoidance of corpse-impurity, 181–184; *miqvaot*, 74–76, 259, 281.

Priorities

Jesus' behaviour, as reconstructed throughout this study, may be understood as indifferent, and there are signs that it was interpreted as such by his adversaries. While this may be a valid understanding on one level, it is neither a satisfactory nor a sufficient interpretation.

One possible way to explain Jesus' seemingly indifferent attitude is to speak of priorities. Jesus' behaviour would express differing priorities as compared to expansionist concerns. The idea of priority is inherent in a relative reading of Mk 7:15, and could easily be applied to the context of the narrative traditions (i.e. Jesus' healing activity) discussed in this study. The idea of different priorities is also applicable to the parabolic and didactic logia which have been previously dealt with. The idea of social justice or humanitarian assistance taking priority over tithing or purity laws, could be understood as part of a prophetic tradition.[4]

This type of explanation might be applied to Jesus' attitude to legal matters in general. If Jesus is seen as setting priorities different to those of his contemporaries on legal issues, this could be understood at in least two ways. Either he made different judgments (perhaps unusual or more lenient?) in cases where various demands of the law came into conflict with others,[5] or he had an essentially different understanding of the will of God (its manifestation or interpretation).[6] In the first case, Jesus will easily be seen as one among several participants in rabbinic debate and dialogue, but any serious conflict would be difficult to account for. In the second case, conflict becomes intelligible, but Jesus runs the risk of becoming an anachronistic Christian construct. It is far too easy to import ideas about new hearts or law and grace, with all their later dogmatic twists, into this suggestion, and in the ensuing wake we tend to find caricatures of Judaism and a denial of ritual, which hardly can be ascribed to the historical Jesus.

While I think that Jesus' behaviour reveals different priorities, and that there is something to the suggestion that his understanding of God's will differed somehow, I am convinced that Jesus' attitude to legal issues must be interpreted within the framework of his contemporary society, with its culture and religion. Hence in my interpretation of how Jesus related to impurity, I have tried to take account of the purity paradigm, which permeated Jewish culture for centuries. By suggesting various "explanatory models" which fit into this paradigm, I have attempted to provide an explanation in a broad sense.[7]

---

[4] Cf. above, 88, 195f, 198, 201, 231, 260.
[5] Cf. Vermes 1993, 11–45.
[6] Cf. the conclusions of Westerholm's study, 1978, 59f, 91, 103, 112f, 123ff.
[7] Cf. the discussion about explanation, causation and "thick description" in Chapter II, 37–39.

VIII.2 Interpreting Jesus' attitude to impurity

The inside: a moral understanding

I have claimed that Jesus' attitude must be interpreted as part of a moral trajectory in which the Israelite prophetic tradition was an important part. We have seen, however, that, although purity language is used in various contexts or for various purposes, and although there are two or three differing purity "systems" in priestly legislation, it is difficult to separate moral and ritual purity in a clear-cut way. The idea that the total "compartmentalization" of the rabbis should have dominated the scene through the Pharisees in Jesus' time is doubtful.

The use of purity language for moral evil and social injustice is not necessarily secondary. When Jesus is seen as part of such a tradition, the sayings contrasting bodily purity with greed fit well into the picture. John's baptism as an alternative to repeated ablution, and in view of the coming judgment, could also be understood within such a purity paradigm.

I have argued that the contrasting pair "inner-outer" is suitable for interpreting tensions between Jesus' and some of his adversaries' views on purity, but that this pair neither corresponds exactly to our distinction between moral and ritual, nor to that between soul and body. Jesus apparently saw moral evil and social injustice as a more serious impurity than bodily defilement, but this must be understood within the context of Hebrew corporeal anthropology, rather than western spiritualization.

We can thus see that the contrast between inner and outer in various strands of the Jesus tradition may be understood not as a later Christian creation, but as part of an intra-Jewish discussion, and that Jesus' ethical ideas are compatible with the current purity paradigm and a moral trajectory.

Galilee: a rural, non-official context

The discussion about regional diversity is perhaps the most speculative part of this study, since there is little concrete evidence for clearly deviating practices in northern Palestine. It is evident that in Jewish Galilee, Judaean traits dominated, including the purity paradigm. There are signs, however, of differing levels of development for various legal matters. A Galilean perspective must take into account rural conditions, economic tensions and pragmatic aspects.

I agree with the judgment that Galilean Jews in general wished to be faithful, and were fairly conservative in their orientation towards Jerusalem as an orthogenetic centre, and the home of "great tradition." At the same time, the development of expansionist interpretation did not provide satisfactory solutions for the ongoing struggle between local social structures and the intrusion of foreign values and changes in economy and ownership patterns, partly associated with the development of heterogenetic cities in the midst of Galilee.

Within such an environment, Jesus cannot be seen simply as a representative of local tradition or popular opinion, but his type of authority (including a differing understanding of the will of God?) and priority (involving a more pragmatic ethics?) was apparently attractive. Although this reconstruction is somewhat uncertain, it makes it possible once more to understand Jesus' attitude to impurity within the framework of a contemporary Jewish purity paradigm.

I would suggest that the idea of Jesus' stance as providing a "way out" of a dilemma caused by conflicting cultural and religious demands, is possible to apply to areas other than purity. When mapping out the various issues, legal or otherwise religious and social, where Jesus stood out from common practice or was opposed by authorities, it will be more fruitful to regard him as suggesting possibilities of remaining faithful to tradition in some ways, albeit different or unusual, rather than breaking with it altogether.

Kingdom: a power perspective

I have argued for obvious and distinct links between demonology and the purity paradigm in ancient Israel, and tried to demonstrate that such links are manifest in various strata of Jewish tradition. Especially on the popular level, demonic aspects to impurity are strong.

Since Jesus' exorcisms are closely associated with God's coming reign, it is possible to examine his attitude to impurity from a power perspective, and to regard his kingdom eschatology as compatible with the purity paradigm. Jesus' exorcisms, as well as his behaviour towards impure people in general, could be seen in the context of a power struggle, in which the power of the kingdom which he proclaimed, mediated or embodied, would overrule demonic influence and impurity.

The interpretations of such an association may differ, however. In the contemporary cultural and religious environment, I do not find it likely that this power perspective caused Jesus to disregard the purity paradigm in the sense that he should have totally scrapped the idea of bodily impurity. The idea of a contagious type of holiness, stronger than impurity and thus overtaking it, is appealing and slightly more convincing, but not sufficiently so, since it lacks clear evidence. It could perhaps be modified somewhat. I suggest that it was not the inherent holiness of his own person, but the power of the coming reign of God, which Jesus believed overpowered demons and impurities. That power was certainly seen as residing with, or mediated by Jesus, but it should not be seen as a warrant for Jesus flouting the impurity concept altogether. It is more likely that this power made it possible for Jesus to relativize and to a certain extent disregard bodily impurity, but still within the framework of a basic purity paradigm. This behaviour pushed the paradigm to the breaking-point, however, at least in the eyes of those who did not subscribe to his power perspective, or views on other issues. To them his attitude was perceived as indifferent.

VIII.3 Jesus then and now

Jesus and purity in his society

During the latest phase of historical Jesus-research, an increasing number of scholars have focused on Jesus' Jewishness. While the counter-cultural Cynic has a number of disciples, and a protestant preacher still lingers in some quarters, the Galilean Jew, Jesus, is more and more taking centre stage.

If Jesus was a first-century Jew he must be interpreted within the Second Temple Judaism of which he was a part. If he was a social and/or religious reformer, an authoritative teacher, or a charismatic healer, intent on communication and response, he must have shared a sufficient number of general concepts and presuppositions belonging to contemporary paradigms.

Such are the conditions under which I have tried to explore Jesus' attitude to impurity. I have suggested that Jesus was part of a moral trajectory which placed relative importance on ethics, that he had a pragmatic, rural or locally based attitude, which did not allow purity rules to intervene with social network, table fellowship and community, and that his eschatological outlook made impurity subordinate to the kingdom. This reconstruction places Jesus clearly within Jewish society. It is nevertheless a picture full of tension. Although remaining somehow within the framework of the purity paradigm, Jesus disregards impurity in a way which may threaten the whole concept and cause its breakdown. Wouldn't it be easier to reconstruct Jesus without any serious conflicts or dissensions?

The problem is that continuity with contemporary society alone does not suffice for a satisfactory historical explanation. There is a *wirkungsgeschichte* too, which must not be cut off from its presumed roots.

Jesus and purity in the early church

Within a few decades, an increasing part (although still not a majority) of the Christian movement was developing standpoints which were far from normal Jewish practice. Not only were purity practices neglected, but forbidden meat was gradually accepted and even circumcision and sabbath-keeping were successively abandoned. The list of practices finally set aside amounts to more or less every important identity marker of Judaism, except monotheism itself.[8]

The early Christians who pulled in this direction apparently took Jesus as an authority for this development. The evidence at their disposal was weak, however. Discussing Mk 7:1–23 in Chapter III, I argued that the food issue in the early church rested on a slender historical base, since the hand-washing tradition did not quite address the problem for which it was appealed to. Likewise, the choice of the story about the Syro-Phoenician woman in Mk 7:24–30, cannot

[8] Cf. Casey 1991, 12f.

be understood except in a context in which arguments in favour of Gentile mission were badly needed, and then as making a virtue out of necessity; this was the best tradition available. At a later stage, Jesus' Sabbath healings were interpreted as an outright abolition of the Sabbath commandment (Jn 5:18), although this is hardly evident from the synoptic accounts. Traditions about Jesus pushing limits or transgressing borders were combined with interpretations of Scripture, and eventually utilized as arguments against a whole paradigm.

As a proof-texting enterprise this does not inspire confidence in modern readers, but neither do the exegeses of contemporary rabbis. More important than the question of how they found support in Scripture and tradition for their standpoints, is the fact that a growing number of Christians believed that this interpretation was *in line with* Jesus' behaviour and attitude.

This process has often been seen as a "spiritualization" which involved not only purity or Sabbath-keeping, but the cultic paradigm in its totality.[9] Spiritualization, however, does not necessarily lead to the abolition of cultic practices, but only to the understanding of their inner meaning, which is evident from Philo or the author of the letter to Aristeas.[10] When we try to describe this process in the early church it would perhaps be better to speak with Dunn about the cultic categories being "transposed,"[11] i.e. they are applied to, or their function is taken over by, other "items."

Jesus' attitude to the cult and the *halakhah* was not one of outright spiritualization, especially not if spiritualization is understood as a metaphorical use of ritual language. In Chapter V, I pointed to the difficulties in strictly separating literal and metaphorical use of language, and noted the corporeal anthropology which permeated moral and spiritual reflection in Judaism.

In my attempt to interpret Jesus' attitude within a Jewish context and in relation to the current purity paradigm, I have looked to a moral trajectory, regional conditions and an eschatological power perspective. I suggest a certain continuity with the early church on these points. It continued the moral trajectory with a relative understanding of bodily impurity. The development took place in a somewhat different context, as the Christian movement encountered various cultural environments and social strata. This created new fellowships and social networks, involving mutual obligation between people of various backgrounds. Although these new social structures were held together by certain common beliefs, they were seriously threatened by conflicting paradigms, and at

---

[9] I.e. the temple cult with its sacrifices and priesthood. Cf. Wenschkewitz 1932. "[Spiritualisierung] bedeutet zunächst, dass die Frömmigkeitsformen geistiger Art die Ausdrucksformen der kultischen Frömmigkeit für sich in Anspruch nehmen, sie in Sinnzusammenhänge ihrer Gestalt einfügen und dadurch umdeuten." Ibid., 8.

[10] *Let.Aris.* 143–171; Allegorization in general can be found all through Philo's works. For an example of spiritualizing interpretation, which is not at all dependent on the rites being carried out, but nevertheless presupposes their literal adherence, see *Spec.Laws* 1: 205–211.

[11] Dunn 1991, 75–97.

times broken apart by some insisting on strict purity practices. In the interest of unity, purity rules were compromized.[12] While Jesus' focus on the "kingdom" was replaced by the "gospel," and imminent eschatology gradually receded into the background, some aspects of a demonic perspective still remained. But since fellowship with Christ, like the reign of God, was considered more powerful than demons, danger and impurity were relativized.[13] The purity paradigm was not totally ignored, but was adapted, as purity rules were relativized and given less priority. The development was partly rationalized by spiritualizing interpretations. The end result looked very different from Jesus' behaviour, but the choices made during the process could be understood as analogous with Jesus' attitude, i.e. as similar judgments and priorities, although in other contexts.

This is a possible interpretation, yet only from the viewpoint of a "western" or predominantly Greek-speaking Christianity. From the viewpoint of "eastern" or Jewish Christians, the development I have sketched cannot have been understood as anything but contrary to Jesus' intentions. In a sense this is plausible, since Jesus hardly denied Jewish identity markers, abolished halakhic custom or scrapped the purity paradigm altogether. Still there were embarrassing traits in Jesus' behaviour which, in view of their interpretation by the increasingly non-Jewish churches, were downplayed by Jewish Christians, since they could give the impression that Jesus was indifferent to legal matters.[14] To these Christians, Jesus was rather a superior rabbinic interpreter of the law, and the distinction between them and other Jews was understood in terms of love versus legalism or honesty versus hypocrisy, resulting in polemic caricatures.[15]

Jesus and purity today

The leap from Jesus to the early church is large enough, although it is only a matter of decades. The leap from Jesus to our own time is a matter of millennia. To the average person in the modern world, purity rules seem strange and remote. Food-restrictions are more familiar to us, mainly through contemporary Judaism and Islam, but also, to some degree, through segments of the Christian church.[16] The non-observer may relate to such restrictions by associating them with other types of contemporary diets based on arguments from health or ethics.

---

[12] Acts 15:19-20, 28-29; 21: 17-26; Rom 14:14; Gal 2:11-14.

[13] Cf. the issue of idol meat and idol worship, and unclean food: 1Cor 8:1–13; 10:1–22; Rom 14:13–23; or marriage with unbelievers and the status of children: 2Cor 6:14–7:1; 1Cor 7:12–14.

[14] Cf. the Matthean variants of Mark's Sabbath traditions (Mt 12:1–14), in which the portrayal of an indifferent Jesus is modified into a responsible interpreter of the law (cf. above, 57ff).

[15] It is interesting that the clearest examples in the New Testament of what is today perceived as a misrepresentation of Judaism and a judgmental attitude are found with Matthew (cf. 22:7; 23; 27:25), not with Paul, unless the latter is read with dogmatic Lutheran glasses.

[16] Cf. various fasting practices during Lent, or the general abstinence from certain foods found with certain Christian sects.

Bodily impurity, however, is a foreign idea in the western world. It is possibly associated with discrimination against women, since those traces which have survived through the centuries until our day have often concerned menstruation and/or childbirth.[17] This is certainly one possible and legitimate angle from which these rules can be studied, but it cannot serve as a sufficient explanation for the conspicuous development, in which the system of bodily impurity successively became obsolete, not only in mainstream Christianity, but also in rabbinic Judaism, except for a few remnants.

This is a different story, which cannot be told here, but some brief reflections are appropriate. To begin with, the demise of purity *halakhah* in rabbinic Judaism is clear not only from various signs of an increasing leniency with regard to rules about "leprosy" and discharges,[18] but also from the fact that the *Talmudim* contain no *Gemara* for any mishnaic tractate belonging to the order of "Purities," except for *Niddah*. The cessation of many purity practices in Talmudic times is often explained as resulting from the loss of the temple. This is argued from the supposition that purity was observed mainly in view of temple visits and the temple service, and from the fact that ashes for purification of corpse-impurity were not infinitely available after the fall of the temple.[19] The arguments are insufficient, since purity during the Second Temple period had an independent value, and was observed not only for the sake of the temple. The reasons for this could be manifold, and the expansionist current was motivated by interpretation of Scripture and a striving for faithfulness.[20] This widespread adherence needs additional explanations: individual piety is one possibility, the increasing endeavour for separation from Gentiles is another.[21] Separation was more difficult in the *diaspora*, however, where a large degree of interaction was necessary, and this became the *Sitz im Leben* for rabbinic Judaism in Talmudic times. Individual piety was expressed increasingly through Torah study and synagogue prayer, and although this development did not originate with the fall of the temple, but at an earlier date, it became a hallmark of rabbinic Judaism.

It is interesting that foot-washing developed into a rite of preparation before prayer during approximately the same period as adherence to other purity rules diminished.[22] It could be questioned whether foot-washing should be defined as a purification rite, relating to bodily impurity, or rather a rite of preparation be-

---

[17] Cf. Meens 2000; Caspers 2000.

[18] *mNeg* 3:1-2; 5:1; *mZab* 2:2; cf. further references and discussion in *EJ* 13: 1412f.

[19] Although originally independent of the temple, the red cow rite was incorporated into the cult, and classified as a *hattat* sacrifice. While the cow was slaughtered outside of the city, its blood was sprinkled by the priest towards the sanctuary (cf. above, 307). According to the Tannaim, only seven or nine cows were burnt all through the history of Judaism, and none after the loss of the temple (*mPar* 3:5).

[20] Cf. Harrington 1993, 261-265.

[21] Cf. Regev 2000, 237-241.

[22] I.e. during Talmudic times; Bar-Ilan 1991; Regev 2000, 239f, n.49.

fore worship.[23] Some suggest that it developed under Islamic influence.[24] However that may be, there is in any case an analogy to Muslim purity rules, which are all geared towards prayer, and exhibit much less of a dynamic or "dangerous" character than did bodily impurity in Judaism during temple times.[25] Traces of purity rules in Christianity are likewise aimed at worship,[26] from the discussions of Dionysios and the *Didascalia* about menstruating women's access to the eucharist,[27] to the medieval practice of churching after child-birth, which survived in some parts of the church well into the twentieth century.[28]

While partly retaining their function as identity markers, at least in Judaism and Islam, the remains of the bodily purity paradigm do not play as important a role today as they did in the past. Other practices have become more important as religious characteristics. The attitude of Jesus as summarized and explained in this study[29] does not seem as relevant when confronted with today's remnant observances of ritual purity as it was in the context of first-century conflicts and dissensions. The purity paradigm played a different role in the past. Today, other things may have similar functions. There are symbols, practices and pieces of dogma in our religions which cause different (or similar?) conflicts and dissensions. There are norms, structures and values in our societies which pose different (or similar?) problems to communities and individuals. Is it possible that Jesus' attitude still has some relevance? Is it reasonable to think that, in view of the huge time leap, the *historical* Jesus would still be significant today? I think so, but my suggestions must be limited to my own religion, Christianity.

The discussion about the relationship between the historical Jesus and Christian faith is inherent in exegetical Jesus research. Already Kähler had pointed to the risk of historical work becoming an ideological tool.[30] Recently, Barry Henaut has argued that the "historical Jesus" must be regarded as a christological construct.[31] John P. Meier, agreeing with Kähler and Bultmann on this point, stresses that "the Jesus of history is not and cannot be the object of Christian

[23] Cf. above, 254f.
[24] Cf. the views of Naphtali Wieder, disputed by Bar-Ilan 1991.
[25] Reinhart 1990.
[26] Cf. the various issues discussed in Browe 1932.
[27] Cf. above, 133, n.243. For examples of various competing views through the Middle Ages, see Meens 2000. However, his idea (292) of ritual purity as so important for third-century Christians that it was no matter for discussion at this early stage is hardly warranted by a reference to Dionysios, in view of opposite opinions from the same period (*Didascalia*).
[28] During the Middle Ages churching developed into a popular feast, and neither early criticism, nor Protestant protests, succeded in restraining this "judaizing" rite. Cf. Caspers 2000.
[29] I.e. representing a moral trajectory, regional conditions, and an eschatological power perspective, leading to different priorities.
[30] Kähler 1988 [1896], 55f.
[31] Henaut 1997.

faith."[32] The historical Jesus is only a scholarly reconstruction, which changes with time and circumstances. The quest for the historical Jesus is useful, however, says Meier, "if one is asking about faith seeking understanding, i.e. theology, in a contemporary context."[33] In the end, however, this distinction between reality and history or faith and theology is difficult to uphold. There is always an interaction between perception and reflection.

Certainly, if historical Jesus research is used as the basis for traditional Christian dogmatics, it will no doubt turn into christological construction. But it is not the task of historical exegetes to provide building blocks for dogmatic theology, but rather to dismantle it, in order to make available the rich diversity and various possibilities residing in so many ancient texts.

From this perspective I suggest that the historical Jesus has a potential significance for both Christian faith and theology. The Christian movement contains an enormous amount of dogmatic variation. We find a number of diverging interpretations of Jesus' death and its meaning, various views on atonement, conflicting ideas about his resurrection. There is no unity, except in the fact that most Christians agree that something crucial was revealed by or through this human being; something about God's being, the divine will, the human condition and/or the possibilities of human co-existence. From such conviction christology evolves, although it takes different paths. While some immediately talk of incarnation, others prefer an approach from below, in which believers are seen as gradually realizing the meaning of their experience: a crucial glimpse of God becoming visible through that person. There is every disagreement on dogmatics, but agreement on Jesus' significance.

This is why the historical Jesus is important for Christian faith. His actions, behaviour and attitude mediated or conveyed an image of God as well as an understanding of humanity to his followers from the very beginning. Interpretation of those actions, that behaviour and attitude, is still the route for followers today, trying to make sense of ancient stories. That is doing theology, and it is done not only by specialists, but by every reflecting person.

Purity is admittedly a narrow subject, but if Jesus' attitude to impurity should be interpreted today, as it was by early Christians, and against the results of an historical investigation, what would that entail? To define the concrete issues is a task for Christian theology which goes beyond the task of this study. A few hints must suffice. I think we would have to discuss the relative priority of moral issues (personal ethics and social justice) as compared with prevailing cultural and religious demands. We would have to wrestle with tensions between conflicting structures, where "local" and diverse "cultures" (in church and society) offering community and network are threatened by official norms

[32] Meier 1991, 197.
[33] Meier 1991, 198.

and policies. We would have to rethink our visions of fellowship and future, and whether they are strong enough to overrule such evil as is allowed to gain ascendancy over people or shut them out from their spiritual or social framework.

In this process of reflection and interpretation, participants may find something revealed in Jesus' behaviour and attitude to impurity, which may be wrought within the bonds of a given social context and cultural paradigm, although not without conflict and tension—something which gives priority to human needs, preference to social fellowship, and power to overcome segregation, and thus has relevance not only in an historical past, but in our contemporary world.

Bibliography

Sources

Jewish Literature

Hebrew Bible

Biblia Hebraica Stuttgartensia. Editio funditus Renovata. Eds. K. Elliger and W. Rudolph. Stuttgart: Deutsche Bibelgesellschaft, 1977.

LXX

Septuaginta: Id est Vetus Testamentum graece iuxta LXX interpretes. 2 vols. Ed. Alfred Rahlfs. Stuttgart: Württembergische Bibelanstalt, 1935.

Vetus Testamentum Graece iuxta LXX interpretes. Ed. Constantinus Tischendorf. 2 vols. Lipsiae: F.A. Brockhaus, 1856.

Apocrypha and Pseudepigrapha

Burchard, Christoph. ed. *Joseph und Aseneth.* Jüdische Schriften aus hellenistisch-römischer Zeit. Band II:4. *Unterweisung in erzählender Form.* Gütersloh: Gütersloher Verlagshaus Gerd Mohn, 1983.

Charlesworth, James H., ed. *The Old Testament Pseudepigrapha.* 2 vols. New York: Doubleday, 1983–1985.

Philonenko, Marc. *Joseph et Aséneth: Introduction. Texte Critique. Traduction et Notes.* Studia Post-Biblica, 13. Leiden: Brill, 1968.

Dead Sea Scrolls

Charlesworth, James H. (ed.).*The Dead Sea Scrolls. Hebrew, Aramaic, and Greek Texts with English Translation.* Vol. 1. *Rule of the Community and Related Documents.* Tübingen: J. C. B. Mohr (Paul Siebeck).

DDR

The Damascus Documents Reconsidered. Ed. Magen Broshi. Jerusalem: The Israel Exploration Society. 1992.

DJD 5

Qumran Cave 4, I: (*4Q158–4Q186*). Ed. John M. Allegro. DJD 5. Oxford: Clarendon, 1968.

DJD 7

Qumrân Grotte 4, III: (*4Q482–4Q520*). Ed. Maurice Baillet. DJD 7. Oxford: Clarendon, 1982.

DJD 10

Qumran Cave 4, V: *Miqṣat Ma'aśe Ha-Torah.* DJD 10. Eds. and tr. Elisha Qimron and John Strugnell. Oxford: Clarendon, 1994.

DJD 18

Qumran Cave 4, XIII: *The Damascus Document (4Q266–273).* DJD 18. Ed. and tr. Joseph Baumgarten. Oxford: Clarendon, 1996.

DJD 35

Qumran Cave 4, XXV*: Halakhic Texts.* Eds. and tr. Joseph Baumgarten et. al. DJD 35. Oxford: Clarendon, 1999.

DSS GM

The Dead Sea Scrolls Translated: The Qumran Texts in English. 2nd ed. Tr. F. García Martínez. Leiden: Brill, 1996.

DSSSE
The Dead Sea Scrolls Study Edition. 2 vols. Eds. F. García Martínez and E. J. C. Tigchelaar. Leiden: Brill, 1997–1998.
TQ
Die Texte aus Qumran: Hebräisch und Deutsch. Ed. and tr. E. Lohse. München: Kösel-Verlag, 1971.
ZD
The Zadokite Documents: I. The Admonition. II. The Laws. Ed. and tr. Chaim Rabin. Oxford: Clarendon Press, 1954.

Josephus and Philo
Josephus. Ed. and tr. H. St. J. Thackeray (vols. 1–5), Ralph Marcus (vols. 5–8) and Louis Feldman (vols. 9–10). LCL. Cambridge, Massachussets: Harvard University Press, 1926–1965.
Philo. Ed. and tr. F. H. Colson and G. H. Whitaker. 10 vols. LCL. Cambridge, Massachussets: Harvard University Press, 1929–1943.
Philo Supplement. Ed. and tr. Ralph Marcus. 2 vols. LCL. Cambridge, Massachussets: Harvard University Press, 1953.

Mishnah
Faksimilie-Ausgabe des Mischnacodex Kaufmann A 50: Mit Genehmigung der Ungarischen Akademie der Wissenschaften in Budapest. 2 vols. Ed. G. Beer. Veröffentlichungen der Alexander Kohut-Gedächtnisstiftung. Haag: Martinus Nijhoff, 1929.
Die Mischna: Text, Übersetzung und ausführliche Erklärung. 6 vols. Eds. Georg Beer, Oscar Holtzmann, Karl Heinrich Rengstorf and Leonhard Rost. Berlin: Walter de Gruyter, 1912–.
Mishna Codex Parma (De Rossi 138): An early Vowelized Manuscript of the Complete Mishna Text. Jerusalem: Kedem Publishing, 1970.
The Mishnah: A New Translation. Tr. J. Neusner. New Haven and London: Yale University Press, 1988.

Tosefta
Lieberman, Saul. *Tosefeth Rishonim: A Commentary.* Part 3–4. *Seder Tohoroth.* New York: The Jewish Theological Seminary of America, 1999 [1939].
The Tosefta: According to Codex Vienna, with Variants from Codex Erfurt, Genizah mss. and Editio Princeps (Venice 1521). The Order of Zera'im. Ed. Saul Lieberman. New York: Jewish Theological Seminary of America. 1955.
Tosefta: al kitve yad Erfurt ve-Vien: im mareh makom ve-hilufe girsaot u-maftehot ve-tsiyur ketav yad Erfurt. Tr. Moses Samuel Zuckermandel. Pazevolk [Trier]: 1881/1882.
Die Tosefta: Text. Ed. Karl Heinrich Rengstorf. Vol. 1. *Seder Zeraim.* Rabbinische Texte. Stuttgart: W. Kohlhammer, 1983.
Die Tosefta: Text / Übersetzung / Erklärung. Eds. Gerhard Kittel and Karl Heinrich Rengstorf. Vol. 1:1, 1–3. *Seder Seraim* [Heft 3: *Zeraim*]. Rabbinische Texte. Erste Reihe. Stuttgart: W. Kohlhammer, 1956–1958.
Die Tosefta: Text. Ed. Karl Heinrich Rengstorf. Vol. 6. *Seder Ṭoharot.* Rabbinische Texte. Erste Reihe. Stuttgart: W. Kohlhammer, 1967.
Die Tosefta: Übersetzung und Erklärung. Ed. Karl Heinrich Rengstorf. Vol. 6:1-3. *Seder Ṭoharot.* Rabbinische Texte. Erste Reihe. Stuttgart: W. Kohlhammer, 1960–1967.
Jerusalem Talmud
Synopse zum Talmud Yerushalmi. Band II/1-4. *Ordnung Mo'ed: Shabbat, 'Eruvin, Pesaḥim und Yoma.* Eds. P. Schäfer and H.-J. Becker. Texts and Studies in Ancient Judaism, 82. Tübingen: Mohr Siebeck, 2001.

The Talmud of the Land of Israel: A Preliminary Translation and Explanation. Tr. Jacob Neusner et.al. 35 vols. Chicago Studies in the History of Judaism. Chicago: University of Chicago Press, 1982–1994.

Yoma: Versöhnungstag. Tr. Friedrich Avemarie. Übersetzung des Talmud Yerushalmi. Eds. H.-J. Becker et.al. Band II/4. Tübingen: J.C.B. Mohr (Paul Siebeck), 1995.

Babylonian Talmud

Der Babylonische Talmud. Tr. Lazarus Goldschmidt. 12 vols. Berlin: Jüdischer Verlag, 1930–1936.

Mekhilta, Sifra and Sifre

Mekhilta: Ein tannaitischer Midrasch zu Exodus. Tr. Jakob Winter and August Wünsche. Leipzig: J.C.Hinrichs'sche Buchhandlung, 1909.

Mekhilta according to Rabbi Ishmael: An Analytical Translation. Tr. Jacob Neusner. 2 vols. Brown Judaic Studies 148, 154. Atlanta, Georgia: Scholars Press, 1988.

Mekilta de-Rabbi Ishmael. Ed. and tr. Jacob Z. Lauterbach. 3 vols. The JPS Library of Jewish Classics. Philadelphia: The Jewish Publication Society of America, 1933-1935.

Sifra. An Analytical Translation. Tr. Jacob Neusner. 3 vols. Brown Judaic Studies, 138–140. Atlanta, Georgia: Scholars Press, 1988.

Sifre Deuteronomium. Tr. Hans Bietenhard. Judaica et Christiana, 8. Bern: Peter Lang, 1984.

Sifre to Deuteronomy: An Analytical Translation. Tr. Jacob Neusner. 2 vols. Brown Judaic Studies, 98, 101. Atlanta, Georgia: Scholars Press, 1987.

Tannaitische Midraschim. Rabbinische Texte, Zweite Reihe, Band 2. *Sifre zu Numeri.* Heft 1–9. Tr. Karl Georg Kuhn. Stuttgart: W. Kohlhammer, 1933–1955.

Tannaitische Midraschim. Rabbinische Texte, Zweite Reihe, Band 3. *Der Midrasch Sifre zu Numeri.* Tr. Dagmar Börner-Klein. Stuttgart: W. Kohlhammer, 1997.

Other rabbinic literature

The Code of Maimonides. Book Ten. The Book of Cleanness. Tr. Herbert Danby. Yale Judaica Series, 8. New Haven: Yale University Press, 1954.

Midrasch Tannaim zum Deuteronomium aus der in der Königlichen Bibliothek zu Berlin befindlichen Handschrift des „Midrasch haggadol" gesammelt und mit Anmerkungen versehen. Ed. D. Hoffmann. Berlin: Druck von H. Itzkowski, 1909.

The Midrash on Psalms. 2 vols. Tr. William G. Braude. Yale Judaica Series, 13. New Haven: Yale University Press, 1959.

Midrash Rabbah. 10 vols. Eds. H. Freedman and M. Simon. London: Soncino Press, 1939.

Pĕsiḳta dĕ-Raḇ Kahăna: R. Kahana's Compilation of Discourses for Sabbaths and Festal Days. Tr. William G. Braude and Israel Kapstein. The Littman Library of Jewish Civilization. London: Routledge & Kegan Paul, 1975.

Targum

The Bible in Aramaic based on Old Manuscripts and Printed Texts. Ed. Alexander Sperber. Vol. 3, *The latter Prophets according to Targum Jonathan.* Leiden: Brill, 1962.

Chilton, Bruce. *The Isaiah Targum: Introduction, Translation, Apparatus and Notes.* The Aramaic Bible, vol. 11. Wilmington, Delaware: Michael Glazier, Inc., 1987.

Greek and Other Ancient Literature

Inscriptions and Papyri

IG

Inscriptiones Graecae. Vol 4. *Inscriptiones Argolidis.* Berolini: Apud Georgium Reimerum, 1902.

PGM

The Greek Magical Papyri in Translation: Including the Demotic Spells. Ed. Hans Dieter Betz. Chicago: The University of Chicago Press, 1986.

Papyri Graecae Magicae: Die Griechischen Zauberpapyri. 2 vols. 2nd ed. Ed. and tr. Karl Preisendanz. Sammlung Wissenschaftlicher Commentare. Stuttgart: Verlag B. G. Teubner, 1973–1974 [1928–1931].

Vandier, Jacques. *Le Papyrus Jumilhac.* Centre National de la recherche scientifique, 1962.

Apuleius

Florida. Ed. R. Helm. *Apulei Platonici Madaurensis: Opera Quae Supersunt,* vol. 2:2. Bibliotheca Scriptorum Graecorum et Romanorum Teubneriana. Lipsiae in Aedibus: B.G. Teubneri, 1959.

Aristophanes

Acharnenses. Ed. and tr. B.B. Rogers. *Aristophanes,* vol. 1. LCL. Cambridge, Massachusetts: Harvard University Press, 1938.

Celsus

On Medicine. 3 vols. Ed. and tr. W.G. Spencer. LCL. Cambridge, Massachusetts: Harvard University Press, 1960–1961 [1935–1938].

Lucian

The Lover of Lies, or the Doubter. Ed. and tr. A.M. Harmon. *Lucian of Samosata,* vol 3. LCL. Cambridge, Massachusetts: Harvard University Press, 1948.

Philostratus

The Life of Apollonius of Tyana. 2 vols. Ed. and tr. F. C. Conybeare. LCL. London: William Heinemann, 1912.

Plato

Laws. 2 vols. Ed. and tr. R.G. Bury. Cambridge, Massachusetts: Harvard University Press, 1961 [1926].

Phaedo. Ed. C.J. Rowe. Cambridge Greek and Latin Classics. Cambridge: Cambridge University Press, 1993.

Pliny

Naturalis Historia: Natural History with an English Translation in Ten Volumes. Ed. and tr. H. Rackham, et. al. LCL. Cambridge, Massachusetts: Harvard University Press, 1938–1971.

Porphyry

Porphyrii Philosophi Platonici. "De abstinentia" in *Opuscula Selecta.* Ed. Augustus Nauck. Bibliotheca Scriptorum Graecorum et Romanorum Teubneriana. Lipsiae: In Aedibus B.G. Teubneri, 1886.

Early Christian Literature

New Testament

Novum Testamentum Graece. Eds. E. and E. Nestle, B. and K. Aland, et. al. 27th ed. Stuttgart: Deutsche Bibelgesellschaft, 1993.

Apostolic Fathers

The Apostolic Fathers. 2 vols. Ed. and tr. Kirsopp Lake. LCL. Cambridge, Massachussets, 1912–1913.

New Testament Apocrypha

New Testament Apocrypha. Vol 1: *Gospels and Related Writings*. Ed. W. Schneemelcher. Tr. R. McL. Wilson. Cambridge: James Clarke & Co., 1991.

Papyrus Egerton 2

Fragments of an Unknown Gospel and other Early Christian Papyri. Eds. and tr. H. Idris Bell and T. C. Skeat. London: Published by the Trustees, 1935.

Kölner Papyri. Papyrologica Coloniensia, vol. 7, band 6. Eds. M. Gronewald, et al. Opladen: Westdeutscher Verlag, 1987.

Papyrus Oxyrhynchus 840

Fragments of an Uncanonical Gospel from Oxyrhynchus. Eds. and tr. Bernard P. Grenfell and Arthur S. Hunt. London: For the Egypt Exploration Fund by Henry Frowde, Oxford University Press, 1908.

The Oxyrhynchus Papyri. Part 5. Eds. and tr. Bernard P. Grenfell and Arthur S. Hunt. London: Egypt Exploration Fund, 1908.

Thomas, Coptic Gospel of

Nag Hammadi codex II, 2–7, together with XIII,2, Brit. Lib. Or. 4926(1), and P.Oxy. 1, 654, 655*. Ed. Bentley Layton. Nag Hammadi Studies 20. Leiden: Brill, 1989.

Didascalia

Didascaliae Apostolorum, Canonum Ecclesiasticorum, Traditionis Apostolicae. Versiones Lainae. Ed. E. Tidner. Texte und Untersuchungen zur Geschichte der Altchristlichen Literatur, 75. Berlin: Akademie-Verlag, 1963.

Didascalia Apostolorum in Syriac, I. Tr. A. Vööbus. Corpus Scriptorum Christianorum Orientalium 402, Scriptores Syri tomus 176. Louvain: Secrétariat du CorpusSCO, 1979.

Dionysius

The Letters and Other Remains of Dionysius of Alexandria. Ed. Charles Lett Feltoe. Cambridge Patristic Texts. Cambrige: University Press, 1904.

John Chrysostom

In Matthaeum Homiliae, 31. *Patrologiae cursus completus. Series graeca*, 57. Ed. J.-P. Migne. Paris: 1860.

Pseudo-Clementine Regognitions

Die Pseudoklementinen. Vol. 2: *Recognitionen in Rufins Übersetzung*. 2nd ed. Ed. B. Rehm and G. Strecker. Die Griechischen Christlichen Schriftsteller der ersten Jahrhunderte. Berlin: Akademie Verlag, 1994.

Tertullian

Tertulliani Opera, Pars I. Opera Catolica. *Adversus Marcionem*. Corpus Christianorum, Series Latina I. Turnholti: Typographi Brepols Editores Pontificii, 1954.

Tertullien: Traité du Baptême [De Baptismo]. Eds. and tr. R.F. Refoulé and M. Drouzy. Sources Chrétiennes. Paris: Cerf, 1952.

Encyclopaediae, Lexica and Concordances

ABD

The Anchor Bible Dictionary. 6 vols. Ed. David Noel Freedman. New York: Doubleday, 1992.

DJBP

Dictionary of Judaism in the Biblical Period, 450 B.C.E. to 600 C.E. Eds. Jacob Neusner and William Scott Green. Peabody, Massachusetts: Hendrickson, 1999 [1996].

EDSS

Encyclopedia of the Dead Sea Scrolls. 2 vols. Eds. L.H. Schiffman and J.C. VanderKam. Oxford: Oxford University Press, 2000.

EJ
Encyclopaedia Judaica. 16 vols. Eds. Cecil Roth and Geoffrey Wigoder. Jerusalem: Keter Publishing House, 1971–1972.
NEAEHL
The New Encyclopedia of Archaeological Excavations in the Holy Land. 4 vols. Ed. Ephraim Stern. Jerusalem: Israel Exploration Society & Carta, 1992.
RGG
Die Religion in Geschichte und Gegenwart: Handwörterbuch für Theologie und Religionswissenschaft. 3rd edition. Eds. H.F.v. Campenhausen, et al. Tübingen: J.C.B. Mohr (Paul Siebeck).
SB
Strack, Hermann L. and Billerbeck, Paul. *Kommentar zum Neuen Testament aus Talmud und Midrasch.* 6 vols. München: C.H. Beck'sche Verlagsbuchhandlung, 1922–1961.
TWAT
Theologisches Wörterbuch zum Alten Testament. 10 vols. Eds. G.J. Botterweck, Helmer Ringgren and H.-J. Fabry. Stuttgart: W. Kohlhammer, 1973–2001.

A Complete Concordance to Flavius Josephus. 4 vols., and supplement. Ed. Karl Heinrich Rengstorf. Leiden: Brill, 1973–1983.

Concordance to the Greek New Testament: An Abridgment from the Edition of Erasmus Schmidt. Ed. W. Greenfield. Athens: "Astir" Publishing Company, Al. & E. Papademetriou, 1977

A Greek-English Lexicon. Compiled by Henry Georg Lidell and Robert Scott. Rev. H.S. Jones. 9th ed. Oxford: Clarendon, 1940.

A Greek-English Lexicon of the New Testament and Other Early Christian Literature. 2nd ed. Walter Bauer. Tr. and adapt. William F. Arndt and F. Wilbur Gingrich. Chicago: University of Chicago Press, 1979.

Konkordanz zum Hebräischen Alten Testament. 2nd ed. Gerhard Lisowsky. Stuttgart: Württembergische Bibelanstalt, 1958.

A Patristic-Greek Lexicon. G.W.H. Lampe. Oxford: Clarendon, 1961.

Synopsis Quattuor Evangeliorum: Locis parallelis evangeliorum apocryphorum et patrum adhibitis edidit. 13th ed. Kurt Aland. Stuttgart: Deutsche Bibelgesellschaft, 1985.

Literature

(To attain simple footnote references, certain sources are listed under this heading as well.)

Adan-Bayewitz, David. 1993. *Common Pottery in Roman Galilee: A Study of Local Trade.* Bar-Ilan Studies in Near Eastern Languages and Cultures. Ramat-Gan: Bar-Ilan University Press.

Ådna, Jostein. 1999. "The Encounter of Jesus with the Gerasene Demoniac." In *Authenticating the Activities of Jesus,* 279–301. Eds. B. Chilton and C. A. Evans. New Testament Tools and Studies 28, 2. Leiden: Brill.

Alexander, Philip S. 1999. "The Demonology of the Dead Sea Scrolls." In *The Dead Sea Scrolls after Fifty Years: A Comprehensive Assessment,* 2: 331–353. Eds. P. W. Flint and J. C. Vanderkam. Leiden: Brill.

Alon, Gedalyahu. 1977. *Jews, Judaism and the Classical World: Studies in Jewish History in the Times of the Second Temple and Talmud.* Jerusalem: The Magnes Press.

Alt, Albrecht. 1953. *Kleine Schriften zur Geschichte des Volkes Israels.* Vol. 2. München: C. H. Beck'sche Verlagsbuchhandlung.

Anderson, Gary A. 1992a. "Sacrifice and Sacrificial Offerings. Old Testament." In *ABD* 5: 870–886.

Anderson, Gary A. 1992b. "The Interpretation of the Purification Offering (חטאת) in the *Temple Scroll* (11QTemple) and Rabbinic Literature." *JBL* 111: 17–35.

André, Gunnel. 1982. "טָמֵא" In *TWAT* 3: 352–366.

Annen, Franz. 1976a. *Heil für die Heiden: Zur Bedeutung und Geschichte der Tradition vom besessenen Gerasener (Mk 5,1–20 parr.).* Frankfurter Theologische Studien, 20. Frankfurt am Main: Josef Knecht.

Annen, Franz. 1976b. "Die Dämonenaustreibungen Jesu in den synoptischen Evangelien." In *Theologische Berichte V,* 107–146. Eds. J. Pfammatter and F. Furger. Zürich: Benziger Verlag.

Appleby, Joyce; Hunt, Lynn and Jacob, Margaret. 1994. *Telling the Truth about History.* New York: W. W. Norton & Company.

Aune, David. E. 1980. "Magic in Early Christianity." *ANRW* II.23.2, 1507–1557. Berlin: Walter de Gruyter.

Aune, David. E. 1997. "Jesus and Cynics in First-Century Palestine: Some Critical Considerations." In *Hillel and Jesus: Comparative Studies of Two Major Religious Leaders,* 176–192. Eds. J.H. Charlesworth and L.L. Johns. Minneapolis: Fortress.

Avi-Yonah, Michael. 1966. *The Holy Land: From the Persian to the Arab Conquests (536 B.C. to A.D. 640): A Historical Geography.* Grand Rapids, Michigan: Baker Book House.

Aviam, Mordechai. 1993. "Galilee: The Hellenistic to Byzantine Periods." In *NEAEHL* 1: 453–458. Ed. E. Stern, A. Lewinson-Gilboa and J. Aviram. Jerusalem: Israel Exploration Society & Carta.

Avigad, Nahman. 1984 [1980]. *Discovering Jerusalem.* Oxford: Basil Blackwell.

Back, Sven-Olav. 1995. *Jesus of Nazareth and the Sabbath Commandment.* Åbo: Åbo Akademi University Press.

Banks, R. 1975. *Jesus and the Law in the Synoptic Tradition.* SNTS Monograph Series 28. Cambridge: Cambridge University Press.

Bar-Ilan, Meir. 1991. "Washing Feet Before Prayer: Moslem Influence or an Ancient Jewish Custom." [In Hebrew: "Rehitzat Raglayim Lifnei ha-Tefila: Hashpa'a Islamit 'o Minhag Yehudi."] *Mahanaim,* 1: 162–169. Cited 11 March 2002. Online: http://faculty.biu.ac.il/~barilm/raglaym.html.

Barrett, C. K. 1978. *The Gospel according to St John: An Introduction with Commentary and Notes of the Greek Text.* 2nd. ed. London: SPCK.

Barslai, Benyamin Z. 1980. *Nidda (Unreinheit der Frau): Die Mischna: Text, Übersetzung und ausführliche Erklärung*. Eds. Georg Beer, Oscar Holtzmann, Karl Heinrich Rengstorf and Leonhard Rost. VI. Seder: Toharot. 7. Traktat: Nidda. Berlin: Walter de Gruyter.

Batey, Richard A. 1991. *Jesus and the Forgotten City: New Light on Sepphoris and the Urban World of Jesus*. Grand Rapids, Michigan: Baker Book House.

Bauckham, Richard. 1998. "The Scrupulous Priest and the Good Samaritan: Jesus' Parabolic Interpretation of the Law of Moses." *NTS* 44: 475–489.

Bauckham, Richard. 1999. "Did Jesus Wash His Disciples' Feet?" In *Authenticating the Activities of Jesus*, 411–430. Eds. B. Chilton and C. A. Evans. New Testament Tools and Studies 28, 2. Leiden: Brill.

Bauernfeind, Otto. 1927. *Die Worte der Dämonen im Markusevangelium*. BWANT 3:8. Stuttgart: Verlag von W. Kohlhammer.

Baumbach, Günther. 1989. "The Sadducees in Josephus. In *Josephus, the Bible and History*, 173–195. Eds. L.H. Feldman and G. Hata. Detroit: Wayne State University Press.

Baumgarten, Albert I. 1991. "Rivkin and Neusner on the Pharisees." In *Law in Religious Communities in the Roman Period: The Debate over* Torah *and* Nomos *in Post-Biblical Judaism and Early Christianity*, 109–125. Eds. P.Richardson and S. Westerholm. Studies in Christianity and Judaism, 4. Waterloo, Ontario: Wilfrid Laurier University Press.

Baumgarten, Albert I. 1997. *The Flourishing of Jewish Sects in the Maccabean Era: An Interpretation*. JSJSup, 55. Leiden: Brill.

Baumgarten, Joseph M. 1967. "The Essene Avoidance of Oil and the Laws of Purity." *RevQ* 21: 183–192.

Baumgarten, Joseph M. 1980. "The Pharisaic-Sadducean Controversies about Purity and the Qumran Texts." *JJS* 31: 157–170.

Baumgarten, Joseph M. 1990. "The 4Q Zadokite Fragments on Skin Disease." *JJS* 41: 153–165.

Baumgarten, Joseph M. 1992. "The Purification Rituals in *DJD 7*." In *The Dead Sea Scrolls: Forty Years of Research*, 199–209. Eds. D. Dimant & U. Rappaport. STDJ, 10. Leiden: Brill.

Baumgarten, Joseph M. 1994. "Zab Impurity in Qumran and Rabbinic Law." *JJS* 45: 273–277.

Baumgarten, Joseph M. 1995a. "The laws about fluxes in 4QTohora[a] (4Q274)." In *Time to Prepare the Way in the Wilderness*, 1–8. Eds. D. Dimant & L. Schiffman. STDJ, 16. Leiden: Brill.

Baumgarten, Joseph M. 1995b. "The Red Cow Purification Rites in Qumran Texts." *JJS* 46: 112–119.

Baumgarten, Joseph M. 1999a. "D. Tohorot." In *Qumran Cave 4, XXV: Halakhic Texts*, 79–122. Eds. and tr. J. Baumgarten et. al. DJD 35. Oxford: Clarendon.

Baumgarten, Joseph M. 1999b. "The Purification Liturgies. In *The Dead Sea Scrolls after Fifty Years: A Comprehensive Assessment,* 2: 200–212. Eds. P. W. Flint and J. C. Vanderkam. Leiden: Brill.

Becker, Carl. 1910. "Detachment and the Writing of History." *Atlantic Monthly* (October): 524–536.

Becker, Jürgen. 1972. *Johannes der Täufer und Jesus von Nazareth*. Neukirchen-Vluyn: Neukirchener Verlag.

Becker, Jürgen. 1998 [1996]. *Jesus of Nazareth*. Berlin: Walter de Gruyter.

Beentjes, Pancratius C. 2000. "'They Saw that his Forehead Was Leprous' (2Chr 26:20. The Cronicler's Narrative on Uzziah's Leprosy." In *Purity and Holiness: The Heritage of Leviticus*, 61–72. Jewish and Christian Perspectives Series, 2. Leiden: Brill.

Belkin, Samuel. 1940. *Philo and the Oral Law: The Philonic Interpretation of Biblical Law in Relation to the Palestinian Halakah*. Harvard Semitic Series, 11. Cambridge, Massachusetts: Harvard University Press.

Bell, H. Idris. 1936. "Noch einmal: Ein bisher unbekanntes Evangelienfragment." *Theologische Blätter* 15 (März/April): 72–74.

Bell, H. Idris. 1949. "The Gospel Fragments P. Egerton 2." *HTR* 42: 53–63.

Bell, H. Idris and Skeat, T. C. 1935a. *Fragments of an Unknown Gospel and other Early Christian Papyri.* London: Published by the Trustees.

Bell, H. Idris and Skeat, T. C. 1935b. *The New Gospel Fragments.* London: Oxford University Press. Cited 15 November 2001. Online: http://alf.zfn.uni-bremen.de/~wie/Egerton/BellSkeat2.html.

Bercé, Yves-Marie. 1990 [1986]. *History of Peasant Revolts: The Social Origins of Rebellion in Early Modern France.* Cambridge: Polity.

Bergen, Wesley J. 1992. "The Prophetic Alternative: Elisha and the Israelite Monarchy. In *Elijah and Elisha in Socioliterary Perspective*, 127–137. Ed. R.B. Coote. Society of Biblical Literature Semeia Studies. Atlanta, Georgia: Scholars Press.

Berger, Klaus. 1972. *Die Gesetzesauslegung Jesu: Ihr historischer Hintergrund im Judentum und im Alten Testament.* Vol 1: *Markus und Parallelen.* Wissenschaftliche Monographien zum Alten und Neuen Testament, 40. Neukirchen-Vluyn: Neukirchener Verlag.

Berger, Klaus. 1988. "Jesus als Pharisäer und Frühe Christen als Pharisäer." *NovT* 30: 231–262.

Bernstein, Moshe J. 1996. "The Employment and Interpretation of Scripture in 4QMMT: Preliminary Observations." In *Reading 4QMMT: New Perspectives on Qumran Law and History*, 29–51. Eds. J. Kampen and M. J. Bernstein. SBL Symposium Series, 2. Atlanta, Georgia: Scholars Press.

Bevir, Mark. 1994. "Objectivity in History." *History and Theory* 33: 328–344.

Blackburn, Barry L. 1991. *Theios Anēr and the Markan Miracle Traditions: A Critique of the* Theios Anēr *Concept as an Interpretative Background of the Miracle Traditions Used by Mark.* WUNT 2: 40. Tübingen: J. C. B. Mohr (Paul Siebeck).

Blackburn, Barry L. 1994. "The Miracles of Jesus." In *Studying the Historical Jesus: Evaluations of the State of Current Research*, 353–394. Eds. B. Chilton and C. A. Evans. Leiden: Brill.

Boccaccini, Gabriele. 1998. *Beyond the Essene Hypothesis: The Parting of the Ways between Qumran and Enochic Judaism.* Grand Rapids, Michigan: Eerdmans.

Böcher, Otto. 1970. *Dämonenfurcht und Dämonenabwehr. Ein Beitrag zur Vorgeschichte der christlichen Taufe.* BWANT 5:10. Stuttgart: Verlag W. Kolhammer.

Böcher, Otto. 1972. *Christus Exorcista: Dämonismus und Taufe im Neuen Testament.* BWANT 5:16. Stuttgart: Verlag W. Kolhammer.

Boer, Martinus C. de. 1988. "Jesus the Baptizer: 1 John 5:5–8 and the Gospel of John." *JBL* 107: 87–106.

Bóid, I. R. Mac Mhanainn, 1989. *Principles of Samaritan Halachah.* SJLA, 38. Leiden: Brill.

Boismard, Marie-Émile. 1964. "Le lavement des pieds (Jn 13:1–17)." *RB* 71: 5–24.

Boismard, Marie-Émile. 1981. "La Guérison du Lépreux (Mc 1, 40–45 et par.)." In *Escritos de Biblia y Oriente: Miscelánea conmemorative del 25.º aniversario del Instituto Español Bíblico y Arquelógico (Casa de Santiago) de Jerusalén*, 283–291. Eds. R. Aguirre and F. G. Lopez. Bibliotheca Salmanticensis, 38. Salamanca: Universidad Pontificia.

Boismard, Marie-Émile. 1990. "Introduction au premier récit de la multiplication des pains. Appendice: La guérison du lépreux." In *The Interrelations of the Gospels*, 254-258. Ed. D. L. Dungan. Leuven: University Press.

Bokser, Baruch M. 1985. "Wonder-Working and the Rabbinic Tradition: The Case of Ḥanina ben Dosa." *JSJ* 16: 42–92.

Bolyki, János. 1998. *Jesu Tischgemeinschaften.* WUNT 2: 96. Tübingen: Mohr Siebeck.

Booth, Roger P. 1986. *Jesus and the Laws of Purity: Tradition History and Legal History in Mark 7.* JSNTSup 13. Sheffield: JSOT Press.

Borg, Marcus J. 1984. *Conflict, Holiness & Politics in the Teachings of Jesus.* Lewiston/Queenston: Edwin Mellen.

Borg, Marcus J. 1987. *Jesus: A New Vision: Spirit, Culture, and the Life of Discipleship.* San Francisco: Harper & Row.

Borg, Marcus. 1994. *Jesus in Contemporary Scholarship.* Valley Forge, Pennsylvania: Trinity.

Boring, M. Eugene. 1992. "The Synoptic Problem, "Minor" Agreements, and the Beelzebul Pericope." In *The Four Gospels 1992. Festschrift Frans Neirynck,* 1: 587–619. Eds. F. Van Segbroeck, et. al. Leuven: University Press.

Börner-Klein, Dagmar (tr.). 1997. *Tannaitische Midraschim.* Rabbinische Texte, Zweite Reihe, Band 3. *Der Midrasch Sifre zu Numeri.* Stuttgart: W. Kohlhammer.

Bornkamm, Günther. 1960 [1956]. *Jesus of Nazareth.* London: Hodder & Stoughton.

Bowie, Ewn Lyall. 1978. "Apollonius of Tyana: Tradition and Reality." In *ANRW* II.16.2, 1652–1699. Berlin: Walter de Gruyter.

Bowker, John. 1973. *Jesus and the Pharisees.* Cambridge: Cambridge University Press.

Bovon, François. 1989. *Das Evangelium nach Lukas.* Vol. 1. EKK 3:1. Zürich: Benziger.

Bovon, François. 1996. *Das Evangelium nach Lukas.* Vol. 2. EKK 3:2. Zürich: Benziger.

Bovon, François. 2000. "*Fragment Oxyrhynchus 840,* Fragment of a Lost Gospel, Witness of an Early Christan Controversy over Purity." *JBL* 119: 705–728.

Boyce, M. 1975. *A History of Zoroastrianism.* Vol. 1. Handbuch der Orientalistik. Leiden: Brill.

Braude, William G. (tr.). 1959. *The Midrash on Psalms.* 2 vols.. Yale Judaica Series, 13. New Haven: Yale University Press.

Braude, William G. and Kapstein, Israel (tr.). 1975. *Pĕsiḳta dĕ-Raḇ Kahăna: R. Kahana's Compilation of Discourses for Sabbaths and Festal Days.* The Littman Library of Jewish Civilization. London: Routledge & Kegan Paul.

Broadhead, Edwin K. 1992a. "Mk 1,44: The Witness of the Leper." *ZNW* 83:257–265.

Broadhead, Edwin K. 1992b. *Teaching with Authority: Miracles and Christology in the Gospel of Mark.* JSNTSup, 74. Sheffield: Sheffield Academic Press.

Broadhead, Edwin K. 1995. "Echoes of an Exorcism in the Fourth Gospel." *ZNW* 86: 111–119.

Broshi, Magen. 1974. "The Expansion of Jerusalem in the Reigns of Hezekiah and Manasseh." *IEJ* 24: 21–26.

Browe, Peter. 1932. *Beiträge zur Sexualethik des Mittelalters.* Breslauer Studien zur historischen Theologie, 23. Breslau: Verlag Müller & Seiffert.

Brown, Raymond E. 1966. *The Gospel according to John.* Vol 1. The Anchor Bible, 29. Garden City, New York: Doubleday.

Brown, Raymond E. 1970. *The Gospel according to John.* Vol 2. The Anchor Bible, 29a. Garden City, New York: Doubleday.

Browne, Stanley G. 1989 [1985]. "The History of Leprosy." In *Leprosy,* 1-14. Ed. R. C. Hastings. Medicine in the Tropics Series. Edinburgh: Churchill Livingstone.

Bultmann, Rudolf. 1952 [1948]. *Theology of the New Testament.* Vol. 1. London: SCM.

Bultmann, Rudolf. 1971. *The Gospel of John: A Commentary.* Oxford: Basil Blackwell.

Bultmann, Rudolf. 1972 [1921]. *The History of the Synoptic Tradition.* Rev. ed. Oxford: Basil Blackwell.

Burchard, Christoph. 1985. "Joseph and Aseneth. A New Translation and Introduction." In *The Old Testament Pseudepigrapha,* 1:177–247. Ed. J.H. Charlesworth. New York: Doubleday.

Burger, Christoph. 1970. *Jesus als Davidssohn: Eine traditionsgeschichtliche Untersuchung.* FRLANT, 98. Göttingen: Vandenhoeck & Ruprecht.

Burkert, Walter. 1977. *Griechische Religion der archaischen und klassischen Epoche.* Die Religionen der Menschheit, 15. Stuttgart: W. Kohlhammer.

Büchler, Adolf. 1908. "The New 'Fragment of an Uncanonical Gospel'." *JQR* 20: 330–346.

Büchler, Adolf. 1968 [1906]. *Der Galiläische 'Am-ha'areṣ des Zweiten Jahrhunderts: Beiträge zur innern Geschichte des palästinischen Judentums in den ersten zwei Jahrhunderten.* Hildesheim: Georg Olms Verlagsbuchhandlung.

Caird, G. B. 1963. *Saint Luke.* The Pelican New Testament Commentaries. Harmondsworth: Penguin Books.

Caird, G. B. 1980. *The Language and Imagery of the Bible.* London: Duckworth.

Carney, Thomas F. 1975. *The Shape of the Past: Models and Antiquity.* Lawrence, Kansas: Coronado.

Carr, Edward. H. 1961. *What is History?* London: Macmillan.

Caspers, Charles. 2000. "Leviticus 12, Mary and Wax: Purification and Churching in Late Medieval Christianity." In *Purity and Holiness: The Heritage of Leviticus*, 295–309. Jewish and Christian Perspectives Series, 2. Leiden: Brill.

Cave, C. H. 1978–1979. "The Leper: Mark 1. 40–45." *NTS* 25: 245–250.

Cerfaux, L. 1936. "Parallèlles canoniques et extracanoniques de 'L'évangile inconnu' (Pap. Egerton 2)." *Le Muséon: Revue d'Études Orientales* 49: 55–77.

Chancey, Mark. 2001. "The Cultural Milieu of Ancient Sepphoris." *NTS* 47: 127–145.

Charlesworth, James H. 1988. *Jesus within Judaism: New Light from Exciting Archaeological Discoveries.* London: SPCK.

Charlesworth, James H. 1995. "The Son of David: Solomon and Jesus (Mark 10.47)." In *The New Testament and Hellenistic Judaism*, 72–87. Aarhus: Aarhus University Press.

Charlesworth, James H. 1997. "Intertextuality: Isaiah 40:3 and the Serek Ha-Yaḥad." In *The Quest for Context and Meaning: Studies in Biblical Intertextuality in Honor of James A. Sanders*, 197–224. Eds. C. A. Evans and S. Talmon. Leiden: Brill.

Charlesworth, James H. 1999. "John the Baptizer and Qumran Barriers in Light of the *Rule of the Community*." In *The Provo International Conference on the Dead Sea Scrolls: Technological Innovations, New Texts, and Reformulated Issues*, 353–375. Eds. D. W. Parry and E. Ulrich. Leiden: Brill.

Chilton, Bruce. 1982. "Jesus *ben David*: reflections on the *Davidssohnfrage*." *JSNT* 14: 88–112.

Chilton, Bruce. 1984 [1979]. "God in Strength." In *The Kingdom of God in the Teaching of Jesus*, 121–132. [= *God in Strength*, 1979, 277–293]. Ed. B. Chilton. Issues in Religion and Theology, 5. Philadelphia: Fortress.

Chilton, Bruce. 1984. *A Galilean Rabbi and His Bible: Jesus' Own Interpretation of Isaiah.* London: SPCK.

Chilton, Bruce. 1992. *The Temple of Jesus: His Sacrificial Program within a Cultural History of Sacrifice.* University Park, Pennsylvania: The Pennsylvania State University Press.

Chilton, Bruce. 1994. *A Feast of Meanings: Eucharistic Theologies from Jesus through Johannine Circles.* NovTSup 72. Leiden: Brill.

Chilton, Bruce. 1996. *Pure Kingdom: Jesus' Vision of God.* Grand Rapids, Michigan: Eerdmans.

Chilton, Bruce. 1999. "An Exorcism of History: Mark 1:21–28." In *Authenticating the Activities of Jesus*, 215–245. Eds. B. Chilton and C. A. Evans. New Testament Tools and Studies 28, 2. Leiden: Brill.

Chilton, Bruce and Evans Craig A. 1997. *Jesus in Context: Temple, Purity, and Restoration.* Arbeiten zur Geschichte des antiken Judentums und des Christentums, 39. Leiden: Brill.

Choksy, Jamsheed K. 1989. *Purity and Pollution in Zoroastrianism: Triumph over evil.* Austin: University of Texas Press.

Christ, Hieronymus. 1977. *Blutvergiessen im Alten Testament: Der gewaltsame Tod des Menschen untersucht am hebräischen Wort* dām. Basel: Friedrich Reinhardt Kommissionsverlag.

Clements, Ronald Ernest. 1989. *Deuteronomy.* Old Testament Guides. Sheffield: JSOT Press.

Cohen, Shaye J. D. 1979. *Josephus in Galilee and Rome: His Vita and Development as an Historian.* Columbia Studies in the Classical Tradition 8. Leiden: Brill.
Cohen, Shaye J. D. 1990. "The Modern Study of Ancient Judaism." In *The State of Jewish Studies*, 55–73. Eds. S. J. D. Cohen and E. L. Greenstein. Detroit: Wayne State University Press.
Cohen, Shaye J. D. 1992. "The Place of the Rabbi in Jewish Society of the Second Century." In *The Galilee in Late Antiquity*, 157–173. Ed. Lee I. Levine. New York: The Jewish Theological Seminary/Harvard University Press.
Cohen, Shaye J. D. 1994. "Judaism at the Time of Jesus." In *Jews and Christians Speak of Jesus*, 3–12. Ed. A. E. Zannoni. Minneapolis: Fortress.
Collingwood, R. G. 1946. *The Idea of History*. Oxford: Oxford University Press.
Collins, John J. 1995. *The Sceptre and the Star: The Messiahs of the Dead Sea Scrolls and other Ancient Literature.* The Anchor Bible Reference Library. New York: Doubleday.
Conzelmann, Hans. 1959. "Jesus Christus." In *RGG* 3: 619–653.
Cook, Edward M. 1996. "A Ritual Purification Center." *BAR* 22 (November–December): 39, 48–51, 73–75.
Coote, Robert B. 1992. *Elijah and Elisha in Socioliterary Perspective.* Society of Biblical Literature Semeia Studies. Atlanta, Georgia: Scholars Press.
Corinaldi, Michael. 1995. "Purity and Conversion Norms among the Falashas." In *Between Africa and Zion: Proceedings of the First International Congress of the Society for the Study of Ethiopian Jewry*, 113–125. Eds. S. Kaplan, T. Parfitt and E. T. Semi. Jerusalem: Ben-Zvi Institute.
Corinaldi, Michael. 1996. "Samaritan Halakhah." In *An Introduction to the History and Sources of Jewish Law*, 57–73. Eds. N. S. Hecht, B. S. Jackson, S. M. Passamaneck, D. Piattelli and A. M. Rabello. Oxford: Clarendon.
Corinaldi, Michael. 1998. *Jewish Identity: The Case of Ethiopian Jewry.* Jerusalem: Magnes Press.
Cotter, Wendy. 1999. *Miracles in Greco-Roman Antiquity. A sourcebook.* London: Routledge.
Countryman, L. William. 1988. *Dirt, Greed and Sex: Sexual Ethics in the New Testament and their Implications for Today.* London: SCM.
Crossan, John Dominic. 1991. *The Historical Jesus: The Life of a Mediterranean Jewish Peasant.* New York: HarperSanFrancisco.
Crossan, John Dominic. 1994. *Jesus, A Revolutionary Biography.* New York: HarperSanFrancisco.
Culpepper, R. Alan. 1983. *Anatomy of the Fourth Gospel: A Study in Literary Design.* New Testament Foundations and Facets. Philadelphia: Fortress.
Cunningham, Graham. 1997. *'Deliver Me from Evil': Mesopotamian incantations 2500–1500 BC.* Studia Pohl: Series Maior. Dissertationes Scientificae de Rebus Orientis Antiqui, 17. Roma: Editrice Pontificio Istituto Biblico.
Daniels, Jon B. 1991. *The Egerton Gospel: Its Place in Early Christianity.* Ann Arbor, Michigan: UMI.
Davies, Stevan L. 1995. *Jesus the Healer: Possession, Trance, and the Origins of Christianity.* London: SCM.
Davies, William David, and Allison, Dale C. 1991. *A Critical and Exegetical Commentary on the Gospel According to Saint Matthew.* Vol. 2, Matthew 8–18. The International Critical Commentary. Edinburgh: T&T Clark.
Deines, Roland. 1993. *Jüdische Steingefässe und pharisäische Frömmigkeit: Ein archäologisch-historischer Beitrag zum Verständnis von Joh 2,6 und der jüdischen Reinheitshalacha zur Zeit Jesu.* WUNT 2:52. Tübingen: J. C. B. Mohr (Paul Siebeck).

Deines, Roland. 1997. Die Pharisäer. Ihr Verständnis im Spiegel der christlichen und jüdischen Forschung seit Wellhausen und Graetz. WUNT, 101. Tübingen: J. C. B. Mohr (Paul Siebeck).

Derrett, J. Duncan M. 1964. "Law in the New Testament: fresh light on the Parable of the good Samaritan." *NTS* 10: 22–37.

Derrett, J. Duncan M. 1979a. "'As a Testimony to them": A Juridical Puzzle in St. Mark." *Studia et Documenta Historiae et Iuris* 45: 582–589. Roma: Pontificia Universitas Lateranensis.

Derrett, J. Duncan M. 1979b. "Contributions to the study of the Gerasene demoniac." *JSNT* 3: 2–17.

Dewey, Joanna. 1994. "The Gospel of Mark." In *Searching the Scriptures*, 2: 470–509. Ed. E. Schüssler Fiorenza. New York: Crossroad.

Dibelius, Martin. 1911. *Johannes dem Täufer.* FRLANT, 15. Göttingen: Vandenhoeck and Ruprecht.

Dibelius, Martin. 1961 [1919]. *Die Formgeschichte des Evangeliums.* 4th ed. Tübingen: J.C.B. Mohr (Paul Siebeck).

Dodd, Charles H. 1936. "A New Gospel." *BJRL* 20: 58–92.

Dodd, Charles H. 1953. *The Interpretation of the Fourth Gospel.* Cambridge: Cambridge University Press.

Dodd, Charles H. 1961 [1935]. *The Parables of the Kingdom.* Rev. ed. Glasgow: Collins.

Dodd, Charles H. 1963. *Historical Tradition in the Fourth Gospel.* London: Cambridge University Press.

Dodd, Charles H. 1971. *The Founder of Christianity.* London: Collins.

Doering, Lutz. 1997. "New Aspects of Qumran Sabbath Law from Cave 4 Fragments." In *Legal Texts and Legal Issues: Proceedings of the Second Meeting of the International Organization for Qumran Studies. Cambridge 1995*, 251–274. STDJ, 23. Leiden: Brill.

Dokka, Trond Skard. 1992. "En fortolkning av Mk 5, 21–43 med synoptisk sammenlikning." *NTT* 93: 149–162.

Donahue, John R. 1994. "Redaction Criticism: Has the *Hauptstrasse* become a *Sackgasse*?" In *The New Literary Criticism and the New Testament*. Eds. E. V. McKnight and E. Struthers Malbon. Valley Forge, Pa.: Trinity.

Douglas, Mary. 1966. *Purity and Danger: An analysis of the concepts of pollution and taboo.* London: Routledge & Kegan Paul.

Douglas, Mary. 1982 [1970]. *Natural Symbols: Explorations in Cosmology.* New York: Pantheon Books.

Douglas, Mary. 1993. *In the Wilderness: The doctrine of defilement in the book of Numbers.* JSOTSup, 158. Sheffield, JSOT Press.

Downing, F. Gerald. 1988. *Christ and the Cynics: Jesus and other Radical Preachers in First-Century Tradition.* JSOT Manuals 4. Sheffield: Sheffield Academic Press.

Downing, F. Gerald. 1992. *Cynics and Christian Origins.* Edinburgh: T&T Clark.

Duling, Dennis C. 1975. "Solomon, Exorcism, and the Son of David." *HTR* 68: 235–252.

Dunderberg, Ismo. 1994. *Johannes und die Synoptiker: Studien zu Joh 1-9.* AASF, Dissertationes Humanarum Litterarum, 69. Helsinki: Suomalainen Tiedeakatemia.

Dunn, James D. G. 1988. "Matthew 12:28/Luke 11:20—A Word of Jesus?" In *Eschatology and the New Testament: Essays in Honor of George Raymond Beasley-Murray*, 29–49. Ed. W. H. Gloer. Peabody, Mass.:Hendrickson.

Dunn, James D. G. 1990. *Jesus, Paul and the Law: Studies in Mark and Galatians.* London: SPCK.

Dunn, James D. G. 1991. *The Partings of the Ways Between Christianity and Judaism and their Significance for the Character of Christianity.* London: SCM.

Dunn, James D. G. 1994. "John the Baptist's Use of Scripture." In *The Gospels and the Scriptures of Israel*, 42–54. JSNTSup, 104. Eds. C.A. Evans and W.R. Stegner. Sheffield: Sheffield Academic Press.

Duprez, A. 1970. *Jésus et les dieux guérisseurs a propos de Jean, V.* Cahiers de la Revue biblique, 12. Paris: Gabalda.

Edwards, Douglas. 1992. "The Socio-Economic and Cultural Ethos of the Lower Galilee in the First Century: Implications for the Nascent Jesus Movement." In *The Galilee in Late Antiquity*, 53–73. Ed. Lee I. Levine. New York: The Jewish Theological Seminary/Harvard University Press.

Eilberg-Schwartz, Howard. 1990. *The Savage in Judaism: An anthropology of Israelite religion and ancient Judaism.* Bloomington: Indiana University Press.

Elliger, K. 1966. *Leviticus.* Handbuch zum alten Testament. Tübingen: J. C. B. Mohr (Siebeck).

Elliott, John. 1995 [1993]. *Social Scientific Criticism of the New Testament.* London: SPCK.

Elman, Yaakov. 1996. "Some Remarks on 4QMMT and the Rabbinic Tradition, Or, When Is a Parallel Not a Parallel?" In *Reading 4QMMT: New Perspectives on Qumran Law and History*, 99–128. Eds. J. Kampen and M. J. Bernstein. SBL Symposium Series, 2. Atlanta, Georgia: Scholars Press.

Erlemann, Kurt. 1996. "Papyrus Egerton 2: 'Missing Link' zwischen synoptischer und johanneischer Tradition." *NTS* 42: 12–34.

Eshel, Esther. 1999. "4QRitual of Purification A." In *Qumran Cave 4: Halakhic Texts,* 135–153. DJD 35. Oxford: Clarendon.

Eshel, Hanan. 1997. "A Note on 'Miqvaot' at Sepphoris." In *Archaeology and the Galilee: Texts and Contexts in the Graeco-Roman and Byzantine Periods*, 131–133. Eds. D. R. Edwards and C. T. McCollough. SFSHJ, 143. Atlanta, Georgia: Scholars Press.

Evans, Christopher Francis. 1990. *Saint Luke*. London: SCM.

Evans, Craig A. 1992. "Opposition to the Temple: Jesus and the Dead Sea Scrolls." In *Jesus and the Dead Sea Scrolls*, 235–253. The Anchor Bible Reference Library. Ed. J.H. Charlesworth. New York: Doubleday.

Evans, Craig A. 1999. "Jesus and the Dead Sea Scrolls." In *The Dead Sea Scrolls after Fifty Years: A Comprehensive Assessment,* 2: 573–598. Eds. P. W. Flint and J. C. Vanderkam. Leiden: Brill.

Fander, Monika. 1992. *Die Stellung der Frau im Markusevangelium: Unter besonderer Berücksichtigung kultur- und religionsgeschichtlicher Hintergründe.* 3rd ed. Münsteraner Theologische Abhandlungen, 8. Altenberge: Oros-Verlag.

Fatum, Lone. 1990. "En kvindehistorie om tro og køn." *DTT* 53: 278–299.

Feldhaus, Anne. 1984. *The Deeds of God in Ṛddhipur:* New York: Oxford University Press.

Feldman, Louis H. 1987. "Introduction." In *Josephus, Judaism and Christianity*, 23–67. Eds. L. H. Feldman and G. Hata. Detroit: Wayne State University Press.

Fiebig, Paul. 1911. *Jüdische Wundergeschichten des neutestamentlichen Zeitalters: unter besonderer Berücksichtigung ihres Verhältnisses zum Neuen Testament bearbeitet: ein Beitrag zum Streit um die „Christusmythe."* Tübingen: J.C.B. Mohr (Paul Siebeck).

Finkelstein, Louis. 1938. *The Pharisees: The Sociological Background of their Faith.* 2 vols. Philadelphia: The Jewish Publication Society of America.

Fishwick, Marshall W. 1982. *Common Culture and the Great Tradition: The Case for Renewal.* Westport, Connecticut: Greenwood.

Fitzmyer, Joseph A. 1981. *The Gospel According to Luke.* Vol. 1. 2nd ed. Anchor Bible. New York: Doubleday.

Fitzmyer, Joseph A. 1985. *The Gospel According to Luke.* Vol. 2. 2nd ed. Anchor Bible. New York: Doubleday.

Flusser, David. 1966. "Qumrân and Jewish 'Apotropaic' Prayers." *IEJ* 16:194–205.

Flusser, David. 1987. *Jewish Sources in Early Christianity.* New York: Adama Books.

Fonrobert, C. 1997. "The woman with a blood-flow (Mark 5.24–34) revisited: Menstrual laws and Jewish culture in Christian feminist hermeneutics." In *Early Christian Interpretation of the Scriptures of Israel: Investigations and Proposals*, 121–140. Eds. C. A. Evans & J. A. Sanders. JSNTSup, 48. Studies in Scripture in Early Judaism and Christianity, 5. Sheffield: JSOT Press.
Fornberg, Tord. 1989. *Matteusevangeliet.* Vol 1. KNT, 1. Uppsala: EFS-förlaget.
Fossion, André. 1980. "From the Bible Text to the Homily. Cure of a Leper (Mk 1, 40–45)." *Lumen Vitae* 35: 279–290.
Fredriksen, Paula. 2000. *Jesus of Nazareth, King of the Jews: A Jewish Life and the Emergence of Christianity.* London: Macmillan.
Freyne, Seán. 1988a. *Galilee, Jesus and the Gospels: Literary Approaches and Historical Investigations.* Dublin: Gill and Macmillan.
Freyne, Seán. 1988b. "Bandits in Galilee: A Contribution to the Study of Social Conditions in First-Century Palestine." In *The Social World of Formative Christianity and Judaism: Essays in Tribute to Howard Clark Kee*, 50–68. Eds. J. Neusner et. al. Philadelphia: Fortress.
Freyne, Seán. 1992. "Urban-Rural Relations in First-Century Galilee: Some Suggestions from the Literary Sources." In *The Galilee in Late Antiquity*, 75–91. Ed. Lee I. Levine. New York: The Jewish Theological Seminary/Harvard University Press.
Freyne, Seán. 1994. "The Geography, Politics, and Economics of Galilee and the Quest for the Historical Jesus." In *Studying the Historical Jesus: Evaluations of the State of Current Research*, 75–121. Eds. B. Chilton and C. A. Evans. Leiden: Brill.
Freyne, Seán. 1995. "Jesus and the Urban Culture of Galilee." In *Texts and Contexts. Biblical Texts in Their Textual and Situational Contexts: Essays in honom of Lars Hartman*, 597–622. Eds. T. Fornberg and D. Hellholm. Oslo: Scandinavian University Press.
Freyne, Seán. 1997a. "Galilean Questions to Crossan's Mediterranean Jesus." In *Whose Historical Jesus?*, 63–91. Eds. W. E. Arnal and M. Desjardins. Studies in Christianity and Judaism 7. Waterloo, Ontario: Wilfrid Laurier University Press.
Freyne, Seán. 1997b. "Town and Country Once More: The Case of Roman Galilee." In *Archaeology and the Galilee: Texts and Contexts in the Graeco-Roman and Byzantine Periods*, 49–56. Eds. D. R. Edwards and C. T. McCollough. SFSHJ, 143. Atlanta, Georgia: Scholars Press.
Freyne, Seán. 1998 [1980]. *Galilee from Alexander the Great to Hadrian 323 B.C.E. to 135 C.E: A Study of Second Temple Judaism.* Edinburgh: T & T Clark [1998 re-issue. Originally Wilmington, Delaware: Glazier, and Notre Dame, Indiana: Notre Dame University Press].
Freyne, Seán. 2000. *Galilee and Gospel: Collected Essays.* Wissenschaftliche Untersuchungen zum Neuen Testament 125. Tübingen: Mohr Siebeck.
Fridrichsen, Anton. 1929. "Jesu kamp mot de urene ånder." *STK* 5: 299–314.
Fuchs, Ernst. 1956. "Die Frage nach dem historischen Jesus." *ZTK* 53: 210–229.
Fuller, Reginald H. 1963. *Interpreting the Miracles.* London: SCM.
Funk, Robert W. 1978. "The Form of the NT Healing Miracle Story." *Semeia* 12: 57–96.
Funk, Robert W. 1993. *The Five Gospels—The Search for the Historical Jesus.* New York: Macmillan.
Funk, Robert W. 1996. *Honest to Jesus: Jesus for a New Millenium.* New York: HarperCollins.
Funk, Robert W. 1998. *The Acts of Jesus: The Search for the Authentic Deeds of Jesus.* New York: HarperSanFransisco.
Gal, Zvi. 1992. *Lower Galilee during the Iron Age.* American Schools of Oriental Research Dissertation Series, 8. Winona Lake, Indiana: Eisenbrauns.
Gånemo, Agneta. 2002. *Hereditary Ichtyosis: Causes, Skin Manifestations, Treatments and Quality of Life.* Comprehensive Summaries of Uppsala Dissertations from the Faculty of Medicine, 1125. Uppsala: Acta Universitatis Uppsaliensis.

García Martínez, Florentino. 1988. "Les limites de la communauté: pureté et impureté à Qumrân et dans le Noveau Testament." In *Text and Testimony: Essays on New Testament and Apocryphal Literature in Honour of A.F.J. Klijn*, 111–122. Eds. T. Baarda et al. Kampen: J.H. Kok.

García Martínez, Florentino and Trebolle Barrera, Julio. 1995. *The People of the Dead Sea Scrolls: Their writings, beliefs and practices.* Leiden: Brill.

Geertz, Clifford. 1973. *The Interpretation of Cultures.* New York: Basic Books.

Geller, Markham J. 1977. "Jesus' Theurgic Powers: Parallels in the Talmud and Incantation Bowls." *JJS* 28: 141–155.

George, Augustin. 1977. "Miracles dans le Monde hellénistique." In *Les Miracles de Jésus selon le Nouveau Testament*, 95–108. Ed. Xavier Léon-Dufour. Paris: Éditions du Seuil.

Gerdmar, Anders. 2001. *Rethinking the Judaism-Hellenism Dichotomy: A Historiographical Case Study of Second Peter and Jude.* ConBNT, 36. Stockholm: Almqvist & Wiksell International.

Gerstenberger, Erhard S. 1993. *Das dritte Buch Mose: Leviticus.* Das Alte Testament Deutsch 6. Göttingen: Vandenhoeck & Ruprecht.

Gnilka, Joachim. 1978. *Das Evangelium nach Markus.* Vol 1. EKK II/1. Zürich/ Neukirchen-Vluyn:Benziger/Neukirchener Verlag.

Goodman, Martin. 1982. "The First Jewish Revolt: Social Conflict and the Problem of Debt." *JJS* 33: 417–427.

Goodman, Martin. 1983. *State and Society in Roman Galilee, A.D. 132–212.* Oxford Centre for Postgraduate Hebrew Studies. Totowa, New Jersey: Rowman & Allanheld.

Grabbe, Lester L. 1997. "4QMMT and Second Temple Jewish Society." In *Legal Texts and Legal Issues: Proceedings of the Second Meeting of the International Organization for Qumran Studies. Cambridge 1995*, 89–108. STDJ, 23. Leiden: Brill.

Green, William Scott. 1979. "Palestinian Holy Men: Charismatic Leadership and Rabbinic Tradition." In *ANRW* II.19.2, 619–647. Berlin: Walter de Gruyter.

Grelot, Pierre. 1977. "Miracles de Jésus et Démonologie Juive." In *Les Miracles de Jésus selon le Nouveau Testament*, 59–72. Ed. Xavier Léon-Dufour. Paris: Éditions du Seuil.

Grenfell, Bernard P. and Hunt, Arthur S. 1908a. *The Oxyrhynchus Papyri.* Part 5. London: Egypt Exploration Fund.

Grenfell, Bernard P. and Hunt, Arthur S. 1908b. *Fragments of an Uncanonical Gospel from Oxyrhynchus.* London: For the Egypt Exploration Fund by Henry Frowde, Oxford University Press.

Groh, Dennis E. 1997. "The Clash Between Literary and Archaeological Models of Provincial Palestine." In *Archaeology and the Galilee: Texts and Contexts in the Graeco-Roman and Byzantine Periods*, 29–37. Eds. D. R. Edwards and C. T. McCollough. SFSHJ, 143. Atlanta, Georgia: Scholars Press.

Gronewald, Michael. 1987. "255. Unbekanntes Evangelium oder Evangelien-harmonie (Fragment aus dem "Evangelium Egerton")." In *Kölner Papyri,* 136–145. Papyrologica Coloniensia, 7, band 6. Eds. M. Gronewald, et al. Opladen: Westdeutscher Verlag.

Gross, Karl. 1985. *Menschenhand und Gotteshand in Antike und Christentum.* Stuttgart: Anton Hiersemann.

Grossouw, W. K. 1966. "A Note on John XIII 1–3." *NovT* 8: 124–131.

Grundmann, Walter. 1940. *Jesus der Galiläer und das Judentum.* Veröffentlichungen des Instituts zur Erforschung des jüdischen Einflusses aur das Deutsche Kirchliche Leben. Leipzig: Verlag Georg Wigand.

Grundmann, Walter. 1971. *Das Evangelium nach Markus.* 5th ed. Theologischer Handkommentar zum Neuen Testament 2. Berlin: Evangelische Verlagsanstalt.

Guijarro, Santiago. 1999. "The Politics of Exorcism: Jesus' Reaction to Negative Labels in the Beelzebul Controversy." *BTB* 29: 118–129.

Hachlili, Rachel. 2000. "Cemeteries." In *Encyclopedia of the Dead Sea Scrolls*, 1: 125–129. Eds. L.H. Schiffman & J. C. VanderKam. Oxford: Oxford University Press.

Haenchen, Ernst. 1984 [1980]. *John 2: A Commentary on the Gospel of John Chapters 7–21.* Hermeneia. Philadelphia: Fortress.

Hahn, Ferdinand. 1963. *Christologische Hoheitstitel: Ihre Geschichte im frühen Christentum.* FLANT, 83. Göttingen: Vandenhoeck & Ruprecht.

Harrington, Hannah K. 1993. *The Impurity Systems of Qumran and the Rabbis: Biblical Foundations.* SBL Dissertation Series 143. Atlanta, Georgia: Scholars Press.

Harrington, Hannah K. 1998. "Biblical Law at Qumran." In *The Dead Sea Scrolls after Fifty Years: A Comprehensive Assessment,* 1: 160–185. Eds. P. W. Flint and J. C. Vanderkam. Leiden: Brill.

Harvey, Anthony E. 1982. *Jesus and the Constraints of History: The Bampton Lectures, 1980.* London: Duckworth.

Hayes, Christine. 1999. "Intermarriage and Impurity in Ancient Jewish Sources." *HTR* 92: 3–36

Henaut, Barry W. 1997, "Is the "Historical Jesus" a Christological Construct?" In *Whose Historical Jesus?*, 241–268. Studies in Christianity and Judaism, 7. Eds. W.E. Arnal and M. Desjardins. Waterloo, Ontario: Wilfrid Laurier University Press.

Hengel, Martin. 1974 [1968]. *Judaism and Hellenism: Studies in their Encounter in Palestine during the Early Hellenistic Period.* 2 vols. London: SCM.

Hengel, Martin. 1985. *Studies in the Gospel of Mark.* London: SCM.

Hengel, Martin and Deines, Roland. 1995. "E. P. Sanders' 'Common Judaism', Jesus, and the Pharisees." *JTS* 46: 1–70.

Herzog, Rudolf. 1931. *Die Wunderheilungen von Epidauros: Ein Beitrag zur Geschichte der Medizin und der Religion.* Philologus, Supplementband 22:3. Leipzig: Dieterich'sche Verlagsbuchhandlung.

Hill, Scott D. 1992. "The Local Hero in Palestine in Comparative Perspective." In *Elijah and Elisha in Socioliterary Perspective*, 37–73. Ed. R.B. Coote. Society of Biblical Literature Semeia Studies. Atlanta, Georgia: Scholars Press.

Hillers, Delbert Roy; Rabinowitz, Louis Isaac; and Scholem, Gershom. 1971. "Demons, Demonology." In *Encyclopaedia Judaica* 5: 1521–1533. Eds. C. Roth and G. Wigoder. Jerusalem: Keter Publishing House.

Himmelfarb, Martha. 2001. "Impurity and Sin in 4QD, 1QS, and 4Q512." *DSS* 8: 9-37.

Hoglund, Kenneth G. and Meyers, Eric M. 1996. "The Residential Quarter on the Western Summit." In *Sepphoris in Galilee: Crosscurrents of Culture*, 39–43. Eds. R. M. Nagy, C. L. Meyers, E. M. Meyers and Z. Weiss. Winona Lake, Indiana: North Carolina Museum of Art / Eisenbrauns.

Hollenbach, Paul W. 1981. "Jesus, Demoniacs, and Public Authorities: A Socio-Historical Study."" *JAAR* 49: 567–588.

Hollenbach, Paul W. 1982. "The Conversion of Jesus: From Jesus the Baptizer to Jesus the Healer." In *ANRW* II.25.1, 196–219. Berlin: Walter de Gruyter.

Holmberg, Bengt. 1990. *Sociology and the New Testament: An Appraisal.* Minneapolis: Fortress.

Holmberg, Bengt. 1995. "Den historiske Jesus—nutida diskussionsläge och bedömning." In *Jesustolkningar idag—tio teologer om kristologi*, 23–54. Stockholm: Verbum.

Holmberg, Bengt. 2001. *Människa och mer: Jesus i forskningens ljus.* Lund: Arcus.

Holmén, Tom. 1999. "Doubts about Double Dissimilarity. Restructuring the Main Criterion of Jesus-of-history Research." In *Authenticating the Words of Jesus*, 47–80. Eds. B. Chilton and C.A. Evans. New Testament Tools and Studies, 28, 1. Leiden: Brill.

Holmén, Tom. 2001. *Jesus and Jewish Covenant Thinking.* Biblical Interpretation Series, 55. Leiden: Brill.

Hooker, Morna D. 1972. "On Using the Wrong Tool." *Theology* 75: 570–581.

Hooker, Morna D. 1991. *The Gospel According to Saint Mark*. Black's New Testament Commentaries. London: A & C Black [Reprint: Hendrickson].
Horsley, Richard A. 1987. *Jesus and the Spiral of Violence*. San Francisco: Harper & Row.
Horsley, Richard A. 1989. *Sociology and the Jesus Movement*. New York: Crossroad.
Horsley, Richard A. 1995. *Galilee: History, Politics, People*. Valley Forge, Pennsylvania: Trinity.
Horsley, Richard A. 1996. *Archaeology, History, and Society in Galilee: The Social Context of Jesus and the Rabbis*. Valley Forge, Pennsylvania: Trinity.
Houston, Walter. 1993. *Purity and Monotheism: Clean and Unclean Animals in Biblical Law*. JSOTSup, 140. Sheffield: JSOT Press.
Hruby, Kurt. 1977. "Perspectives Rabbiniques sur le Miracle." In *Les Miracles de Jésus selon le Nouveau Testament*, 73–94. Ed. Xavier Léon-Dufour. Paris: Éditions du Seuil.
Hultgren, Arland J. 1979. *Jesus and His Adversaries*. Minneapolis: Augsburg.
Humphries, Michael. 1993. "The Kingdom of God in the Q Version of the Beelzebul Controversy. Q 11:14–26." *Foundations and Facets Forum* 9: 121–150.
Hübner, Hans. 1986 [1973]. *Das Gesetz in der synoptischen Tradition: Studien zur These einer progressiven Qumranisierung und Judaisierung innerhalb der synoptischen Tradition*. 2nd ed. Göttingen: Vandenhoeck & Ruprecht.
Hulse, E. V. 1975. "The Nature of Biblical 'Leprosy' and the Use of Alternative Medical Terms in Modern Translations of the Bible." *PEQ* 107: 87-105.
Iggers, Georg G. 1962. "The Image of Ranke in American and German Historical Thought." *History and Theory* 2: 17–40.
Jacobs, Martin. 2000. "Pagane Tempel in Palästina—rabbinische Aussagen im Vergleich mit archäologischen Funden." In *The Talmud Yerushalmi and Graeco-Roman Culture*, vol. 2, 139-159. Eds. P. Schäfer and C. Hezser. Texts and Studies in Ancient Judaism, 79. Tübingen: Mohr Siebeck.
Jeanrond, Werner G. 1991. *Theological Hermeneutics. Development and Significance*. Dublin: Macmillan.
Jeffers, Ann. 1996. *Magic and Divination in Ancient Palestine and Syria*. Studies in the History and Culture of the Ancient Near East 8. Leiden: Brill.
Jeremias, Joachim. 1936. "Ein bisher unbekanntes Evangelienfragment. Untersuchung des Textes." *Theologische Blätter* 15.2: 38–45. Eds. K. L. Schmidt and H. Strathmann. Leipzig: Verlag der J. C. Hinrichs'schen Buchhandlung.
Jeremias, Joachim. 1947. "Der Zusammenstoss Jesu mit dem pharisäischen Oberpriester auf dem Tempelplatz. Zu Pap. Ox. V, 840." *Coniectanea Neotestamentica XI in honorem Antonii Fridrichsen sexagenarii*. Lund/Köpenhamn: C. W. K. Gleerup/Ejnar Munksgaard.
Jeremias, Joachim. 1958 [1923]. *Jerusalem zur Zeit Jesu: Kulturgeschichtliche Untersuchung zur neutestamentlichen Zeitgeschichte*. 2nd ed. Göttingen: Vandenhoeck & Ruprecht.
Jeremias, Joachim. 1963. *Unbekannte Jesusworte*. 3rd ed. Gütersloh: Gütersloher Verlagshaus Gerd Mohn.
Jeremias, Joachim. 1971. *New Testament Theology*. Vol. 1. London: SCM.
Jeremias, Joachim. 1972 [1947]. *The Parables of Jesus*. 3rd ed. London: SCM.
Jeremias, Joachim. 1980. *Die Sprache des Lukasevangeliums: Redaktion und Tradition im Nicht-Markusstoff des dritten Evangeliums*. KEK. Göttingen: Vandenhoeck & Ruprecht.
Juusola, Hannu. 1999. *Linguistic Peculiarities in the Aramaic Magic Bowl Texts*. Studia Orientalia, 86. Helsinki: Finnish Oriental Society.
Kahl, Brigitte. 1996. "Jairus und die verlorenen Töchter Israels. Sozioliterarische Überlegungen zum Problem der Grenzüberschreitung in Mk 5, 21–43. In *Von der Wurzel getragen: Christlich-feministische Exegese in Auseinandersetzung mit Antijudaismus*, 61–78. Eds. L. Schottroff & M.-T. Wacker. Biblical Interpretation Series, 17. Leiden: Brill.

Kahl, Werner. 1994. *New Testament Miracle Stories in their Religious-Historical Setting*. FRLANT, 163. Göttingen: Vandenhoeck & Ruprecht.

Kähler, Martin. 1988 [1896]. *The So-called Historical Jesus and the Historic Biblical Christ*. Philadelphia: Fortress.

Kampen, John and Bernstein, Moshe J. (eds.) 1996. *Reading 4QMMT. New Perspectives on Qumran Law and History*. Atlanta, Georgia: Scholars Press.

Käsemann, Ernst. 1954. "Das Problem des historischen Jesus." *ZTK* 51: 125–152.

Käsemann, Ernst. 1965 [1954]. *Essays on New Testament Themes*. London: SCM.

Kaufmann, Yehezkel. 1960 [1937–1948]. *The Religion of Israel: From Its Beginnings to the Babylonian Exile*. [תולדות האמונה הישראלית מימי קדם עד סוף בית שני. Vols. 1–7. Translated and abridged by Moshe Greenberg. Tel-Aviv: Bialik Institute-Dvir, 1937–1948.] Chicago: The University of Chicago Press.

Kazmierski, Carl R. 1992. "Evangelist and Leper: A Socio-Cultural Study of Mark 1.40–45." *NTS* 38: 37–50.

Kee, Howard Clark. 1967–1968. "The Terminology of Mark's Exorcism Stories." *NTS* 14: 232–246.

Kee, Howard Clark. 1983. *Miracle in the Early Christian World: A Study in Sociohistorical Method*. New Haven and London: Yale University Press.

Kee, Howard Clark. 1986. *Medicine, Miracle and Magic in New Testament Times*. SNTSMS, 55. Cambridge: Cambrige University Press.

Kertelge, Karl. 1970. *Die Wunder Jesu im Markusevangelium*. SANT 23. München: Kösel-Verlag.

Kieffer, René. 1986–1987. "Judiska reningar och det dop som Jesus kommer med." *SEÅ* 51–52: 116–126.

Kieffer, René. 1988. *Johannesevangeliet 11–21*. KNT 4B. Uppsala: EFS-förlaget.

Kieffer, René. 1991. *Nytestamentlig Teologi*. Stockholm: Verbum.

Kieffer, René. 1995. "Traditions juives selon Mc 7,1–23." In *Texts and Contexts. Biblical Texts in Their Textual and Situational Contexts: Essays in honor of Lars Hartman*, 675–688. Eds. T. Fornberg and D. Hellholm. Oslo: Scandinavian University Press.

Kieffer, René. 1998. "Fottvagningens tolkning mot dess judiska bakgrund." *SEÅ* 63: 217–223.

Kiilunen, Jarmo. 1985. *Die Vollmacht im Widerstreit: Untersuchungen zum Werdegang von Mk 2,1–3,6*. AASF, Dissertationes Humanarum Litterarum, 40. Helsinki: Suomalainen Tiedeakatemia.

Kister, Menahem. 1999. "Demons, Theology and Abraham's Covenant (CD 16:4–6 and Related Texts)." In *The Dead Sea Scrolls at Fifty: Proceedings of the 1997 Society of Biblical Literature Qumran Section Meetings*, 167–184. Eds. R. A. Kugler and E. M. Schuller. Atlanta, Georgia: Scholars Press.

Kister, Menahem. 2001. "Law, Morality, and Rhetoric in Some Sayings of Jesus." In *Studies in Ancient Midrash*. Ed. J. L. Kugel. Harvard: Harvard University Center for Jewish Studies.

Kittay, Eva Feder. 1987. *Metaphor: Its Cognitive Force and Linguistic Structure*. Oxford: Clarendon.

Kiuchi, N. 1987. *The Purification Offering in the Priestly Literature: Its Meaning and Function*. JSOTSup, 56. Sheffield: JSOT Press.

Klausner, Joseph. 1925. *Jesus of Nazareth: His Life, Times, and Teaching*. London: George Allen & Unwin.

Klawans, Jonathan. 1997a. *Impurity and Sin in Ancient Judaism*. Ann Arbor, Michigan: UMI.

Klawans, Jonathan. 1997b. "The Impurity of Immorality in Ancient Judaism." *JJS* 48: 1–16.

Klawans, Jonathan. 1998. "Idolatry, Incest, and Impurity: Moral Defilement in Ancient Judaism." *JSJ* 29: 391–415.

Klawans, Jonathan. 2000. *Impurity and Sin in Ancient Judaism*. Oxford: University Press.

Kloppenborg, John S. 1987. *The Formation of Q: Trajectories in Ancient Wisdom Collections.* SAC. Philadelphia: Fortress.

Kloppenborg Verbin, John S. 2000. *Excavating Q: The History and Setting of the Sayings Gospel.* Minneapolis: Fortress.

Klutz, Todd E. 1999. "The Grammar of Exorcism in the Ancient Mediterranean World. Some Cosmological, Semantic, And Pragmatic Reflections on How Exorcistic Prowess Contributed to the Worship of Jesus." In *The Jewish Roots of Christological Monotheism: Papers from the St. Andrews Conference on the Historical Origins of the Worship of Jesus*, 156–165. Eds. C. C. Newman, J. R. Davila and G. S. Lewis. Supplements to the Journal for the Study of Judaism 63. Leiden: Brill.

Knibb, Michael. 1987. *The Qumran Community.* Cambridge commentaries on writings of the Jewish and Christian world, 200 BC to AD 200, 2. Cambridge: Cambridge University Press.

Knohl, Israel. 1995. *The Sanctuary of Silence: The Priestly Torah and the Holiness School.* Minneapolis: Fortress.

Knox, Wilfred L. 1953. *The Sources of the Synoptic Gospels.* Vol. 1. *St. Mark.* Cambridge: Cambridge University Press.

Koester, Helmut. 1980. "Apocryphal and Canonical Gospels." *HTR* 73: 105–130.

Koester, Helmut. 1982 [1980]. *Introduction to the New Testament.* 2 Vols. Hermeneia Foundations and Facets. Philadelphia: Fortress.

Koet, Bart J. 2000. "Purity and Impurity of the Body in Luke-Acts." In *Purity and Holiness: The Heritage of Leviticus*, 93–106. Eds. M. J. H. M. Poorthuis & J. Schwartz. Jewish and Christian Perspectives Series, 2. Leiden: Brill.

Kollmann, Bernd. 1996. *Jesus und die Christen als Wundertäter.* FRLANT, 170. Göttingen: Vandenhoeck & Ruprecht.

Koskenniemi, Erkki. 1994. *Apollonios von Tyana in der neutestamentlichen Exegese.* WUNT 2:61. Tübingen: J. C. B. Mohr (Paul Siebeck).

Kuhn, H.-W. 1971. *Ältere Sammlungen im Markusevangelium.* Studien zur Umwelt des Neuen Testaments 8. Göttingen: Vandenhoeck & Ruprecht.

Kümmel, Werner Georg. 1953. *Verheißung und Erfüllung: Untersuchungen zur eschatologischen Verkündigung Jesu.* Abhandlungen zur Theologie des Alten und Neuen Testaments, 6. Zürich: Zwingli-Verlag.

Lambrecht, J. 1977. "Jesus and the Law. An Investigation of Mk 7, 1–23." *ETL* 53: 24–82.

Lane, William L. 1974. *The Gospel of Mark.* NICNT. Grand Rapids: Eerdmans.

Lapin, Hayim. 1995. *Early Rabbinic Civil Law and the Social History of Roman Galilee: A Study of Mishnah Tractate Baba' Mesi'a'.* Atlanta, Georgia: Scholars Press.

Lazarus-Yafeh, Hava. 1984. "Some Differences Between Judaism and Islam as Two Religions of Law." In *Religion* 14: 175–191.

Légasse, Simon. 1977. "L'historien en quête de l'événement." In *Les Miracles de Jésus selon le Nouveau Testament*, 109–145. Ed. Xavier Léon-Dufour. Paris: Éditions du Seuil.

Léon-Dufour, Xavier. 1977. "Structure et fonction du récit de miracle." In *Les Miracles de Jésus selon le Nouveau Testament*, 289–353. Ed. Xavier Léon-Dufour. Paris: Éditions du Seuil.

Leslau, Wolf. 1951. *Falasha Anthology.* Yale Judaica Series, 6. New Haven: Yale University Press.

Leslau, Wolf. 1957. *Coutumes et Croyances des Falashas (Juifs d'Abyssinie).* Université de Paris. Travaux et mémoires de l'institut d'éthnologie, 61. Paris: Institut d'éthnologie.

Levine, Baruch A. 1974. *In the Presence of the Lord: A study of Cult and some Cultic Terms in Ancient Israel.* Leiden: E.J. Brill.

Levine, Baruch A. 1993. *Numbers 1–20.* Anchor Bible. New York: Doubleday.

Levine, Lee I. (ed.) 1992. *The Galilee in Late Antiquity.* New York: The Jewish Theological Seminary/Harvard University Press.
Lieberman, Saul. 1999 [1939]. *Tosefeth Rishonim: A Commentary.* Vols. 3–4. *Seder Tohoroth.* New York and Jerusalem: The Jewish Theological Seminary of America.
Loader, William R. G. 1997. *Jesus' Attitude towards the Law: A Study of the Gospels.* Tübingen: J. C. B. Mohr (Paul Siebeck).
Lohmeyer, Ernst. 1937. *Das Evangelium des Markus.* Kritisch-exegetischer Kommentar über das Neue Testament begründet von Heinr. Aug. Wilh. Meyer. Göttingen: Vandenhoeck & Ruprecht.
Lövestam, Evald. 1972–1973. "Davids-son-kristologin hos synoptikerna." *SEÅ* 37–38: 196–210.
Lührmann, Dieter. 1987. *Das Markusevangelium.* Handbuch zum Neuen Testament, 3. Tübingen: J.C.B. Mohr (Paul Siebeck).
Luz, Ulrich. 1997. *Das Evangelium nach Matthäus.* Vol. 3. EKK 3:2. Zürich: Benziger.
Maccoby, Hyam. 1982. "The Washing of Cups." *JSNT* 14: 3–15.
Maccoby, Hyam. 1998. "Corpse and Leper." In *JJS* 49: 280–285.
Maccoby, Hyam. 1999. *Ritual and Morality: The Ritual Purity System and its Place in Judaism.* Cambridge: Cambridge University Press.
Macintyre, Alasdair. 1976. "Causality and History." In *Essays on Explanation and Understanding: Studies in the Foundations of Humanities and Social Sciences*, 137–158. Eds. Juha Manninen and Raimo Tuomela. Synthese Library, 72. Dordrecht:D. Reidel.
Mack, Burton L. 1988. *A Myth of Innocence: Mark and Christian Origins.* Philadelphia: Fortress.
Mack, Burton L. 1993. *The Lost Gospel: The Book of Q & Christian Origins.* New York: HarperSanFrancisco.
Mack, Burton L. 1997. "Q and a Cynic-Like Jesus." In *Whose Historical Jesus?*, 25–36. Eds. W. E. Arnal and M. Desjardins. Studies in Christianity and Judaism 7. Waterloo, Ontario: Wilfrid Laurier University Press.
Magen, Yitzhak. 1994. "Jerusalem as a Center of the Stone Vessel Industry during the Second Temple Period." In *Ancient Jerusalem Revealed*, 244–257. Ed. H. Geva. Jerusalem: Israel Exploration Society.
Malina, Bruce J. 1996. *The Social World of Jesus.* London: Routledge.
Mann, Jacob. 1915–1916. "Jesus and the Sadducean Priests: Luke 10. 25–37." In *JQR* 6: 415–422.
Manns, Frédéric. 1981. "Le Lavement des Pieds. Essai sur la Structure et la Signification de Jean 13." *RevScRel* 55: 149–169.
Marcus, Joel. 1995. "Jesus' Baptismal Vision." *NTS* 41: 512–521.
Marcus, Joel. 1999. "The Beelzebul Controversy and the Eschatologies of Jesus." In *Authenticating the Activities of Jesus*, 247–277. Eds. B. Chilton and C. A. Evans. New Testament Tools and Studies 28, 2. Leiden: Brill.
Marcus, Joel. 2000. *Mark 1–8: A New Translation with Introduction and Commentary.* Anchor Bible. New York: Doubleday.
Marmorstein, A. 1914. "Einige Bemerkungen zum Evangelienfragment in Oxyrhynchus Papyri, vol. V. n. 840, 1907." *ZNW* 15: 336–338.
Marshall, I. H. 1978. *The Gospel of Luke: A Commentary on the Greek Text.* NIGTC. Exeter: Paternoster.
Marshall, John W. 1997. "The *Gospel of Thomas* and the Cynic Jesus." In *Whose Historical Jesus?*, 37–60. Eds. W. E. Arnal and M. Desjardins. Studies in Christianity and Judaism 7. Waterloo, Ontario: Wilfrid Laurier University Press.
Martin, Raymond. 1995. "Forum: Raymond Martin, Joan W. Scott, and Cushing Strout on *Telling the Truth about History.*" *History and Theory* 34: 320–329.

Marxsen, Willi. 1969 [1956]. *Mark the Evangelist: Studies on the Redaction History of the Gospel.* Nashville, Tennesse: Abingdon.

Mason, Steve. 1991. *Flavius Josephus on the Pharisees: A Composition-Critical Study.* Studia Post-Biblica, 39. Leiden: Brill.

Mayeda, Goro. 1946. *Das Leben-Jesu-Fragment Papyrus Egerton 2 und seine Stellung in der urchristlichen Literaturgeschichte.* Bern: Paul Haupt.

Mazar, Benjamin. 1975. *The Mountain of the Lord.* Garden City, New York: Doubleday.

McCasland, S. Vernon. 1939. "The Asklepios Cult in Palestine." *JBL* 58: 221–227.

McCullagh, C. Behan. 1998. *The Truth of History.* Routledge: London.

Meens, Rob. 2000. " 'A Relic of Superstition:' Bodily Impurity and the Church from Gregory the Great to the Twelfth Century Decretists." In *Purity and Holiness: The Heritage of Leviticus*, 281–293. Jewish and Christian Perspectives Series, 2. Leiden: Brill.

Meier, John P. 1991. *A Marginal Jew: Rethinking the Historical Jesus.* Vol. 1. Anchor Bible Reference Library. New York: Doubleday.

Meier, John P. 1994. *A Marginal Jew: Rethinking the Historical Jesus.* Vol. 2. Anchor Bible Reference Library. New York: Doubleday.

Meier, John P. 2001. *A Marginal Jew: Rethinking the Historical Jesus.* Vol. 3. Anchor Bible Reference Library. New York: Doubleday.

Metso, Sarianna. 1997a. "The Textual Traditions of the Qumran *Community Rule.*" In *Legal Texts and Legal Issues: Proceedings of the Second Meeting of the International Organization for Qumran Studies. Cambridge 1995*, 141–147. Eds. M. Bernstein, F. García Martínez, and J. Kampen. STDJ, 23. Leiden: Brill.

Metso, Sarianna. 1997b. *The Textual Development of the Qumran Community Rule.* STDJ, 21. Leiden: Brill.

Metso, Sarianna. 1999. "In Search of the *Sitz Im Leben* of the *Community Rule.*" In *The Provo International Conference on the Dead Sea Scrolls: Technological Innovations, New Texts, and Reformulated Issues*, 306–315. STDJ, 30. Eds. D. W. Parry and E. Ulrich. Leiden: Brill.

Meyer, Ben F. 1979. *The Aims of Jesus.* London: SCM.

Meyer, Ben F. 1992. "'Phases' in Jesus' Mission." *Gregorianum* 73: 5–17.

Meyer, Ben F. 1994. "Jesus' Ministry and Self-Understanding." In *Studying the Historical Jesus: Evaluations of the State of Current Research*, 337–352. Eds. B. Chilton and C. A. Evans. Leiden: Brill.

Meyer, Robert. 1999. "Magical Ascesis and Moral Purity in Ancient Egypt." In *Transformations of the Inner Self in Ancient Religions*, 45–64. Studies in the History of Religions (*Numen* Book Series), 83. Leiden: Brill.

Meyers, Eric M. 1985. "Galilean Regionalism: A Reappraisal." In *Approaches to Ancient Judaism.* Vol. 5: *Studies in Judaism and Its Greco-Roman Context*, 115–131. Ed. W. S. Green. Brown Judaic Studies, 32. Atlanta, Georgia: Scholars Press.

Meyers, Eric M. 1992. "Roman Sepphoris in Light of New Archaeological Evidence and Recent Research." In *The Galilee in Late Antiquity*, 321–338. Ed. Lee I. Levine. New York: The Jewish Theological Seminary/Harvard University Press.

Meyers, Eric M. 1997. "Jesus and His Galilean Context." In *Archaeology and the Galilee. Texts and Contexts in the Graeco-Roman and Byzantine Periods*, 57–66. Eds. D. R. Edwards and C. T. McCollough. SFSHJ, 143. Atlanta, Georgia: Scholars Press.

Michaels, J. Ramsey. 1999. "The Itinerant Jesus and His Home Town." In *Authenticating the Activities of Jesus*, 177–193. Eds. B. Chilton and C. A. Evans. New Testament Tools and Studies 28, 2. Leiden: Brill.

Milgrom, Jacob. 1971a. "Sin-Offering or Purification-Offering?" *VT* 21: 237–239.

Milgrom, Jacob. 1971b. "'Eglah 'Arufah." In *Encyclopaedia Judaica* 6:475–477. Eds. C. Roth and G. Wigoder. Jerusalem: Keter Publishing House.

Milgrom, Jacob. 1976a. *Cult and Conscience: The* Asham *and the Priestly Doctrine of Repentance.* SJLA, 18. Leiden: Brill.
Milgrom, Jacob. 1976b. "Two Kinds of *Ḥaṭṭā't*." *VT* 36: 333–337.
Milgrom, Jacob. 1978. "Studies in the Temple Scroll." *JBL* 97: 501–523.
Milgrom, Jacob. 1981. "The Paradox of the Red Cow (Num. xix)." *VT* 31: 62–72.
Milgrom, Jacob. 1983. *Studies in Cultic Terminology.* SJLA, 36. Leiden: Brill.
Milgrom, Jacob. 1989. "The Qumran cult: its exegetical principles." In *Temple Scroll Studies*, 165–180. Ed. G. J. Brooke. JSPSUP 7. Sheffield: JSOT Press.
Milgrom, Jacob. 1990a. "The Scriptural Foundations and Deviations in the Laws of Purity of the *Temple Scroll*." In *Archaeology and History in the Dead Sea Scrolls: The New York University Conference in Memory of Yigael Yadin*, 83–99. Ed. L. H. Schiffman. JSPSup, 8. JSOT/ASOR Monographs, 2. Sheffield: JSOT Press.
Milgrom, Jacob. 1990b. *Numbers במדבר*. The JPS Torah Commentary. Philadelphia, New York: The Jewish Publication Society.
Milgrom, Jacob. 1991. *Leviticus, 1–16: A New Translation with Introduction and Commentary.* Anchor Bible, 3. Garden City, New York: Doubleday.
Milgrom, Jacob. 1993a. "On the Purification Offering in the Temple Scroll." *RevQ* 61: 99–101.
Milgrom, Jacob. 1993b. "The Concept of Impurity in *Jubilees* and the *Temple Scroll*." *RevQ* 61: 277–284.
Milgrom, Jacob. 1994. "Confusing the Sacred and the Impure: A Rejoinder." *VT* 44: 554–559.
Milgrom, Jacob. 1995. "4QTohora[a]: An unpublished Qumran text on purities." In *Time to Prepare the Way in the Wilderness*, 59–68. Eds. D. Dimant & L. Schiffman. STDJ, 16. Leiden: Brill.
Milgrom, Jacob. 2000a. *Leviticus, 17–22: A New Translation with Introduction and Commentary.* Anchor Bible 3a. Garden City, New York: Doubleday.
Milgrom, Jacob. 2000b. *Leviticus, 23–27: A New Translation with Introduction and Commentary.* Anchor Bible 3b. Garden City, New York: Doubleday.
Milgrom, Jacob & Wright, David P. 1986. "נִדָּה." In *TWAT* 5: 250–253. Eds. G. J. Botterweck, H. Ringgren & H.-J. Fabry. Stuttgart: Verlag W. Kohlhammer.
Miller, Stuart S. 1992. "Sepphoris, the Well Remembered City." *BAR* 18 (June): 74–83.
Montgomery, James A. 1913. *Aramaic Incantation Texts from Nippur.* University of Pennsylvania. The Museum. Publications of the Babylonian Section, 3. Philadelphia: University Museum.
Moxnes, Halvor. 1995. "Den historiske Jesus: Mellom modernitet og postmodernitet?" *NTT* 96:139–156.
Moxnes, Halvor. 2002. "Jesus the Jew: Dilemmas of Interpretation." In *Fair Play: Diversity and Conflicts in Early Christianity: Essays in Honour of Heikki Räisänen*, 83–103. Eds. I. Dunderberg, C. Tuckett and K. Syreeni. Leiden: Brill.
Murray, Oswyn, ed. 1990. *Sympotica: A Symposium on the* Symposion. Oxford: Clarendon.
Naveh, Joseph and Shaked, Saul. 1993. *Magic Spells and Formulae: Aramaic Incantations of Late Antiquity.* Jerusalem: Magnes Press, Hebrew University.
Neirynck, Franz. 1985. "Papyrus Egerton 2 and the Healing of the Leper." *ETL* 61: 153–160.
Neirynck, Franz. 1989. "The Apocryphal Gospels and the Gospel of Mark. 5: Papyrus Egerton 2." In *The New Testament in Early Christianity: La Réception des écrits néotestamentaires dans le christianisme primitif,* 161–167. Ed. J.-M. Sevrin. Bibliotheca Ephemeridum Theologicarum Lovaniensium, 86. Leuven: University Press.
Neirynck, Franz. 1990. "Response to the Multiple-Stage Hypothesis. II: The Healing of the Leper." In *The Interrelations of the Gospels*, 94–107. Ed. D. L. Dungan. Leuven: University Press.

Netzer, Ehud. 1982. "Ancient Ritual Baths *(Miqvaot)* in Jericho." In *The Jerusalem Cathedra: Studies in the History, Archaeology, Geography and Ethnography of the Land of Israel*, 2: 106–119. Ed. L. I. Levine. Jerusalem: Yad Izḥak Ben-Zvi Institute.

Neusner, Jacob. 1970. *Development of a Legend: Studies on the Traditions concerning Yoḥanan ben Zakkai.* Studia Post-Biblica 16. Leiden: Brill.

Neusner, Jacob. 1971. *The Rabbinic Traditions about the Pharisees before 70.* 3 vols. Leiden: Brill.

Neusner, Jacob. 1973a. *The Idea of Purity in Ancient Judaism.* The Haskell lectures 1972–1973. Leiden: Brill.

Neusner, Jacob. 1973b. *Eliezer ben Hyrcanus: The Tradition and the Man.* 2 vols. SJLA, 3–4. Leiden: Brill.

Neusner, Jacob. 1974–1977. *A History of the Mishnaic Law of Purities.* 22 vols. SJLA, 6. Leiden: Brill.

Neusner, Jacob. 1979. *From Politics to Piety: The Emergence of Pharisaic Judaism.* 2nd ed. New York: KTAV.

Neusner, Jacob. 1981–1983. *A History of the Mishnaic Law of Appointed Times.* 5 vols. SJLA, 34. Leiden: Brill.

Neusner, Jacob. 1982. *Formative Judaism: Religious, Historical, and Literary Studies.* Brown Judaic Studies, 37. Chico, California: Scholars Press.

Neusner, Jacob. 1985. *Formative Judaism: Religious, Historical, and Literary Studies.* 5th Series: *Revisioning the Written Records of a Nascent Religion.* Brown Judaic Studies, 91. Chico, California: Scholars Press.

Neusner, Jacob. 1987. "Josephus' Pharisees: A Complete Repertoire." In *Josephus, Judaism and Christianity*, 274–292. Eds. L. H. Feldman and G. Hata. Detroit: Wayne State University Press.

Neusner, Jacob. 1988. *Judaism: The Evidence of the Mishnah.* 2nd ed. Brown Judaic Studies, 129. Atlanta, Georgia: Scholars Press.

Neusner, Jacob. 1993a. *Judaic Law from Jesus to the Mishnah: A Systematic Reply to Professor E. P. Sanders.* SFSHJ, 84. Atlanta, Georgia: Scholars Press.

Neusner, Jacob. 1993b. *The Judaism Behind the Texts: The Generative Premises of Rabbinic Literature. I. The Mishnah. A. The Division of Agriculture.* SFSHJ, 89. Atlanta, Georgia: Scholars Press.

Neusner, Jacob. 1994. *Purity in Rabbinic Judaism: A Systematic Account.* SFSHJ, 95. Atlanta: Scholars Press.

Neusner, Jacob and Green, William Scott, eds. 1999 [1996]. *Dictionary of Judaism in the Biblical Period, 450 B.C.E. to 600 C.E.* Peabody, Massachusetts: Hendrickson.

Newton, Michael. 1985. *The Concept of Purity at Qumran and in the Letters of Paul.* Cambridge: Cambridge University Press.

Nineham, D. E. 1963. *The Gospel of St Mark.* The Pelican New Testament Commentaries. Harmondsworth: Penguin Books.

Novick, Peter. 1988. *That Noble Dream: The "Objectivity Question" and the American Historical Profession.* Cambridge: Cambridge University Press.

Oppenheimer, Aharon. 1977. *The 'Am Ha-Aretz: A Study in the Social History of the Jewish People in the Hellenistic-Roman Period.* Arbeiten zur Literatur und Geschichte des Hellenistischen Judentums 8. Leiden: Brill.

Overholt, Thomas W. 1996. "Elijah and Elisha in the Context of Israelite Religion." In *Prophets and Paradigms: Essays in Honor of Gene M. Tucker,* 94–111. Ed. S. B. Reid. JSOTSup, 229. Sheffield: Sheffield Academic Press.

Overman, J. Andrew. 1997. "Jesus of Galilee and the Historical Peasant." In *Archaeology and the Galilee: Texts and Contexts in the Graeco-Roman and Byzantine Periods*, 67–73. Eds. D. R. Edwards and C. T. McCollough. SFSHJ, 143. Atlanta, Georgia: Scholars Press.

Palm, Jonas. 1976. *Om Filostratos och hans Apollonios-biografi.* Acta Universitatis Upsaliensis Studia Graeca Upsaliensia, 10. Uppsala: Almqvist & Wiksell International.
Parker, Robert. 1983. *Miasma: Pollution and Purification in early Greek Religion.* Oxford: Clarendon.
Paschen, Wilfried. 1970. *Rein und Unrein: Untersuchung zur biblischen Wortgeschichte.* SANT 24. München: Kösel-Verlag.
Pasto, James. 1999. *Who Owns the Jewish Past? Judaism, Judaisms, and the Writing of Jewish History.* Vol. 1. Ann Arbor, Michigan: UMI.
Penney, Douglas L. and Wise, Michael O. 1994. "By the Power of Beelzebub. An Aramaic Incantation Formula from Qumran (4Q560)." *JBL* 113: 627–650.
Perrin, Norman. 1963. *The Kingdom of God in the Teaching of Jesus.* New Testament Library. London: SCM.
Perrin, Norman. 1967. *Rediscovering the Teaching of Jesus.* New York: Harper & Row, Publishers.
Perrin, Norman. 1969. *What is Redaction Criticism?* Guides to Biblical Scholarship. New Testament Series. Philadelphia: Fortress.
Perrin, Norman. 1976. *Rediscovering the Teaching of Jesus.* New York: Harper & Row, Publishers.
Perrot, Charles. 1979. *Jésus et l'histoire.* Paris: Desclée.
Pesch, Rudolf. 1970a. "Jaïrus (Mk 5,22 / Lk 8,41). *Biblische Zeitschrift,* Neue Folge 14: 252–256.
Pesch, Rudolf. 1970b. *Jesu Ureigene Taten? Ein Beitrag zur Wunderfrage.* Freiburg: Herder.
Pesch, Rudolf. 1972. *Der Besessene von Gerasa: Entstehung und Überlieferung einer Wundergeschichte.* Stuttgarter Bibelstudien, 56. Stuttgart: KBW.
Pesch, Rudolf. 1976. *Das Markusevangelium.* Vol. 1. Herders theologischer Kommentar zum Neuen Testament, 2. Freiburg: Herder.
Péter-Contesse, R. 1993. *Lévitique 1–16.* Commentaire de l'Ancien Testament IIIa. Genève: Labor et Fides.
Pfann, Stephen J. 1999. "The Essene Yearly Renewal Ceremony and the Baptism of Repentance." In *The Provo International Conference on the Dead Sea Scrolls: Technological Innovations, New Texts, and Reformulated Issues*, 337–351. Eds. D. W. Parry and E. Ulrich. Leiden: Brill.
Piattelli, Daniela and Jackson, Bernard S. 1996. "Jewish Law during the Second Temple Period." In *An Introduction to the History and Sources of Jewish Law*, 19–56. Eds. N. S. Hecht, B. S. Jackson, S. M. Passamaneck, D. Piattelli and A. M. Rabello. Oxford: Clarendon.
Qimron, E. 1991. "Notes on the 4Q Zadokite Fragment on Skin Disease." *JJS* 42: 256–259.
Rabin, Chaim. 1954. Ed. and tr. *The Zadokite Documents: I. The Admonition. II. The Laws.* Chaim Rabin. Oxford: Clarendon Press.
Rad, Gerhard von. 1975 [1957]. *Old Testament Theology.* Vol. 1. London: SCM.
Räisänen, Heikki. 1986. *The Torah and Christ: Essays in German and English on the Problem of the Law in Early Christianity.* Publications of the Finnish Exegetical Society, 45. Helsinki: Finnish Exegetical Society.
Räisänen, Heikki. 1990. *The 'Messianic Secret' in Mark.* Studies of the New Testament and its world. Edinburgh: T. & T. Clark.
Räisänen, Heikki. 1996. "Exorcisms and the Kingdom: Is Q 11:20 a Saying of the Historical Jesus?" In *Symbols and Strata: Essays on the Sayings Gospel Q.* Ed. R. Uro. Publications of the Finnish Exegetical Society 65. Helsinki/Göttingen: The Finnish Exegetical Society/Vandenhoeck & Ruprecht.

Ranke, Leopold von. 1874 [1824]. *Geschichten der romanischen und germanischen Völker von 1494 bis 1514*. 2nd ed. Sämmtliche Werke, 33–34. Leipzig: Verlag von Duncker und Humblot.

Rappaport, Uriel. 1992. "How Anti-Roman Was the Galilee?" In *The Galilee in Late Antiquity*, 95–102. Ed. Lee I. Levine. New York: The Jewish Theological Seminary/Harvard University Press.

Redfield, Robert. 1953. *The Primitive World and Its Transformations*. Ithaca, New York: Cornell University Press.

Redfield, Robert. 1955. *The Little Community: Viewpoints for the Study of a Human Whole*. The Gottesman Lectures, Uppsala University, 1955. Uppsala & Stockholm: Almqvist & Wiksells Boktryckeri.

Redfield, Robert. 1956. *Peasant Society and Culture: An Anthropological Approach to Civilization*. Chicago & London: The University of Chicago Press.

Redfield, Robert and Singer, Milton B. 1956 [1954]. "The Cultural Role of Cities." *Man in India* 36: 161–194 [First publ. in *Economic Development and Social Change* 3 (1954): 53–73].

Reed, Jonathan. 2000. *Archaeology and the Galilean Jesus: A Re-examination of the Evidence*. Harrisburg, Pennsylvania: Trinity.

Regev, Eyal. 2000. "Non-Priestly Purity and its Religious Aspects according to Historical Sources and Archaeological Findings." In *Purity and Holiness: The Heritage of Leviticus*, 223–244. Jewish and Christian Perspectives Series, 2. Leiden: Brill.

Reich, Ronny. 1980. "*Mishnah Sheqalim* 8:3 and the Archaeological Evidence." In *Jerusalem in the Second Temple Period — Abraham Schalit Memorial Volume*, 225–256 (Hebrew; English summary p. xiv). Eds. A. Oppenheimer, U. Rappaport and M. Stern. Jerusalem.

Reich, Ronny. 1981. "Archaeological Evidence of the Jewish Population at Hasmonean Gezer." *IEJ* 31: 48–52.

Reich, Ronny. 1984. "A *Miqweh* at 'Isawiya near Jerusalem." *IEJ* 34: 220–223 + plate 28.

Reich, Ronny. 1988. "The Hot Bath-House (balneum), the Miqweh and the Jewish Community in the Second Temple Period. *JJS* 39: 102–107.

Reich, Ronny. 1993. "The Great Mikveh Debate." *BAR* 19 (March–April): 52–53.

Reinhart, A. Kevin. 1990. "Impurity / No Danger." In *History of Religions* 30: 1–24.

Rengstorf, Karl Heinrich (ed.). 1967. *Die Tosefta: Text.*. Vol. 6. *Seder Ṭoharot.* Rabbinische Texte. Erste Reihe. Stuttgart: W. Kohlhammer.

Rengstorf, Karl Heinrich (ed.). 1960–1967. *Die Tosefta: Übersetzung und Erklärung*. Ed. Karl Heinrich Rengstorf. Vol. 6:1-3. *Seder Ṭoharot.* Rabbinische Texte. Erste Reihe. Stuttgart: W. Kohlhammer.

Rentería, Tamis Hoover. 1992. "The Elijah/Elisha Stories: A Socio-cultural Analysis of Prophets and People in Ninth-Century B.C.E. Israel. In *Elijah and Elisha in Socioliterary Perspective*, 75–126. Ed. R.B. Coote. Society of Biblical Literature Semeia Studies. Atlanta, Georgia: Scholars Press.

Riches, John K. 1980. *Jesus and the Transformation of Judaism*. London: Darton, Longman & Todd.

Riches, John K. 1990. *The World of Jesus: First-Century Judaism in Crisis*. Understanding Jesus Today. Cambridge: University Press.

Riches, John K. 1993. *A Century of New Testament Study*. Valley Forge, Penns.: Trinity.

Riedel, Manfred. 1976. "Causal and Historical Explanation." In *Essays on Explanation and Understanding: Studies in the Foundations of Humanities and Social Sciences*, 3–25. Eds. Juha Manninen and Raimo Tuomela. Synthese Library, 72. Dordrecht: D. Reidel.

Ringgren, Helmer. 1982. "טָהַר" In *TWAT* 3: 306–315.

Rivkin, Ellis. 1978. *A Hidden Revolution: The Pharisees' Search for a Kingdom Within*. Nashville: Abingdon.
Robinson, James M. 1959. *A New Quest of the Historical Jesus*. London: SCM.
Rofé, Alexander. 1988. *The Prophetical Stories: The Narratives about the Prophets in the Hebrew Bible. Their Literary Types and History*. Jerusalem: Magnes Press, Hebrew University.
Rordorf, Willy. 1962. *Der Sonntag: Geschichte des Ruhe- und Gottesdiensttages im ältesten Christentum*. Abhandlungen zur Theologie des Alten und Neuen Testaments, 43. Zürich: Zwingli Verlag.
Rouwhorst, Gerard. 2000. "Leviticus 12–15 in Early Christianity." In *Purity and Holiness. The Heritage of Leviticus*, 181–193. Jewish and Christian Perspectives Series, 2. Leiden: Brill.
Runesson, Anders. 2001a. *The Origins of the Synagogue: A Socio-Historical Study*. CONBNT, 37. Stockholm: Almqvist & Wiksell International.
Runesson, Anders. 2001b. "Water and Worship: Ostia and the Ritual Bath in the Diaspora Synagogue." In *The Synagogue of Ancient Ostia and the Jews of Rome: Interdisciplinary Studies,* 115–129. Eds. B. Olsson, D. Mitternacht and O. Brandt. Acta Instituti Romani Regni Sueciae, Series in 4°, 57. Stockholm: Paul Åströms Förlag.
Ruzer, Serge. 1999. "The Seat of Sin in Early Jewish and Christian Sources." In *Transformations of the Inner Self in Ancient Religions*, 367–391. Studies in the History of Religions (*Numen* Book Series), 83. Leiden: Brill.
Safrai, Shmuel. 1981. *Die Wallfahrt im Zeitalter des Zweiten Tempels*. Forschungen zum jüdisch-christlichen Dialog, 3 [Hebrew original 1965]. Neukirchen-Vluyn: Neukirchener Verlag.
Saldarini, Anthony J. 1977. "'Form Criticism' of Rabbinic Literature." *JBL* 96: 257–274.
Saldarini, Anthony J. 1988. *Pharisees, Scribes and Sadducees in Palestinian Society: A Sociological Approach*. Wilmington, Delaware: Michael Glazier.
Saldarini, Anthony J. 1994. "Pluralism of Practice and Belief in First-Century Judaism." In *Jews and Christians Speak of Jesus*, 13–34. Ed. A. E. Zannoni. Minneapolis: Fortress.
Sanders, Ed P. 1977. *Paul and Palestinian Judaism: A Comparison of Patterns of Religion*. London: SCM.
Sanders, Ed P. 1985. *Jesus and Judaism*. London: SCM.
Sanders, Ed P. 1990. *Jewish Law from Jesus to the Mishnah: Five Studies*. London: SCM.
Sanders, Ed P. 1992. *Judaism: Practice and Belief 63 BCE – 66 CE*. London: SCM.
Sanders, Ed P. 1993. *The Historical Figure of Jesus*. London: Penguin.
Sanders, Ed P. 1996. "Jesus' Relation to Sepphoris." In *Sepphoris in Galilee: Crosscurrents of Culture*, 75–77. Eds. R. M. Nagy, C. L. Meyers, E. M. Meyers and Z. Weiss. Winona Lake, Indiana: North Carolina Museum of Art / Eisenbrauns.
Sanders, Ed. P. 2002. "Jesus' Galilee." In *Fair Play: Diversity and Conflicts in Early Christianity: Essays in Honour of Heikki Räisänen*, 3–41. Eds. I. Dunderberg, C. Tuckett and K. Syreeni. Leiden: Brill.
Sariola, Heikki. 1990. *Markus und das Gesetz: Eine redaktionskritische Untersuchung*. AASF, Dissertationes Humanarum Litterarum, 56. Helsinki: Suomalainen Tiedeakatemia.
Sawyer, John F. A., ed. 1996. *Reading Leviticus: A Conversation with Mary Douglas*. JSOTSup, 227. Sheffield: Sheffield Academic Press.
Schiffman, Lawrence H. 1975. *The Halakhah at Qumran*. SJLA, 16. Leiden: Brill.
Schiffman, Lawrence H. 1989. "The Temple Scroll and the Systems of Jewish Law of the Second Temple Period." In *Temple Scroll Studies*, 239–255. Ed. G. J. Brooke. JSPSUP 7. Sheffield: JSOT Press.
Schiffman, Lawrence H. 1990. "The Impurity of the Dead in the *Temple Scroll*." In *Archaeology and History in the Dead Sea Scrolls: The New York University Conference in Memory*

of Yigael Yadin, 135–156. Ed. L.H. Schiffman. JSPSup, 8. JSOT/ASOR Monographs, 2. Sheffield: JSOT Press.

Schiffman, Lawrence H. 1992a. "Laws Pertaining to Women in the *Temple Scroll*." In *The Dead Sea Scrolls: Forty Years of Research*, 210–228. Eds. D. Dimant & U. Rappaport. STDJ, 10. Leiden: Brill.

Schiffman, Lawrence H. 1992b. "Was There a Galilean Halakhah?" In *The Galilee in Late Antiquity*, 143–156. Ed. Lee I. Levine. New York: The Jewish Theological Seminary/Harvard University Press.

Schiffman, Lawrence H. 1994. "Pharisaic and Sadducean Halakhah in Light of the Dead Sea Scrolls. The Case of Ṭevul Yom." *DSD* 1: 285–299.

Schiffman, Lawrence H. 1995. *Reclaiming the Dead Sea Scrolls: The History of Judaism, the Background of Christianity, the Lost Library of Qumran*. The Anchor Bible Reference Library. New York: Doubleday.

Schmidt, Karl F. W. 1936. "Ein bisher unbekanntes Evangelienfragment. Einblicke in die Arbeitsweise eines alten Evangelisten." *Theologische Blätter* 15.2: 34–38. Eds. K. L. Schmidt and H. Strathmann. Leipzig: Verlag der J. C. Hinrichs'schen Buchhandlung.

Schmidt, Karl Ludwig. 1919. *Der Rahmen der Geschichte Jesu: Literarkritische Untersuchungen zur Ältesten Jesusüberlieferung*. Berlin: Trowitzsch & Son.

Schnackenburg, Rudolf. 1982. *The Gospel according to St John*. Vol. 3. Herder's Theological Commentary on the New Testament. London & Tunbridge Wells: Burns & Oates.

Schneemelcher, Wilhelm (ed.). 1991. *New Testament Apocrypha*. Vol 1: *Gospels and Related Writings*. Tr. R. McL. Wilson. Cambridge: James Clarke & Co.

Schwartz, Daniel R. 1983. "Josephus and Nicolaus on the Pharisees." *JSJ* 14: 157–171.

Schwartz, Daniel R. 1986. "Viewing the Holy Utensils (P. Ox. V, 840)." *NTS* 32: 153–159.

Schwartz, Daniel R. 1992. *Studies in the Jewish Background of Christianity*. WUNT, 60. Tübingen: J. C. B. Mohr (Paul Siebeck).

Schwartz, Daniel R. 1996. "MMT, Josephus and the Pharisees." In *Reading 4QMMT: New Perspectives on Qumran Law and History*, 67–80. Eds. J. Kampen and M. J. Bernstein. SBL Symposium Series, 2. Atlanta, Georgia: Scholars Press.

Schwartz, Joshua. 2000. "On Birds, Rabbis and Skin Disease." In *Purity and Holiness: The Heritage of Leviticus*, 207–222. Jewish and Christian Perspectives Series, 2. Leiden: Brill.

Schweitzer, Albert. 1936 [1906]. *The Quest of the Historical Jesus: A Critical Study of its Progress from Reimarus to Wrede*. 2nd ed. London: A. & C. Black.

Schweizer, Eduard. 1971 [1967]. *The Good News According to Mark: A Commentary on the Gospel*. London: SPCK.

Scott, James C. 1977. "Protest and Profanation: Agrarian Revolt and the Little Tradition." *Theory and Society* 4: 1–38, 211–46.

Segal, Alan F. 1990. *Paul the Convert: The Apostolate and Apostasy of Saul the Pharisee*. New Haven: Yale University Press.

Segovia, Fernando F. 1982. "John 13 1–20, The Footwashing in the Johannine Tradition." *ZNW* 73: 31–51.

Sellew, Philip. 1988. "Beelzebul in Mark 3. Dialogue, Story, or Sayings Cluster?" *Foundations and Facets Forum* 4: 93–108.

Selvidge, Marla J. 1984. "Mark 5:25–34 and Leviticus 15:19–20: A Reaction to Restrictive Purity Regulations." *JBL* 103: 619–623.

Selvidge, Marla J. 1990. *Woman, Cult, and Miracle Recital: A Redaction Critical Investigation on Mark 5:24–34*. Lewisburg: Bucknell University Press.

Semi, Emanuela Trevisan. 1985. "The Beta Israel (Falashas): From Purity to Impurity." *JJSoc* 27: 103–114.

Shirock, Robert. 1992. "Whose Exorcists are They? The Referents of οἱ υἱοὶ ὑμῶν at Matthew 12.27/Luke 11.19." *JSNT* 46: 41–51.

Sievers, Joseph. 1997. "Who Were the Pharisees?" In *Hillel and Jesus: Comparative Studies of Two Major Religious Leaders*, 137–155. Eds. J. H. Charlesworth and L. L. Johns. Minneapolis: Fortress.

Singer, Milton. 1972. *When a Great Tradition Modernizes: An Anthropological Approach to Indian Civilization.* London: Pall Mall.

Smith, D. Moody. 1996. "What Have I Learned about the Gospel of John?" In *"What is John?" Readers and Readings of the Fourth Gospel*, 217–235. Ed. F.F. Segovia. SBL Symposium Series, 3. Atlanta, Georgia: Scholars Press.

Smith, Dennis E. 1987. "Table Fellowship as a Literary Motif in the Gospel of Luke." *JBL* 106: 613–638.

Smith, Jonathan Z. 1978. "Towards Interpreting Demonic Powers in Hellenistic and Roman Antiquity." In *ANRW* II.16.1, 425–439. Berlin: Walter de Gruyter.

Smith, Morton. 1973. *Clement of Alexandria and a Secret Gospel of Mark.* Cambridge, Massachusetts: Harvard University Press.

Smith, Morton. 1981 [1978]. *Jesus the Magician.* San Francisco: Harper & Row.

Steele, E. Springs. 1984. "Luke 11:37–54—a Modified Hellenistic Symposium?" *JBL* 103: 379–394.

Stegemann, Hartmut. 1998 [1993]. *The Library of Qumran: On the Essenes, Qumran, John the Baptist, and Jesus.* Grand Rapids, Michigan: Eerdmans.

Stemberger, Günter. 1995 [1991]. *Jewish Contemporaries of Jesus: Pharisees, Sadducess, Essenes.* Minneapolis: Fortress.

Sterling, Gregory E. 1993. "Jesus as Exorcist: An Analysis of Matthew 17:14–20; Mark 9:14–29; Luke 9:37–43a." *CBC* 55: 467–493.

Stolz, Fritz. 1999. "Dimensions and Transformations of Purification Ideas." In *Transformations of the Inner Self in Ancient Religions*, 211–229. Studies in the History of Religions (*Numen* Book Series), 83. Leiden: Brill.

Strange, James F. 1992. "Some Implications of Archaeology for New Testament Studies." In *What Has Archaeology to Do with Faith?*, 23–59. Eds. J. H. Charlesworth and W. P. Weaver. Philadelphia: Trinity.

Strange, James F. 1997. "First Century Galilee from Archaeology and from the Texts." In *Archaeology and the Galilee: Texts and Contexts in the Graeco-Roman and Byzantine Periods*, 39–48. Eds. D. R. Edwards and C. T. McCollough. SFSHJ, 143. Atlanta, Georgia: Scholars Press.

Stroumsa, Guy G. 1999. "Purification and its discontents: Mani's Rejection of Baptism. In *Transformations of the Inner Self in Ancient Religions*, 405–420. Studies in the History of Religions (*Numen* Book Series), 83. Leiden: Brill.

Svartvik, Jesper. 2000. *Mark and Mission: Mk 7:1–23 in its Narrative and Historical Contexts.* ConBNT 32. Stockholm: Almqvist & Wiksell International.

Syreeni, Kari. 1987. *The Making of the Sermon on the Mount: A Procedural Analysis of Matthew's Redactoral Activity.* Part 1: Methodology & Compositional Analysis. AASF, Dissertationes Humanarum Litterarum, 44. Helsinki: Suomalainen Tiedeakatemia.

Syreeni, Kari. 1999. "Wonderlands: A Beginner's Guide to Three Worlds." In *SEÅ* 64: 33–46.

Syreeni, Kari. 2000. "Characterization, Ideology and History in the Gospels: Narrative Criticism as a Historical and Hermeneutical Approach." In *A Bouquet of Wisdom: Essays in Honour of Karl-Gustav Sandelin*, 171–196. Eds. K.-J. Illman, T. Ahlbäck, S.-O. Back, R. Nurmela. Religionsvetenskapliga skrifter, 48. Åbo: Åbo Akademi.

Tagawa, Kenzo. 1966. *Miracles et Évangile: La Pensée personelle de l'Évangeliste Marc.* Études d'Histoire et de Philosophie religieuses, 62. Paris: Presses Universitaires de France.

Taylor, Joan E. 1997. *The Immerser: John the Baptist within Second Temple Judaism.* Studying the Historical Jesus. Grand Rapids, Michigan: Eerdmans.

Taylor, Vincent. 1935 [1933]. *The Formation of the Gospel Tradition.* 2nd ed. London: Macmillan.

Taylor, Vincent. 1966. *The Gospel According to St. Mark: The Greek Text with Introduction, Notes, and Indexes.* 2nd ed. London: Macmillan.

Theissen, Gerd. 1973. "Wanderradikalismus: literatursoziologische Aspekte der Uberlieferung von Worten Jesu im Urchristentum." *ZTK* 70: 245–271.

Theissen, Gerd. 1978 [1977]. *Sociology of Early Palestinian Christianity.* Philadelphia: Fortress.

Theissen, Gerd. 1983 [1972]. *The Miracle Stories of the Early Christian Tradition.* Edinburgh: T & T Clark.

Theissen, Gerd. 1987 [1986]. *The Shadow of the Galilean: The Quest of the Historical Jesus in Narrative Form.* London: SCM.

Theissen, Gerd and Merz, Annette. 1998 [1996]. *The Historical Jesus: A Comprehensive Guide.* Minneapolis: Fortress.

Theissen, Gerd and Winter, Dagmar. 1997. *Die Kriterienfrage in der Jesusforschung: Vom Differenzkriterium zum Plausibilitätskriterium.* Novum Testamentum et Orbis Antiquus, 34. Freiburg, Schweiz: Universitätsverlag.

Thiering, Barbara. 1980. "Inner and Outer Cleansings at Qumran as a Background to New Testament Baptism." *NTS* 26: 266–277.

Thomas, John Christopher. 1991. *Footwashing in John 13 and the Johannine Community.* JSNTSup, 61. Sheffield: Sheffield Academic Press.

Thomas, Joseph. 1935. *Le Mouvement Baptiste en Palestine et Syrie.* Gembloux: J. Duculot.

Thompson, R, Campbell. 1908. *Semitic Magic: Its Origins and Development.* Luzac's Oriental Religions Series, 3. London: Luzac & Co.

Thraede, Klaus. 1969. "Exorzismus." In *Reallexikon für Antike und Christentum: Sachwörterbuch zur Auseinandersetzung des Christentums mit der antiken Welt*, 7: 44–117. Ed. T. Klauser. Stuttgart: Anton Hiersemann.

Todd, Judith A. 1992. "The Pre-Deuteronomistic Elijah Cycle." In *Elijah and Elisha in Socioliterary Perspective*, 1–35. Ed. R.B. Coote. Society of Biblical Literature Semeia Studies. Atlanta, Georgia: Scholars Press.

Torstendahl, Rolf. 1971. *Introduktion till historieforskningen: historia som vetenskap.* 2nd ed. Stockholm: Natur & Kultur.

Trummer, Peter. 1991. *Die blutende Frau: Wunderheilung im Neuen Testament.* Freiburg: Herder.

Trunk, Dieter. 1994. *Der Messianische Heiler: Eine redaktions- und religionsgeschichtliche Studie zu den Exorzismen im Matthäusevangelium.* Herders Biblische Studien 3. Freiburg: Herder.

Turner, Eric B. 1987 [1970]. *Greek Manuscripts of the Ancient World.* 2nd ed. Institute of Classical Studies Bulletin Supplement, 46. London: Institute of Classical Studies.

Twelftree, Graham H. 1993. *Jesus the Exorcist: A Contribution to the Study of the Historical Jesus.* WUNT 2:54. Tübingen: J. C. B. Mohr (Paul Siebeck).

Uro, Risto. 1996. "Apocalyptic Symbolism and Social Identity in Q." In *Symbols and Strata. Essays on the Sayings Gospel Q*, 67–118. Ed. R. Uro. Helsinki: Finnish Exegetical Society.

Uro, Risto. 1998. "*Thomas* and oral gospel tradition." In Thomas *at the Crossroads: Essays on the* Gospel of Thomas, 8–32. Ed. R. Uro. Studies of the New Testament and Its World. Edinburgh: T&T Clark.

Uro, Risto. 2000. " 'Washing the Outside of the Cup': *Gos. Thom.* 89 and Synoptic Parallels." In *From Quest to Q: Festschrift for James M. Robinson*, 303–322. Eds. J. Ma. Asgeirsson, K. De Troyer and M. W. Meyer. BETL, 146. Leuven: University Press.

Vaage, Leif E. 1994. *Galilean Upstarts: Jesus' First Followers According to Q*. Valley Forge, Pennsylvania: Trinity.
Valtink, Eveline. 1996. "Feministisch-christliche Identität und Antijudaismus." In *Von der Wurzel getragen: Christlich-feministische Exegese in Auseinandersetzung mit Antijudaismus*, 1–26. Eds. L. Schottroff & M.-T. Wacker. Biblical Interpretation Series, 17. Leiden: Brill.
VanderKam, James C. 1994. *The Dead Sea Scrolls Today*. Grand Rapids, Michigan: Eerdmans.
Vandier, Jacques. 1962. *Le Papyrus Jumilhac*. Centre National de la recherche scientifique.
Vermes, Geza. 1972. "Ḥanina ben Dosa. A Controversial Galilean Saint from the First Century of the Christian Era." *JJS* 23: 28–50.
Vermes, Geza. 1973a. "Ḥanina ben Dosa. A Controversial Galilean Saint from the First Century of the Christian Era (II)." *JJS* 24: 51–64.
Vermes, Geza. 1973b. *Jesus the Jew: A Historian's Reading of the Gospels*. London: Fontana/Collins.
Vermes, Geza. 1983. *Jesus and the World of Judaism*. London: SCM.
Vermes, Geza. 1993. *The Religion of Jesus the Jew*. London: SCM.
Vermes, Geza. 1996. "Jesus the Jew." In *Jesus' Jewishness: Exploring the Place of Jesus within Early Judaism*, 108–122. Ed. J. H. Charlesworth. Shared Ground Among Jews and Christians. A Series of Explorations, 2. New York: Crossroad.
Vledder, Evert-Jan. 1997. *Conflict in the Miracle Stories: A Socio-Exegetical Study of Matthew 8 and 9*. JSNTSup 152. Sheffield: Sheffield Academic Press.
Wagenvoort, Hendrick. 1947. *Roman Dynamism: Studies in ancient Roman thought, language and custom*. Oxford: Basil Blackwell.
Wassén, Cecilia. 1991. "Sadducees and *Halakah*." In *Law in Religious Communities in the Roman Period: The Debate over* Torah *and* Nomos *in Post-Biblical Judaism and Early Christianity*, 127–146. Eds. P.Richardson and S. Westerholm. Studies in Christianity and Judaism, 4. Waterloo, Ontario: Wilfrid Laurier University Press.
Weaver, Walter P. 1999. *The Historical Jesus in the Twentieth Century. 1900–1950*. Harrisburg, Pennsylvania: Trinity.
Weber, Otto. 1906. *Dämonenbeschwörungen bei den Babyloniern und Assyrern: Eine Skizze*. In *Der alte Orient* Jhrg 7, heft 4. Leipzig: J. C. Hinrichs'sche Buchhandlung.
Webb, Robert L. 1991. *John the Baptizer and Prophet: A Socio-Historical Study*. Sheffield: JSNTSup, 62. JSOT Press.
Webb, Robert L. 1994. "John the Baptist and his Relationship to Jesus." In *Studying the Historical Jesus: Evaluations of the State of Current Research*, 179–229. Eds. B. Chilton and C. A. Evans. Leiden: E.J. Brill.
Weeden, T. J. 1971. *Mark—Traditions in Conflict*. [PB ed. 1979] Philadelphia: Fortress.
Wegner, Judith Romney 1998. "'Coming before the LORD': לפני יהוה and the Exclusion of Women from the Divine Presence." In *Hesed ve-Emet: Studies in Honor of Ernest S. Frerichs*, 81–91. Eds. J. Magness and S. Gitin. Brown Judaic Studies, 320. Atlanta, Georgia: Scholars Press.
Weill, Raymond 1920. *La Cité de David: Compte rendu des fouilles exécutées, à Jérusalem, sur le site de la ville primitive: Campagne de 1913–1914*. Paris: Librairie Paul Geuthner.
Weinreich, Otto 1909. *Antike Heilungswunder: Untersuchungen zum Wunderglauben der Griechen und Römer*. Giessen: Verlag von Alfred Töpelmann.
Weiss, Herold. 1979. "Foot Washing in the Johannine Community." *NovT* 21: 298–325.
Weiss, Johannes. 1892. *Die Predigt Jesu vom Reiche Gottes*. Göttingen: Vandenhoeck & Ruprecht.
Weiss, Johannes. 1900. *Die Predigt Jesu vom Reiche Gottes*. Zweite, völlig neubearbeitete Auflage. Göttingen: Vandenhoeck & Ruprecht.
Wenham, Gordon J. 1979. *The Book of Leviticus*. NICOT. London: Hodder and Stoughton.

Wenschkewitz, Hans. 1932. *Die Spiritualisierung der Kultusbegriffe: Tempel, Priester und Opfer im Neuen Testament.* Angelos. Archiv für neutestamentliche Zeitgeschichte und Kulturkunde, 4. Leipzig: Verlag von Eduard Pfeiffer.

Westerholm, Stephen. 1978. *Jesus and Scribal Authority.* CONBNT 10. Lund: CWK Gleerup.

Wilder, Amos N. 1950 [1939]. *Eschatology and Ethics in the Teaching of Jesus.* Rev. ed. New York: Harper & Brothers.

Wilkinson, John. 1977. "Leprosy and Leviticus: The Problem of Description and Identification." *SJT* 30: 153–169.

Wilkinson, John. 1978. "Leprosy and Leviticus: A Problem of Semantics and Translation." *SJT* 31: 153–166.

Willker, Wieland. 2001. "The Papyrus Egerton 2 Bibliography." No pages. 1 November 2001. Online: http://alf.zfn.uni-bremen.de/~wie/Egerton/egerton-biblio.html.

Wink, Walter. 1968. *John the Baptist in the Gospel Tradition.* Cambridge: Cambridge University Press.

Winninge, Mikael. 1995. *Sinners and Righteous: A Comparative Study of the Psalms of Solomon and Paul's Letters.* CONBNT 26. Stockholm: Almqvist & Wiksell International.

Wojciechowski, Michal. 1989. "The Touching of the Leper (Mark 1,40–45)." *BZ* 33: 114–119.

Wolff, Hans Walter. 1974 [1973]. *Anthropology of the Old Testament.* London: SCM.

Woolf, Jeffrey Robert. 2000. "Medieval Models of Purity and Sanctity: Ashkenazic Women in the Synagogue." In *Purity and Holiness: The Heritage of Leviticus*, 263–280. Jewish and Christian Perspectives Series, 2. Leiden: Brill.

Wright III, Benjamin G. 1997. "Jewish Ritual Baths—Interpreting the Digs and the Texts: Some Issues in the Social History of Second Temple Judaism." In *The Archaeology of Israel: Constructing the Past, Interpreting the Present*, 190–214. Eds. N.A. Silberman and D. Small. JSOTSup, 237. Sheffield: Academic Press.

Wright, David F. 1985–1986. "Papyrus Egerton 2 (the *Unknown Gospel*)—Part of the *Gospel of Peter*?" *Second Century* 5: 129–150.

Wright, David P. 1985. "Purification from Corpse-Contamination in Numbers XXXI 19–24." In *VT* 35: 213–223.

Wright, David P. 1987. *The Disposal of Impurity: Elimination Rites in the Bible and in Hittite and Mesopotamian Literature.* SBL Dissertation Series 101. Atlanta, Georgia: Scholars Press.

Wright, David P. 1992. "Unclean and Clean." In *ABD* 6: 729–741. Ed. D. N. Freedman. New York: Doubleday.

Wright, David P. & Jones, R. N. 1992. "Discharge." In *ABD* 2: 204–207. Ed. D. N. Freedman. New York: Doubleday.

Wright, Georg Henrik von. 1971. *Explanation and Understanding.* International Library of Philosophy and Scientific Method. London: Routledge & Kegan Paul.

Zohar, Noam. 1988. "Repentance and Purification: The Significance and Semantics of חטאת in the Pentateuch." *JBL* 107: 609–618.

Indices

Author Index

Subject Index

This is basically a word index. However, **bold types** indicate a major discussion on the subject.

Source index

For the reader's convenience references in footnotes are *italicized*. Plain numbers refer to the main text. This does not indicate relative importance, since footnote references may correspond to detailed discussions in the text. Major analyses of central texts are indicated by **bold types**.

Jewish Literature

Hebrew Bible

(including LXX references)

Apocrypha and Pseudepigrapha

Dead Sea Scrolls

Tosefta

Jerusalem Talmud

Babylonian Talmud

Mekhilta

Sifra

Sifre

Other Rabbinic literature

Targum

Samaritan Literature

Greek and other Ancient Literature

Inscriptions and Papyri

Ancient Authors

Early Christian Literature

New Testament

Extracanonical Gospel Traditions

Apostolic Fathers

Other NT Apocrypha

Christian Authors

Itero

www.ehs.se/itero

1. Åke Viberg, *Symbols of Law: A Contextual Analysis of Legal Symbolic Acts in the Old Testament.* 2021. First published 1992 by Almqvist & Wiksell International.
2. Thomas Kazen, *Jesus and Purity* Halakhah*: Was Jesus Indifferent to Impurity?* 2021. First published 2002 by Almqvist & Wiksell International. Corrected reprint edition published 2010 by Eisenbrauns.
3. Åke Viberg, *Prophets in Action: An Analysis of Prophetic Symbolic Acts in the Old Testament.* 2021. First published 2007 by Almqvist & Wiksell International.
4. Thomas Kazen, *Issues of Impurity in Early Judaism.* 2021. First published 2010 by Eisenbrauns.
5. Rikard Roitto, *Behaving as a Christ-Believer: A Cognitive Perspective on Identity and Behavior Norms in Ephesians.* 2021. First published 2011 by Eisenbrauns.